Microsoft® BizTalk Server 2004 UNLEASHED

Scott Woodgate, Stephen Mohr, Brian Loesgen,
Susie Adams, Alex Cobb, Benjamin Goeltz,
Brandon Gross, Chris Whytock, Erik Leaseburg,
Gavin Islip, Imran Aziz, Kevin Smith, Michael Roze,
Naveen Goli, Puru Amradkar, and Stephen Roger

800 East 96th Street, Indianapolis, Indiana 46240

Microsoft BizTalk Server 2004 Unleashed

International Standard Book Number: 0-672-32598-5

Library of Congress Catalog Card Number: 2003116631

Printed in the United States of America

First Printing: November 2004

07 06 05 4 3

Trademarks

All terms mentioned in this book that are known to be trademarks or service marks have been appropriately capitalized. Sams Publishing cannot attest to the accuracy of this information. Use of a term in this book should not be regarded as affecting the validity of any trademark or service mark.

Warning and Disclaimer

Every effort has been made to make this book as complete and as accurate as possible, but no warranty or fitness is implied. The information provided is on an "as is" basis.

Bulk Sales

Sams Publishing offers excellent discounts on this book when ordered in quantity for bulk purchases or special sales. For more information, please contact

U.S. Corporate and Government Sales

1-800-382-3419

corpsales@pearsontechgroup.com

For sales outside of the U.S., please contact

International Sales

international@pearsoned.com

Associate Publisher
Michael Stephens

Acquisitions Editor
Neil Rowe

Development Editor
Songlin Qiu

Managing Editor
Charlotte Clapp

Project Editor
George E. Nedeff

Copy Editor
Barbara Hacha

Indexer
Erika Millen

Proofreader
Tracy Donhardt

Technical Editor
Bob Schmidt

Publishing Coordinator
Cindy Teeters

Multimedia Developer
Dan Scherf

Interior Designer
Gary Adair

Cover Designer
Alan Clements

Contents at a Glance

Table of Contents

About the Author

Scott Woodgate is a Lead Product Manager for BizTalk Server at Microsoft corporate campus in Redmond. Scott has been a member of the product team since the heady days when BizTalk Server was merely a code name. He currently manages the BizTalk Server technical product management team. His team provides worldwide technical readiness, competitive analysis, and plans future versions of the product on the basis of customer, partner, and analyst feedback. Scott has contributed to two previous BizTalk Server books; he holds five university degrees, including a PhD in Organometallic Chemistry specializing in osmabenzenes, and he is a huge fan of his native country New Zealand's major sport, rugby.

"To my wife, Artemiza, for her support, all members of the BizTalk Server Team past and present for your inspiration, and all our customers for choosing BizTalk Server 2004."

Stephen Mohr is a senior software systems architect with Omicron Consulting and XMLabs in Philadelphia, USA. He has more than 15 years of experience developing software and systems for various platforms. Stephen is the author of numerous books for Wrox and Que and has spoken at a variety of international conferences. He has research interests in distributed computing using service-oriented architectures. Stephen holds BS and MS degrees in computer science from Rensselaer Polytechnic Institute.

"To my wife, Denise, who came along on this ride."

Based in San Diego, **Brian Loesgen** is a principal consultant with Neudesic, a firm that specializes in .NET development and Microsoft Server integration. Brian is a Microsoft MVP for BizTalk Server 2004. Brian has more than 18 years of experience in building advanced enterprise and mobile solutions. He is a coauthor of the *Professional XML, Professional ASP/XML, Professional Windows DNA, Professional ASP.NET Web Services,* and *Professional VB.NET Web Services* books from Wrox. In addition, Brian has written technical white papers for Intel, Microsoft, and others. Brian has spoken at numerous major technical conferences worldwide. Brian is a cofounder and President of the International .NET Association (`ineta.org`). He is the President of the San Diego .NET user group, leads the San Diego Software Industry Council Web Services SIG, and is a member of the Editorial Board for the .NET Developer's Journal.

In his spare moments, Brian enjoys outdoor activities such as geocaching (see `geocaching.com`), cycling, hiking in the mountains, kayaking, camping in the desert, or going to the beach with his wife, Miriam, and children Steven and Melissa. Brian can be reached at `brian.loesgen@ineta.org`.

Susie Adams is a MTC Technical Director with Microsoft Corporation. She has more than 18 years of application integration and development experience and currently focuses her attention on the architecture, design, and integration of service-oriented enterprise Web applications as well as traditional Enterprise Integration (EAI) using .NET and BizTalk Server. She has contributed to several industry technical journals, was the lead author of *BizTalk Server Unleashed*, a contributing author of *Visual InterDev Unleashed*, both published by Sams, and a contributing author of Microsoft Press's *Visual InterDev 6.0 Enterprise Developer's Workshop*. She has spoken at several industry trade show conferences, including the Visual Basic Insider Technical Summit (VBITS), Microsoft Developer Days, and Microsoft TechEd. Susie can be reached at `susiea@microsoft.com`.

"I'd like to thank the many members of the BizTalk product group, Scott Woodgate, Anil Balakrishnan, Joe Klug, John Ballard, and Zach Jason, who put up with my never-ending questions and who took the time out of their insane schedules to review content for accuracy! Without you guys I would have been up a creek!"

Alex Cobb is a Senior Technical Product Manager in the Business Process and Integration division of Microsoft Corporation. He has been a member of the BizTalk Server team for four years. Alex is a frequent speaker at Microsoft events and conferences. Prior to joining Microsoft, Alex held both technical and business positions in the financial services and international trade industries. Alex received a Bachelor of Science degree in Business Management from the University of Colorado.

Benjamin Goeltz is a system architect specializing in the enterprise application integration space. He has designed and implemented solutions for each version of BizTalk Server and was heavily involved with prerelease versions of BizTalk Server 2004 and its associated adapters. Ben's work has been focused in the energy, professional sports, manufacturing, and food processing and distribution industries, where he has deployed solutions integrating both internal (EAI) and external (B2B) systems to support mission-critical business processes. In addition to his client work, Ben has authored content used in BizTalk Server 2004's help file, as well as a published white paper on the product. Ben works for the Bellevue, WA branch of the Interlink Group (`www.ilg.com`), which is a Microsoft Gold Partnered consulting firm headquartered in Denver, CO.

Brandon Gross is a solution architect for the services company Interlink. He received a degree in Information Systems and Accounting from the University of Washington. Since graduation, Brandon has worked on Microsoft-based integration projects for medium-to-large enterprise clients in a wide range of industries, including government, resources, high-tech manufacturing, and the software industry. He has experience in a breadth of Microsoft technologies, including Com+, .NET, BizTalk 2002, and most recently, BizTalk 2004. He also has experience with industry business-to-business standards, including RosettaNet and OAGIS.

Chris Whytock works as a software engineer in Microsoft's business process and integration division. In his seven years of professional engineering, he has developed applications in a wide range of fields, including graphics, precision measurement, audio/video processing, and business processes. He has also written for MSDN and has a bachelor's degree in mathematics from the University of Waterloo.

When not working, Chris is happiest when wandering a foreign country, most recently the Amazon forest in Brazil, with his father.

"To my father, Kim, my mother, Cheryl, and Anil and Kristen, each of whom has made me a better person than I would have otherwise been."

Erik Leaseburg has been a consultant with Microsoft Premier Services for the past five years. He works with .NET and BizTalk Server early adopter partners and customers to provide training, support, consulting, and architectural guidance. Erik's technical focus areas include .NET and COM-based architectures, BizTalk Server 2000/2002/2004, .NET integration, deployment, operations, monitoring, support, and .NET development/migration. He has been a consultant for 10 years developing applications, Web sites, and EAI architectures that span multiple operating systems and environments.

"Erik thanks his loving wife, Kristy, and three amazing children, Alex, Emma, and Michael, for their support. Thank you Mom and Dad for sending me to computer camp. And thank you God for all life's blessings."

Gavin Islip is a consultant with the Microsoft Services Partner Advantage group based in Issaquah, Washington. He works with major Microsoft partners, including Independent Software Vendors and System Integrators, to help them develop solutions based on Microsoft technology. He is currently working at the Unisys Microsoft Innovation Center in Redmond where he helped develop the BizTalk Server 2004 Certification Program. Gavin has been a software development consultant for eight years, spending the last four years working at Microsoft. In his previous life he worked as a professional trombonist with the Orquesta Sinfonica de Tenerife in the Canary Islands.

"Gavin would like to thank his wife, Karin, and children Emma and Nathaniel for their love and support."

Imran Aziz has a bachelor's degree in computer science and engineering from the University of Wisconsin, Madison. He has worked in the software industry for more than eight years in varying roles, such as software design engineer, development consultant, and program management. He is currently working at Microsoft as a lead program manager in the business process and integration division.

"Thanks to my late dad, Dr. Abdus Salam, for his kind words and advice throughout my education and career."

Kevin Smith has worked for Microsoft for the past six and a half years. He worked as a software design engineer in the core engine team for BizTalk Server 2000 and 2002 and was the Technical Lead SDE for the Messaging Sub-Service for the BizTalk Server 2004 release. He now works for Microsoft Consulting Services in the U.K., helping customers architect enterprise solutions using BizTalk Server 2004.

Michael Roze is a Software Design Engineer with Microsoft Corporation and Redmond, USA. He has worked on the BizTalk team for over 2 years with expertise in Performance, Scalability, High Availability and distributed computing. He has over 14 years experience developing software and systems for various platforms. He has also consulted on Microsoft and other competitive technologies.

Naveen Goli is a Test Lead with Microsoft Corporation in Redmond, USA. He is currently working with the BizTalk Server product unit at Microsoft Corporation. He has more than 12 years of experience developing software and systems on Unix and Windows platforms. Naveen holds a postgraduate Diploma in International Trade from Bharatiya Vidya Bhavan in India and a MS degree in computer science from Monmouth University.

"For my wife, Veena, and kids Sohan and Sahas for their support and understanding as always; for Sangram Mohapatra, Ravi Annepu, Jason Arbon, and others in the BizTalk product unit who have helped me immensely with the content and editing. For my Dad and Mom, who gave inspiration and support all through my life."

Puru Amradkar is currently working as Program Manager on the BizTalk team with Microsoft Corporation.

"I would like to thank Eamon O'Reilly and Hans-Peter Mayr for encouragement. Also I would like to dedicate this book to my family. Thanks to Vinay Balasubramaniam."

Stephen Roger is a director with Interlink in Seattle, Washington. He has more than 15 years of experience in developing business applications, with a current focus on solutions based on integration technologies such as BizTalk Server. Interlink has been designing and building solutions with BizTalk Server since its initial release in December 2000.

Conventions Used in This Book

The following typographic conventions are used in this book:

- Code lines, commands, statements, and variables are in a `monospace` typeface. **`Bold monospace`** typeface is used to indicate user input.
- *Italic* type highlights technical terms when they're being defined.
- If a line of code is too long to fit as a single line on the printed page, it is broken into multiple lines. The ➥ character signifies that the continued code should appear on the preceding line.

CAUTION

Cautions alert you to common pitfalls that you should avoid.

TIP

Tips are used to highlight shortcuts, convenient techniques, or tools that can make a task easier. Tips also provide recommendations on best practices you should follow.

NOTE

Notes provide additional background information about a topic being described, beyond what is given in the chapter text. Often, notes are used to provide references to places where you can find more information about a particular topic.

Sidebars

A sidebar provides a deeper discussion or additional background to help illuminate a topic.

What's On the Web For This Book

The sample source code described throughout this book, and Appendix C, "Using BizTalk Native Adapters" are available on Sams website at `http://www.samspublishing.com`. Enter this book's ISBN 0672325985 in the Search box and click Search. When the book's title is displayed, click the title to go to a page where you can download the code and Appendix C.

We Want to Hear from You!

As the reader of this book, *you* are our most important critic and commentator. We value your opinion and want to know what we're doing right, what we could do better, what areas you'd like to see us publish in, and any other words of wisdom you're willing to pass our way.

As an associate publisher for Sams Publishing, I welcome your comments. You can email or write me directly to let me know what you did or didn't like about this book—as well as what we can do to make our books better.

Please note that I cannot help you with technical problems related to the topic of this book. We do have a User Services group, however, where I will forward specific technical questions related to the book.

When you write, please be sure to include this book's title and author as well as your name, email address, and phone number. I will carefully review your comments and share them with the author and editors who worked on the book.

Email: feedback@samspublishing.com

Mail: Michael Stephens
Associate Publisher
Sams Publishing
800 East 96th Street
Indianapolis, IN 46240 USA

For more information about this book or another Sams Publishing title, visit our Web site at `www.samspublishing.com`. Type the ISBN (0672325985) or the title of a book in the Search field to find the page you're looking for.

PART I

Introducing BizTalk Server 2004

IN THIS PART

CHAPTER 1

An Overview of BizTalk Server 2004

IN THIS CHAPTER

- The Need for Integration Architecture
- Feature Overview of BizTalk Server 2004
- Plugging in the Business User

This chapter provides an overview of the integration product BizTalk Server 2004, with a particular emphasis on new features in this release. However, before we introduce you to the product itself, it is important to understand the challenges of integration and the requirements that drive the need for an integration architecture.

The Need for Integration Architecture

For many years, businesses have both purchased and written computer applications. Fifteen years ago, access to the information stored within each of these applications was sufficient to address important business initiatives. However, as a result of the significant explosion of IT assets within companies, today there is a strong need to integrate applications to fulfill core business initiatives. Coupled with the need for better internal integration is a need for better external integration to trading partners driven by the global economy.

Over the past few years, companies have attempted to create custom-coded solutions that directly integrate applications on a tactical project-by-project basis. Initially, these custom integrations involved direct object calls between applications, which required an intimate knowledge of the inner workings of both applications and were subject to breakage each time an application interface changed.

The first step in the definition of integration architecture is the recognition of the need for a more decoupled approach which was more resilient to interface change. A message–based solution where important application data is represented in a serialized message *format* abstracting the specifics of the target applications provides a more decoupled approach than an object-based model. The format of each of these messages was once proprietary to each application, which caused further complexity, but it is now becoming ubiquitously standardized as XML for new applications.

After message definition is complete, the next challenge in integration architecture is managing the message flow in and out of applications. The architecture has at least four layers of complexity, which we will address one at a time.

Integration Architecture Tier 1: Connecting Two Applications

Let's start with the most basic need: messages generated from one application must be sent to another application and vice versa.

It is a *transport* that fulfills this requirement. Broadly speaking, transports can be categorized as the following:

- Standard-based—SMTP, HTTP/S, FTP, for example
- Pseudo-standards—MQSeries, MSMQ for example
- Application specific—BAPI for SAP, sockets, and the like

This myriad of transports clearly leads to complexity. Unfortunately, none of the previously listed transports is suitable for all integration scenarios, because each was defined to solve a particular problem: HTTP was originally for Web browsing, MQSeries for reliable queuing, and BAPI for SAP.

On the other hand, a key goal of Web services is to provide a singular, consistent, and normalized transport stack that is built on open standards, widely implemented across platforms, and deeply integrated into applications. Just as the goal of XML is to reduce message complexity, the goal of the Web services stack is to reduce transport complexity.

Although XML and Web services are clearly strong technologies in the integration space, offering message, transport, and to some extent security solutions, the reality is that most businesses will have assets that are non-XML and non-Web services for many years. An integration architecture needs to support both the large variety of existing technologies and newer technologies that attempt to simplify the issue. As you will learn, although XML and Web services do simplify the message format and transport aspects of an integration architecture, there are many more aspects to an integration architecture than format and transport.

The integration of two applications requires a transport and manipulation of data that may be described by two different message formats. Why two message formats? There is a message being sent from one application and a message being received into the other application. Even if both applications use XML, it is unlikely that the metadata representation required for these two applications will be identical. Different applications have different schema with elements and attributes in different order, with different names, and often with different granularities of information. The message from a source application must be mapped to the format of a target application. This problem is even more profound if we relax our assumption that both messages are XML and explore connecting application A, which sends flat-file messages to application B, which receives XML messages. In this case, it is useful to homogenize the message format with code that sits between the two applications—for example, converting the flat-file format to XML so that both messages are in XML. When that is completed, standard XML mapping techniques using XSLT can be used to map the data from one message to another message.

Yet another core requirement for integration services is to manage security issues. There are many aspects of security, including transport and message-format security. Transport security is often independently configurable per transport—for example, using HTTP/S to secure HTTP transport. Message-format security often requires message encryption, and commonly utilized methods include the SMIME standard or PGP. In addition, there is a fundamental need to authenticate credentials with a source or target application prior to message exchange. For example, an application request for payroll information should be secured so that only a particular user's payroll is available given a set of credentials. Although Kereberos is probably the most common mechanism to fulfill this requirement, many applications and operating systems provide their own custom mechanisms, such as SSH login into a Unix machine, or the custom authentication scheme used in SAP. Integration services must manage the complexity of the multiple authorization schemes in an automated manner to securely connect two applications without human intervention. The complete set of tier 1 requirements, including messages, transports, mapping, and security is shown in Figure 1.1.

Earlier, we stated that connecting applications was a multilayer problem. Thus far, we have discussed connecting a single application directly to another application; next we will examine the requirements for connecting multiple applications.

Integration Architecture Tier 2: Connecting Multiple Applications

The second layer of integration services manages connectivity between multiple applications—such as sending a message from application A and receiving that message into applications B and C.

Let's briefly delve into some history to expose some key requirements and best-practice design patterns for connecting multiple applications. Initially, customers exploring integration architectures built connections directly from one application to another in a pattern described as point-to-point integration. For each connection, code was written to manage transports, message formats, and mappings. Although scoping the problem at this level of complexity was often successful in that it worked fine when only two applications were involved, the so-called point-to-point approach was fraught with issues as additional connections were developed. In a small organization with five applications, the number of possible ways to directly connect these five applications is n*(n-1)/2 = 10 as depicted in Figure 1.2.

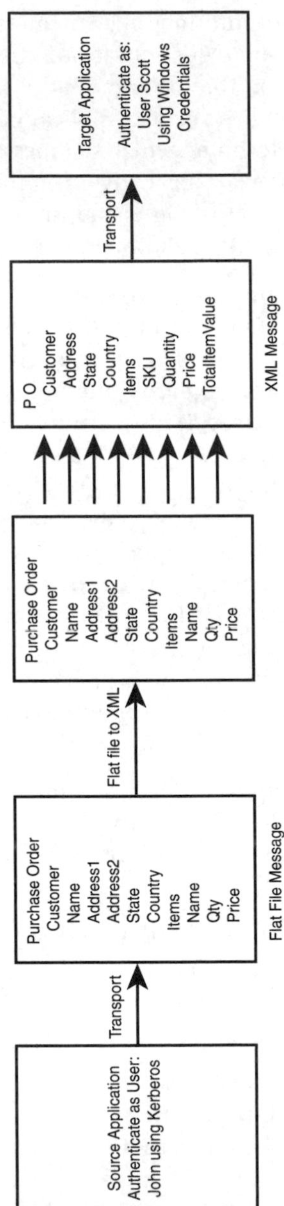

FIGURE 1.1 Requirements for direct application connectivity.

As you can see from Figure 1.2, point-to-point integration leads to the so called "spaghetti" problem. Each of these connections had its own custom code providing transport, message, and format services. Further, it was common that each of these point-to-point integrations was developed independently over time, such that each of the lines in the diagram had no consistent design principles; management was an afterthought. Even worse, little thought was applied to the longer-term business requirements, such as the need to replace applications within the ecosystem with newer applications over time. Probably the most common example of this type of development in a Microsoft platform context is the proliferation of "VBScript and FTP" integration pseudo-architectures that attempt to glue multiple applications together and rapidly become tedious to develop and manage.

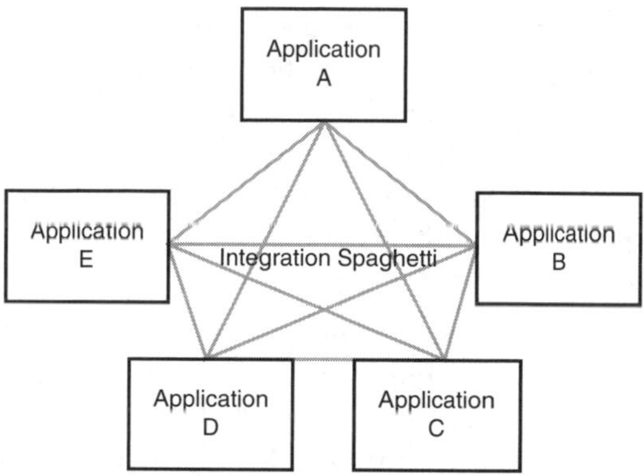

FIGURE 1.2 Point-to-point integration spaghetti.

Clearly, there must be a better way to integrate applications, and the key is providing a level of indirection between the applications by placing integration services topologically in the middle, as shown in Figure 1.3. Immediately, this architecture reduces the complexity of application integration from n*(n-1)/2 to a simpler linear problem. In our example, five applications require five connections to the integration services.

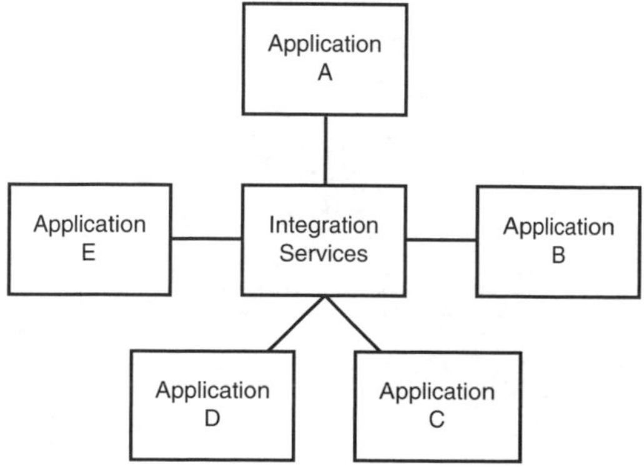

FIGURE 1.3 Simplifying the integration problem with "centralized" integration services.

This topology places a requirement on the integration services to be able to receive messages from a source application and deliver them to multiple target applications. This functionality is often called *message routing,* which has a number of potential implement patterns. The simplest is to create a rule specifying that when a message is received from application A, it be delivered to applications B and C. The challenge with this simplistic routing approach is that it is tied to the applications themselves, and when the applications change, the rules must also be modified.

Another approach provides an abstraction layer, isolating the rules from the individual applications. To illustrate this, let's return to our example. Application A sends purchase orders, and applications B and C receive purchase orders. The abstract definition of business called a purchase order is shared metadata between these three applications, and this information, rather than the application names, can be used for routing. The purchase-order metadata is more resilient to change than the application name. If application D replaces application A, as long as application D is sending purchase orders to the integration services, they will be automatically picked up by applications B and C with no additional changes.

The behavior of routing messages based on metadata properties is called *publish and subscribe.* Application A publishes a purchase order, which is described by the purchase order metadata, and applications B and C subscribe to the messages conforming to the purchase order metadata. The subscription rules may be as simple as we have described, where all messages conforming to a particular metadata are retrieved by a subscription but a more complex subscription is often required. For example, application E processes all purchase orders from trading partner F with a total value greater than $5,000. In this scenario, the rule is composed by the combination of the metadata of the message, a purchase order, and a specific data element inside the message, the total value. The basic publish and subscribe process is illustrated in Figure 1.4:

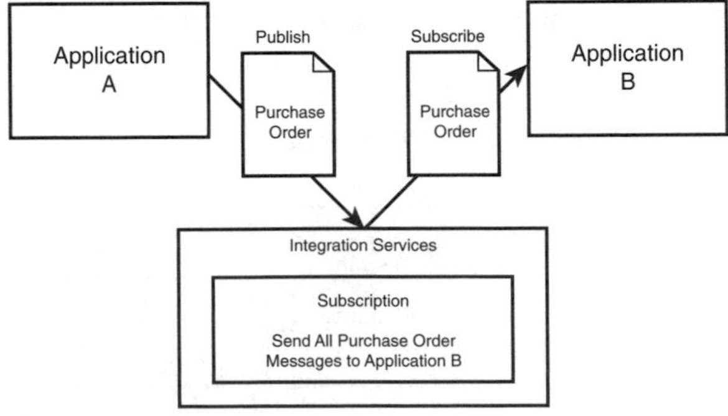

FIGURE 1.4 Publish and subscribe.

In this model, when a single connection point to the central services is added, removed, or replaced, there is potentially no additional effect on any of the other remaining applications.

How do applications connect to the integration services? This code is called an adapter. *Adapters* manage communication between the integration services and the application, sending and receiving messages over a particular transport.

The integration architecture we have defined thus far fits very nicely into the generic service-oriented architecture model. The four canonical tenets of service-oriented architecture and how they map to our integration architecture are described in the following list:

- Boundaries are explicit—Each application in our architecture explicitly has a boundary around it.
- Services are autonomous—Each of the applications connecting to the integration infrastructure performs a specific function in its own right. Indeed, each application is completely independent of other applications as a result of the publish and subscribe methodology described earlier.
- Share schema and contract, not implementation—In the architecture, we have defined messages, or schema, which are shared between applications and hide internal implementation issues.
- Service compatibility is based on policy. The integration services use policies such as publish and subscribe rules to route between services and metadata to describe expected message formats. Compatibility of services is greatly assisted by abstracting away the transport, message, and security requirements with the integration services.

As a result of the architecture we have described, each of these applications interact with the integration services in a manner that is similar to the "plug and play" technology in the device world.

Additional requirements exist for a truly manageable service-oriented architecture; such visibility into the messages passed between the applications. This visibility is important to handle exceptions that may occur on any particular connection and provide aggregate analysis across multiple connections. The integration approach described thus far enables these requirements because all messages passing through a centralized set of integration services can save the messages for later analysis and troubleshooting. This set of services is often called the *tracking services*.

Now that we have described some of the key functional services such as message, transport, and publish and subscribe, let's examine the physical layout of integration services. Integration services need not be a single, at the center of a business, although this is one potential design pattern. In the network device world, subnets manage their own internal packets and pass packets on to external parts of the network. Similarly, integration services can be instantiated at a departmental or regional office level to manage departmental integration, and these departmental integration services may interact with each other or with a centralized environment, as shown in Figure 1.5.

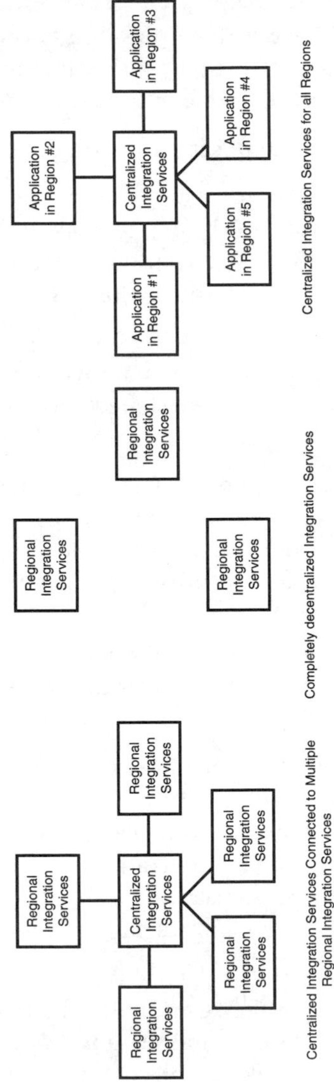

FIGURE 1.5 Potential integration services physical layouts.

Now that we have discussed some of the key integration services, including adapters, routing, mapping, and tracking, and briefly touched on centralized versus departmental or regional deployments, let's explain in more detail how these services can be packaged and deployed on physical hardware. There are two stereotypical approaches for instantiating integration services on hardware. The first is called *hub and spoke*, and the second is described as *message bus*.

The Hub and Spoke Model

Hub and spoke integration services got their name because architecturally they are centralized processing machinery, the hub, that accept requests from multiple applications, the spokes. Applications interact with the hub through adapters deployed on the hub, and as such, hub and spoke does not require any modification to the existing applications and supports a wide variety of transports. The hub manages routing, mapping, and tracking of messages between applications. A typical hub and spoke deployment is depicted in Figure 1.6, with a single hub machine managing connections across multiple spokes.

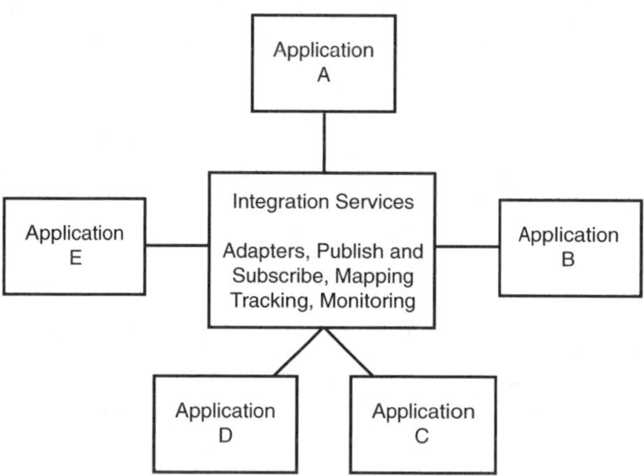

FIGURE 1.6 Hub and spoke model.

Although the hub and spoke model provides strong total cost of ownership by reducing the cost to add and remove connections and through centralized management, the hub and spoke model is not without challenges. In particular, hub and spoke models historically predicated a single hub machine, and so scalability was limited to the scalability of the central machine resource. Likewise, the central machine was a single point of failure. To avoid these issues, multiple implementations of hub and spoke were often tied together. Sometimes this was appropriate, such as when independently managed and connected to global hubs. On other occasions, what was required was more scale and reliability at the central hub, and this proved to be more problematic.

The Message Bus Model

On the other hand, the message bus model got its name because it consisted of a network of message-processing functionality interlinked through a common bus-specific protocol. Although message buses still reduce connections between applications to a linear factor, message bus architectures provided high-throughput multicast capabilities utilizing an ethernet-based network of nodes, as shown in Figure 1.7.

However, a message bus is not without a different set of issues and complexities. For example, the network is composed with multiple nodes, and management of these nodes is more complex. Routing between the nodes in the network typically employs a proprietary bus protocol and format so that customers are restricted to a homogeneous integration technology across the whole bus. Further routing on the bus is typically implemented by sending packets out to each of the nodes over the ethernet. This ethernet routing mechanism uses considerable bandwidth and causes a security risk on the bus; every node had access to the other messages in routing, and eventually the network becomes overloaded. This issue can be addressed by applying a layered security protocol, which increases complexity. Likewise, transmissions on ethernet are not reliable without the addition of a layered reliability protocol on top of the message packets.

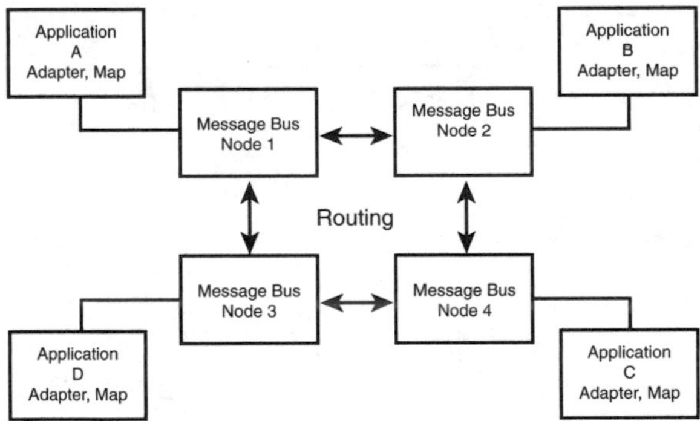

FIGURE 1.7 Message bus model.

The per-application integration costs for message bus are greater than hub and spoke because each application that talks to the message bus needs to adapt data from its own format to the proprietary bus format and transport. This leads to a considerable expense in adding additional applications because transformation logic must be applied locally at each application node, rather than being centralized as adapters, as described in the hub and spoke architecture.

Indeed, the integration services offered by the bus were limited by its decentralization across multiple processing nodes. Even logging or monitoring information across the bus created considerable challenges because it typically involved either broadcasting logging packets to centralized logging machinery, which further clogged bandwidth, or browsing individual log files across multiple nodes.

Message bus design patterns have not been commonly used for application integration. Edge-case scenarios of high value, such as stock-market ticker applications technically do not require the message bus architecture. They provide simultaneous multicast capabilities and throughput, require the message bus architecture, and are not well suited to typical integration scenarios for the reasons detailed above.

Given that neither hub and spoke nor message bus provide the 100% solution, an ideal solution is a combination of the two technologies. That solution provides hub-and-spokelike management, with the scale-out and performance of a message bus. This architecture will be described in more detail in the section titled "BizTalk Server 2004 Hub-bus Hybrid Model."

Interestingly, the set of integration services and the architecture applicable for internal integration are equally useful for external integration to trading partners. However, some key issues must be more fully evaluated when undertaking an external integration effort.

Trading partner integration is typically through the Internet or a VAN, so a subset of transports (FTP, HTTP, HTTP/S, Web services, and SMTP) that cross firewalls and span across platforms are most suitable. Similarly, EDI and XML are more predominately used in trading partner scenarios because of their ubiquity across platforms.

When connecting to trading partners, businesses often have little capability to demand that a message should conform to a specific format or demand a specific transport for each trading partner connection. Businesses need to provide flexibility to their trading partners so that the integration technology doesn't block the success of the trading relationship. Having a single message format and transport for all trading partners, although theoretically interesting, is practically not possible. Even the largest companies in the world often can't force all their trading partners to deliver messages that conform to a specific format. However, they are successful if they demand connectivity and provide options for the format that is used to describe the messages and the transports they are delivered on. It is the integration services that manage this complexity and normalize the messages for internal use. These large-scale environments managing multiple trading partners place additional management and architectural requirements on the integration services.

In concluding our discussion of second-tier integration services, note that security both at the transport and the message layer becomes more important in a trading partner scenario because messages are commonly sent across the Internet.

Integration Architecture Tier 3: Business Process

Now let's address the third level of complexity within an integration architecture by taking a step back from the details and examining the bigger picture. From a business perspective, integration is about taking applications, trading partners—and possibly people—and applying them to solve an important business initiative. This initiative is often expressed in terms of optimizing a particular business process, such as the need to reduce the time it takes to process a customer's order for merchandise and ship it. A business process typically involves a sequence of steps that integrates messages across applications, trading partners, and people, as shown in Figure 1.8.

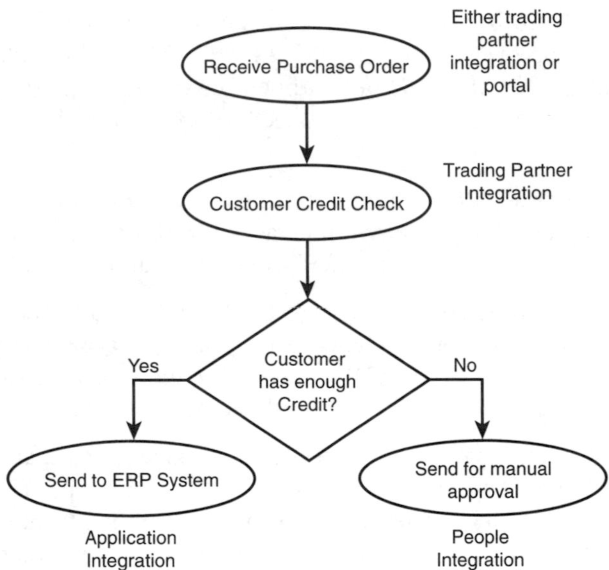

FIGURE 1.8 A simple business process.

Historically, these processes have been represented in functional specifications, but they have not been represented as distinct entities in the resulting software. Rather, most engineering efforts intermingle the business process logic with the code for business objects. Although the integration architecture we have described thus far provides a significant set of useful services, it has no notion of integration over time. Publish and subscribe is about integration at a point in time, yet a *business process* is about multiple interactions among applications, trading partners, and people. Although formally representing a business process as part of an integration architecture does help the business user understand the process better, as a developer don't be fooled into thinking that this is a tax you pay to keep the business user happy. Many deep technical aspects of integration are also solved by business process technology, as we will describe next.

At the heart of business process management is *state* management. State is commonly shared by entities within a business process. For example, a purchase order is received and then sent to the ERP system, and several steps later, information on that purchase order is used to determine the shipping address. The issue is how you manage the state of the purchase order throughout the life cycle of the process so that it is available to future steps in the process. One inelegant approach is to modify all the messages passing between the business objects to carry the state through the system. This approach is impractical in most cases because it requires modification of not just the messages themselves but the business objects that consume them. A more practical approach is to recognize that business process services should provide a "centralized" state container that business objects within a particular process can use to either update state based on their actions, such as adding purchase order information into the state container, or receive information, such as receiving a purchase order.

A key challenge with managing state is the duration of business processes. Business processes are often long lived, and managing state for a significant period of time generates a number of technical challenges, such as how to scale a stateful system and manage resources such as memory. Leaving state in memory in the form of objects for extended periods simply doesn't scale, and a core requirement for integration services is to manage this state in a scaleable manner. This can be achieved by persisting the state when the business process flow is blocked—for instance, when it is awaiting the arrival of a message. When that message is received, the state can be retrieved from the persistence container. This approach also relies on an appropriately scalable persistence store.

Other important issues exist that an architecture including business process must take into consideration. After a few business processes have been triggered and are persisted, what happens when a message arrives for a particular instance of a business process? How does it know to which existing business process instance it should deliver the message? This is the notion of message *correlation*. A number of techniques can solve this problem:

- One method is to stamp the outgoing message with a unique identifier and then match on that unique identifier. The challenge with this approach is that it pollutes messages with unnecessary technical information from the business perspective.
- Another more elegant approach associates the message with a unique business process instance, through an existing field on the message, such as a purchase order number of a purchase order message. The integration services persists both the business instance and the unique information from the message and uses it to correlate messages back to the process.

Figure 1.9 demonstrates business-process state management and correlation techniques.

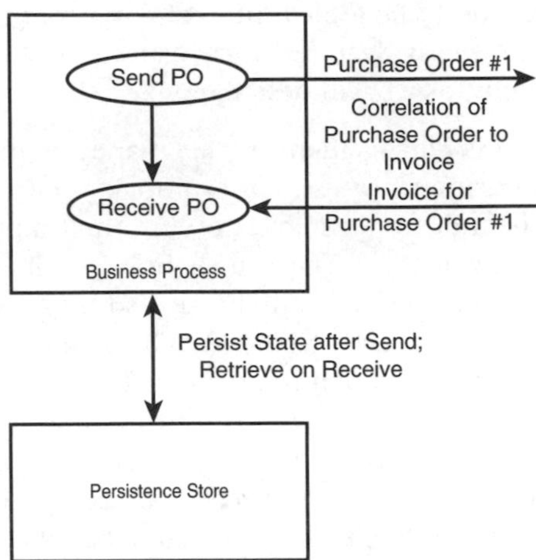

FIGURE 1.9 State management in a business process.

Business processes shouldn't replace business objects themselves; rather, they should maintain the state, and in doing so, manage the transitions between the steps of the business process at a macro level. For example, a business process for procurement defines the need to receive a purchase order, call a business object, application, or service that determines whether the customer has credit, and then, on the basis of the result, make a decision about which path in the business process to take. The specifics of the credit-card business logic are stored in a business object.

State management is a core architectural runtime requirement for business process, whereas a graphical representation is important because it makes the business process easier to understand, modify, and manage. A graphical representation of the business process provides a consistent design-time context for communication between business people and developers and also makes it easier for new developers to understand the "big picture." Further, this graphical representation can be used at runtime or for debugging to rapidly troubleshoot a particular step in the process that has failed. After a business process is codified, it effectively becomes a manageable unit within the system.

Closely related to state management is transaction management. Traditional component-oriented transaction management uses resource controllers (such as MSDTC) to provide data isolation within a transaction, such as updating two databases. These transactional semantics are still appropriate for business processes, but additional requirements exist because of the long-running nature of the business processes.

For example, a purchase order is sent to a trading partner and the trading partner has 27 days to respond with a payment. This is a transaction that either completes because an invoice is received, or aborts and fails after 27 days. A component-oriented transaction is inappropriate because the message was sent out to a trading partner over a nontransactional transport such as email. Even if that data was local, there is no guarantee that both systems support a transaction dispenser model. Even if they did, this type of solution would not scale, because the transaction would potentially lock thousands of rows in the database for a long duration, 27 days. When this transaction aborts, a corrective course of action isn't a rollback because it isn't possible to transactionally cancel an email sent 27 days earlier. Rather, it is another set of steps, such as sending a second escalation mail to the customer and one to an internal clerical worker to pursue the matter. This set of steps, or mini business process, that may be executed when a long-running transaction is aborted is called a *compensation block*. Business process services should manage both short-running transactions and long-running transactions, including the capability to nest transactions within larger transactions, as shown in Figure 1.10.

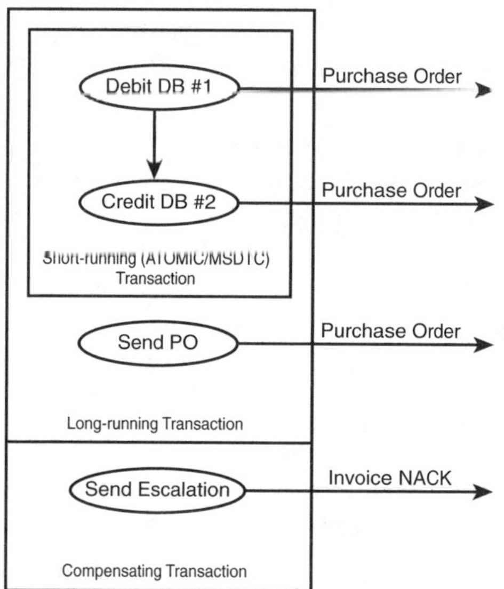

FIGURE 1.10 Short- and long-running transactions within a business process.

Another potential benefit from codifying business processes is that tracking infrastructure can be layered on top of a business process to collect relevant business data, such as how long it takes for my overall procurement business process, or a step inside it such as shipping, or how many invoices are not yet paid, or the total dollar amount of the purchases this month, all directly from the business process. Technically, this information can be obtained by placing tracking markers inside the business process. These tracking points record information specific to the data moving inside the business process or the process itself. This data can then be analyzed on a per instance or an aggregated view to answer interesting business questions. This business process service is often called *business activity monitoring*.

Security is an ubiquitous concept that should be applied to all elements of a software stack, and business process is no exception. One important security requirement in a business process context is to authenticate a message entering a business process for a known set of credentials to ensure that only trusted systems or partners can access the business process. Another is giving business processes different levels of execution privilege, depending on the resources they require.

The examples we have described thus far have been focused on interapplication integration; however, in a service-oriented architecture, applications themselves may be composed of services. Each of those services may be distributed across the network, and the need to visualize the interactions between these services as part of a codified business process becomes even more important.

Business processes often include human interaction, and although the goal of optimizing a particular business process is often to reduce the involvement of people and to increase automation across trading partners and applications, this is not always the right solution. For example, even in a highly automated procurement scenario, a manager may be required to approve a purchase order over a set limit, or potentially override a low-credit warning to allow a customer order. Integration services should allow people to be part of the business process. In some ways, integrating people into the process is similar to integrating applications, except that a message is delivered to a portal, an email inbox, or some other user interface where a person can make a decision and return the message back into the business process. In some cases, additional requirements exist for integrating people, such as the need to send a message to a group of people and manage a rather unstructured workflow between the individuals.

By codifying the notion of a business process, there are significant benefits in ease of management, modification, tracking, and troubleshooting, as well as business-level visibility. The third layer of integration provides business process services. With this in mind, we close our discussion on the third tier of integration services and explore the fourth tier—namely, business rules.

Integration Architecture Tier 4: Business Rules

As more people began codifying business processes in their integration architectures, it became apparent that an additional layer of abstraction was required. The business process flow—that is, the sequence between the steps—absolutely changes over time. However, the rules inside process decisions also change, and they sometimes change more frequently than the process itself. For example, in a particular business process, gold-card customers are determined by a formula based on the total value of purchases that have been made in the past 12 months. Subsequently, the business decides to create additional criteria, examining not only the total value, but also the number of individual purchases, and changes the gold-card discount from 15% to 10%. This change does not affect the flow of the business process. Rather, it affects decisions, specifically whether this customer is a gold-card customer and what discount should be applied, inside the flow.

Traditionally, the rules syntax was hard-coded into business objects, or more recently, into the process. Neither of these are particularly suitable choices. Rules implicitly hard-coded into business objects are both hard to discover and require recompilation and versioning of the business objects for every modification. Rules embedded inside a process are somewhat more discoverable, but why should a process be recompiled when the process flow itself doesn't change? An integration architecture should have a rules service that integrates with both the business objects and the business process. Figure 1.11 shows a business process with a step to execute a generic rule. That rule can be independently modified without modification of the business process or business objects.

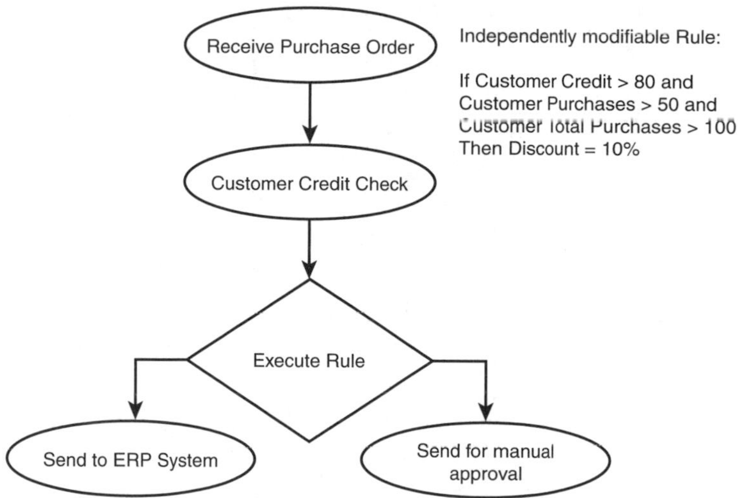

FIGURE 1.11 Business rules.

In this section, we have described requirements for an architecture that provides multi-tiered integration services, as shown in Figure 1.12. Although it is possible to use these tiers independently, the most value is obtained when they are used together.

At this point, you probably realize that the requirements for integration are complex, and an implementation of this architecture with a toolset that reduces development complexity will be beneficial. Microsoft's packaged set of integration services is delivered in the BizTalk Server product, and the purpose of the remaining sections in this chapter is to introduce you to BizTalk Server 2004.

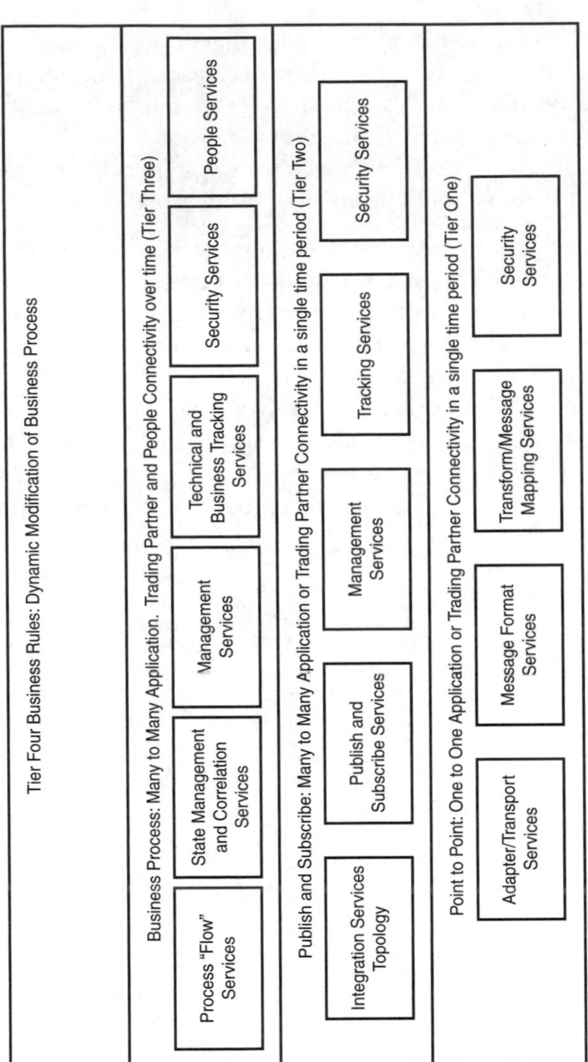

FIGURE 1.12 Multitier integration services architecture.

Feature Overview of BizTalk Server 2004

BizTalk Server 2004 is the third-generation integration product from Microsoft. In this section, you will learn how BizTalk Server implements the integration services architecture described earlier in the chapter, and along the way we will briefly examine the product feature set with a particular emphasis on new features in BizTalk Server 2004.

BizTalk Server 2004 is a significant release that includes key innovations in the architecture of the product, the developer toolset, business process management, and the capabilities it provides business users.

BizTalk Server 2004 has a completely reengineered architecture built on top of the .NET Framework. In fact, BizTalk Server 2004 is currently the largest server application shipping from Microsoft built on the .NET Framework. The managed code base is no less than 1.6 million lines of C#. As a result of these investments, business processes now execute five times faster than previous versions of the product, and security is improved. BizTalk Server's physical deployment topology has been centralized on SQL Server 2000 and tweaked to handle extreme scale-out and message-throughput scenarios.

The BizTalk Server 2004 developer toolset is deeply integrated inside Visual Studio .NET, providing seamless integration with your favorite toolset, including the notion of a BizTalk Server project with integrated designers for message schema, maps, business processes, called *orchestrations*, and the like. The Visual Studio .NET integration offers full support for IntelliSense and source-code control.

Management of business processes has also been reexamined with BizTalk Server 2004. New features include end-to-end tracking of business processes through a Health and Activity Tracking tool, a simplified deployment methodology based on .NET assemblies and XML manifests, and more centralized management of scale-out scenarios.

The business user, commonly left out in integration architectures, is a new area of emphasis with BizTalk Server 2004. BizTalk Server 2004 provides an entire gamut of tools for business process life cycle support, including business process design through the Visio modeling surface, participation in business processes through form-based experiences in InfoPath and collaboration with SharePoint, and business process analysis through business activity monitoring inside Excel.

The following sections will provide you with a basic level of understanding of these features, and the remainder of this book will progressively go into more depth in each of the individual areas.

BizTalk Server 2004 Architecture and Topology Improvements

BizTalk Server is designed to be an intermediary between applications. Thus, it avoids the point-to-point spaghetti issue described earlier so that the services in the first two tiers can be thought of jointly as messaging services. BizTalk Server provides services across all four tiers of the integration architecture in a single consistent manner that is suitable for both internal and external integration, including business process and rules as shown in Figure 1.13.

First, let's address the services in tier one and two of the integration architecture, focusing on messaging-based integration.

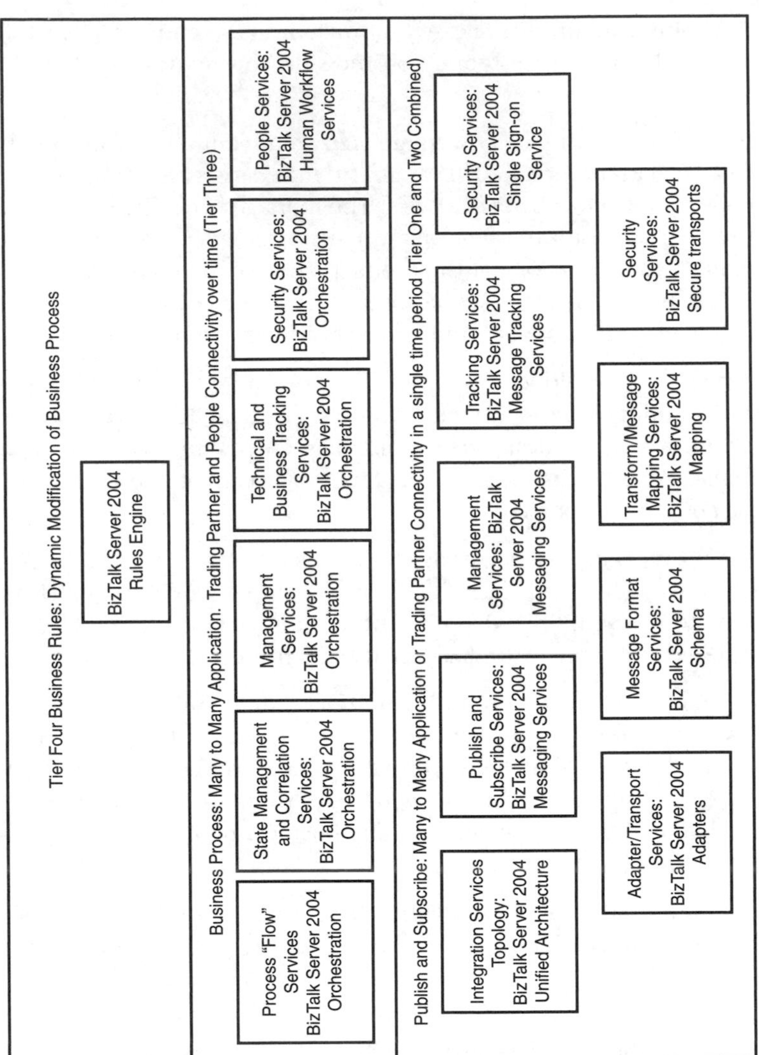

FIGURE 1.13 BizTalk Server as an integration services architecture.

BizTalk Server 2004 ships with a set of adapters to manage transport normalization, including Web services, FTP, HTTP/S, MSMQT, SQL, , EDI, SMTP, File adapters on the product CD-ROM, and Web downloads for MQSeries, traditional MSMQ, and WSE 2.0 (WS-Security and WS-Policy support) adapters.

Additional adapters, such as an adapter to send and retrieve information to and from SharePoint document libraries and a direct submission adapter enabling input of documents through .NET code, are available as samples on the CD-ROM or as Web downloads.

Microsoft also sells an adapter that connects to SAP, using the SAP-specific IDOC and BAPI formats. A large set of additional adapters are available for the majority of ERP, CRM, standard line of business applications, and other technologies such as Java through partners including certified adapter vendors such as IWay.

Even with an extensive adapter library, businesses that have invested in creating their own proprietary applications may need to create their own adapters to those applications. BizTalk Server 2004 ships with an advanced adapter framework that enables development, configuration, and management of all adapters in a consistent manner. The adapter framework gives customers the same set of interfaces that Microsoft uses internally, providing high-performance adapters. These adapters can interact with applications in simple patterns, such as sending or receiving a message, as well as more complex patterns, such as request/response or solicit/response.

After a message is received through an adapter, it is often passed into a serial set of stateless business logic components, known as a *receive pipeline*, that performs a set of user-defined message manipulations such as decryption of a S/MIME encoded message, parsing, and validation of the message. Developers can create their own pipeline components using the BizTalk Server SDK to perform any custom business logic, such as modification of the message, support for compression methods such as unzipping, and so on.

A key step inside the receive pipeline is *parsing*. Parsing takes the incoming message regardless of format and creates an XML representation. Parsing is completed by executing business logic against the message with the assistance of a user-defined schema that describes its metadata. Important *properties* from the document are retrieved and stored separately from the message in a property bag called the *message context*. The schema for an XML message is simply an XML schema with additional BizTalk Server specific annotations describing important information in the schema, useful for populating the message context. The schema for a flat-file message also includes annotations describing key flat-file properties, such as the layout of information within the flat file, using delimiters, positional separators, or a combination of these two methods. The parsing, also known as *disassembling*, step is important because it allows any input or output data format to be received by BizTalk Server but normalizes all these data to XML, which means all operations performed within BizTalk Server are XML based. BizTalk Server provides parsers for XML, flat files, and EDI as part of the product, and Microsoft ships parsers for HL7, HIPPA, SWIFT, and RosettaNet messages as part of add-ons called accelerators. Like most of the components of the product, additional parsers, although often not particularly simple to write, can be written using the BizTalk Server SDK that is included with the product.

As messages are parsed and passed through the receive pipeline, they are streamed rather than being read in memory all at once, which enables support for a significant new feature in BizTalk Server 2004—very large messages. Most larger messages are actually collections of smaller messages, and using a technology called enveloping, the BizTalk Server parsers can effectively break apart these large messages into the smaller messages.

After transport and data format normalization, the message may then be passed into a mapping component. The BizTalk Server mapping infrastructure is built on XSLT. Mapping provides a methodology to normalize different message schemas that may have been sourced for different transports or indeed different data formats, and as such, it gives users the flexibility to provide for many input message options and yet have a single internal representation of a particular message for a particular business function, if required. The mapping technology in BizTalk Server 2004 has been enhanced with support for calling .NET Framework-based functions within maps.

After mapping is complete, the message is always persisted into a set of SQL database tables, called the MessageBox, to ensure transactional reliability of the system, to guarantee no message loss inside the BizTalk Server itself, and because this is a useful way of building a scalable architecture. Information such as properties on the adapter used to receive the message and any information promoted into the message context itself as part of parsing are also persisted to the MessageBox. This persistence step is often called *publishing* of the message because it is the first step in using the new publish and subscribe architecture built in to BizTalk Server 2004. When a message is published into BizTalk Server, the published message context properties are compared against a list of preconfigured subscriptions, typically set through the tools we will describe later, that will fire when a message with the matching details in its context is published into the system. This generic publish and subscribe mechanism provides a flexible integration architecture with the capability to subscribe to one message by one or multiple target applications and plug and play-end end-points with the minimum changes to the overall ecosystem in a manner described earlier in this chapter.

BizTalk Server 2004's architecture is relatively symmetrical in the sense that the operations performed for a message receive and a message send are similar, albeit in the reverse order of execution. After a subscription is fired, the user-defined send-side logic is executed (including a send pipeline that performs stateless business logic steps, such as transforming the message meta-data format required by the target application or technology using a second map). The message is then serialized into a target message format or encrypted using S/MIME; finally, the message is delivered to the target application using a send adapter.

As the message passes through the system, BizTalk Server can track the whole message at several steps in the process, as well as track specific pieces of the message that may be important. The complete message flow from the point of entry, a receive adapter, to the final send adapter function is persisted into a separate set of SQL Server tracking tables for viewing with the provided tool or a custom-built tracking tool.

Single-sign-on security services are a new feature of the BizTalk Server 2004 messaging layer. Often it is useful to restrict access to information on the basis of a set of user credentials. The challenge is transferring those credentials between applications of different technology bases. Single sign on allows authenticated credentials to be passed or mapped between two target applications. For example, a user on a portal application submits a message to BizTalk Server 2004 as user: Redmond\scottwoo and password: password. This user is then mapped to the correct credentials on the SAP system subscribing to the message, in this case user: scott and password: SAP. The BizTalk Server 2004 single-sign-on technology is designed to work with custom authentication schemes that are implemented in adapters and stores the mapped credentials in a securely encrypted database. Indeed, regardless of whether the user is taking advantage of this functionality, BizTalk Server 2004 uses single sign on internally to encrypt sensitive information, such as the URIs of target applications configured using its user interface.

Before we describe the physical architecture, how these logical services map to hardware, let's examine the services provided in the business process layer. A new feature of BizTalk Server 2004 is a single consistent architecture for both business process and messaging services, and a singular treatment of the physical architecture is appropriate.

The business process, or orchestration, technology in BizTalk Server 2004 is a radical improvement on previous versions in terms of both features, performance, and scale. The BizTalk Server 2004 business process engine includes many flow control capabilities such as sequence, parallels, loops, and event handlers that model the flow of the business process. In addition, business processes can both call and be called from other business processes, enabling business process encapsulation and reuse. Layered on the flow control is a transaction and exception component that provides for both short-running and long-running nested transactions and exception handling. In addition, BizTalk Server provides complete correlation functionality with the set of services described in the earlier section. Given that business processes may "run" on the BizTalk Server infrastructure for anywhere between a few seconds and numerous months, BizTalk Server 2004 provides a fully scalable business-process architecture. BizTalk Server derives much of its scalability from the capability to persist business processes that are currently idle or waiting for messages into SQL Server; it then retrieves them when appropriate. The publish and subscribe engine in BizTalk Server 2004 is not limited to messaging functionality. Business processes are started, or continued, using the subscription mechanism described earlier. A message is published to the MessageBox and a business process subscribes to this message and thus begins executing or continues from its last persisted state.

One interesting new feature in BizTalk Server 2004 that we haven't discussed in much detail is the notion of *role links* and *parties* within business processes. To understand why these are important, let's think of a simple trading partner scenario. A buyer wants to trade with 20 sellers in a procurement process. Previous implementations of this requirement would require 20 different business processes, one for each seller. However, the reality is that in this case, each seller is involved in exactly the same business process except for some parameters. Specifically, the message formats, transports, and so on are modified. Using the notion of role links, a business process can be abstracted from a specific implementation by labeling a set of input and output operations constituting the buyer role or belonging to the seller. Then at deployment time, this generic business process can be specialized, enlisting a particular buyer or a particular seller and configuring the inputs they require. For example, seller #1 will send a PO as a flat file using

HTTP/S, and seller #2 will send a PO as an XML file using a Web service. The addition of new participants, called parties, does not require an additional business process, merely configuration of the existing business process, and so the cost of maintenance of this mechanism is much lower than previous approaches.

Just as for the message-based services, orchestration persists tracking information into a SQL Server database. System administrators and developers can use this information to obtain end-to-end visibility into running business processes, including the capability to inspect variables and set breakpoints. Although technical tracking of the running business process is useful, business-level tracking of information is also possible using the new business activity monitoring (BAM) infrastructure. This will be described in more detail in the section "Plugging In the Business User."

An additional layer on top of the business process engine supports human-based ad hoc interactions. This new API layer is called *human workflow services*.

BizTalk Server provides support for standards wherever possible. In addition to those already mentioned, such as XML, W3C XML Schema, and XSLT, BizTalk Server 2004 has excellent support for Web services using SOAP and WSDL. Indeed, just as the messaging engine translates all messages into XML, the business process engine exposes input and output as WSDL ports and messages, regardless of whether the source or target application actually uses Web services. This provides a simple paradigm to manage many complex interactions. Business processes can consume multiple Web services and manage the interactions between them. Conversely, business processes can be exposed as Web services, enabling clients on any platform to submit messages to them. In addition, support is available for WS-Security and WS-Policy features through the WSE 2.0 adapter.

BizTalk Server 2004 provides support for an upcoming Web services business process interoperability standard called *business process execution language (BPEL)*. BPEL is most useful for business process interoperability across platform boundaries in the same way as WSDL provides business operation interoperability across platform boundaries. In a similar manner as WSDL, BizTalk Server supports import and export of BPEL as part of its design. One difference is that BPEL is a least–common-denominator standard, and as such, business process modeled in BPEL is most appropriately the public business process shared by two parties rather than the private implementation. The BPEL committee at Oasis is currently finalizing the standard, and BPEL will no doubt play a significant role in the future of these types of technologies given its broad industry support.

The final tier in our architecture is business rules. BizTalk Server 2004 includes a brand-new business-rules engine, coded entirely in C#, hostable within a business process or your custom server application.

The rules engine provides rapid in-memory business rules evaluation and can be used for both abstraction of simple business rules, as an expression evaluator, and as a fully fledged forward-inferencing rules engine.

The logical architecture we have described thus far is illustrated in Figure 1.14.

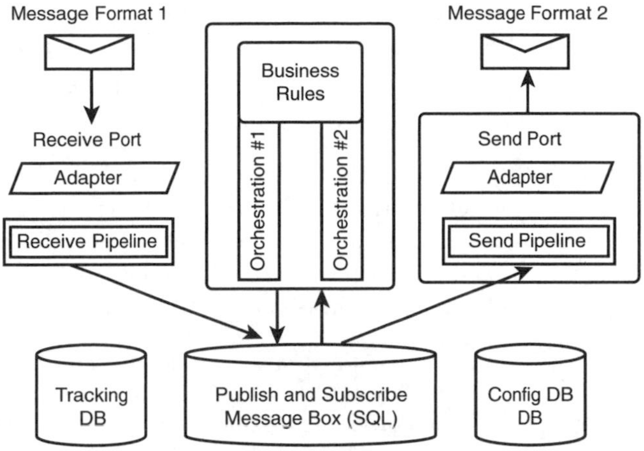

FIGURE 1.14 BizTalk Server logical architecture.

Now that we have briefly addressed logical architecture in the integration tiers, let's examine the physical architecture.

BizTalk Server 2004 Hub-bus Hybrid Model

The new BizTalk Server 2004 topology goes beyond traditional integration paradigms of hub and spoke and message bus described earlier. BizTalk Server provides a hybrid architecture that takes advantage of key aspects of both models, namely scale-out for throughput and centralized management. The key is that although BizTalk Server 2004 includes hublike properties such as adapters, transformation, tracking, and centralized management, its internal architecture is buslike. Innovations in this architecture revolve around the concepts of a MessageBox, used for state persistence, and the host, where actual execution occurs.

The MessageBox is a set of one or more distributed SQL Server databases that provide all the state services required for integration. The MessageBox hides the complexity of its potentially distributed nature by appearing as a single "virtual" MessageBox at the user level, making scale-out a trivial effort. Adding an additional MessageBox requires only an additional SQL Server database and registration with the integration services. The integration services will take advantage of this functionality immediately without any change to the applications. Configuration information for all the SQL Server databases is stored in a centralized master MessageBox database, which simplifies system management.

The MessageBox acts in a somewhat similar manner to the ethernet component of the message bus model described in the previous section. In a message bus, messages are sent into the ethernet, which routes them to one or more endpoints. In the MessageBox model, messages are delivered to the MessageBox, which routes them to one or more endpoints. Using the physical storage of SQL Server rather than ethernet to persist and manage this state results in a transactional, never lose a message system. By adding clustering to the SQL databases, the MessageBox has no single point of failure.

Now that we have addressed the state persistence provided by the MessageBox layer, let's examine the host and host instance notions that are used for the machines actually processing messages.

The host and host instance model are used for the processing nodes, or machines. A host is an *abstract* container for processing resources—effectively a collection of integration services. For example, an abstract host may contain transport services such as an HTTP adapter, a receive pipeline, and a business process that expects a message over HTTP and sends it to SAP.

Host instances are the physical incarnation of hosts, meaning the actual HTTP adapter, receive pipeline, and business process physically deployed on a particular machine as a Windows service.

Why the abstraction? Two or more machines in a physical topology may run the same set of processing resources for fault tolerance or scale-out. With the host model, a single host is defined and managed, yet instances of that host are seamlessly deployed to multiple nodes in the network. Depending on the scenario, customers can create networks of receive host instances, processing host instances, and send host instances within the larger "hub bus." Key to the host and host instance model is that the host instances do not persist state locally; instead, they use the MessageBox for this task. This means that should the power supply fail on any host instance, assuming there are two or more host instances of any host, another host instance will automatically pick up the workload and continue. This architecture provides strong resilience to failure conditions.

No explicit relationship exists between a particular MessageBox node and a particular host instance node at runtime. This means that MessageBox nodes can be added, and immediately any of the non-MessageBox nodes can take advantage of the functionality they provide without any configuration change on the Host Instance nodes. It also means that Host Instances can be added without adding additional SQL Server functionality.

Although this description might seem a little unclear, future chapters will drill into the details. However, this architecture effectively avoids flaws in ethernet-based bus topologies because intelligent self-adjusting load balancing and throttling are inherently part of the infrastructure. The host instances can adjust their interactions with the MessageBox in times of peak volume to avoid flooding issues, while providing the advantage of hub and spoke simplicity.

For development purposes, you will probably start with a single machine running one host instance, called the BizTalkServerApplication, and a single MessageBox database.

The various BizTalk Server artifacts are deployed inside .NET assemblies on one or more host instances. The product includes new support for multiple artifact versions, leveraging the .NET assembly versioning methodology, enabling either side-by-side scenarios or in-place upgrades.

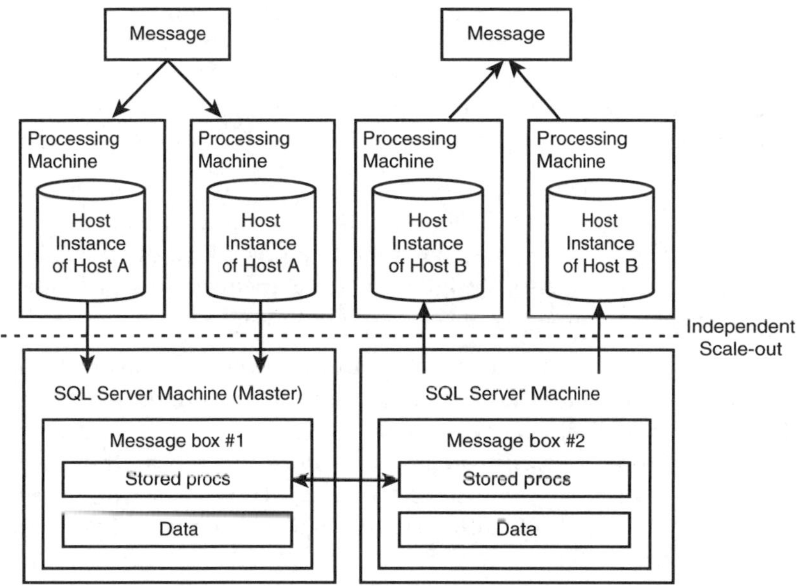

FIGURE 1.15 BizTalk Server physical architecture.

With that primer on the BizTalk Server architecture and topology improvements complete, let's move on to the development tools.

BizTalk Server 2004 Development Tools

To ease development, the BizTalk Server toolset is now deeply integrated into Visual Studio .NET with the key addition of a BizTalk Server project. Within a single Visual Studio .NET solution, developers can include C# projects, VB projects, and BizTalk Server projects. BizTalk Server projects can contain the following:

- Schema—The BizTalk Schema Editor plug-in models the message schema used by the parsers to load incoming messages and the serializers to save outgoing messages. The BizTalk Schema Editor is a graphical tool with a tree hierarchy for designing schema and property pages for setting attributes on the schema, such as the type of a node.
- Property schema—The BizTalk Property Schema Editor is an advanced editor used to create properties that publish and subscribe messages, especially for correlation. In many cases, the BizTalk Schema Editor can be used directly to create these properties.

- Maps—The BizTalk Mapper tool plug-in allows graphical creation of maps upon selection of a source and a target schema. The mapping tool provides an intermediate surface between the two schema where lines can be drawn to represent copying data between one message or another, or additional functions—such as converting data to uppercase—may be used. These additional functions are called *functoids* and BizTalk Server ships with many useful functoids in the Mapper toolbox, including a functoid to call a .NET assembly or inline .NET code and a functoid to roll your own XSLT as part of the map. You can add functoids to the toolbox using the SDK.
- Receive or send pipelines—The receive and send pipeline plug-ins design the set of steps executed by each of the pipeline infrastructures. Components shipped in the product, such as the XML parser, or written to a predefined interface can be dragged and dropped into the pipeline designer to create a sequential set of stateless business logic that executes on inbound and outbound messages.
- Orchestration—The BizTalk Orchestration Designer plug-in enables the design of business processes. The toolbox includes actions representing the sending and receiving of messages as well as branches, loops, decisions, and transformations. Also available is the capability to encapsulate business processes and call them synchronously or asynchronously from other business processes. The orchestration designer has its own view in Visual Studio where WSDL-based ports and messages can be defined and added to the surface.

The following chapters of the book will show you each of these tools in more detail, and the next chapter will walk you through a simple end-to-end example that uses many of the tools.

In addition to the standard BizTalk Server project, there are several other project types:

- BizTalk Server Migration Project—This enables migration of messaging-based applications from previous versions of BizTalk Server to BizTalk Server 2004.
- BPEL Import—This enables import of BPEL processes from other BPEL-compliant sources.
- BizTalk Server Human Workflow Project—This enables creation of Human Workflow Services (HWS) specific templates.

Additionally, several useful sample projects have been released since the product shipped, including an adapter project that includes a wizard to make the job of creating adapters simpler and a pipeline wizard to expedite pipeline component creation. Both are available for download from the Web and are referred to in `http://blogs.msdn.com/scottwoo`.

The project system's primary purpose is to create the design-time artifacts. When a project is built, all the artifacts are compiled into an assembly.

There is another new tool called the BizTalk Explorer. Whereas the project system is targeted at building assemblies containing artifacts to be used across one or more implementations, BizTalk Explorer provides the user with a means to configure the BizTalk Server runtime to use these artifacts.

The BizTalk Explorer is modeled on the Server Explorer, which ships in Visual Studio .NET and uses a list paradigm. The key nodes in the BizTalk Explorer are the following:

- The Assemblies node—This node lists all assemblies deployed, including their version.
- The Receive Port node—A *receive port* contains all the information BizTalk Server needs to receive a document and publish the document to the MessageBox. Specifically, the adapter used to receive, its properties, the pipeline used, and the maps used are configured on the receive port as well as the host. The schema required is often referenced in the pipeline, unless it is XML, in which case BizTalk Server uses the namespace conventions in XML to look up the correct schema automatically.
- The Send Port node—The *send port* is the complement of the receive port and contains the subscription configuration information. Specifically, it includes the send adapter to deliver the message on, the send pipeline to use, the maps to use to transform the data, if necessary, as well as the host.
- The Send Port Groups node—This node makes it possible to treat a collection of target endpoints as a single logical entity. A *send port group* contains multiple send ports and thus when the subscription for a send port group is fired, all send ports transmit the outbound message.
- The Parties node—This node configures the role-link information described earlier, linking it to one or more port nodes.

There are a couple of tools not inside Visual Studio .NET:

- The debugging functionality is included inside the Health and Activity Tracking tool because it is shared by the IT Professional.
- The Microsoft Business Rules Composer tool, which is used for designing the English-language-like rules executed by the rule engine is also not inside Visual Studio because it was originally targeted at the business analyst. Although this tool does not require coding skills, it is probably most suited for a developer skill set or an advanced technical business analyst. The rules engine API is extensible, and so simpler, but necessarily less generic, clients for the rules engine design can be written and provided to business analysts.

BizTalk Server 2004 Management Tools

Management tools are a critical integration service and immediately differentiate quality product from custom-coded solutions that typically are lacking in all aspects of management. BizTalk Server provides specific tools for scale-out server management, monitoring, and deployment, and there are samples available for impact analysis and documentation.

BizTalk Server 2004 provides a centralized Microsoft Management Console (MMC) to manage a single-box installation or a highly scaled-out installation topology. The MMC provides for the following:

- Adding new BizTalk Servers to a farm providing scale-out of the processing machines.
- Adding new SQL Server MessageBoxes providing scale-out of the database machines.
- Mapping hosts to create host instances across one or more physical machines for performance and reliability.
- Configuring adapters across one or more machines.
- Stopping and starting various artifacts, such as receive ports, send ports, and orchestrations.

BizTalk Server 2004 includes a new Health and Activity Tracking (HAT) tool. This tool provides for both real-time reporting and historical reporting, drawing its information from the tracking database. The HAT tool includes the capability to

- Examine all the running artifacts and trace their paths of execution end to end.
- Visualize orchestrations, save out tracked messages inside orchestrations, and set breakpoints.
- Create custom SQL queries over the tracking data.
- Set properties that determine what level of granularity will be used for the message-tracking system.
- Stopping and starting various artifacts such as receive ports, send ports, and orchestrations.
- Examine errors, such as suspended messages and orchestrations.

With the introduction of .NET assemblies as the unit of deployment, deployment has been simplified in BizTalk Server 2004. In addition to copying the assembly itself, the BizTalk Server 2004 Deployment Wizard provides the capability to retrieve configuration information and persist it in an XML manifest. This manifest can be edited for differences between environments, such as changing an HTTP location or a certificate. Then the manifest can be imported into the target environment. A similar methodology exists for transferring business rules written using the rules engine from one environment to the next.

Additional samples that have shipped after the product include

- The capability to use the SQL Reporting Services functionality that is part of the required SQL Server 2004 database to generate reports detailing which artifacts rely on which artifacts for impact analysis.
- An especially useful tool that creates a help file of a BizTalk Server installation providing for automatic documentation.

Both of these tools can be found on `http://blogs.msdn.com/scottwoo`.

Plugging in the Business User

Microsoft provides a set of tools based in Microsoft Office that empower the business user inside business processes. These tools span the business process life cycle from design of the process to participation in the running process and, finally, analysis of the process for further optimization. Figure 1.16 describes this life cycle.

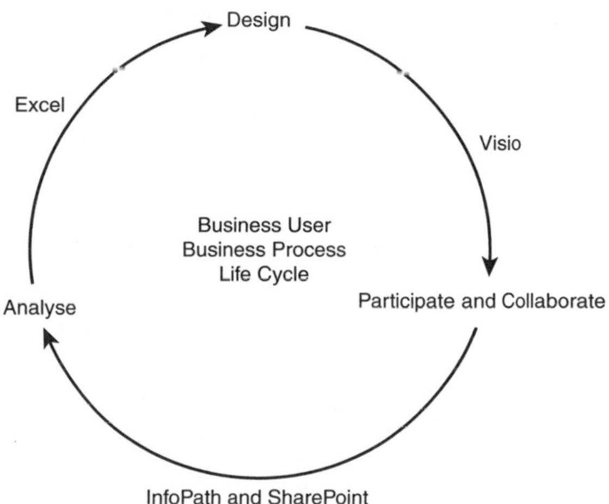

FIGURE 1.16 Business process design life cycle tools.

Business process design is often a collaborative process between a business analyst, with knowledge of the business itself, and a developer with the skills to implement this process in software. Previous versions of BizTalk Server provided a singular design tool inside Visio for the purpose of both documenting and implementing business process. The approach proved neither particularly satisfactory for the developer, who wanted a more technical surface, nor the business analyst who wanted a less technical surface. BizTalk Server 2004 addresses this issue by providing one surface for each role and import/export functionality between them. We have already described the developer experience; for the business analyst, BizTalk Server 2004 includes the Orchestration Designer for Business Analysts

(ODBA). This product is not on the product CD and does not require any of the BizTalk Server footprint to reside on the business analyst's desktop. The product can be downloaded from Microsoft Office Online (`http://office.microsoft.com/home/default.aspx`) and installed on a business analyst computer that has Visio 2002/3 available.

The ODBA provides a simple, nontechnical palette of shapes where business analysts can document process flow. This process flow can be exported from the Visio-based tool and delivered to the developer, who can import the rendition in the Visual Studio-based Orchestration Designer to continue implementing the business process. Although this tool is not designed to be a comprehensive business process modeling surface, it is useful for collaboration between developers and business users. The tool is shown in Figure 1.17.

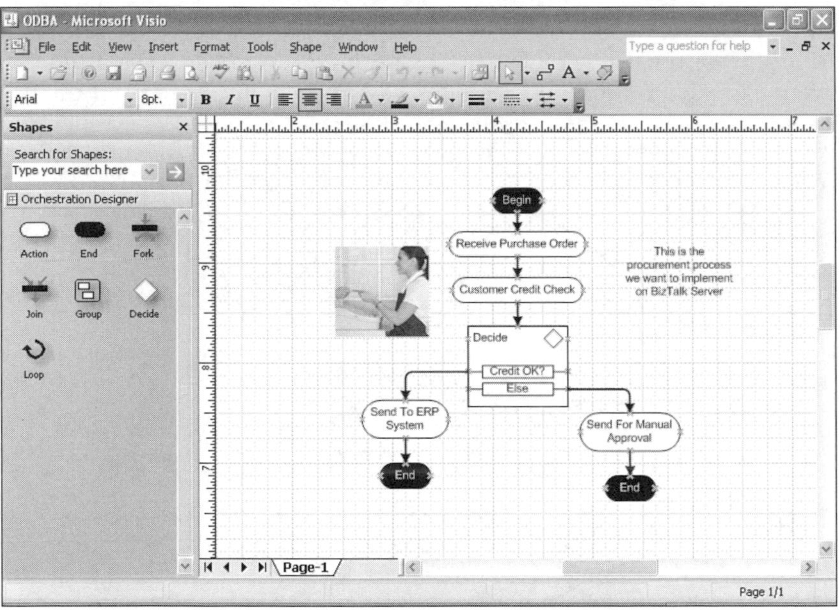

FIGURE 1.17 Orchestration Designer for Business Analysts (ODBA).

Participation of people in the business process is significantly enhanced in this version. BizTalk Server 2004 provides strong integration with the new form package shipping in Microsoft Office 2003 called InfoPath. With InfoPath, structured XML from BizTalk Server can be rendered for people to view and change before returning the XML to the process. Although InfoPath has strong support for both XML and Web services, these facets are insulated from the user, who is presented with a familiar Office interface. BizTalk Server 2004 continues support for sending email, but additional support for SharePoint is available in two forms:

- The SharePoint adapter—Available on the Web, InfoPath forms or other structured data can be uploaded into a SharePoint document library and that information, in turn, can be retrieved into BizTalk Server as part of a business process. Integration between SharePoint Web part technology and BizTalk Server also provides secure access to information stored in business processes through the portal user interface.

- Business Activity Services—A heavily modified Windows SharePoint services site provides a trading partner management facility, including the capability to create a share agreement between trading partners, send and receive messages, and manage them through the SharePoint infrastructure.

After a business process is designed and has been running for some time, it is often useful to measure the effectiveness of the process. BizTalk Server 2004 provides a technology called Business Activity Monitoring (BAM) that enables real-time collection of process and data events. This information is incredibly useful for making business decisions. BizTalk Server 2004 provides a direct integration between BAM's information and Microsoft Excel. With Microsoft Excel, business users without knowledge of processes or integration technologies can view real-time or aggregated graphs, charts, and pivot tables that describe the behavior of a business process and can be used to further optimize the business process in a second iteration through the business process life cycle. BAM is complementary to an existing business intelligence strategy, especially one using SQL Server. This technology is enabled by setting tracking points in the business process and then persisting these business events in a SQL OLTP or OLAP database for analysis with tools such as Excel. Some sample real-time pivot tables and charts depicted in Excel are shown in Figure 1.18.

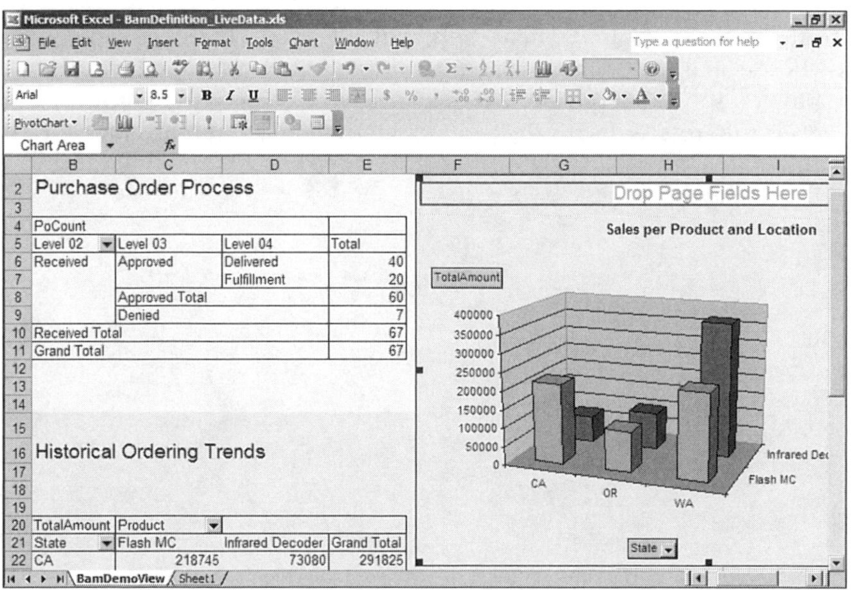

FIGURE 1.18 Business Activity Monitoring.

Summary

This chapter described the requirements for an integration architecture and the key services and tools provided in BizTalk Server 2004 for such an architecture.

The next chapter in this book will provide more insight into the runtime architecture of BizTalk Server and teach by example how to use the tools to build your first integration solution. The remaining chapters will then provide you with the deep technical drill-downs into the various parts of the BizTalk Server product.

Make sure you download the latest product updates. The help file has been substantially revised, several times, since the product was shipped and is an important download. Also available are additional SDK samples, the Orchestration Designer for Business Analysts, the MOM management pack, and the Adapter Migration Toolkit. You should also install the latest service packs or roll-ups when they become available. Your best starting point to obtain these is the downloads link from `http://www.microsoft.com/biztalk`.

TIP

In addition to this book, there are many sources of information on the Internet that you will find helpful, including numerous blogs. Mine, at `http://blogs.msdn.com/scottwoo`, indexes many others, as well as online videos, samples mentioned in this chapter, training materials, and classes. In particular, the BizTalk Server community in the Microsoft newsgroups is a good starting place to get your questions addressed by Microsoft employees, MVPs, and other customers.

When it comes to your first implementation, which is probably the reason you bought this book, choose an appropriately scoped but important business problem and use BizTalk Server to help you solve that problem. This way, you can demonstrate value to the business and also get up to speed with the product with the maximum likelihood of project success.

CHAPTER 2

Your First BizTalk Server Integration

IN THIS CHAPTER

- Architecture 101—How BizTalk Organizes Things
- BizTalk Developer Tools Overview
- Your First Integration Project

Integration projects in Microsoft BizTalk Server 2004 use so many different concepts that it can be difficult to know where to start. BizTalk Server is best used in applications that combine messaging with a business process. These applications have their own concepts and components, so it can be hard to know where to begin with the product. We'll start your journey through BizTalk Server with a basic application integration project. This project will be too simple for a real-world application, but it will introduce you to all the main ideas needed to create an integration project using BizTalk Server.

We'll start by examining the basic architecture of a BizTalk project. In particular, you need to learn about the following:

- Messages
- MessageBox databases
- Ports and pipelines for messaging
- Process orchestration
- BizTalk rules
- Adapters

Next, we'll provide a quick introduction to the tools you'll use to create the needed components. We'll cover the finer points and advanced features of these tools in the chapters to come, but you need to know the basics first. Finally, we'll tie everything together with a simple integration project.

Architecture 101—How BizTalk Organizes Things

BizTalk Server architecture is divided into two main ideas: messaging and orchestration. Messaging is a low-level concept involving the exchange of structured data, whereas orchestration is the high-level view of a sequence of messaging exchanges. Let's begin with BizTalk messaging. Consider the architecture depicted in Figure 2.1.

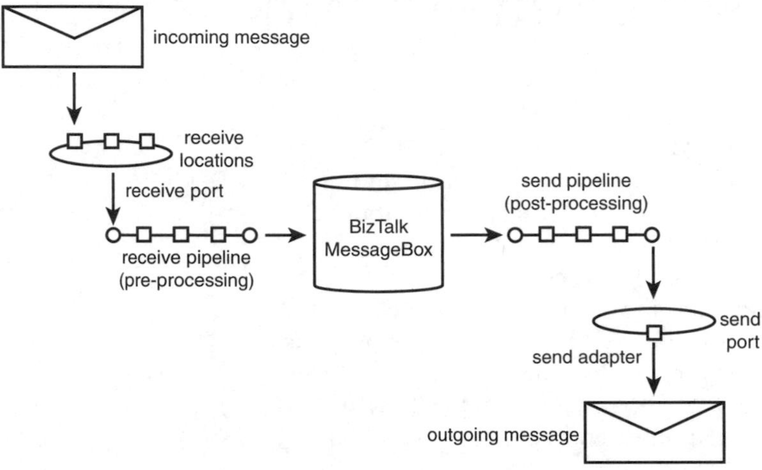

FIGURE 2.1 BizTalk messaging involves several important steps performed in sequence.

A message arrives at a receive location from an application or business partner. The receive location is a particular URL that is being actively monitored by a listener for the protocol involved. The listener is the component that grabs the message and introduces it into the BizTalk runtime environment. Some postreceipt processing occurs in the form of a receive pipeline. The incoming message might be encrypted and signed, for example, in which case the pipeline is responsible for decrypting it and verifying the signature. If the actions in the receive pipeline are successful, the message is entered into the BizTalk MessageBox.

The MessageBox is the heart of BizTalk messaging. It is a SQL Server database that allows for reliable messaging and simple clustering for scalability. We'll go into more detail in a moment. For now, think of this as a post office for messages. They are stored in the MessageBox, awaiting sorting and delivery. Messages are stored with identifying properties, such as the type of message and the originating source of the message. These properties are known as the *context* of a message.

Applications subscribe to messages based on their context. For example, they might subscribe to all messages from a particular business partner, or they might restrict themselves to purchase-order messages from any partner.

The MessageBox compares a message's context with the subscriptions it has on hand. A message is sent to each send port whose subscription information matches the context of the message. The process at this point is essentially the reverse of message reception. A send pipeline performs any pretransmission preparation needed; then the message is handed off to a send adapter. This is a component that performs the actual protocol-specific transmission of the message to a recipient. Receive and send ports are configured independently. Send ports, as we shall see when we look at messaging in detail, subscribe to messages from receive ports based on various criteria. This gives us the flexibility to create one-to-one, one-to-many, and even many-to-many messaging configurations without requiring the creation of new receive configurations every time we add a send port.

Messaging, though, ignores the fact that business activities are more than simple exchanges of messages. They involve a process. A procurement process, for example, might involve circulating a request for proposal, receiving bids, selecting one, sending a purchase order, and receiving confirmation. Each of these actions involves the receipt or transmission of a message. An organization is interested in the overall logical flow of the process, and messaging handles the exchange of data that implements each step of the process. Processes are the concern of BizTalk orchestration. The name comes from the view of a process as organizing, or orchestrating, a sequence of messaging actions. BizTalk messaging and BizTalk orchestration, then, are complementary, with orchestration providing the process and messaging providing the actions within the process. There is some overlap, of course, because orchestrations need some knowledge of messaging concepts.

The procurement example is highly simplified. Real-world processes may involve logical decisions, parallel operations, and transactions of various sorts. For example, an orchestration for an order fulfillment business process will need to treat a messaging operation accepting the order and a messaging operation to the internal inventory application as a transaction. If both messages succeed, the confirmation message is sent and the inventory is correctly updated. If either fails, the order cannot be accepted and the inventory must remain unchanged. Long-running business processes and application-integration scenarios introduce complexities that are not present in the familiar world of database transactions. Orchestration offers powerful tools for handling those complexities.

That's the very quick and necessarily very vague overview of BizTalk architecture and organization. Each of these pieces will be treated at length in subsequent chapters. Before we go on to the details of implementing messages and orchestrations, however, let's turn our attention to each of these pieces in turn and try to fill in a few of the details so you can have a better understanding of what is possible in BizTalk Server.

Messages

Messages are just an abstract way of looking at structured data. Any sort of structured data, such as XML, CSV flat files, or positional files, qualifies as a message in BizTalk messaging.

BizTalk brings a formal view of processing structured data to the idea of messaging, but the structure of data is the key idea that lets us integrate applications.

BizTalk is designed with XML in mind, and, indeed, converts all messages to its own XML format inside the messaging engine to simplify processing. It can also handle flat-file formats. These would be delimited—for example, comma-separated variable (CSV) format, positional, or some combination of the two. Most legacy applications you will encounter are set up to export data in flat-file format. If you can create a formal specification of the data format, BizTalk can process it. Creating such specifications is the purpose of the BizTalk Editor. In the next section, we'll briefly describe this tool and all the other tools needed for BizTalk projects.

There are many ways to structure the same data. As soon as you begin integrating applications and business partners, you will encounter the problem of two parties talking about the same thing but using differing schemas. An important part of BizTalk messages is message mapping. You can describe how two message schemas—even two in dissimilar formats such as CSV and XML—are related by specifying a mapping from one to another. With that information, BizTalk is able to perform a runtime translation from a message received in the source format to an equivalent message in the destination format. With this feature, applications and partners are able to continue working with their native formats while still participating in an integrated environment. The mapping effort is driven by a file that is easily changed.

The BizTalk MessageBox

As stated earlier, BizTalk messaging separates the stateful part of messaging, messages and their context information, from the stateless part, the actual processing and delivery of messages. The MessageBox is a SQL Server database, and much of the functionality of BizTalk messaging is implemented as stored procedures. Messages are the irreplaceable part of BizTalk. If you interrupt the message flow, the rest of the architecture falls apart. Because the MessageBox is a SQL Server database, we can protect messaging using well-understood techniques, chiefly failover clusters and RAID storage. All the stateless machines in a BizTalk cluster draw from a single MessageBox database, thereby implementing a simple clustering mechanism for performance and load balancing.

Send ports and orchestrations connect to a source of data by subscribing to a particular type of message. These subscriptions take the form of predicates and service information. Predicates are queries against the context data stored with any particular message. In addition to the standard context data provided by BizTalk Server, a message designer can specify, or promote, additional properties from the body of the message into the context. When a message is received, its context is compared to stored subscription information. When a predicate matches the context data, the service information for the subscription is consulted to see how to process the message. The message is then passed to the appropriate message adapter or orchestration instance running on an available server in the messaging cluster.

Of course, there is much more to the MessageBox than that. Messages may fail to be delivered. Messages might not match specifications, the context might not match any available subscription predicates, or any other sort of software or hardware failure might occur. Messages that fail in delivery are suspended pending action by a system administrator.

MessageBoxes can also be associated for scalability. The first MessageBox database created is designated the master database. You can then establish secondary MessageBoxes to receive some designated portion of the message traffic. The master MessageBox routes incoming messages to the appropriate MessageBox instance for processing.

NOTE

Readers familiar with previous versions of BizTalk Server will note a number of differences. Whereas earlier versions had tables directly related to each of four queues, BizTalk Server 2004 features a reorganized database schema for the MessageBox. Rather than seeing a listing for each queue in the Administration tool, queues are in the background in this version. You will refer to the Health and Activity Tracking tool and find a status for each message that was received by the MessageBox. The concept of multiple, cooperating MessageBoxes is also new.

Messaging Ports and Pipelines

Receive ports and send ports are the originating and terminal endpoints, respectively, of BizTalk messaging. A message enters the BizTalk world through a receive port and leaves through a send port. Receive ports are logical arrival points that aggregate one or more receive locations. Each receive location is associated with a messaging protocol—for example, HTTP and a specific URL. A receive location uses a protocol-specific adapter to monitor the specified URL for arriving messages. A send port uses its specified URL and an adapter to send the message. Should the transmission fail, additional attempts may be made if a backup protocol and URL has been specified. You can also specify how many retry attempts to make and at what interval.

One innovation BizTalk Server 2004 introduces is the idea of port binding. Ports in an orchestration must be bound, as appropriate to the direction of message flow, to a receive location or a send port. An orchestration designer might not know the specific URL at design time or might be creating a general orchestration pattern for use throughout an enterprise. In these cases, she will specify the direction of flow and message type, but defer binding the orchestration to a physical messaging port (receive or send port) until deployment. Upon deployment, the administrator responsible for the cluster on which the orchestration is being deployed will create the physical ports, with specific URLs, and bind the logical orchestration ports to the physical messaging ports. It is important to note that the administrator can make this configuration without recompiling the orchestration. This allows the same orchestration, representing a logical business process, to be deployed to a number of physical servers with differing port configurations.

Introducing a message into BizTalk or sending it out into the world is a bit more complicated then simply plucking it off the wire or shooting it off using a particular protocol. Real-world messages may require security and may therefore be encrypted or digitally signed. Context properties must be captured. Messages must be converted into the internal XML format used by BizTalk. Additional processing may be required by your particular messaging needs. The pre- and post-processing involved is handled by message pipelines. A port is assigned a pipeline to specify how the port will handle the message. BizTalk includes several default pipelines for handling routine tasks, as well as a pipeline design tool for creating custom pipelines. These pipelines and their uses are the following:

- Pass through receive—Performs no processing and contains no components; used when BizTalk is being used to route messages without manipulation.
- Pass through send—The transmission complement to the pass through receive pipeline.
- XML receive—Performs disassembly of incoming XML messages without validation.
- XML send—Performs basic assembly of outgoing XML messages.

The default pipelines cannot be modified by designers.

A pipeline organizes COM and .NET components into stages to accomplish message processing. Components in a stage can be executed in one of two modes. All components in a stage can be executed in the sequence they are specified in the pipeline.

Common pipeline tasks include MIME encoding/decoding and message assembly/disassembly. MIME components allow BizTalk to handle various encodings as well as SMIME encryption. An incoming message will be in plain-text form following MIME decoding, and an outgoing plain-text message will be properly encoded and encrypted following a MIME encoding stage.

Assembly and disassembly is a concept specific to BizTalk. This is the stage where inbound XML or flat-file messages are broken apart into their constituent parts, the context information is captured, and data is properly readied for the MessageBox. Messages can be bundled for transmission using an envelope. In this case, a disassembler component must be used to recognize the envelope and the boundaries of the messages within it. After a message is extracted from the bundle (called an *interchange*), context properties are captured for the MessageBox. Message assembly components reverse the process, adding context data from the MessageBox back into message fields and combining multiple messages into a single interchange.

Many types of port binding can be accomplished using the default pipelines provided by BizTalk. Custom pipelines are the topic of Chapter 5, "Building Pipelines."

Process Orchestration

An orchestration can be thought of as a flowchart that represents a particular business process. Like a classic flowchart, an orchestration diagram has action shapes and flow-of-control shapes. Action shapes send and receive BizTalk messages or call other orchestrations. Flow-of-control shapes include launching another orchestration, branching on logical conditions (decisions), looping, and terminating an orchestration.

Orchestrations also have some functional items that are unique to orchestration. Transactions are supported in two forms: atomic and long-running. Atomic transactions are similar to the database transactions with which you are probably familiar. These begin and end within a short span of time and respect the properties of atomicity, consistency, isolation, and durability that are at the heart of database transaction processing. BizTalk orchestrations may model long-running processes, some of which involve human intervention. These actions may also require transactions, but they either cannot tie up resources for the relatively long periods of time involved or they involve resources, such as human intervention or Web services, which are not inherently transactional in the database sense. For these situations, BizTalk provides long-running transactions. These provide a lesser degree of transactional integrity (specifically respecting consistency and durability, but not atomicity and isolation). An attempt at atomicity is provided through compensation. In compensation, an orchestration designer specifies an alternative workflow to execute in the event that completed workflow tasks need to be "backed out." This is similar to rolling back a transaction in a database, but it relies on the cooperation of the parties to the messaging provided in the original workflow. For example, you might send a message and subsequently have to undo the effect because other actions have failed. There is no way to roll back a sent message, but you could send a message canceling the action directed by the previous message.

Orchestrations are saved as XML documents using the XLANG/s vocabulary. The XLANG/s vocabulary is an extension of the language used by earlier versions of BizTalk. Not only have new features been added to the language, but efforts are proceeding toward a standard workflow language, called the Business Process Execution Language for Web Services, or BPEL4WS. The Orchestration Designer tool supports exporting orchestrations that adhere to the BPEL4WS subset to BPEL4WS format.

> **NOTE**
>
> The constructs of XLANG/s mirror nearly all of the BPEL4WS vocabulary. XLANG/s also contains many features that depend on the .NET Framework.

As you might suspect, orchestration is both a fascinating and complex subject. Consequently, we devote all of Part III, Developing with BizTalk Server: Studio-Business Processes, in this book, a total of four chapters, to BizTalk orchestration and its related topic, BizTalk rules.

BizTalk Rules

Earlier versions of BizTalk orchestration support the decision-making shape that is still available in BizTalk Server 2004. This shapes relies on a scripted expression that evaluates to a logical true or false. But business processes embody complicated rules involving business objects and rules related to the business environment. BizTalk Server 2004, therefore, separates rules from orchestration so that rules can be developed outside orchestrations. Business analysts may therefore capture important business logic that orchestration designers can refer to in their workflows. BizTalk uses the BizTalk Rules Framework as the architecture for an entire rule-based engine. Orchestrations use a new shape to invoke these rules, but do not incorporate the rules themselves. That way, business analysts are free to modify the content of rules without requiring a recompile of orchestrations that use those rules.

BizTalk rules begin with conditions, facts, and actions. Facts are evaluated by if-then conditions to result in a logical true or false condition. Actions are the tasks executed based on the results of this evaluation. Facts and actions are represented in the Framework as .NET components or their properties. Facts may be implemented by complex bindings, such as a SQL query. To make things easier for designers and analysts, facts are given friendly names. A collection of related fact definitions and their friendly names is called a vocabulary.

Rules that are related by some underlying business domain knowledge are grouped together into policies. Policies are the basic unit of development, testing, deployment, and execution in the Framework. As such, they are a reusable element of business-specific knowledge available to BizTalk orchestration. BizTalk Server provides a runtime inference engine, or rule executor, that takes policies and their rules, evaluates facts, and executes actions. The engine is supported by a .NET class library and a SQL Server database for policies and their rules.

Orchestration makes use of the Framework by invoking a policy and submitting facts based on data in messages to the rule engine. The results of the policy inference process are returned to the orchestration and used to compose and control messages in the orchestration.

The BizTalk rules are discussed in Chapter 11, "Developing Rules."

Messaging Adapters

Before we leave our discussion of BizTalk architecture for a look at the tools you will use in BizTalk development, we need to look at an essential component of BizTalk messaging: adapters. Recall that our ports are endpoints that connect BizTalk with a particular URL and protocol. Adapters are the software components that handle the reception or transmission of messages on specific protocols. BizTalk ships with the following standard adapters:

- File—Disk-based file exchange
- HTTP—Messaging using HTTP
- MSMQT—BizTalk Message Queuing, an enhancement of MSMQ shipped with BizTalk Server 2004
- SMTP—Email messaging
- SOAP—Messages exchanged via Web services
- SQL—Messages retrieved and transmitted via database

Because adapters are software components, we can use them to encapsulate any well-known API, thereby opening the reach of BizTalk messaging to important third-party software applications such as ERP or CRM packages.

MSMQT and the development of custom messaging adapters using the BizTalk adapter interfaces is the topic of Chapter 7, "Working with Adapters."

BizTalk Developer Tools Overview

Programmers and designers use a series of add-ins to Microsoft Visual Studio .NET 2003 to design and implement integration projects with BizTalk Server 2004. The tools are

- Editor—Design tool for specifying message schemas
- Mapper—Design tool for specifying the translation of one message schema into another
- Pipeline Designer—Design tool for building message processing pipelines from a palette of components
- Orchestration Designer—Graphical tool for designing orchestration workflows
- Explorer—Administrative tool for exploring and managing a BizTalk configuration database

Editor

The BizTalk Server architecture relies on exchanging structured data as messages, as you have seen, so you would be correct in assuming that specifying message formats is the first and most important task of a BizTalk project. To perform this task, we rely on the BizTalk Editor, a Visual Studio add-in that is opened whenever a schema project item is added to or opened in a BizTalk Visual Studio solution.

Message formats are specified using an annotated and augmented version of the World Wide Web Consortium (W3C) XML Schema Recommendation. All message structures, flat file as well as XML, are specified using this format. If you are familiar with the schema designer from earlier versions of Visual Studio, you will quickly become acquainted with the Editor.

The Editor is organized into four views, depicted in Figure 2.2.

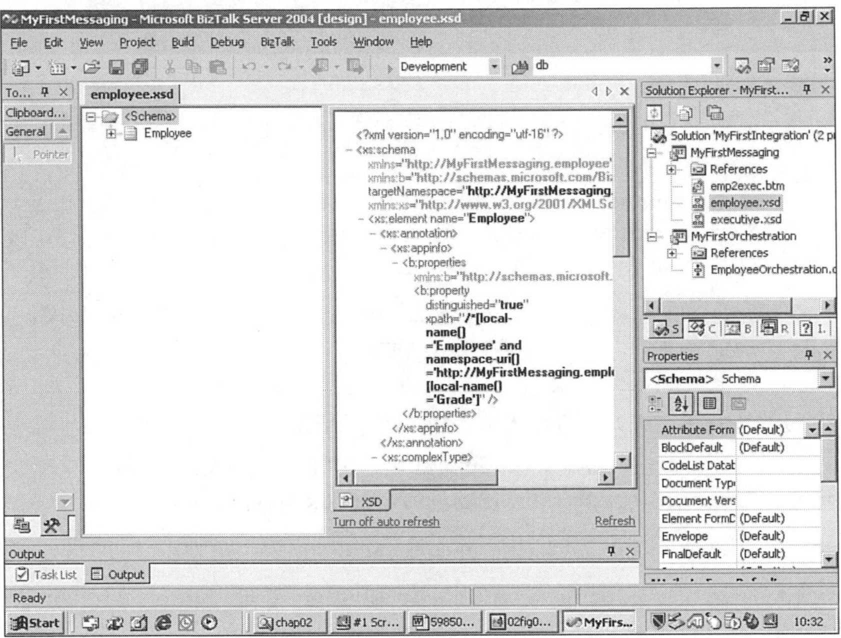

FIGURE 2.2 The four views of BizTalk Editor in Visual Studio.

The tree view on the left of Figure 2.2 is the Schema view. It provides a visual representation of the hierarchy of a BizTalk message. Because messages can be either XML or flat file in format, Editor uses the concept of fields and records for message schemas. Nodes in the schema tree that contain other nodes are records, and individual data elements are fields. You use the Schema view to construct schemas by adding nodes or moving them around within the node tree.

Like most Visual Studio tasks, you continue your process of specifying a message structure by setting properties for each node in the schema tree. The properties for the selected node in the Schema view are presented in the standard Visual Studio Properties window, depicted in the lower-right part of Figure 2.2. You enter the value of a property or select from a list to configure that node.

The large text pane dominating the center of Figure 2.2 is the XSD Schema view. This view displays the source text of the XSD Schema document the Editor is creating for the message. This is a read-only view and is intended to familiarize designers with the XSD syntax. Experienced XML developers can also use this view to ensure that they are correctly specifying the message in accordance with their wishes.

Editor also permits you to check your work in several ways. You may validate a message schema to ensure that you have set all the properties required to correctly specify a message schema. You can also generate a sample instance of a message conforming to the schema under development, or even validate a sample instance. These latter two features are valuable when you have an existing legacy format requiring the creation of a BizTalk message schema or when you have a specific structure in mind for your message. You can then generate samples to see if they look as you desire, or validate existing sample data against the schema to ensure that your schema will correctly describe the data your legacy application is currently generating. The results of these tasks are depicted in the Visual Studio Task List and Output windows shown at the bottom of Figure 2.3.

The output of a message schema is an XSD Schema document, which is compiled into a .NET assembly. Creation of BizTalk message schemas is the topic of Chapter 3, "Building Message Specifications."

Mapper

Application data comes in a variety of formats. Before BizTalk, integrating applications required the addition of sometimes extensive amounts of code within each application to perform the translation to and from each application's format. The BizTalk messaging engine eliminates this code by providing runtime data translations during messaging or orchestration. To do this, BizTalk needs to know not only the schema for each message, but also how the data from the incoming message is mapped to fields in the outgoing message. Schemas developed using the Editor provide the incoming and outgoing structures; maps designed using BizTalk Mapper provide the messaging engine with the correspondence needed to transform data from the form specified by one schema to that specified by the other.

Figure 2.3 shows a typical BizTalk Mapper session.

When you create a new map in BizTalk Mapper, you will be prompted to specify source and destination schemas for the map. These schema documents will either be included in the current project or in an assembly referenced by the current project. The schemas for the source and destination message schemas are depicted in the tree views on the left and right sides of the central area of Figure 2.3 and are identical to the Schema views for these messages in BizTalk Editor. As with Editor, the properties of the node currently selected in one of the schema trees are listed in the Visual Studio Properties view. In Figure 2.3, this appears in the lower-right portion of the window.

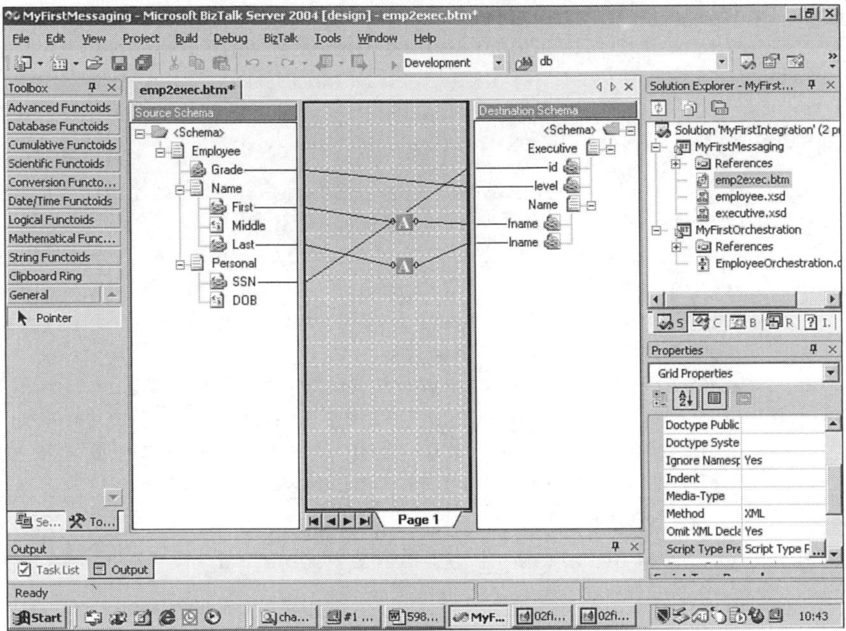

FIGURE 2.3 Typical BizTalk Mapper layout in Visual Studio.

Basic data translation is accomplished by establishing links between source fields and records and the equivalent fields and records of the destination schema. These are depicted as lines crossing the lightly gridded area between the two Schema views. This area is the Map Zone view. More complicated data manipulation is handled by functoids. A functoid is a .NET component that accepts input from the source message at runtime and generates output for the destination message based on the input. BizTalk ships with an extensive array of functoids for string handling, arithmetic manipulation, database tasks, and other data manipulation functions. Programmers can also extend the Mapper by creating custom functoids. Functoids are organized by category in the Visual Studio toolbox, shown on the left of Figure 2.3.

To use functoids with maps, you drag a functoid from the toolbox to the map zone, add a link from the appropriate source field or fields to the functoid, and then add a link from the functoid to the proper destination field or fields. Earlier versions of BizTalk Mapper placed all functoids and links on a single map zone. Maps could become quite confusing to read for complex messages with many links and functoids. BizTalk Server 2004 helps you organize maps by providing for multiple layers in the map zone. You select a layer using the tabs at the bottom of the Map Zone view.

As with the Editor, you can test the validity of your map or generate sample output. In either case, the result is a temporary document that you can view by following the link in the Visual Studio Output view. You test a map by adding sample data to one of the properties for source nodes and then select the Test Map menu item from the context menu in the Solution Explorer. Mapper uses the sample data you provided to create a source message and then applies the translations and transformations specified by the map to generate a sample destination message.

Maps, like schemas, are compiled into assemblies that are used by the runtime messaging engine. The creation of maps and functoids is the topic of Chapter 4, "Mapping Messages."

Pipeline Designer

The processing of messages following reception or prior to transmission is the responsibility of receive and send pipelines. Although BizTalk includes two basic pipelines, more complicated messaging scenarios require you to use the BizTalk Pipeline Designer to construct a pipeline that fits your needs.

The Pipeline Designer follows the pattern of the design-time tools we have looked at so far. As you can see in Figure 2.4, when a pipeline item is open, Visual Studio displays a toolbox (left), a graphical design surface (center), and the Properties view (lower right).

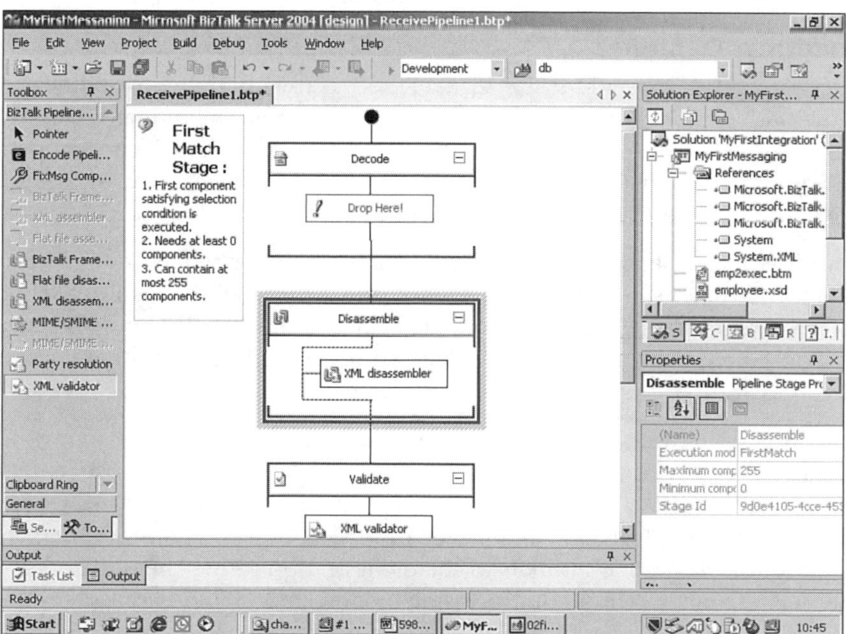

FIGURE 2.4 Receive pipeline from the SDK open in the Pipeline Designer.

When you add a pipeline to a BizTalk project, you select the template for either a receive pipeline or a send pipeline. The new item appears in the design surface with a start symbol, the stages appropriate to the template, and a terminal symbol. You proceed by dragging pipeline components from the toolbox to a stage and setting properties for each stage and component. The toolbox is populated with symbols for the components available to the designer, but only those components appropriate to the pipeline template type (send or receive) are enabled. BizTalk comes with a number of components, and programmers can create new pipeline components and add them to the toolbox by implementing specific interfaces in COM or .NET. The properties for the stage or component currently selected in the design surface are displayed in the Properties view.

Pipeline components are implemented as COM or .NET components. Components are designed for use within a particular stage, and stages will not accept a component intended for another stage. In addition to general properties such as the name and the assembly in which the component is implemented, components may have properties specific to them. For example, the XML Validator component has a Document Schemas property that is a collection of XSD Schemas the component should consult when validating incoming documents.

The use of the Pipeline Designer for the creation of specialized pipelines is the topic of Chapter 5.

Orchestration Designer

The Orchestration Designer add-in for Visual Studio is used to design workflows for use by the runtime orchestration engine. Like the Pipeline Designer, the interface features a toolbox, a design surface, and a Properties view. It also features the Orchestration view for the types and variables in an orchestration. In Figure 2.5, this view is at the bottom of the window with the Orchestration Variables tab selected.

The activities you can perform in an orchestration are represented by the symbols available in the toolbox. This is a rather rich palette, and a thorough discussion of it must wait for Chapter 9, "Introducing Orchestration." For now, remember that these include typical flowchart constructs, such as loops, as well as symbols specific to BizTalk processing, such as message transformation.

When you add an orchestration to a BizTalk project, an empty template appears in the design surface. This template consists of start and end symbols with a large, gray box between them. You build an orchestration by dragging symbols to the box between the start and end symbols. The first symbol to be dropped on the design surface replaces the gray box placeholder. Adding symbols to the orchestration causes them to appear sequentially. You may change the order of processing by dragging symbols around on the design surface.

Although Orchestration Designer connects symbols as you add them, you still have to establish some links yourself. The symbols we have been talking about so far populate the central portion of the design surface. Orchestrations rely on the flow of messages in and out of the orchestration, which implies ports. Areas to the left and the right of the design surface are reserved for ports and are labeled Port Surface. You drag port symbols onto either surface and then connect them to send and receive symbols in the central portion of the design surface.

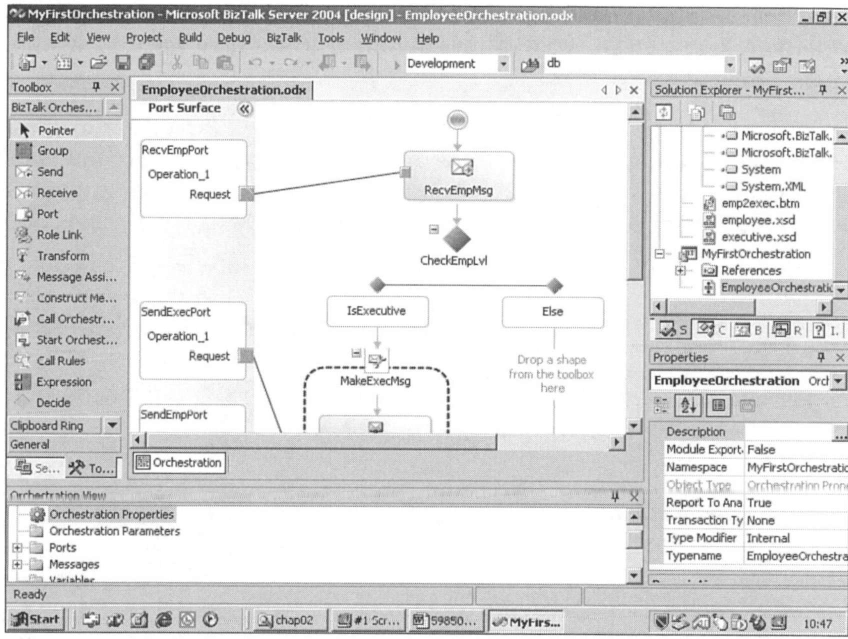

FIGURE 2.5 Visual Studio showing a typical view of the Orchestration Designer.

Types in an orchestration refer to types you create, most commonly for ports. As you add actual ports and messages to your orchestration, you will use wizards to configure instances that are listed in the Orchestration Variables view. You may also define variables for use within an orchestration much as you would in a programming language (which XLANG/s is, in fact). These variables are typed. BizTalk predefines the usual atomic types—Boolean, for example—but you can also refer to a .NET class and use that software during the execution of an orchestration.

After you design an orchestration, you build it by building the solution in which it resides. This causes the orchestration to be compiled into an assembly. Any errors are noted in the Visual Studio Output view. Basic use of the Orchestration Designer is covered in Chapter 9 with additional coverage as we investigate the advanced features of orchestration in Chapter 10, "Orchestrating Web Services and Correlation," and Chapter 12, "Orchestrating—Advanced Concepts."

Explorer

The BizTalk Explorer is a departure from the BizTalk add-ins for Visual Studio we have discussed so far. It is not a design tool so much as a programmer's view of BizTalk administration. Explorer gives programmers a view of the BizTalk configuration database. It is similar to the BizTalk Server Administration tool installed with and prominently displayed on the BizTalk Server 2004 group of the Windows Start menu. You can use it from within Visual Studio to perform administrative tasks that you routinely encounter in the course of developing a BizTalk solution. It is not intended to be the primary tool for BizTalk administrators; instead, it allows programmers to get their job done without leaving Visual Studio.

There is no project template associated with Explorer, because it is an administrative tool, not a project type. It is similar in appearance to the Server Explorer view and appears in the same window when visible. To make the BizTalk Explorer visible, go to the Visual Studio View menu and select BizTalk Explorer. Figure 2.6 shows a typical view of the Explorer.

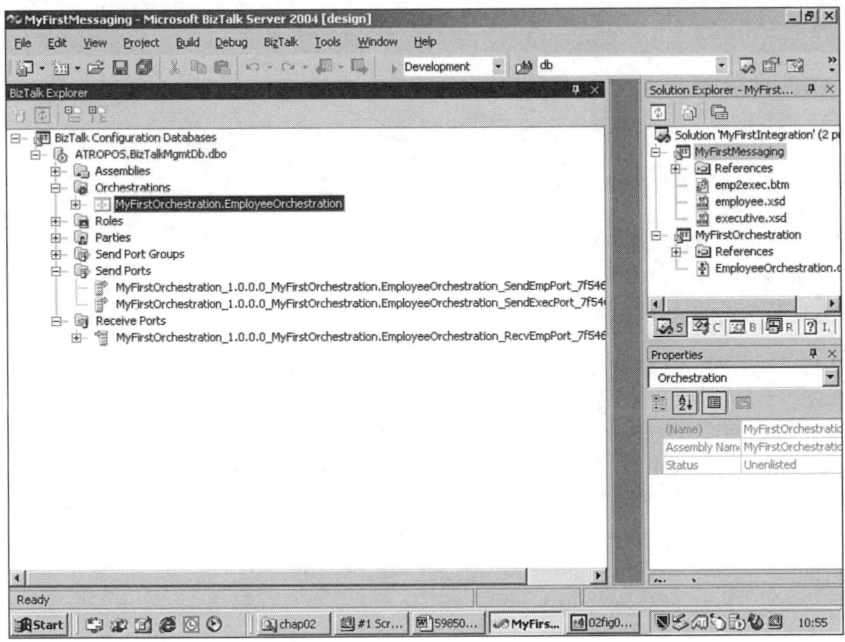

FIGURE 2.6 BizTalk Explorer provides programmers with a view of BizTalk configurations.

Explorer provides a tree view of the configuration databases visible to your computer. It has a node for each such database instance. Figure 2.6 depicts an installation with a single configuration database on a single machine. Each such instance has nodes for the following items:

- Assemblies—.NET assemblies deploying BizTalk items
- Orchestrations—Deployed orchestration

- Roles—Roles defined for the interaction of business partners in BizTalk
- Parties—External business partners and the configuration for sending messages to them
- Send Port Groups—Collections of send ports grouped so as to implement a distribution list
- Send Ports—All send ports created for use with BizTalk messaging
- Receive Ports—All receive ports created for use with BizTalk messaging

Note that some nodes, such as send and receive ports, permit you to create the entities they list as well as configure or remove them. Others, like assemblies and orchestrations, are primarily for the modification or removal of their entities. For example, you can use the Assemblies node to view all assemblies deployed for the implementation of BizTalk projects. Over time, particularly on a development server, this configuration will become cluttered. Explorer allows you to remove a deployed assembly when it is no longer needed.

The Orchestrations node is a bit more powerful. For each deployed orchestration, you can view all the roles used, roles implemented, and orchestrations invoked by that orchestration. You may enlist or unenlist an orchestration, optionally enlisting or unenlisting its dependencies, such as ports. Enlistment is the process by which an orchestration is associated with the runtime physical environment. This is where you specify the protocol and specific URL used in communicating with the orchestration and tell the server which application process will host the orchestration at runtime. Equally important is starting and stopping an orchestration. Once enlisted, an orchestration must be started. While an orchestration is stopped, messages arriving for that orchestration will be queued by the messaging system for delivery when the orchestration is started. Orchestration instances are activated either through invocation from another, running orchestration schedule, or through the receipt of a message at a receive location in the schedule. To monitor for the latter and activate the schedule, BizTalk has to keep a list of things to watch for. This consumes server resources, so you want to start orchestrations only when they are needed. The capability to start and stop orchestrations and send ports allows an administrator to perform maintenance without losing messages and without wasting resources on retry attempts to deliver messages.

Explorer also provides an object model for .NET or COM development. Although this is not properly a task of the Explorer tool, it allows programmers to create new administrative and operational tools. You'll encounter the Explorer in more detail in the course of developing BizTalk solutions throughout this book.

Your First Integration Project

This chapter has introduced a lot of different topics, as was our intention. You are, hopefully, beginning to develop a picture of how BizTalk works as a whole, as well as a roadmap for the tasks that go into a BizTalk development project. Nothing clarifies things like a concrete example, though, so let's tackle your first integration project using BizTalk Server.

> **NOTE**
>
> Our aim is to illustrate the concepts involved, not bury you in the details of advanced features or practical solutions. Rest assured, we will develop increasingly sophisticated solutions throughout the course of this book. For now, though, it is useful to create a simplified and somewhat contrived example so that you can focus on the underlying concepts. We'll walk you through the development process in checklist format, providing explanation of the underlying topics in just enough detail for you to understand what you are implementing.

Let's assume you have an application that collects information about new employees. Your company's Human Resources department has an application that tracks and manages staff. Additionally, another application elsewhere in the company manages executive-level employees. Your task is to integrate the three applications by taking the output of the collection application and passing it on to the HR application. In the process, when a new employee is an executive, you must also send the employee information to the application that manages executive resources.

To simplify matters, we'll use the file transport protocol. Everyone has a file system, and use of the protocol consists of dropping files into folders or picking them up from disk. It's also extremely easy to see the outcome of file-based messaging. Just to make things interesting, though, we'll assume that the data collection and HR applications share a common XML message schema, but the executive management application uses a different XML Schema. This will necessitate the use of a message map.

Following are the tasks we will have to accomplish to make this work:

- Specify message schemas.
- Specify the mapping between the two schemas.
- Design the orchestration that implements our business process.
- Deploy the .NET assemblies implementing our project and configure them for use.

Let's start by creating a new BizTalk project in Visual Studio to organize our assemblies. To do so, follow these steps:

1. Start Visual Studio .NET.
2. Create a new solution by selecting the New Blank Solution menu item on the File menu.

3. In the New Project dialog box, select the Blank solution template from Visual Studio Solutions and name it MyFirstIntegration. Browse to the location on disk where you want to create and maintain your project files.

4. Click OK to close the dialog box. The new solution opens in Visual Studio with zero projects.

We'll organize our solution into one project for messaging (including maps) and one for workflow, which is where the orchestration schedule will reside. Let's create those projects right now. To do so, follow these steps:

1. In the Solution Explorer view, right-click the node labeled `Solution 'MyFirstIntegration'` and select Add New Project.

2. From the Project Types list, select the BizTalk Projects folder, and then from the Templates list, select the Empty BizTalk Server Project template.

3. Change the project name from `BizTalk Server Project1` to `MyFirstMessaging` and click OK.

4. Repeat steps 1–3 to create a project called MyFirstOrchestration.

Message Formats

Now we need to create two message schemas, one for the initial data collection application that starts our workflow and one for the executive management application. Begin with the former:

1. In the Solution Explorer, select the MyFirstMessaging project, right-click, point to Add, and then select Add New Item from the context menu.

2. Select the Schema template and name the new item `employee.xsd`. Note that when the BizTalk Project Items root node is selected, all BizTalk templates are displayed. You may also get to the Schema template by expanding that node and selecting the Schema Files folder.

3. Click Open. BizTalk Editor opens, displaying the shell of a new schema.

4. Set the name of the document element by right-clicking the node named Root (immediately under the `<Schema>` node), click Rename, and then type **`Employee`** and press the Enter key.

5. Right-click the `Employee` node, point to `Insert Schema` node, and then click Child Field Attribute.

6. Type **`Grade`** as the field name and then press Enter.

7. Ensure `Grade` is selected and then go to the Properties view. Scroll until you find Data Type, and then select `xs:positiveInteger` from the list of data types.

8. Right-click `Employee`, point to `Insert Schema Node`, and click Child Record.
9. Type **`Name`** for the name of the new record, and then press Enter.
10. Right-click `Name` and insert a child field element. Name it **`First`**.
11. Repeat step 10 two more times, creating field elements named **`Middle`** and **`Last`**.
12. Right-click `Employee` and insert a child record. Name it **`Personal`**.
13. Right-click `Personal` and insert child field elements named `SSN` and `DOB`.

The results should look like the structure in Figure 2.2. Don't worry about the XSD source for now. Figure 2.2 includes an important annotation we'll make in a little while. Listing 2.1 shows what a sample employee message should look like.

LISTING 2.1 Sample XML Employee Message

```
<?xml version="1.0" encoding="utf-8" ?>
<e:Employee xmlns:e="http://MyFirstMessaging.employee" Grade="1">
     <Name>
          <First>MBig</First>
          <Middle>Big</Middle>
          <Last>Boss</Last>
     </Name>
     <Personal>
          <SSN>111-22-3344</SSN>
          <DOB>1960-04-01</DOB>
     </Personal>
</e:Employee>
```

Of course, this is a greatly simplified schema. Names can be a good deal more complicated, and we would want to capture a lot more information. This is good enough for the purposes of our application, however. Note that this structure is oriented to representing data as nested elements in XML. We'll deliberately take a different approach with the next schema.

Now we need a schema for messages going to the executive management application.

1. In the Solution Explorer, select the MyFirstMessaging project, right-click, point to Add, and select Add New Item from the context menu. Name the new item `executive.xsd` and click Open.
2. Rename the root node **`Executive`** using the Rename item from the context menu.
3. Right-click `Executive` and insert child field attributes named **`id`** and **`level`**.
4. Right-click `Executive`, point to Insert Schema Node, and click Child Record.

5. Enter **Name** for the new record name and then press Enter.
6. Right-click Name and insert a child field attribute named **fname**.
7. Repeat step 6, inserting a child field attribute named **lname**.

A sample for this message schema that is equivalent to our Employee sample is shown in Listing 2.2. Note that we've leaned toward representing data as attributes, and we've dropped the executive's middle name entirely.

LISTING 2.2 Sample XML Executive Message

```
<?xml version="1.0" encoding="utf-8" ?>
<x:Executive xmlns:x="http://MyFirstMessaging.executive"
➥id="111-22-3344" level="5">
    <Name fname="MBig" lname="Boss"/>
</x:Executive>
```

There is one final task to perform before we compile our solution. Our business process calls for us to conditionally send a message to the executive management application based on the employment level of the employee. This is represented by the Grade attribute in the employee schema and the level attribute in the executive schema. We'll check this condition in the orchestration for this project. Orchestration, however, rides above messaging. Orchestration schedules can only "see" data in message contexts; they cannot operate on the body of messages themselves. Because our schemas are custom to our project, there is no way that Grade and level could possibly be in the context by default. We have to get the messaging system to extract the data during processing and put it into the message context for orchestration. The task for specifying this is called promoting the properties. This is done with the Editor. Because property promotion is unique to BizTalk, the specification is recorded in the XSD Schema document under an appinfo element. The W3C Schema Recommendation provides this element expressively for the purpose of recording application-specific data. Perform the following steps to accomplish property promotion:

1. Open employee.xsd if it is not already open.
2. Right-click the <Schema> node, point to Promote, and click Show Promotions. The Promote Properties dialog box appears.
3. Expand the Employee node.
4. Select Grade, ensure the Distinguished Fields tab is active, and click the Add button. Grade appears in the property column and an XPath expression locating it within the document appears in the Node Path column.
5. Click OK.

NOTE

Note that an `appinfo` element appears in the XSD source containing a child `b:properties` element. The node path you just created through property promotion is recorded in the body of a child `b:property` element. This element, and the namespace it belongs to, is proprietary to Microsoft BizTalk.

6. Repeat steps 1–5 with `executive.xsd` to promote the `level` attribute.

Message Map

We are going to need to send an executive message to the executive management application whenever an employee message representing an executive arrives at our orchestration schedule from the data collection application. BizTalk will create the executive message by mapping the data in the employee element into the equivalent executive form. BizTalk will need our guidance in the form of a message map. It is useful to put the message map in the same assembly as the schemas. You add the needed map with the following steps:

1. In the Solution Explorer, right-click the MyFirstMessaging project, click Add, and then click Add New Item.
2. In the Add New Item dialog box, from the BizTalk Project Items folder, select the Map template. Give the new item the name `emp2exec.btm` and click Open.
3. BizTalk Mapper appears with an empty map. Click the Open Source Schema link in the source schema pane.
4. In the BizTalk Type Picker dialog box, expand the Schemas node and double-click the `myFirstMessaging.employee` node. The employee schema appears in the source schema pane.
5. Repeat steps 3 and 4 from the destination schema pane, opening `MyFirstMessaging.executive`.
6. Expand `Employee` in the source pane and `Executive` in the destination pane.
7. Drag from the `Grade` node in the source to the `level` node in the destination. A line appears between the two, and chain link icons appear on each node. You have established a link mapping the value of the `Grade` attribute to the value of the `level` attribute. At runtime, BizTalk will create the `level` attribute and fill it with the value in the source message's `Grade` attribute.
8. Expand `Name` and `Personal` in the source schema and `Name` in the destination schema.
9. Repeat step 7 to create a link between `SSN` and `id`.
10. To illustrate the use of functoids, let's assume we want to force the employee's name to uppercase for the executive message. Expand the String Functoids category in the toolbox.

11. Drag the Uppercase functoid (capital A icon) to the map zone on the design surface.
12. Drag from `First` in the source to the Uppercase functoid to create a link. After releasing the mouse, drag again from the functoid to `fname` in the destination.
13. Repeat steps 11 and 12 to establish a link through the Uppercase functoid between `Last` and `lname`.

We're finished with the messaging side of the solution, but there is one more task to perform before we can properly build the assembly and move on to the orchestration project. The .NET assemblies we build will have to be accessible to the various BizTalk runtime engines, which means that we will have to move them to the .NET global assembly cache, or GAC. This makes the assemblies globally accessible to any process on the machine, provided they have access rights. Assemblies in the GAC must be what are called strong named assemblies. A discussion of this is outside the scope of a book on BizTalk Server, but it involves digital code signing. Fortunately, Visual Studio includes tools that let us do this. Let's create a key file, associate it with our messaging assembly, and build the project. Later, when we've completed the orchestration project, we'll move both assemblies into the global cache as part of deployment.

1. Open a Visual Studio command prompt window from the Start menu, switch to the MyFirstIntegration folder (this is the parent of the folder, MyFirstMessaging, where your source code files for this project reside).
2. At the command prompt, type **`sn -k MyFirstIntegration.snk`**. You will receive a message that a key pair was written to `MyFirstIntegration.snk`.
3. In Visual Studio, in the Solution Explorer, right-click the MyFirstMessaging project and click Properties.
4. In the project Properties dialog box, select Assembly from the Common Properties folder.
5. Scroll down in the right pane. The last category should be Strong name. Select the Assembly key file property and click the ellipsis to its right.
6. Browse to the key-pair file you created in step 2 and click Open to select it as the value of the project's Assembly key file property.
7. Click OK to apply the property selection and close the project Properties dialog box.
8. In the Solution Explorer, right-click the MyFirstMessaging project node and click Build. The Output view should indicate successful completion with 1 succeeded, 0 failed, 0 skipped.

Process

Now we're going to create an orchestration schedule to implement the business process we outlined at the beginning of this example. We've already created a project, MyFirstIntegration, for this purpose. Because it must work in cooperation with our newly completed messaging project, we must create a reference in our integration project to our messaging project.

1. In the Solution Explorer under MyFirstIntegration, right-click References and click Add Reference.
2. In the Add Reference dialog box, click the Projects tab.
3. Double-click the entry for MyFirstMessaging to add it to the Selected Components list.
4. Click OK to close the dialog box.

Now we're going to create the flow of logic for the workflow. We'll add in the messaging details we need in a later step.

1. Right-click MyFirstIntegration, point to Add, and click Add New Item.
2. From the BizTalk Project Items folder, select the BizTalk Orchestration template.
3. Name the new item **`EmployeeOrchestration.odx`** and click Open. Orchestration Design appears with an empty schedule.
4. Drag a Receive shape from the toolbox to the design surface. In the Properties view, change the Name property to **`RecvEmpMsg`**.
5. Change the Activate property for the receive shape to `True`. This will cause the orchestration engine to launch an instance of this schedule whenever an Employee message is received.
6. Drag a Decide shape to the design surface and drop it on the line immediately below `RecvEmpMsg`.
7. Change the Decide shape's Name property to **`CheckEmpLvl`**.
8. The Decide shape consists of a rectangle (now labeled `CheckEmpLvl`) with two subordinate rectangles. Select the one named `Rule_1` and change its Name property to `IsExecutive`.
9. Immediately below the `IsExecutive` rectangle is a box labeled Drop a Shape from the Toolbox Here. Drag a Transform shape from the toolbox and drop it onto this box.
10. Select the enclosing `ConstructMessage_1` shape and change its Name property to **`MakeExecMsg`**.

11. Select the enclosed rectangle named `Transform_1` and change its Name property to **`TransformEmpMsg`**.
12. Drag a Send shape from the toolbox and drop it onto the line immediately below the enclosing `MakeExecMsg` shape.
13. Change the Send shape's Name property to **`SendExecMsg`**.
14. Drag a Send shape and drop it onto the line just below the gray rectangle that joins the two sides of the decision tree. We will use this to send an Employee message to the HR application regardless of Employee level.
15. Change the name of the new Send shape to **`SendEmpToHR`**.

The schedule so far should look like Figure 2.7.

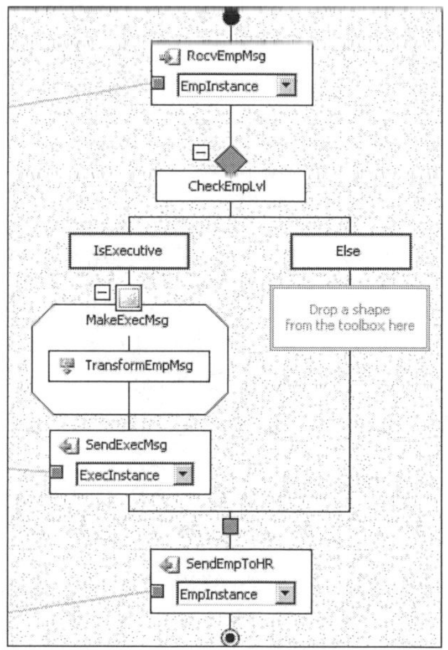

FIGURE 2.7 Logical flow for the employee orchestration schedule.

There's a lot left to configure. We currently have no rule for the decision and no messages for the Send and Receive shapes. Because the rule depends on checking a promoted property (also known as a distinguished field) from the messages, we should define our messages for the schedule. Do this using the following steps:

1. Refer to the Orchestration view.
2. Right-click Messages and click New Message.
3. Change the name to **`EmpInstance`** and press Enter. Focus shifts to the next column.

4. Press Alt+Down, expand Schemas, and click Select from Referenced Assembly.
5. In the Select Artifact dialog box, expand MyFirstMessaging, select the child MyFirstMessaging node (preceded by the braces icon), and then select the entry for `employee` under the Type Name column in the right pane.
6. Click OK.
7. Repeat steps 2–6 to create a message instance variable for the `executive` message type. Name this variable **`ExecInstance`**.

Now that we have messages, let's create logical ports to go with them. We know that we want to use the file protocol. We also know that this is a sample application that isn't going to be deployed on multiple machines, so we can go ahead and select specific file folders for our messaging. This lets us go ahead and bind the ports to physical locations at design time. You won't usually do this in production because you lose the flexibility of deferred binding, but it is a useful shortcut for a sample like this that will not be deployed to other servers.

1. Drag a Port shape onto the Port Surface so that it is level with the Receive shape we constructed previously. The Port Configuration Wizard opens.
2. Click Next.
3. Under Port Properties, change Name to `RecvEmpPort` and click Next.
4. Under Select a Port Type, ensure Create a New Port Type is checked, and enter **`InEmpType`** for the Name. Retain the defaults of One-Way and Private for Communication Pattern and Access Restrictions.
5. Click Next.
6. Ensure that I'll Always Be Receiving Messages on This Port is selected for Port Direction in the Port Binding page.
7. Select Specify now from the list labeled Port binding on that page. The page expands.
8. Select File from the transport list, and enter **`c:\MyFirst\In\*.xml`**. When the receive location is activated during deployment, any file ending in the `.xml` extension dropped in that folder will be taken as an arriving employee message.
9. Ensure the default `XMLReceive` pipeline is selected.
10. Click Next, and then click Finish to close the Port Configuration Wizard.
11. Drag Port shapes onto the Port Surface so that they are level with the Send shapes created earlier. Use the information in Table 2.1 to configure these ports using the Port Configuration Wizard. Note that you will be specifying the port binding now, at design time, in both cases.

TABLE 2.1 Send Port Configuration Settings

Port Properties (Name)	Type Name	Direction	URI and Transport
`SendExecPort`	`OutExecType`	Send	URI: `c:\MyFirst\ExecOut\Exec%MessageID%.xml` Transport: File
`SendEmpPort`	`OutEmpType`	Send	URI: `c:\MyFirst\EmpOut\Emp%MessageID%.xml` Transport: File

NOTE

The string `%MessageID%` in the preceding URIs is a macro that expands to a unique message identifier at runtime. Using this allows us to send multiple messages to the same file folder without conflict.

Now that we have messages and ports, we can establish the flow of data in and out of the orchestration by specifying the message instances used with each Send and Receive shape and connecting them to the appropriate Port shape.

1. From the drop-down list in the `RecvEmpMsg` shape, select `EmpInstance`.
2. Establish an incoming connection by dragging from the green handle on `RecvEmpPort` to the green handle on `RecvEmpMsg`.
3. From the drop-down list in the `SendExecMsg` shape, select `ExecInstance`.
4. Drag from the green handle on `SendExecMsg` to the green handle on `SendExecPort`.
5. From the drop-down list in `SendEmpToHR`, select `EmpInstance`.
6. Drag from the green handle on `SendEmpToHR` to the green handle on `SendEmpPort` to establish an outgoing link.

If you look at the orchestration schedule diagram now, you will see yellow caution icons on `IsExecutive`, `MakeExecMsg`, and `TransformEmpMsg`. This means that all we have left to configure are, respectively, the expression to determine if we have to construct and send an executive message, the message type we want to construct, and the map used to construct the message.

1. Select `IsExecutive` and click the Caution icon smart tag. Text describing the incomplete configuration appears. Click this text to open the BizTalk Expression Editor.
2. Type **`EmpInstance.Grade > 5`** into the text box. Note that expressions are case sensitive. Note also that smart help is available after you enter the name of the message variable.

3. Click OK to close the Expression Editor. Note that the caution smart tag is gone from IsExecutive.
4. Select the `MakeExecMsg` shape.
5. In the Properties view, find Messages Constructed and select `ExecInstance`.
6. Click the smart tag adjoining `TransformEmpMsg`, and then click on the explanatory text to open the Transform Configuration dialog box.
7. Select Existing Map.
8. Select the `<Select from referenced assembly...>` entry from the list under Fully Qualified Map Name.
9. In the Select Artifact Type dialog box, select MyFirstMessaging, and then select `emp2exec` from the list of type names.
10. Click OK to close the Select Artifact Type dialog box.
11. In the left tree under Transform, select the source entry.
12. Under Variable Name for the Source Transform, select EmpInstance.
13. Repeat steps 11 and 12 to specify `ExecInstance` for the Destination Transform.
14. Ensure that Launch BizTalk Mapper is unchecked, and then click OK.

We are finally ready to compile the orchestration project. As with the messaging project, we have to make this a strongly named assembly. We can use the same key file we employed in that project.

1. In the Solution Explorer, right-click MyFirstIntegration and then click Properties.
2. Click assembly under Common Properties in the project Properties dialog box.
3. Scroll down to the Assembly Key file property under the Strong name category.
4. Click the ellipsis and browse to `MyFirstIntegration.snk`. Click Open to close the Assembly Key File dialog, and then click OK to close the project Properties dialog box.
5. In the Solution Explorer, right-click the project and click Build.

Deployment and Testing

It is finally time to deploy our assemblies to the global cache of the BizTalk server. BizTalk provides a wizard for this, the BizTalk Deployment Wizard, which may be started from the Programs item on the Windows Start menu. Start this wizard, found in the BizTalk Server 2004 group, and perform the following steps.

1. Click Next on the Welcome page.
2. Check Deploy BizTalk Assembly to database for the Deployment Task.
3. Click Next to accept the defaults on the Configuration Database page.
4. On the Deploy BizTalk Assembly page, browse to the `MyFirstIntegration\MyFirstOrchestration\bin\Development` folder and select `MyFirstMessaging.dll`. Click Open.
5. Make sure the check box Install Assembly to the Global Cache on This Computer is checked, and then click Next.
6. Click Next on the ready page.
7. After the deployment task completes, check Run This Wizard Again on the final page and click Finish.
8. Repeat steps 1–6 to locate and deploy `MyFirstOrchestration.dll`. On the final page, uncheck the check box and click Finish.

If you had left any port specifications in the orchestration for later, you would now use BizTalk Explorer to bind the logical ports to the physical file locations. Because we performed this task during the design process, we are ready to move on to some administrative tasks. Remember, we did this as a shortcut in this sample. In a production environment, you will usually have to go on and perform the binding process.

1. Use the Windows Start menu to locate the BizTalk Server group and launch BizTalk Server Administration.
2. Expand the Hosts node for the server in question. Select the `BizTalkServerApplication` node. If it is stopped, right-click the entry and click Start. If the status remains Start Pending, click Refresh. If the status does not change and you are running Message Queuing (MSMQ) on the same server, shut MSMQ down using the Services in the Administrative Tools folder of the Windows Control Panel, and then try to start `BizTalkserverApplication` again.
3. Select Orchestrations, then right-click `MyFirstOrchestration.EmployeeOrchestration` and click Enlist to start the Enlistment Wizard.
4. Click Next on the Welcome page.
5. Click Next on the Receive Locations page. You fully configured the receive location at design time.
6. Click Next on the Orchestration Enlistment page, leaving the default selection in place.
7. Click Finish on the final page.

8. In the left pane, select Send Ports.
9. Locate the long names ending in `SendEmpPort` and `SendExecPort` in the right pane. Right-click each in turn and click Enlist.
10. Right-click each send port again, this time clicking Start. The send ports are now active.
11. Return to the left pane and select Orchestrations. In the right pane, right-click `MyFirstOrchestration.EmployeeOrchestration` and click Start Processing. Click Yes when prompted to start the receive location associated with the schedule.

You are now ready to test the integration solution. For simplicity, the download for this chapter includes two sample files, `sample_employee_grade2.xml` and `sample_employee_grade7.xml`, which test both sides of the decision tree. The former has a value of 2 for the employee's Grade attribute, whereas the latter has a value of 7. You may also compose your own messages based on these files.

1. If you have not already done so, create the test folder structure corresponding to the configurations performed in the Orchestration: a folder named `MyFirst` off the root of the C drive, with child folders In, `ExecOut`, and `EmpOut`.
2. Copy `sample_employee_grade2.xml` and paste the copy into the In folder. After a few seconds, the file should disappear.
3. Check `ExecOut` and ensure that it remains empty.
4. Open the file that appeared in `EmpOut` and note that it is a copy of the message you dropped.
5. Repeat steps 2–4 with `sample_employee_grade7.xml`. This time, both outbound folders will have a message. Open the one in `ExecOut` and note that it is an executive instance whose data corresponds to that in the original employee message. Note that the `fname` and `lname` attributes have uppercase values.

Summary

BizTalk Server 2004 has an extensive architecture that rests, as you have seen in this chapter, on two core runtime engines. Messaging handles low-level message exchanges with data transformation and protocol-switching capabilities. Orchestration is a sophisticated and powerful workflow processing engine that relies on the messaging engine for the implementation of the individual actions in the workflow.

Designers and developers working with BizTalk Server 2004 rely on a series of add-ins to Visual Studio .NET for their development tasks. This is a consolidation of the tools from earlier versions of BizTalk Server and represents a considerable improvement in that developers are able to stick with a single, familiar IDE.

You completed your overview of this product with a basic sample integration project that exercised messaging, message transformation, and orchestration. You saw that BizTalk projects can be organized into projects that track the architecture of BizTalk Server, splitting functionality and resources into messaging and orchestration assemblies. You learned how to use the Deployment Wizard to move assemblies into the global cache and update the BizTalk Configuration database. Finally, you used the BizTalk Administration console to start your solution and run it.

Much of the rest of this book is an in-depth amplification of the tools and features you have seen. The next few chapters refine and extend the topics to which you were introduced in this chapter. With that in mind, let us proceed to Chapter 3.

PART II

Developing with BizTalk Server 2004—Messaging

IN THIS PART

CHAPTER 3

Building Message Specifications

IN THIS CHAPTER

- Editor Details
- Flat-File Specifications
- Property Promotion and Property Schemas
- Using InfoPath Documents with BizTalk

Messaging is the foundation of BizTalk Server, and message schemas are the bedrock on which messaging is built. Schemas are used by the messaging runtime to understand the structure of data messages and find specific fields. The property fields specified by schemas can be used to help route a message to its destination. Messaging is the exchange of structured data, and schemas are where that structure is defined.

BizTalk Server makes use of XML Schemas to describe a wide range of message structures. Messages in BizTalk encompass the full range of features supported by XML and can also include positional and delimited flat-file formats. Because the same tool is used for both XML and flat-file formats, BizTalk abstracts messages into records and fields. This is a common notion that will be familiar to many programmers. Visually, BizTalk Editor treats both as nodes in a tree. We will begin by looking at how you can use Editor to visually describe a textual structure as nodes in this tree. After you've mastered that, we'll move on to see how various XML structures are described as the properties of these nodes. Then we'll move to the slightly more difficult task of doing the same thing for flat-file formats. Finally, we'll see how BizTalk's use of XML Schemas allows us to prepare the messaging system for use with another technology that uses forms in Microsoft Office as Web service clients.

Editor Details

Recall from Chapter 2, "Your First BizTalk Server Integration," that BizTalk Editor has three principal views: the Schema tree view, the XSD Source view, and the Property view. Because the XSD Source view is read-only, you'll be spending your time in the other two views. Because a lot of the properties you'll set and the options available to you depend on the type of the schema (XML or flat file), we'll concentrate on the basics of navigating the user interface and building a general document structure in this section.

Schema Properties

The first thing you see when you open a new schema is a `<Schema>` node with a single child node named Root. `<Schema>` is something of a metanode and as such is really a placeholder for the document as a whole. You'll set two kinds of properties for this node: properties that pertain to the schema as part of an overall BizTalk project and properties that pertain to the schema itself. The former are found and set in a properties dialog box that you open, whereas the latter are manipulated through the Properties window that is typically open throughout your Visual Studio session.

In the Solution Explorer node, right-click the schema file entry and click Properties. You'll see the Property Pages dialog box depicted in Figure 3.1.

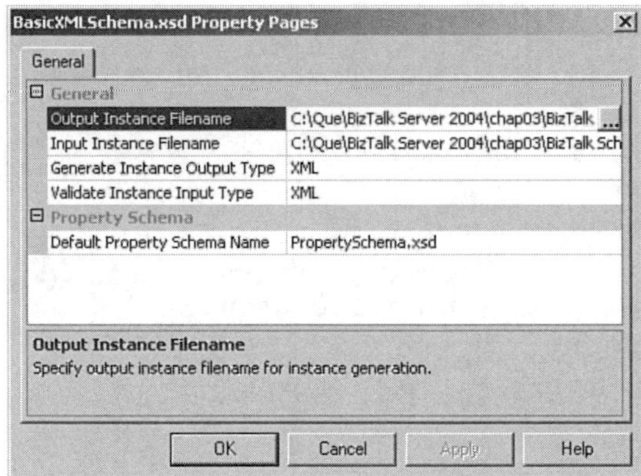

FIGURE 3.1 Schema item properties for the project are set in the Property Pages dialog box.

There are four properties you can set, but they pertain to two features: Instance Document Interaction and Property Promotion. Editor lets you generate sample instance documents from the schema or validate sample instance documents. These are useful features that let you compare your schema to the sort of instance document you envision. Without setting instance document filenames, Editor can generate a temporary file for output, but you need an actual input document to use the validation feature. If you need a bit more permanence in output, you'll need to set the following properties:

- Output Instance Filename—The name and location of the sample instance document generated by Editor from the schema.
- Input Instance Filename—The name and location of the sample input document you provide for validation against the schema.

When generating instance documents, you may also need to set the Create Instance Output Type property. This defaults to XML, but when you are dealing with flat files, you'll need to set it to Native. You generate an instance document by right-clicking the schema document in Solution Explorer and clicking Generate Instance. When you want to validate the existing document pointed to by the Input Instance Filename property, you right-click as before and click Validate Instance.

The remaining property, Default Property Schema Name, refers to a schema that is used in conjunction with the property promotion feature we discuss in the "Property Promotion and Property Schemas" section later in this chapter. This property defaults to `PropertySchema.xsd`. Note that unlike the Filename properties we set for instance files, this is an unqualified filename.

Close the Property Page dialog box now and turn your attention to the Visual Studio Property window. With the schema file selected in the Solution Explorer, the Property window displays a variety of properties, mostly names and file locations. The Namespace property is a .NET-style namespace and differs from the Schema node's Target Namespace property. It turns up throughout the tools when qualifying .NET types. Similarly, the Type Name property is derived from the filename and is the unqualified typename.

If you select the `<Schema>` node in the tree view, however, you find a richer set of properties. In this view you can declare a namespace for the schema, indicate whether you are specifying a message or an envelope used to enclose messages, specify the standard for the schema, and even specify a root node to use when you are sending a message with multiple top-level nodes.

NOTE

This may seem curious if you are an XML programmer. An XML document will not be well formed if it has more than one top-level node. You do not have this restriction with flat-file formats. It is not uncommon to encounter a situation where you want to work with a subset of data exported by a legacy application. Rather than change the code and modify the export (which may not even be possible for your project), you can specify which top-level node BizTalk should use to begin processing. The data anchored by other top-level nodes will be ignored during message processing.

You can usually accept the defaults for Schema node properties, particularly when writing a schema for an XML message. There is one property, however, which may seem curious to you, especially if you have experience with previous versions of the Editor. If you peruse the Schema node properties for a newly created schema, you will not find a property that permits you to declare a flat file. Experienced BizTalk programmers will look at the Standard property without success. The answer to this dilemma lies in the fact that Editor is now composed of an XML subset plus extensions. To declare a flat-file schema, go to the Schema Editor Extensions property, click the ellipsis button, and check Flat File Extension in the Schema Editor Extensions dialog box. This dialog box also lets you load the Human Workflow extension. After the flat-file extension is loaded, new properties appear in the Property view, and new property values are added to the standard property list box. One of these is Flat File.

Adding Records and Fields

After you've created a schema and renamed the root node, you're ready to add some content. The commands to do this are found on the BizTalk menu off the main menu bar or directly through right-clicking and selecting from the context menu. Regardless of which menu you use, you point to Insert Schema Node and make a selection from the submenu.

The first distinction you have to worry about is whether to insert a record node or a field node. This distinction is easy when you are solely concerned with structure. Records can contain other records and fields or can have values directly. Fields take only values. This is directly analogous to database design. When you move into schemas for XML messages, you have another choice to make. Only elements can have child content, so they have to be implemented as elements. Both elements and attributes can have values, so BizTalk message fields can be implemented as either XML node type.

Now that you've decided what sort of node to add, you need to think about where the node is going. Your choices are all relative to the node currently selected in the tree view. Consequently, the Insert Schema Node menu has choices for Child Record, Child Field Attribute, and Child Field Element as well as Sibling Record, Sibling Field Attribute, and Sibling Field Element. After child content is created, you can change the order of the child nodes by dragging them within the tree view.

The XSD Schema format includes several kinds of group constructs. BizTalk takes advantage of this. By default, child content for a node is presumed to occur in order in the sequence provided. You can get the same effect explicitly by using the Sequence Group menu item, in which case a `sequence` element is created in the XSD Source view. Sometimes, though, you want to specify a series of records or fields from which to choose in creating a message instance. If you had a message schema representing this chapter, for example, you'd need to be able to select from a choice of paragraphs, figures, notes, and tables at any given point under the chapter record. To do this in BizTalk Editor, you insert a Choice group. The node in the tree view is labeled `<Choice>`, and the available choices are specified as the child nodes of this node. You control the number of times the message instance can choose from these options with the `Min Occurs` and `Max Occurs` properties of the `<Choice>` node.

XSD format schemas also allow you to specify an element that acts as a wildcard placeholder. At some point in the schema you know that you will have some element, and you know what the child content of that node will be, but you do not know in advance what the node itself will be. A family of applications might have various specialized views of an individual, but you are concerned only with some subset of the content. For example, a hospital information system might embrace Nurse, Doctor, and Other Staff types of employees, but all have a common substructure for the purposes of employee benefits. An HR application, then, might use a schema that ignores `Nurse`, `Doctor`, and `OtherStaff` elements while paying attention to the child content. This is the purpose of the All Group type of node. This option appears only when the selected node meets the constraints of the XSD Schema Recommendation for the use of the `all` element. To use this in BizTalk Editor, insert a child record, set the record's `Content Type` property to `ComplexContent`, and then point to Insert Schema Node and click All Group.

The final type of group you can create in Editor is an Attribute Group. You might have a series of field attributes that you need to apply to multiple records, and you want to avoid respecifying them every time you use them. You can do this by inserting an Attribute Group node and then inserting child field attribute nodes. When you want to reuse the group in another record, insert an Attribute Group node and then change the Group Name property value from what Editor generated to the value in the first attribute group. All the field attributes you defined there will automatically appear in the new group node.

Continuing our tour, you'll see that BizTalk Editor offers two singleton node types that, like the All Group node, allow you to inject some degree of ambiguity into a schema to accommodate uncertainty. The first is created with the Any Element command on the Insert Schema Node menu. When created, it inserts an `<Any>` node into the tree view and an XSD Schema `any` element into the schema source view. Like the All Group, the `Any` node accommodates some unknown well-formed element content. In contrast to the `All Group` node, it cannot have child content specified for it. The schema allows child content, but that content will be ignored for validation purposes. If you are specifying a schema for a very complex schema, you might, for example, want to skip specifying content for areas of the message that you know will never be used by the receiving application or partner. Similarly, if you are modeling an element that you know will have some unknown attributes (that you don't care about), you may use the `Any` Attribute command to insert an `<AnyAttribute>` node into the tree view. An XSD Schema `anyAttribute` element is added to the source view. Like the `Any` node, `AnyAttribute` is used to provide for the existence of content while ignoring its particulars.

Sample Schema: Structure

We've given you all the commands BizTalk Editor provides for creating structure, and that's a lot of material for one sitting. Let's ground this in a practical sample. You can examine this schema in the file `BasicXMLSchema.xsd` in the chapter download, or you can use the steps that follow to create it from scratch. The purpose of this message schema is to model a single person who serves as a point of contact, possibly as part of a customer management system. Each message instance must model the contact's name as well as a list of one or more home or office addresses. For simplicity, we'll assume United States style postal addresses and SSNs and ignore electronic means of contact.

1. Within a BizTalk project, right-click the project node in Solution Explorer, point to Add, then click Add New Item. From BizTalk Project Items, select the Schema template to create a new schema file.
2. Change the root node's Node Name property to `Contact`. Enter `ContactType` for the value of Data Structure Type.

3. Right-click Contact in the tree view, point to Insert Schema Node, and then click Sequence Group. Set the Max Occurs and Min Occurs properties of this new node to `1`.
4. Right-click `<Sequence>`, point to Insert Schema Node, and then click Child Record. Change the Node Name property to `Person` and the Min Occurs and Max Occurs properties to `1`.
5. Right-click Person and insert a Sibling Record. Name this `Locations` and set Min Occurs and Max Occurs to `1`.
6. Return to Person and insert a Child Field Attribute. Name it `SSN`. Set the Use Requirement property to `Required`.
7. Return to Person and insert a Child Field Element. Name it `FirstName` and set Min Occurs and Max Occurs to `1`.
8. Repeat step 7, inserting `MiddleName` (Min Occurs = `0`, max Occurs = `1`) and `LastName` (Min occurs = `1`, Max Occurs = `1`).

NOTE

Locations is intended to be a collection of one or more instances of home and or office addresses. These can occur in any order and any number, provided that at least one instance of an address record occurs. We'll model this with a Choice Group. Further, we note that home and office addresses have something in common: the street address. They differ in that a home address can have an apartment number, whereas an office can have a room number or mailstop. We can therefore create a reusable type to model addresses.

9. Right-click Locations, point to Insert Schema Node, and then click Choice group. Set the Min Occurs property to `1`. This will ensure that at least one selection must be made from the permissible choices.
10. Right-click `<Choice>` and then insert a Child Record. Change the Node Name property to `Home`.
11. Right-click `Home` and insert a Child Field Attribute. Name this node `apt`.
12. Right-click `apt` and insert a Sibling Record. Name it `Address` and then type **`AddrType`** into the Data Structure Type property field. `AddrType(ComplexType)` appears in bold.
13. Insert a Sequence Group node as a child of Address. Set Min Occurs and Max Occurs to `1`.
14. Select the `<Sequence>` node and insert the following five Child field Elements, setting their properties as shown in Table 3.1.

TABLE 3.1 Child Field Elements for the AddrType Global Type

Node Name	Min Occurs	Max Occurs
Street1	1	1
Street2	0	1
City	1	1
State	1	1
ZIP	1	1

15. Under Locations, select `<choice>`, and then insert a Child Record. Set Node Name to `Office`.
16. Right-click Office and insert a Child Field attribute. Name it `room`. Set Use Requirement to `optional`.
17. Repeat step 16 to create `mailstop`.
18. Right-click `Office` and insert a Child Record. Set Node Name to `Address`. Select AddrType (ComplexType) from the list in the Data Structure Type property. Note that the child content previously declared in step 14 appears.
19. Save your work as `BasicXMLSchema.xsd`, then right-click the Schema node in Solution Explorer and click Validate Schema. The Output window should indicate `Validate Schema succeeded`.

At this time, the tree view should look like Figure 3.2.

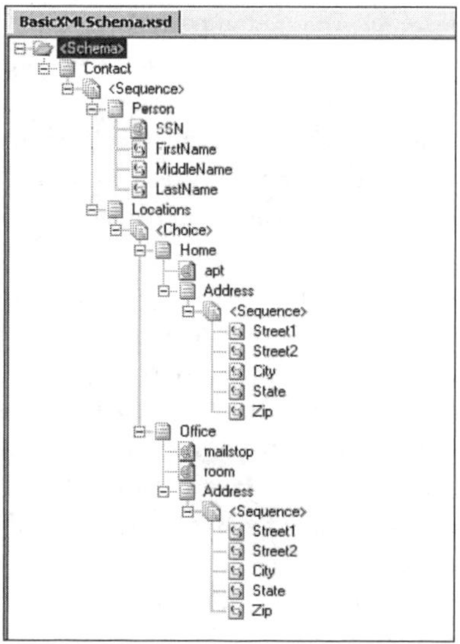

FIGURE 3.2 Final structure for your first sample schema.

Node Properties

We've covered a few of the properties of various nodes in the course of our previous discussion and introductory structural sample. The online documentation for BizTalk covers node properties in exhaustive detail. You need to know a bit more about node properties. Rather than repeat the BizTalk topics on node properties in their entirety, we'll cover the properties you are most likely to use in normal BizTalk development projects.

Schema Node Properties

Starting at the top, we should first consider the `<Schema>` metanode. Schema nodes are commonly configured with the properties in Table 3.2, although we'll be discussing several more properties when we get to flat-file schemas.

TABLE 3.2 Commonly Used Schema Node Properties

Property Name	Meaning and Usage
FinalDefault	Specifies how types in the schema can be used to create derived types using common XSD techniques. The value of this property is mapped to an XSD `finalDefault` attribute. Permissible values are `(Default)`—Removes the `finalDefault` attribute if present and makes normal derivation mechanisms available through the schema. `All`—Permits new types to be derived from any type declared in the schema using any XSD technique. `Restriction`—Allows derivation from all types in the schema using restriction. `Extension`—Permits derivation throughout the schema using extension. `List`—Permits a new type to be derived such that it is a space-delimited list of values permitted to the base type. `Union`—Permits a new type to be declared such that it is a value permitted to any one of a list of base types. Restriction, Extension, List, and Union may be chosen in combination by using the check boxes associated with each value.
Imports	Manages the schemas and namespaces used by this schema. Only schemas that are part of the current project may be imported. By default, the target namespace for the current schema, the W3C XSD namespace, and the core BizTalk namespace are members of this collection property.
Schema Editor Extensions	Specifies Editor extensions to be loaded. These extensions add node properties specific to a given class of messages. An example is the Flatfile extension that ships with BizTalk. Developers can create their own extensions.
CodeList Database	Locates the mdb format database that contains code lists.
Promote Properties	Used to promote fields in message instances as properties in the message context.
Node Name	Name of the node. This is read-only and fixed to `<Schema>` for the Schema node.

TABLE 3.2 Continued

Property Name	Meaning and Usage
Schema File Location	Location of the annotated schema document persisted by the Editor for the message schema. This property is read-only for the Schema node and may be changed only through the File, Save As menu item.
Target Namespace	Namespace URI identifying the declarations in the schema (limited to 255 characters).
Case	Controls character case conversion in message instances during processing by the BizTalk messaging engine. Permissible values are (Default)—Removes any prior case annotations from the schema. Characters will be unchanged during processing. Uppercase—Messages will be forced to uppercase. Lowercase—Characters in messages will be forced to lowercase.
Code Page	Used with flat-file schemas to define the character code page to use for message parsing.
Document Type	Used to specify an arbitrary identifier defining the type of document being specified. This identifier should be meaningful to your application and is chiefly used with flat-file schemas.
Document Version	Value of an arbitrary, application-specific version identifier. Usually used for flat-file schemas.
Envelope	Denotes whether the schema represents an envelope specification. Permissible values are `Yes`—The schema defines an envelope. `No`—The schema does not define an envelope. `(Default)`—Equivalent to `No`, this value also removes the attribute used to persist this property in the schema document.
Receipt	Indicates that messages associated with this schema are incoming receipts for previously sent messages. Values are `Yes`—The schema defines a receipt message. `No`—The schema does not define a receipt. `(Default)`—Equivalent to `No`, this value also clears the attribute used to persist this property in the schema document.
Root Reference	Used to indicate which of several top-level nodes to use to anchor message processing. The default value is sufficient for schemas defining XML messages because well-formed XML documents may have but a single top-level element. You can select a record node name from a list of top-level nodes when defining other types of messages.
Schema Type	Denotes whether this is a document or a property schema. Values are `Document`—This schema defines message instances. `Property`—This schema is used for property promotion. `(Default)`—Same as `Document`, this value also removes the attribute used to persist this property in the schema document.

TABLE 3.2 Continued

Property Name	Meaning and Usage
Specification Name	An arbitrary string meant to be a human-friendly name for the schema.
Standard	Denotes the format used for the message. Values are `XML`—XML syntax is used. `(Default)`—Same as `XML`, but also removes the attribute used to persist this property in the schema document. Other string—Arbitrary string denoting the standard syntax used; for example, `X12` or `EDIFACT`.
Standard Version	Version of the syntax (specified by the Standard property) used; for example, `1.0` when Standard has the value `XML`.

Some of the properties discussed previously require further discussion. Schema importation is an important mechanism for structuring your schemas and reusing common constructions. We deal with this issue in the section on building schemas from existing schemas. Property promotion is a very important topic for BizTalk messaging. We alluded to this in Chapter 2 when we promoted some properties from message instances into the message context. We discuss property promotion and property schemas later in this chapter. Envelopes are useful for message routing. Envelopes are processed by pipelines, so we shall go into greater depth on the topic of envelopes in Chapter 5, "Building Pipelines."

Record Node Properties

Record nodes, which include the document root element, are most important nodes after the Schema metanode because they are the foundation of message structure. The most commonly used record node properties in XML messages are listed in Table 3.3. We'll be adding additional properties when we get to flat-file formats.

TABLE 3.3 Commonly Used Record Node Properties

Record Node Property Name	Meaning and Usage
Base Date Type	When inheriting from a globally declared type, you select the global type from which you are deriving this record from the list provided in Editor.
Content Type	Defines the type of content the record may contain. Values are `(Default)`—Clears the property in the schema. `SimpleContent`—Prevents the record from containing record and field element nodes. `ComplexContent`—Allows the record to contain child records and/or field element nodes.

TABLE 3.3 Continued

Record Node Property Name	Meaning and Usage
Derived By	If the content type property is set to `ComplexContent`, this property may be used to control how the record inherits from a global type. Permissible values are `(Default)`—Clears the persisted property and clears inheritance for this record. `Extension`—The record derives by extension (child content is added to that declared in the global type). `Restriction`—The record derives by restriction, forming a subset of the base type; property value ranges for properties in the global type are restricted from the ranges declared in the global type.
Form	Defines whether elements from the target namespace of this schema (that is, elements declared in the schema) must be qualified with a namespace prefix in message instances. Although typically set for the document as a whole, you may set this property on a record-by-record basis. Permissible values are `(Default)`—Removes the attribute used to persist this property in the schema document. Records with this property value may be unqualified in messages. `Qualified`—Instances of this record must be qualified in messages. `Unqualified`—Instances of this record need not be qualified (but are allowed to be qualified).
Group Max Occurs	Controls the maximum number of times a child group node may appear in a message instance. Permissible values are any positive integer or the literal string `unbounded` (also abbreviated with a literal asterisk character). Defaults to `1`.
Group Min Occurs	Indicates the minimum number of times a child group node may appear in a message instance. Must be less than or equal to Group Max Occurs. Permissible values are zero or any positive integer. Defaults to `1`.
Group Order Type	Used to control the ordering of child element groups. Permissible values are `All`—Marks the child group as an All Group. Permissible only for top-level record nodes. `Choice`—Marks the child group as a Choice Group. `Sequence`—The child group is a Sequence Group; all content must appear in the order specified. This is the default value for this property. `None`—Selecting this value clears any prior choice. You may not select this value if the record node has child records defined for it.
Mixed	If `True`, this record may have textual content, child records, or both. If `False` (default), this record must have either content or child records, but not both.
Notes	This property is used for user-defined comments or notes.
Block	Controls how the type defined by this node may be extended in an instance message. The mechanisms used are the ones provided by the XSD Schema recommendation for type derivation. Permitted values of this property are `(Default)`—Lifts all restrictions and removes the attribute used to persist this property in the schema document.

TABLE 3.3 Continued

Record Node Property Name	Meaning and Usage
	`All`—Explicitly denies all forms of derivation. `Restriction`—Denies derivation through the restriction mechanism. `Extension`—Denies extension. `Substitution`—Denies substitution. `Restriction`, `Extension`, and `Substitution` may be used in any combination by using the check boxes provided in the drop-down list for this property.
Data Structure Type	Used when defining or referencing a reusable type. You may enter a string to name a new type or select from a list of declared types when declaring a record node to be an instance of a reusable type.
Final	Controls how the type declared by the record node may be used to derive new types elsewhere in this schema. Permissible values are `(Default)`—Clears this property and the attribute used to persist it in the schema file. `All`—Blocks all further derivation from this type. `Restriction`—This type may not be used to derive a new type using the restriction mechanism. `Extension`—Denies the use of extension for the derivation of new types. `Restriction` and `Extension` may be combined by checking their restrictive check boxes in the drop-down list for this property.
Max Occurs	The maximum number of times the element represented by this node may occur in a message. Permitted values are any positive integer, the string unbounded (also abbreviated as an asterisk), or blank. If left blank, the property value defaults to `1`.
Min Occurs	The minimum number of times this element may occur in a message. This value must be less than or equal to the value provided for Max Occurs. Permitted values are the integer zero, any positive integer, or blank. If left blank, the property defaults to `1`.
Namespace	This read-only property displays the namespace of the node.
Node Name	Name of the node. Limited to 255 characters.

Field Node Properties

Field nodes have a greater number of commonly used properties. Because they represent data fields in your messages, field nodes need properties to specify and constrain the permitted values of that data. XSD Schemas provide rich mechanisms for type restriction, specification, and extension. This is reflected in BizTalk Editor's Property view for field nodes. Table 3.4 describes the properties you will most commonly use when working with message schemas.

TABLE 3.4 Commonly Used Field Node Properties

Field Node Property	Meaning and Usage
Base Data Type	When the Derived By property is set to Restriction, you can select one of the XSD simple types as the base data type from which this field node is derived.
Derived By	Specifies what XSD mechanism is used to derive the type of this node. Permissible values are `(Default)`—Clears this property and its attribute in the schema document. `Restriction`—The new type is derived by placing constraints on the value of the base data type. When this value is selected, the properties Enumeration, Length, MaxFacet Type, MaxFacet Value, MinFacet Type, MinFacet Value, Maximum Length, Minimum Length, and Pattern become available to you for defining simple constraints. `List`—The value of this node is constrained to be a space-delimited list of simple types. The type of each item in the list is set to be the value of the Base Data Type property. `Union`—The node is defined as having a value taken from any of a list of types. When this value is selected, the Member Types property is added to the Property view to enable you to select the types for the union.
Final	Used to control further derivation of this type elsewhere in the schema. Values are `(Default)`—Clears the property. `All`—Prevents all further derivation. `Restriction`—Prevents derivation through restriction. `List`—Prevents derivation through the List mechanism. `Union`—Prevents derivation through the Union mechanism. `Restriction`, `List`, and `Union` can be combined by selecting the appropriate check boxes in the drop-down list for this property.
Fixed	Specifies a fixed value to be used in all instances of this node. This property conflicts and may not be used with Default Value.
Item Type	When Derived By is set to List, the simple type chosen for this property's value is the data type of each item in the list.
Member Types	When Derived By is set to Union, this property specifies the list of permissible types for the field node's values.
Nillable	When True, the field node may have an XSD nillable attribute and must then be empty. False otherwise. Not available for attribute field nodes.
Code List	Used to indicate the code list to use for the allowable range of values for this field. Typically, the value of this property is an integer.
Notes	User-defined notes or comments.
Data Type	Used to specify the XSD simple type of this field node. The xs:long type is not recommended for messages that will be processed on Windows 2000 systems, because the related operating system data type is not supported.

3

TABLE 3.4 Continued

Field Node Property	Meaning and Usage
Default Value	Used to specify a default value that will be used for this field when one is not explicitly provided by the message. Conflicts with Fixed.
Field Type	Denotes whether this field is an element or an attribute. Read-only.
Max Occurs	Maximum number of times the field may occur. Not available for field attribute nodes. Permissible values are any positive integer, the literal string `unbounded`, or the literal character `*`, which is the abbreviation for `unbounded`. Defaults to `1`.
Min Occurs	Minimum number of times the field may occur. Not available for field attribute nodes. Must be less than or equal to Max Occurs. May be `0` or any positive integer. Defaults to `1`.
Node Name	Name of the field node.
Namespace	Namespace of the field node. Read-only.
Required	When `Yes`, the field must appear in message instances. When `No`, the field is optional. Defaults to `No` (also represented as a blank value).
Enumeration	A linefeed-delimited list of permissible values for the field node.
Length	When the Base Data Type property is a string-related type and Derived By is set to `Restriction`, you can use this to set the exact length of the field's value. Conflicts with MaxLength and MinLength.
MaxFacet Type	When Base Data Type is a numeric simple type and Derived By is `Restriction`, the value of this property controls how MaxFacet Value is applied. Permissible values are `Inclusive`—The permitted range for the field includes the value specified in MaxFacet Value. `Exclusive`—The permitted range does not include the value of MaxFacet Value. `(Default)`—Clears the property in the schema, signifying that there is no maximum value for this field.
MaxFacet Value	Specifies the maximum value of the field when the node is a numeric type and derived through restriction.
MinFacet Type	When Base Data Type is a numeric simple type and Derived By is `Restriction`, the value of this property controls how MinFacet Value is applied. Permissible values are the same as for MaxFacet.
MinFacet Value	Specifies the minimum value of the field when the node is a numeric type and derived through restriction.
Maximum Length	When deriving a string type through restriction, this property indicates the maximum length of the string. The permissible values are any positive integer or blank (to remove the upper limit).
Minimum Length	When deriving a string type through restriction, the value of this property denotes the minimum length of the string. This may be `0`, any positive integer less than or equal to the value of Maximum Length, or blank (to remove the lower bound).

TABLE 3.4 Continued

Field Node Property	Meaning and Usage
Pattern	When Derived By is `Restriction`, you may specify a regular expression to constrain the values of this field. The syntax for the regex is specified by the W3C Schema Recommendation.
Restriction Type	When `True`, inheritance from an XSD simple or built-in type through restriction is permitted. `False` otherwise.

This list—which, remember, is only the list of commonly used properties—is somewhat lengthy, but most of the list pertains to type derivation. This is a complex and powerful topic. An exhaustive treatment is found in the W3C Recommendation XML Schema: Datatypes (`http://www.w3.org/TR/xmlschema-2/`). Type derivation is a useful technique, so we'll go over the basic ideas in the "Inheritance and New Types" section that follows.

Inheritance and New Types

You can go a very long way defining message schemas without once worrying about global types and type derivation. Business applications in the real world, however, frequently deal with objects that are variations on the same underlying idea. You will look at people, for example, in various ways, recording different attributes depending on whether they are employees, managers, customers, prospective customers, or vendor contacts. You can sell a physical good or perform a service, yet both are products. Each has slightly different attributes, but also have some things in common. Type inheritance in schemas is a useful tool for meeting the need of these variations while still capturing their commonality. Creating schemas from other schemas (multiple namespaces) is another tool, but that will have to wait for the "Creating Schemas from Existing Schemas" section.

Our basic XML sample defined a global type, `AddrType`, to capture common address fields. We used this as the data type for the `Address` child record in `Home` and `Office`. This was typing, though, not inheritance. `Home` and `Office` were variations on the idea of a place. We inserted what they had in common, `Address`, and then added the fields that made them unique. This met our admittedly simple needs but left no room for further refinement. Let's modify that schema to take advantage of inheritance.

Make a copy of your finished `BasicXMLSchema.xsd` file. In the download for this chapter, the file is called `DerivedXMLSchema.xsd` and it reflects the changes we are about to make. Now perform the following steps:

1. Select the Home record node. In the Properties view, select AddrType from the list provided for the Base Data Type property.
2. Click Yes to dismiss the dialog box warning you that you have performed an action that will delete structures defined in the schema.
3. Note that the Content Type property has the value `ComplexContent` and the Derived By property defaults to `Extension`.

4. Enter **`HomeType`** for the value of Data Structure Type.
5. Note that `Home` now has a sequence node that contains another sequence node. The latter node contains the field element nodes for the actual information defined in `AddrType`.
6. Select the sequence node that is the immediate child of Home. Right-click, point to Insert Schema Node, and then click Sibling Attribute.
7. Name the new node `apt`.
8. Repeat steps 1–3 for the Office record node.
9. Enter **`OfficeType`** for the value of the Data Structure Type property.
10. Repeat step 6 twice and name the new attribute field nodes `room` and `mailstop`.

At this point, you have the same message structure you had at the end of our basic XML schema, and you may be wondering what all the fuss is about. After saving your work, select any record node and insert a new record. Select either `HomeType` or `OfficeType` as the Data Structure Type property. When you do so, all the fields defined for the type, including the ones we added to differentiate Home and Office from `AddrType`, appear. We can now derive from these new types to create variations, perhaps to differentiate between a primary residence and a vacation home, or between primary and satellite offices.

Schema type derivation is about more than simply creating new types in the sense of class inheritance in an object-oriented programming language. The W3C Schema Recommendation devotes a considerable amount of space to deriving types through restriction. BizTalk Editor reflects a lot of this, mainly through the Pattern property and the Min and MaxFacetValue properties for numeric types.

> **NOTE**
>
> Facets in XML Schemas are more flexible than what BizTalk permits. They are abstract properties for characterizing the permissible range of values for some derived type, and new facets may be defined. BizTalk's message schemas are somewhat more focused, restricting facets to ranges for numeric types and patterns for string types.

Any application that includes a data entry form should include code for field-level data validation. BizTalk is integration middleware, though, so we have no idea whether the applications that are generating the messages flowing through BizTalk have checked their data thoroughly. Tightening up message schemas through the use of restriction is a very good way to ensure that bad data does not spread from one poorly written application to the rest of your system.

You make use of restriction by selecting Restriction for the value of the Derived By property of a node. When you do this, the value of Data Type is moved to the Base Data Type property. If you are working with a numeric type, you can then use MinFacetValue and MaxFacetValue to set lower and upper bounds, respectively. MinFacet Type and MaxFacet Type let you control whether the permissible range for your new type includes these boundary values.

Anyone who has used regular expressions in programming knows that regular expressions are a way to pack a lot of validation information into a compact expression. In general terms, the expression (or expressions) you provide for the value of the Pattern property is a string that specifies what can appear at any given point in the input data value. At runtime, the data in the message field must match the pattern expression for the message to be considered valid.

NOTE

Although the W3C borrowed liberally from Perl and other scripting languages when developing their regular expression syntax, differences exist and you should refer to Part 2 of the Schema Recommendation (`http://www.w3.org/TR/xmlschema-2/`)for a complete treatment of the syntax used.

Our message schema includes a field for U.S. Social Security Numbers (SSNs). These numbers have a definite format, so the SSN field is an ideal candidate for demonstrating the use of restriction for string types. Perform the following steps using `DerivedXMLSchema.xsd`:

1. Select the SSN attribute field node.
2. Select Restriction from the drop-down list in the Derived By property.
3. Select the Pattern property and click the ellipsis button that appears.
4. Enter **`[0-9]{3}-[0-9]{2}-[0-9]{4}`** into the Edit field of the Pattern Editor dialog box.
5. Click OK to close the dialog box.

The regular expression that you entered says that an acceptable value for this field will be a string consisting of 3 digits selected from the range 0–9, followed by a literal hyphen character, then 2 digits from the same range, another hyphen, and then 4 digits, again from the same range. After you save the schema, you can experiment with instance validation and different values for this field to test your pattern.

Creating Schemas from Existing Schemas

The same concepts usually occur in many places throughout an organization, and this is reflected in the data structures in the organization's applications. Consequently, when you develop more than a few message schemas for a system, you'll probably find yourself repeating the same structures over and over. A better approach is to create individual schemas for these frequently recurring structures and then import the schema into more complicated message schemas.

BizTalk Editor offers three mechanisms for doing this, all adopted from XML Schemas. These mechanisms are import, include, and redefine. All three make the types in an external schema available to the schema on which you are working. Include requires that the two schemas either have the same target namespace or that the included schema must come from the empty namespace. Both include and import prevent you from deriving new types from the included or imported schema. Redefine works like import, except that you are free to derive from the external types. BizTalk Editor restricts you to including, importing, or refining schemas that are part of your current project or that are part of the project references.

Let's assume, for the sake of illustration, that you need to write a schema for messages describing projects. You quickly realize a need for describing a project contact and decide to borrow the Contact structure we created in `DerivedXML.xsd`. To do this, perform the following steps:

1. Add a new schema item to your current BizTalk project. Name it `ProjectContactXML.xsd`.
2. Rename the root node `Project`.
3. Add a child element field and name it `Name`. We'll leave other, non-Contact specifications as an exercise for the reader.
4. Select the `<Schema>` node.
5. Select the Imports property and click the ellipsis button.
6. Ensure that `XSD Import` is selected from the list for Import New Schema, as shown in the Imports Dialog window (see Figure 3.3).
7. Click Add.
8. Select `DerivedXMLSchema` from the Schemas branch in the BizTalk Type Picker dialog box that appears. This type will be qualified by the value of the Namespace property for the schema.
9. Click OK to close the type picker; then click OK again to close the Imports Dialog window.
10. Select the Project record node, insert a child record node, and name it `Contact`.
11. Select ns0:ContactType from the list of values for Data Structure Type property.

The Imports dialog box is shown in Figure 3.3. When you complete step 11, you'll see the nodes you defined in `DerivedXML.xsd` appear under the new node.

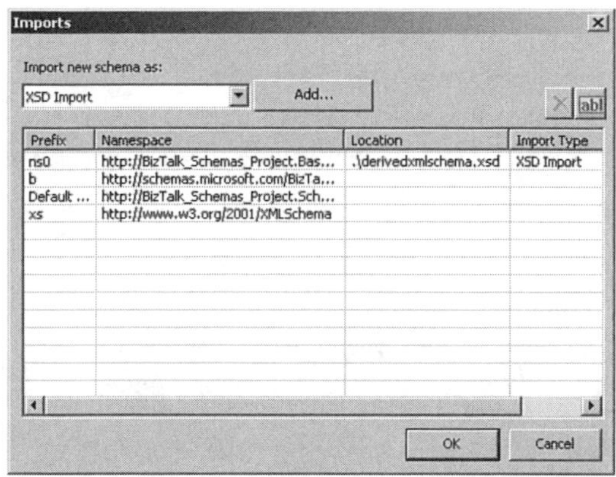

FIGURE 3.3 The BizTalk Type Picker enables you to select a schema to import, include, or redefine.

Creating a Schema from an Instance Document

BizTalk enables you to make use of any of several types of existing resources you may have for the specification of messages. Earlier versions of BizTalk used the XDR schema syntax proprietary to Microsoft. Before we had XSD Schemas as a standard, XML metadata was specified in document type definitions (DTDs). Without a prior definition, you can always compose a well-formed XML document or generate one from an existing application. You can use any of these to generate a new message schema for your BizTalk project.

To do this, you right-click the project node in the Solution Explorer, point to Add, and then click Add Generated Items. The Add Generated Items dialog box appears. Select the Generate Schemas folder under the Generated Schema Files folder in the categories pane, and then select the BtsImportSpecifications template in the templates pane and click Open. When that dialog box closes, the Generate Schemas dialog box appears. A typical view of this is shown in Figure 3.4.

By default, the software to import XDR schemas is loaded when you install BizTalk Server, but not the software for DTDs or well-formed XML documents. This is easily remedied. Execute the InstallDTD.vbs script (for DTDs) or InstallWFX.vbs script (for well-formed XML) as needed to install these components. These scripts are found in the SDK\Utilities\Schema Generator folder under your BizTalk installation.

When you have the proper components loaded, you select the type of resource from the Document type list, browse to the resource itself, and then click OK in the Generate Schemas dialog box. Visual Studio will then generate a message schema and add it to the project.

To get an idea of the process, we'll import the XML document shown in Listing 3.1 (found in the code download as sample_proj.xml).

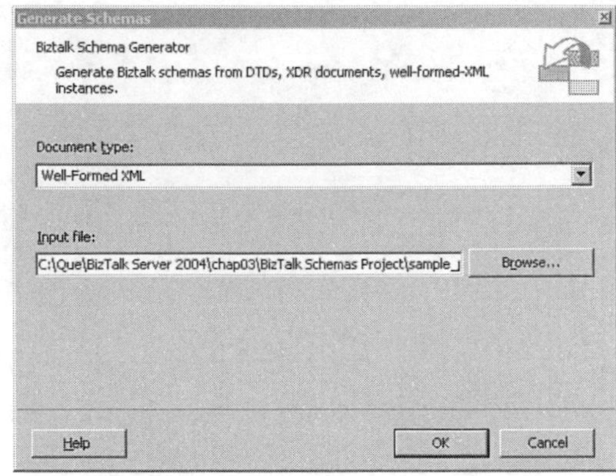

FIGURE 3.4 You can select existing resources to generate a new schema using the Generate Schemas dialog box.

LISTING 3.1 Sample XML for Schema Import

```
<?xml version="1.0" encoding="utf-8" ?>
<Project xmlns="http://project.xsd">
    <Name>Project 1</Name>
    <Start priority="3">2003-08-01</Start>
</Project>
```

Referring to Listing 3.1, you should take note of three items: First is a default namespace, denoted by the xmlns attribute on the Project element; second is a numeric type for the attribute priority; and third is an ISO 8601 format date we've inserted as the textual content of the Start element. How does the importer handle these? Keep this in mind as we examine the schema over the next few paragraphs.

When the schema is generated (`sample_proj.xsd` in the code download), select the `<Schema>` node and examine the value of the Target Namespace property in the Properties view. The default namespace in the document was taken for this value in the schema. This will likely differ from the naming convention Visual Studio uses by default when you create a new schema, but if you have taken the trouble to declare namespaces in your documents, you are either pointing to a schema, in which case you don't need to import the instance document, or you have a meaningful scheme for creating namespace URIs.

Now if you look at the value assigned to the `Start` element, which had textual content in the sample, you'll see that the schema generator recognized the possibility that we meant to enter a date and therefore assigned `Start` the XSD date type as its data type. The `priority` attribute was recognized as a numeric type and was assigned the smallest type consistent with the value found. Unsigned byte might not have been what we had in mind.

NOTE

There is a lesson in this. First, check generated schemas carefully. The generator code is good, but it cannot read your mind. Equally important, make sure you have a representative sample instance. If you have optional attributes or elements, make sure they appear in the sample code. It is easier to change the cardinality of a generated item than to insert a missing item.

Flat-File Specifications

Although BizTalk is based on the use of XML message formats internally, and you are strongly encouraged to use XML for the creation of new messages, it also works with flat files. There is such an installed base of legacy flat-file data formats, moreover, that you will likely find yourself dealing with one in your first BizTalk project. Happily, you already learned much of what you need to know to work with flat-file schemas.

Everything we said earlier about creating structure applies to flat files, as does the information regarding record and field node properties. But where data fields in XML messages are known to be delimited with tags and attributes of known syntax, we know little more about delimited and positional files than that they follow certain conventions. For example, consider the following fragment of a comma delimited message:

```
C
Sam,,Brown,29
C
Sarah,J,Adams,42
...
```

This sample constitutes two contact records, each of which consists of a first name, an optional middle initial, a last name, and an age. Each record starts with the literal C followed by a newline character. Each field within the record is delimited by a comma. The comma is inserted between fields, which is called infix notation. Unlike XML, the delimiters are dictated by our schema and there are no tags. Clearly, our BizTalk schemas for delimited files will require some additional information to initialize the parser.

Now consider the positional equivalent to the last message fragment:

```
Sam        Brown          29
Sarah     JAdams          42
```

This is actually a hybrid delimited-positional flat file. For clarity, we delimit the records with a new line (the literal record indicator character has been dropped), and each field occupies a fixed area. The first name is allotted 10 characters, the middle initial gets 1, the last name is allowed 15 characters, and the age takes 2 characters. Fields that do not fill the allotted space are left justified and padded with spaces. Everything we've just told you has to be communicated to BizTalk if the flat-file parser is to be able to make sense of an incoming message or compose an outgoing message. Let's take a quick look at the additional properties needed; then we'll go on and create a couple of sample flat-file schemas.

Schema Node Additions

Before diving into the additional properties, we should define three terms. Many of the new properties pertain to delimited format flat files. Delimiters can go in three places with respect to records and fields: before the item it is delimiting, after the item it delimits, and between two items. The last is a special case of the second one; they differ in that when the delimiter follows an item, it always appears, even if no item follows it. In the last case, when the delimiter comes between items, the delimiter will not appear following the last field in a record or after the last record in the message. The terms for these positions are prefix (before), postfix (after), and infix (between).

The Schema node adds the properties found in Table 3.5 to the most commonly used properties listed in Table 3.2. Because this node is a sort of umbrella for everything in the schema, these properties are mostly related to setting defaults for the rest of the schema.

TABLE 3.5 Commonly Used Flat-File Schema Node Properties

Schema Node Property Name	Meaning and Usage
Default Child Delimiter Type	Configures how the default child delimiter for the schema will be specified in the Default Child Delimiter property. Values are `Character`—The delimiter is specified as a character string. `Hexadecimal`—The default delimiter is specified as a hexadecimal value. `None`—Clears the property in the schema document (default property value).
Default Child Delimiter	Specifies the value of the Default Child Delimiter for the entire schema. This property is not available until the Default Child Delimiter Type property is set. The value of this property may be any string of characters or hexadecimal values, depending on the Child Delimiter Type property.
Default Child Order	Specifies the default delimiter position used throughout the schema. Permissible values are `Prefix`, `Postfix`, and `Infix`.
Default Decimal Character Type	Specifies how the Default Decimal Character property is expressed. Values are `Character`, `Hexadecimal`, and `None`.
Default Decimal Character	Specifies the decimal character (separating integral and fractional values in a numeric value) used as a default. Values are restricted to any of the predefined characters in the drop-down list (international characters), any single character (or hexadecimal value), or blank to remove this property from the schema.
Default Escape Character Type	Configures how the Default Escape Character property is expressed. Permissible values for this property are `Character`, `Hexadecimal`, or `None` to clear this property setting.

TABLE 3.5 Continued

Schema Node Property Name	Meaning and Usage
Default Escape Character	Specifies the default character used to escape reserved characters so that they may be used as literals in a message. This property may be any of the characters in the drop-down list, any single character, or blank to clear the property setting.
Default Repeating Delimiter Type	Denotes whether the value of the Default Repeating delimiter property is a character string (`Character`), hexadecimal value string (`Hexadecimal`), or `None` to clear this property.
Default Repeating Delimiter	Specifies the character or hexadecimal string used as the default delimiter for repeating fields.
Default Wrap Character Type	Denotes how the value of the Default Wrap Character property is expressed. Values for this property are `Character`, `Hexadecimal`, and `None`.
Default Wrap Character	Specifies, for the entire schema, the default wrap character. This property may take a value from the predefined drop-down list, any single character you provide, or a blank value to clear this property.
Count Positions in Bytes	Indicates whether to count positions within fields in a positional message in bytes. Values are `Yes` (to count by bytes) or `No` (to count by character).
Restricted Characters	This property is a collection of character ranges that may not appear in messages specified by this schema.

Record Node Additions

Record nodes also add a number of commonly used properties to those mentioned earlier. Many of these are identical to those listed for the Schema node, except that they establish defaults for the scope of the record rather than the entire document. These properties are Child Delimiter Type, Child Delimiter, Child Order, Escape Character Type, Escape Character, Repeating Delimiter Type, and Repeating Delimiter. In addition, record nodes in flat-file message schemas add the properties found in Table 3.6.

TABLE 3.6 Commonly Used Properties Unique to Flat-File Records

Record Property Name	Meaning and Usage
Ignore Record Count	When `Yes`, this record is ignored when records are accumulated. When `No`, this record is counted for the total. When left blank, the property is cleared.
Preserve Delimiter for Empty Data	Specifies whether delimiters are used when the fields they delimit are empty. By default, BizTalk preserves delimiters for empty fields and suppresses them for empty records. Permissible values are `Yes` to preserve the delimiter, `No` to suppress a delimiter, and blank to clear the property. When a record is optional, the delimiter will be suppressed regardless of the value of this property.

TABLE 3.6 Continued

Record Property Name	Meaning and Usage
Suppress Trailing Delimiters	Indicates whether to suppress the delimiter for trailing records (`Yes`) or retain them (`No`). `No` is the default value.
Tag Identifier	A character string used to identify a tag for the record.
Tag Offset	Specifies the starting position of the record's tag relative to the preceding sibling node or delimiter. This value must be nonzero or blank (default).

Field Node Additions

Schema and record nodes convey the structure of the document but do not give us any data (with the significant but rare exception of mixed-content records). From the point of view of an application, field nodes are the valuable part of the message. In addition to the common properties described for XML message schemas and the obscure, advanced properties in the product documentation), field nodes in flat-file messages also use the properties listed in Table 3.7. Note that in contrast to records, most of these properties are meaningful to positional message formats.

TABLE 3.7 Commonly Used Field Node Properties Specific to Flat-File Schemas

Field Property Name	Meaning and Usage
Custom Date/Time Format	Specifies a character string indicating the format of date/time fields. The drop-down list provides a number of preconfigured formats, but you can specify a custom format string of your own. Allowable separators are dashes, periods, and slashes. Julian dates may not be specified because of their similarity to nondate numeric types.
Justification	Indicates how data in a positional field is justified when it is shorter than the defined field length. Values are `Left` and `Right`.
Minimum Length with Pad Character	Controls how the BizTalk serializer will add pad characters to a positional field to achieve the proper overall length for the field. This property may be set only if Pad Character has been configured.
Pad Character Type	Denotes how the pad character is expressed. Values are `Character`, `Hexadecimal`, and `(Default)`. The latter value clears the property in the schema.
Pad Character	Defines a single character that is used by the serializer to pad field values shorter than the space allotted in a positional schema to achieve the proper overall field length. You may select any of the predefined characters in the list box for this property, enter any other single character, or leave the field blank to clear the property in the schema document.

TABLE 3.7 Continued

Field Property Name	Meaning and Usage
Positional Offset	Specifies the start of the field as an integer offset from the previous sibling or delimiter. Any positive integer less than or equal to the value of Positional Length is acceptable.
Positional Length	Specifies the length of the field starting from the end of the preceding sibling or delimiter. Any positive integer is accepted.

The Positional Offset and Positional Length properties may seem confusing at first. Look at things from the parser and serializer's viewpoint, however. It will see a stream of characters and must do something with them whether you think they are meaningful or not. If there is junk data between one field and the next, perhaps a series of fields you don't want to configure, you want to be able to instruct the parser (and its complementary serializer for outgoing messages) to skip over them and not treat them as part of the next field. Positional Length includes those characters so that the overall message is a series of contiguous fields. Positional Offset tells the parser when to start treating the characters as real data that is a meaningful part of the current field.

Sample Delimited Specification

You should be well-acquainted with the techniques for creating a schema structure by now. But although creating an XML message schema is no trouble at all when you know about specifying structure, a flat-file format requires a bit more. We'll demonstrate the techniques for creating a delimited flat-file in this section. We'll show how to nest records and insert header information.

Suppose that we want to record basic information for a project: namely, the project name, deadline, and team composition. Here's a sample message instance:

```
Project
Massive Confusion
2004-01-01
Team
Member,Larry Loki,021D
Member,Esther Morris,A234H
Member,Lucretia Borgia,A91R
```

We start with a header tag, Project, followed by the name and deadline, which is in turn followed by the team composition. The name and deadline constitute a header, and the team has structure of its own. We denote the team record with the tag Team and then list an individual member on each line thereafter. Each member is itself a record composed of the tag Member, followed by the full member name and an employee ID.

As you can see, this message is delimited in several ways. Most of our entries are delimited with a carriage return, but the member information is comma delimited. The tags act to unambiguously indicate what record is appearing at any given time. Consider, for a moment, writing your own parser to handle this message type. You would need to specify tags when there is no convention similar to XML's angle brackets, and you would have to specify different delimiter characters at different points in the message. We're beginning to appreciate what BizTalk offers.

To begin building this schema, add a new Schema item to the project named `ProjectDelimited.xsd`. Select the Schema node and select the Schema Editor Extensions property. Click the ellipsis and select the Flat File Extension. Note that the value of the Standard property is automatically set to Flat File.

Rename the root node `Project` and add two child field elements, `Name` and `Deadline`. Set the Data Type property for `Deadline` to xs:date. Next, add a child record to `Project` and name it `Team`. Add a child record, `Member`, to team. Set Min Occurs to `0`, and Max Occurs to `*`. Add child field elements `Fullname` and `EmpID` to member. This gives us the structure we need: a root node with two fields, followed by a record composed of a repeating record. All that remains is to set the delimiters and tags. These are given in Table 3.8.

TABLE 3.8 Tag and Delimiter Properties for the Delimited Schema

Node/Tag Name	Child Delimiter Type	Child Delimiter Character	Child Order
Project	Hexadecimal	0x0A (CR)	Prefix
Team	Hexadecimal	0x0A	Prefix
Member	Character	, (comma)	Prefix

The carriage return delimiters are expressed as hexadecimal because there is no way to express the carriage return as a character. The order of all the delimiters might seem counterintuitive. Most people start out with postfix because they expect their data to be followed by the delimiter. As soon as they see a trailing delimiter, they modify it to be infix. That takes care of the trailing delimiter (which may also be handled with the Suppress Trailing Delimiters property), but puts our first field right after the tag identifier without a delimiter. By preceding our fields with delimiters, we get the message format we desire.

TIP

A couple of common pitfalls might be troubling you if you are following along with the sample. First, if you generate an instance of a flat file, you might be surprised to see an XML document. If this is the case, open the Properties dialog box for the schema and set the Create Instance Output Type to Native. BizTalk likes XML and sometimes needs to be coaxed into seeing things our way. Second, if you are having trouble getting a sample instance to validate because of the record delimiters, you'll find that Visual Studio inserts extra characters. The easiest way to get the single 0x0A carriage return is to open a generated instance in Notepad and edit it, being careful not to change the record delimiters.

Sample Positional Specification

Now let's turn that last schema into a positional message schema. In fact, we'll be making a hybrid delimited-positional schema because that is the form virtually all legacy flat-file formats take when dealing with positional data. As soon as a programmer has to look at the raw data stream, she starts inserting linefeeds for clarity.

This process will be very simple. Perform the following steps:

1. Copy `ProjectDelimited.xsd` and rename the copy `ProjectPositional.xsd`. Add it to the current project.
2. Select `Member` and change the Structure property's value to `Positional`.
3. Select `Fullname` and set Justification to `Right`, Pad Character Type to `Hexadecimal`, Pad Character to `0x20`, and Positional length to `50`.
4. Repeat step 3 with `EmpID`, but this time make the Positional Length value `10`.

Left justification is far more common, but it is easier for us to demonstrate fixed length fields on the page if the actual data appears at the end of the field. Here's what a sample message instance looks like:

```
Project
More Confusion
2004-06-01
Team
                                                        Sam . Am      A219
                                                      Jay Gatsby      Q002
```

Property Promotion and Property Schemas

In Chapter 2 we briefly demonstrated the use of distinguished fields as a mechanism for promoting properties into the message context. Property promotion is used in a number of places throughout BizTalk, such as custom receive components, message routing, and orchestration. The messaging engine doesn't worry about the internal values of message fields unless you tell it. Messages are merely a chunk of data to be passed along. Property promotion identifies what should be specifically examined for use by the engine. There are two ways to do this. Distinguished fields are the easiest because they do not require a separate schema for promoted properties. Unfortunately, fields promoted through distinguished fields cannot be used for routing. Promotion using property schemas requires more work, but the properties identified therein can be used for routing.

Property schemas are a good deal simpler than message schemas. There is only one level of structure. The Schema node may only contain a series of field elements. They are also shorter. Typically, you specify only one or two fields. Property schemas record only those fields that are being promoted, so you will typically see only a small number of nodes in a property schema.

The easiest way to create a new property schema is to use the Quick Promotion menu item on the context menu inside a message schema. Right-click a node and select this, and the Editor will prompt you to see if you want a property schema. Otherwise, to explicitly create a property schema ahead of time, select the Property Schema template from the Add New Item dialog box. Let's do this, creating a new schema named `ContactProperties.xsd`. We're going to specify a property for the derived version of the contacts message schema. When the new schema appears, note that the Schema node's Schema Type property is set to `Property`. If you forgot and selected the basic Schema template, you could recover by setting this property manually.

Next, rename the root node `ContactID`. We plan to promote a unique identifier for routing purposes. Leave the data type as `xs:string`. Save the property schema and open `DerivedXMLSchema.xsd`.

Select the Schema node and scroll down until you find the Promote Properties property for that node. Click the ellipsis button to open the Promote Properties dialog box. This is the same one you saw in Chapter 2. This time, however, we want to click the Property Fields tab. The Property Schemas List is initially empty. Click the Open Folder button, then browse to and select ContactProperties from the Schemas folder. This schema will be prefaced with the name of your BizTalk project. After it is selected, it appears in the Property Schemas List.

Now turn your attention to the tree view to the left. Expand the tree until the SSN field is visible and selected. Click Add, and the field appears on the right in the Property-Fields dictionary. This is a list of all fields in the message schema that have been associated with a field in the property schema associated with the current message schema. Because our property schema has but the one field, ContactID, it is the default for the Property column entry for the newly promoted property. You can inspect the Node path column and see an XPath expression pointing to SSN. Click OK to close the dialog box, and you'll see some annotations added to the message schema to record the association. The SSN field node's graphic changes to add a gold and blue ribbon to indicate the promoted status.

The effect has been to associate the SSN field in the message schema with the ContactID field in the property schema. Any component or pipeline that requires the property in the message context will be configured with the name of the property schema. The value will be pushed into the message context as the message arrives. Anything that needs the information, such as an orchestration, can inspect it there.

Using InfoPath Documents with BizTalk

We've spent a lot of time creating message schemas with the intention of using them to process inbound and outbound messages. Little thought has been given to how the information will enter BizTalk. It's just been assumed that some application will submit messages. To show you that it need not be a matter of endless custom development, we'll take a very brief look at Microsoft Office InfoPath, a tool that takes standard schema or

Web service metadata and creates client forms that can submit XML or Web service messages via HTTP.

InfoPath is a brand new addition to the Microsoft Office 2002 suite. The basic concept is to create forms that are backed by generated code that turns form input into HTTP messages. Of course, we've been doing that for years using HTML and script. The benefit that InfoPath brings to Web development is its capability to consume metadata in some standard form and offer a palette of form controls that are compatible with the information presented.

The metadata may be in the form of an XSD document or a WSDL document, the "schema" for a Web service. Having just created a host of XSD schemas, we are in an ideal position to create an InfoPath form.

Opening the InfoPath design time editor, we look to the right palette and find New from Data Source under the Design a New Form heading. We use the wizard to browse to `DerivedXMLSchema.xsd`, which you'll recall pertains to Contact messages. We are prompted to make some selections, namely how many times we want the Choice group repeated and which choice—Home or Office—to make. We can modify this later, but for now, we choose a single instance of Office. When we close the wizard, the right control palette looks like Figure 3.5. We can then drag the controls onto the design surface to create the form shown in the view to the left of that figure.

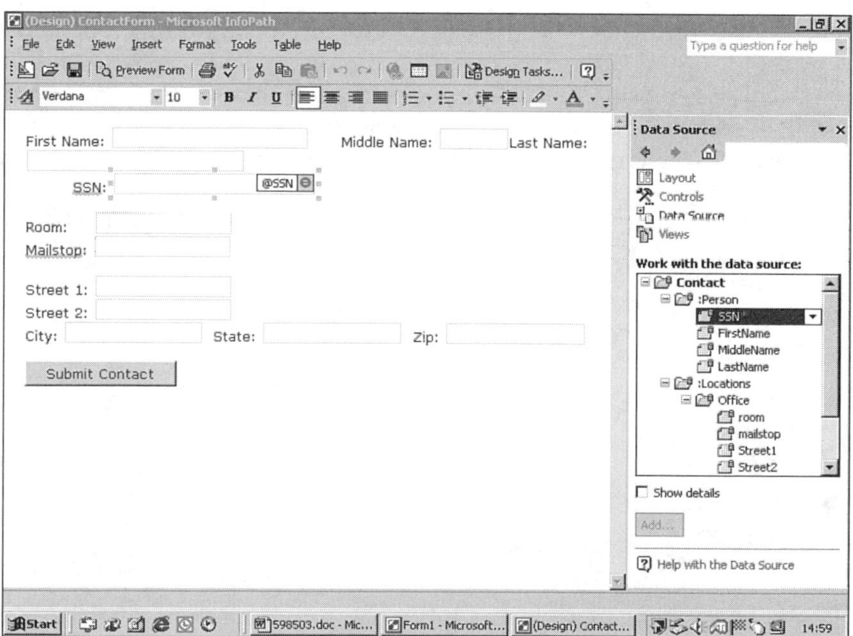

FIGURE 3.5 Sample InfoPath form submits a Contact message via HTTP.

We can save the form to a Web server. Persons who want to submit a contact enter the URL for the form, receive it in their Web browser, and fill it out. When they click the Submit button, an XML message conforming to our schema is generated and submitted to the URL configured into the form. In later chapters, we'll use InfoPath to create data entry clients for orchestrations. By virtue of the fact that BizTalk works with open standards, we are able to leverage another application to generate applications that can talk to BizTalk using standard messaging protocols.

Summary

This chapter showed you how to get started in BizTalk messaging by specifying message schemas. We started with structure, which give us the basic tools to create XML schemas. These are by far the most common sorts of schemas for BizTalk messaging. We demonstrated records and fields, which abstract BizTalk schemas away from XML-specific terms such as elements and attributes. An important part of XML Schemas, as specified by the W3C, is type extension, and this chapter showed how BizTalk Editor supports the mechanisms for reuse and extension.

After a discussion of the more common node properties, we proceeded to demonstrate how to compose flat-file schemas. These are used in BizTalk projects chiefly to embrace legacy formats, because they are less flexible and unambiguous than XML-formatted messages.

We rounded out the information we presented in Chapter 2 regarding property promotion to show how that information may be captured in property schemas. We will see these again when we discuss pipelines and custom components. Finally, we demonstrated Microsoft Office InfoPath. The tool illustrated the benefits of open standards for Web development even though both it and BizTalk are proprietary applications. Because both embrace XSD-format schemas, the output of BizTalk Editor easily became the input for InfoPath, and the output of that application will become the point of entry for message instances to BizTalk.

CHAPTER 4

Mapping Messages

IN THIS CHAPTER

- Purpose and Scope of Mapping
- Mapper Basics
- Functoids in BizTalk
- Custom Functoids

A major consideration of integration projects, whether they are internal application-to-application projects or external projects between business partners, is reconciling differing data formats. The fact that different applications or partners are being integrated indicates that they are dealing with the same concepts. Unfortunately, the actors in a project have differing views resulting in different data structures. Sometimes, the problem is as simple as different programming teams coming up with different structures that solve the same problem. This is evident in the wide range of legacy message formats for commonly encountered problems. The end result is the same: data must be mapped from one form to another in order to be useful.

BizTalk mapping is a data-driven approach to this problem. In Chapter 2, "Your First BizTalk Server Integration," the sample showed you how to graphically establish links that were persisted in an XML document used by the messaging runtime to dynamically drive the mapping process. In this chapter, we'll investigate the BizTalk Mapper in more depth to gain an understanding of how it may be used to manage the mapping aspect of a BizTalk project. In addition, we'll survey the functoid library provided with the product to gain an appreciation of the range of tasks that can be solved with functoids. Finally, we'll construct a custom functoid using the relevant APIs and integrate it into a mapping project.

Purpose and Scope of Mapping

A curious problem with mapping is not that it can't solve the problems of data transformation, but that it is too powerful and encourages some bad practices. The authors have seen some perfectly legitimate and workable solutions that used mapping to perform tasks best left to other aspects of BizTalk. Although this is to some extent a matter of design philosophy, a good architecture should be easy to read and understand. If a bad choice buries the solution to a problem in an obscure area, the overall project will be hard to maintain. In short, we really want you to solve the right problems in the right place with BizTalk. What, then, is the purpose and scope of mapping?

Simply stated, mapping is intended to manipulate the form of data, not its content. You might be skeptical of this assertion if we showed you a lengthy XML message transformed into a brief flat file, but we maintain the data values themselves have not really changed. The structure is markup and syntax surrounding the data, which is really what messages are about. Mapping is intended to change that structure so that it is recognizable to another application. If you translated a weather forecast from English to Italian, you'd be doing mapping on a human scale. If you added a discussion of the effect of weather on the economy during the translation, you'd be applying business rules and processing. That task might need to be done in the overall solution, but no one would be expecting to find it in the translation task. A rough general rule is this: If you are changing formats, mapping is the right place to be. If you are processing data, you should be looking to orchestration or the applications themselves.

Design and architecture are, of course, subject to interpretation and discussion. There are gray areas where experienced programmers may disagree. Indeed, a category of functoids exists that let you pull information from a database. Some would argue that doing so verges on processing, whereas others (including the authors) would say that it depends on what you are doing with the database. Mapping in BizTalk is powerful, but it is a low-level activity. Strive to keep your maps as simple as possible in the interest of performance.

Mapper Basics

Mapping is all about links. You will be pointing to sources and establishing links right from the start. In contrast to the process of creating schemas, there are relatively few properties to set. There are basically four ordered steps to creating a BizTalk map:

1. Creating a map file
2. Specifying links
3. Setting test properties
4. Validating and testing the map

Creating a Map File

A shell map file is created by pointing to a BizTalk project in the Solution Explorer, selecting Add New Item, selecting Map from the Biztalk Project Items folder, and giving the new item a filename.

TIP

It is typical but not essential to group maps in the same project with your document schemas if all the schemas are being created at the same time. On the other hand, if you are adding a map to deal with a legacy format for which a schema was previously created, it is better to group the map with the new schemas or orchestrations to indicate that it is new and not an original part of the legacy material.

You saw this process in Chapter 2. When the Map view appears, you see an empty grid flanked by two links, one each for selecting the source and destination schemas. When you click these links, the BizTalk Type Picker dialog box appears as shown in Figure 4.1. You have the option of selecting a schema from any schema appearing under the References or Schemas nodes.

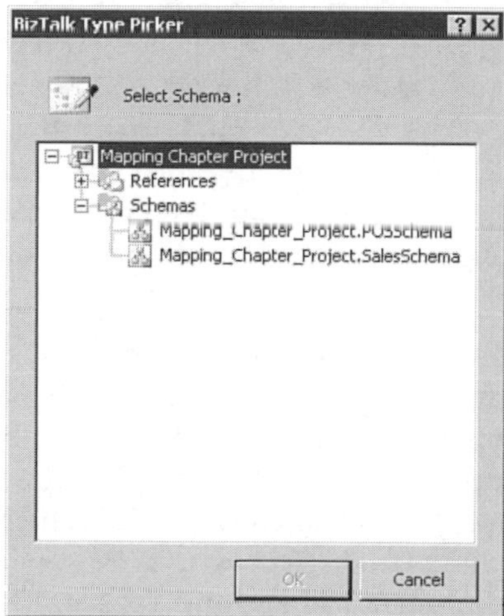

FIGURE 4.1 Select source and destination schemas from the schemas in the project.

A tree view of the selected schema replaces the link when either a source or a destination schema is selected. At this point, you have the foundation of a map, but no links. A typical map specification effort can proceed directly to the link task. Before proceeding to links, however, let's take a quick look at the properties you can set for the map as a whole.

A Quick Look at the Map Properties

If you select the map item in the Solution Explorer, the Properties view displays some properties you would expect to find, such as File Name, Full Path, Fully Qualified Name, and Namespace. The remaining two properties bear mention. The first, Build Action, controls what Visual Studio will do with the map when building the project in which it resides. The choices are Compile and None. Compiling is the process of generating an XSLT stylesheet that implements the transformation specified by the map. If you select None, the item will be skipped in the build. The final property, Type Name, is initialized with the filename of the map minus the file extension. The Namespace and Type Name properties are used together to create the qualified name of the .NET class that wraps the XSLT generated by a map. When you pick a map from a list—for example, when selecting a map in an orchestration, it is this qualified name that you will see and select.

If you right-click the map in the Solution Explorer and select Properties, the Property Pages dialog box for maps appears. It has one tab, Test Map, which contains five properties that control what happens during testing. We'll cover testing a little bit later, but basically Visual Studio invokes the map component with sample input and generates an output document. The first two properties, Validate TestMap Input and Validate TestMap Output, are Boolean values that instruct Visual Studio whether to attempt to validate the input and output documents against their respective schemas. You will generally want to accept the default value of `True`, but if you are working on a particularly tricky map, you might want to set the value of these properties to `False` initially. If the map output fails validation, no output document is generated. If you suppress validation, the Output view will include a link to an output file deep inside your temporary files folder (you may need to scroll to the right to see this link. You may then inspect the file to gauge how you are progressing.

The next property, TestMap Input Instance, enables you to select a sample input document on disk to use when testing the map. This selection may be overridden with the value of the next property, TestMap Input. The choices for this property are `Generate Instance`, `XML`, and `Native`. If you select the first, any file selected as the input instance is ignored. Visual Studio will generate an input document from the schema and submit it to the map. `XML` is the default value, but you should select Native for any flat-file input file. The final property, TestMap Output, has the choices `XML` and `Native`. If you select `XML`, the output of the map test will always be an XML document, regardless of the expected output format. `Native` is used when you are mapping to a flat-file format and you want to see what Biztalk will generate at runtime.

Specifying Links

Now that you have created a map file, you need to specify the links in that file that map values in an incoming document into the corresponding outbound document. Establishing a link between two fields (or a mixed content record) seems simple enough. You drag the mouse from the source node to the destination. A line appears linking the two, and the node icons change to include two chain links. There are, however, a few linking techniques to discuss now that make things slightly more complicated.

TIP

You can link entire substructures with one mouse-drag operation. If you hold the Shift key down while dragging between two records, the Mapper will create simple links between the records and all subordinate nodes if the content of the source and destination nodes is the same. This is a useful shortcut if you have identical structures contained within differing parent formats. If the two subtrees are slightly different, links will be created automatically only for those nodes with identical names. This can be changed by changing the setting of the grid's Autolink By property discussed in Table 4.1.

Properties of links and the grid itself affect how links operate. There is a lengthy list of properties you can set for the grid, thereby affecting the operation of the map as a whole and links in particular, but the most commonly used properties are given in Table 4.1.

TABLE 4.1 Commonly Used Grid Properties

Grid Property Name	Meaning and Usage
CDATA Section Elements	Lists the names of elements whose textual content should be output wrapped in CDATA sections.
Indent	If Yes, the output is indented for readability. No, or Blank, otherwise.
Method	Specifies the XSLT method for generating output: `xml`—Output is assumed to be XML (default). `html`—Output is HTML markup. `text`—Output is plain text, not markup. This should be used for flat-file outputs.
Autolink By	Controls how links are automatically generated when linking two records: `Structure`—Links by identical or similar child content structure without regard to node names. `Node Name`—Creates automatic links only if two names have the same name.
Ignore Namespaces for Links	If `Yes` (default), the XSLT generated refers to links solely by their local name. If `No`, the namespace of the node is considered as well.

The Ignore Namespaces for Links property becomes a concern when the schemas you are mapping are composed of nodes from several namespaces. One of the purposes of namespaces is to prevent two nodes from interfering with one another if they have the same name. When you start to compose schemas through importation, you may find that the same names occur in two namespaces that are used in the same document. When that happens, you should set this property to `No`. The minor increase in the complexity of generated XPath expressions is worth being sure that you are mapping the data you intend to transfer and not something from elsewhere in the document.

NOTE

Links themselves have fewer properties. To view them in the Mapper, click a link in the grid. It will be bounded on either end with rectangles and will change color to denote its selection. The properties then appear in Visual Studio's Property view.

Links themselves have five properties. These are Link Source, Link Target, Label, Source Links, and Target Links. Two, Link Source and Link Target, are read-only and display the XPath expression locating the source and destination nodes of the link. Label allows you to assign a friendly name to the link to help you make sense of what you are doing in the context of the link.

The remaining two properties, Source Links and Targets Links, are somewhat more complicated because they control how data is moved from the source to the target. The Source Links property controls what gets copied to the output from the source. There are three values for this property:

- `Copy Name`—The name of the source node is copied.
- `Copy Text Value`—The textual child content of the source node is copied (default).
- `Copy Text and Subcontent Value`—All child content, nodes and text alike, are copied to the output document.

The Target Links property affects what happens to the copied data when it arrives in the destination document:

- `Flatten Links`—Any source hierarchy is flattened into a single destination node (default).
- `Match Links Top Down`—The compiler will match nodes and generate XSLT from the top of the schema to the bottom.
- `Match Links Bottom Up`—The compiler will start at the bottom of a schema's node hierarchy and match links from there up.

Test Properties and the Validation and Testing Process

After you've established some links, you're ready to check the validity of the map you've created. To do this, right-click the map item in the Solution Explorer and select Validate Map from the context menu. The Editor will examine the map and provide errors and warnings in the Output view. Warnings can arise when the types of linked nodes disagree or when functoids have an incorrect number of inputs or outputs.

Testing is where things can get interesting. This is your opportunity to see what will happen in the runtime messaging engine when your map is applied to a message. Thorough testing at this stage will help avoid errors at runtime—errors that are hard to diagnose because the process is hidden from view. If you have set the map's TestMap Input Instance property, you have the opportunity to create any challenging source data you want. If you rely on generated data entirely, BizTalk Editor will create some strings based on the name and type of the input node. If you want more challenging input but don't want to go to the trouble of creating your own input document, you still have one option.

When you select a node in either the source or destination schema, its properties appear in the Property view. All but two of these properties carry over from the schema and are therefore read-only. One of the two, Notes, is simply a documentation field. Value, however, lets you set a value to be used during testing. An entry for the Value property of a source field will be submitted to the mapping process. A similar entry for a destination field forces the output field value to whatever you specify. This might seem odd to you, but we'll find a use for it in our next sample.

Direct Links Sample

Suppose we want to report on book sales. Listing 4.1 shows what an input message would look like.

LISTING 4.1 Sample Sales Message

```
<ns0:Sales xmlns:ns0="http://Mapping_Chapter_Project.SalesSchema">
  <Sale bookID="BU1032" qty="10" saleDate="2003-07-30" price="10.50" />
  <Sale bookID="PS3333" qty="8" saleDate="2003-07-30" price="19.95" />
</ns0:Sales>
```

This message is specified in the schema `SalesSchema.xsd` in the chapter download. Each `Sale` element pertains to a particular title identified by the value of the `bookID` property. The `qty` attribute tells how many copies were sold on `saleDate`, whereas `price` gives the per-copy retail price. Now suppose we are integrating this information with another application that takes data in the form shown in Listing 4.2.

LISTING 4.2 Sample BookSales Message

```
<ns0:BookSales xmlns:ns0="http://Mapping_Chapter_Project.POSSchema">
  <Item pubID="AX2190">
    <Title>A Theory of Everything</Title>
    <TransInfo listPrice="10.95" transPrice="8.95"
➥transRoyalty="895" transDate="1999-05-31"
➥transTotal="8950" transQty="100" />
  </Item>
</ns0:BookSales>
```

The `pubID` attribute is the same as `bookID` in the source message schema, but the actual book title is included as well. This message gives the list price from the publisher's catalog, but it also gives the retail per-copy price charged in that day's transactions. The `transTotal` attribute is the total dollar value of the day's sales, whereas `transRoyalty` is the estimated dollar value of the royalties due the author based on the day's transactions. Clearly, we're going to need some information that is not explicitly listed in the source message.

Let's start with the information we've got in the source message. We'll revisit the map as we work through functoids. For right now, perform the following steps:

1. Create a new BizTalk solution.
2. Within the default project, create two schemas—one for each of the previous message instances. Name the source `SalesSchema.xsd` and the destination `POSSchema.xsd` (for Point of Sale). Establish the following data types and required fields:
    - `qty` and `transQty` are `positiveInteger` types.
    - `Item` and `Sale` have `minOccurs = 1` and `maxOccurs = *`.
    - `saledate` and `transDate` are `date` types.
    - `price`, `transPrice`, `listPrice`, and `transtotal` are `decimal` types.
    - `Title` has `minOccurs = 1` and `maxOccurs = 1`.
    - `Sale` and `Item` have `minOccurs = 1` and `maxOccurs = *`.
3. Add a BizTalk map item to the same project, naming it `Sales2POS.btm`.
4. Select `salesSchema.xsd` as the source schema and `POSSchema.xsd` as the target of the map.
5. Create the following links:
    - `Sale` record to `Item` record
    - `bookID` field to `pubID` field
    - `qty` field to `transQty` field
    - `saleDate` field to `transDate` field
    - `price` field to `transPrice` field

    All the links except the first one exist to copy a value from a source field to its counterpart in the destination message. The first link, `Sales` to `Item`, might seem strange. Neither record contains any text, so there is nothing to copy. The map is data-driven, though, and won't create any item in the destination without some sort of prompt from the source message. If we didn't include the link, `Item` would never be created and the output message would fail validation. Because there is a link, though, the mapping process will create the Item record, and the rest of our field copying links can proceed. There is one final step to perform, and it is needed as a placeholder to make our map work until we can grab some of the other fields from another source.

6. Select the `Title` field element in the destination schema. Set its Value property to any string value.

   Because `Title` is required, we have to force the map to create it. In the following section, we'll retrieve a value from a database and that will be sufficient to create it. Right now, though, we have nothing in the source that will force its creation, yet it is a required field. Setting the Value property will suffice to create the output field.

At this point, your map should look like Figure 4.2. You can validate it and test it successfully.

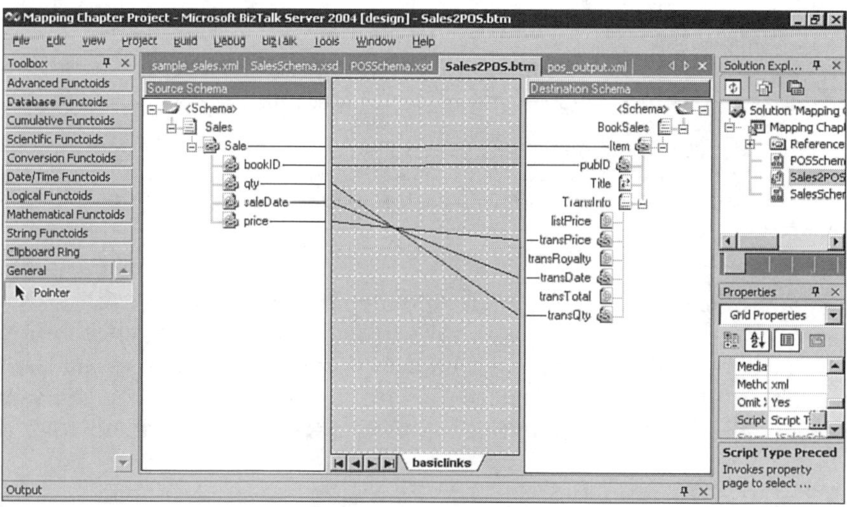

FIGURE 4.2 Direct links between Sales and POS messages in the map.

Functoids in BizTalk

Functoids provide map designers with chunks of code for manipulating data during the mapping process. We saw a very simple example of this in Chapter 2 when we used a functoid to force a field value to uppercase. The standard functoid toolbox that comes with BizTalk is very rich, providing you with the tools for string, mathematical, date and time, and scientific functions. Additionally, you may retrieve data from relational sources, perform cumulative operations over repeating fields, and even write your own script code in any .NET-compliant language. If these features aren't sufficient, BizTalk provides an interface for writing your own functoids and integrating them into the Mapper functoid toolbox.

Standard Functoids

BizTalk Mapper comes with 79 functoids grouped into nine categories. These categories are

- String—Basic string manipulation, including substrings, concatenations, and case conversions.
- Math—Basic arithmetic operations such as addition, multiplication, square roots, and modulo.
- Logical—Boolean operators.
- Date/Time—Extract date and time information from the system.
- Conversion—Character representation conversions.
- Scientific—Scientific operations such as logarithms and trigonometric functoids.
- Cumulative—Functoids that operate over a number of fields to give cumulative concatenations, sums, averages, minima, and maxima.
- Database—Functoids for retrieving values from relational databases during mapping.
- Advanced—Advanced operations, including a functoid for inserting your own .NET code.

As always, the product documentation provides the definitive reference to the exact behavior and parameters of each functoid. We are going to cover the general use and configuration of functoids in maps and then demonstrate the use of the database functoids in a practical sample. Later, in the section on custom functoids, you will gain some insight into the internal operation of functoids when we create several functoids of our own.

Using Functoids

Functoids are executed during the mapping process and are used to help generate the outgoing message from the source message. It is only natural, then, that they are added to a map by dragging them from the toolbox onto the design grid that stands between the source and destination schemas. After they are on the grid, you may move them around by dragging them or clicking them and using the arrow keys. A selected functoid is displayed with a series of rectangular control handles around it. Functoids have to be connected to the stream of information, so we must make links from the source schema or other functoids to the functoid, and from the functoid to other functoids or the destination schema.

When you establish a link from a source schema field to a functoid, you are making the value of that field one of the input parameters of the functoid. You create the link in the same way you create a link directly between fields: drag from the source node to the left side of the functoid. Not all functoids work with all types of nodes. Some, for example, cannot be connected to records, whereas others can be connected only to numeric type fields. The functoid communicates its requirements to Mapper; if you try to establish a prohibited link, your cursor will change from a crosshair symbol to a circle with a slash through it. If the link is allowed, however, releasing the mouse button causes a line to be drawn between the input node and the functoid, and a circular connection point appears on the functoid. The process for connecting a functoid's output—the right side of the functoid—to a node in the destination schema is similar.

Functoids may also be cascaded. Sometimes, the output of one functoid is not quite in the right form for your destination message. In that case, you can connect the output of the first functoid to another functoid as one of its inputs. Mapper does not impose any limit on the number of functoids that can be cascaded in this way, but you should keep processing considerations in mind. Each cascaded functoid represents some chunk of code that must execute in sequence, and the overall process is occurring during the mapping of the source message into an outgoing target message. If you expect a great deal of traffic, or incoming messages are going to a number of sources, you will want to keep your maps as simple as possible in the interests of performance.

Configuring Functoid Parameters

Just connecting nodes and functoids may not be enough to properly configure a functoid in the map. A functoid is very similar to a function call in a programming language. It expects a specific list of parameters in a certain order. If more configuration is necessary, you will need to resort to the Configure Functoid Inputs dialog box. Each functoid feeds information to the Mapper allowing the Mapper to set up this dialog. An example is shown in Figure 4.3. The figure shows a functoid taking exactly four inputs, so the appearance of the dialog box will vary depending on which functoid is being configured. The buttons and operation of the dialog box remain the same, however. Starting from the left of the toolbar, the button with an ellipsis on it is the Edit Selected Parameter button. Clicking this brings up another dialog box with a text box containing the value of the parameter. The next button is the Insert New Parameter button. When clicked, it merely adds an empty item to the end of the list. The third button from the left bears a stylized X; this is the Delete Selected Parameter button.

The next two buttons will be somewhat more important to you than they might first appear. They are, respectively, the Move Up Selected Parameter and Move Down Selected Parameter buttons. Clicking these buttons moves the selected parameter up and down in the list. These are important because Mapper enters parameters in the order in which you create links or click the Insert New Parameter button, but the functoid expects the parameters in a particular order, just like the parameter signature of a function in a programming language. Functoids, as you shall see, are implemented by code functions, so you must move parameters around until your data is in the correct order.

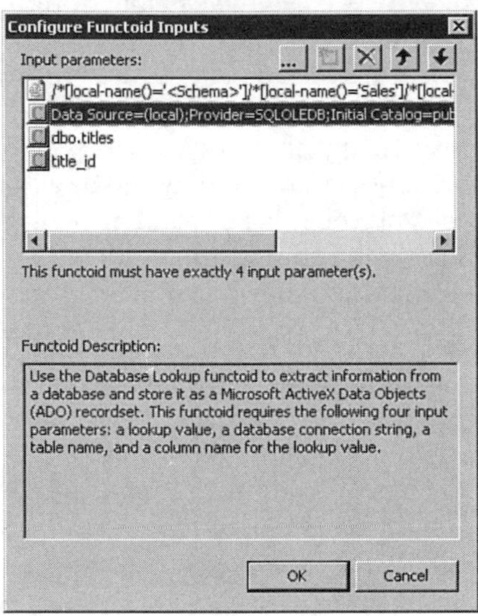

FIGURE 4.3 The Configure Functoid Inputs dialog box allows you to enter, delete, and reorder parameters specific to each functoid.

Revised Sample: Table Extractor

When we left our Sales to POS map, we had a few fields left unfilled. Specifically, `Title`, `listPrice`, `transRoyalty`, and `transTotal` are in need of data—data not immediately expressed in the source message. We do, however, have `bookID`. For the purposes of this exercise, we will assume that all the books being sold are represented in the venerable SQL Server sample database, pubs. The value of the `bookID`, then, is the identifier `title_id` used throughout that database to uniquely identify individual books. The database functoids, then, will be the key to extracting information on file in the database.

This may seem to violate our design rule regarding not doing any business processing in a map. In fact, the book's ID is a pointer to additional information. Resolving that pointer into specific fields is more a matter of transforming the data than processing it. After all, we are not modifying any values, merely looking them up. The issue of performance, however, is a real one. In an actual deployment, we would want to look at the average time needed to connect to the database and do the lookup, estimate or measure the expected frequency of Sales messages, and decide if our system could handle the overhead of the database activity.

Continuing where we left off with the links sample and the map Sales2POS.btm, you should now perform the following steps:

1. Delete the simple link between Sale and Item. The additional inputs we create will force the creation of the Item record.

2. From the main menu, select BizTalk Add Page. When a new grid page appears, select Biztalk Rename Page and enter `functoids`. We'll be adding some links and four functoids, so adding a page lends clarity.

3. Drag a Database Lookup functoid from the Database Functoids palette of the toolbox. Establish a link between `bookID` in the source message and the new functoid instance.

   The Database Lookup functoid retrieves one or more records from a relational table given some identifier. Value Extractor functoids are subsequently used to extract individual values from the records retrieved by the Database Lookup functoid. If there is more than one record returned, the first one will be used. In our example, that's not a problem. Now let's configure the Lookup functoid to point it to the titles table of the pubs database.

4. Select the Database Lookup functoid and click the ellipsis button to the right of the Order Input Parameters property. The button bears the label Reorder Functoid Inputs. The Configure Functoid Inputs dialog appears.

   The Database Lookup functoid takes four parameters: lookup value, database connection string, table name, and the name of the column in which to search for the lookup value. Dragging the link from `bookID` to the functoid gives us the lookup value in the form of an XPath expression. The remaining four parameters are entered by clicking the Add Parameter button (second button, with a rectangle and flash bitmap) and entering the following values into the Input Parameters list:

   - connection string: `Data Source=(local);Provider=SQLOLEDB;Initial Catalog=pubs;UID=sa;pwd=;`
   - table name: `dbo.titles`
   - lookup column name: `title_id`

NOTE

Your connection string will vary depending on the location and configuration of your database.

5. Drag two Value Extractor functoids onto the grid and then create links from the Database Lookup functoid to each of the extractor functoids, in turn.

The Value Extractor functoids take two parameters: a connection to the Database Lookup and the name of a column to extract.

6. Use the Configure Functoid Inputs dialog box as in step 4 to add a second parameter to the first Value Extractor, proving the column name price. Click OK to close the dialog box.
7. Drag a link from this functoid to the listPrice field in the destination message.
8. Repeat step 6, providing the second extractor functoid with the column name title.
9. Create a link between this functoid and the element field Title in the destination message.

TIP

If you have database problems, as I did, you may want to drag an error return functoid onto the grid, connect it to the Database Lookup, and link its output to the Title field in lieu of the connection to the Value Extractor. Any error messages returned by ADO then turn up in the output message.

Now we need to get a value for `transTotal`. This, as you'll recall, is the total dollar value of the transaction. We'll leave out details such as discounts and sales tax and simply assume that this is calculated as the value of the `price` field in the source message times the value of the `qty` field. Open the Mathematical Functoids palette and proceed.

10. Drag a Multiplication functoid onto the grid.
11. Create a link from `qty` to the functoid, and then a second incoming link from `price`.
12. Create a link from the Multiplication functoid to `transTotal` in the destination message. No further configuration of the functoid is required.

That leaves `transRoyalty`, the estimated dollar amount due the book's author based on the sale. The pubs database has a quantity-based royalty schedule, as well as a known advance paid value, but we'll ignore all that for the sake of getting a simple estimated value. The royalty percentage is expressed as a numeric value between 0 and 100 in the database, so the formula should be: `royalty/100 * price * qty`. We could do all that using math functoids, but things might get busy in the grid. It would also leave us without a reason to create a custom functoid in the next section, so let's leave `transRoyalty` empty for now. Save your map, right-click the map item in the Solution Explorer, and select Test Map from the context menu. When the test concludes, you can follow the link in the Output view to inspect the results of your map as applied to the values of input fields or a specific sample input message. The chapter download includes a sample input message, `sample_sales.xml`, in the parent folder of the project. At this point, your map should look like Figure 4.4.

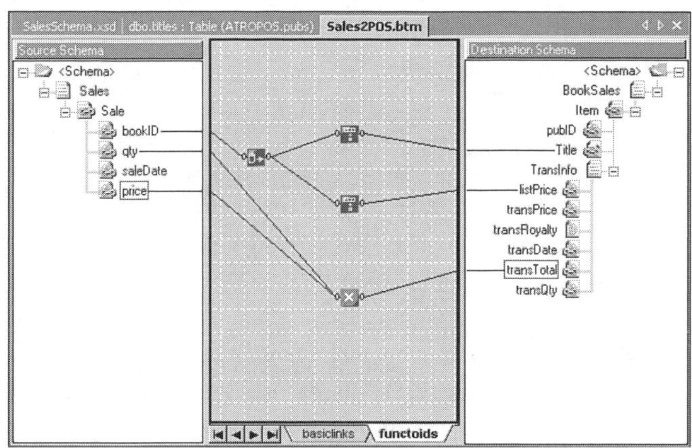

FIGURE 4.4 Links in the Sales2POS map.

Custom Functoids

Functoids are like consumer electronic devices: no matter how many you have, it never seems to be enough. Although BizTalk provides a fairly full toolbox of functoids, you will encounter occasions where you can't find just the right operation for your needs. That is where custom functoids come in. Custom functoids are class library projects that reside in a .NET assembly. You create a custom functoid by deriving from the `Microsoft.BizTalk.BaseFunctoid` class (implemented by `Microsoft.BizTalk.BaseFunctoids.dll` in the Developer Tools folder) and overriding certain methods. If you inspect this base class in the documentation or by creating a reference to the assembly in Visual Studio, you will see that it has an extensive interface. Happily, the number of methods you will have to override is fairly limited for the typical functoid project.

Deployment Choices

Functoids in earlier versions of BizTalk were COM components that worked by exposing a chunk of script code, either VBScript or JScript, which Mapper copied into the body of a map. BizTalk Server 2004 functoids are .NET components, and they offer two choices for deployment. One is very similar to the old method. A functoid may offer .NET source code in any .NET-compliant language. In that case, Mapper will retrieve the source code and incorporate it into the map. This has the advantage of making the map independent of the functoid component at runtime. Your custom functoid, then, need not be deployed to every machine in the BizTalk cluster. It has the disadvantage, however, of revealing your source code.

If you don't want to expose .NET source code, you may elect to have the map reference the functoid component at runtime. If your functoid is so referenced, you will need to deploy the functoid assembly to the global assembly cache of every server expected to process the map.

Functoid Basics

Your functoid must perform two prime tasks. First, it has to describe itself to Mapper. Later, during map testing or runtime mapping, it must provide some implementation of your functionality. As we've seen, this is either a chunk of source code as a string or a public function BizTalk can call by name.

The most important thing you will do is override the class constructor. You'll call the `BaseFunctoid` class constructor, but you must also provide your own class constructor. This is where you tell Mapper everything it needs to know to use your functoid. At a minimum, you need to provide the following information:

- Specify the location of the assembly resources, such as bitmaps and strings, with a call to `SetupResourceAssembly`.
- Specify the resource ID of the string that provides the name of your functoid with a call to `SetName`.
- Specify the resource ID of the string containing the ToolTip for your functoid with a call to `SetTooltip`.
- Specify the resource ID of the string describing your functoid through a call to `SetDescription`.
- Specify the resource ID of the 16×16 pixel bitmap Mapper should place in the toolbox through a call to `SetBitmap`.
- Specify the kinds of nodes that can be connected as inputs to the functoid by passing an enumerated value or a bitwise combination of enumerated values in a call to `AddInputConnectionType`.
- Set an ID for your functoid by setting the `ID` property of the class.
- Indicate which functoid category (from the existing toolbox palettes) your functoid belongs to by setting the `Category` property of the class.
- Indicate which types of nodes can be connected to the functoid to accept its output by setting the `OutputConnectionType` property of the class.

There are other methods you can call, depending on the nature of your functoid. If you opt to deploy your assembly to the GAC and have BizTalk call into it, you must call `SetExternalFunctionName`. The parameters for this method name the assembly to call, the class within the assembly implementing the functoid, and the name of the method of the class that implements the functoid behavior. If you will be providing .NET source code for inclusion in the map body, you must override `SetScriptBuffer`. If your script calls global functions in script, you must override `SetGlobalScriptBuffer`. If your script relies on commonly used functions, such as IsNumeric, that are implemented elsewhere in the .NET Framework, you will set the `RequiredGlobalHelperFunctions` property with a bitwise combination of the enumerated identifiers for those functions. That lets BizTalk know what else it has to copy into the map.

There are still more functions to call and properties to set if your functoid can have a variable number of parameters, such as optional inputs. You will always need to set the `HasVariableInputs` property to `true`. After that, you'll call the `SetMinParams` and `SetMaxParams`, passing an integer to indicate the upper and lower bounds on the parameter list. If you are developing a functoid that must be placed in the global cache and called into at runtime, you are set. The normal language support for variable length parameter lists in .NET languages kicks in and works for you. If you are providing script code, however, you have to provide the correct source code. In that case, you will override the overloaded version of `GetInlineScriptBuffer` that takes a parameter for the number of parameters being passed to the functoid. Your implementation must examine this parameter and pass the correct functional signature.

Cumulative functoids present a special case. This is a category of functoids designed to loop through a series of recurring fields or records and perform some action, such as taking a cumulative sum of numeric fields. If you are writing one of these functoids, you need to provide three functions: one to initialize your operation, one to execute inside the loop, and one to retrieve the final value for output to the destination document. For functoids that will be deployed to the global assembly cache, the function named in `SetExternalFunctionName` is the initialization function. The other two functions are specified with calls to `SetExternalFunctionName2` and `SetExternalFunctionName3`. Inline script functoids, by contrast, call `SetInlinescriptBuffer` three times, but it is an overloaded version of the method that includes a third parameter, functionNumber. This parameter takes the value `0` for the initialization function, `1` when you specify the looping function, and `2` when naming the retrieval function.

Custom Functoids Sample

Writing custom functoids is actually easier than it sounds from the foregoing discussion. We had one field left to map when we last left our sample project, and that is the `transRoyalty` field. This field requires a database lookup to obtain the royalty rate paid the author, followed by a calculation involving the rate and the `price` and `qty` fields in the source message. We'll implement this as a functoid, first as a functoid for the global assembly cache, and then as an inline script functoid.

Setting Up the Project

Add a C# class library project to the solution and name it `QueFunctoids`. After Visual Studio finishes its work and gives you a project shell, open the file `AssemblyInfo.cs`. We need to edit it to make it ready for global use on your machine.

The first thing to do is give it a unique identifier because Mapper needs this to unambiguously refer to functoids in map files. You do this by adding a guid assembly directive. This requires the following reference at the top of the file:

```
using System.Runtime.InteropServices;
```

After you have that reference, add the following line at the start of the generated assembly references:

```
[assembly: Guid("F0857CF6-F8A8-4b58-B52A-15D0D27456A4")]
```

CAUTION

You should use the Tools Create guid item off the Visual Studio menu to generate your own guid and copy it to the clipboard. Be sure to remove the curly brackets the tool creates when you paste it into the assembly information file.

One of our functoid classes will not expose inline script code, so our assembly will eventually have to be moved to the global assembly cache. This requires a keyfile for signing the assembly. Open the Visual Studio Command Prompt (*not* the Windows Command Prompt) and change directories so that you are in the project folder where the source code resides. Execute the following command line to create a strong name key file:

```
sn -k QueFunctoids.snk
```

Now go back to the `AssemblyInfo.cs` file and find the line (near the bottom of the generated file) that refers to the AssemblyKeyFile attribute and edit so that it looks like this:

```
[assembly: AssemblyKeyFile("..\\..\\QueFunctoids.snk")]
```

Note that the path is relative to the output directory, not the source code project folder.

Now move to the Solution Explorer. Our custom functoid classes must derive from the base class, so we have to add a reference to the project and browse to Microsoft.BizTalk.BaseFunctoids.dll assembly in the Developer Tools folder under the BizTalk Server 2004 installation. Import the proper system packages by inserting the `using` statements in Listing 4.3:

LISTING 4.3 Packages Imported for the Custom Functoid

```
using System;
using Microsoft.BizTalk.BaseFunctoids;
using System.Text;
using System.Reflection;
using System.Globalization;
```

The reference to `Microsoft.BizTalk.BaseFunctoids` is needed for the class derivation, and the others are needed for various tasks in the class implementation.

When you created the class library project, Visual Studio created names for the namespace and class. First, revise the namespace so that it reads `QueFunctoids`. This is arbitrary, of course, but it should be more descriptive than what is automatically generated. Now revise the generated class declaration to reflect our own name for the class, as well as the derivation from the base class:

```
public class GlobalRoyaltyFunctoid : BaseFunctoid
```

We're ready to proceed with the class implementation. The first thing to do is to override the class constructor so that our functoid will properly register itself with Visual Studio.

Required Resources

A functoid project requires a handful of resources to integrate into Visual Studio. These resources belong in a resource file (resx extension) within the functoid library project. The needed resources are

- Name—Label that appears beneath the functoid icon in the toolbox
- Tooltip—String displayed in the ToolTip when hovering over the functoid icon
- Description—String resource describing the functoid that is displayed in the functoid configuration dialog box
- Bitmap—16×16 pixel bitmap resource displayed in the toolbox and on the grid surface to denote the functoid

It is a good idea to include a list of any parameters your functoid takes in the description string so that designers have a bit of help when configuring the functoid's inputs. Similarly, keep the name and ToolTip strings as brief as possible to avoid cluttering the interface. The functoid category is displayed on the toolbox tab, so you don't need to repeat this information.

A convenient tool for creating the resource file is ResEdit.exe, which is available in the globalization SDK. The native resource editor that opens in Visual Studio when you double-click in the Solution Explorer will not let you add external bitmap files. The best way to proceed is to create your bitmaps in a tool such as Windows Paint, and then open ResEdit and add them. Strings may be entered directly. The identifiers for each resource are arbitrary strings, although I have followed the convention of beginning with `IDB` for bitmaps and `IDS` for strings, followed by `CACHEDFUNCTOID` to identify which implementation the resource applies to, followed by a string indicating the use; for example, `NAME`. The resource file for this sample is found in the chapter download and is named `QueFunctoidResources.resx`. When you are finished, go to the Visual Studio Solution Explorer and use Add Existing Item to add the resource file to the functoid project.

Class Constructor

The functoid class constructor we implement works to report information about the functoid to Mapper so that Visual Studio can correctly populate the toolbox and reference the proper code when a designer actually uses our functoid. Examine the first few lines of the constructor in Listing 4.4.

LISTING 4.4 Class Constructor for the Globally Cached Functoid Sample

```
public class GlobalRoyaltyFunctoid : BaseFunctoid
{
   public GlobalRoyaltyFunctoid() : base()
   {
         this.ID = 6045;
         SetupResourceAssembly("QueFunctoids.QueFunctoidResources",
➥Assembly.GetExecutingAssembly());
         SetName("IDS_CACHEFUNCTOID_NAME");
         SetTooltip("IDS_CACHEFUNCTOID_TOOLTIP");
         SetDescription("IDS_CACHEFUNCTOID_DESCRIPTION");
         SetBitmap("IDB_CACHEFUNCTOID_BITMAP");
       this.SetMinParams(3);
       this.SetMaxParams(3);
         SetExternalFunctionName(GetType().Assembly.FullName,
➥"QueFunctoids.GlobalRoyaltyFunctoid", "CalcRoyalty");
         this.Category = FunctoidCategory.Math;
         this.OutputConnectionType = ConnectionType.AllExceptRecord;
         AddInputConnectionType(ConnectionType.AllExceptRecord);
}
```

We first assign an ID to the functoid. Microsoft reserves the range 100–4000 for itself and then recommends that you use anything beyond 6000 for your own work. The selection of 6045 in this case complies with those guidelines but is otherwise arbitrary. Your Identifiers should be unique within your functoid library, but Mapper will use the guid you provided in the assembly information file to ensure that your functoid and the classes within it are globally unique.

Now we need to point to the resource assembly that holds the strings and bitmaps for our functoid. Because the resource file is compiled into our functoid assembly, we use the .NET Assembly class `GetExecutingAssembly` method to point to our assembly, which will be the currently executing assembly when the call to the `BaseFunctoid` class `SetupResourceAssembly` method is made. The first parameter points to the resources. In Visual Studio projects, that string must take the form *`project_name.resource_filename`*.

After Mapper knows about the resource assembly, we can tell it about the individual resources through calls to `SetName`, `SetTooltip`, `SetDescription`, and `SetBitmap`. That takes care of integrating the functoid with the Visual Studio IDE. Now we have to make sure Mapper can actually get at the functoid's implementation when it is used.

Functoids designed for deployment to the global assembly cache are distinguished by a function that is called from Mapper or the runtime environment when the functoid's behavior is needed. A call to `SetExternalFunctionName` takes care of registering a private class method with Mapper so that the proper references can be made in the map's XSLT file. This method takes three parameters: the full name of the assembly, the name of the functoid's implementing class, and the name of the function to call. `Assembly.FullName` takes care of the first parameter. We provide literal strings for the other two. Note that the class is properly qualified with the namespace we created when creating the project.

The BaseFunctoid `Category` property takes an enumerated value that tells Mapper which tab of the toolbox should display the functoid bitmap. There is an enumerated value for each tab. These values are defined in the BaseFunctoids DLL.

Inputs can come from all sorts of different source nodes, and the output can go to a similar variety of destination nodes. The base class DLL provides the `ConnectionType` enumeration to denote these nodes. In addition to field and record nodes, it further designates various sorts of functoids that might be cascaded into or out of your functoid. The `OutputType` property and the `AddInputConnectionType` method take a bitwise combination of these enumerated types. Mapper makes use of this information to change the cursor when you are trying to link to a prohibited node or functoid.

NOTE

I've taken a very loose approach to qualifying the inputs and outputs for this functoid by using the `AllExceptRecord` enumerated value. In a real-world functoid implementation, however, you would be well advised to think carefully about what nodes and functoids can reliably be used with the behavior you are implementing.

Implementation Function

Now we come at last to the heart of the functoid, the method that implements the behavior of our functoid. This is shown in Listing 4.5. From the perspective of creating custom functoids in general, the most important thing to look at is the first line where we declare the method and its signature. The method must be public because it will be called either by the Mapper or the runtime messaging engine, not the functoid class itself. Next, the method must return a string, and all input parameters must be strings. The mapping process itself does not make use of the schemas and so cannot perform type conversions for you.

LISTING 4.5 Implementation Function for the Globally Cached Functoid

```
public string CalcRoyalty(string rate, string price, string qty)
{
   decimal dRate, dPrice, dRetVal;
   int iQty;

   if (IsNumeric(rate) && IsNumeric(price) && IsNumeric(qty))
   {
      dRate = Convert.ToDecimal(rate,
➥System.Globalization.CultureInfo.InvariantCulture);
      dPrice = Convert.ToDecimal(price,
➥System.Globalization.CultureInfo.InvariantCulture);
      iQty = Convert.ToInt32(qty,
➥System.Globalization.CultureInfo.InvariantCulture);

      dRetVal = dRate/100 * dPrice * (decimal)iQty;
      return dRetVal.ToString();
   }
   else
      return "0.0";
}
```

The first thing to do, then, is to test the parameters and make sure they can be converted to a numeric type. The messaging runtime engine should take care of this for us by checking the message against the schema, but it is good practice not to rely on another layer of a distributed system for data integrity. The `IsNumeric` function performs the test for us and also handles any exceptions that may be generated. If the tests return true, we can proceed to convert the data.

We handle the conversion of the decimal types with `Convert.ToDecimal`. The `System.Globalization` package is used to take care of the different characters cultures use for the decimal point. `ToInt32` performs the integer conversion. When we are done, `dRate`, `dPrice`, and `iQty` contain numeric values and we perform the actual calculation in the next line. We have to return a string, not a number, so the `ToString` method of our dRetVal decimal type variable is called. We do not pass the string literal C (for a localized conversion to a currency representation) even though we know we are dealing with money, because the currency symbol will violate the destination schema's typing of `transRoyalty` as a decimal.

Inline Script Functoid

The inline script version of this functoid will be easier than you think, so let's complete the implementation before we try to use our custom functoid in the map we created earlier in the chapter.

We add another class to our class library, again deriving from BaseFunctoid. The constructor follows the same pattern as our previous example with some notable additions. The constructor is shown in Listing 4.6.

LISTING 4.6 Class Constructor for an Inline Scripting Functoid

```
public class InlineRoyaltyFunctoid : BaseFunctoid
{
   public InlineRoyaltyFunctoid() : base()
   {
        this.ID = 6046;
        SetupResourceAssembly("QueFunctoids.QueFunctoidResources",
➥Assembly.GetExecutingAssembly());
        SetName("IDS_INLINEFUNCTOID_NAME");
        SetTooltip("IDS_INLINEFUNCTOID_TOOLTIP");
        SetDescription("IDS_INLINEFUNCTOID_DESCRIPTION");
        SetBitmap("IDB_INLINEFUNCTOID_BITMAP");
       this.SetMinParams(3);
       this.SetMaxParams(3);
        SetScriptBuffer(ScriptType.CSharp, ScriptSource());
        this.Category = FunctoidCategory.Math;
        this.OutputConnectionType = ConnectionType.AllExceptRecord;
        this.RequiredGlobalHelperFunctions =
➥InlineGlobalHelperFunction.IsNumeric;
        AddInputConnectionType((~ConnectionType.FunctoidCumulative)
➥&(~ConnectionType.FunctoidDateTime)&ConnectionType.AllExceptRecord);
}
```

The initial portion is the same as before. We point to the resources for the assembly and then specify the various descriptive strings and the bitmap. The first difference comes with the call to `SetScriptBuffer`. This tells Mapper what language we are using and what method will provide the script source code. The enumeration for the first parameter (denoting the language) provides values for all the commonly used .NET languages. When the map is compiled, the method we specify will be called. Mapper will take the source returned by this method and insert it into the map file, calling the appropriate compiler in the process. If a problem exists with the source code, an error will be reported in the output pane of Visual Studio.

Our functoid implementation used the external function `IsNumeric`. In the globally cached version, this was compiled into the final assembly. Because the inline version must stand by itself in the map file, without referencing the assembly, we have to tell Mapper to copy the script for this function into the map file. This is done by setting the `RequiredGlobalHelperFunctions` property. The value is a bitwise combination of enumerated values for each of the available global functions.

We would be done with new code at this point and could simply repeat what we did regarding input nodes in the globally cached version. Instead, I've provided a little more detail regarding inputs. We still want to accommodate all nodes other than records, but this time I've added the negation of some incompatible functoids in case a designer tries to cascade the output of some incompatible functoids. The functoid will not work with a datetime type, nor should it accept the result of a cumulative functoid. We negate the enumerated values for these types and use a bitwise `AND` to combine them to get the parameter for `AddInputConnectionType`.

Now we need to write the method to which we referred in the call to `SetScriptBuffer`. This method is shown in Listing 4.7.

LISTING 4.7 Method Providing the Inline Script Source Code

```
private string ScriptSource()
{
   StringBuilder source = new StringBuilder();

   source.Append("public string CalcRoyalty(string rate, string price,
➥string qty)\n");
   source.Append("{\n");
   source.Append("     decimal dRate, dPrice, dRetVal;\n");
   source.Append("     int iQty;\n");
   source.Append("     if (IsNumeric(rate) && IsNumeric(price) &&
➥IsNumeric(qty))\n");
   source.Append("     {\n");
   source.Append("          dRate = Convert.ToDecimal(rate,
➥System.Globalization.CultureInfo.InvariantCulture);\n");
   source.Append("          dPrice = Convert.ToDecimal(price,
➥System.Globalization.CultureInfo.InvariantCulture);\n");
   source.Append("          iQty = Convert.ToInt32(qty,
➥System.Globalization.CultureInfo.InvariantCulture);\n");
   source.Append("          dRetVal = dRate/100 * dPrice *
➥(decimal)iQty;\n");
   source.Append("          return dRetVal.ToString();\n");
   source.Append("     }\n");
   source.Append("     else\n");
   source.Append("          return \"0.0\";\n");
   source.Append("}\n");


   return source.ToString();
}
```

Because we need to compose a lengthy string, the StringBuilder class is a natural type to use. The method, therefore, is simply a matter of creating a string builder, then appending each line of the source we used in the globally cached functoid, providing whitespace and newline characters for clarity. This is one of the advantages of using .NET rather than one of the older scripting languages. We can use the same source we used and tested in our prior example. When we've finished building the string, we return the output of the StringBuilder's `ToString` method, completing the implementation of the inline script version of the Royalty Estimator functoid.

Adding a Custom Functoid to the Toolbox

Before we can use the functoid in a map, we have to get BizTalk Mapper to recognize the assembly as a functoid. When Mapper starts, it checks a folder named Mapper Extensions under the BizTalk Developer Tools folder and tries to load any assemblies it finds. This folder is usually not created by the product installation process, so you will probably have to create this manually. After you have done so, copy your assembly QueFunctoids.dll into the folder. If you have just built the assembly, Visual Studio is open and you will have to force a refresh. Open the map from earlier in the chapter and then select Tools, Add/Remove Toolbox Items. When the Customize Toolbox dialog box opens, click the Functoids tab, and then click the Reset button. When this process eventually finishes (all the components on all the toolbox tabs are interrogated and updated) click OK to close the dialog box. Our two functoids now appear on the Mathematical Functions tab of the functoids toolbox.

The assembly also has to be in the global assembly cache to make use of the first functoid we created. Map tests will try to call into the assembly, as will the BizTalk runtime messaging engine. To do this, open the Visual Studio command prompt and switch to the folder containing your newly built assembly. Invoke gacutil.exe with the `-if` switch and the name of the assembly:

```
gacutil -if QueFunctoids.dll
```

You will need to remove the old assembly on subsequent builds before you can install the new one:

```
gacutil -uf QueFunctoids
```

Note the lack of the .dll extension. When you are removing an assembly, you are referring to a package name. The file extension might be mistaken for part of the package qualified name.

Using the Custom Functoid in a Map

Now we can finish off our map. Open `Sales2POS.btm` and click the functoids grid layer. We need to get the value of the `royalty` column in the database, so drag another Value Extractor functoid onto the grid. Connect it to the existing Database Lookup functoid and then open the configuration dialog box and add the second parameter, a string literal with the value royalty.

Open the Mathematical Functions tab of the toolbox and scroll down to the bottom. Our two custom functoids are represented. Drag the GAC version onto the grid and then make a connection from the new Value Extractor to the Royalty functoid. Complete the configuration of the functoid by dragging links from `price` and `qty` to the functoid. Finally, make a link from the output of the functoid to the `transRoyalty` field of the destination schema. Your map should look like Figure 4.5.

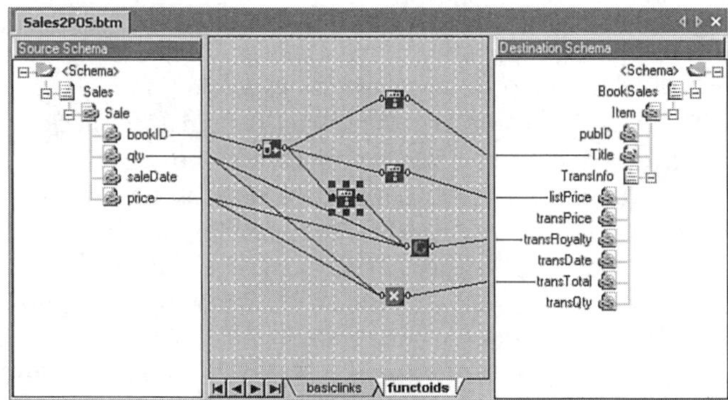

FIGURE 4.5 If you test the map now, the *transRoyalty* attribute appears with a correctly calculated value.

Summary

Mapping lets us build on the schemas you learned to specify in the previous chapter and begin with the work of integration. Although we are a long way from bridging applications and business partners, the tools provided in this chapter allow us to transform data from one schema to another. It will be the task of succeeding chapters to examine how to bring that data together in a meaningful way.

We first reviewed how to work with BizTalk Mapper to create maps with direct links between source and destination nodes. Next, we looked at the standard functoids BizTalk provides and how to use them in maps. The standard functoids provide a wide ranging variety of functions that perform tasks commonly encountered in message mapping and data integration. Using them is only slightly more complicated than using direct node-to-node links. Often, they are no more complicated and you simply link source nodes to functoids and functoid outputs to destination nodes. Occasionally, though, you will need to configure a functoid directly. We demonstrated functoid cascading when we used the database functoids to retrieve important information for us from a relational database.

No matter how useful the standard functoids are, though, there are times when you will need to resort to creating your own custom functoids. You do this to implement specialized logic for mapping. We examined the two implementation types: functoids that are added to the global assembly cache and called directly and those that export script source to a map file at design time. Finally, we integrated our sample functoids with the Visual Studio development environment and used them to complete our map.

Mapping completes the internal details of message construction. There is one final area that needs to be covered before we get back to actually exchanging messages, though, and that is pipelines, the topic of the next chapter.

CHAPTER 5

Building Pipelines

IN THIS CHAPTER

Pipelines are the interface between protocol-specific adapters that send and receive messages and the messaging engine, which is responsible for overall processing of those messages. Pipelines provide BizTalk developers with an opportunity to put an inbound message into proper form for the messaging engine or prepare an outbound message for delivery. The messaging engine assumes certain things about messages. All inbound messages arriving from a receive location will be converted into an internal XML format regardless of whether their native format is XML, and all messages will be in the clear, that is, decrypted and in the proper character encoding when they reach the messaging engine. Having pipelines, then, simplifies the internal workings of the messaging engine, but still lets us have such features as digital encryption and signing.

Pipeline development takes two forms:

- Assembling pipelines from pipeline components using pipeline templates
- Developing custom pipeline components to provide features that are not available in the standard pipeline components that come with BizTalk Server

In this chapter you will become familiar with basic pipeline concepts, the standard features and components available to pipeline developers, and how to use the BizTalk pipeline interfaces to create your own custom pipeline components.

Pipeline Concepts

You might think of a pipeline as an assembly line. An inbound message arrives on the loading dock—the receive adapter—and proceeds down the line. Along the line, individual operators perform specific tasks before passing the message along. These operators are organized into related stages and work under the control of some supervisor. A BizTalk pipeline is simply an organized sequence of .NET or COM components that manipulate messages before or after processing by the messaging engine. A pipeline is organized into stages. Each stage is where a series of related components perform a certain type, or stage, of work in the processing. The BizTalk messaging engine acts as the supervisor, transferring the message from one component to another. Within a stage, components can be executed in sequence, or the stage can be configured to execute only the first component that matches some criteria before transferring control to the next stage. The latter mode, called FirstMatch mode, lets a designer specify a group of components to handle a variety of scenarios. At runtime, the messaging engine will pass control to each component in turn until one of them recognizes the message. That component processes the message and the engine passes control to the next stage, bypassing other component candidates.

Two kinds of pipelines exist: receive pipelines and send pipelines. Receive pipelines take a raw inbound message, decode and decrypt it as needed, disassemble it into parts, and translate it into an internal XML format. Send pipelines perform the complementary tasks. They receive an XML-format message from the runtime engine, convert it to a flat-file format if necessary, assemble multiple messages into a batched form, and then encrypt the message, if desired.

BizTalk Server enforces this sequence in two ways. First, two default pipelines are provided to accommodate truly routine types of processing. We took advantage of these defaults in the sample in Chapter 2, "Your First BizTalk Server Integration." Next, pipeline templates are provided for use in the Visual Studio Pipeline Designer. A template exists for each type of pipeline, receive and send. This ensures that every stage of message processing is represented and that only the proper kind of component is allowed into each of the stages. Thus, a receive pipeline is assured that the decode stage occurs before the disassembly stage, and only components that perform decoding tasks are allowed into that stage.

Default Pipelines

BizTalk Server provides four default pipelines out of the box, but because they are send/receive pairs, they account for the two most common messaging situations. The first is the pass-through, in which a message arrives, passes through the messaging engine, and is sent on its way without any sort of processing. The receive pass-through pipeline requires that the source and destination of the message be known and that the message is in clear-text and does not require validation. Its send counterpart, meanwhile, takes the message and sends it along to its known destination without any sort of post-processing. The pass-through pipelines are very simple and exist to let you do basic messaging without resorting to the Pipeline Designer. They are almost always associated with a secure environment and are most useful for accommodating legacy formats and applications that have already been integrated to some extent in the past.

The other pair of default pipelines handles basic messaging with XML-format messages. The default XML receive pipeline breaks the message down into its component parts so that it will be ready for the runtime engine. It also invokes a standard component that looks at the message and resolves the identity of the message source. The default XML send pipeline takes a message from the messaging engine, assembles it for transmission, and hands it off to the outbound adapter for transmission. As with the pass-through pipelines, this pair of pipelines is best suited to a secure environment, but it does permit a bit more sophistication in processing. You can use it to verify basic message handling in an all-XML system before developing your own pipeline with more robust features.

Types of Pipeline Development

BizTalk developers who work with any nontrivial system will develop pipelines starting from one of the templates. Like the BizTalk development tasks we have seen, you work with a toolbox, a design surface, and a Property view in Visual Studio. The toolbox is populated with the standard pipeline components, which are then dragged onto the design surface in one of the stages provided by the template. Components and stages are configured by setting their properties in the Property view. For most BizTalk projects, this will be the sum of pipeline development.

In special cases, however, you may need features not provided by the standard pipeline components. BizTalk Server specifies a number of interfaces that allow .NET developers to create their own custom components, much as we created a custom functoid in the last chapter. Custom pipeline components must still respect the stages specified for send and receive pipelines, however. Still, custom pipeline components allow developers to add any low-level message pre- or post-processing tasks required by their specific environment or system. Custom pipeline development is a classic programming task in which you use one of the .NET languages to build a class library assembly.

Receive Pipelines

Now that you have a general idea of what goes into a pipeline, we can look at the details. We'll start at the beginning, with a message arriving at a receive port via a receive adapter. The messaging engine is confronted with a raw message and turns it over to the receive pipeline configured for the receive port. All receive pipelines consist of four stages: decode, disassemble, validate, and party resolution. If the features of a particular stage are not needed, they can be left empty. Let's consider each stage in a bit more depth.

Decode Stage

The first thing you might want to do with a message is get it into a form that BizTalk can recognize. S/MIME decoding can occur here to get the message into unencrypted form. Decryption components can be invoked to decrypt a secure message into plain text. The decode stage will always execute all components in sequence. This stage can accept as many as 255 components. Throughput would suffer, but you could have quite a party going on in this stage! The output of the decode stage is a single message in plain text.

Disassemble Stage

You might wonder what disassembly is in terms of message processing. As designers, we are accustomed to thinking of messages as the smallest element of processing. The BizTalk messaging engine goes deeper. Message disassembly is parsing a message into one or more messages. This stage is configured with zero or more parsing components. The messaging engine gives each component a chance. When one of the components recognizes the format of the incoming message, it will parse the message. Custom components may modify the contents of the message in the process.

An incoming message can consist of a number of discrete messages bundled together within an envelope that lets them be transferred in a single operation, a configuration known as a *message interchange*. In such a case, the parser recognizing the interchange is responsible for breaking the message into multiple messages that the runtime engine will process individually. This is a common situation with legacy systems that have slow links. It was not uncommon just a few years ago to accumulate the day's processing into one large transaction file that was sent overnight via a slow dial-up link. BizTalk is designed for individual message transactions; this step bridges the gap.

An alternative situation is one in which a message is composed of a header, trailer, and message body, each of which we want to process and specify separately. Again, the parsing component that handles such a configuration is responsible for breaking the raw message down into its parts and passing them to the messaging engine.

This stage began with a single clear-text message in XML or flat-file format. It ends with one or more messages that are always in XML form so that the runtime engine never has to deal with flat-file formats directly.

Validate Stage

After the violence done by the disassemble stage, a prudent programmer might want to check the integrity of the messages that come whizzing out of that stage. The validation stage gives us this chance, stopping any malformed messages before they can pollute the rest of the messaging stream. This stage can be configured with as many as 255 validator components, and every component in this stage will be invoked. If this stage has any components at all, the stage will be repeated once for each message emerging from the disassembly stage. Assuming that the messages pass validation, the output of this stage will be as many clear-text, XML-format messages as came into the stage. The contents of the messages are not altered in any way.

Party Resolution Stage

This stage has but one function—to determine who sent the message and to populate the `SourcePartyID` context property with this information. There is a standard pipeline component called the Party Resolution pipeline component that applies a bit of business logic to information passed along from earlier stages. All components in the stage are executed, and as many as 255 instances of the Party Resolution component may be added to this stage.

The protocol-specific adapter that receives the original, native-format message either knows the Windows ID of the sender (and passes this along) or marks the message as belonging to the anonymous user ID. If S/MIME decoding took place in the first stage of the receive pipeline, the thumbprint of the digital certificate used to sign the message is used to look up the sender in the certificate repository. This identity is used in preference to the Windows user because a digital signature explicitly marks a message with an identity, whereas the Windows user ID may simply reflect the ID under which the message was received (including the anonymous user ID).

Send Pipelines

We're halfway through the messaging engine. A message has come in, has been prepared for the engine by the receive pipeline, and the engine has performed any routing needed. Depending on who has subscribed to the message, multiple messages may be coming out of the engine. Regardless, BizTalk has a message ready to send and is calling on a send pipeline to perform the final steps for transmission. The stages in send pipelines are largely complementary to their receive counterparts. There are, however, only three stages to the send pipeline template: preassemble, assemble, and encode.

Preassemble Stage

The default pipelines do nothing with this stage. BizTalk provides it as a place where designers can create custom components that manipulate a message prior to serialization. Because of this, the stage executes all components in it. The stage will be invoked by the messaging engine exactly once. As with the other stages we have seen so far, the preassemble stage can hold as many as 255 component instances.

Assemble Stage

This stage exists to take the XML format the messaging engine turns out and convert it to a flat-file format, if needed, or to add an envelope to an outgoing message. This stage will accept no more than one component, however. An assembler component is configured with one or more message schemas. It accepts the XML-format message coming from the runtime engine without validation and uses the schema to generate the output format. We'll get into the specifics of configuring assemblers in a later section when we discuss the default pipeline components provided by BizTalk.

Encode Stage

When a message reaches this stage, it is a complete message in the format desired for transmission. Only one general task remains, and that is to convert the logical form of the message to the wire format required. This may involve S/MIME encoding or some custom encryption. The logical message is the format demanded by the business requirements of the system. This may be sensitive information, so we can invoke encoding and encryption components in this stage to secure it. The business case is unaffected, but the transmission environment may call for additional security, such as when sending a purchase order to a business partner over the public Internet. Components in this stage are invoked exactly once, and all components in the stage will be executed.

Pipeline Components

You've seen how send and receive pipelines are organized into stages, and we've referred to components in the course of describing what those stages do. The different stages perform different tasks, and they execute differently. Some invoke all components in a stage, whereas others search for the appropriate component for a particular message. As you might imagine, this behavior means there are different types of components, each suited to a particular stage or type of processing. In this section, we'll discuss the different kinds of pipeline components BizTalk supports, then we'll look at the default components that are provided out of the box with BizTalk Server 2004.

General Components

This is the most basic class of pipeline components. A general pipeline component takes a single message, performs some processing, and emits zero or more messages. If it does not produce any message output, it is called a consuming component. This is a fairly rare situation, but it might be necessary to preserve the integrity of the system. The Validation component that comes with BizTalk, for example, is a general component that produces no message output if the message it processes is invalid.

Because of the broad nature of general components, their complexity depends on the task they are performing. BizTalk requires only that they implement four interfaces: `IBaseComponent`, `IComponent`, `IComponentUI`, and `IPersistPropertyBag`. (We'll discuss these interfaces more in the section on custom pipeline components.) Four interfaces may seem like a lot, but there isn't much to them. `IBasecomponent` has three read-only properties to the entire interface, `IComponent` has a single method, and `IComponentUI` has a read-only property and a single method. `IPersistPropertyBag` is a utility interface defined by the .NET Framework and isn't terribly complicated, either. If your requirements can be satisfied by taking an entire message, performing some unit of work, and passing the output along, then a general component is a good, low-cost choice for implementation. It is possible for a general component to also be a probing component, which can complicate matters. You would implement probing functionality when you want the flexibility to throw a lot of different types of messages through the same pipeline but want to perform essentially the same task on each. In this situation, you'd write several general components, each performing the same broad task, but specialized to the individual nature of a single schema. You could then drop one instance of each type into a pipeline stage and allow them to probe incoming messages so that the messaging engine could select the right component for the arriving message type.

General components may be placed in the decode, encode, preassemble, and validate stages of message pipelines.

Assembling Components

These components belong in one place, the assembling stage of send pipelines. With such specificity, you might think that they would be very easy to develop. They are responsible for a number of potentially complicated tasks, however. They take an XML message coming out of the message engine and convert it to the flat-file output format using the message schema. You can see that this mapping could be complicated. Because the messaging engine operates on XML data, an assembling engine also has to create an XML envelope for a flat-file message and insert the message so that the engine can forward it to a send adapter. If the message schema has promoted properties, the assembler takes these properties from the message context and inserts them into the field designated by the XPath expression associated with the property. This is why there is an XML Assembler component in BizTalk in spite of the fact that no conversion from XML is required in that case.

Assemblers implement `IBaseComponent`, `IAssemblerComponent`, `IComponentUI`, and `IPersistPropertyBag`. The only change from general components is the replacement of `IComponent` with `IAssemblerComponent`. This is not a derivation. The latter interface has two methods and is slightly more complicated than the `IComponent` interface. One method is called by the messaging engine to add message parts to a list, and another is called to actually assemble the parts into a whole message interchange.

Disassembling Components

Disassemblers are complementary and belong to the disassemble stage of receive pipelines. The first thing they do is convert flat-file messages into an XML format so that the messaging engine can handle them. Because BizTalk supports the concept of batching multiple messages within a single envelope, a disassembler may be configured with schemas for envelopes and messages. In that case, the disassembler inspects the incoming message and splits it into its constituent parts for further processing. Each separate message will then be processed individually.

Now the disassembler has to tell BizTalk about the message. The most important property it sets is the type of the message. The value of this property is the namespace of the message, a literal pound sign (#), and the name of the root element (or top-level equivalent for flat files) concatenated into a string. The messaging engine uses this property to determine what subscriptions apply to this message. Next, the disassembler sets properties of the message context.

If the message is being passed through without manipulation or submission to an orchestration, and the message is encoded in a character set other than UTF-8, the disassembler performs the character set conversion so that the message can be persisted in the MessageBox database. Otherwise, if the pipeline is a pass-through, the disassembler will skip this step, leaving it for the complementary assembler to check the message against the outgoing schema and perform any needed conversions.

Disassemblers are naturally very similar to assemblers in terms of required interfaces. In addition to the familiar `IBaseComponent`, `IComponentUI`, and `IPersistPropertyBag` interfaces, disassemblers add `IDisassmblerComponent`. This interface has two methods: one that splits a message into its constituent parts and another that is called by the messaging engine to iterate through the resulting list of message parts.

Probing Components

This isn't so much a separate class of components as an additional characterization of some types of components. By implementing the `IProbeMessage` interface, a general component, assembler, or disassembler can first check a message to see whether it, the probing component, is suitable for use. If it is, the component can then go ahead and process the message. Any stage that supports the `FirstMatch` mode of execution can make use of this capability.

A few rules apply to how the messaging engine utilizes probing components in such a stage. If the stage has no components, the stage is skipped and pipeline processing continues with the next stage. If the stage has one or more components, the engine retrieves the next component. If the component does not support `IProbeMessage`, the component is assumed to be appropriate and is invoked. When it is through processing, the messaging engine transfers control to the next stage. If, however, the component supports `IProbeMessage`, the `Probe` method of the interface is called with the message and its context as parameters. If the method returns true, the component is invoked by the messaging engine to complete processing of the message at that stage. Control then passes to the next stage. If the messaging engine gets through the entire list of components for the stage without finding a match, an error is generated.

Default Components

Much of your work with pipelines will be accomplished with the default components found in the Pipeline Designer toolbox. Now that you know a bit about the kinds of components and how they are built, it is worth briefly examining the default components to see what is provided.

General Components

The Pipeline Designer in Visual Studio provides the following general components:

- XML Validator—Checks XML messages in receive pipelines against one or more schemas and raises an error if they do not conform.
- Party Resolution—Attempts to determine the sender of a message in receive pipelines based on Windows user IDs and digital certificates.

- MIME/SMIME Decoding—Provides MIME-type decoding in the decoding stage of receive pipelines. This component can also provide SMIME decryption and signature checking when a received message is so signed and/or encrypted.
- MIME/SMIME Encoding—Provides the complementary encoding, signing, and encryption services in the encoding stage of send pipelines.

Assemblers

Message assembly is an important task for BizTalk pipelines. Although earlier versions of BizTalk supported message maps in channels, the precursor to pipelines, BizTalk Server 2004 puts message mapping into orchestrations.

TIP

If you need mapping but do not require an orchestration, you may configure a send or receive port to invoke a map. This is done using the property dialog box for the desired port in BizTalk Explorer. A send port has a node named Outbound Maps in the Filters and Maps folder. Clicking an empty row displays a list of installed maps from which to make a selection. In use, this map will be applied as the message departs the port. For receive ports, the top-level folder has nodes labeled Inbound Maps and Outbound Maps. In use, these are applied as the message arrives or departs the port, respectively.

If you need to translate message formats in a simple messaging scenario, you need to use message assemblers to construct the output message in the format you desire. Even if you are not translating messages, you will still need an assembler if you are using envelopes for reliable messaging, routing, or as a container for batching and handling multiple discrete messages. Pipeline Designer provides the following default assemblers:

- XML Assembler—Builds envelopes as needed and appends XML messages within the envelope. In addition, this component moves the value of message context properties into distinguished fields in envelopes and message bodies.
- Flat File Assembler—Converts XML messages to a designated flat-file format. This component also builds message headers and trailers (the flat-file equivalent of XML envelopes) as required and batches individual messages.
- BTF Assembler—Supports the BizTalk Framework (BTF) by building BTF envelopes and inserting messages. BTF was an application-level effort to provide reliable, exactly-once message delivery based on standard envelope properties specified by the BTF. The Framework was supported in earlier versions of BizTalk Server. The BTF assembler also provides some of the reliable messaging semantics (message receipt and retransmission) mandated by BTF. This component requires an orchestration to support it.

Disassemblers

The Pipeline Designer also provides the following disassemblers to complement the assemblers found in the toolbox by default. These provide parsing, disassembly, and property promotion services.

- XML Disassembler
- Flat File Disassembler
- BTF Disassembler

Building a Pipeline

Constructing a pipeline is very similar to designing an orchestration. Like the Orchestration Designer we saw in Chapter 2, the Pipeline Designer uses a Visio add-in to Visual Studio to let you specify a pipeline by dragging shapes onto a design surface and configuring the properties of the pipeline and the shapes.

To create a new pipeline, invoke the Add New Item dialog box from Solution Explorer. Now specify the type of pipeline you want to construct by selecting the Receive Pipeline or Send Pipeline item from the BizTalk Project Items folder.

When you create a new pipeline, you are presented with empty shapes for each stage of the pipeline. As you attempt to drag shapes from the palette to the design surface, the Designer will indicate whether you can drop the shape onto the stage shape over which you are dragging the component shape. You then set the properties for each stage, shape, and the pipeline itself. There is no code to write. Upon compilation, the pipeline is added to the assembly that is the end result of your project. After the assembly is added to the global cache, the pipeline becomes available for use in the BizTalk Explorer for use in configuring send and receive ports.

The best way to demonstrate this is with a sample. We'll start with a simple sample that uses the standard pipeline components to perform a simple processing task. Then, after you learn how to build custom pipeline components, you'll modify the pipeline to do more sophisticated processing. We'll begin the sample by specifying a schema for a message the pipeline is meant to handle.

Creating the Activity Message Schema

Let's suppose that different organizations want to send a message to one another to indicate the occurrence of some activity, much in the way we fire events in a program and inspect the event arguments to find out what happened. The first step is to create a message for our pipeline to process.

Listing 5.1 shows a sample Activity message.

LISTING 5.1 Sample Activity Message

```
<?xml version="1.0" encoding="utf-8" ?>
<ns0:Activity type="5" xmlns:ns0="http://Pipeline_Chapter_Project.Activity">
  <Location>Philadelphia</Location>
  <Timestamp>1999-05-31T13:20:00.000-05:00</Timestamp>
  <Notes>Notes_0</Notes>
 </ns0:Activity>
```

The organizations share a great deal of knowledge of their activities, so we don't have to communicate too much. The `type` attribute is a numeric code denoting which activity has taken place, and each organization knows what these codes mean. This gives us some meager degree of confidentiality in the event the message is intercepted. The `Location` element's textual content is the geographic location of the organization experiencing the activity. The `Timestamp` element is an ISO 8601 datetime value representing the time the activity occurred, and `Notes` gives us a place to add comments regarding the event.

To specify the schema for this message, create a new BizTalk project and add a Schema item to the project. Give it the filename `Activity.xsd`, the namespace `Pipeline_Chapter_Project`, and the TypeName `ActivitySchema`. Name the root node Activity. Create the `type`, `Location`, `Timestamp`, and `Notes` fields, remembering to make `type` an attribute and the rest elements. Table 5.1 shows how to configure the schema.

TABLE 5.1 Activity Schema Properties

Field Name	Base Data Type	Constraints
Type	xs:nonNegativeInteger	Derived by restriction, minFacet 1, maxFacet 10, inclusive, use Required
Location	xs:string	minOccurs 1, maxOccurs 1, nillable false
Timestamp	Xs:dateTime	minOccurs 1, maxOccurs 1, nillable false
Notes	xs:string	minOccurs 1, maxOccurs 1

NOTE

The sample code for this chapter includes two Activity messages. The file ActivityTest.xml complies with the schema. ActivityTestBad.xml is an Activity message with a validation error and may be used to check the schema. We will use both to check the proper operation of our pipeline.

Validating Receive Pipeline

As we saw in Chapter 2, BizTalk comes with several default pipelines so that you can get started with common messaging solutions. One of these processes XML messages like the one we just created. Our first pipeline will replicate this behavior, but we're going to demonstrate the use of pipeline components to validate XML messages with schemas. We'll assume that the system administrator wants to check incoming activity messages against the activity schema and reject them if they do not validate properly.

Add a receive pipeline item to the same project within the solution that contains the schema. You will see the shell of a receive pipeline, with stage shapes for Decode, Disassemble, Validate, and ResolveParty. The first thing to remember is what BizTalk's messaging system is looking for in terms of pipeline processing. Every incoming message needs to be converted into an internal BizTalk format. The standard pipelines we've seen do that for us, which is why we selected the XMLReceive pipeline in Chapter 2: We needed a pipeline that knew how to break an XML message down into BizTalk's internal format. Before we dash off to accomplish our task-related processing (in this case, validation), then, we need to add the proper disassembler to our pipeline.

Drag the XML Disassembler component shape from the toolbox to the Disassemble stage shape. When your mouse cursor is over the body of the shape, the cursor will change from the slashed circle to an arrow with a gray rectangle. This indicates that the component can be dropped into this stage. Drop the component into the stage. The pipeline is now ready to turn our activity messages into a format BizTalk can use.

Now, turn your attention to the properties pane. You might think our next step is to drop an XML validator component into the validation stage, but an inspection of the disassembler component's properties will reveal that we can accomplish validation right here. Configure the following properties as indicated:

- Allow unrecognized message—Set to `false`.
- Document schemas—Click the ellipsis button and select Pipeline_Chapter_Project.ActivitySchema from the list in the Schema Collection Property Editor dialog box.
- Validate document structure—Set to `true`.

The effect of the first and third settings is to force the pipeline to throw an exception if a message can't be matched to a schema and successfully validated. Because the document schema and envelope schema properties are collections, you can open your pipeline to a series of message types and require the disassembler to match the incoming message to the appropriate schema. Because we are forcing it to do validation, we have to provide at least one schema. Our activity schema, being part of the current project, was automatically added to the somewhat lengthy list of available schemas. The diagram in Figure 5.1 shows what the pipeline should look like.

At this point you can save your project and build it. You will need to generate a key file and deploy the resulting assembly to the global cache as we have done in previous chapters.

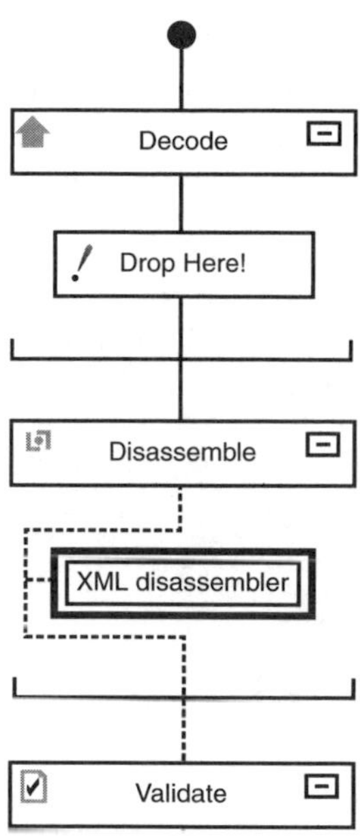

FIGURE 5.1 The heart of the ReceiveActivity pipeline, showing an XML Disassembler component in the disassemble stage.

Deploying and Using the Solution

If you worked through the introductory sample in Chapter 2 you might now expect to construct an orchestration in order to use our new pipeline. Instead, we will anticipate the next chapter and discover that we can use the messaging system directly. With the assembly deployed to the global cache on our server, the remainder of our sample is reduced to configuration.

The first step is to prepare to receive a message. That involves creating a port and associating our new pipeline with the port. We'll use the file reception protocol for our testing. The goal for right now is to be able to drop an activity message into a folder on the file system and have BizTalk move it to a specified destination, performing validation en route.

First, create two folders on your local hard drive. On my system, I created a folder named PipelineSample containing folders named Source and Destination. Anything will do, provided you use two distinct folders.

Next, turn to the BizTalk Explorer in Visual Studio. If it is not visible, open it from the View menu. Right-click the Receive Ports node and select Add Receive Port. In the Create New Receive Port dialog box that results, make sure One-Way Port is selected and click OK. Click OK to accept the defaults in the Port Properties dialog box. Name the new node `receiveActivityPort`.

> **NOTE**
>
> You may find it useful, as I have, to preface port names with the direction of message travel and include some indicator of the expected message type in the name. As you create more ports and receive locations, it is easy to become lost and uncertain of the purpose of each.

Now we have a logical port, but it is not tied to any actual messaging protocol. To fix this, expand the port node, right-click the subordinate Receive Locations node, and select Add Receive Location from the context menu. Set the properties in the Receive Location Properties dialog box as indicated in Table 5.2.

TABLE 5.2 Receive Location Properties

Property	Setting
Name	receiveActivityLocation
Transport Type	FILE
Address (URI)	C:\PipelineSample\Source*.xml or other location ending in the .xml mask to denote your expected source folder
Receive Handler	BizTalkServerApplication
Receive Pipeline	Pipeline_Chapter_Project.ReceiveActivity

The dialog box should look like Figure 5.2 when you are finished.

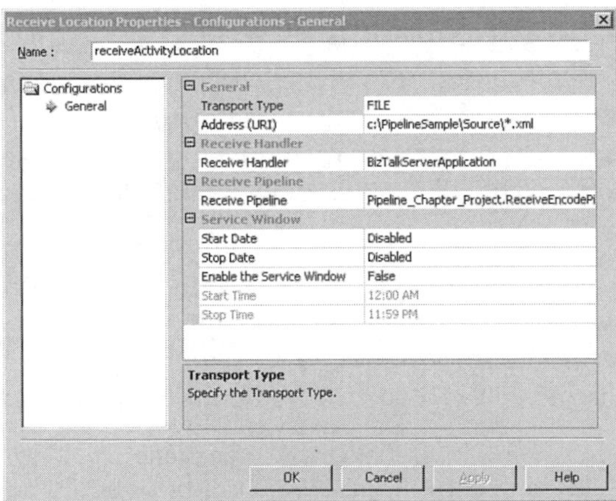

FIGURE 5.2 Receive Location Properties dialog box configured for use with activity messages and our new pipeline.

Now turn your attention to the Send Ports node in BizTalk Explorer. We need to add a port so that BizTalk will have somewhere to send the activity messages it receives. Following the previous steps, add a new send port, selecting Static One-Way Port for the type and setting the port properties as shown in Table 5.3.

TABLE 5.3 Send Port Properties

Property	Setting
Transport	
Transport Type	FILE
Address (URI)	C:\PipelineSample\Destination\%MessageID%.xml
Send	
Send Pipeline	Microsoft.BizTalk.DefaultPipelines.XMLTransmit

The macro `%MessageID%` instructs the messaging engine to use the unique message identifier it generates for its own use as a unique name for the message filename. The send pipeline we have selected is one of the default pipelines and simply serves to take an XML message from the engine, convert it from the internal representation back to XML, and pass it through the associated send port. It is the functional complement to the pipeline we created, minus validation.

There is one final setting to make in the send port properties. At this point, we have a receive port and a send port, but nothing associating the two. We need to establish a link, called a subscription, between the send port and the receive port. As you shall see in the next chapter, send ports subscribe to incoming messages through filters on various properties in the messaging system. When the messaging system receives a message, it runs through its list of filters and sends the message through any send port whose filter criteria match the characteristics of the incoming message.

Select the Filters and Maps node in the configurations list of the port properties dialog box and expand it. Select Filters. In the right pane, you will see three column headings: Property, Operator, and Value. Click the label to create a new row, and then select the Property cell. Scroll down until you can select `BTS.ReceivePortName`. Select == under Operator, and then select the Value cell and enter `receiveActivityPort`. Click OK to complete the configuration. The send port is now subscribed to any message arriving at the receive port named `receiveActivityPort`. Now, whenever a message arrives through that port, BizTalk will transmit it through this send port.

To test this messaging configuration, we need to start things through the BizTalk Server Administration console. Remember, that's the MMC snap-in you can access from the Microsoft BizTalk Server 2004 folder in the Start Programs menu. First, select the Receive Locations node in the left pane, then right-click `receiveActivityLocation` in the right pane and click Enable on the context menu. Now select SendPorts in the left pane of the console and right-click `sendActivityPort`. Click Enlist on the context menu to bind the port to the physical environment. Right-click again and select Start to activate the port. Finally, expand the Hosts node in the left pane and select the node for `BizTalkServerApplication`.

NOTE

`BizTalkServerApplication` is the default name established during installation for the server host process. If you chose a different name, select that node.

5

In the right pane, locate the machine name of your server. If its running status is stopped, right-click and select Start from the context menu. At this point, your ports are bound to the physical runtime environment and the host process is started. Your receive location is regularly polling the source folder.

Drop a valid activity message into that folder. If you are working with the download for this chapter, you may copy the file `ActivityTest.xml`. After a brief interval, the file will disappear from the source folder and an identical file will appear in the destination folder with a unique name. Now take the file `ActivityTestBad.xml`, or modify the message you used in such a way as to invalidate it, and drop it into the source folder. The file will disappear (the messaging system consumes it), but no message appears in the destination folder.

NOTE

If you run the Health and Activity Tracking application from the Microsoft BizTalk Server 2004 folder in the Start Programs menu, you can use the Operations Messages menu item to search for the message, see that it is suspended, and discover that the message had a validation error. This procedure is covered in detail in Chapter 16, "BizTalk Health and Activity Tracking." For a simpler, though less-detailed check, you can inspect the Application Log in the Windows Event Viewer to detect the problem.

The first test indicates that our pipeline can accept a message and pass it successfully to the messaging engine. The second test verifies that the pipeline is, in fact, performing message validation using the schema you created.

You can accomplish a lot of messaging processing using the standard pipeline components. One of the beauties of having pipelines is the capability to insert needed bits of functionality into the message-processing behavior of BizTalk. Another is that pipelines, like BizTalk Server in general, support extensibility through their support for custom components. If you cannot find what you need in the standard set of pipeline components, you can create your own. Custom pipeline component creation is our next, and final, topic for consideration in our study of messaging pipelines.

Custom Pipeline Components

The idea of pipelines and pipeline components at Microsoft goes back at least to Commerce Server. The basic ideas originated there have been carried forward in BizTalk. Broadly speaking, a pipeline is a sequential series of stages through which a message passes. At each stage, as we just saw, components take the message out of the pipeline, perform some specific act of processing on it, and return it to the pipeline. Each component makes minimal assumptions about the activities of other components and stages, and each component must respect some minimum rules of pipeline processing. This lets components specialize in one specific task without breaking the overall pipeline processing model.

The common rules are codified in four interfaces each pipeline component must implement. These interfaces are as follows:

- IBaseComponent—Communicates basic descriptive information to the operating environment.
- IComponentUI—Provides services needed to allow the component to function well in a design-time environment such as Visual Studio.
- IPersistPropertyBag—Permits persistence of custom properties for the component.
- IComponent—The heart of pipeline processing, this interface provides a common, well-known interface that the messaging engine uses to communicate with components and invoke their functionality.

IBaseComponent Members

This interface is a bit of boilerplate that enables various tools to interrogate the component to furnish information to other applications or the tool user. It has just three members, each of which is a read-only string property. These properties are

- Description—User-friendly explanation of the purpose of the component.
- Version—Arbitrary string denoting the component version. This is typically formed using the "major dot minor" convention.
- Name—User-friendly component name or title.

IComponentUI Members

Like `IBaseComponent`, this interface exists to make the component work well in a design-time environment like Visual Studio. It consists of two members: a read-only property and a method.

The property is called `Icon` and it returns a `System.IntPtr`. The programming contract implied by this interface understands this pointer to be the handle of a bitmap the design environment can use in a toolbox to represent the component.

Because components exist to extend the core functionality of pipelines, there is no way Visual Studio (or BizTalk, for that matter) can be expected to "know" what custom properties the component supports. Visual Studio will populate the properties pane with these properties (obtained through another interface) and let programmers change them, but it has no way of checking their values and enforcing any interdependencies. The method, `Validate`, is called when a component's properties are committed and lets the component enforce dependency checks to make sure the component is left in a valid state. `Validate` takes a single parameter, an object that contains the configuration properties in question, and returns an instance of the `IEnumerator` interface. The enumerator is a list of strings representing errors.

CAUTION

If Visual Studio finds that the enumerator is not empty upon return from the method invocation, it will display the strings as compiler errors.

IPersistPropertyBag Members

This interface pops up throughout the .NET Framework, so you might have some previous experience with it. The particular definition BizTalk uses is defined in the `Microsoft.BizTalk.Component.Interop` namespace, so there are some minor differences from its definition elsewhere in Windows. Moreover, there is some legacy overlap designed so that our pipeline components can interoperate with unmanaged code. It is a general purpose container class that lets you read in or save out an arbitrary number of name-value pairs. The names are strings, and all values are treated as being of type object by the interface, thereby allowing it to deal with any value in the .NET environment. It is presumed the implementing class knows the names and types of values with which it is dealing and will cast the values accordingly.

This interface consists of four public methods: `GetClassID`, `InitNew`, `Load`, and `Save`. `GetClassID` exists primarily to let our components interoperate with unmanaged code. It returns void but takes a single out parameter of type `System.Guid`. On return, the parameter should be a globally unique value so that any application can determine which implementation of `IPersistPropertyBag` it is dealing with.

`InitNew` takes no parameters and returns void. It is your component's opportunity to initialize any structures, caches, or other data and objects it might need to properly use the persisted properties. `Load` and `Save` are the core of this interface. They let pipeline components retrieve saved property values for configuration purposes, as well as write them out for later retrieval.

`Load` takes two parameters and returns void. The first parameter is an `IPropertyBag` interface. You may think of the latter as a lightweight version of the interface we are implementing. Behind the scenes, Visual Studio will deal with the physical storage of your property values and hand you an instance of this interface. It has two methods, `Read` and `Write`, which mirror the `Load` and `Save` methods we are discussing. The second parameter of `Load` is an `Int32` value that is the address of an error log object. This is a departure from other declarations of the interface outside BizTalk that use an interface pointer.

`Save` returns void and takes three parameters: an `IPropertyBag` interface and two Booleans. The Booleans allow the caller to fine-tune the property storage by communicating the nature of the desired operation. The first Boolean indicates whether the implementing object should clear its dirty flag (true) or whether the caller intends to save a copy (false) of the object, in which case the dirty flag should be left unchanged. The second Boolean instructs the implementing class to save all property values if the value is true. If it is false, the implementing class may decide what to save based on internal considerations such as the dirty flag.

IComponent Members

This is the most important interface for pipeline components because it is the one BizTalk calls during message processing. It consists of a single method, the aptly named `Execute`. `Execute` is BizTalk's way of saying "do whatever it is you do." It takes two parameters: an `IPipelineContext` describing the pipeline surrounding the component and an `IBaseMessage` that represents all the parts of the message on which the component is operating. `Execute` returns an `IBaseMessage` representing the message following component processing. Your implementation can use the first parameter to decide what it wants to do or to locate the component's place in the pipeline, and it will use the second parameter to get the message out of the pipeline. The return value is the component's way of putting the message back into the pipeline.

What is the difference between a pipeline context and a message, and how is a message structured?

The `IPipelineContext` interface tells about the environment in which the component is executing. It has properties that will tell us the guid of the executing pipeline, the name of the pipeline, the ID of the stage in which the component is operating, and even the index of the component within the stage. It also provides access to any schemas that are in use. Recall that we configured a component with a schema in our previous pipeline. A custom component designer cannot know about this at design time if he is building a component for general use, but the component can be programmed to interrogate the pipeline context at runtime to obtain the schema. There is another aspect to `IPipelineContext` that is of some importance. The `ResourceTracker` property is an object that allows the pipeline to take control of non-CLR resources created in the component and ensure their proper recovery later, thereby conserving system resources.

The second parameter is an interface that lets us deal with multipart messages and their context. Although a message can have only one main, or body, part, it can have numerous other parts to act as headers or envelopes. The `IBaseMessage` interface lets us read and write parts, determine the message ID assigned by BizTalk, obtain the overall size of the message, and read and write error information. In addition, the `Context` property gives us access to the message context. This should not be confused with the pipeline context we just described. You'll recall that we promoted a property in the employee schema so that the orchestration could use a rule involving the value of that property without having to read the message itself. Similarly, our component can read and write the value of promoted properties through the `Context` property.

This method is where you implement the feature or function that is the component's reason for existing, your custom processing or functionality. Whereas the other interface implementations are largely (but not entirely) the same from component to component, this interface method is the one where you have to do some real work. This will become more apparent from our sample component.

Building a Custom Component for Our Sample Pipeline

In the course of running our messaging configuration from the previous example, our fictional organization identified a serious security concern. The use of a numeric code to identify the specific type of event secures that information so long as the sender and receiver share the secret of the code values and their meanings. The timestamp doesn't need to be concealed, because it would readily be discovered by noting the time of message transmission. The physical location of the activity originator, however, is transmitted in the clear. We could apply digital encryption to the message, but such encipherment can be broken with enough time and resources. Our organization wants another layer of security. It wants to code the location rather than encipher it. That is, it wants to replace the physical name—New York, for example—with an arbitrary code name—Tall Pine—with the code names and their meanings being a secret akin to the `type` attribute values.

Ideally, the sending and receiving applications (whatever is generating and consuming these messages) would perform the coding/decoding process. Assume, however, that we cannot modify the legacy applications. The solution is to create a custom pipeline component that will open a received message, replace the clear-text name with the proper code value, and replace it in the pipeline. A similar component would provide the complementary service at the destination. Although not ideal, it ensures that the information is protected from the point at which we receive it through to the final application.

For sample purposes, we will create the encoding component and use it to modify our pipeline. To get started, you must create an entirely new solution, a component library. You can't very well include it in your pipeline solution, because you want the component in the BizTalk toolbox when you are working with that solution. We need to create the component, add it to the global cache, and then return to the pipeline solution to use it.

Declarations and References

After creating the solution, you need to turn to the source code file (`EncodeActivity.cs` in the download) and add the references for your project. Listing 5.2 shows how our component begins:

LISTING 5.2 References

```
namespace EncodeComponent
{
   using System;
   using System.Resources;
   using System.Drawing;
   using System.Collections;
   using System.Reflection;
   using System.ComponentModel;
   using System.Text;
```

LISTING 5.2 Continued

```
    using System.IO;
    using Microsoft.BizTalk.Message.Interop;
    using Microsoft.BizTalk.Component.Interop;
    using System.Xml;
    using System.Xml.XPath;
```

The reference to `System.Drawing` lets us handle the bitmap for our toolbox icon. The two BizTalk references are needed so that our project understands pipelines and messages. We are going to use the XML document object model to inspect activity messages and XPath to locate the `Location` element within the document, hence the final two references.

TIP

Strictly speaking, a streaming approach to XML would be a better choice in the real world to keep resource usage to a minimum. In our sample, however, we know our component is working with very small messages, and the XML DOM classes let us implement our component with fewer lines of code. This choice, then, is for convenience and clarity of teaching and is not a prescription for production code.

Before we get to the interface implementations, we need to include a few .NET attributes. These declare a guid (for unmanaged code interop) and tell Windows and Visual Studio that this is a pipeline component and what stages are appropriate homes for the component. Listing 5.3 shows these declarations and the basic class declaration with its ancestry.

LISTING 5.3 Class Attributes

```
[ComponentCategory(CategoryTypes.CATID_PipelineComponent)]
[ComponentCategory(CategoryTypes.CATID_Decoder)]
[System.Runtime.InteropServices.Guid("ACC3F15A-C389-4a5d-8F8E-2A951CDC4C19")]
public class EncodeLocation :
    IBaseComponent,
    Microsoft.BizTalk.Component.Interop.IComponent,
    Microsoft.BizTalk.Component.Interop.IPersistPropertyBag,
    IComponentUI
```

The two `ComponentCategory` attributes use the `CategoryTypes` enumeration found in the `Microsoft.BizTalk.Component.Interop` namespace. The first tells Windows that this is a pipeline component, and the second will tell the Pipeline Designer that this component is suitable for the decode stage. We have decided to restrict our component to that stage so that the encoding takes place at the earliest point in processing so as to avoid having the clear-text location turn up in the tracking system. The `CategoryTypes` enumeration also includes a catch-all CATID_Any for those situations where your component may safely be used in any stage. The `Guid` attribute allows the legacy COM subsystem of Windows (and all COM/COM+ components) to uniquely identify the component class. The value should be unique to your implementation and may be generated using the Visual Studio Tools Create Guid menu item.

Properties and Logic

With all our discussion of implementing required interfaces, you could be forgiven for forgetting that this is a custom component that will probably need some properties and logic of its own. We use such custom items. One is a static instance of a `ResourceManager` to facilitate getting the icon bitmap out of the assembly. The other is task specific.

An actual encoding component would use a database or some sort of in-memory cache to record all the location values and their corresponding code words. We will hard-code these pairs for a few locations just to keep the sample manageable. However, real-world storage would require us to have some sort of connection string or other means of connecting to the code book, and this is an excellent way to demonstrate the use of custom, persistent properties. You could well imagine a pipeline designer entering the value of a database connection string while configuring the component in the Pipeline Designer. Listing 5.4 shows the declarations for these component-specific members as well as the public accessor for the connection string property.

LISTING 5.4 Class Member Declarations

```
private string connectString = null;
static ResourceManager resManager =
➥new ResourceManager("EncodeComponent.EncodeLocation",
➥Assembly.GetExecutingAssembly());
public string ConnectionString
{
   get {return connectString;}
   set {connectString = value;}
}
```

Take a look at the resource manager declaration. The string identifier consists of the namespace, `EncodeComponent`, followed by the classname, `EncodeLocation`, so that the resource manager can locate the appropriate resources in the assembly. We have added a bitmap to the component resource file using the methods described in Chapter 4, "Mapping Messages," when we built a custom functoid.

Implementing IBaseComponent

This interface is easily implemented. Continuing with the class implementation in `EncodeActivity.cs`, we have to write three get-accessors that return fixed strings. Listing 5.5 illustrates the process for the `Name` property.

LISTING 5.5 Declaring the Component Name

```
public string Name
{
   get
   {
      return "Encode Pipeline Component";
   }
}
```

The process for `Description` and `Version` is identical.

Implementing IComponentUI

This interface has two parts: implementing the `Icon` property and implementing the `Validate` method. First, let's tackle the easier of the two by retrieving and returning the toolbox icon for this component. Listing 5.6 shows the code. At startup, Visual Studio scans the components in the Pipeline Components folder found immediately under the BizTalk Server installation directory. It calls each of the component's Icon property and populates the BizTalk toolbox with the bitmaps returned.

LISTING 5.6 Icon Property Implementation

```
public System.IntPtr Icon
{
   get
   {
      return
➥((Bitmap)resManager.GetObject("IconBitmap")).GetHicon();
   }
}
```

Recall that when we declared custom members for the class, we created a static instance of a `ResourceManager` object under the name `resManager`. That way, all instances of the component have ready access to the resources of the host assembly. The `Icon` accessor merely asks that object to retrieve the resource named `IconBitmap` (the label we assigned when we added the bitmap to the resource file) and get its icon handle.

If you are less than artistically inclined and merely want to experiment with pipeline components with a minimum of fuss, you can return `null`. Visual Studio .NET 2003 is considerate enough to insert a placeholder into the toolbox when that happens.

Next, implementing `Validate` is a bit harder. Because we have only a single custom property and it is not actually used, we have nothing to perform in our implementation. The body of our implementation simply returns `null`. However, if you have actual validity checks to perform, you can create an ArrayList object. This class supports IEnumerator. You call the Add property to add your error messages, if any, and then call GetEnumerator and return the result.

Implementing IPersistPropertyBag

We have one last task before turning to the heart of the component—implementation of IPersistePropertyBag. GetClassId is very simple and requires no explanation other than to remind you to generate a unique guid using Visual Studio for each component. Our sample has one simple property that requires no special handling, so the implementation of InitNew is empty. If we populated a code book in memory from a database, we could perform access checks here and populate the in-memory cache. Listing 5.7 shows the implementation of IPersistPropertyBag.

LISTING 5.7 IPersistPropertyBag Implementation

```
public void InitNew()
{
}
public void GetClassID(out Guid classID)
{
    classID = new
➥Guid ("ACC3F15A-C389-4a5d-8F8E-2A951CDC4C19");
}

public void Load(IPropertyBag propertyBag, int errorLog)
{
   object val = null;
   try
   {
      propertyBag.Read("ConnectionString", out val, 0);
   }
   catch (ArgumentException)
   {
   }
   catch (Exception ex)
   {
      throw new ApplicationException("Error reading
➥propertybag: " + ex.Message);
   }

   if (val != null)
      connectString = (string)val;
   else
```

LISTING 5.7 Continued

```
        connectString = "";
}

public void Save(IPropertyBag propertyBag, bool clearDirty,
➥ bool saveAllProperties)
{
    object val = (object)ConnectionString;
    propertyBag.Write("ConnectionString", ref val);
}
```

`Load` and `Save` are the methods you must master. Fortunately, they are complementary. After you understand one, the other falls into place easily.

Implementing IComponent

Now we come to the interface that justifies custom components. The `Execute` method is where we are going to grab the Activity message from the pipeline, find the Location element, replace its value with the corresponding code word, and hand the altered message back to the pipeline for delivery. Most of our implementation is straightforward XML DOM programming using the .NET classes, but you'll also learn a few tricks regarding getting messages in and out of the pipeline. Listing 5.8 shows the entire body of the Execute method implementation.

We start by creating a new `XmlDocument` object to parse and hold the body of the message. To get at it, we go to the message parameter `pInMsg` and get the value of the `BodyPart` property. This will be an `IBaseMessagePart` representing the entire text of the Activity message, but it is not just a string. The part object has a bunch of information regarding the type of data, the character set, and so forth. To get the data stream itself, we turn to the Data property, which is an instance of System.IO.Stream. Fortunately for us, one of the overloaded variants of the document object's Load method can accept a stream, so we can cause `bodyDoc`, the DOM object, to load and parse our message by passing Data to Load. We wrap this in a try block to catch any XML exceptions that might get thrown.

LISTING 5.8 Execute Method Implementation

```
public IBaseMessage Execute(IPipelineContext pContext, IBaseMessage pInMsg)
{
    XmlDocument bodyDoc = new XmlDocument();
    IBaseMessagePart bodyPart = pInMsg.BodyPart;
    if (bodyPart != null)
    {
        try
        {
```

LISTING 5.8 Continued

```
            bodyDoc.Load(bodyPart.Data);
        }
        catch (XmlException ex)
        {
            throw new ApplicationException(ex.Message);
        }
        try
        {
            XmlNamespaceManager nsmgr =
➥new XmlNamespaceManager(bodyDoc.NameTable);
            nsmgr.AddNamespace("ns0",
➥"http://Pipeline_Chapter_Project.Activity");
            XmlNode locNode =
➥bodyDoc.DocumentElement.SelectSingleNode("/ns0:Activity/Location",
➥nsmgr);
            string val = locNode.InnerText;
            switch (val)
            {
                case "New York":
                    locNode.InnerText = "Homeplate";
                    break;
                case "Philadelphia":
                    locNode.InnerText = "Pooltable";
                    break;
                case "Chicago":
                    locNode.InnerText = "Thunderball";
                    break;
            }
        }
        catch (XPathException ex)
        {
            throw new ApplicationException("Probable wrong
➥document type: " + ex.Message);
        }
        try
        {
            Stream strm = new MemoryStream();
            bodyDoc.Save(strm);
            strm.Position = 0;
            bodyPart.Data = strm;
            pContext.ResourceTracker.AddResource(strm);
        }
```

LISTING 5.8 Continued

```
        catch (Exception ex)
        {
            throw new ApplicationException("Error trying to write
➥ encoded doc: " + ex.Message);
        }
    }
    return pInMsg;
}
```

At this point, we know we have a well-formed XML message. We expect to have an activity message, but we can't assume it. Because a namespace is associated with activity messages, we need to create a namespace manager object and associate the namespace with a prefix we can use in an XPath query. With that done, we can call the document object's `SelectSingleNode` method, passing it an XPath expression and the namespace manager. If we have a valid activity message, we'll get a single node representing the single, expected `Location` element. If we throw an XPath exception, we can safely assume that we're looking at the wrong class of document. When that happens, we throw an Application exception, which BizTalk will put into both its own tracking system message and the Windows event log for applications.

Because we fully expect to get an activity message, the interesting processing goes on outside the exception `catch` block. This is where we would reach into a database or cached code book in a real implementation. For demonstration purposes, though, we enter a `switch` statement based on the value of the text inside the Location element. Note that in each of the supported cases, we simply change the `InnerText` property of the node to the arbitrary code word we've assigned.

That's basic DOM and XPath programming in the .NET Framework, but we still haven't updated the message. We've updated only a DOM model in memory. The stream underlying the message object's `Data` property (as well as the results of calling `GetOriginalDataStream` on the message part object) is read-only. We need to write the updated document to some sort of stream and then assign that stream to `Data`. The `MemoryStream` class fits our requirements. After creating such a stream in the variable `strm`, we pass that into the `Write` method of the document object. This is where you run into a small quirk of BizTalk's. If you do not rewind your stream, the pipeline processor will not attempt to do so and will throw an exception. The error system, however, will do so. In consequence, you will be in the interesting position of having a suspended message in which BizTalk tells you it does not have a message, but will show you the text of a perfectly good activity message with your encoded `Location` element! It's always good practice to rewind your streams, so we do that by setting `Position` to zero and then passing `strm` to the `Data` property. Finally, we add `strm` to the resource tracker to ensure proper clean-up and return from `Execute`. The message has been modified and is back in the pipeline.

Our component implementation is complete. Create a keyfile for the project as with any global component project, build the solution, and drop the resulting assembly into the Pipeline Components folder under the BizTalk installation directory. Finally, add the assembly to the global cache.

Modifying the Receive Pipeline

Now close Visual Studio and reopen it with the pipeline project from our first sample. When it reopens, Visual Studio checks for pipeline components, finds our new custom component, and drops an icon for it into the toolbox when a pipeline file is in focus.

TIP

If Visual Studio fails to load the new component for any reason, you will need to right-click the toolbox, select Add/Remove New Items, and select your component.

You can continue with the pipeline we built previously. The sample project in the download for this chapter includes two pipelines so you can see each form, but we are going to add only to the preceding pipeline.

Find the icon and name you gave your component in the BizTalk Pipeline Components palette of the toolbox (mine has a black code book icon bearing the letter "e" and the name Encode Pipeline Component). Drag the icon to the decode stage. Ironically, we're going to perform what cryptographers call encoding in the stage where BizTalk is expecting us to do what programmers call decoding. The former is a word-for-word replacement, whereas the latter is a low-level, symbol-for-symbol operation. Our intent is to make the switch as early as possible in the pipeline to maximize security.

After the component appears in the stage, make sure it is selected, and then refer to the properties pane. You should see `ConnectionString`, our custom property, appear in its alphabetical place among the standard properties. Although we won't use it, you can enter a string value and see that it is persisted from session to session. Rebuild the project. Figure 5.3 shows you what the updated pipeline should look like.

If you have created a new version of the pipeline, as is the case in the sample, you have to go into the BizTalk Explorer and edit the `Receive Pipeline` property for the receive location (`receiveActivityLocation`). Regardless, it is worth restarting the host application from BizTalk Administration to ensure that the changed pipeline assembly is loaded properly. Now drop a sample message into the source folder. If the value of Location is one of the three supported locations, the message that arrives at the destination folder will reflect the change.

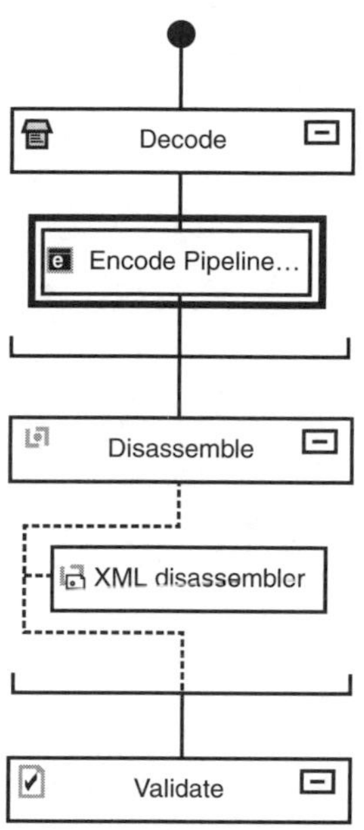

FIGURE 5.3 Activity receive pipeline with custom component.

Summary

Pipelines are the key link between a message at a protocol-specific port and the messaging engine. Many messaging scenarios can be implemented with one of the standard pipelines that are built into BizTalk Server, but the Pipeline Designer in Visual Studio gives you an easy means of building the exact message-handling features your solution requires. The basic details that previous versions of BizTalk handled in channels can be accomplished in BizTalk Server 2004's pipelines using the standard pipeline components provided.

When unique processing is required, BizTalk offers the interfaces needed to create custom component assemblies that plug into both Visual Studio and the messaging engine. This brings the entire scope of the .NET Framework and your imagination to bear on the problem. Custom processing can be packaged in a reusable component and deployed easily to development desktops and servers.

As a bonus, we saw that orchestrations are not always required. We set up a basic messaging configuration without one. We also peered briefly into the structure of messages and their context. Hopefully, you are becoming curious about the scope, features, and operation of the messaging engine. Message exchanges, after all, are the basic building block of BizTalk solutions. The messaging system is the topic of our next chapter.

CHAPTER 6

Receiving and Sending Messages

IN THIS CHAPTER

- Receive and Send Ports in Detail
- Message Security
- Subscription Filters
- Messaging Solution Sample

The previous few chapters have brought you to the verge of the BizTalk Server messaging system. Adapters gave you the means to bring messages into the system from a particular protocol and send messages out from BizTalk into a protocol. Pipelines drew us closer to the center, standing between ports (and their associated adapters) and the messaging system. Now we're going to turn our attention squarely to the messaging system itself. This chapter will give you full coverage of the methods and settings by which a messaging solution is configured.

We'll start with incoming messages and cover receive ports and receive locations. We'll explain how they differ, why they complement one another, and how to specify and configure all aspects of receiving an incoming message. Next, we'll turn our attention to the other end of the messaging stream—send ports and send port groups. With the concepts in place, we'll move on to a reference section detailing all the available configuration settings for ports and receive locations.

With the basics of messaging in place, we'll take a step back and discuss security. BizTalk Server is a serious enterprise application, and you need to know how to apply security to the messaging system. This includes securing access, authenticating messages, and encrypting data.

Finally, we touch on the publish–subscribe mechanism. This is the means by which messages flow from receive ports to send ports. As such, they are the last detail needed to turn pieces of messaging configuration into a messaging solution. We'll show you how to use property promotion with the messaging system for robust message routing. The final part of the chapter will tie together everything you've seen. We'll take a message in from one protocol, map it to another format, and deliver it conditionally to several locations on a second protocol. When you are done with this chapter, you should have a firm grasp of the messaging system and be ready to move on to business processes and orchestration.

Receive and Send Ports in Detail

Ports are the points of contact between BizTalk Server's messaging system and the outside world. They are a logical construct, combining details of protocol, location, and delivery. When a message arrives at a receive port, it is handed off to a receive pipeline so that it can be prepared for the messaging runtime engine. When a message completes final processing in a send pipeline, it is flung through one or more send ports into the world for delivery via a communications protocol. In this section, we'll refine the concept of ports by taking up receive locations and send port groups. We'll cover the general tasks needed to configure and manage ports and their associated entities, but we'll defer the necessarily dry recitation of available port settings until after we've provided an overview of ports.

Receive Ports

Receive ports are the logical boundary and security border for incoming messages. Matters are complicated a bit by the provision of receive locations. Most of what you typically think of in terms of configuring inbound messaging is actually done in the receive locations. By providing an additional layer, BizTalk Server lets you specify message authentication and tracking details that can then be shared across several receive locations belonging to a single receive port. A receive port, then, is a generalized container for receive locations. It is a completely logical construct, requiring the creation of one or more receive locations before a single message may be accepted by the messaging system. Besides allowing you to share some configuration details across multiple receive locations, receive ports are the lowest level that orchestrations deal with. All the receive locations belonging to a receive port are hidden. Thus, orchestrations are shielded from the details of protocol and location. You can therefore accept conceptually related messages from a variety of sources and treat them the same way. For example, you might receive purchase orders from some customers via HTTP and from others via SMTP, but you could group all your purchase orders under the same receive port. Similarly, you can configure a receive port with a map. If one of the customers in the preceding example uses a different format from the rest, you would want to keep the translation out of the orchestration by doing this. Otherwise, you would have to complicate the orchestration with a conditional branch just so you could perform the translation in the one case.

Configuring Receive Ports

Receive ports are created and configured in Visual Studio through the BizTalk Explorer. You right-click the Receive Ports node in BizTalk Explorer and select Add Receive Port from the context menu. You are first presented with the Create New Receive Port dialog box, pictured in Figure 6.1. The only thing you configure here is the direction of messaging. This may seem odd to you—isn't the direction implied by the "receive" part of receive port? There are two kinds of receive ports: one-way and request-response. One-way ports are for applications that drop off a message and do not wait synchronously for a reply. An application making use of a request-response port, by contrast, will block and wait for BizTalk to offer a response to this message. Because the response requires processing, request-response is usually not used for elaborate processing in highly scalable solutions. Instead, it is used for simple processing or, more likely, a simple acknowledgement to receipt of a message. As far as BizTalk is concerned, the direction of travel is inbound, but a response message is expected to emerge in the case of a request-response port. A receive port of either type, however, will always have a message coming in.

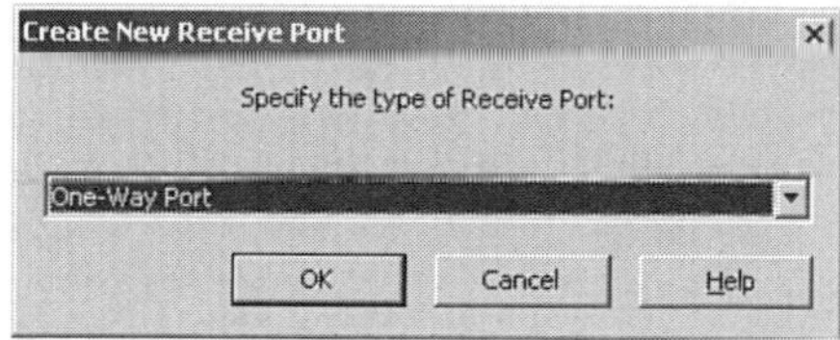

FIGURE 6.1 Choosing the Receive Port type.

After selecting a port type, the Port Properties dialog box appears. The settings available in this dialog box differ slightly depending on which type of port you selected, but the dialog box is substantially the same in both cases. Figure 6.2 depicts the properties dialog box. Both types of port ask for a port name and give you the option of configuring authentication and tracking requirements; you may specify message maps for inbound messages. Request-response ports also ask you to specify a send pipeline for the response and give you the option of specifying outbound maps, as well. In fact, you may specify a collection of maps, with as many maps in the collection as there are schemas in the schema collection. When a message passes through a port, BizTalk checks the schema type against the maps in the collection. If a match is found, the translation is performed before passing the message along.

Receive Locations

Now that you've created a logical port of arrival for messages coming into BizTalk, you really want to get specific about locations. If BizTalk ports were physical maritime ports, such as New York and San Francisco, receive locations would be the piers within those ports. The traffic is substantially similar throughout the port, but just as each pier is particular about the kind of shipping it can receive, so each receive location is particular about the URL and protocol on which it will look for messages.

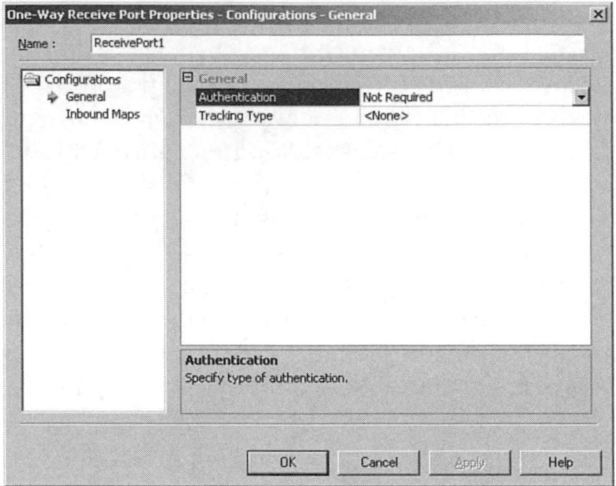

FIGURE 6.2 The Receive Port Properties for one-way ports.

Configuring Receive Locations

You create a new receive location by expanding a receive port node in BizTalk Explorer, right-clicking the Receive Locations node, and selecting Add Receive Location from the context menu. The Receive Location Properties dialog box appears in response. This dialog box, shown in Figure 6.3, is also what you see if you double-click an existing receive location node in BizTalk Explorer to edit its properties. This dialog box enables you to configure the transport protocol, URL, receive handler, and pipeline. You can also establish a service window, enabling you to specify when BizTalk will look for messages at this location.

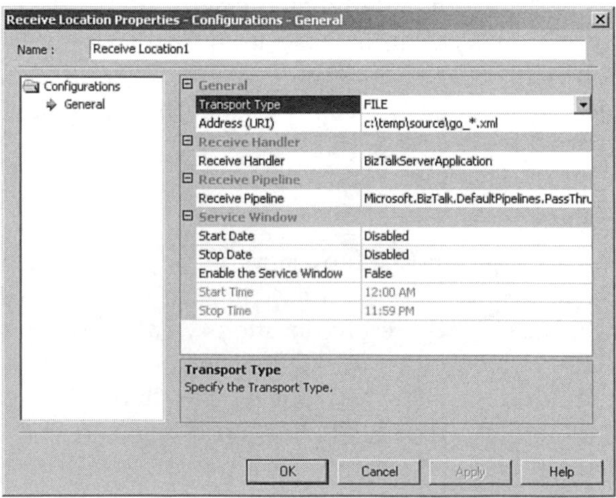

FIGURE 6.3 Configuring properties for a receive location.

Managing and Operating Receive Locations

The configuration we just described, which uses BizTalk Explorer, is the design-time configuration used to create and edit a receive location. Even when you are done, it cannot be used by the messaging engine to receive messages. You will need to enable the port using the context menu item for the port node in BizTalk Explorer, or go to the BizTalk Administration Console and enable the receive location there. When you specified a receive handler in BizTalk Explorer, you associated the location with a BizTalk process (such as the default application or isolated host). If BizTalk immediately started listening or polling on that transport at that location, it would consume system resources whether you were expecting traffic or not. By giving an administrator the capability to enable and disable receive locations at runtime, the messaging system enables you to fine-tune your performance. To enable or disable a receive location, expand the Receive Ports node in BizTalk Explorer, find the receive port associated with the desired receive location, and expand the port and its Receive Locations node. Right-click the receive location you want to enable and select Enable from the context menu.

In addition to enabling receive locations, some location settings may be specified or edited at runtime. The BizTalk Administration Console lets you access these properties through a property page, as shown in Figure 6.4. To access this property page, select Receive Locations in the left pane and then select a specific receive location from the list in the right pane. Right-click the location entry and select Properties from the context menu.

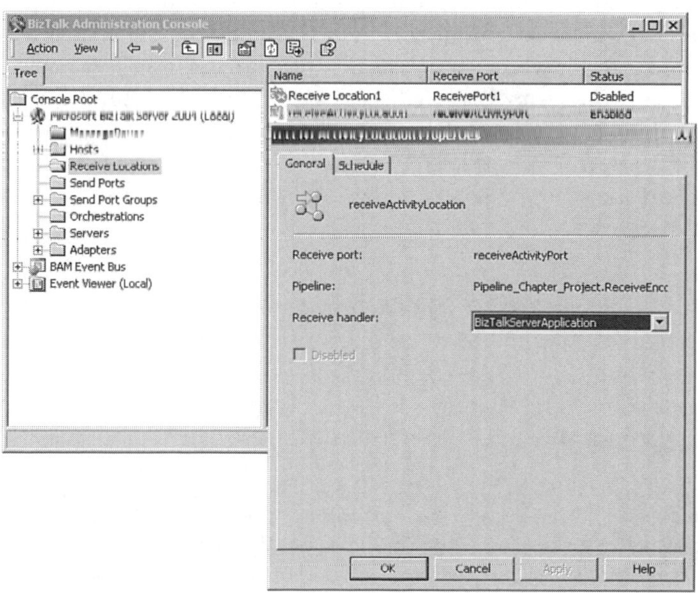

FIGURE 6.4 Managing an existing receive location.

Send Ports

Send ports are analogous to receive ports. They are the outgoing boundary for security and message transmission. They take a message emerging from the messaging engine and fire it off to the outside world through a send pipeline. Unlike receive ports, which act as containers for one or more receive locations, send ports are collected into send port groups when you need to send the same message to more than one location. We'll have more on send port groups a little later.

Send ports have a few more configuration options than receive ports. There are four types of send ports:

- Static one-way—A preconfigured send-only port.
- Static solicit–response—A preconfigured send port that waits for a reply from the target application.
- Dynamic one-way—A send-only port that can be bound to a protocol at runtime based on message properties.
- Dynamic solicit–response—A send port that waits for a reply and can be bound to a protocol and location at runtime based on message properties.

Other configuration options involve communications. Like receive ports, send ports are associated with a transmission protocol and location (URL). Like receive ports, send ports can be associated with a service window, which is useful when you have an intermittent connection to the target or when you want to shift transmission loads to off-peak times. Send ports have a few differences, as well. Because BizTalk is in control of transmission for send ports, you can specify the number of times BizTalk should attempt to send the message. Most important, you can specify a back-up protocol and URL. If the send port fails all attempts on the primary protocol, BizTalk will switch to the secondary protocol and try to send the message.

The life cycle of a send port has three stages. Once specified, it is said to be bound. The next stage is to enlist it into the BizTalk environment. This is the process by which the subscription filter(s) you specify are verified against the available receive ports and the subscriptions are created in the MessageBox database. Until the send port is enlisted, its subscription is not active and therefore it has no source of messages. Following enlistment, the send port must be started to put it into operation.

NOTE

Messages arriving for an enabled send port that is not yet started will be held in the MessageBox for later delivery. This isn't significant for new send ports because you would not expect to start sending messages to a port that is not yet part of a complete solution. If, however, the application that is the target of a send port is taken offline for maintenance, you can stop the send port without losing any traffic and without having to shut down the application (or business partner) that is the original source of the messages.

Configuring Send Ports

You create send ports much the same way as you create receive ports. Right-clicking the Send Ports node in BizTalk Explorer and selecting Add Send Port brings up the Create New Send Port dialog box. This is almost identical to the analogous dialog box for receive ports (refer to Figure 6.1) and is where you select the type of send port desired. After you've made a selection, the Send Port Properties dialog box appears. It is similar in appearance and function to the Receive Ports property dialog box in Figure 6.2, albeit with a slightly different set of properties.

Managing and Operating Send Ports

When you configure a send port through BizTalk Explorer, it is said to be bound to your set of configurations, even if it is a dynamic port. To be able to make use of it, you must enlist and start it.

To enlist a send port from Visual Studio, you expand the Send Ports node in BizTalk Explorer and select the desired send port node. Right-click and select Enlist from the context menu. After this is done, you can right-click and select Start to put the port into service.

Send Port Groups

Sometimes you want to be able to send the same message to multiple recipients. If you were sending a request for proposal message to all your vendors, for example, each vendor would be represented by a port, and each port would have its own details of transport and mapping. You, on the other hand, want to perform the same action for each—throw the message at the target—without getting bogged down repeating the configuration for each vendor. The solution is send port groups. These groups are collections of static ports that may be treated as a static entity for the purposes of a messaging configuration. The ports themselves continue to operate as independent entities. Any subscriptions you have established continue in force. However, you can create filters for the send port group, and any messages that fit the expression are then sent to each send port assigned to the group.

> **NOTE**
>
> Use care when adding send ports to a send port group. If the subscription for the group duplicates an existing subscription belonging to a send port, that port will receive multiple copies of the same message.

To create a new send port group, right-click the Send Port Groups node in BizTalk Explorer and select Add Send Port Group from the context menu. Unlike when you create ports, you go directly to a Send Port Group Properties dialog box. This dialog box is similar to the port properties dialog box with which you are familiar. You may specify a name for the send port group, as well as create filters to subscribe to messages. What distinguishes the dialog box is the capability to add send ports to a list from the ports available to BizTalk.

You add a send port to a port group by opening the send port group's property dialog box, selecting the Send Ports node in the pane at the left of the dialog box, and then clicking in the Send Port list on the right. A drop-down list populated with the available send ports appears. When you select a port, it is added to the list and a new row is added to the list. To delete a port from the send group, select the row in the list of send ports and press the Delete key. There is no menu item for deleting ports. Note that adding and deleting ports from a port group does nothing to the port's status in the BizTalk database. A port that is deleted from a port group still exists and continues to function as a messaging location.

Settings

As we've covered ports, receive locations, and port groups, we've made mention of dialog boxes used to configure the properties of these BizTalk artifacts without going into specifics. Now it's time to go into detail regarding their properties.

> **NOTE**
>
> This will be a fairly dry section, heavy on tables, but it is necessary. In many cases, it is possible to determine the settings for simple BizTalk configurations largely by inspection of the dialog box itself, so feel free to skip ahead to the sample. Just don't forget to come back and fill in the gaps with this section and the following one on security before you attempt more complicated solutions.

Receive Port Properties

All receive ports are either one-way or request–response. Only ports using HTTP or SOAP as the transport for the associated receive location can be request–response, because the other protocols do not support a reply. Be careful to consider your planned protocols when specifying direction.

If you refer back to Figure 6.2, you'll recall that the Receive Port Properties dialog box, like most of the dialog boxes in messaging, consists of a node tree on the left that summarizes the major categories of properties and a table on the right that contains the minor categories and the individual properties. In the right pane, you make actual property selections. The receive port properties node tree has a single root node, Configurations. That root has two major categories, General and Inbound Maps. Request–response ports have a third category—Outbound Maps. The minor categories and their properties for the General category of properties are laid out in Table 6.1.

TABLE 6.1 Receive Port Properties, General Category

Property	Values
General	
Authentication	Whether authentication should be performed, and what happens to messages that fail authentication (select one): Not required Required (drop messages) Required (keep messages, but suspend if authentication fails)
Tracking Type	When messages are captured for the Health and Activity Tracking database (select zero or more): Before Receive After Receive For request–response ports, you can also select: Before Send After Send
Request - Response	
Send Pipeline	Name of the pipeline associated with the request-response port

You will configure a receive pipeline when you configure a receive location. Because a request–response port involves two-way communication, however, you need to specify a send pipeline at the port level. When you click the Value column of the Send pipeline property, a drop-down list of available send pipelines appears. Select one to configure this property.

You configure maps for the Inbound Maps and (request–response ports only) Outbound Maps categories by clicking the column titled Map to Apply. If maps have been deployed as part of a solution, a drop-down list of available maps is provided. After you select a map, the source and target documents are named in their respective columns. These values are read-only because they are established by the map itself.

Receive Location Properties

Receive locations have more specialized properties. This is appropriate because you are taking the generalized properties of the port, which apply to all receive locations under it, and are specializing them to a single, specific location. To extend our request for proposal analogy for send ports earlier in the chapter, you would have a single receive port for all the vendor proposal messages and one receive location for each specific vendor replying.

The Receive Location Properties dialog box has a single major category, General. The minor categories and their properties and values are detailed in Table 6.2.

TABLE 6.2 Receive Location Properties

Property	Values
General	
Transport Type	Communications protocols: EDI File FTP HTTP SOAP SQL
Address (URI)	Click to invoke a protocol-specific configuration dialog box.
Receive Handler	
Receive Handler	Name of configured hosts (limited to in-process or out-of-process hosts, as appropriate to the protocol).
Receive Pipeline	
Receive Pipeline	Name of the receive pipeline chosen from a list.
Service Window	
Start Date	Disabled or select from a calendar.
End Date	Disabled or select from a calendar.
Enable the Service Window	True or false (defaults to false).
Start Time	Select from a spin control when the window is enabled and a Start Date is selected.
End Time	Select from a spin control when the window is enabled and an End Date is selected.

Transport protocols carry their own protocol-specific properties. These are configured when you click the value cell for the Address (URI) property. As noted in Table 6.2, a protocol-specific dialog box appears. The properties displayed in that dialog box will be familiar to you provided you are familiar with the nature of the protocol in question. For example, HTTP properties include firewall information. FTP asks you to specify the batch information, firewall configuration, account information, and pre- and post-GET FTP commands to execute. Figure 6.5 shows the dialog box for the FILE transport.

The choice of which hosts are available to you as receive handlers is restricted by the protocol you select. This is driven by the technology BizTalk uses to implement the protocol listener. Most installations have two hosts: BizTalkServerApplication and BizTalkServerIsolatedHost. The former host is for all handlers that operate in the BizTalk Server process. Because they are part of BizTalk, they readily have access to the BizTalk management database. Some handlers, principally SOAP and HTTP, build on existing, non-BizTalk technology—in this case, ASP.NET. The isolated host is provided to give such handlers access to the database with Windows-integrated security.

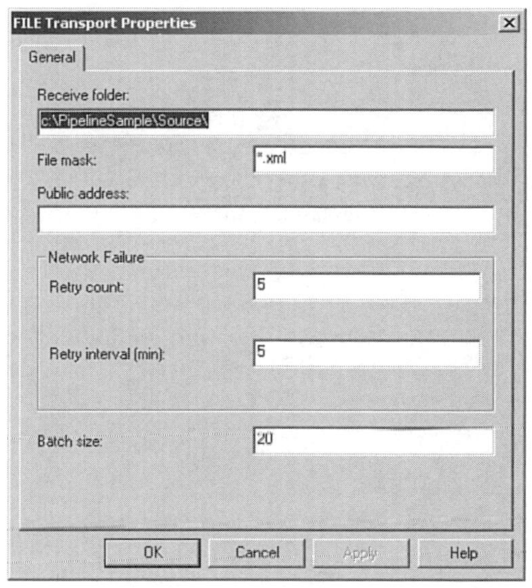

FIGURE 6.5 Configuring transport-specific properties for file reception.

Send Port Properties

The Send Port Properties dialog box is more involved than what we have seen so far because there are more categories of properties to consider. The node tree for send ports is rooted by Configuration and has nodes, or major categories, for Transport, Send, and Filters and Maps.

The Transport node expands to reveal Primary and Secondary nodes (also major categories). The properties for both nodes are the same and are listed in Table 6.3.

TABLE 6.3 Transport Properties

Property	Values
General	
Transport Type	Communications protocols: EDI File FTP HTTP SOAP SQL
Address (URI)	Click to invoke a protocol-specific configuration dialog box.
Retry Count	Integer number of transmission attempts to make.
Retry Interval	Integer number of minutes to wait between transmission attempts.
Ordered Delivery	Indicates whether messages must be transmitted in order; values are true or false (default is false).

TABLE 6.3 Continued

Property	Values
Service Window	
Enable the Service Window	True or false (defaults to false).
Start Time	Select from a spin control.
End Time	Select from a spin control.

The Send category of properties expands to reveal a General category under it. When selected, the minor categories and properties listed in Table 6.4 are displayed in the right pane.

TABLE 6.4 Send Category Properties

Property	Values
General	
Tracking Type	None, or one or both of the following: Before Send After Send
Priority	1–10 (descending order list, defaults to 5)
Outbound Encryption	
Certificate Name	Select from a list of certificates in storage
Long Name	Long name of the certificate
Usage	Signing or encryption (dictated by the certificate)
Send Pipeline	
Send Pipeline	Select from a list of pipeline names

We'll have more to say on certificates and which certificate stores are used by BizTalk when we take up the topic of security later in this chapter.

Returning to the node tree in the dialog box, note that the Filters and Maps node expands to reveal the Filters and Outbound Maps categories. Maps operate the way they did for receive ports. Filters are new. They are expressions that establish a subscription to received messages on behalf of the send port. A *filter expression* consists of three things: a message property, an operator, and a value to compare the property to. We'll discuss filter expressions in a later section.

Send Port Group Properties

Happily, send port groups are simpler and have fewer properties to configure. The Configurations node has categories named Send Ports and Filters. Send Ports is merely a list of named send ports, which we've discussed previously. Filters is a list of filter expressions. They are constructed just like the expressions for send ports, but apply to the group as a whole and do not supercede the filters configured for each port in the list of send ports.

Message Security

Security is a vital concern for messaging solutions. We need to be able to establish the identity of message senders and provide similar information to those who receive messages from us. We need to protect the data in our messages from disclosure to unauthorized parties. These tasks occur on the boundaries of the messaging system—ports and pipelines. Within the messaging system itself, as messages flow through the MessageBox and hosts send and receive messages, we need to ensure that only authorized processes are given access to messages. The issues, then, are identity authentication, data integrity, and authorization.

Not surprisingly, authorization is handled through Windows security. Each host operates under a Windows login account, typically a service account. You establish the least possible rights for each account. When you create a host, you assign it to an account and either check the Authentication Trusted check box in the Create New Host dialog box to mark it as trusted or leave it unchecked to designate an untrusted host. This is a matter of checking a box in the Create New Host dialog box when you create a host. If the host is trusted, all messages coming into BizTalk through the host retain the party ID and Windows account ID, if established, when they go into the MessageBox. If the host is not trusted, the message is marked "guest" and the login account ID is set to the service account of the host. This information is used inside messaging to determine what hosts can have which messages and whether some send ports may have a message for transmission. Send ports are associated with hosts just like receive ports are. If a message matches a send port's subscription filter but the send port's host is not authorized to receive messages from the sender, the message will not be turned over to the send port.

The identity of the message sender may be established several ways. First, adapters can use protocol-specific mechanisms for establishing identity. If the protocol does not permit this or is not configured for identity authentication (think anonymous HTTP access), you will need to resort to digital certificates. In this case, your receive pipeline needs a decoding component (either the standard MIME/SMIME decoder or a custom component) in the Decode stage to look at the certificate thumbprint in the message context, retrieve the related public key (for signature verification) or private key (for decryption), and then verify the signature and decrypt the message. Signature verification not only establishes the identity of the sender, it helps with data integrity by proving that the message has not been altered after signing. Decryption ensures data integrity by shielding the message contents from entities other than the sender and the recipient.

On the transmission side, the process is reversed. You control the certificate used for outbound encryption by selecting a certificate suitable for encryption using the properties in the Outbound Encryption minor category of the send port's properties. An encoder component in the associated send pipeline will use this for encryption. If signing is indicated by the properties of the encoder component, the certificate assigned to the BizTalk Server Group will be used for signing. You configure the group for signing using the BizTalk Administration Console by opening the Properties dialog box for the BizTalk

Server 2004 node. In the Properties dialog box that appears, click the General tab and find the Signing Certificate group. Enter the certificate thumbprint, grouping the Thumbprint field within that group.

If you have experience with certificate management under Windows, you are probably wondering what certificate stores BizTalk is using to get certificates. You choose from a list box in a property dialog box, but BizTalk has to populate that list. To obtain public key certificates for the decryption and signature verification of incoming messages, BizTalk looks in the Address Book certificate store in Windows Server 2003. If you are running Windows Server 2000, this store is called Other People. If you have thrown caution to the winds and are using Windows XP for your server, the store is named Trusted People. Before you can employ security when communicating with an outside organization, you must obtain a public key certificate (X.509 v.3) from them and import it into this store. For signing and outbound encryption, the private key certificates are drawn from the MY certificate store created for the host service account. You must obtain an appropriate certificate (not all certificates are designed for encryption) from a certificate authority, log in to Windows using the host's login account, and import the certificate into the MY store.

Subscription Filters

We said that send ports are associated with incoming messages through a subscription. That is, an incoming message is "published" by its receive port, and the message is given to any send port whose subscription filter expression evaluates to true based on the properties of the message. More than one send port can receive a given message, and one send port can obtain messages from more than one receive port. We also said that the subscription took the form of one or more rules called filter expressions (sometimes simply referred to as filters) that were created for the send port or send port group. When a message arrives, the messaging engine runs through all the filters in its configuration database and hands out the message accordingly.

You use BizTalk Explorer in Visual Studio to work with filters. Open the properties dialog box for a send port or send port group. Expand the Filter and Maps folder in the left pane and select the Filters category. The right pane will be set up with four columns: Property, Operator, Value, and Group By. Any existing filters will be displayed as rows in this pane. Beneath the grid is a read-only text box displaying the text of the overall filter expression. This expression is composed by concatenating the text of the individual filters in the filter list in the order in which they appear using the logical operators specified in the Group By column. The order of filters may be altered using the up and down arrow buttons above the grid, and individual filters can be deleted by clicking the button with the graphical X. This view is shown in Figure 6.6.

A new filter is created by clicking the next empty row. Clicking in the Property cell opens a drop-down list that is populated rather extensively with properties. Properties are qualified by namespace and name using dots for delimiters. Right out of the box, we find the 15 namespaces listed in Table 6.5. Each namespace has several properties specific to it.

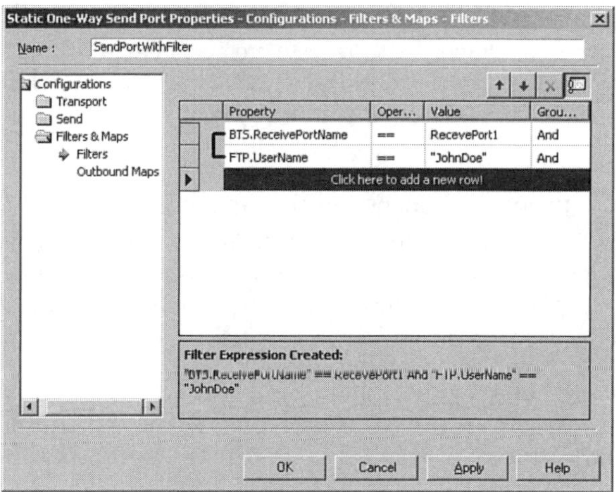

FIGURE 6.6 Working with filters in send port properties.

TABLE 6.5 Standard BizTalk Filter Property Namespaces

Namespace	Meaning
BTF2	BizTalk Framework 2.0
BTS	BizTalk Server 2004 message context
FILE	Local file system protocol
FTP	File Transfer Protocol specific
HTTP	HTTP protocol specific
LEGACY	BizTalk Server properties for versions prior to 2004
MessageTracking	Message-tracking properties
Microsoft.BizTalk.Hws	Human Workflow Services properties
Microsoft.BizTalk.KwTpm	Knowledge Worker properties
Microsoft.BizTalk.XLANGs	Orchestration
MIME	MIME encoding properties
MSMQT	MSMQT adapter properties
SMTP	SMTP protocol-specific properties
SOAP	SOAP-specific properties
XMLNORM	Message-map properties

We made use of the BTS namespace in Chapter 2, "Your First BizTalk Server Integration," by subscribing a send port to all messages published by our receive port. As you can see by browsing the list, you can create surprisingly complex filter expressions using the standard properties.

> **NOTE**
>
> Like almost everything else about BizTalk, however, you can extend this list. In our discussion of schemas in Chapter 3, "Building Message Specifications," we mentioned that there are two types of schemas: those for messages and those describing promoted properties. When you deploy an assembly that includes one or more schemas with promoted properties and their attendant promotion schemas, the promoted properties are added to the list of available properties. This lets you use values found in specific fields of your messages to perform dynamic routing.

After you've selected a property, you click in the Operator cell and select an operator used to evaluate the property value. The operators are equals (==), not equal to (!=), less than (<), greater than (>), less than or equal to (<=), greater than or equal to (>=), and exists. The last operator is used to indicate simply that the property exists for the particular message being routed.

Next, unless you are using the exists operator, you must provide a value to compare to the value found in the message. You enter this by typing in the cell. String values are delimited by quotation marks, except for names of BizTalk entities such as port names, which are not delimited.

Finally, you click in the Group By cell and select the operator used to concatenate your new filter. Filters grouped by the `AND` operator are linked by a thick line between their rows to the left, whereas filters joined by a logical `OR` are not shown as linked. As you enter filters in the list, you can watch Visual Studio build the overall filter expression by inspecting the text beneath the grid.

Messaging Solution Sample

This sample is basic in terms of code and schema complexity but still shows the following messaging features:

- HTTP receive
- Translation from the receive protocol (HTTP) to the FILE transmission protocol
- Message mapping without orchestration
- One-to-many messaging with send port groups

  Content-based routing using promoted message properties

Recall the `Activity` message schema from the preceding chapter. It represents some event or action generated within the organization. Now imagine that we want to build a solution that publishes these messages within the organization. Assume all applications generating `Activity` messages send them via HTTP to a central location. Now suppose that messages whose `type` attribute value is `1` must go to an application that will handle those messages exclusively. To make things more complicated, we'll have to map those messages to an attribute major format that looks like the sample in Listing 6.1.

LISTING 6.1 Sample Event Message

```
<?xml version="1.0" encoding="us-ascii"?>
  <ns0:Event id="1" site="Philadelphia"
    time="2004-01-18T13:48:35" xmlns:ns0="http://Que.Event">
   Test 1
</ns0:Event>
```

We've just taken all the elements in the `Activity` message except `Notes` and mapped them to an attribute in the `Event` element. The contents of `Notes` get mapped to the textual content of `Event`.

Activity messages with any other type—`2` through `10`—have to go to two other applications. One might be the principal actor and the other might be some sort of audit trail. Regardless of their purpose, we'd like to configure both destinations with one subscription.

To accomplish this, we need to set up an HTTP receive port and location and three file folders, each associated with a send port. I've established a file folder named `MessagingTargets` off the root of my C drive, and under that I've created a folder named `Single` to receive messages whose `type` attribute has the value `1`. The other two applications are represented by file folders named `GroupA` and `GroupB`, also under `MessagingTargets`. Using the file protocol and putting the destination folders in the same parent folder makes it easy to check the outcome of a message interchange.

Begin the sample by creating a new BizTalk solution named Messaging Project. The embedded project should be named Schemas and Maps.

Message Schemas

As with any BizTalk project, we begin with the message schemas. Copy the Activity schema from the pipeline project into your new project folder and add it to the solution. To make things more compact, and to distinguish between this instance and the one in the pipeline chapter, I've changed the namespace for this schema to `http://que.activity`, but this step is optional.

Now, create a new project item, a properties schema. Name the file `ActivityProperties.xsd`. Select the Schema node and enter **`http://Schemas_and_Maps.ActivityProperties`** for the target namespace. Add an element field off the Schema root and name it **`type`**. Give it the type **`xs:nonNegativeInteger`**. This gives us a placeholder for the promoted property. At runtime, the messaging engine refers to this schema to find the XPath expression that will locate the value within the Activity message to use for routing.

All that is left is to provide the location of the type attribute in the Activity message. Return to that schema now. Right-click the type field, select Promote, and then select Show Promotions from the context menu. Select the Property Fields tab.

The Property schemas list should be empty. Click the first row of the list and then click the Folder button immediately above the list. The BizTalk type picker dialog box appears. Expand the Schemas node, select Que.ActivityProperties, and then click OK. This links the property schema to the message schema and allows us to promote properties of the message schema.

Select the type field in the schema tree on the left side of the dialog box and click the Add button. A new row appears in the Property fields list. The property will be given as `ns0:type` and the XPath expression locating type within the message will be listed for Node Path.

The result of all this will be to add a new property to the global list of properties when we deploy this assembly. In addition to all the namespaces in Table 6.5, the Que namespace will appear with a single property, `Que.type`. When we add filters to send ports, we can use this property to build subscriptions based on the value of this attribute, thereby satisfying the routing business rule.

Before we are ready to do that, though, we need to create a schema for Event messages and a map that will convert Activity messages into Event messages. Add a schema to the project, Event.xsd, with the namespace `http://Que.Event`. Change the root node to **`Event`** and set the Base Data Type property to `xs:string`. This gives us an element that can have textual content. Now add three attribute fields to Event: id, site, and time. Each should have the data type of the corresponding element in Activity. The `id` attribute will stand in for `type` in `Activity`, `site` will be paired with `Location`, and `time` will take on `Timestamp`'s value.

Now add a map to the project and name it `Activity2Event.btm`. Make Activity the source schema and Event the destination. Create simple links as specified in Table 6.6. There are no functoids in this map.

TABLE 6.6 Links for the Activity to Event Map

Source Field	Destination Field
`type`	`id`
`Location`	`site`
`Timestamp`	`time`
`Notes`	`Event`

NOTE

When you compile this map, you will get a warning that the destination Node `Event` is required, but the source node `Notes` is optional. Because `Event` is the message's document element, and because it bears required attributes linked to required source fields, `Event` will always be created so long as there is an incoming `Activity` message.

Sending Application Stub

We don't really care about the initiating application from a strictly BizTalk perspective so long as something sends an Activity message via HTTP. We need something with which to test our solution, however, so we've elected to create a very simple Web form application. Add a C# project of this type to the overall solution. Mine is named `HTTPSender`. It consists of a single page, default.aspx, shown in Figure 6.7. When you click the Submit button, the values from the Type, Location, and Notes controls will be used to generate an Activity message. The current system time will be determined and used for the Timestamp element. After it is created, the message is sent to the receive handler via an HTTP POST. One control that is not visible in this illustration is a Label named `Status`. It is configured without any text so as to be invisible when the form is first presented. We will use it to display the results of the submission process. Although we will use a one-way receive port, the HTTP protocol is two way, so the receive handler will have to generate some response. A two-way port would be called for if we wanted an application-level response, but even a one-way port will give us a protocol-level response. Using a Label control in lieu of a text box ensures that anything we display will not be posted as part of a subsequent submission.

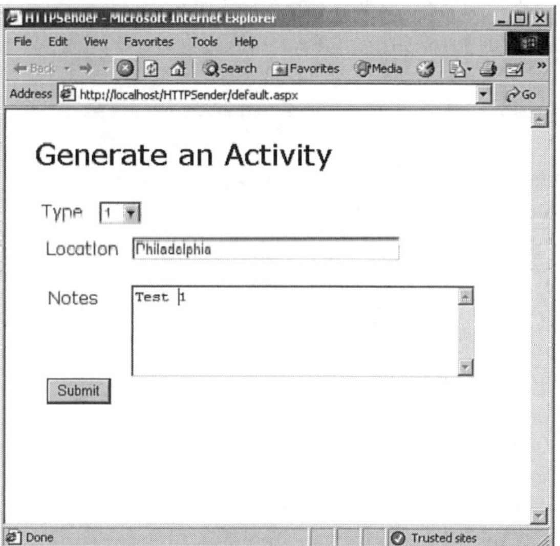

FIGURE 6.7 A simple ASP.NET Web form application is the source of Activity messages sent via HTTP POST to the receive location.

All the action in our HTTP stub application occurs in the Click event handler for the Submit button. Listing 6.2 shows the code. You will need to add using directives for `System.Xml` and `System.Net`. The former gives us the classes we need to create the message, and the latter allows us to perform the HTTP POST operation. To support the latter, you will also add a directive for `System.Text` because of some encoding issues. The code prior to the `try` block is largely XML DOM code.

> **NOTE**
>
> You should pay particular attention to the namespaces provided in calls to `CreateNode`. BizTalk will reject your messages if you do not get the namespaces right. Additionally, note the use of the `System.DateTime` class to get the current system time through that class's `Now` member property.

The `Now` property is also of type `DateTime`, so we convert it to a string using the `ToString` method. The BizTalk `dateTime` type is an ISO 8601 format. The preset `SortableDateTimePattern`, denoted by the character code `s`, is based on that format, so we can get the appropriate string value merely by passing the character value `s` as the sole parameter of `ToString`. Fans of GMT (which would be better for a dispersed solution) should note that the `UniversalSortableDateTimePattern` does not give an ISO 8601 string.

LISTING 6.2 HTTPSender Submit Button Event Handler

```
private void Submit_Click(object sender, System.EventArgs e)
{
  string requestLocation = "http://atropos/HTTPSender/BTSHTTPReceive.dll";
  Status.Text = "";
  XmlDocument xmlDocument = new XmlDocument();
  xmlDocument.PreserveWhitespace = true;

  XmlNode tempXmlNode =
➥xmlDocument.CreateNode(XmlNodeType.Element, "Activity",
➥"http://que.activity");
  xmlDocument.AppendChild(tempXmlNode);

  tempXmlNode = xmlDocument.CreateNode(XmlNodeType.Attribute,
➥"type", "");
  tempXmlNode.Value = TypeList.SelectedItem.Text;
  xmlDocument.DocumentElement.Attributes.Append(
➥(XmlAttribute)tempXmlNode);

  tempXmlNode = xmlDocument.CreateNode(XmlNodeType.Element,
➥"Location", "");
  tempXmlNode.InnerText = Location.Text;
  xmlDocument.DocumentElement.AppendChild(tempXmlNode);

  tempXmlNode = xmlDocument.CreateNode(XmlNodeType.Element,
```

LISTING 6.2 Continued

```
➥"Timestamp", "");
  DateTime now = DateTime.Now;
  tempXmlNode.InnerText = now.ToString("s");
  xmlDocument.DocumentElement.AppendChild(tempXmlNode);

  tempXmlNode = xmlDocument.CreateNode(XmlNodeType.Element,
➥"Notes", "");
  tempXmlNode.InnerText = Notes.Text;
  xmlDocument.DocumentElement.AppendChild(tempXmlNode);
  try
  {
    HttpWebRequest request = (HttpWebRequest)
➥HttpWebRequest.Create(requestLocation);
    request.Method = "POST";
    ASCIIEncoding encoding = new ASCIIEncoding();
    byte[] requestData =
➥encoding.GetBytes(xmlDocument.OuterXml);

    request.ContentType="application/x-www-form-urlencoded";
    request.ContentLength = xmlDocument.OuterXml.Length;
    Status.Text += "Submitting activity message";
    Stream requestStream = request.GetRequestStream();
    requestStream.Write(requestData,0,requestData.Length);
    requestStream.Flush();
    requestStream.Close();
    HttpWebResponse response = (HttpWebResponse)
➥request.GetResponse();
    StreamReader responseData = new StreamReader(
➥response.GetResponseStream());
    Status.Text = System.Web.HttpUtility.HtmlEncode(
➥responseData.ReadToEnd()) + "<br>";
  }
  catch (WebException wex)
  {
   Status.Text = "Unable to complete web request. Web Exception
➥ error: " + wex.Message;
  }
}
```

Now that we've built a message, we have to send it. The `HttpWebRequest` class lets us do this, but we have to consider all the issues of encoding and HTTP property configuration that are a part of that protocol. We create a new request by passing the class the URL of the receive handler. We then specify POST as the HTTP operation. Next, we have to give our XML, found in `xmlDocument.OuterXml`, an ASCII encoding using the class `ASCIIEncoding` and its `GetBytes` method. As far as HTTP is concerned, we're sending a form, so we set the request object's ContentType to the standard string `application/x-www-form-urlencoded` and `ContentLength` to the length of the XML message.

At this point, we are ready to send an appropriate HTTP message, but we have not written the XML into the request. We can do this by getting the stream underlying the request via the request object's `GetRequestStream` method. We then use the stream's `Write` method, passing it the encoded request data, starting location, and overall length of the stream. Flushing and closing the stream sends the POST to the receive handler.

After the receive handler has submitted the message, it will generate a context token in the form of an XML message. If there is any problem, it will feed back an HTTP error message. We get the results of the POST operation by querying the request object's `response` property. This is an instance of `HttpWebResponse`. After we read the response stream, we want to set the `Status` Web form label control's `Text` property to whatever is in the stream. Because this is going to appear in an HTML page viewed in a browser, we need to encode it using the utility class `System.Web.HttpUtility` and its `HtmlEncode` method.

At this time, you can build the project and deploy the assembly containing the three schemas and the map. Check the Assemblies node in BizTalk Explorer to ensure that the assembly was properly deployed to the configuration database.

HTTP Receive Location

That's all the code we need to write. Everything else in our solution is a matter of configuration. First, we need to put the HTTP receive adapter out there somewhere. To make things easy, I've put it in the same folder as `HTTPSender`, but this is not necessary. In fact, in a real system in which messages are going from dispersed sources to a central handler, this would not be the case. Wherever you decide to put the handler, you simply copy `BTSHTTPReceive.dll` from the `HttpReceive` folder under the BizTalk installation to the target location. Using the Component Services application in the Windows Control Panel's Administrative Tools folder, configure the `HTTPSender` application (or the Web application you create, if you elect to put the HTTP handler assembly in another location) to use the identity of a member of the BizTalk Users group to ensure that the handler will have access to the MessageBox.

Now create a one-way receive port named `activityRecvHttpPort` and accept the defaults. Create a receive location named `activityRecvHttpLocation`. Select the HTTP protocol and `BizTalkServerIsolatedHost` as the receive handler. Select `XMLReceive` from the default pipelines as your receive pipeline. Click the Address (URI) cell and configure the resulting HTTP Transport Properties dialog box with **`/HTTPSender/BTSHTTPReceive.dll`** as the virtual directory plus ISAPI extension property and **`http://localhost /HTTPSender/BTSHttpReceive.dll`** as the Public address property. Click OK, and then click OK to close the receive location property dialog box. Right-click the receive location in BizTalk Explorer and select Enable from the context menu.

File Send Ports

We have a port to receive a message, but nowhere to send it. We'll create three send ports to match the business scenario we set forth in our description of the sample.

The send port that sends messages with the type code `1` is created by going into BizTalk Explorer and creating a new send port named `SendEventPort`. Make this a one-way port because our application is not sending back a response. Select the FILE transport. Configure the Address with **`c:\MessagingTargets\Single\`** as the folder and **`%MessageID%.xml`** as the filename. Under Send General, select the default `XMLTransmit` pipeline for the send pipeline.

Leave the port property dialog box open and expand the Filters and Maps node. In the next section you will configure the translation between message schemas.

Mapping

Select the Outbound Maps category. We want to point to the map we created so that when an `Activity` message is passed through this port, the map will be applied to create an equivalent `Event` message for transmission. Click the first cell under Map to Apply and select `Que.Activity2Event` from the drop-down list. The source and destination document cells will be populated on the basis of this selection.

Subscription with Property Promotion

We've done everything but connect this send port to a message source. This is done by creating a subscription filter. Select Filters in the left pane. Remember that we want only Activity messages whose type property has the value `1`. Because we promoted the type property, we can configure a filter expression based on that. Click the first Property cell and find `Que.type` in the drop-down list. This appears because we deployed a property schema with this .NET-style type namespace and property. Now click the adjacent Operator cell and select the == operator. Then click Value and enter `1`. Because this is the only filter we need, we can ignore the value of Group By. Click OK to complete the configuration of this send port.

Find the port in BizTalk Explorer and use the context menu to enlist and start the port.

Group Publish and Subscribe

We have two more send ports to configure. These represent the two applications or organizations that receive Activity messages when the value of type is greater than one. In BizTalk Explorer, create a new send port and name it `SendActivityAPort`. In the properties dialog box, choose the file protocol, access the protocol configuration dialog box, and specify your file folder and the filename **`%MessageID%.xml`**. For the file structure I created and described earlier, the file path is **`c:\MessagingTargets\GroupA`**. Click OK to dismiss the protocol-specific dialog box and return to the send port properties dialog box. Expand the Send category and select the default `XMLTransmit` pipeline.

You no doubt recall that we plan to send `Activity` messages through unchanged, so you know we don't need to configure an outbound map. We do need to establish a subscription, but we won't do that quite yet. Click OK to close the properties dialog box.

Return to BizTalk Explorer and follow the same procedure to create and configure a send port named `SendActivityBPort`. The only difference will be the file path. On my machine, that's **`c:\MessagingTargets\GroupB`**. After you are sure you've configured the protocol and selected the pipeline, click OK.

Now go to the Send Port Groups node in BizTalk Explorer. We're going to create a send port group for the two ports we just created and then use that to specify a subscription that will do what we want—route the appropriate `Activity` messages to these two ports. Right-click the Send Port Groups node and select Add Send Port Group from the context menu. In the dialog box that results, name the new group **`SendABPortGroup`**. Under Configurations, select Send Ports, then click the empty row and select `SendActivityAPort` from the drop-down list. Click the next row and select `SendActivityBPort`.

Now select the Filters category. Note that it does not say Filters and Maps. We can have one subscription for the entire group while still performing different mapping operations at the port level. In the grid, create a filter just like the one for `sendEventPort`, except you want the greater than operator. The finished filter expression should be `Que.type > 1`. Click OK. Enlist and start the send ports, then do the same for the send port group using the context menu.

Test the Solution

You are now finished with design and development. There are just a few administrative tasks to perform before we can test the solution. Open the BizTalk Administration Console application. Make sure your receive location is enabled, or enable it if it is not. Also make sure the BizTalk Application host is started. You will not be able to ascertain the status of the isolated host, but that is okay. You need the other host, however, because that is the host application for the file protocol. If you sent Activity messages without starting that host, the HTTP receive would work, but the messages would be suspended. If you allowed that to happen and then started the host application for the file protocol, the messages would be delivered.

After you've verified that everything is running, open a browser window and open the `HTTPSender` page. Use the controls to fill out an Activity message with a value of `1` for type. Click Submit. You can verify that a message was delivered to the Single folder. If you open it, you will see that it is an Event message whose attributes bear the values you entered in `HTTPSender`. Now change type to some other value and click Submit again. You should see two `Activity` messages, one in the `GroupA` folder and one in `GroupB`.

Summary

BizTalk Server 2004 puts much more emphasis on orchestration than earlier versions did, largely due to the success and popularity of orchestrations in those versions. Because of this, orchestration sometimes eclipses the messaging system. You might easily conclude that you can't do any messaging in BizTalk without orchestration. As we have just shown, however, messaging remains the bedrock of BizTalk Server. You can do message routing and mapping without resorting to orchestration. With some careful consideration when you design your messages, you can promote the right properties to let you implement runtime message routing strictly as a matter of configuration.

In this chapter, we tied up all the different pieces of messaging. We saw how the two types of schemas work together to expose properties to the messaging engine and the design time tools. We showed you how to create ports and send port groups, and how send ports subscribe to messages published by receive ports. Using filters on send ports, you can create one-to-one, one-to-many, and many-to-one messaging configurations.

Our sample application gave you some practical experience with HTTP receive locations, as well as exposure to subscriptions and send port groups. Although you can experiment much more with the different messaging settings, you can now say that you have seen the entire breadth of BizTalk messaging.

CHAPTER 7

Working with Adapters

IN THIS CHAPTER

- Adapter Overview
- Adapter Design-Time Configuration
- Native Adapters
- Developing Custom Adapters
- Adapter Design-Time Development
- Adapter Runtime Development
- Adapter Registration

This chapter covers how adapters fit into the BizTalk Server 2004 architecture, how to deploy and configure existing adapters, and how to write your own adapters.

You will first learn how to use the adapters that ship with BizTalk Server 2004 and then learn how to build your own adapters for BizTalk Server 2004.

Adapter Overview

Adapters play a vital role in connecting BizTalk Server 2004 with target applications or technologies. There are three categories of adapters:

- Application adapters—These adapters connect to both packaged applications, such as your ERP or CRM system and proprietary applications that you may have written in-house. Common examples of application adapters to packaged systems include SAP, JDE, PeopleSoft, and Siebel. Although BizTalk Server 2004 is not bundled with any application adapters, Microsoft separately sells an SAP adapter.
- Technology adapters—These adapters bridge heterogeneous technologies and protocols. BizTalk Server 2004 ships with support for .NET API, EDI, File, FTP, HTTP, MSMQ, SMTP, and Web services. Microsoft also sells an MQSeries adapter.
- Data Adapters—These adapters connect BizTalk Server to databases such as SQL Server, Oracle, or DB2. BizTalk Server ships with a data adapter for SQL Server.

BizTalk Server 2004 has a symmetric adapter model exposing the same capabilities to both send and receive adapters.

Although the adapter framework does not require it, most adapters include the functionality to both send and receive messages.

> **NOTE**
>
> Previous versions of BizTalk Server have support for adapters through application integration components (AICs). These AIC interfaces provide support for the sending of messages to target systems but lack interfaces for building adapters to receive messages. Receive-side adapters are just one of a large number of enhancements in the adapter framework for BizTalk Server 2004. Existing adapters are not compatible with the new enhancements in the adapter framework; however, Microsoft provides a Web download that contains shims between the new adapter framework and existing AICs so that you can reuse existing code. You should decide whether the new features in the adapter framework merit porting your adapters to the new framework.

All adapters perform activities associated with transport normalization, such as taking a message from BizTalk Server and delivering it to a target using a specific target-dependent protocol. Examples of this include the SQL Server adapter, which sends messages to SQL Server using the TDS protocol, the SOAP adapter, which sends messages using the SOAP protocol, and the SAP adapter, which sends messages using the RFC protocol.

Additionally, some adapters perform activities associated with data normalization. For example, the SQL Server adapter represents the SQL table structure in XML, and the SAP adapter represents an SAP IDOC in XML. It is important to point out that data normalization should be used only where necessary inside adapters because BizTalk Server's mapping infrastructure provides rich support for data normalization.

BizTalk Server 2004 supports adapters that run either in the BizTalk Server process or in an independent process. In-process adapters, such as the File adapter, execute in the BizTalk Server 2004 process space, called a *host instance*, which manifests itself as the Windows NT service BTSNTSVC.exe. Isolated adapters execute in their own process space. You may choose to create Isolated adapters for security reasons or for design reasons. For example, the BizTalk Server 2004 SOAP adapter is implemented as an IIS extension and runs inside the ASP.NET process space rather than the BizTalk Server process space.

Figure 7.1 illustrates how adapters fit inside the overall BizTalk Server 2004 architecture.

One of the key decisions in any integration project is which adapters to buy and which adapters to write. Writing adapters can be a time-consuming exercise because it often requires domain knowledge of the target technology. Typically, but not always, the total cost of ownership associated with hand-coding an adapter is greater than the cost of purchase. Both Microsoft and Microsoft adapter partner ISVs provide a set of prebuilt, pretested adapters for purchase. The Microsoft BizTalk Server 2004 Web site (`http://www.microsoft.com/biztalk`) provides a complete list of available adapters.

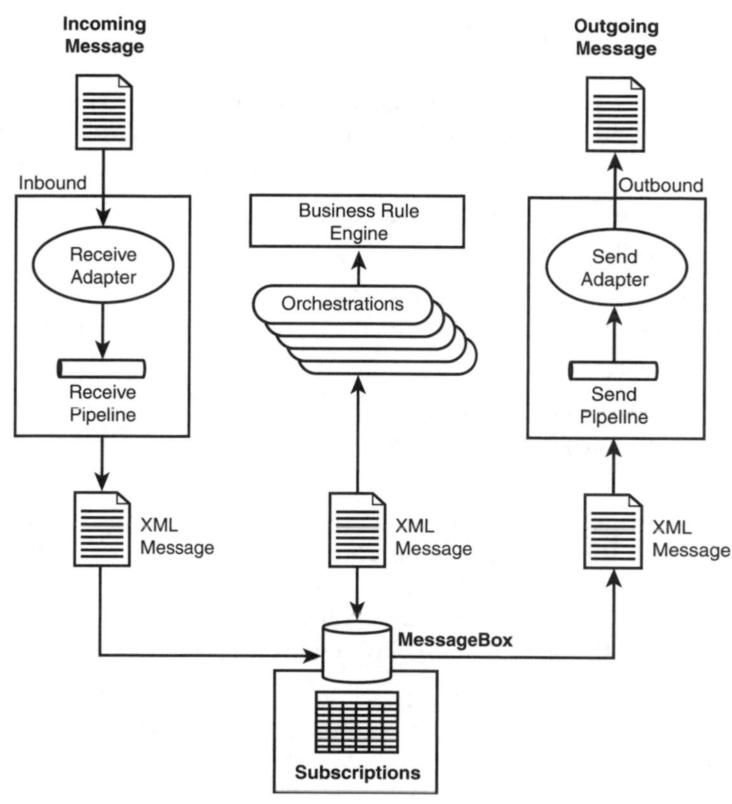

FIGURE 7.1 Adapters inside the BizTalk Server 2004 architecture.

Adapter Design-Time Configuration

No doubt your primary interaction with BizTalk adapters will be to configure them as part of a receive or send port. If you have done this already, you'll notice that when configuring a port, you are usually required to specify an adapter (transport) at design time. Therefore, let's spend some time getting used to the adapter design time configuration.

Adapter configuration in previous versions of BizTalk could be challenging because of the lack of standard APIs to develop the AIC. In many cases, an AIC would require separate tools for configuration, management, and setup. Therefore, in an EAI project requiring three AICs, the project administrator might need to learn and use nine tools. The Microsoft BizTalk Server 2004 Adapter framework addresses this issue with a set of standard interfaces ensuring that all design-time configuration for any adapter is confined to the BizTalk Administration Console and the BizTalk Explorer in Visual Studio .NET.

Adapter Communication Patterns

Before we delve too far into the details of configuring adapters, it is important for you to understand the way in which an adapter can communicate with BizTalk and other external applications. This will make some of the configuration choices more meaningful when it comes to configuring receive and send ports in the next section.

The BizTalk adapter framework provides a number of communication patterns that can be supported by an adapter, as follows:

- One Way Receive—BizTalk receives a message from a wire protocol (File, HTTP, and so on) and passes it off to a receive pipeline, which then persists it to the MessageBox database.
- One Way Send—BizTalk picks up a message from the MessageBox database and passes it through a send pipeline, which then sends it out to the appropriate endpoint.
- Request Response—BizTalk receives a message in the same way as a One Way Receive, but then the requesting application waits for a response from BizTalk. An example of this type of interaction is exposing an orchestration as a Web service via the SOAP adapter. In this case, a client application sends a request into the SOAP adapter, bound to the orchestration, and then waits for a response.
- Solicit Response—BizTalk sends a message to an application in the same way as a One Way Send, but then it waits for a response from the external application. An example of this type of interaction is consuming a Web service within an orchestration via the SOAP adapter. In this case, the orchestration makes a request out to the Web service and then waits for a response.

NOTE

You may hear the term *sync on async*, which is synonymous with the Request Response pattern. This term refers to a synchronous message exchange that has been built on top of a number of correlated asynchronous message exchanges. For example, a Web page that checks inventory may make a SOAP request to a BizTalk orchestration, exposed as a Web service, that aggregates a number of other Web services and returns the resulting data in a SOAP response. To the client, this appears to be a synchronous operation.

Handlers and Ports

Essentially, adapter configuration is achieved via handlers and ports. Adapter handlers come in two varieties: a send handler and one or more receive handlers. A handler is a way of associating an adapter with a host. Handlers, hosts, and host instances are all managed in the BizTalk Server 2004 Administration Console, as shown in Figure 7.2.

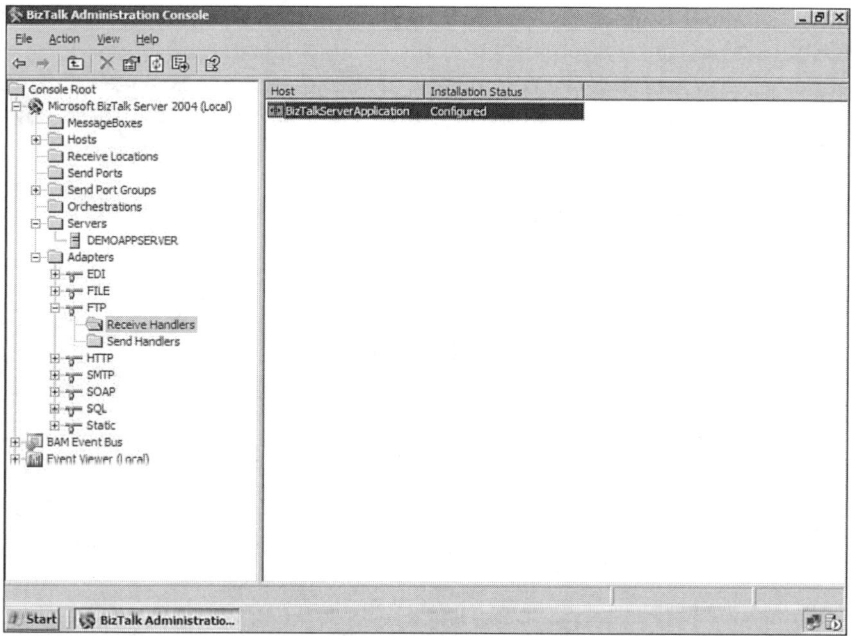

FIGURE 7.2 Handlers and hosts in the BizTalk Administration Console.

Handlers allow send ports and receive locations to be partitioned across multiple machines via the host configuration and so facilitate scalable and fault-tolerant architectures. For example, a receive handler host that contains multiple host instances running on separate machines can be associated with an adapter and ultimately be used as the Receive Handler for a specific receive location. In Figure 7.3, the receive location is being associated with the AdapterHost Receive Handler that is, in fact, pointing to host instances running on three separate machines.

In the case of a machine failure, BizTalk continues to use the other two machines for processing. Likewise, when the message volume increases, we can balance the load over multiple host instances running on three different machines, as shown in Figure 7.4.

The actual configuration of the adapter for both the handler and port are dependent on whatever properties the adapter needs to function and are presented to the user via a property browser. Any properties defined at the send port or receive location will take precedence over the properties defined at the adapter's handler.

Dynamic Send Ports

Up to now, the adapter configuration that we have described has been implemented via the design-time user interface. When you're defining send ports, this approach is termed as being *static*. However, on occasion there is a need for the adapter and ultimate endpoint to be configured at runtime via properties contained within a message to be sent. This approach is termed as being *dynamic*. For example, consider the scenario whereby an orchestration sends a message, the destination of that message is extracted at runtime from the contents of a document, perhaps from a tag that is marked as the receipt address. This would be a dynamic send.

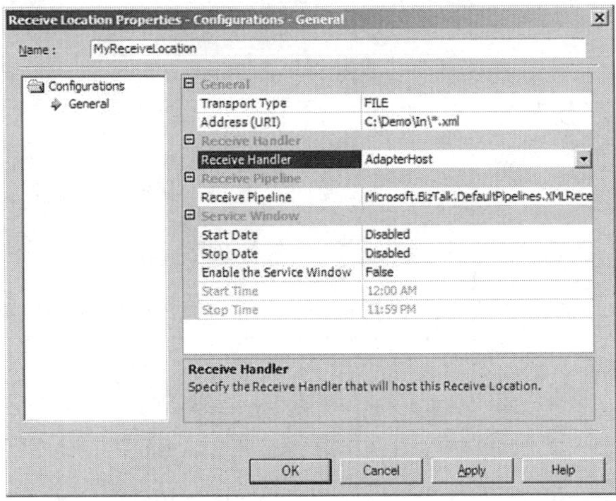

FIGURE 7.3 Receive location pointing to a Receive Handler.

Add Adapter Wizard and Metadata Harvesting

In the case of application and database adapters, you may need to import supporting schemas that describe message types and port types needed by the adapter in the BizTalk project. This can be accomplished by using the Add Adapter Wizard, which is available by right-clicking your chosen BizTalk project in Visual Studio .NET, selecting Add, Add Generated Items, and then opening the Add Adapter template. Figure 7.5 shows the Add Adapter Wizard user interface.

At this point, you can select the adapter that you want to use and go through its set of steps to add the appropriate schemas. In the case of application adapters, this can involve querying the back-end server to see what services the application server supports—a process known as metadata harvesting. The BizTalk adapter framework provides a set of APIs that can be used to import the required schemas for the adapter. This will be explained in greater detail in the "Developing Custom Adapters" section of this chapter.

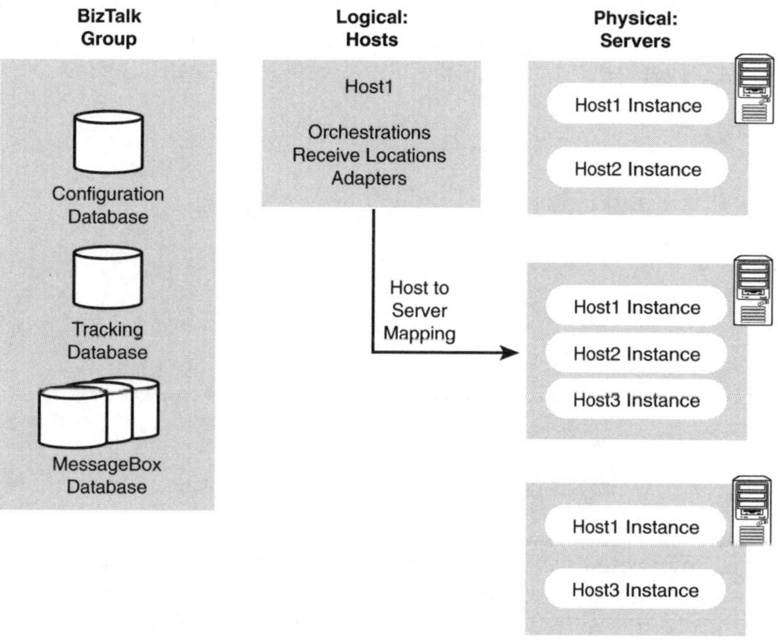

FIGURE 7.4 Host with host instances on separate machines.

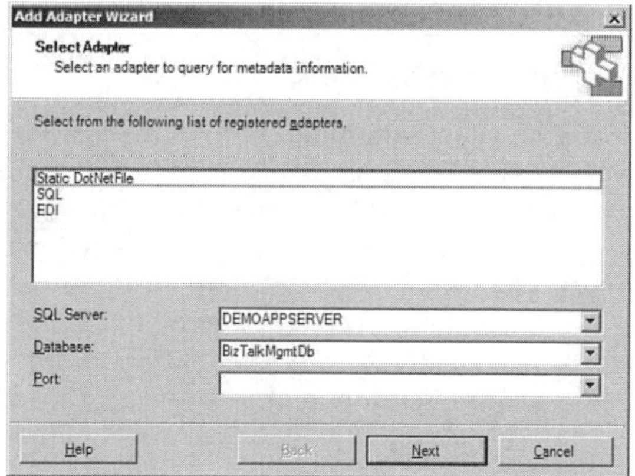

FIGURE 7.5 Add Adapter Wizard.

Native Adapters

Now that you understand a little more about how adapters can be configured, please refer to the online Appendix C, "Using BizTalk Native Adapters," for details on using each of the BizTalk Native Adapters that ship with BizTalk Server 2004. In all, there are eight native adapters:

- FILE
- Hypertext Transport Protocol (HTTP)
- File Transport Protocol (FTP)
- Microsoft Message Queue Transport (MSMQT)
- Simple Mail Transfer Protocol (SMTP)
- Simple Object Access Protocol (SOAP)
- Microsoft SQL Server (SQL)
- Electronic Data Interchange (EDI)

All the native adapters are developed using the BizTalk adapter framework. Each adapter is available for use after the BizTalk Server 2004 installation has been completed, with the exception of the MSMQT adapter. In this case, the MSMQT binaries will have been installed to the server machine, but for security reasons, the additional step of adding the MSMQT adapter to the BizTalk Administration Adapters folder will be required for it to be functional.

Developing Custom Adapters

Up to now we have focused on the design-time configuration of the native adapters that ship with Microsoft BizTalk Server 2004. As already mentioned, a number of other BizTalk adapters developed by third parties could be leveraged in your integration project. But what happens if the adapters available do not support the functionality that your solution requires? What if you have your own custom server application that you want to integrate with BizTalk? At this point, you may want to consider building a custom BizTalk adapter using the Microsoft BizTalk Server 2004 Adapter framework. In this section we look at the three main areas of custom adapter development:

- Design time
- Runtime
- Registration

NOTE

The BizTalk Server 2004 Adapter framework is an extensible API that sits on top of the underlying BizTalk messaging engine. It provides design-time and runtime interfaces that allow the developer to build a BizTalk adapter. The framework is a COM API that is accessible to managed code via a .NET Primary Interop assembly. The recommended approach for adapter development is to use managed code; therefore, all code samples in this section will be in C#.

Adapter Design-Time Development

Recall that the adapter design time refers to handler configuration in the BizTalk Administration Console, port configuration in the BizTalk Explorer, and the metadata harvesting capabilities of an adapter via the Visual Studio .NET Add Adapter Wizard. Each of these areas of the design time allow for custom adapter extensibility. Let's take a look at how you can use the BizTalk adapter framework to integrate the configuration requirements of your custom adapter.

Property Browser

Receive Handler properties, Send Handler properties, receive location properties, and send port properties can all be configured via a property browser, as shown in Figure 7.6, which shows the FTP adapter Receive Handler properties.

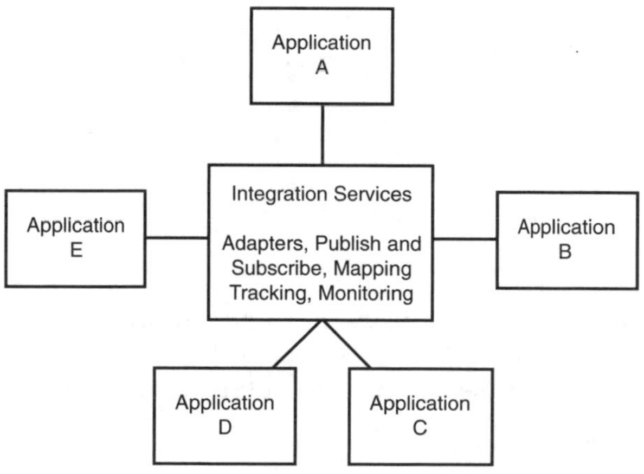

FIGURE 7.6 Receive Handler property browser.

To access the Receive Handlers for an adapter, open the Adapters folder in the BizTalk Server 2004 Administration Console and double-click a listed adapter; for example, FTP. The Adapter's tree view will expand to show a Receive Handlers folder, which can be opened to reveal the available hosts for the adapter. Right-click a related host and select the Properties menu option. You can then select the Properties tab, which will display a Property Browser with the relevant properties for the adapter's Receive Handler.

The underlying process for displaying the properties is driven by the mandatory interface IAdapterConfig that uses a predefined XML Schema to define the properties that should be presented to the user. This same process is used to present properties for the corresponding send handler, accessed in a similar way to the Receive Handler, a send port, and a receive location. Adapter properties for ports are accessed by clicking the button marked with an ellipsis, which is part of the Address URI property for a send port or receive location, as shown in Figure 7.7.

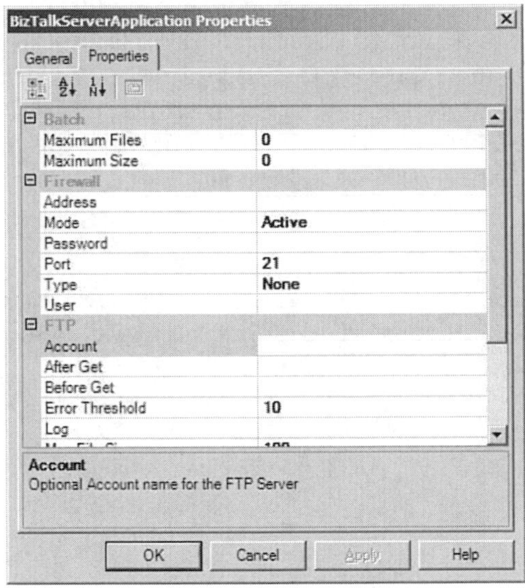

FIGURE 7.7 Receive location address (URI).

Potentially, a receive handler, a send handler, a receive location, and a send port could all have different schemas that define different properties, in which case four different schemas would be needed. Each schema is loaded by the `IAdapterConfig.GetConfigSchema()` method based on the value of the `ConfigType` enum, as follows:

```
Public enum ConfigType
{
   ReceiveLocation = 0,
   TransmitLocation = 1,
   ReceiveHandler = 2,
   TransmitHandler = 3
}
```

The following code is based on the BizTalk SDK sample File adapter and demonstrates the implementation of `GetConfigSchema()`. `GetResource()` is a helper function that loads the schema from the associated resource that is part of the assembly.

```
public string GetConfigSchema(ConfigType type)
   {
     switch (type)
     {
        case ConfigType.ReceiveHandler:
          return GetResource("AdapterManagement.ReceiveHandler.xsd");
        case ConfigType.ReceiveLocation:
          return GetResource("AdapterManagement.ReceiveLocation.xsd");
        case ConfigType.TransmitHandler:
          return GetResource("AdapterManagement.TransmitHandler.xsd");
        case ConfigType.TransmitLocation:
          return GetResource("AdapterManagement.TransmitLocation.xsd");
        default:
          return null;
     }
   }
```

Add Adapter Wizard Integration

The Add Adapter Wizard enables you to display available adapter services and ultimately import required port and message types to a BizTalk project. You can also leverage this tool to harvest metadata applicable to your own custom adapter via the `IStaticAdapterConfig` or `IDynamicAdapterConfig` interfaces. For example, to display the services that your custom adapter exposes within the Add Adapter Wizard, you would need to construct an XML file that describes those services and then load it into the design time using the `IStaticAdapterConfig.GetServiceOrganization()` method, as shown in the following code excerpt:

```
public string GetServiceOrganization(IPropertyBag endPointConfiguration,
string NodeIdentifier)
   {
     string result = GetResource("AdapterManagement.CategorySchema.xml");
     return result;
   }
```

This method will, in effect, generate the appearance of the Services Organization tree, an example of which is shown in Figure 7.8.

After the required services have been chosen, an array of service descriptions, in Web Service Definition Language (WSDL), can be loaded by BizTalk via the

`IStaticAdapterConfig.GetServiceDescription()` method, as shown in the following code excerpt:

```
public string[] GetServiceDescription(string[] wsdlRefs)
   {
     string[] result = new string[1];
     result[0] = GetResource("AdapterManagement.service1.wsdl");
     return result;
   }
```

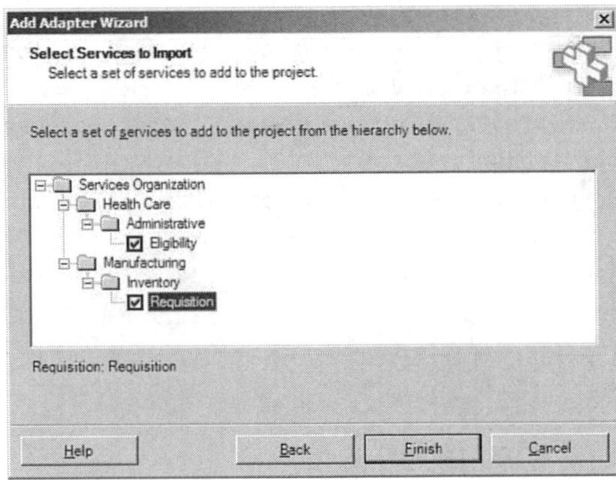

FIGURE 7.8 Services Organization tree.

The `wsdlRefs` parameter is an array of unique WSDL references that correspond to the WSDL references in the source XML loaded by `GetServicesOrganization()`. In this code excerpt, the WSDL description is returned with a hard-coded WSDL reference. The returned set of WSDL descriptions will be used to generate the port types and message types for the BizTalk project. You will need to call the `IAdapterConfig.GetSchema()` method to load a schema if your WSDL has only schema references. You may find that the Services Organization tree user interface is not appropriate for your adapter and that you require a more flexible user interface to generate the required array of service definitions. This can be achieved by using the `IDynamicAdapterConfig` interface, instead of `IStaticAdapterConfig`, and calling the `DisplayUI()` method, which has the following signature:

```
Result DisplayUI(IPropertyBag     endPointConfiguration,
    IWin32Window     owner, out string[]     serviceDescriptionFiles )
```

The `endPointPointConfiguration` parameter contains the configuration for the adapter. This parameter may be null if an endpoint is not specified in the Add Adapter Wizard. If an endpoint has been specified, `endPointPointConfiguration` will have a root element of CustomProps and a property named `AdapterConfig` that holds an XML instance of the endpoint configuration for the adapter.

The owner parameter contains a handle to the parent window, allowing for interaction with the custom user interface.

The `serviceDescriptionFiles` parameter is the array of WSDL service definitions that must be returned to BizTalk after the custom user interface has been displayed.

Adapter Runtime Development

Having covered the design time, you now have an understanding of what it takes to store the configuration data for your custom adapter in BizTalk Server 2004. In the next section, we will take a look at the BizTalk runtime APIs that can be used to exchange messages between your application and BizTalk Server 2004.

The Messaging Architecture

To give you an idea of some of the concepts that we will cover in this section, Figure 7.9 illustrates how a message is received into BizTalk via the File adapter.

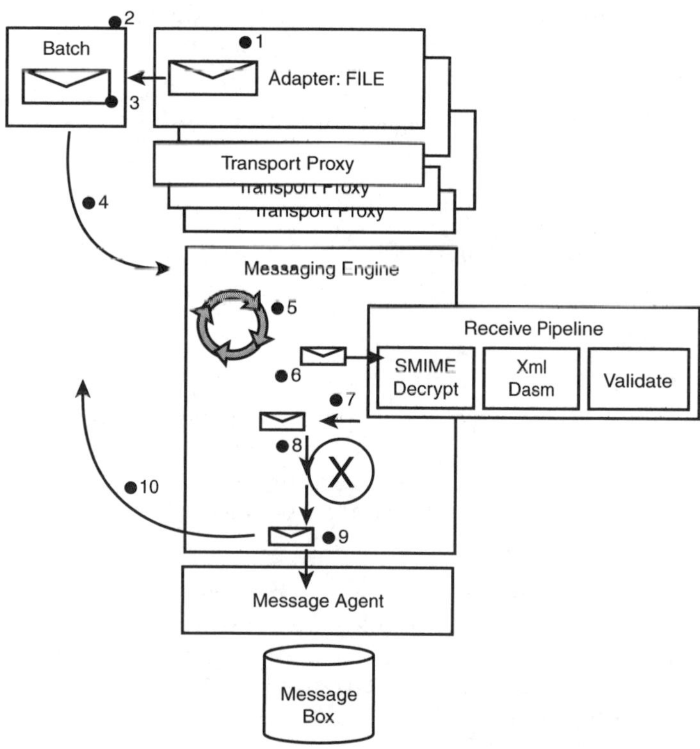

FIGURE 7.9 BizTalk Server 2004 Messaging Architecture.

Each Adapter has its own instance of a Transport Proxy object that it uses to interact with the messaging engine. Adapters perform work against the messaging engine in batches, which will be described later. Essentially, a batch is a collection of "operations," such as

SubmitMessage, SuspendMessage, and DeleteMessage, among others; the processing of a batch is atomic.

The following is the sequence of events outlined in Figure 7.9 whereby an Adapter submits a message to the messaging engine:

1. The Adapter creates a new message, connecting the data stream to the message.
2. The Adapter requests a new batch from the messaging engine via its Transport Proxy.
3. The Adapter adds a message to the batch to be submitted.
4. The batch is committed, which causes it to be posted to the messaging engine's thread pool.
5. The messaging engine's thread pool starts processing the new batch.
6. The message is processed by the receive pipeline.
7. Zero or more messages will be produced by the receive pipeline. Pipelines can consume messages providing they do not return any errors; receive pipelines can produce more than one message, typically when the dissassembler component disassembles a single interchange into many messages. Usually, the receive pipeline will normalize the message submitted into XML.
8. The message(s) produced by the pipeline may be processed in the mapper if mapping is configured.
9. The message(s) will be published to the Message agent and MessageBox.
10. The Messaging Engine will call back the adapter to notify it of the outcome of that batch of work.

A BizTalk Message

The interface on which BizTalk messages are implemented is the `IBaseMessage` interface. Each message has one or more message parts, of type `IBaseMessagePart`. Each message part has a reference to its data, which is exposed through the IStream interface. Each message also has a message context, of type `IBaseMessageContext`. Figure 7.10 illustrates the BizTalk message object model.

The message context is a dictionary that is keyed on a combination of the property name and the property namespace, preventing collisions between similarly named properties from different sources—for example, BizTalk system properties and custom adapter properties. The values for these properties are of type object in .NET. Under the covers, however, these properties are of type VARIANT.

Properties may be written to the message context, in which case they are metadata that flows with the message. Alternatively, properties may be promoted to the context from the body of the message, in which case they may be used for message routing. After a promoted property has been used for routing, it will be demoted to prevent cyclic subscription matches.

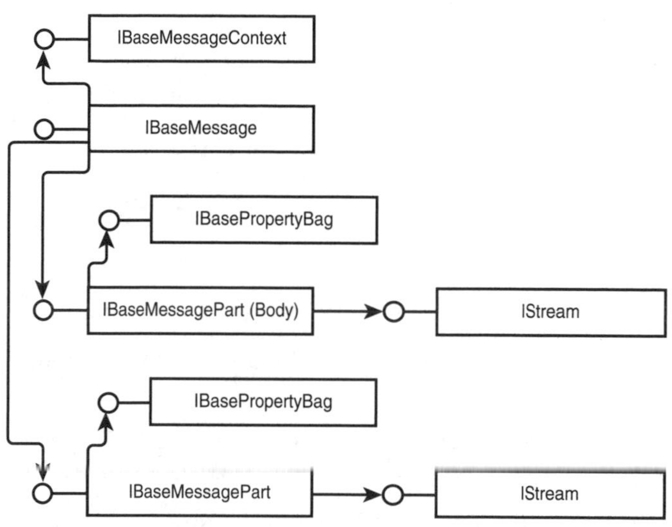

FIGURE 7.10 BizTalk Server 2004 Message object model.

Message context properties are loaded into memory at runtime. Therefore, very large pieces of data should not be written to the message context, because this could potentially break the BizTalk large message support. Objects may be written to the message context providing they implement `IPersistStream`.

The message factory should always be used to create new messages. The following code excerpt illustrates how to create a new BizTalk message:

```
using Microsoft.BizTalk.Message.Interop;
IBaseMessage CreateMessage (Stream s, IBaseMessageFactory msgFactory)
{
   IBaseMessage msg = null;
   IBaseMessagePart part = msgFactory.CreateMessagePart();
   part.Data = s;
   msg = msgFactory.CreateMessage();
   msg.AddPart("body", part, true);
   return msg;
}
```

Message Engine Interfaces

The messaging engine has three public interfaces used by adapters:

- `IBTTransportProxy`—Adapters always talk to the messaging engine via their own Transport Proxy. The Transport Proxy is used to create batches, get the message factory, and register isolated receivers with the engine.

7

- `IBTTransportBatch`—The interface exposed by the messaging engine's batch. Work done against the engine is performed using a batch; batches are processed asynchronously.
- `IBTDTCCommitConfirm`—Adapters using DTC transactions on batches must notify the engine of the outcome of the transaction using this interface.

Adapter Interfaces

All adapters must implement the following interfaces:

- `IBaseComponent`—Plumbing interface detailing the Name, Version, and the Description of the Adapter.
- `IBTTransport`—Plumbing interface detailing the Transport Type and the ClassID of the Adapter.
- `IBTBatchCallback`—Callback interface on which the adapter will be notified of the outcome of a batch of work that it has submitted to the engine.

The following interfaces are provided but not required when developing a custom adapter:

- `IPersistPropertyBag`—Configuration interface on which handler configuration will be delivered to the Adapter. This interface is not required for Adapters that do not have handler configuration.
- `IBTTransportControl`—Used to initialize and terminate an Adapter, the Adapter's Transport Proxy is passed as a parameter to the `Initialize()` method on this interface. This interface is not required for isolated adapters.

Receive Interfaces

In addition to the standard Adapter interfaces, Receive Adapters need also to implement `IBTTransportConfig`. This is the interface on which receive location configuration will be delivered to the adapter and is covered in further detail later in this chapter.

Request-response adapters need to implement `IBTTransmitter`, as shown in Figure 7.11.

Send Interfaces

Send Adapters need to implement either `IBTTransmitter`, if they are nonbatched, or `IBTBatchTransmitter`, if they are batched, as shown in Figure 7.12.

Adapter Initialization

On service startup, all the receive adapters that have one or more active receive locations are created. By default, send adapters are lazily created; that is, they are not created until the messaging engine finds the first message to be sent via that send adapter. The capability of `InitTransmitterOnServiceStart` may be specified to direct the messaging engine to create the send adapter on service startup, rather than using the default lazy creation. The default approach helps to reduce the amount of system resources used when certain adapters are not configured on any endpoints.

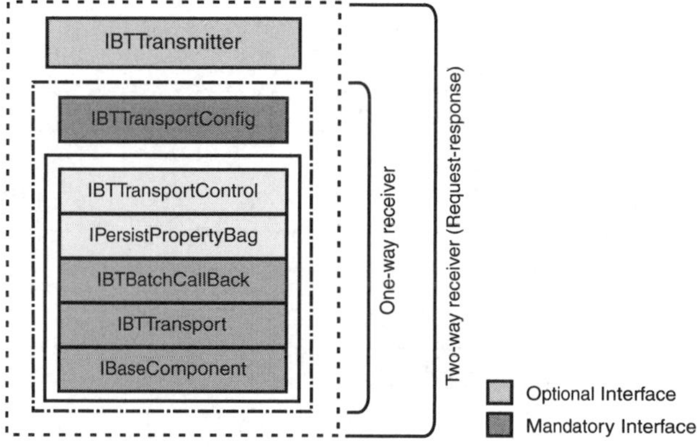

FIGURE 7.11 Receive Adapter interfaces.

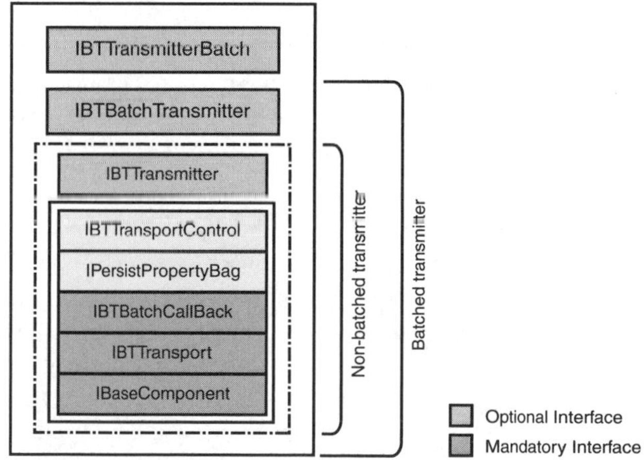

FIGURE 7.12 Send Adapter interfaces.

Receive Adapter Initialization

After a receive adapter is created, it is initialized. First the Messaging Engine will `QueryInterface()` for the mandatory interface `IBTTransportControl`. Next it will `QueryInterface()` for `IPersistPropertyBag`. If the adapter implements the interface, the handler configuration will be passed to the adapter in the `Load()` method call. Next, the

Engine will `QueryInterface()` for `IBTTransportControl` and the engine will then call `Initialize()`, passing in the Adapters Transport Proxy. The final stage of initializing a receive adapter involves passing the endpoint configuration to the adapter. During this phase the engine will call `IBTTransportControl.AddReceiveEndpoint()` once for each active endpoint passing in the URI for the endpoint, the adapter specific configuration for the endpoint, and the BizTalk configuration for that endpoint.

Figure 7.13 illustrates this sequence of API calls.

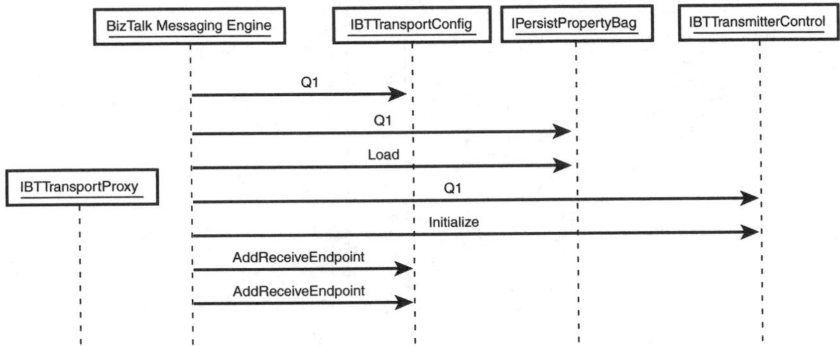

FIGURE 7.13 Receive Adapter initialization.

In general, adapters should not block the engine in calls such as `IBTTransportControl.Initialize()`, `IPersistPropertyBag.Load()`, and `IBTTransportControl.AddReceiveEndpoint()`. Performing excessive processing in these calls will have an adverse impact on service startup time.

Send Adapter Initialization

When the engine initializes send adapters, it will first `QueryInterface()` for `IPersistPropertyBag`. If the adapter implements the interface, the handler configuration will be passed to the adapter in the `Load()` method call. Next, the engine will `QueryInterface()` for `IBTTransportControl`, and the engine then calls `Initialize()` passing in the Adapters Transport Proxy. The engine will then `QueryInterface()` for IBTTransmitter. If this interface is discovered, the adapter will be treated as a batch-unaware transmitter. If this interface is not discovered, the engine will `QueryInterface()` for `IBTBatchTransmitter`, discovery of which will indicate that the adapter is a batch-aware transmitter. If neither of these interfaces are discovered, an error will be raised, causing the initialization to fail and canceling any further discovery of mandatory interfaces.

Figure 7.14 illustrates this sequence of API calls.

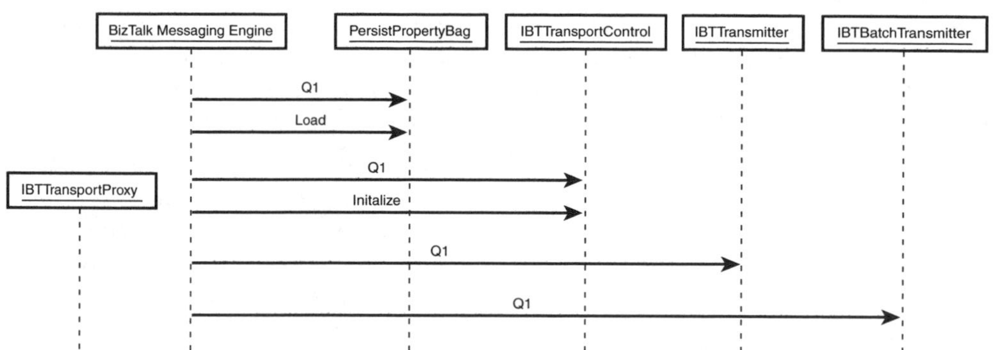

FIGURE 7.14 Send Adapter initialization.

Adapter Termination

When the messaging engine is shutting down, it will call `IBTTransportControl.Terminate()` on each adapter. After this method returns, the adapter will be destroyed. For managed adapters this is less deterministic because of the Garbage Collector. Regardless, the adapter should block in `Terminate()` until it is ready to be destroyed. Any cleanup work should be done in the `Terminate()` method, and the adapter should block until this work has been completed.

Isolated receive adapters will not have `Terminate()` called on them, because they are not hosted in the BizTalk service. Instead, they should call `IBTTransportProxy.TerminateIsolatedReceiver()` to notify the messaging engine that they are about to shut down.

Loading Configuration

Adapter configuration data is stored in the SSO database after creation via the design-time property browser discussed earlier. At runtime, the messaging engine retrieves the configuration for the Adapter and delivers it to the Adapter. Four types of configuration are delivered to adapters:

- Receive handler configuration
- Receive location (endpoint) configuration
- Send handler configuration
- Send port (endpoint) configuration

Loading Handler Configuration

As previously mentioned, the handler configuration is delivered to an adapter by its implementation of the Load method on the `IPersistPropertyBag` interface. The handler configuration is delivered only once; the adapter is not updated if the handler configuration is changed after the BizTalk service has started. In general, the common model is for the adapter to treat the handler configuration as the default configuration. Endpoint configuration overrides the handler configuration on a per-endpoint basis.

The following code excerpt demonstrates parsing the configuration. The code assumes that the adapter uses the Adapter Framework design time, the adapter's configuration will be in the property passed in to the Load call in the string property `"AdapterConfig"`, and this property value will contain an XML document representing the adapter's configuration. The adapter needs to load this configuration into a DOM or an XML Reader so that it can utilize XPath expressions to retrieve the individual properties.

```
public class MyAdapter : IBTTransport,
             IBTTransportConfig,
             IBTTransportControl,
             IPersistPropertyBag,
             IBaseComponent
{
   // Handler configuration properties...
   private int defaultBatchSize = 0;
   private string defaultHeader;
   // IPersistPropertyBag.Load() implementation...
   public void Load(IPropertyBag pb, int pErrorLog)
   {
     //The adapter configuration is in the property
     // "AdapterConfig" in the form of an Xml blob...
     object obj = null;
     pb.Read("AdapterConfig", out obj, 0);
     // Create a DOM and load the Xml blob...
     XmlDocument dom = new XmlDocument();
     string adapterConfig = (string)obj;
     dom.LoadXml(adapterConfig);
     // XPath the individual properties...
     XmlNode node = document.SelectSingleNode("/Config/batchSize");
     defaultBatchSize = int.Parse(node.InnerText);
     node = document.SelectSingleNode("/Config/header");
     defaultHeader = node.InnerText;
   }
}
```

Loading Endpoint Configuration

Receive location configuration is delivered to an adapter on its implementation of `IBTTransportConfig`. This interface has three methods: `AddReceiveEndpoint`,

UpdateEndpointConfig, and RemoveReceiveEndpoint. The messaging engine will notify the adapter for which endpoints it needs to listen on, and when the configuration for an endpoint is changed, the adapter will be notified of the change for that endpoint. Similarly, the adapter does not need to worry about service windows. Endpoints will be added and removed as service windows become active or inactive.

When an Adapter needs to begin listening on an endpoint, the engine will call IBTTransportConfig.AddReceiveEndpoint(), passing in the receive location's URI, a property bag containing the adapter's configuration for that endpoint, and a second property bag containing BizTalk specific configuration for that endpoint.

Reading the receive location properties from the adapter's property bag is no different from reading the handler configuration as detailed previously.

When the configuration of a receive location that is already active is changed, the engine will notify the adapter that it needs to use a different configuration via the API UpdateEndpointConfig(). All of the configuration will be delivered to the adapter, including the BizTalk specific configuration.

When a receive location is no longer active, the adapter will be notified via RemoveReceiveEndpoint(), and after the adapter returns from this method, it will no longer be allowed to submit messages into the engine using that receive location's URI.

The messaging engine writes the configuration for a send port on the message context in the adapter's namespace before delivering the message to the adapter. It is the adapter's' responsibility to read and validate that configuration, which it will subsequently use to control the transmission of the message. For send adapters that support batched sends, messages destined for different send ports may be in the same batch, so the adapter will need to handle these "mixed" batches.

7

The following code excerpt illustrates first how to read the OutboundTransportLocation, which is the URI for the outbound message, then how to read the XML blob containing the adapter's configuration, and subsequently, how to read the individual properties.

```
private static readonly PropertyBase UriProperty = new BTS.
➥OutboundTransportLocation();
private string propertyNamespace =
➥"http://schemas.mySchemas.com/MyAdapter/myadapter-properties";
private string uri;
private string headers;
private int timeOut = 1000;
private void ReadSendPortConfig(IBaseMessage msg)
{
   // Read the OutboundTransportLocation,
   // i.e. the send port uri....
   uri = (string)msg.Context.Read(UriProperty.Name.Name, UriProperty.Name.
➥Namespace);
```

```
    // Read the adapters configuration Xml blob from
    // the message...
    XmlDocument locationConfigDom = null;
    object obj = msg.Context.Read("AdapterConfig", this.propertyNamespace);
    // If this is a dynamic send there will not be
    // any configuration...
    if ( null != obj )
    {
      locationConfigDom = new XmlDocument();
      locationConfigDom.LoadXml((string)obj);
      this.headers = Extract(locationConfigDom, "/Config/headers", true);
      this.timeOut = ExtractInt32(locationConfigDom, "/Config/timeOut", true);
    }
}
// Helper method to XPath string properties...
private static string Extract(XmlDocument document, string path, bool required)
{
    XmlNode node = document.SelectSingleNode(path);
    if (!required && null == node)
    return String.Empty;
    if (null == node) throw new
         ApplicationException(string.Format("No property was found at {0}", path));
    return node.InnerText;
}
// Helper method to XPath int32 properties...
private static int ExtractInt32(XmlDocument document, string path, bool required)
{
    string s = Extract(document, path, required);
    return int.Parse(s);
}
```

Transport Proxy Batch

Adapters perform work against the engine using a Transport Proxy batch. There is a fixed set of allowed operation types that can be performed within a batch; these operations are defined by the enumeration `BatchOperationType`. Batches are processed asynchronously, which means that when an Adapter calls `Done()` on a batch, the batch is posted to the messaging engine, the calling thread returns to the Adapter, and the batch will be processed in the engine's thread pool. After processing of the batch has completed, the Adapter will be notified of the outcome via a callback.

Batch Callback

Because batches are processed asynchronously, the Adapter needs a mechanism to tie a callback to some state in the Adapter so that it can perform necessary cleanup actions. The callback semantics are flexible so that Adapters can use one or a combination of two approaches:

- All callbacks are made on the same object intance that implements `IBTBatchCallBack`. The cookie passed into the engine when requesting a new batch is used to correlate the callback to the state in the Adapter.
- Provide a different callback object for each batch that implements `IBTBatchCallBack`. Each object holds all the state necessary for cleanup actions associated with that batch.

The Adapter is called back on its implementation of `IBTBatchCallBack.BatchComplete()`. The overall status of the batch is indicated by the first parameter, status. This is an HRESULT because batches are atomic; if this value is greater than or equal to zero, the batch was successful. Success means that the engine has ownership of the data and the Adapter is free to delete that data from the wire. A negative status indicates that the batch failed; this means that none of the operations in the batch were successful and the Adapter is responsible for handling the failure.

If the batch failed, the Adapter may need to know which item in which operation failed. For example, if the Adapter was reading 20 files from disk and submitting them into BizTalk using a single batch, and the tenth file was corrupted, the Adapter would need to suspend that one file and resubmit the remaining nineteen. This information is available to the adapter in the second and third parameters, opCount of type short and operationStatus, which is of type `BTBatchOperationStatus[]`. The operation count indicates how many operations were in the batch (the size of the `BTBatchOperationStatus` array). Each element in the operation status array corresponds to an operation in the batch. Using the `BTBatchOperationStatus`, the Adapter can determine which item failed by looking at `BTBatchOperationStatus.MessageStatus[]`. In this particular scenario, the adapter would then need to create a new batch containing nineteen submit operations and one suspend operation. The MessageStatus array is again an array of HRESULT's meaning that a failure code will be negative.

The following code excerpt illustrates how an Adapter would request a new batch from the engine via its Transport Proxy and submit a single message into the engine; this excerpt uses the cookie approach:

```
using Microsoft.BizTalk.TransportProxy.Interop;
using Microsoft.BizTalk.Message.Interop;

public class MyAdapter :
          IBTTransport,
```

```
            IBTTransportConfig,
            IBTTransportControl,
            IPersistPropertyBag,
            IBaseComponent,
            IBTBatchCallBack
{
   private IBTTransportProxy _tp;
   public void BatchComplete(Int32 status,
                 Int16 opCount,
                 BTBatchOperationStatus[] operationStatus,
                 System.Object callbackCookie)
   {
     // Use cookie to correlate callback with work done,
     // in this example the batch is to submit a single
     // file the name of which will be in the
     // callbackCookie
     string fileName = (string)callbackCookie;
     if ( status >= 0 )
        // DeleteFile from disc
        File.Delete(fileName);
     else
        // Rename file to fileName.bad
        File.Move(fileName, fileName + ".bad");
   }

   private void SubmitMessage(IBaseMessage msg, string fileName)
   {
     // Note: Pass in the filename as the cookie
     IBTTransportBatch batch = tp.GetBatch(this, (object)fileName);
     // Add msg to batch for submitting
     batch.SubmitMessage(msg);
     // Process this batch
     batch.Done(null);
   }
}
```

NOTE

The BizTalk SDK, at the time of writing, includes three Adapter samples: FILE, HTTP, and MSMQ. All three of these Adapters are built on top of a common building block called the BaseAdapter. In the BaseAdapter you will find all the relevant code to parse the batch operation status array and rebuild a new batch to submit.

One-Way Receive

For a receive adapter to submit a message into the engine, it first needs to create a new IBaseMessage BizTalk message. The stream that the Adapter sets as the message body should typically be a forward-only stream, meaning that it should not cache the data that it has previously read in memory. Before the Adapter submits the message into the engine, it must write two mandatory message context properties in the system namespace onto the BizTalk message. These are the `InboundTransportLocation` and the `InboundTransportType` properties, illustrated in the following code excerpt:

```
using Microsoft.BizTalk.Message.Interop;
using Microsoft.XLANGs.BaseTypes;

private static readonly PropertyBase InboundTransportLocationProp =
        new BTS.InboundTransportLocation();
private static readonly PropertyBase InboundTransportTypeProp =
        new BTS.InboundTransportType();

private void StampMsgCtxProps(IBaseMessage msg, string uri, string adapterType)
{
   msg.Context.Write(InboundTransportLocationProp.Name.Name,
            InboundTransportLocationProperty.Name.Namespace,
            uri);
   msg.Context.Write(InboundTransportTypeProp.Name.Name,
            InboundTransportTypeProperty.Name.Namespace,
            adapterType);
}
```

In addition, the adapter may define its own property schema and write message context properties pertaining to the endpoint over which it received the message. For example, an HTTP adapter may want to write the HTTP headers to the message context, and an SMTP receiver may want to write the subject of the mail to the message context. This information may be useful to components downstream, such as pipeline components, orchestrations, or a send adapter.

After the messages are prepared, they can be submitted into the engine; the code sample in Batch Call Back indicates how a one-way receive Adapter submits a message into the engine.

Figure 7.15 illustrates the API interaction for a one-way receive.

Request Response

Two-way receive adapters may be used on a one-way or a two-way receive port, and the adapter determines whether the receive location it is servicing is a one-way or two-way port by inspecting the BizTalk configuration property bag, as detailed in `AddReceiveEndpoint`.

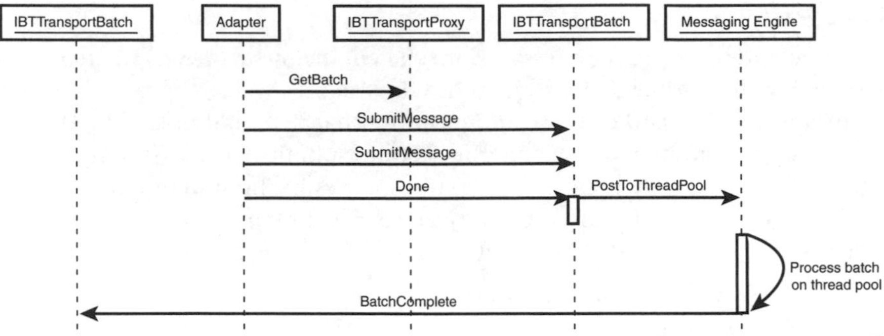

FIGURE 7.15 One-way receive sequence diagram.

Figure 7.16 illustrates the process of performing a request-response operation. The Adapter requests a new batch from its Transport Proxy and calls the API `SubmitRequestMessage()`, passing in its reference to an `IBTTransmitter` interface. The engine will deliver the response message on this interface. The response message should be transmitted using a nonblocking transmission.

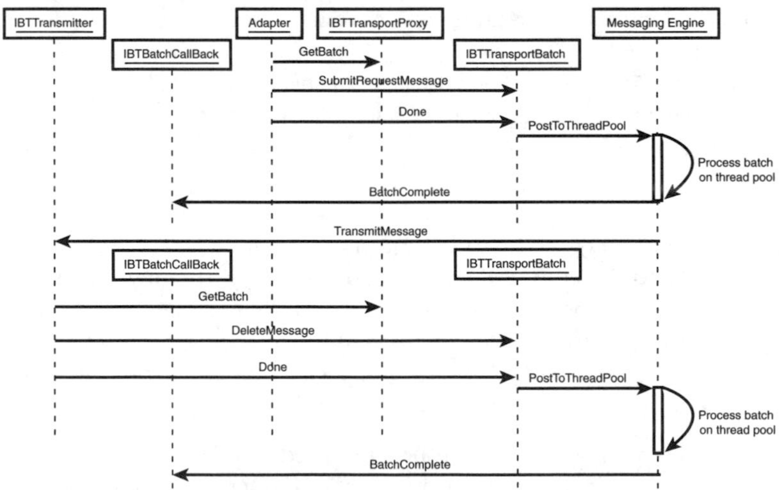

FIGURE 7.16 Request-response sequence diagram.

NOTE

Because the engine is processing messages asynchronously, it is possible for the `BatchComplete()` callback to take place before `Done()` has returned, and the call to `TransmitMessage()` on the IBTTransmitter could be made before `BatchComplete()` and even `Done()`. Although both of these scenarios are rare, the Adapter should protect itself against this scenario.

One-Way Send

The messaging engine will deliver messages to the send adapter either in `IBTTransmitter.TransmitMessage()` or `IBTTransmitterBatch.TransmitMessage()`, depending on whether the adapter is batch aware. Both methods have a Boolean return value that indicates whether the adapter sent the message.

If the adapter returns true, the engine will delete the message from the application queue on behalf of the adapter. If, however, the adapter returns false, the adapter is responsible not only for deleting the message from the application queue, but also for handling any send failures that, for example, require the message to be retried for transmission, suspended, and so on.

For adapters returning false, the `TransmitMessage()` implementation should be a nonblocking call and should therefore add the message to a logical queue of messages ready to be sent. The adapter should have its own thread pool, which will service the queue, send the messages, and then notify the engine of the outcome of the transmission.

The message engine threads are typically more CPU bound than the threads used to send data over the wire. Mixing these two types of threads has a negative impact on performance. Nonblocking send adapters enable the decoupling of these two types of thread usage and yield a significant performance improvement (see Figure 7.17).

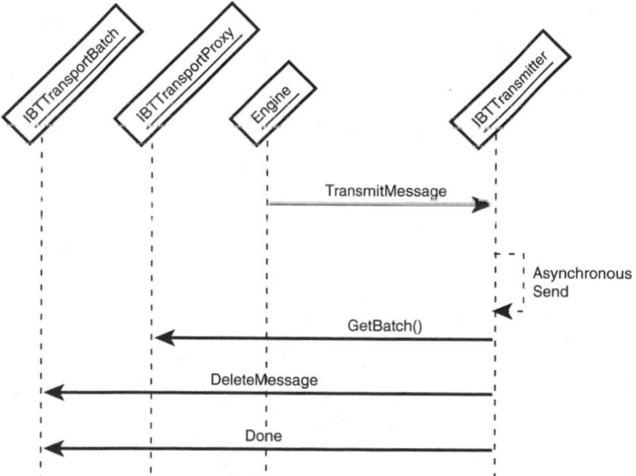

FIGURE 7.17 One-way send sequence diagram.

For the best performance, send adapters should be nonblocking and batch aware. When the BizTalk FILE adapter was changed from blocking and nonbatch aware to nonblocking and batch aware, a threefold performance gain was realized.

Blocking transmits can cause a performance degradation of an entire host instance because if the send adapter does excessive blocking in `TransmitMessage()`, it will be preventing engine threads from delivering messages to other adapters.

Solicit Response

Two-way send adapters typically support both one-way and two-way transmissions. The adapter determines whether a specific message should be transmitted as a one-way or a two-way send by inspecting the `IsSolicitResponse` system context property in the message context.

The following code excerpt demonstrates this:

```
private bool portIsTwoWay = false;
private static readonly PropertyBase IsSolicitResponseProperty =
        new BTS.IsSolicitResponse();
...
   // Port is one way or two way...
   object obj = this.message.Context.Read(IsSolicitResponseProperty.Name.Name,
                          IsSolicitResponseProperty.Name.Namespace);
   if ( null != obj ) this.portIsTwoWay = (bool)obj;
```

During a solicit-response transmission, the adapter will transmit the solicit message, wait for a response, submit that response, and finally delete the original solicit message from the application queue. The action of deleting the message from the application queue should be performed in the same Transport Proxy batch as the submission of the response message; this ensures atomicity of the delete and submission of the response. For complete atomicity, the adapter should use a DTC transaction whereby the transmission of the solicit message, submission of the response message, and the deletion of the solicit message are all in the context of the same DTC transaction. As always, it is recommended that the solicit message is transmitted using a nonblocking send. Figure 7.18 illustrates the API calls used for Solicit Response.

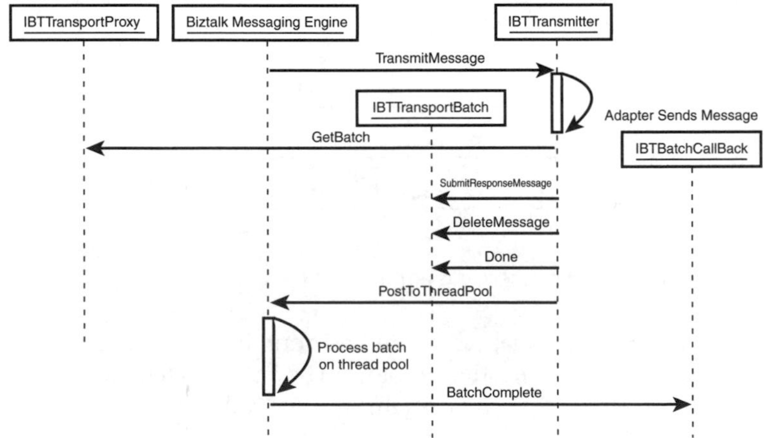

FIGURE 7.18 Solicit-response sequence diagram.

The following code excerpt illustrates the main aspects of a two-way send. When `IBTTransmitter.TransmitMessage()` is called by the engine, the adapter enqueues the message to be transmitted to an in-memory queue. The adapter then returns false to indicate that it is performing a nonblocking send. The adapter's thread pool services the in-memory queue, `WorkerThreadThunk()`. It will dequeue a message and hand it off to a helper method that is responsible for sending the solicit message and receiving the response message, the implementation of which is outside of this excerpt. The response message is submitted into the engine, and the solicit message is deleted from the application queue.

```
using System.Collections;
using Microsoft.XLANGs.BaseTypes;
using Microsoft.BizTalk.Message.Interop;
using Microsoft.BizTalk.TransportProxy.Interop;

static private Queue _transmitQueue = new Queue();
static private IBTTransportProxy _transportProxy = null;

// IBTTransmitter
public bool TransmitMessage(IBaseMessage msg)
{
   // Add message to the transmit queue...
   lock(_transmitQueue.SyncRoot)
   {
     transmitQueue.Enqueue(msg);
   }
   return false;
}
// Threadpool worker thread...
private void WorkerThreadThunk()
{
   try
   {
     lock(_transmitQueue.SyncRoot)
   {
     IBaseMessage solicitMsg = (IBaseMessage)_transmitQueue.Dequeue();
   }
   IBaseMessage responseMsg = SendSolicitResponse(     solicitMsg );
   Callback cb = new Callback();
   IBTTransportBatch batch = _transportProxy.GetBatch(cb, null);
   batch.SubmitResponseMessage( solicitMsg, responseMsg );
   batch.DeleteMessage( solicitMsg );
   batch.Done(null);
```

7

```
    }
    catch(Exception)
    {
        // Handle failure....
    }
}
static private IBaseMessage SendSolicitResponse(IBaseMessage solicitMsg )
{
    // Helper method to send solicit message and receive
    // response message...
    IBaseMessage responseMsg = null;
    return responseMsg;
}
```

Dynamic Send

Dynamic send ports do not have adapter configuration associated with them; they use handler configuration for any default properties that the adapter needs in order to transmit messages on a dynamic port. For example, an HTTP adapter may need to use a proxy; the username, password, and port could be specified in the handler configuration that the adapter caches at runtime.

For the engine to determine the right send adapter for a message being sent over a dynamic port, the `OutboundTransportLocation` context property will be prefixed with the adapter's alias. An adapter can register one or more aliases with BizTalk at installation time, and the engine parses the `OutboundTransportLocation` at runtime to find a match and therefore determine the adapter to deliver the message to. For example, the native HTTP adapter has HTTP:// and HTTPS:// registered as aliases. It is the adapter's responsibility to handle the `OutboundTransportLocation` with or without the alias prepended to it. For example, a File adapter should be able to send messages whose OutboundTransportLocation is set to either FILE://C:\Foo\Bar.xml or C:\Foo\Bar.xml.

Adapter Registration

After the design-time and runtime custom adapter code has been successfully built, it is time to register the adapter with BizTalk. This is done by updating the registry with the appropriate adapter settings via a registry file or the Adapter Registration Wizard. Table 7.1 describes each available setting.

TABLE 7.1 Adapter Registration Settings

Name	Type	Description
TransportType	REG_SZ	Name of the Adapter.
Constraints	REG_DWORD	The capabilities supported by the adapter; for example, request-response, solicit-response, isolated adapter.

TABLE 7.1 Continued

Name	Type	Description
OutboundProtocol_PageProv	REG_SZ	Property page for send handler configuration.
InboundProtocol_PageProv	REG_SZ	Property page for receive handler configuration.
ReceiveLocation_PageProv	REG_SZ	Property page for receive locations.
TransmitLocation_PageProv	REG_SZ	Property page for send port.
InboundEngineCLSID	REG_SZ	Class ID of the receiver; for COM adapters this will be the CLSID, for .NET adapters this will be a unique GUID.
InboundTypeName	REG_SZ	The .NET type name of the class that implements receiving part of the adapter.
InboundAssemblyPath	REG_SZ	Path to the .NET assembly that implements receiving part of the adapter.
ReceiveHandlerPropertiesXML	REG_SZ	SSO registration of the adapter framework property page for receive handler.
ReceiveLocationPropertiesXML	REG_SZ	SSO registration of the adapter framework property page for receive location.
OutboundEngineCLSID	REG_SZ	Class ID of the sender, for COM adapters. This will be the CLSID; for .NET adapters this will be a unique GUID.
OutboundTypeName	REG_SZ	The .NET type name of the class that implements sender part of the adapter.
OutboundAssemblyPath	REG_SZ	Path to the .NET assembly that implements sender part of the adapter.
AliasesXML	REG_SZ	URL prefixes used for dynamic port transport resolution.
SendHandlerPropertiesXML	REG_SZ	SSO registration of the adapter framework property page for send location.
SendLocationPropertiesXML	REG_SZ	SSO registration of the adapter framework property page for send location.
PropertyNameSpace	REG_SZ	Namespace of the adapter properties. The properties will be stored on message context under this namespace.
AdapterMgmtTypeName	REG_SZ	Type name of the class that provides UI for adapter property pages.
AdapterMgmtAssemblyPath	REG_SZ	Path to the assembly that implements UI for adapter property pages.

Adapter Registration Wizard

To make registration of an adapter more user friendly, the Adapter Registration Wizard has been included as part of the BizTalk Server 2004 SDK refresh available at `http://www.microsoft.com/biztalk/techinfo/productdoc/2004/default.asp`. This tool provides an intuitive user interface that prompts you for your adapter's settings and ultimately registers the adapter with BizTalk. The Adapter Registration Wizard can be found at `<Installation Path\SDK\Utilities\AdapterWizard\`.

Add Adapter to BizTalk

The final stage in being able to use a custom adapter in BizTalk is to add it to the BizTalk Server Administration Console. This can be done by going to the BizTalk Administration Console and locating the Adapters folder underneath the Microsoft BizTalk Server 2004 root tree node. Right-click the Adapters folder and select New, Adapter, which will open the Add Adapter dialog box as shown in Figure 7.19.

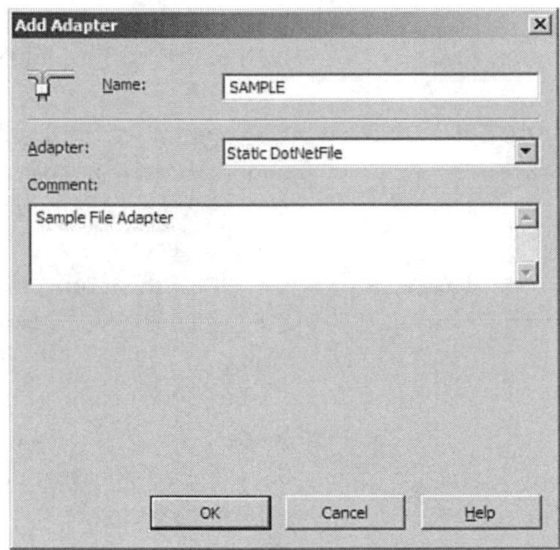

FIGURE 7.19 Add Adapter dialog box used for adding adapters to BizTalk.

Select your new adapter from the drop-down list of registered adapters, give the adapter a name, and add any pertinent comments to describe the adapter's capabilities. When you click OK, your adapter will then be available as a transport to BizTalk.

Summary

Adapters play an integral part in allowing BizTalk to integrate disparate systems. They can support sending and receiving messages in various communication patterns, including one-way receive, request-response, one-way send, and solicit response. Adapters are configured as part of receive handlers, send handlers, receive locations, and send ports via a property browser.

A number of native adapters are shipped with BizTalk, including File, HTTP, FTP, MSMQT, SMTP, SOAP, SQL, and EDI. Handlers allow an adapter to be configured in association with a host, which is made up of one or more host instances that can potentially run on separate machines. This architecture enables fault tolerance and load balancing for receive locations and send ports.

The BizTalk Server 2004 Adapter framework is a COM API that enables the development of custom adapters. The API can be categorized into design time, runtime, and registration elements. Design-time development is concerned with the customization of the property browser and harvesting metadata such as service descriptions, port types, and message types via Web Service Definition Language (WSDL). The runtime API deals with loading a configuration for the adapter and then using this data to send and receive messages per the relevant communication pattern. The final step in using the adapter is to register it with BizTalk via a registration file or the Adapter Registration Wizard.

CHAPTER 8

Using Single Sign-On

IN THIS CHAPTER

- What Is Single Sign-On?
- Enterprise Single Sign-On Scenarios
- The Enterprise Single Sign-On System

In traditional enterprise environments, information workers and automated business processes often require access to heterogeneous systems, most of which have not been designed to leverage a common authentication mechanism. Common authentication solutions provide services to request and verify your credentials upon logon to the network. Those credentials are then used to determine the actions you can perform and applications you can assess based on your user privileges. For example, you can use Windows Integrated Authentication (WIA) to pass the credentials of the logged on Windows user to any application that supports WIA and Active Directory. This is a very common practice for applications that provide access to Microsoft SQL Server databases.

When common authentication mechanisms are not in place, applications most often utilize multiple credential stores and authentication protocols, making it very difficult to securely synchronize and exchange credentials between applications and platforms. To gain access to each application, the user or business process must present a different set of user credentials for each. Although somewhat tedious for the users when they are manually accessing these systems, it becomes even more challenging for an automated business process. In these cases, developers have traditionally written custom business logic that either requires the hard-coding of these credentials or the mapping and management of user credentials for each application. On platforms using different authentication protocols, developers must also rely on middleware products to assist with the exchange of the credentials between the two platforms.

In this chapter we will discuss a software solution named BizTalk Enterprise Single Sign-On (SSO), which provides services that business applications and developers can use to assist them with authentication to multiple disparate applications that do not have access to a common authentication mechanism.

NOTE

Additional information on Web services, SOAP, and the ws_* specifications can be found at `http://msdn.microsoft.com/webservices`.

What Is Single Sign-On?

In the perfect world, a common federated model for user identity exchange and verification using industry standard protocols would exist to allow seamless identity integration between platforms. Today, a number of emerging technologies are moving toward this goal, including WS-Security, a specification that VeriSign, Microsoft, and IBM coauthored. WS-Security is an XML security specification that defines a standard set of Simple Object Access Protocol (SOAP) extensions or message headers for exchanging secure, signed messages in a Web services environment. This and the many other emerging Web service ws_* specifications provide a foundation on which to build platform–independent, federated, and interoperable Web services. These new standards, along with future products and platforms that support them, could and will most likely provide a foundation on which to build a standards-based solution for identity management. Until then, developers will need to leverage software and middleware to help them address these challenges.

The term *single sign-on* is usually associated with three general categories of authentication: common authentication, as discussed earlier, Web authentication, and Enterprise Application Integration (EAI) authentication. Web-based authentication services usually refer to mechanisms that allow you to use a single set of credentials to access multiple Web sites. Two examples of this type of single sign-on are Microsoft .NET Passport and WebSSO solutions, such as Microsoft SharePoint Portal Server SSO.

EAI single sign-on authentication services are slightly more complex and involve the integration of multiple heterogeneous systems residing on sometimes disparate platforms. For example, you may need to integrate a Windows application that uses Windows Integrated Authentication (WIA) and Active Directory with an application running on an IBM mainframe using IBM's Resource Access Control Facility (RACF) as its authentication store. To accomplish this, you would need to utilize a middleware platform such as Microsoft Host Integration Server (HIS) to communicate the credentials between the platforms as well as a credential store to map the Windows credentials to the IBM credentials. BizTalk Server 2004 Enterprise Single Sign-On (SSO), BizTalk Adapters, and Host Integration Server together provide an end-to-end solution for the EAI single sign-on scenario.

BizTalk's Enterprise Single Sign-On (SSO) is a standalone service that allows administrators to map a Windows user account to one or more alternative Windows or non-Windows accounts. These accounts are mapped per application so that they can be used to securely access applications that require credentials other then those originally provided by the end user. These credentials are stored and encrypted in a secure database and then retrieved when requested by the SSO to access the external application. After users are authenticated in the Windows domain, they are not required to provide additional credentials to access the disparate back-end application. These credentials could be provided securely to external applications via a variety of protocols. Today, BizTalk Server 2004 SSO supports credential mapping and retrieval using both the HTTP and SOAP transport protocols.

BizTalk's SSO service is a standalone service and can be easily integrated into middleware applications using custom BizTalk 2004 adapters. You construct custom BizTalk adapters using the BizTalk Server 2004 Adapter framework. Adapters built using this framework can take advantage of SSO services natively allowing authentication to back-end systems with mapped credentials. For example, you could write a custom Oracle adapter that implements the BizTalk SSO services interfaces. Developers could then leverage those services to authenticate to the Oracle DB with the mapped credentials. The SSO services and the Credential Data Store are together referred to as the *SSO System*.

Enterprise Single Sign-On Scenarios

We have discussed several categories of SSO solutions and now know that BizTalk Server 2004 SSO was designed to support EAI SSO requirements. There are, however, multiple EAI SSO scenarios that must be considered. Several of these scenarios are described in the sections that follow. The first two, Windows Initiated SSO and Configuration Store, are currently supported in BizTalk Server 2004.

Windows Initiated SSO

In the Windows Initiated SSO scenario, SSO services are used to map credentials from a Windows application to a non-Windows application. The following is an example of this scenario:

A user attempts to view an ASP.NET Web page that displays information retrieved from a back-end system such as SAP. The Web site is using WIA to authenticate the user. The request is received by an SSO-aware HTTP BizTalk Server 2004 adapter. That adapter makes a request to the SSO system for an encrypted ticket based on the Windows credentials. The SSO system creates the ticket and places it in the message header as it is passed back to the HTTP adapter. The message is then processed by an orchestration and passed to a BizTalk Server 2004 SAP send port. The SSO-aware SAP adapter makes a second request to SSO system with the encrypted ticket to validate and redeem the ticket for the corresponding back-end (affiliate application) credentials. These credentials are then provided to the SAP adapter for authenticated access to the back-end SAP system. Figure 8.1 displays a diagram of this scenario.

To configure SSO for this scenario, an administrator defines a logical entity representing the application or back-end system, called an *affiliate application*. The administrator then defines the credential mappings for each affiliate application. These mappings are retrieved as previously described at runtime by the corresponding SSO services.

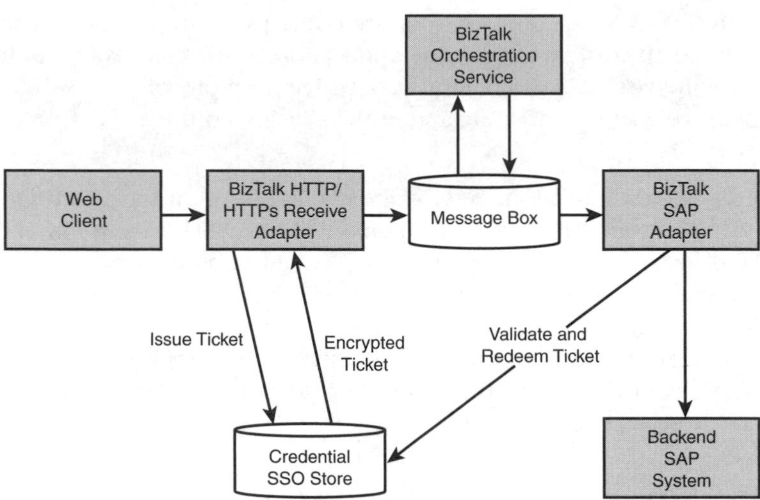

FIGURE 8.1 Windows Initiated Single Sign-On.

The diagram in Figure 8.1 shows a very simplistic picture of the SSO process. Details about the SSO system, ticket issuance and redemption, and the underlying SSO architecture will be covered in the Enterprise Single Sign-On section that follows.

Configuration Store

In addition to allowing administrators to securely store credential mapping information, BizTalk Server 2004 SSO also allows administrators to store application configuration information securely. In this scenario, the data is associated with an applications configuration, in contrast to an end-user credential. In effect, SSO provides services that developers can leverage to securely store and access dynamic configuration information.

The data in a typical credential mapping is associated with an affiliate application. In a configuration store, the data is maintained in a different type of affiliate application called a *config store*. The general concept is the same with all data encrypted and stored in the configuration database; however, with this type of affiliate application, the data is encrypted and stored in the configuration database with a UniqueID in contrast to a UserId. When an application calls the SSO service to look up this information, it provides this UniqueID.

A good example of this is the use of the configuration store by BizTalk Server 2004 to store custom configuration information for BizTalk adapters. The information required to configure BizTalk adapters is usually very dynamic in nature and is configured at deployment time. To store this information, BizTalk creates two affiliate applications—one for both the handler and port associated with each direction, send and receive, of an adapter. The set of properties associated with each of these affiliate applications is dependent on the adapter type and is defined by the developer of the original adapter code. When you configure an end point (send port or receive location) either manually or using the BizTalk Explorer, the SSO system automatically creates a mapping for a UniqueID to the configuration properties or values for that end point.

CAUTION

The BizTalk adapter SSO config store implementation requires the installation of SSO services on a BizTalk Server.

We discussed the supported scenarios, so now let's quickly discuss a few of the currently unsupported scenarios.

Unsupported Scenarios

The following services and scenarios are not supported in this version of BizTalk Server 2004 SSO:

- Single sign-on from a non-Windows system to Windows
- Windows password synchronization
- Non-Windows password synchronization
- Full password synchronization

Using single sign-on from a non-Windows system to a Windows system would allow users on non-Windows systems, such as an AS/400 or IBM mainframe, to access and retrieve data from a Windows server by mapping their non-Windows credentials to their Windows credentials. An example of this scenario follows:

A user on an SAP system wants to retrieve data from a SQL Server database running on a Windows server using Basic SQL authentication. The user would be able to log on to the non-Windows system, and SSO would retrieve the username and password for the SQL database based on the account provided by the non-Windows system.

Windows and non-Windows password synchronization would ensure that Windows user credential changes and updates are automatically reflected in the SSO credential database, and vice versa. This enables the Windows system to continue to access the non-Windows system without manually updating the SSO database. Full password synchronization ensures that user modifications to credentials on both systems are automatically reflected and updated when modified.

Throughout the remainder of this chapter, we will discuss the details of the SSO architecture and the specifics of how messages flow through the SSO system. You can find an SSO solution example in the <drive:>\Program Files\Microsoft BizTalk Server 2004\SDK\Samples\SSO\HTTPSSO Directory.

The Enterprise Single Sign-On System

The BizTalk Server 2004 SSO system provides the core services needed to store, map, and transmit encrypted user credentials to back-end affiliate applications using standard Internet transport protocols. This allows an end user to provide non-Windows credentials to back-end applications based on the end-user's original Windows credentials. To accomplish this, the Windows application provides the Windows domain\user id to the SSO server. The lookup component of the SSO server obtains the corresponding non-Windows user id and password credentials from the SSO credential database and then passes them on to the back-end affiliate application.

The SSO system contains the following artifacts: a credential database, a master secret server, and one or more SSO servers. The core functionality of the SSO service is divided into four subservices: mapping, lookup, administration, and secret. When configuring SSO mappings, an administrator creates an affiliate application and then maps one or more user credentials to that application. The administration service provides services that allow administrators to add, edit, and delete these affiliate applications and their mappings. The mapping service provides the capability to add, edit, and delete mappings of the affiliate application user accounts to Windows accounts.

After the mappings are created and configured, an end-user application can request affiliate application credentials based on a Windows user id. The SSO lookup service runtime processes this request returning the mapped credentials for the specified affiliate application and Windows user id combination.

Finally, the secret service generates the master secret key that encrypts the data when it is stored and read from the credential database. In a distributed environment, it provides services for the distribution of the key to the other SSO servers in the BizTalk cluster.

The master secret server can function as the lookup, mapping, and admin server; however, there can be only one master secret server in the SSO system (see Figure 8.2). This server is also the only server that can run the secret service.

BizTalk Server 2004 provides a set of APIs and utilities that allow you to access and configure the information managed by each of the four SSO subservices. The administration (management) API allows the administrator to enable and disable the SSO server as well as create, modify, and delete affiliate applications and their mappings. The configuration API allows administrators to create a new SSO database or to associate the SSO server with an existing SSO database. It is also used to execute master secret server procedures, such as backing up and restoring the master secret and generating a new master secret. A client API is provided that allows users to modify their credential information without contacting an administrator.

NOTE

A more in-depth look at the SSO architecture components and their associated APIs can be found in the next section and in the section titled "SSO Command-Line Utilities and APIs."

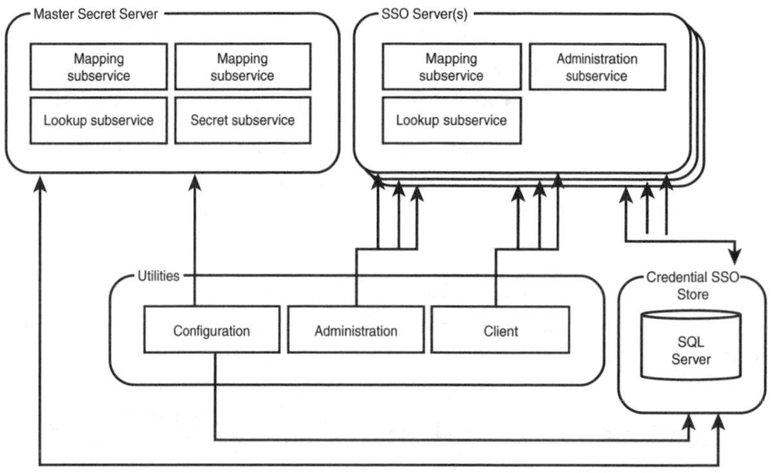

FIGURE 8.2 Enterprise SSO system.

SSO Architecture

A component-level view of the BizTalk Server 2004 Enterprise Single Sign-On architecture is displayed in Figure 8.3.

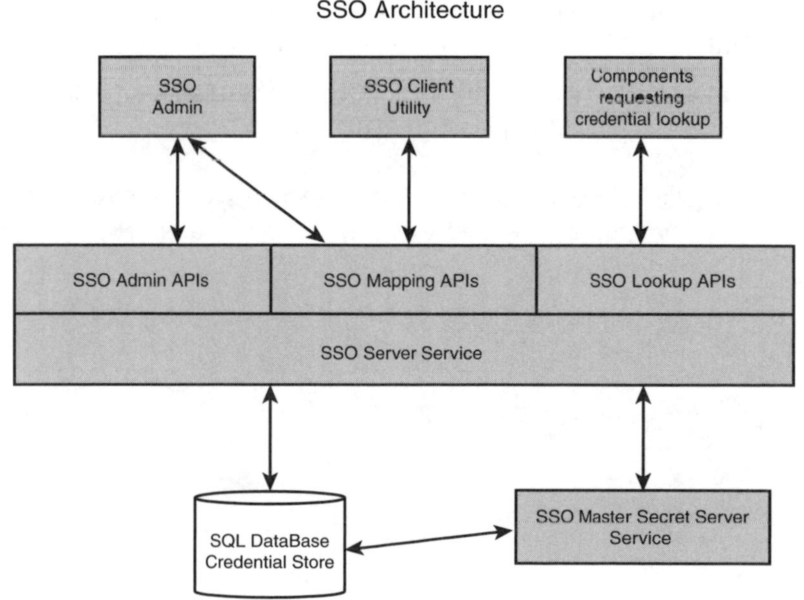

FIGURE 8.3 Enterprise SSO architecture.

8

The basic SSO system consists of the following components and objects:

- Credential Store—A SQL Server database that securely stores information about the affiliate applications' configuration information and/or credential information.
- SSO Service—The primary SSO service that allows administrators to configure and manage the SSO service as well as manage credentials, mappings, and affiliate applications. The SSO service can be configured to provide administration, mapping, and lookup services and/or provide master secret server services.
- SSO Master Secret Server—Stores the master secret. All SSO servers in a BizTalk Server cluster retrieve the master secret from this server to encrypt configuration and or credential data.

NOTE

There can be only one master secret server in a BizTalk configuration.

- SSO Admin Object—Provides management and administration interfaces for the SSO services. The SSO Manage and SSOConfig command-line utilities call this object.
- SSO Client Utility—A command-line utility that allows users to configure their user mappings. This can be installed on a user's desktop as a standalone utility.
- SSO Lookup Object—Gives end-user applications the capability to look up affiliate application credentials based on provided Windows UserIds or configuration data based on unique ids.
- SSO Mapping Object—Provides the capability to create, edit, and delete configuration and credential affiliate application mappings.

The following APIs enable you to create custom components and scripts to facilitate the administration and configuration of the SSO system. The six interfaces are

- `ISSOAdmin`
- `ISSOConfigStore`
- `ISSOLookup1`
- `ISSOMapper`
- `ISSOMapping`
- `ISSOTicket`

Three command-line utilities provided by SSO wrap the administration and mapping APIs, allowing administrators and users to perform SSO tasks without writing code:

- `SSOConfig`
- `SSOManage`
- `SSOClient`

Finally, there are four Windows users groups, each with defined SSO configuration privileges, required to administrate an SOS configuration:

- SSO Administrators
- SSO Affiliate Administrators
- SSO Application Administrators
- SSO Application Users

SSO Application Administrators and SSO Application Users groups are assigned for each affiliate application created.

Before we delve further into the configuration of SSO using its APIs and command-line utilities, let's first take a look at several scenarios that employ the use of the SSO services so that we can get a better understanding of the flow of information through the SSO system. To learn more about the SSO APIs and command-line utilities, refer to the section titled "SSO Command-Line Utilities and APIs" later in this chapter.

How Single Sign-On Works

BizTalk Server 2004 supports SSO on incoming and outgoing messages that use the HTTP and SOAP send and receive adapters. When using the HTTP or SOAP adapters on a receive location, the developer specifies whether to use SSO (see Figure 8.4). On receipt of a message, the receive adapter calls the SSO system to retrieve a ticket for the Windows user who submitted the message.

The ticket is composed of an encrypted string containing the domain/user id of the submitting user, expiration time (2-minute default), and flags that determine the type of ticket issued. This ticket is then put into the context properties of the message by the receive adapter with the property name SSOTicket.

The HTTP and SOAP send adapters require you to specify the use of SSO as well as select the affiliate back-end application you need to redeem the credentials for (see Figure 8.5). When the send adapter receives the message, it makes a `ValidateandRedeemTicket` request to the SSO service using the ticket to retrieve the user credentials mapped to that specific affiliate application. The message is then submitted to the back-end application using the credentials retrieved from the SSO store.

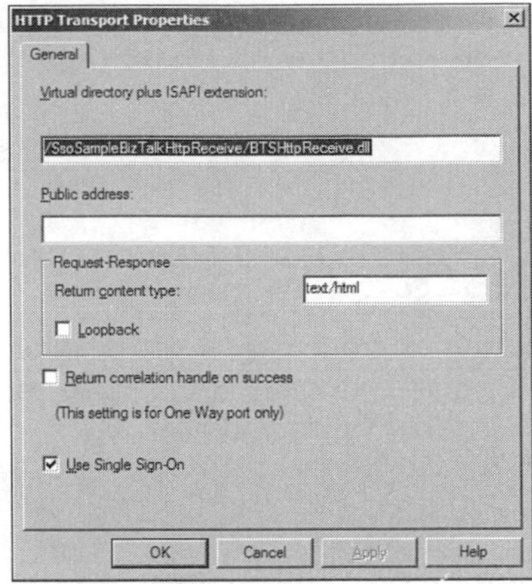

FIGURE 8.4 HTTP Receive Adapter Configuration dialog box.

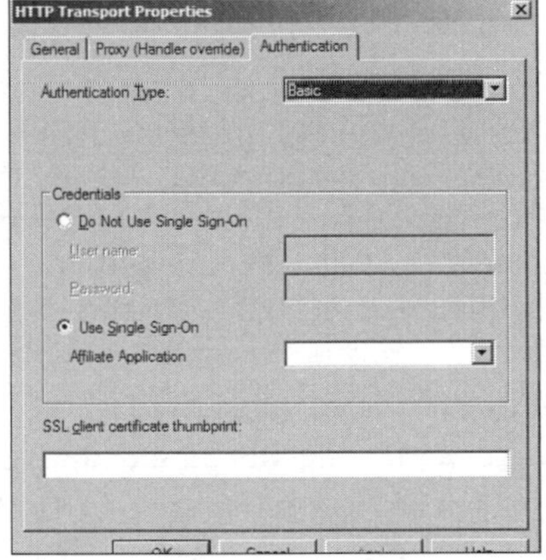

FIGURE 8.5 HTTP Send Adapter Configuration dialog box.

There are several ways to employ the use of SSO. You can use SSO in conjunction with BizTalk Messaging, BizTalk Orchestration, and as a standalone service. The following sections contain detailed descriptions and a walk through of each of these scenarios.

SSO with BizTalk Orchestration

In this example there are two ASP.NET Web sites: A and B. A uses WIA and allows a user to create a request for data. Web site B uses Basic Authentication and returns data based on a request from application A. Although both applications are running on the Windows platform and could leverage WIA, you could also choose to employ SSO to retrieve Web application B's Basic Authentication credentials from the SSO store based on the initial user's Windows credentials. A diagram of this scenario is shown in Figure 8.6.

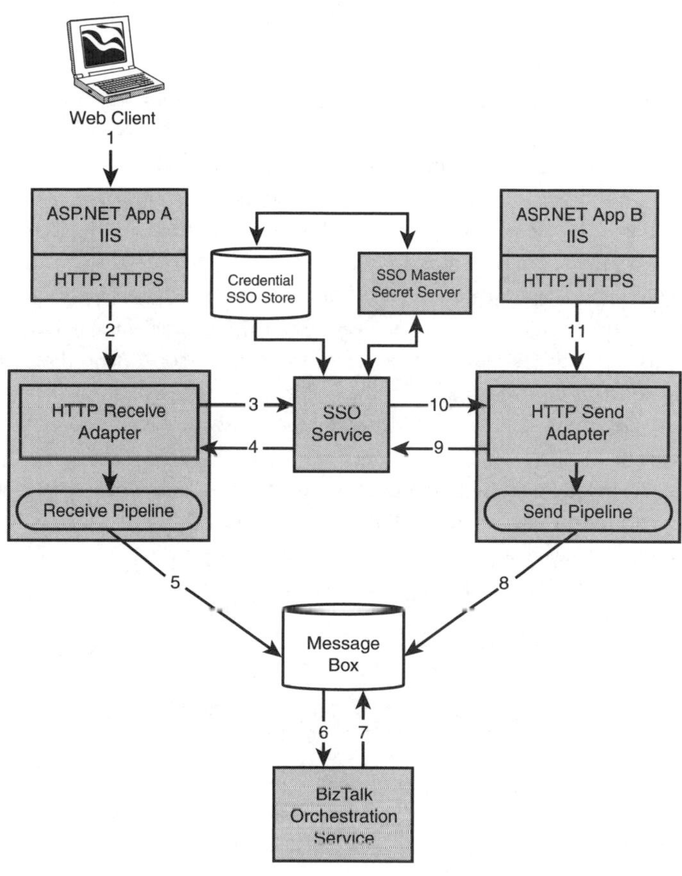

FIGURE 8.6 SSO with BizTalk Orchestration.

A detailed description of each of the numbered steps is described in Table 8.1.

TABLE 8.1 BizTalk Orchestration SSO Processing Steps

Step #	Description
1	The Web client browser makes an HTTP request to the BizTalk HTTP receive adapter URL.
2	The BizTalk HTTP receive adapter responds to the request and begins to process the message.
3	The HTTP receive adapter makes an SSO ticket request to the SSO service using the authentication credentials provided. These credentials were passed to the adapter from the IIS Web site by means of WIA.
4	The SSO service responds with an SSO encrypted ticket for the Windows user.
5	The receive pipeline puts the ticket and `OriginatorSID` into two message context properties, `SSOTicket` and `OriginatorSID`, and submits the message to the `MessageBox` for subscription fulfillment.

TABLE 8.1 Continued

Step #	Description
6	The subscribing orchestration schedule picks up the message with the ticket in the message `SSOTicket` context property.
7	The orchestration processes the message, being careful to leave the ticket context properties `SSOTicket` and `OriginatorSID` untouched, and places the resultant message back onto the message box. If a new message is created by the orchestration, the ticket context properties must be added to the new message.
8	The HTTP send adapter reads the ticket and makes a ValidateandRedeemTicket ticket call to the SSO service. Credentials are retrieved from the SSO credential database if the validation succeeds. Validation is done by comparing the `OriginatorSID` and the user in the encrypted SSO ticket. This needs to match for the validation to succeed. This validation is to ensure a trusted subsystem—that is, only trusted BizTalk hosts can be used for end-to-end SSO scenarios to work.
9	This SSO service reads the ticket, unencrypts the ticket credentials, and then looks up the credentials for the affiliate application.
10	The mapped affiliate application credentials are passed back to the HTTP send adapter.
11	The HTTP send adapter uses the affiliate application credentials to make the request to Web application B.

NOTE

In orchestration, two context properties need to be copied over when creating a new message that would be consumed by a send adapter: `SSOTicket` and `OriginatorSID`. Only trusted hosts have permission to submit a message to the `MessageBox` with any `OriginatorSID`. Therefore, all services that need to pass messages to the `MessageBox` with the `OrginatorSID` must run within a Trusted Host in BizTalk Server.

BizTalk Messaging integration with SSO is very similar and is described in the following section.

SSO with BizTalk Messaging

Using the same basic scenario described previously, we are going to assume this time that no requirement exists for business process logic in an orchestration. BizTalk simply receives the message and routes it to Web application B, as shown in Figure 8.7.

As you can see, the general steps are the same. The only thing missing is the call to and from the orchestration. Refer to Table 8.1 for a description of these steps.

SSO as a Standalone Service

Because SSO is a standalone component of BizTalk Server 2004, we could also revise this same scenario to exclude BizTalk Server 2004 Orchestration and Messaging and provide SSO services independently of them. In this scenario, we would use the SSO APIs to programmatically integrate our two Web applications with BizTalk SSO. A diagram of the steps involved in this process is shown in Figure 8.8.

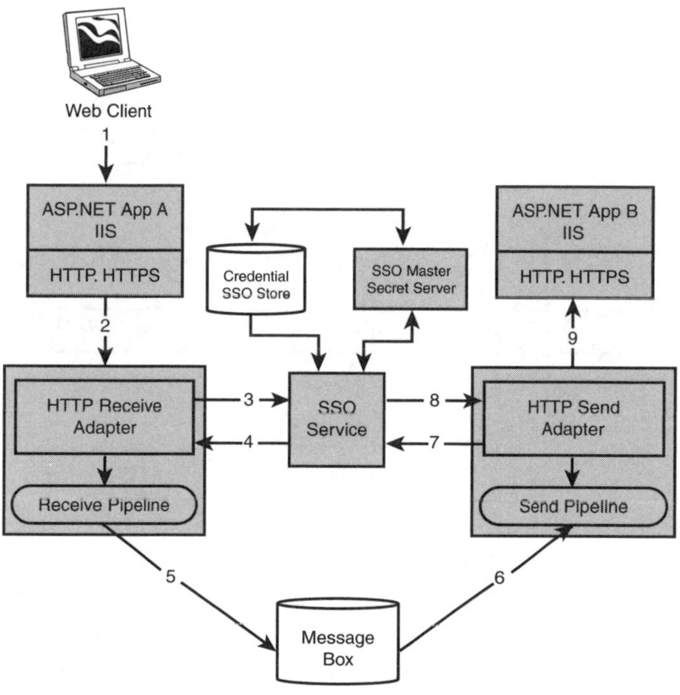

FIGURE 8.7 SSO with BizTalk Messaging.

A detailed description of the numbered steps is described in Table 8.2.

TABLE 8.2 Single Sign-On Processing Without BizTalk

Step #	Description
1	Web client makes a request to Web application A.
2	Application A uses the SSO APIs to request a ticket for the Windows user.
3	The SSO service returns the encrypted SSO ticket.
4	Application A makes a request to the SSO service to validate and redeem the ticket.
5	SSO looks up the Windows credentials in the SSO credential database and returns the affiliate applications mapped credentials.
6	Application A now makes the request to Application B using the affiliate application credentials.

As you can see from the preceding three similar scenarios, the general steps required to use SSO services are the same. You must request a ticket from the SSO server and then look up and redeem that ticket to pass the mapped credentials to an affiliate application.

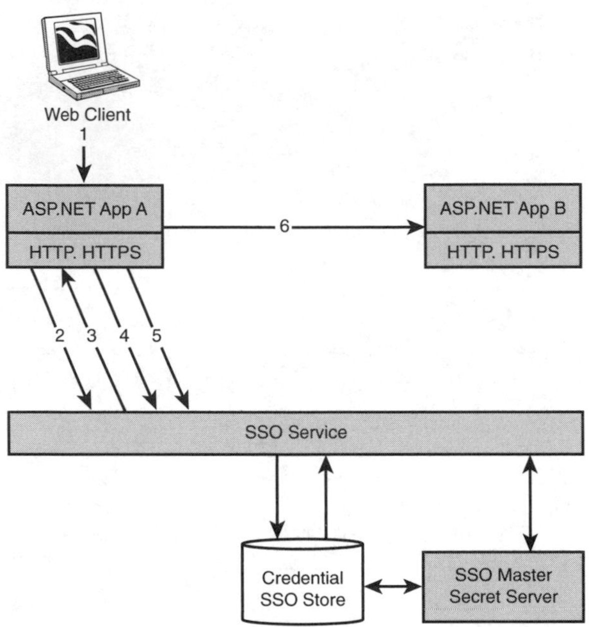

FIGURE 8.8 Windows Initiated SSO without BizTalk services.

Now that you are familiar with SSO processing, let's take a look at the configuration requirements for the SSO services, affiliate applications, and their associated mappings.

Single Sign-On Windows Accounts

To manage and configure the Enterprise Single Sign-On (SSO) system, you must create four Windows accounts: SSO Administrators, SSO Affiliate Administrators, SSO Application Administrators, and SSO Application Users. You can designate them as either a domain or as local accounts, but it is strongly recommended that you use domain accounts. Local account support is provided only for standalone SSO configurations and is not supported for SSO affiliate application users and mappings. Local account support is provided to accommodate scenarios where the SSO service is providing configuration store services for applications and adapters. If you need to use SSO credential mapping services, you must use domain accounts.

You usually create these groups prior to installation. The installation process then designates these groups to their associated SSO role during the configuration process. You can, however, also manually modify these settings using the `ssomanage -updatedb <filename>` command-line utility. A sample XML input file for this command follows:

```
<sso>
<globalInfo>
<ssoAdminAccount>Domain\Accountname</ssoAdminAccount>
```

```
<ssoAffiliateAdminAccount>Domain\Accountname</ssoAffiliateAdminAccount>
</globalInfo>
</sso>
```

When you are defining SSO accounts, it is best to remember these two things:

- Always use domain groups and accounts.
- Even though you can use domain accounts for each of the four groups, it's better to use domain groups. Domain groups give you the capability to add and delete users from a role without modifying the SSO configuration.

Each group has the capability to perform a specific set of SSO management functions. The group with the highest level of user access is the SSO administrator. The SSO administrator has full control over all SSO administration and configuration tasks. The service account running the Enterprise SSO service must be a member of this group.

The next Windows group in the hierarchy is the SSO Affiliate Administrators group. This group has the capability to manage the SSO system's affiliate applications and their mappings.

Under the SSO Affiliate Administrators is the SSO Application Administrator. SSO Application Administrators manage individual affiliate application users and their mappings. There is one SSO Application Administrators group per affiliate application. Because this group has configuration store responsibilities, including storage of BizTalk Server adapter configuration data, it must also have BizTalk Server administrator user rights associated with it.

The forth and final group is the SSO Application Users group. This group contains user accounts that have affiliate application mappings. There is one SSO application user's group account for each affiliate application. Members of this group have the right to manage the credentials of their affiliate application mappings only.

Master Secret Server

All SSO system configurations are limited to one and only one master secret server. The master secret server stores the master secret encryption key and is responsible for the encryption and decryption of credentials. This secret is stored in the Windows Registry of a master secret server as a Local Security Authority (LSA) Secret. Administrators can generate the master secret by using the BizTalk Server 2004 Configuration Wizard during the installation of SSO or by using the SSOConfig command-line utility. SSO administrators are the only SSO group that has privileges to access and generate a master secret. The master secret must be created and configured on the master secret server before you can create an affiliate application.

After you have created the master secret, you should back it up and store it in a safe location. If a secret becomes corrupt and it has not been backed up, all data stored in the SSO credential database may become inaccessible. This secret can be restored at any time from a backup by an SSO administrator.

Because you can have only one master secret server, it is also recommended that you cluster the master secret server using Microsoft Cluster Server in active/passive mode. This will ensure that the SSO system can continue to process requests even if the active master secret server encounters an unexpected outage. In this case, the passive master secret server would take over and begin to process master secret requests.

To enable the encryption and decryption of credentials, SSO servers read and cache the master secret from the master secret server every 30 seconds. If the master secret has been updated, the new secret will be retrieved and then cached on the SSO server that requested the secret. In certain situations, SSO administrators may also want to periodically regenerate the master secret. When a request is made to the master secret server to regenerate the secret, it will go through all its mappings, decrypt them using the old master secret key, and then reencrypt them with the new secret.

To manually generate a new master secret key, you can execute the `ssoconfig -generatesecret <backup file name>` command-line utility located in the default SSO installation directory. The default SSO installation directory can be found at <drive>:\Program Files\Common Files\Enterprise Single Sign-On. When you execute this command, you will be prompted for a password.

As discussed earlier, if the master secret server key becomes corrupted or the server itself crashes, you won't be able to retrieve configuration information stored in the credential database. This includes affiliate applications and mapped credentials as well as adapter configuration information stored in the credential database. Therefore, it is highly recommended that you back up the master secret.

To back up the master secret, execute the command-line utility`ssoconfig -backupsecret <backup file>` from the command prompt in the SSO default directory. When you execute this command, you are prompted automatically for a password. Remember this password you were prompted for; you will need it to restore the secret. To execute this command, you must be a member of the SSO administrators group.

In the next section, we will discuss the SSO command-line utilities and APIs.

SSO Command-Line Utilities and APIs

BizTalk 2004 supplies three command-line utilities for configuring and managing the SSO database. These utilities provide an easy-to-use wrapper interface for the SSO APIs discussed later in this section. There is no user interface (UI) included with BizTalk Server 2004 SSO. All the command-line utilities for SSO can be found in the default installation directory: <drive>:\Program Files\Common Files\Enterprise Single Sign-on.

ssoconfig.exe, the first command-line utility, is used to create a new SSO database or to associate the SSO server with an existing SSO database. It also is used to perform master secret procedures such as backing up the master secret, generating a new master secret, and restoring a master secret.

The ssoconfig.exe commands are displayed in Table 8.3.

TABLE 8.3 SSO Config Commands

Command	Description
`-setdb`	Set the SQL Server and SQL database names.
`-showdb`	Show the SQL Server and SQL database names.
`-createdb`	Create the SSO database.
`-generatesecret`	Generate the new SSO master secret.
`-backupsecret`	Back up the current SSO master secret.
`-restoresecret`	Restore the SSO master secret.

SSOManage.exe is used to manage the SSO server. The SSO administrator can use this utility to enable and disable the SSO server as well as create applications and password mappings for those applications. The command-line options are divided into three categories: Administration functions, Application functions, and Mapping functions, as displayed in Table 8.4.

TABLE 8.4 SSOManage Command-Line Options

Commands	Description
`-server`	Set SSO server name (for current user).
`-serverall`	Set SSO server name (for all users).
`-showserver`	Show the SSO server name(s).
`-auditlevel`	Set SSO server audit level.
Administration Functions	
`-updatedb`	Update SSO database.
`-enablesso`	Enable SSO.
`-disablesso`	Disable SSO.
`-tickets`	Control SSO ticket behavior.
`-displaydb`	Display current SSO database settings.
Application Functions	
`-listapps`	List existing applications.
`-displayapp`	Display application information.
`-createapps`	Create new applications.
`-deleteapp`	Delete an existing application.
`-updateapps`	Update existing applications.
`-enableapp`	Enable application.
`-disableapp`	Disable application.
`-purgecache`	Purge the credential cache for an application.

8

TABLE 8.4 Continued

Commands	Description
Mapping Functions	
`-listmappings`	List mappings for user.
`-createmappings`	Create mappings for user.
`-deletemappings`	Delete mappings for user.
`-enablemapping`	Enable a mapping for user.
`-disablemapping`	Disable a mapping for user.
`-deletemapping`	Delete a single mapping for user.
`-setcredentials`	Set credentials for user.

The third and final command-line utility is named SSOClient.exe. This utility allows a user to set credentials for affiliate applications they have privilege for. An administrator could also use the `SSOManage` command-line utility to set the credentials for the user. The `SSOClient` commands are listed in Table 8.5.

TABLE 8.5 SSO Client Commands

Command	Description
`-server`	Set the SSO server name.
`-showserver`	Show the SSO server name.
`-listapps`	List available applications.
`-enablemapping`	Enable a mapping.
`-disablemapping`	Disable a mapping.
`-deletemapping`	Delete a mapping.
`-listmappings`	List all mappings for a user.
`-setcredentials`	Set external credentials.

The command-line utilities allow you to avoid creating custom scripts and business logic to configure SSO servers, master secrets, applications, and mappings. There may, however, be an occasion when you want to have programmatic access to SSO. As discussed earlier in the section titled "SSO Architecture," a set of APIs is provided. These API interfaces allow you to create custom components and scripts to facilitate the administration of the SSO system. The six APIs and their public methods are listed in Table 8.6.

TABLE 8.6 SSO API Public Methods

Command	Description
`CreateApplication`	Creates an application.
`CreateFieldInfo`	Creates field information for an application.
`DeleteApplication`	Deletes an application.
`GetApplicationInfo`	Gets the application information.
`PurgeCacheForApplication`	Purges the cached credentials for an application on all SSO servers.
`UpdateApplication`	Updates the application information.
`UpdateGlobalInfo`	Returns the SSO configuration information.
ISSOConfigStore	
`DeleteConfigInfo`	Deletes the configuration information from a configuration store.
`GetConfigInfo`	Gets the configuration information from a configuration store.
`SetConfigInfo`	Sets the configuration information in a configuration store.
ISSOLookup1	
`GetCredentials`	Retrieves the user credentials for an application.
ISSOMapper	
`GetApplications`	Retrieves the available applications for a user.
`GetFieldInfo`	Retrieves the field information for an application.
`GetMappingsForExternalUser`	Retrieves the mappings for an external user.
`GetMappingsForWindowsUser`	Stores a set of external credentials in the SSO database.
`SetExternalCredentials`	Stores a set of external credentials.
ISSOMapping	
`Create`	Creates the mapping.
`Delete`	Deletes the mapping.
`Disable`	Disables the mapping.
`Enable`	Enables the mapping.
ISSOTicket	
`IssueTicket`	Issues an SSO ticket.
`RedeemTicket`	Redeems an SSO server ticket.

Auditing SSO Services

Auditing services are provided for two SSO components: the SSO service and the SSO credential database. The auditing of both components is configured using SSO command-line utilities that accept audit level parameters. There are two arguments for the SSO service audit level:

- Current positive level
- Current negative level

Current positive level sets the successful audit level and is defaulted to 0. The current negative level sets the unsuccessful audit level and is defaulted to 1. To configure the maximum audit-level logging, you specify a positive level of 3 and negative level of 3. All audit messages are written to the Windows application event log.

To set the auditing levels for the SSO server, you use the ssoconfig –auditlevel command-line utility. The command-line utilities can be found in the default SSO installation directory. You can use the following command from the command line in that directory to accomplish this: ssoconfig -auditlevel <positive level> <negative level>

To enable or change the credential database auditing level, you use a similar command-line utility, but this time you must provide an XML file containing the settings. A sample XML file is shown next:

```
<sso>
<globalnfo>
<auditDeletedApps>1000</auditDeletedApps>
<auditDeletedMappings>1000</auditDeletedMappings>
<auditCredentialLookups>1000</auditCredentialLookups>
</globalInfo>
</sso>
```

The command-line utility required to update the credential database audit level is named ssomanage –updatedb. To configure the audit levels for the SSO credential database, execute the ssommanage -updatedb <update file> command from the command-line within the SSO default installing directory.

Managing Affiliate Applications

SSO affiliate applications are logical entities that represent the back-end systems using SSO. To create an affiliate application, the user must be an SSO affiliate administrator. When you define a new affiliate application, you must make a number of configuration decisions. First, you must decide who the administrator of the application (SSO application administrator) is going to be and who the users (SSO application users) of the application will be; then you create the network groups and accounts with these users. Next, you need to decide what type of credentials the application requires and whether you want to use individual or group mappings (see the section titled "Managing Mappings" for more details on mapping types).

To create the application, you use the ssomanage –createapps <XML file name> command-line utility. An example of a createapps XML file is displayed next:

```
<sso>
<application name="SAP">
<description>The SAP application</description>
<contact>someone@example.com</contact>
```

```
<appuserAccount>domain\AppUserAccount</appuserAccount>
<appAdminAccount>domain\AppAdminAccount</appAdminAccount>
<field ordinal="0" label="User Id" masked="no" />
<field ordinal="1" label="Password" masked="yes" />
<flags groupApp="no" configStoreApp="no" allowTickets="no"
       validateTickets="yes" allowLocalAccounts="no" timeoutTickets="yes"
       adminAccountSame="no" enableApp="no" />
</application>
</sso>
```

After the application has been created, there are several parameters that cannot be modified. These parameters are listed next:

- Name
- Fields associated with the affiliate application
- Affiliate application type
- Administration account

NOTE

Additional information on the flags and associated command properties can be found in the BizTalk Server 2004 online documentation.

There are two ways to manage affiliate applications. You can use the ssomanage command-line utility or the ssoclient utility. These utilities can be found in the default SSO installation directory. The `ssomanage` and `ssoclient` command-line options are detailed in the section titled "SSO Command-Line Utilities and APIs." You can perform the following affiliate application configuration tasks using either the `ssomanage` or `ssoclient` utilities:

- Create an affiliate application.
- Delete an affiliate application.
- Update the properties of an affiliate application.
- Enable an affiliate application.
- Disable an affiliate application.
- List affiliate applications.
- List the properties of an affiliate application.
- Clear the application cache.

As we discussed earlier in the SSO architecture section, BizTalk Server adapters depend on the SSO credential database to store configuration data in a configstore affiliate application. Because adapters depend on the SSO infrastructure, they also require certain SSO infrastructure user privileges. For example, the BizTalk administrator responsible for the management of send and receive adapters must be a member of the SSO affiliate administrator group. The SSO system will automatically assign the BizTalk Server Administrators group as the application administrator for an adapter affiliate application when a BizTalk administrator creates a send port or receive location. The BizTalk Server host instance service account that the adapter runs in must also be a member of the SSO affiliate application users group for the adapter.

Managing Mappings

Mappings can contain information about credentials or application configuration data. Credential mappings usually provide a direct mapping of a Windows account to a non-Windows back-end application credential. An application configuration mapping maps a unique identifier to a piece of configuration data stored in the SSO configuration database.

When using credential mappings, you have the choice of two basic types of mappings: individual and group. In many circumstances you may want to limit user access to credential data, permitting individual users to modify only their credential mappings. In this case, you would want to employ individual mappings. Individual mappings provide a one-to-one mapping between a Windows user and back-end applications credentials. With this type of mapping, users can manage credentials only for their own mappings.

SSO group mappings, on the other hand, map a Windows group, containing multiple users to a single back-end application account. The downside to this type of mapping is that all members of the group now have access to the credential information for the group.

NOTE

You need to be an SSO administrator or SSO affiliate application administrator to create a group mapping.

You can create mappings using the ssomanage or ssoclient utilities. The `ssomanage -createmappings <filename>` command requires an XML file containing its configuration data. The example of a create mappings XML file is shown next:

```
<sso>
<mapping>
<windowsDomain>domain</windowsDomain>
<windowsUserId>WindowsUserName</windowsUserId>
<externalApplication>Application name1</externalApplication>
<externalUserId>App1UserName</externalUserId>
```

```
</mapping>
<mapping>
<windowsDomain>domain</windowsDomain>
<windowsUserId>WindowsUserName</windowsUserId>
<externalApplication>Application name2</externalApplication>
<externalUserId>App2UserName</externalUserId>
</mapping>
</sso>
```

After the mapping has been created, you must enable it and then set the credentials for the mapping. You can set the credentials using either `ssomanage -setcredentials <domain>\<username> <applicationname>` or the ssoclient utility. If any of the mapping details change, you must delete the mapping and create a new one.

You can perform the following mapping tasks using the ssomanage and ssoclient command-line utilities:

- List user mappings.
- Create user mappings.
- Delete user mappings.
- Set credentials for a user mapping.
- Enable a user mapping.
- Disable a user mapping.

A complete list of ssomanage and ssoclient command-line options is defined in the section titled "SSO Command-Line Utilities and APIs."

Using Tickets

Throughout this chapter we have skirted around a detailed description of the concept of "tickets" and why BizTalk Server 2004 employs them. So far you have learned that you must request a ticket and then redeem it when you want to retrieve the credential or configuration information stored in the SSO configuration database. But why do we need tickets? To better understand, let's walk through a scenario without tickets, using instead the authenticating user's credentials as the primary lookup key when retrieving data from the credential database.

In this scenario, we have a long-running business process that accesses multiple Windows and external non-Windows applications. When automating long-running business processes, it's usually very difficult to maintain the original requesting user's identity throughout the lifetime of the process. In these scenarios the processes are usually running under the context of a service id or a system logon. When this occurs, the initial user's identity is almost always lost or undeterminable, making it very difficult—if not impossible—to use it to define mappings in the BizTalk Server 2004 SSO configuration database. In this SSO scenario, the initiating user context is required to determine the mapped credentials.

To solve this credential mapping problem, SSO uses a ticketing scheme similar in concept but not the same as Kerberos tickets. SSO provides a service that issues an encrypted ticket to a valid user and then allows applications to redeem the ticket to obtain mapped credentials to an affiliate application. The ticket consists of an encrypted string that contains the Domain\UserId of the user, expiration time, and flags that determine the type of ticket that was issued.

NOTE

All tickets, by default, have a timeout of two minutes, which can be configured at the SSO system level by an SSO administrator.

After an application has a ticket, it can redeem it at any time to retrieve the securely stored mapped credentials or configuration data from the SSO credential database. Ticket redemption can occur in one of two ways using the redeem only method or the validate and redeem method.

A simple example of the ticketing process is shown in Figure 8.9.

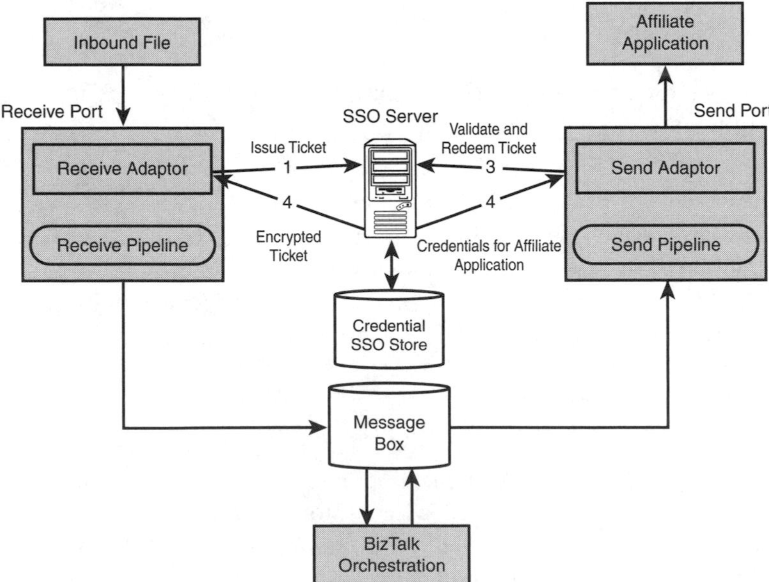

FIGURE 8.9 SSO ticketing.

In the example in Figure 8.9, a message is received through a BizTalk receive adapter. The receive adapter in this case is configured for SSO and therefore requests a ticket based on the Windows Domain\UserId of the user submitting the document from the SSO server. The ticket that's received is placed in the `SSOTicket` context property of the message and the message is placed on the BizTalk Server message box. An orchestration schedule that subscribes to this message picks it and begins to process it carefully, ensuring the ticket is placed in the outbound message if the original message has been modified. A send port then retrieves this message from the message box and makes a request to an SSO server to validate and redeem the ticket and the credentials for the mapped affiliate application.

SSO Caching

BizTalk Server 2004 SSO provides caching to help improve the performance of credential lookups on the SSO server. The first time a credential lookup is requested, SSO calls into the database to obtain the credentials and then stores them in the SSO cache. The next time a lookup is requested for the same credentials, the credentials are returned from the cache instead of the configuration database. If the credentials are not available, it then retrieves them from the SSO credential database. The default timeout for the cache is set to 60 minutes and is configurable at the SSO system level by an SSO administrator.

Integrating SharePoint SSO

SharePoint Portal Server (SPS) also provides SSO services. In fact, the architecture is conceptually very similar to BizTalk 2004's Enterprise SSO solution. Although the underlying code is somewhat different, they share a very similar ticketing and secure credential store implementation.

Today BizTalk Server 2004 supports SPS/SSO using the SOAP receive adapter. There are two basic SPS/SSO—BTS/SSO integration options:

- Use only BizTalk SSO services.
- Use BizTalk SSO and SPS/SSO services.

8

In a typical SPS BizTalk integration scenario, an SPS Web part would make a SOAP request to a BizTalk orchestration exposed as a Web service. This orchestration would then make calls to external applications as needed, returning a resultset to the Web part.

In the first scenario, SPS would rely on the BTS/SSO implementation of SSO. The Web part would send a SOAP request to a local or remote BizTalk Web service adapter. The Web service adapter needs to be configured to use SSO. To enable SSO on the Web service adapter, you must check the Enable SSO check box on the receive location properties during configuration. The Web services adapter would then request a ticket based on the original authenticated user placing it in the SSOTicket context property of the message. The Web services adapter also sets the OriginatorSID context property to the original authenticated user. To obtain a ticket, the Web services adapter impersonates the caller prior to making the call to the BTS/SSO service to get a ticket for the end user (Web client user).

For this scenario to work, you must either install the Web service adapter and BizTalk runtime on the same server as the SPS Web part or enable delegation. BizTalk adapters cannot be installed on a machine without the BizTalk runtime. Because the SOAP adapter is an out-of-process adapter, running in the context of an IIS process, you don't need a BizTalk service running on the SPS machine. You just need the BizTalk runtime pieces installed to enable the routing of messages to the message box.

Delegation, on the other hand, doesn't require the installation of the BizTalk runtime or SOAP adapter on the SPS server. It will pass the original authenticated user's credentials to the Web service. When the Web part calls the Web service adapter, the Web service adapter will receive an impersonation level token of the Windows user that originated the request on the SPS server. This will then allow the BTS/SSO service to issue the ticket for the originally authenticated user. When a send adapter, configured to use SSO, receives the request it will call the `ValidateAndRedeemTicket` SSO API method to redeem the ticket and obtain the external credentials from the BTS/SSO credential database. Credentials are retrieved from the SSO credential database if the validation succeeds. Validation is done by comparing the `OriginatorSID` and the user in the encrypted SSO ticket. This needs to match to succeed the validation. This validation is to ensure a trusted subsystem; that is, only trusted BizTalk hosts can be used for end-to-end SSO scenarios to work. In this scenario you need to manage only the BTS/SSO service and SSO credential database. A diagram of this scenario with delegation is shown in Figure 8.10. A diagram of this scenario with the BizTalk runtime installed on the SPS server is shown in Figure 8.11.

Using the second scenario, the Web part would utilize SPS SSO to obtain an SSO ticket for the authenticated user. This ticket would be placed in the SOAP header of the SOAP request that is sent to the BizTalk Web service adapter. To configure the Web service adapter for this scenario, you need to configure support for SPS SSO using the BizTalk Web Services Publishing Wizard. When you run the BizTalk Web Services Publishing Wizard, you will see a check box on one of the pages for using SharePoint Portal Server SSO. When this is checked, the Web service will expect an SSO ticket from an SPS Web part. The Web service adapter will then recognize the SPS/SSO ticket and place it in the SSOTicket context property of the message before it is placed on the message box. When the message is sent to a BizTalk send adapter, the adapter configured to support BTS/SSO will call the BTS/SSO `ValidateAndRedeemTicket` method. This method will evaluate the ticket and forward the redemption request to the SPS SSO service.

The biggest problem with this scenario is that you need to manage and configure both SPS/SSO and BizTalk Enterprise SSO. In this particular case, SPS/SSO must be installed on the BizTalk Server requesting the ticket redemption. The Web service adapter can live on either the SPS server or a remote server.

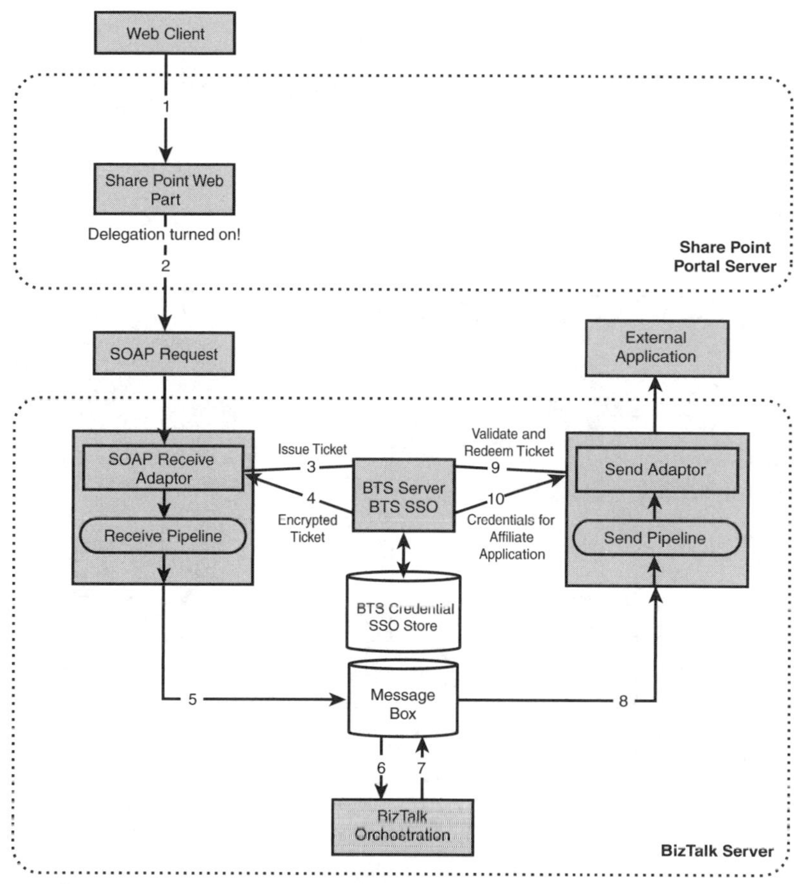

FIGURE 8.10 SPS integration without the BTS runtime on the SPS server.

TIP

The Windows 2003 platform supports constrained delegation.

At the time of the writing of this book, Microsoft was preparing to release an updated component that would allow BizTalk and SPS to reside on separate servers. The Microsoft SharePoint Single Sign-On component, when installed on a BizTalk Server, will allow this scenario to work without requiring the installation of SPS SSO on the BizTalk Server. The component is an NT service that redeems SPS SSO tickets from the SPS SSO database. It will come with a UI that will let you configure the SPS SSO server and database names. Figure 8.12 displays a diagram of this solution.

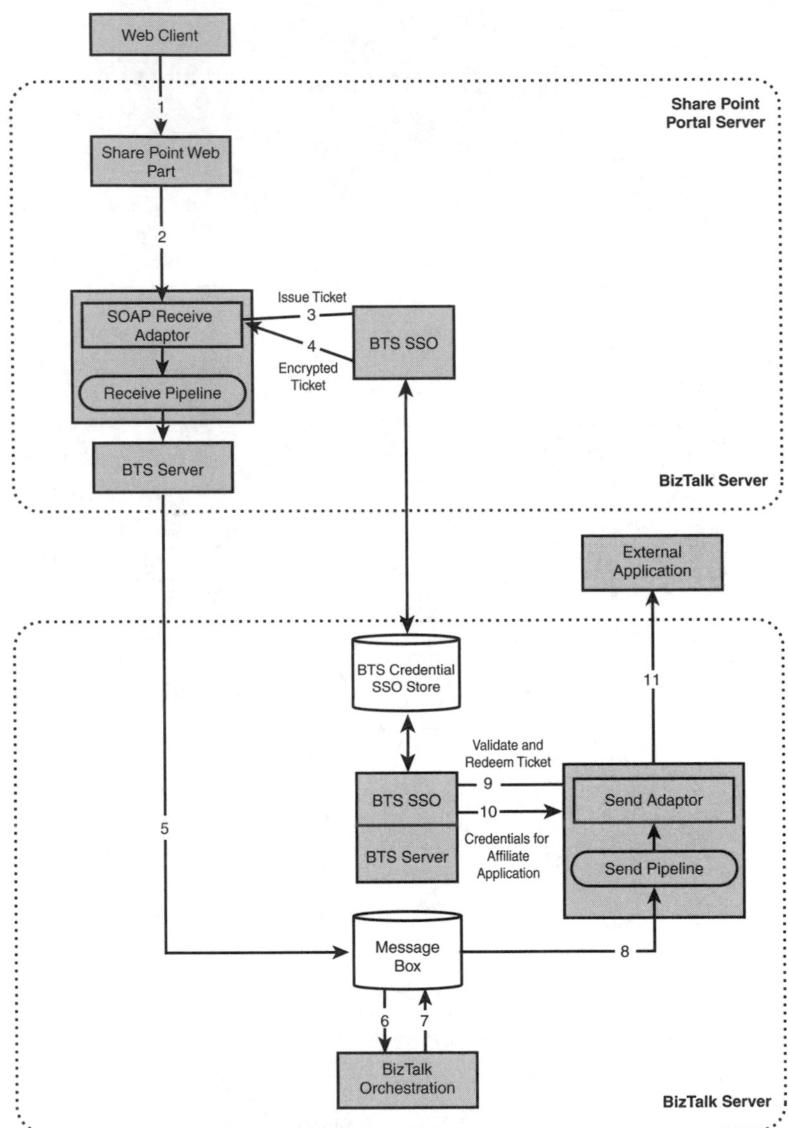

FIGURE 8.11 SPS integration with the BTS runtime.

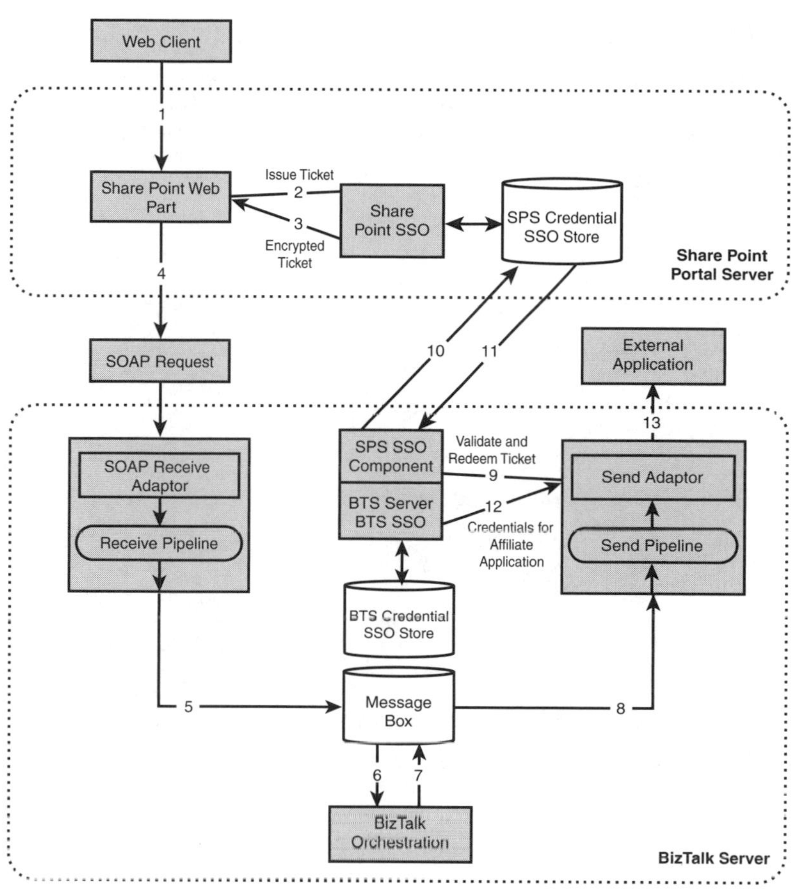

FIGURE 8.12 SPS integration using the SPS component on BTS server.

Summary

BizTalk Server 2004 Enterprise SSO provides a standalone service that allows administrators to map Windows users' accounts to multiple back-end applications that would normally expect credentials other then the user's Windows credentials. The credentials are stored and encrypted in a secure credential database and then retrieved though the issuance and redemption of encrypted tickets. These services can be deployed independently of BizTalk Server or seamlessly integrated with both BizTalk Messaging and Orchestration services. To configure SSO services, you are provided with both a command-line interface as well as a programmatic COM/.NET API.

NOTE

Future versions of BizTalk SSO will extend the current product to include the password synchronization feature that will be available in Host Integration Server 2004. The version of SSO that will ship with HIS 2004 will be completely compatible with BizTalk Server 2004 SSO.

PART III

Developing with BizTalk Server 2004 —Business Processes

IN THIS PART

CHAPTER 9
Introducing Orchestration

IN THIS CHAPTER

- Business Processes and Orchestration Defined
- Orchestration Designer
- Using .NET Components
- Deployment
- Sample Orchestration Solution
- Orchestration and BPEL

As powerful as BizTalk messaging is, orchestration is what defines BizTalk Server 2004 as a robust tool for enterprise-level development. Message exchanges are point-to-point interactions and BizTalk makes sure the details of those interactions are taken care of at the level of communications. Mission-critical systems, by contrast, are highly concerned with operations at a much higher level—the business process. They are all about process and procedure, flow, and business logic. No single message serves to capture this, so BizTalk messaging cannot be the answer all by itself.

Orchestration is the tool that addresses this issue. A business process is triggered or supported by messaging operations. The overall process, then, orchestrates—there's the origin of the name—a series of message exchanges. Of course, a real-life business process is seldom a straight-line flow of logic. There are decision points and error checking. The orchestration technology in BizTalk Server arms developers with the tools to model robust business processes, right down to error recovery, flow of control, and nested processes.

As you might imagine, orchestration is a very big topic. This chapter introduces you to the basics. It is a fuller treatment of the topics you were exposed to briefly in Chapter 2, "Your First BizTalk Server Integration." You will learn about the technology and concepts behind orchestration, and you will get a full tour of the Orchestration Designer tool in Visual Studio. You will learn how to use Orchestration Designer to model a business process and deploy the model in a form that can be executed by the orchestration engine. Although we will cover the full scope of orchestration in this chapter, we will delve only into the basics. Chapter 10, "Orchestrating Web Services and Correlation," takes a closer look at a new feature of orchestration in BizTalk Server 2004, orchestration and Web services, and Chapter 12, "Orchestrating—Advanced Concepts," rounds out our coverage of orchestration with discussion of more advanced topics. At the end of this chapter, we present a basic BizTalk orchestration solution. When you have completed it, you will be ready to implement your own orchestration solutions that are sufficient for the majority of problems addressed by current day BizTalk deployments.

Business Processes and Orchestration Defined

Any business application embodies some sort of logical sequence of operations that constitutes a complete business process. Monolithic applications, however, have several drawbacks for enterprise applications. They are inflexible—any change in the sequence requires recoding. Unless extensive effort has been put into documenting the application, it is opaque and requires programmers reading the code to discern the process. Monolithic applications are generally constructed from the top down, in one big effort. The best approach to an enterprise development project, conversely, is from the bottom up, solving small problems in a reusable way and then integrating them to form successively larger processes.

The state most organizations find themselves in today is one in which they have a well-defined business process, but a collection of isolated applications. The applications solve individual parts of the process and have been proven through years of operation. The goal is to automate the process without losing the investment in the legacy applications.

A SUPPLY CHAIN BUSINESS PROCESS

Consider a supply chain process. The process starts when an order arrives at a supplier. The purchaser's credit status must be checked with a financial application. The customer's pricing data is consulted to see whether any special terms are in effect. Next, the purchase order might be split up with some orders being forwarded to a subcontractor or remote warehouse for direct fulfillment. An inventory application is checked for the items that will be shipped from the supplier. If sufficient stock is available, inventory is updated, a warehousing application is notified to prepare a shipping manifest, and a bill is prepared for the customer. If any items are unavailable, a message is sent to the customer while the inventory data is updated to indicate a backorder status. Additional activities may be required to order parts from other suppliers and to schedule manufacturing activities.

A business process is a well-ordered sequence of operations, just like an application. There are well-defined inputs, entry points, and exit conditions. Transition from one operation to another obeys specific business rules. Although the process might be linear, it is more likely to involve branches and even loops. If applications implement specific operations or steps in the process, how might we connect them into a larger application without writing one large application?

Orchestration provides a solution using a loosely structured system model based on communicating actors. Each actor, whether an application or a business partner, performs a discrete unit of processing. The system as a whole is interested in the input to and output from the actor, but the internal workings of the actor are opaque to the rest of the system. Actors are integrated by passing messages that represent the state of the system or that convey an intention between actors. This works as a solution to our systems integration problem in several ways:

- Protection of investment—The legacy applications become actors in the system, with no need to have common code or technology.
- Scalability—Execution may proceed in parallel in some cases, and messages may often be queued to smooth spikes in the processing load.
- Fit with BizTalk messaging—Communicating state can take the form of passing messages through the messaging engine. With support for file and FTP transports, even very old applications can usually be fit into the BizTalk processing scheme.

An orchestration, then, is a coordinating layer above the messaging system. An orchestration does not perform major chunks of processing directly. Instead, it receives messages from some applications and sends messages to others. Any processing it does internally is primarily in support of messaging operations. The orchestration directs the activities of the applications. It incorporates the analyst's knowledge of the process, whereas the applications themselves know how to perform individual steps but do not understand the overall process. Without the applications, orchestration cannot work. With orchestration, the applications become more valuable because they have been integrated to implement an automated process that is faithful to the business rules and concepts of the organization.

NOTE

BizTalk Server did not always include integration. The original plans for the first version extended only to messaging. Feedback from marketing and Microsoft business partners indicated a need to include a business-process solution if the new product was to be competitive. The resulting orchestration engine is easily the most popular and important part of the product.

Developing a BizTalk integration involves business analysts and programmers. Analysts provide the model, drawing the basic flowchart that describes the business process. Rules governing the flow of processing through the model also are provided by the analyst. Programmers take over from there. They know the interfaces to the various programs that make up the steps in the process. They know what transports are available to move the data in and out of the applications, and they know the details of the network. An old, well-established application may be able to communicate only by reading and writing files to a known location on a batch basis. A more recent application, written with scalability, reliability, and mobile workers in mind, may be structured to support MSMQ. The analyst has no knowledge of these details and little interest in them. He or she may have only a general knowledge of the message and file structures involved in communicating with the applications. The programmers, for their part, are well versed in these details but do not have the business expertise to model the enterprise process. Orchestrations are designed so that the two groups can collaborate.

After an orchestration is in place, changes in the business process can be easily accommodated. The internal workings of the individual steps rarely change. Checking inventory or pricing items is important, but fairly simple. It is the overall sequence or the rules governing the flow of the process that change most often. An orchestration exposes this information in a visual model. Changing the process is usually a matter of moving processing steps or modifying rules. Analysts can perform this, and programmers can update transport configurations to reflect changes in the network. The orchestration is compiled—which is much less complicated than compiling a complex application—and deployed to the BizTalk Server group. The applications that have been integrated to form the process do not require recoding and compiling. Legacy applications can remain unchanged so long as the basic building blocks and message schemas of the business are unchanged.

Orchestration Designer

The tool for developing BizTalk orchestrations, as we saw in Chapter 2, is the Orchestration Designer. This is a graphical add-in to Visual Studio .NET that lets programmers and business analysts model processes and configure the messaging operations to implement them. Figure 9.1 depicts an orchestration under development with the major user-interface elements visible. The Visual Studio toolbox is on the left, with the BizTalk Orchestrations tab visible. The items visible in that tab are the shapes used to create orchestrations. Shapes from the toolbox are dragged onto the visual surface in the main part of the window. On closer inspection, you will note that the surface is actually composed of three surfaces. In the center is an untitled area known as the *Orchestration Surface*. This is where most of the shapes are dropped and where the logic of the process is modeled. It is flanked on either side by two port surfaces. Note that these may be collapsed to free up space in the window, as we have done with the port surface on the right. Clicking the circle with the double arrow expands and collapses the port surface.

The port surfaces are where we drop, not surprisingly, port shapes to define the interface between orchestration and messaging. These orchestration ports are the portals through which messages enter and leave the orchestration.

Closer inspection of the bottom part of the Visual Studio window reveals a few more items for our consideration. First, the Orchestration window has two tabs. The one that is visible is labeled Orchestration. This is the main view of the process. The tab next to it is marked Compensation. Certain orchestrations can be configured with a complementary process intended to reverse, or compensate for, the successfully completed actions of the main process in the event of an error higher in the call stack. If you click the Compensation tab, you see another window complete with port and orchestration surfaces. Compensations are constructed the same way we build the main process of an orchestration, by dragging shapes to construct a flow chart pattern.

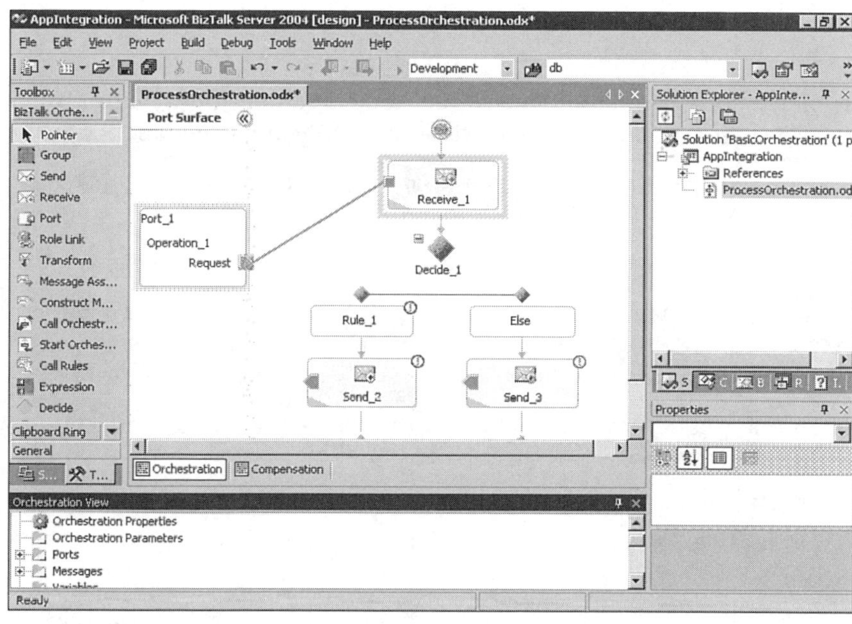

FIGURE 9.1 Orchestrations are developed using the various panes of the Orchestration Designer in Visual Studio.

Finally, at the bottom, where we normally expect to find the task list and output panes, you see the Orchestration view. For users of earlier versions of BizTalk, this fulfills the function of the Data view. This is a greatly enhanced version of that view, reflecting the increased feature set of orchestrations in BizTalk Server 2004. This view presents a tree whose nodes represent all the nonvisual items in an orchestration. This includes messages, ports, variables and parameters, the types declared in the orchestration, as well as other constructs we discuss in this and subsequent chapters.

Shapes

The shapes are the basic building blocks through which orchestrations are implemented. Each has a specific visual appearance that represents the item and resizes it as needed. As you add shapes to the flow chart, Orchestration Designer takes care of connecting them to the main flow. Some shapes require you to connect them, such as connecting send and receive shapes to ports for messaging. Smart shapes are new to orchestration shapes in this edition of BizTalk. As you can see in Figure 9.1, a shape that has not been completely configured displays a red exclamation mark in the upper-right corner. If you hover over the mark with the cursor, a box with a down arrow appears around the exclamation mark. Clicking that arrow displays a message summarizing which shape properties remain to be configured.

The shapes available for building orchestrations, listed in Table 9.1, may be loosely categorized as follows:

- Flow of control—Programming constructs that determine how control will be transferred between operations; these include conditional branches and loops.
- Messaging—Shapes that govern the passage of messages between applications and the orchestration.
- Data—Shapes that construct or transform messages or alter the data within them.
- Error handling—Shapes that extend transactional processing concepts from the database world to loosely coupled, long-running processes, or implement exception handling for orchestrations.
- Abstraction—Shapes that aid analysts in the construction of orchestrations by provided abstraction mechanisms.

TABLE 9.1 Shapes Available in the Orchestration Designer Toolbox

Shape Name	Purpose
Group	Combines selected shapes into a collapsible block for visual clarity.
Send	Sends an outbound message.
Receive	Receives an inbound message.
Port	Interface between the messaging system and orchestration; messages are sent and received through ports.
Role Link	Collects specified ports, allowing the orchestration to group several ports into a role that is played by a single logical partner. The link is between a BizTalk role for the orchestration and a BizTalk role for the external entity.
Transform	Performs message mapping.
Message Assignment	Used within the Construct message shape, this shape allows you to assign one message instance to another, assign message parts, or call a .NET class to create a message instance.
Construct Message	Composes a new message instance.
Call Orchestration	Makes a synchronous call to another orchestration.
Start Orchestration	Makes an asynchronous call to another orchestration.
Call Rules	Allows you to call a business policy using parameters from the orchestration (see Chapter 11).
Expression	Executes .NET expressions. This may be used to assign values to orchestration variables or call external code.
Decide	Implements a conditional branch in the flow of control.
Delay	Causes the orchestration to pause for a specified interval.
Listen	Introduces a conditional branch based on receipt of a message or expiration of a delay shape. The first branch condition satisfied causes the termination of the other branches and transfers the flow of control to the satisfied branch.

TABLE 9.1 Continued

Shape Name	Purpose
Parallel Actions	Allows operations to be executed in parallel.
Loop	Implements a while loop.
Scope	Specifies a boundary for transactions or exception handling.
Throw Exception	Throws an exception that may be caught within an enclosing scope or a calling orchestration.
Compensate	Explicitly invokes a compensation handler to reverse the effects of a completed transaction.
Suspend	Generates an error and halts orchestration execution without altering the state of the orchestration until an administrator intervenes and resumes processing of the orchestration.
Terminate	Terminates execution of the orchestration and generates an error.

Flow of Control

Because an orchestration is all about coordinating the activities of different applications, it stands to reason that orchestrations need shapes that govern how control (and by implication, messages and data) passes between calls to and from these applications. Some of these shapes are directly analogous to flow-of-control statements in programming languages. The Decide shape works like an if-elseif-else statement, and the Loop shape works like a while loop, for example. Others, such as Start Orchestration, Call Orchestration, and Listen are peculiar to BizTalk. Expression and Call Rules shapes, moreover, fall somewhere between this category and the Data category because they serve to introduce data and state information into the system by evaluating expressions or calling on the rule engine. However we sort shapes into our arbitrary categories, some shapes are necessary to control the flow of data through an orchestration. They start, stop, and organize orchestrations.

Let's start with an easy shape. The Decide shape works like an if-then-else expression, and its visual symbol is the diamond shape made popular by flowcharting. The shape introduces a conditional branch into the flow. When you drag a Decide shape onto the orchestration surface, each branch is connected to the flow line. Below the diamond-shaped symbol, the flow branches toward two shapes, one for a rule and one labeled Else. Below these shapes are labels indicating where you can drop additional shapes, and then the flows from each branch are joined together.

The shape for the rule has a smart tag attached to it signaling that you need to provide an expression for evaluation. This will be a snippet of code that evaluates to a logical true or false value. You provide this expression through the BizTalk Expression Editor, which will be discussed later in greater detail in the section "Rule Expression Basics." You can get to this dialog box in several ways: by clicking the smart tag, from the context menu for the rule shape, or by clicking the Expression property's value cell in the Property view.

As you might imagine, any shapes on the branch coming out of the Rule shape are executed if the expression evaluates true, whereas shapes following the Else shape execute if the expression is false. We can make the situation even more complicated. If you right-click the Decide shape diamond, you'll see that the context menu offers a New Rule Branch option. If you select that, a new rule shape and its associated branch appear. A Decide shape will evaluate its rules left to right until one evaluates to true, at which time control is transferred to that rule's branch. If all rules are false, the Else branch is executed.

Several other shapes use the Expression Editor, chief among them the Loop shape. This shape implements a while loop. You enter a Boolean expression using the Expression Editor. So long as that expression is true, the shapes dropped onto the loop's line of control are executed. When the expression is false, the loop terminates and execution passes to the shapes that follow the loop construct.

The Delay shape, as its name implies, causes the orchestration to wait for a given period (or more if the engine is under stress) before resuming execution. You might be surprised, however, to learn that this shape also takes an expression. Instead of a Boolean value, however, the expression used by a Delay shape must return `System.DateTime` or `System.TimeSpan` object. The use of expressions gives you more flexibility than specifying a fixed interval. You might, for example, get the delay interval value from a message field.

Listen shapes are a novel hybrid of the familiar Delay concept and the notion of waiting for receipt of a message. Like a Decide shape, a Listen shape has two or more branches. Instead of using an expression, however, the orchestration engine will wait until the condition on one of the branches is satisfied. Each branch contains either a Receive shape or a Delay shape. You can either drag one of these shapes to the Listen shape branch or click the Listen shape's smart tag and select a type, in which case the appropriate shape is added to the branch for you. No shapes may be dropped onto a branch before one of these shapes. A Receive branch will wait until a message of the type specified for the Receive shape is received. If no such message is received before the Delay shape interval expires, the actions on the Delay branch are executed. If a message is received in time, the Receive branch is executed. Like the Decide shape, a Listen shape can have more than two branches. Right-clicking the shape and selecting the New Listen Branch option creates a new branch.

The Parallel shape executes all its branches concurrently. Control does not leave the shape until all branches have completed their actions. Processing on all branches occurs concurrently. There is one exception to the normal operation of the Parallel shape. If a Terminate shape is encountered on a Parallel branch, the orchestration will terminate regardless of the status of the other branches. You must be very careful to specify actions so that all branches will complete or the entire orchestration will block. The usual problems of concurrent access to data (in this case, messages and orchestration variables) apply to the Parallel shape and are managed through synchronized scopes.

The Suspend and Terminate shapes are fairly drastic. If you have detected an unrecoverable error condition, you can call on the features offered by these shapes. Suspend halts execution without terminating the orchestration. You might, for example, have waited for receipt of a critical message. Without this message you cannot continue processing. Unfortunately, because of an unreliable legacy application or a loss of network connectivity, the message does not arrive before the expiration of a Listen shape. After expiration, a Decide shape is used to check for the existence of the message. If it is not found, you use a Suspend shape. An administrator will find the orchestration suspended by using the Health and Activity Tracking application and correct the problem. He may then resume the orchestration, at which time the orchestration resumes where it left off with all state information intact. A Terminate shape, in contrast, is fatal. It ends all processing and permanently halts the running instance of the orchestration. Both shapes take an expression whose return type is a string. The string is used as an error message displayed by the Health and Activity Tracking application.

The Expression shape is a sort of utility catchall. Like the Decide and Delay shapes, it uses the Expression Editor. Unlike those shapes, though, it is not looking for a single return type. Instead, the expression is more like a brief script to be run. You may execute .NET code and assign values to orchestration variables.

BEST PRACTICES FOR EXPRESSION SHAPES

The purpose of the Expression shape is to perform some processing that is best handled by procedural code and that does not implement the business process directly. For example, I have a component class that calculates the Julian date number for a given date. This is a useful way to perform date calculations. Rather than set this up as a Web service and call it via messaging, I can instantiate an instance of the component and call it via the Expression shape. The return value could be used to populate a field in a message, or I could use it in an orchestration variable to perform calculations or as the basis of a Decide shape expression. By contrast, I would not want to do extended business processing, such as accessing a database, to check a customer's credit terms. Although that would work, it would hide a key part of the business process, thereby sacrificing the transparency and ease of reconfiguration that are important benefits of orchestration.

The Call Rules shape is orchestration's gateway to the BizTalk rule processing engine, which is the topic of Chapter 11, "Developing Rules." For now, let's just say that business entities may be coded as .NET components. Rules are then constructed by a business analyst and grouped into policies using the Business Rule Composer. These policies codify business practices that are to be applied across the enterprise. We can make use of these policies in orchestration using the Call Rules shape. The alternative is to code the policies and rules directly into the orchestration as a series of shapes. This would be highly transparent, but ultimately self-defeating because we would have to repeat the construction time and time again in various orchestrations. You invoke the Call Rules Policy

Configuration dialog box by clicking the shape's smart tag. Within the dialog box, you select a deployed policy from a drop-down list and then specify parameterized values to pass to the policy. At runtime, the policy is executed using the parameters, resulting in side effects in components and the calling orchestration's variables. These changes can be used to guide Decision, Delay, and Listen shapes.

Nesting

Orchestrations may be nested by calling one orchestration from another using the Call Orchestration and Start Orchestration shapes. You can use these shapes either to reuse existing orchestrations or to modularize complex processes much in the manner that complicated programs are broken into functions and objects. Each orchestration can implement a specific process or subprocess. From the standpoint of the outer process, these nested processes are black boxes. You can get a high-level view of the complex process by looking at the outer orchestration and then diving down into the details by inspecting the called orchestrations.

Call Orchestration invokes the called orchestration synchronously. The called orchestration is said to be nested within the calling orchestration. The calling orchestration may optionally pass parameters to the nested orchestration. Because Call Orchestration is synchronous, you may not call an orchestration whose first shape is a Receive shape that is configured as activating the orchestration. Such a shape is designed to trigger an orchestration. If it were permitted to be callable, it would block the calling orchestration. In short, then, activation implicitly launches an orchestration in response to an event, whereas callable orchestrations are an explicit launch as part of another orchestration.

Start Orchestration is asynchronous. The shape launches a specified orchestration, optionally passing parameters to the started orchestration. In addition to the traditional uses of parameters in programming, these orchestration parameters might take the form of a port reference, identifying a port on a specific orchestration instance the started orchestration should call, or a correlation set. Correlation sets will be important when we discuss Web services and orchestration in Chapter 10. For now, it is sufficient to know that a correlation set is a collection of properties and their values that the orchestration engine may use to uniquely identify a specific instance of an orchestration.

Both Call Orchestration and Start Orchestration pass parameters to the called or started orchestration. You can configure parameters for an orchestration in the Orchestration view. You right-click the Orchestration Parameters node and select New Type Parameter options, in which Type is Message, Correlation Set, Variable, or some other parameter type. You then select the basic type of the parameter in the Properties view when the parameter is selected under the Orchestration Parameters node. After you have done this, the orchestration is associated with a series of one or more parameters, much in the way we pass parameters to a function or method.

After an orchestration has parameters, you can configure a Call or Start Orchestration shape using a configuration dialog box. The two dialog boxes are essentially the same, and the version for Start Orchestration is depicted in Figure 9.2. In each, you select an orchestration from a list of available orchestrations and then select variables from the current orchestration to pass as parameter values to the nested orchestration.

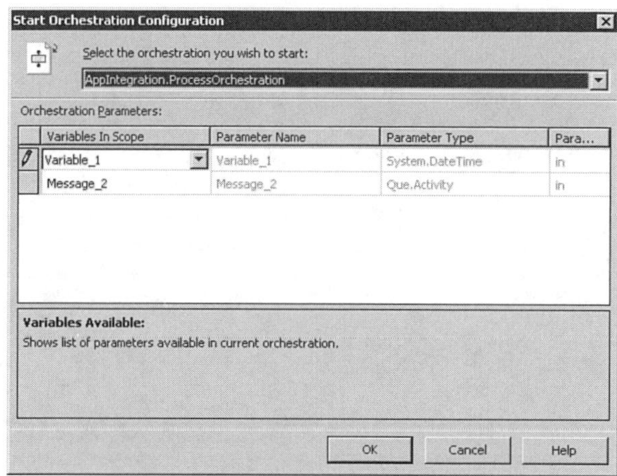

FIGURE 9.2 Parameters for a Start Configuration shape are specified in the configuration dialog box by selecting variables from the current orchestration to pass as parameters.

You have the greatest flexibility in selecting parameters when using Call Orchestration. Because the nested call is synchronous, parameters may have the direction of the parameters typed as In, Out, or Reference. You may pass in data by copy (In), receive results by copy (Out), or pass a variable by reference for direct manipulation. Parameters passed via Start Orchestration must be In types only. If you want to get results back from the started orchestration, you will need to have the started orchestration call a port or send a message using a correlation set. The direction of a parameter is read-only in the configuration dialog box. It is set in the Properties view when the parameter is defined in the called or started orchestration using the Orchestration Parameters node in the Orchestration view.

Rule Expression Basics

Many shapes, as we have seen, require expressions. Most use single expressions to determine what to do next (Decide, Loop) or how long to do something (Delay). The Expression shape must be configured with a lengthy expression that specifies some procedural processing you want performed. The language syntax is quite similar to C#. What sorts of things can you reference in your code? If you reference a .NET assembly in your orchestration project, you may call on an object that can be instantiated from those packages. In Figure 9.3, for example, the expression assumes an object named Customer that has a method for obtaining the customer's credit line. You can also reference any parameters or variables established through the Orchestration view for the orchestration, and you can reference the promoted properties and distinguished fields of any messages in the orchestration. The left side of the expression in Figure 9.3 presumes a purchase order message in which the TotalPrice property has been promoted.

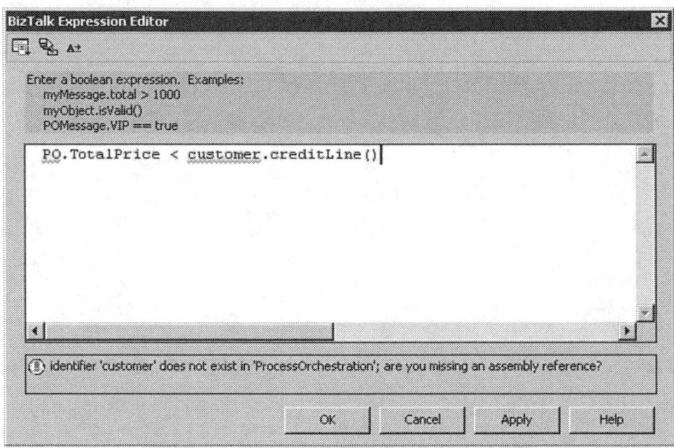

FIGURE 9.3 Using the Expression Editor with .NET classes

The Expression Editor also uses IntelliSense. Red squiggles appear under the names in the expression in Figure 9.3 because neither purchase order nor customer has been declared yet. We'll discuss how to work with messages and .NET classes a little later in this chapter. The usual IntelliSense word completion and parameter information mechanisms you have in a source code window in Visual Studio are available in the editor dialog box, as well.

Transaction Basics

Programming languages over the years have developed, refined, and used the concepts of transactions and exception handling as mechanisms for guaranteeing the integrity of data when several operations need to be performed. The classic example is transferring money from one bank account to another. The process requires a debit from the losing account and a credit to the gaining account. To maintain the integrity of the accounts, either both operations must complete successfully or neither must complete. Classic, database-style transactions provide us with a way to roll back the individual operations when a failure is detected.

This is relatively easy to do within a single database because the database engine controls all the resources. The Windows Distributed Transaction Coordinator (DTC) extended this concept to COM+ applications. As long as all the participants in a transaction controlled by the DTC exposed certain interfaces, the DTC could use those interfaces to roll back a transaction. The DTC monitored the progress of the operations and called on the participating components to commit or roll back operations as necessary.

BizTalk orchestration is much more loosely coupled than relational or DTC-style processing. Rather than taking place over a period of seconds on a single machine or within a small network, BizTalk processing may occur over hours or days across the public Internet as integrated business partners perform different tasks.

Transaction Types

To provide transactional integrity to orchestrations, BizTalk offers two kinds of transactions: atomic and long-running. Atomic transactions are very similar to DTC transactions—in fact, if you restrict yourself to DTC-compatible components, the atomic transaction will be a DTC transaction. Regardless, atomic transactions are guaranteed by BizTalk to preserve the four classic transactional properties: atomicity, consistency, isolation, and durability. Although you can obtain a full explanation of these properties from any database text, the short form for our purposes is that any changes to an orchestration's state—variables, messages, parameters, and objects—will not be visible outside the transaction until the transaction is committed.

Long-running transactions, by contrast, offer less rigorous protection but are better suited to operations that span business partners. If you are relying on action taken in response to a message sent to a remote partner, some of the resources involved are not under your control, and the duration of the transaction is likely to be long. Whereas an atomic transaction, particularly a DTC-style transaction, can control resources and tightly control the visibility of data modified within the transaction, a long-running transaction cannot offer the same protection, because it is has no control over the resources or cannot afford to maintain a lock on resources for the duration of the transaction.

The advanced details of transactions will be covered in Chapter 12. Following, however, are the basic mechanics of working with transactions in orchestration. A scope shape is used to define the boundaries of a transaction. You may set the transaction property of a scope shape to None, Atomic, or Long-Running. When you select either of the latter, a transaction begins when control enters the shape and ends when control leaves the scope. Transactions end when all actions are complete, if an exception occurs during the transaction, when a transactional component fails during a DTC-style atomic transaction, or when a long-running transaction exceeds its timeout interval.

Compensations and Exceptions

Two control blocks are associated with scopes. If you configure the Compensation property of a scope to be Custom, a compensate block is created. If you right-click a scope and select New Exception Handler, an exception block is created. A scope can have only one compensate block, but many exception blocks. The key to understanding the two is to realize how they are called. A custom compensate block will execute whenever the scope finishes its actions or when it is explicitly called from a Compensate shape in another scope. The idea of a compensate block is to manually design the actions needed to undo the activities that took place in the body of the transaction. Whereas a database or the DTC can perform automatic rollback to maintain the integrity of its resources, the compensate block provides you with the opportunity to provide the same service, though you must work out the implementation yourself. The block will be executed only if you explicitly call it from an outer scope, and the nested scope to which the compensation applies has completed successfully. Suppose you have a scope that inserts a row into a database table nested inside another scope. The nested scope completes successfully. Following completion of that scope, a send message shape in the outer scope fails to send a message to a partner. The outer scope may compensate by deleting the newly inserted row. If, instead of inserting data into a table, the inner scope had sent a message placing an order, the appropriate action in the nested scope's compensation block would be to send another message canceling the order.

Exception blocks, by contrast, are called only when an exception occurs. They work like the catch blocks in a try-catch-finally construction in .NET. Each block is associated with an exception type. The runtime compares the block type against the thrown exception and executes the block that matches types.

Scope Synchronization and Nesting

Scopes may be synchronized. This is useful when two or more branches of a Parallel shape will be working with shared data. By synchronizing a scope, you direct the runtime to obtain a lock on any data that must be manipulated within the scope. This prevents one scope from writing to a variable while another is reading it, or prevents two scopes from writing to the same message or variable at the same time. Care must be exercised, however, to avoid a deadlock condition. This occurs when two scopes require locks on the same resources. Each obtains locks on some resources, but cannot complete because the other holds locks on resources it needs.

Scopes, like orchestrations, may be nested. There are a few rules, though. Synchronized scopes cannot contain other scopes, nor can atomic transactions contain other scopes. Transactional scopes cannot be nested within nontransactional scopes. When nesting is used, there are important rules regarding how compensation and exception handling blocks are invoked. We will explore this in greater depth in Chapter 12.

Messages

Messages are the fundamental elements of communication in orchestration, just as they are in BizTalk messaging. Messages in orchestration are treated as chunks of data that flow into, through, and out of an orchestration. Like all other orchestration variables, messages are typed.

There are a variety of ways to type a message. If you create a message in the Orchestration view, you can select a type for it in the Properties view. You can select from schemas, .NET classes (whose use we discuss fully in the "Using .NET Components" section that follows), any existing multipart message types, or any Web service request types. If you are planning ahead and creating the type before the message instance, you can expand the Types node in the Orchestration view, right-click the Multipart Message Types node and select

New Multipart Message Type from the context menu. A new message type node is created with a single message part node. You type the message part by selecting its node and then configuring its Type property in the properties pane by selecting a .NET class or schema. You can add a new message part by right-clicking the node for the multipart type and selecting New Message Part.

Multipart message types also have a Type Modifier property that defines the scope of the type. The values for this property are the following:

- Private—The type is restricted to orchestrations in the same namespace.
- Internal—The type is accessible to other orchestrations in the same project.
- Public—The type is visible to any orchestration interacting with the declaring orchestration.

Messages are built in the Construct Message shape. This shape contains one or more Transform Message or Message Assignment shapes. A very simple orchestration, such as we saw in Chapter 2, creates messages simply by applying a mapping to a message it has received. This is done with the Transform Message shape. More complicated orchestrations may need to construct a new message instance entirely from scratch or may need to directly manipulate some field values in an existing message. That is the purpose of the Message Assignment shape. Message Assignment shapes also provide a positive signal to the compiler regarding what messages are constructed at what points in the orchestration. This allows the compiler to catch such errors as trying to send a message before it is built. We will explore the use of this shape to create messages from .NET classes in the "Using .NET Components" section later in this chapter. If you have an existing message—for example, one that you received through a port—you may read and write the values of any distinguished fields. This allows your business process to override values and calculate new ones based on accessing Web services or applying business rule policies. The Message Assignment shape is configured with an expression using the BizTalk Expression Editor we described earlier.

Ports

Because orchestrations involve the coordination of different applications through the exchange of messages, we need a way to get messages in and out of orchestrations. This is where ports come in. Ports are the interface between the messaging system and the orchestration engine. By configuring them, we tell the orchestration what is passing in or out of the process, where it is going, and what the pattern of communication looks like.

Ports, like messages, are typed. The discussion of port types as they relate to ports can be a little confusing. Ports have a type, a communication direction, and a binding. Port types consist of a communication pattern, and a set of operations with a message type. There are only two communication patterns: request-response and one-way. Each operation is a request (one-way pattern) or a request-response pair (request-response pattern). Each request or response is given a message type. Port types also have a Type Modifier property to control the scope of the type. The values and meanings for this property are identical to those listed previously for messages. Note that the port type says nothing about the direction of messaging or the address of the messages sent and received.

When you place a port on one of the port surfaces, you select the direction by selecting a Send or Receive for the port's Communication Direction property. Visually, the port is a rounded rectangle containing a rectangle for each operation defined for the port type. These operations have connection points that may be connected to Send and Receive shapes on the orchestration surface. If you double-click a Port shape, you invoke the Port Configuration Wizard. You may also right-click on the port surface and select Add Configured Port. The Port Configuration Wizard lets you configure a new port and its port type over the course of several dialog boxes. In addition, you may specify the binding for the port, the one item of configuration we have not yet discussed.

Business analysts work with programmers to devise orchestrations that faithfully model and implement a business process. Orchestrations are deployed to servers to execute that process. Because it might be nice to implement such processes throughout an organization, ports are designed with a level of abstraction built in. If you know all the details of transport and address for a port, you can configure the binding through the Port Configuration Wizard at design time. If, however, you are going to use the orchestration in multiple places, you can defer this specification until later. All you have to do is tell BizTalk at design time what sort of binding you are going to use:

- Direct—A type of binding we discuss in Chapter 12 that bypasses the messaging system to communicate between two orchestrations running on the same server.
- Specify Later—Used when you want the administrator deploying the orchestration to complete the binding.
- Specify Now—When you know all the binding details at design time.

Although it is not part of port configuration, there is an additional useful bit of information to know. When a Receive shape is the first shape in an orchestration, you have the option of setting its Activate property to true. In that case, the arrival of a message at the port feeding that shape will cause the runtime engine to load and run a new instance of the orchestration.

TIP

This is an architectural pattern that I like to use because it makes my orchestrations simple and event driven. Orchestrations set up this way do not reside in memory-consuming resources until I need them.

Using .NET Components

You can use .NET components in orchestrations in several ways. Earlier versions of BizTalk included calls to COM components as a messaging protocol for orchestration ports. This is no longer necessary in the current version. You can create and use any .NET class referenced in the project in expressions. Expressions are used in quite a few shapes, so this feature brings .NET components right into the flow of an orchestration. It also requires much less configuration than it took to configure a COM port in older versions of orchestration.

You can instantiate a .NET object in an orchestration in several ways. If you create a variable in the Orchestration view and give it a .NET type, you may be able to instantiate it right there. If the class has a default constructor, you can set the Use Default Constructor property to true. The object will be instantiated by calling the default constructor. If you do not set this property that way, you must call a constructor using the new operator somewhere in an expression in the orchestration.

BizTalk Server 2004 introduces a new feature that makes standard practice out of a useful technique developed by programmers in earlier versions. This involves the creation of messages in an orchestration. If a message is received by an orchestration, you can set its distinguished properties and send it through a port. This modifies a message but does not create a new one. If you need a completely new message, the easiest way is to use a Transform shape. But what if you need a wholly new message—one that is not simply a transformation of an equivalent message received by the orchestration?

In earlier versions, we created a string variable whose value was a message template, and then set its fields in the Data view. That view has been replaced by expressions and the Construct Message shape. The documentation for the current version of BizTalk Server shows a similar technique in which the template is stored on disk and loaded by a .NET component in a Construct Message shape. This is largely an adaptation of the earlier technique, however, and it is hardly elegant.

A key feature of the .NET Framework, however, is serialization of objects to and from XML documents. The default shape of the document is governed by the property names and types, but it is possible to override this using attributes. Regardless of the details, though, serialization gives us a way to generate XML documents without resorting to XML APIs, and XML documents are a key message format in BizTalk. With this realization, it is no great leap to making it possible for .NET serializable classes to create BizTalk messages with distinguished fields.

You must do two things to take advantage of this. The first is to adorn your class with the Serializable attribute. The second is to include a reference to the Microsoft.XLANGs.BaseTypes package. That package gives you access to a host of attributes, one of which is `DistinguishedFieldAttribute`. A class property adorned with that attribute is promoted when serialized into a message in orchestration. The orchestration itself gets a reference to your class. From there, you create a message type in the

Orchestration view. In a Construct Message shape, you add a Message Assignment shape and configure it by writing an expression that instantiates a new instance of your class and assigns it to the message variable. You are then free to set the distinguished fields. When the class is serialized, the result is a new message instance you can send whose fields you set in the Message Assignment expression. We'll make use of this elegant technique in the chapter sample.

Deployment

After you have successfully built an orchestration solution, it is time to deploy it. If you are deploying this as part of development and testing, you can select the Deploy Solution item from Visual Studio's Build menu. An administrator deploying a finished assembly to his BizTalk Server group would use the BizTalk Deployment Wizard as described in Chapter 2. Either way, there are a few steps to keep in mind.

Deployment puts the assemblies for the solution into the global cache and the BizTalk configuration database. Before you can run an orchestration, you must complete the binding process and enlist the orchestration into a host.

If you specified your port binding at design time, no further configuration of ports is needed. Any required physical ports will be created for you during deployment. If, however, you deferred binding until deployment, you need to configure physical ports that mirror the logical ports you configured in the orchestration. After you have done this, open the BizTalk Administration Console application and locate the orchestration. Right-click it in the right pane and select Bind from the context menu. If all ports were bound at design time, no further intervention is necessary. If port binding was deferred, you will be given the opportunity to select the physical port to associate with the logical port or ports.

After the orchestration is bound, right-click its entry again and select Enlist. The Orchestration Enlistment Wizard appears. You select a host on the Select Host page and proceed through the rest of the wizard. When you are ready to begin processing, right-click the orchestration's entry one more time and select Start Processing. If the host is running, you are ready to test and run your orchestration.

Sample Orchestration Solution

We'll construct a simplified purchasing process orchestration for our chapter sample. We specifically want to accept a purchase order, check the customer's credit line, and approve the order if the cost is covered by the credit line. If approved, we need to send a message to manufacturing to schedule the order. Regardless of the credit decision, we also have to pass a message back to the customer indicating the status of the order.

Although this is a greatly simplified view of an actual purchasing chain, it gives us a chance to demonstrate a number of the techniques presented in this chapter. A Decision shape will be in there to direct execution down one of two paths based on the credit line. Because the credit check is a potentially complex process—with varying credit lines depending on who is approving the purchase order, conditional discounts, and checks against pending orders—we want to segregate that logic in a parameterized orchestration of its own and call it from the main purchasing orchestration. Because message assembly has changed somewhat in this version of BizTalk, we also want to exercise that feature to some extent. We'll insert a status message into the original purchase order for return to the sender, and we'll use a .NET component to generate the message to manufacturing. This gives the IT people in manufacturing the chance to offer their own component interface to the rest of the organization. The component could contain various business rules or utility code, but we will focus on its capability to create an XML message and serialize it for BizTalk.

To begin, create the file folder structure for messaging. You can establish anything you want so long as there are three separate folders, but the sample presumes a folder off the root named `BasicOrchestrationsMsgs`, with child folders `POIn`, `POOut`, and `PlaceOrders`. Now create a new BizTalk project and name it **`BasicOrchestration`**. The orchestrations and the message schema will go in the initial solution, named `OrderSystem`. Later, we'll add another project for a component to handle the manufacturing order placement message.

Messages

Because we're programmers, not purchasing specialists, we'll use a very simple schema for our purchase order. It should have enough information to identify the customer, a single item for purchase along with a price, and a status line. Listing 9.1 depicts a sample purchase order.

LISTING 9.1 Sample Purchase Order Message

```
<ns0:PO xmlns:ns0="http://OrderSystem.BasicPO">
  <OrderNumber>3456</OrderNumber>
  <ItemNo>12345</ItemNo>
  <CustID>M1911</CustID>
  <Qty>10</Qty>
  <Price>10500</Price>
  <Status>Requested</Status>
</ns0:PO>
```

By now you should have no difficulty creating a schema for this message. Everything is a string type with the exception of `Qty`, which is an `xs:int`, and `Price`, which is typed as `xs:decimal`.

We do need all the fields to be visible within an orchestration, however. `CustID` and `Price` will be needed as parameters for the credit check, and we'll need all the fields to compose the acknowledgement and the manufacturing order message. In Chapter 6, "Receiving and Sending Messages," we used a property schema to promote fields, but that leads to an interesting, collection-oriented syntax in orchestration expressions—for example, `Message(Field)`, whereas a `Message.Field` syntax is more familiar to programmers. To get this, we use distinguished fields. This has the happy side effect of eliminating the need for a property schema. We can get away with this because we are not using the fields to perform message routing. Only promoted fields can be used for that purpose. In the schema editor, select one of the fields you want to promote, right-click, and select Promote Show Promotions from the context menu. Make sure the Distinguished Fields tab is selected. Click Add for each field in the schema and ensure the fields are added to the list of distinguished fields, then click OK. The field nodes will be decorated with the icon indicating a distinguished or promoted field. Save this schema as `BasicPO.xsd`.

Manufacturing orders have a good deal of overlap with purchase orders, as you might expect. Listing 9.2 shows a sample order. There are differences, of course. Manufacturing, at least in our plant, doesn't care about the ultimate customer. They need the order number and the item ID and quantity, but they don't care about the customer's cost. They do, however, care about the date of order placement because they are evaluated on their average time to fulfill an order.

LISTING 9.2 Sample Order Placement Message for Manufacturing

```
<MfgOrder xmlns:xsd="http://www.w3.org/2001/XMLSchema"
➥xmlns:xsi="http://www.w3.org/2001/XMLSchema-instance">
  <OrderID>3456</OrderID>
  <Qty>10</Qty>
  <DatePlaced>2004-01-26T22:43:27</DatePlaced>
  <ItemNo>12345</ItemNo>
</MfgOrder>
```

Because we are planning to produce this message exclusively through .NET serialization, we do not need a BizTalk message schema. Orchestration Designer will use reflection to examine the component library and determine its distinguished fields. Because we can't do much without messages, let's put the orchestration project on hold for a moment and implement our manufacturing component.

Manufacturing Component

At this time you need to go to the Solution Explorer and add a new project to the `BasicOrchestration` solution. The type is a C# Component Library. Name it **`Manufacturing`** and rename the created source code file **`Order.cs`**. For BizTalk to work with the component, it needs a strong name and eventual transfer to the global cache. Follow the procedure we've used before to create a keyfile, **`keyfile.snk`** in the BasicOrchestration folder, and then modify the `AssemblyInfo.cs` file to reflect the name and location of that file.

LISTING 9.1 Continued

`Order.cs` is shown in its entirety in Listing 9.3. We are interested only in the capability to serialize a message, so there are no business rules, no utility code, and all properties are public and without accessor functions. We have implemented a constructor that sets the order placement date to the current system date and time and sets a default quantity of one.

LISTING 9.3 Source Code for the Manufacturing Component

```
using System;
using Microsoft.XLANGs.BaseTypes;

namespace Manufacturing
{
 [Serializable]
  public class MfgOrder
  {
   public MfgOrder()
        {
     DateTime dtNow;
     dtNow = DateTime.Now;
     DatePlaced = dtNow.ToString("s");
     Qty = 1;
        }

   [DistinguishedFieldAttribute]
     public String OrderID;
   [DistinguishedFieldAttribute]
     public int Qty;
   [DistinguishedFieldAttribute]
     public String DatePlaced;
   [DistinguishedFieldAttribute]
     public String ItemNo;
  }
}
```

There are four important points to notice in this listing:

- Namespace and class name—BizTalk will reference this component as `Manufacturing.MfgOrder`.
- References—The `System` Package gives us basic component behavior, and `Microsoft.XLANGs.BaseTypes` gives us access to the specialized attribute needed for promoting our properties.

- `Serializable` attribute—This is the standard .NET Framework attribute that enables serializing this class as an XML message. All structure and element names are generated from the names and organization in the source code by the Framework.
- `DistinguishedFieldAttribute`—This attribute causes our properties to be emitted as distinguished fields in the `MfgOrder` message so that we will have access to them in the orchestration.

Go ahead and build this component now. BizTalk deployment won't push this component to the global cache for us, so go to a Visual Studio command line and use the command `gacutil -i manufacturing.dll` to place the component assembly in the global cache. Then go to the OrderSystem project and add a reference to this assembly so that we can use it as a type in our orchestration.

Orchestrations

Now we can go back to building orchestrations. Because we've broken off the credit check function into a separate orchestration called from the main process, let's begin with that. This task could be quite complicated. In fact, it is a prime candidate for a policy such as we discuss in Chapter 11. Our purpose in this chapter, however, is simply to demonstrate how orchestrations can be nested, at least at an elementary level. Consequently, this orchestration will be a stub. It will set a flat credit limit of $50,000 for everyone.

Add a new orchestration to the OrderSystem project and name it **`CreditCheck.odx`**. In the Properties view, set the Namespace to **`OrderSystem`** and the Typename to **`CreditCheck`**. The first step is to establish the parameters that this orchestration accepts. One of the examples in the BizTalk SDK takes a message as the input parameter, and it would be easy enough to pass in the entire purchase order. This would limit the utility of the credit check orchestration by tying it to one particular message type, however. Instead, we'll use two variable parameters. These would be a customer ID as an in parameter and a credit amount as an out parameter for return to the calling orchestration. Select the Orchestration Parameters node in the Orchestration view, right-click it, and select New Variable Parameter. A new variable is added to the tree. Select this node and then go to the properties pane. Change the name to `CustID`, verify that the Direction is `In`, and select `System.String` as the type. Repeat the process to create a variable parameter named `CreditLimit`, whose Direction property is `Out` and whose type is `System.Decimal`.

Now drag an Expression shape onto the design surface. Double-click it to expose the Expression Editor. Enter the expression `CreditLimit = 50000;` and then name the shape `GetCreditLimit` in the Properties view. That's the entire orchestration.

> **NOTE**
>
> Notice that there is absolutely no messaging passing. This orchestration is useful only when it is called from some other orchestration.

That orchestration is the heart of this sample. Add a new orchestration item to the project, naming it `AcceptPO.odx`. In the Properties view, set the Namespace Property to **`OrderSystem`** and the Typename to **`ProcessOrchestration`**.

> **NOTE**
>
> I like to work in a top-down approach, so we'll begin by setting up the messages and variables for this orchestration.

We will work with three messages: an incoming purchase order, a purchase order passed back out to the customer, and a manufacturing order message sent out to the manufacturing operation. Right-click the Messages node in the Orchestration view and select New Message. Select the node that is created in response and turn to the Properties view. Enter `POIn` as the Identifier property and then click the value of the Message Type property and open the drop-down list. Expand the Schemas node and select `OrderSystem.BasicPO` to type this message as a purchase order according to the schema we created. Repeat the process to create another Message variable, named `POAck`, of the same type.

Now create a new message variable named `MfgOrder`. We don't have a schema for this. Instead, in the Type list box, expand the .NET Classes node, and then click the entry labeled <Select from Referenced Assembly>. The Select Artifact Type dialog box will appear as shown in Figure 9.4. Find the node for the Manufacturing assembly near the top of the References list. When you expand it, select the Manufacturing package. The type `MfgOrder` will appear in the grid on the right. Select it and click OK. This types the message variable as `Manufacturing.MfgOrder`, but does nothing to create or otherwise initialize the message variable.

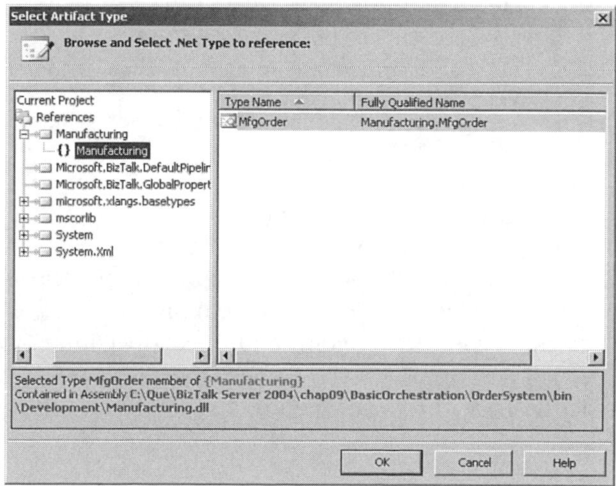

FIGURE 9.4 Typing a message using a .NET class.

Now we need two variables. These will be used to pass in the customer ID and accept the credit limit from the credit check orchestration. Although these will be taken from the incoming purchase order message, Orchestration Designer will not offer distinguished fields as options when configuring a Call Orchestration shape. Instead, we will create appropriate variables and assign the customer ID value after we have a message. Right-click the Variables node in Orchestration view and select New Variable. Select the newly created variable node and go to the Properties view. Give the variable the Identifier `cust_id` and the type `System.String`. Repeat the process for a variable named `credit_limit` typed as `System.Decimal`.

Now we can begin to design the process flow in earnest. Drop a Receive shape onto the design surface immediately below the Start shape. Name it **`ReceivePO`** and ensure the Activate property is set to `True`. This allows the messaging system to direct the runtime engine to launch a new instance of this orchestration when a purchase order message arrives. In the drop-down list for the Message property, select `POIn`.

Now drag a Port shape onto the Port Surface to the left of the new Receive shape. Use the Port Wizard to set the properties listed in Table 9.2.

TABLE 9.2 Receive Port Settings

Property Name	Setting
Name	RecvPOPort
Create New Port Type	Create now
Communication Pattern	One-way
Access	Internal
Port Type	OrderSystem.POPortType
Port Binding	Specify Now
Transport	File
URI	C:\BasicOrchestrationMsgs\POIn*.xml (or whatever other location you created on your local drive)
Receive Pipeline	XMLReceive

Go to the Orchestration view. Find the POPortType node in the Port Types node in the Types area. Expand it and select the Operation node that appears under it. In the Properties view, rename it `ListenForOrders`. Select the Request node under `ListenForOrders`, then return to the Properties view and select `OrderSystem.BasicPO` as the Message Type property's value. Now return to the design surface and drag a connection between this operation's connection point and the connection point for the Receive shape. We've established a port by which the orchestration is launched and through which a purchase order message enters our orchestration. This also initializes the `POIn` variable.

Calling the CreditCheck Orchestration

Now we need to get ready to call the credit check orchestration. First we'll set up the parameters. Add an Expression shape directly beneath the Receive shape and name it `SetParms`. Use the Expression Editor to enter the expression **`cust_id = POIn.CustID;`**, which sets up the In parameter. Now drag a Call Orchestration shape to the flow beneath the Expression shape. In the Properties view, give it the Identifier `CallCreditCheck` and the Name `CallCreditCheckOrch`. Double-click the shape to open the Call Orchestration Configuration dialog box. The `OrderSystem.CreditCheck` orchestration should be selected, with `cust_id` and `credit_limit` as the parameters. These selections are correct simply because we have only one other orchestration in the project and the only variables we have happen to match the types of the parameters for that orchestration. If we had more options from which to choose, you'd have to make some selections. Click OK to accept the defaults.

Assembling Messages

When this shape returns control to the `AcceptPO` orchestration, `credit_limit` will be initialized with the value passed back from `CreditCheck.odx`. We can use this to branch the flow, with one branch handling the case in which the purchase order is approved and the other handling the rejection. Drag a Decide shape onto the surface and name it `CanPay`. Select the Rule shape that appears on the left and give it the name **`CreditSufficient`**. Use the Expression Editor to enter **`POIn.Price <= credit_limit`**. Note that there is no semicolon at the end of the expression. The orchestration is beginning to look like Figure 9.5.

This side of the branch is where the purchase order is approved. We need to set up an outgoing purchase order message with an approval string in the Status field and create a `MfgOrder` message using the component. To begin, drag a Construct Message shape onto the branch. This is shown in collapsed form in Figure 9.5 as `ReplyAccepted`. Drag a Message Assignment shape into it. Give it the name **`SetStatusOK`** and enter the code shown in Listing 9.4.

LISTING 9.4 Message Assignment Expressions for Approving a Purchase Order

```
POAck = POIn;
POAck.Status = "Accepted";
```

The first line initializes our outgoing message with all the values from the purchase order we received. The second line overrides the Status field with the literal value we use to denote acceptance.

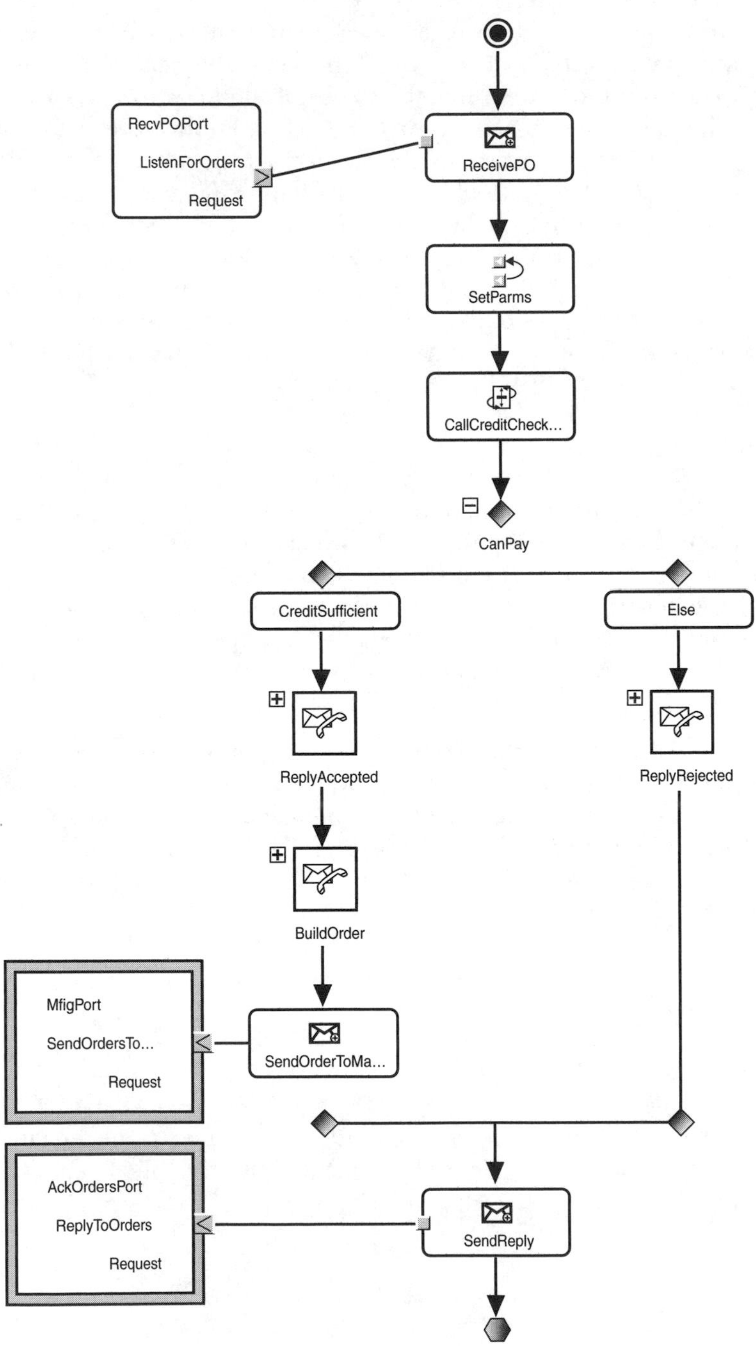

FIGURE 9.5 AcceptOrder process flow.

Now add another Construct Message shape, name it **BuildOrder**, and add a Message Assignment shape inside. Add the code from Listing 9.5. Note how we call the constructor to create a new object and then set the various fields based on what we received in the purchase order. We can bypass the DatePlaced field because the constructor sets that up for us.

LISTING 9.5 Creating a Manufacturing Order with a Component

```
MfgOrder = new Manufacturing.MfgOrder();
MfgOrder.ItemNo = POIn.ItemNo;
MfgOrder.OrderID = POIn.OrderNumber;
MfgOrder.Qty = POIn.Qty;
```

Now go over to the Else branch and drop a Construct Message shape on that flow. Name it **ReplyRejected**. We need to create only an outbound purchase with a rejection Status. Because the purchase order is rejected, there is no need for a manufacturing order message. Drag a Message Assignment shape into the construction and enter code just like Listing 9.4, except the value for POOut.Status should be **Rejected - insufficient credit**.

All our messages are properly assembled at this time. On the acceptance branch, add a Send shape and name it **SendOrderToManufacturing**. Select MfgOrder as the value of the Message property. Now drag a Port shape onto the Port surface. Follow the process we demonstrated for the receive port to create a port named MfgPort with a single operation SendOrdersToManufacturing. Like the earlier port, this is a one-way port using the File transport. Set the URI to c:\BasicOrchestrationMsgs\PlaceOrders\%MessageID%.xml, or wherever you decide to send your PO replies.

Regardless of the outcome of the credit-check decision, we will have a purchase order acknowledgement message to send. Drag another Send shape onto the surface and drop it onto the flow after the two branches are joined following the decision. This shape is named SendReply and uses POAck for its message. Configure a port like the others, named AckOrdersPort, with an operation named ReplyToOrders. Use the File transport and the URI c:\BasicOrchestrationMsgs\POOut\POReply_%MessageID%.xml.

Deployment and Testing

Build the OrderSystem project and then use Deploy Solution from the Build menu. This will put the orchestration and schema assembly into the global cache and create the three ports specified in our orchestration. You still need to enlist the ports and ensure that the host is started, however.

Open the BizTalk Administration Console application. Make sure BizTalkServerApplication (or whatever your default in-process host is named) is started. Examine the Receive Locations list. At the end you will see a new location that begins

`OrderSystem`, followed by the version and `ProcessOrchestration`, with `RecvPOPort` near the end of the concatenated name. Enable this location.

Now go to the Send Ports list. Two `OrderSystem` ports will have been added, one for each of the send ports in the orchestration. Enlist and start both ports. At this time, your messaging artifacts are ready to go, but your orchestrations are not yet ready.

Select the Orchestrations node. `OrderSystem.ProcessOrder` and `OrderSystem.CreditCheck` appear. You must start with `CreditCheck` because `ProcessOrchestration` is dependent upon it and will report an error if you attempt to configure it first. Right-click `CreditCheck` and select Enlist. Accept the defaults in the Enlistment Wizard, ensuring `BizTalkServerApplication` is the host. Right-click again and select Start processing. This does not launch an instance of the orchestration. It simply directs the orchestration engine to monitor the orchestration's ports, if any, and be ready to load an instance. Now repeat the process for `ProcessOrchestration`.

You are ready to test the system. Create an instance of `BasicPO` or use the sample document `SamplePO.xml` in the chapter download. Drop this into the folder `c:\BasicOrchestrationMsgs\POIn` (or wherever you created a folder to receive purchase orders). If your message has a `Price` field with a value less than or equal to $50,000, a new Manufacturing order message appears in PlaceOrders. A purchase order acknowledgement will always appear in `POOut`. You can open it and inspect the value of the Status field to determine which branch of the orchestration was executed. The chapter download also includes a sample, `SamplePO_Reject.xml`, whose `Price` field exceeds the fixed credit limit.

Orchestration and BPEL

Orchestration provides a powerful mechanism for execution of business processes on the Windows platform. Businesses with heterogeneous environments may have the need for business processes on a variety of platforms to work well together. It is for this reason that Microsoft, IBM, Siebel, BEA and many others are currently creating a standard specification called Business Process Execution Language (BPEL). The name of the BPEL specification is a little misleading. As we will discuss in more detail, BPEL is targeted at business process interop, rather than cross-platform execution. This is consistent with other web services specification such as WSDL which targets business logic interop rather than cross-platform execution.

The BPEL draft specification from May 2003 that is being standardized at OASIS is available here: `http://msdn.microsoft.com/library/default.asp?url=/library/en-us/dnbiz2k2/html/bpel1-1.asp`.

Key scenarios that BPEL addresses include:

- A large organization such as a retailer or manufacturer may wish to specify the process its suppliers must implement to sell to it. This kind of hub-and-spoke arrangement, common in business-to-business (B2B) interactions, can be made easier by using BPEL. The large buyer at the hub may use BPEL to describe the business process that its suppliers must implement, then distribute this definition to those suppliers. The BPEL definition precisely specifies the required interactions with the hub organization, and each supplier can use it as a starting point for implementing its side of the process.

- An organization may wish to implement an internal business process that relies on several existing applications, but allows this process to be deployed on several different integration servers. To allow this kind of enterprise application integration (EAI), the organization could define the basics of the process in BPEL, then use the common definition as a starting point for implementing the process on servers from one or more vendors.
- Libraries of best-practice business processes can be created, allowing intellectual property to be captured and reused more effectively. For organizations building a process from scratch, standard BPEL solutions like these can be a useful starting point.
- An industry-specific standards organization could provide BPEL templates to its members to help ensure industry-wide support for agreements on how to conduct electronic business.

BPEL is not a one-for-one replacement for Orchestration. It is a least common denominator specification for business process interop and is purely based on web services and XML Schema types to create a process language. As such, it coordinates a series of actions that are web service operations described in WSDL documents. Orchestration is a superset of BPEL, adding key features for business process execution on the Windows platform with the .NET Framework.

BizTalk Server allows you to export a properly designed orchestration to BPEL. So long as your orchestration does not use any features that are not in BPEL, you may export the orchestration as complementary[md]BPEL, WSDL, and XSD documents.

NOTE

NotThe Orchestration Designer provides support for building BPEL-exportable orchestrations. You can set the Module Exportable property for the orchestration as a whole to true in the properties pane. If you do so, any construct that is not BPEL-compliant will result in a compile-time error. Similarly, you can set the BPEL Compliance flag in the project properties to true to ensure that generated code is compliant. This flag is found in the Code Generation section of the Configuration Properties Build page in the project's property pages.

The BPEL specification is still in draft and BizTalk Server was the first product from a major vendor to provide support for the specification. As more and more product vendors adopt BPEL in mainstream products it will become increasingly more useful for business process interop.

Summary

This chapter covered a lot of ground. Even programmers with experience with previous versions of BizTalk Server will find much that is new to them. The familiar flow control shapes are here, although there are some subtle refinements. New shapes have been added for nesting orchestrations. The single greatest change has been in Orchestration support for .NET. The expressions used in the various shapes are no longer script code.

This latter feature was highlighted when we used a .NET component to generate and serialize a message without using schemas, maps, or string types. BizTalk makes use of .NET's serialization support and reflection to provide this new and powerful feature. This allows architects to blend orchestration and any component infrastructure in the enterprise to create enterprise process solutions.

Another new feature to which we alluded is BizTalk's support for Web services. This has several facets and is the topic of our next chapter.

CHAPTER 10

Orchestrating Web Services and Correlation

IN THIS CHAPTER

- Correlating Messages in Orchestration
- Calling Orchestrations
- Web Services and Orchestration
- Orchestration Debugging

BizTalk Server is a tool for building enterprise solutions, and orchestrations are the top-level building blocks in that product. Recent years have seen a parallel trend toward the adoption of Web services as a way to integrate applications and build critical solutions across the enterprise. Processes above the level of functions and methods are folded into discrete modules accessible to any Web service client. BizTalk and Web services could have become competitors. Instead, the two have become cooperative, offering enterprise developers and architects more implementation choices.

BizTalk Server 2004 is the first release of BizTalk that embraces Web services. The implementation is far more than simply adding a new transport protocol. The first, and obvious, feature is the capability of an orchestration to act as a Web service client. You can make a Web service request to implement a step of your schedule in the same way you would send or receive a message. This can be done in one of two ways. Either a synchronous, send/receive call or an asynchronous, send-only call can be made. Another feature performs the complementary act: a Web service facade can be placed over an orchestration schedule. A client application can make a SOAP call to an orchestration, causing the XLANG/s runtime engine to launch an instance of that schedule. The results of the orchestration form the contents of the SOAP response.

An existing feature of BizTalk, correlation, takes on increased importance in this realm and has been strengthened. In our samples so far, we've launched a single instance of an orchestration schedule at a time. We've called one schedule from another, but have done so synchronously. Getting the response back to the right place has been simple. All this changes when we move to asynchronous calls, and when schedules, under the guise of Web services, become implementation tools for mission-critical solutions. Hundreds of schedule instances may be active simultaneously in a production BizTalk server group. An application replying BizTalk with an invoice in response to a purchase order for automobiles had better return its results to the orchestration that generated the purchase order for automobiles, not the one requesting the purchase of a box of pencils. Correlation is the technique that keeps our orchestrations organized.

This chapter ties together some more advanced orchestration concepts. You will learn all about correlation, an important concept when you are running multiple orchestrations in parallel and need to keep related messages together with the orchestrations that are operating on them. You will also learn about two of the most exciting new features in BizTalk Server 2004, Web services, and orchestration. Orchestrations can call on web services as if they were just another messaging protocol, but orchestrations can also be exposed to the outside world as Web service methods. These complementary additions to BizTalk orchestration make it possible to use BizTalk in service-oriented architectures, which are becoming a popular strategy for enterprise development. You will see practical samples of both features.

Correlating Messages in Orchestration

The orchestration runtime engine keeps track of different instances of orchestrations and routes messages to the proper instance, provided we give it a hint with correlation sets. Like almost everything else, correlation sets are typed. You can think of correlation types as being similar to primary keys in a database. For example, the correlation set for a purchase order orchestration could be the ID from the purchase order message. You identify one or more promoted properties that uniquely identify a schedule instance. A correlation type, then, is just a list of properties. These properties may be from the message data or the surrounding message and orchestration context.

Just as orchestration instances deal with instances of message types, they also work with specific instances of correlation types, called *correlation sets*. A correlation set is initialized from the underlying correlation type when a message is sent or received based on a set of values in the message. These values come from properties in the message that the orchestration designer specifies. A correlation type may be initialized only once, which makes sense when you think about it. It wouldn't be helpful to have schedules changing their identity midway through execution.

Creating a Correlation Type

A correlation type is created in the Orchestration view by right-clicking the Correlation Types node (in the types tree) and selecting New Correlation Type from the context menu. As soon as you do that, the Correlation Properties dialog box depicted in Figure 10.1 appears. The available properties appear in a tree in the left pane of the dialog box. Each available namespace roots its own subtree. Note that all the predefined namespaces in the

BizTalk environment are represented and provide access to context properties. Additionally, any promoted properties in your project namespace appear as well. These must be promoted using a property schema; distinguished fields do not appear. In Figure 10.1 we have added the order number from the Purchase Order schema in the previous chapter to a property schema and selected that as our correlation property. Selecting a property and clicking Add moves the property to the pane labeled Properties to correlate on. Clicking OK adds the new type to the Orchestration view. You can rename and describe the new type in the Properties view for that node. The vast majority of cases are handled with a single property.

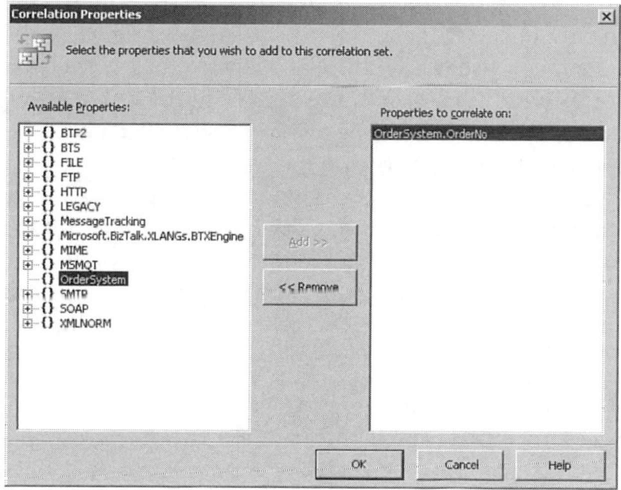

FIGURE 10.1 Promoted properties are added to correlation types using the Correlation Properties dialog box.

Creating a Correlation Set

After you have a correlation type, you are ready to use it with an orchestration. You create correlation sets for an orchestration the same as you create other variables. Go to the Orchestration view and right-click the Correlation Sets node in the project's orchestration tree (the top tree in the view). Select New Correlation Set from the context menu. A new node is created. In the Property view for that set, you rename and describe the set. More importantly, though, you select a Correlation Type using a drop-down list in the value cell for the property. You have the option of creating a new type, selecting a correlation type from a referenced assembly, or picking from the list of types previously defined in your orchestration.

The purpose of a correlation set is to ensure that messages are properly routed to the correct instance of an orchestration schedule. Imagine a system in which a purchase order moves through several steps in an orchestration. The purchase order is received from a purchaser, sent to an application for pricing, sent to another application for approval, and so forth. At each step, we want to make sure that the orchestration presents to receive ports only those purchase order messages that bear the correct purchase order number. The first message received initializes the correlation set using an ID we've identified in the message. After that, orchestration will present messages to orchestration instances only if the purchase order ID matches the ID in the correlation set for that instance. If any of the messages are incorrect, the execution of the schedule will be wrong. Ensuring integrity in a schedule, then, consists of two tasks: initializing a correlation set and designating those Send and Receive shapes that participate in the convoy.

The first thing to do is to identify the first place that unique values for the correlation properties appear in the schedule. If the schedule originates the values, this will be a Send shape that transmits a message bearing those property values. If the value originates outside the schedule, as was the case with the sample purchase order schedule in Chapter 9, "Introducing Orchestration," this will be a Receive shape that accepts the first message bearing an initialized set of values. After you have done this, you select that shape in the design surface and go to its Property view. Send and Receive shapes have two properties that pertain to the task at hand: Initializing Correlation Sets and Following Correlation Sets. The first Send or Receive shape in the schedule will have only the former property. After you have found the shape that initializes a correlation set, select that set or sets from the drop-down list of defined correlation sets next to the Initializing Correlation Sets property for the shape.

Now find the other shapes that participate in the correlation scenario. Add them to the correlation set by selecting it from the list next to the Following Correlation Sets property for the shape. As you add shapes to the set, they appear as children of the correlation set's node in the Orchestration view. When this is done, you've completed the tasks needed to ensure integrity using correlation sets. The messages used in the Receive shape that initializes the correlation set and the subsequent shapes that follow the correlation set share the same property schema that identifies the property or properties used to correlate messages and schedules. In the purchase order example we gave earlier, all the messages received under the correlation set would have to share a property schema that promotes the purchase order ID we want to use for correlation.

Correlation sets may be used with nested orchestrations. You may pass correlations sets as parameters when you invoke a schedule using the Call Orchestration or Start Orchestration shapes. When a correlation set is passed as a parameter, however, orchestrations that receive it must pass it in its entirety and without modification to any orchestrations they invoke.

There are a few ways to get into trouble with correlation in orchestration. Initializing a correlation set in several shapes in the same Parallel shape can lead to inconsistent data when conflicting initializing values arrive or originate on parallel branches. That might seem fairly obvious, but there is a more subtle restriction on correlation sets. The orchestration engine will not guarantee proper correlation when messages in a convoy arrive at ports following the initializing shape before the initializing message has been processed.

Until the correlation set has been initialized with a unique set of values, the runtime engine cannot properly route messages and protect ports. The best way to avoid this condition is to ensure that the semantics of your process are such that messages subsequent to initialization cannot be sent by their originator before the set has been initialized. A good example is a process in which each step is a response to the step before it. An originating PO, for example, triggers action by the estimating application. The PO received from the estimating application with a complete price list triggers action from the approval application, and so forth. This is much harder to accomplish when dealing with multiple shapes on parallel branches, so proceed with care with such orchestrations. An alternative is to ensure that each parallel branch begins with a Receive shape that is designated as initializing the correlation set.

Calling Orchestrations

We briefly discussed nested orchestration in the previous chapter when we described and later used the Call Orchestration shape. We could do that then because there was no difficulty with correlation. Because Call Orchestration works synchronously, the out parameters from the called orchestration are guaranteed to be returned to the proper instance of the schedule. Start Orchestration, however, is asynchronous. Correlation is very important if we want to do more than simply spawn independent schedules. Replies have to have a way of getting back to the right schedule and arriving at the proper port much in the way that an object in a conventional programming language might provide a callback function.

Any correlation sets passed as parameters to an orchestration as part of a Start Orchestration shape call serve to share the correlation set with the child orchestration. If you need to send a message from the child back to the parent, you can pass in port references or role links (a logical collection of ports we discuss in Chapter 12, "Orchestrating—Advanced Concepts") to identify where in the parent schedule to send the reply message. Because the correlation set is shared between the two, any message sent from the child with the proper value for the correlation property in the message will be automatically routed to the proper schedule instance—that is, the parent that called the child. Because we are launching the dependent schedule asynchronously, the Start Orchestration shape can be configured only within type parameters. Start Orchestration uses the same configuration dialog box as Call Orchestration.

Web Services and Orchestration

Web services, like orchestrations, tend to fit into enterprise architectures as the implementation of medium-to-large modules of processing. The overhead inherent in these technologies works against selecting them for small, possibly stateful, tasks such as are implemented in conventional application code. The choice of which technology to use depends on several factors. If you have a lot of legacy code that pre-dates .NET and is under the control of one organization, a Web service wrapper is a good way to preserve your investment. On the other hand, if the task involves loosely coupled applications that may span organizations, you should choose orchestration. Because programming is frequently a matter of compromise between what we'd like to do and what we must live with, it makes good sense that orchestration and Web services should be capable of interoperating in BizTalk Server 2004.

Orchestrations can make use of Web services in two ways. First, an orchestration can use SOAP as a transport protocol for a port and invoke an external Web service the same as it would send a message and receive a response from a conventional application using a two-way port. The orchestration makes use of the Web service's processing to implement part of the business process.

Other applications in your organization (or a business partner's organization) may be committed to Web services. An outside partner might not have BizTalk as part of their infrastructure, or an application in your organization may be configured for Web services. Your orchestration then becomes the implementation of a task that the outside entity calls as a Web service client. In architectural terms, we provide a Web service façade for the orchestration so that the SOAP standard becomes a platform-neutral integration technique. In BizTalk terms, we expose an orchestration as a Web service. This is the second way that orchestrations can use Web services.

Using Web Services in Orchestration

Making use of a Web service as a transport protocol within an orchestration is similar to adding a reference to a component. So long as the service publishes a WSDL document describing its types, ports, and operations, Orchestration Designer will be able to do most of the detail work for you.

The first and most important task when using a Web service is to add a Web reference to your orchestration project. This is accomplished in the Solution Explorer by right-clicking the project node and selecting Add Web Reference from the context menu or by selecting the same option from the Project menu on the Visual Studio main menu. In response, the Add Web Reference window, shown in Figure 10.2, appears.

You can point directly to a Web service by entering the appropriate URL in the URL box, or you can select an option from the drop-down list that searches your local HTTP host for Web services. After you have selected a particular Web service, the Web reference window interrogates the Web service for its WSDL description. The results are displayed in a human-friendly form in the browser window. You click Add Reference to add a reference to your selected Web service operation to your project.

Doing so causes Visual Studio to go into the lengthy process of parsing the WSDL and generating new types for your project. All the types show up in the Type tree in Orchestration view as read-only nodes. A port type will be added for a request-response port for the Web service. Two multipart message types will be added: one for the SOAP request message and one for the SOAP response. You can use these types in an orchestration to configure port and message instances.

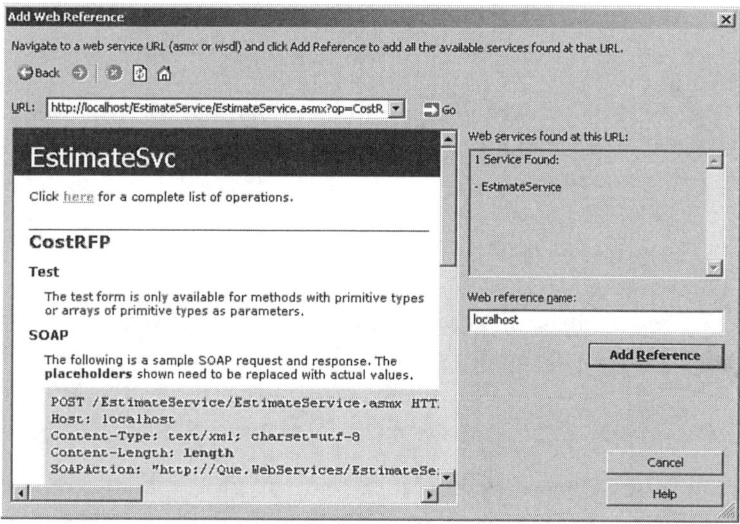

FIGURE 10.2 Adding a Web reference to an orchestration project adds message and port types to the orchestration.

Calling a Web service operation involves four steps:

1. Creating a SOAP request message
2. Sending the SOAP message to the request part of a Web service port with a Send shape
3. Receiving the SOAP response from the response part of the same Web service port with a Receive shape
4. Optionally converting the response message to a local message type

The first and fourth tasks may seem a bit odd when you first look at the message types in Visual Studio .NET. After you add the Web reference, Visual Studio .NET exposes the request and response message types to the BizTalk Mapper and the Orchestration Designer by revealing only the payload or body of the message. The SOAP header is omitted. If you are planning to send data from a locally defined message to the Web service, you might be tempted to think you can configure the Send shape to use that message. If you do, you will not only lack the SOAP header, but you will likely have namespace issues. You must construct a new instance of the SOAP request message type using either message assignment or transformation.

The request-response nature of the SOAP call is reflected in the fact that you will create a single port for each SOAP invocation, but you need to connect Send and Receive shapes to the difference connectors on the Port shape. After the call completes, you will have a new instance of the SOAP response message type in your Receive shape.

At this point, you run into the complementary problem of turning a SOAP response message into something your orchestration can deal with. You could use message assignment to inspect and use the SOAP response fields, but if you want to pass the data obtained from the service to any other application or partner, you will need to map the response or use message assignment to create a new instance of some message type defined in a schema or component.

Using a Web Service Sample

Let's illustrate this process by creating a Web service and building an orchestration that uses it. The concept is that we are receiving a request for proposal (RFP) from a prospective customer. He would like to contract with us to provide a particular service, which is described in an RFP message, and wants us to return the RFP with our proposed cost inserted. Estimating a proposal can be an involved process, and we have a Web service to do that for us. Our customers, however, do not have access to the Web service. Instead, we want them to drop the RFP message into a file folder (typically in a network demilitarized zone for security), where we will pick it up with an orchestration. After we have a reply from the Web service, we drop the completed RFP document into another file folder for pick up by the customer.

Estimate Web Service Implementation

The first step is to create the Web service. Our orchestration, hence our Web service, will perform estimates based solely on the number of hours the customer proposes to contract for our services. Based on that, it would be easy enough to create a Web method that takes a numeric type (hours) and returns another numeric type (cost). In the real world, though, you would want to use a longer list of parameters, and the parameters might vary depending on the service. It is far more flexible, then, to define an RFP schema and pass an instance of such a document into the Web method. Upon return, the updated document is passed into the response. This takes advantage of the SOAP specification's message encoding format for the SOAP message body, which is the preferred format.

Because we are working in .NET, we can take advantage of the .NET Framework's serialization support to define our message by creating a class to represent RFPs. Our RFP class source code is given in Listing 10.1. It is within the namespace that includes the Web service class, but it is not within the class itself. A sample in the BizTalk SDK shows a similar example in which the document class is embedded within the Web service class, but this is not necessary.

LISTING 10.1 .NET Class Implementing RFP Documents

```
public class RFP
{
  public String ID;
  public String ServiceName;
  public Decimal Hours;
```

LISTING 10.1 Continued

```
  public Decimal Cost;

  public void calculateCost()
  {
   if (Hours > 0)
     Cost = 150 * Hours;
   else
     Cost = 150;
  }
}
```

There are several points to make regarding this listing. First, you should note that we did not add the [Serializable] attribute to the class, as was necessary in the last chapter when we constructed a component library. The serialization support in .NET for Web service classes will take care of that for us when we pass an instance of this class as a parameter. Next, any public properties of the class show up in the SOAP message as XML elements. Finally, we take advantage of object-oriented code to encapsulate the estimating algorithm as a method of the class. Our documents are wholly contained entities that can take care of estimating themselves.

Now turn your attention to the Web method implementation in Listing 10.2. This method accepts an instance of our RFP class and returns an instance of the same class. The Web service infrastructure in .NET deserializes the SOAP body into the parameter object. We call the calculateCost method to do the calculation and set the Cost property, and then return the object. The SOAP infrastructure serializes the updated object into the body of the SOAP response message. Using classes to represent messages is a helpful technique when you have complicated business entities to model. You can establish a library of classes representing those entities and their capabilities and then rely on .NET to convert between objects and SOAP messages.

LISTING 10.2 Web Method Implemented for Estimating an RFP

```
[WebMethod]
public RFP CostRFP(RFP RFPDocument)
{
   RFPDocument.calculateCost();
  return RFPDocument;
}
```

Go ahead and build the Web service. It is independent of the orchestration that we are about to create.

NOTE

If you are working with the code download for this chapter, go ahead and create a virtual directory in IIS for this service and then drop the code into that folder. If you use the orchestration provided in the download, be sure to change the Web reference to reflect your local Web service deployment.

Creating the RFP Orchestration

Now create a new BizTalk project and name it **`RFPConsumeWS`**. Add a new orchestration item to the project and name it **`RespondToRFP.odx`**. Besides an orchestration, you will need a Web reference, a schema, and two maps. Begin by adding a Web reference to the Web service we just created using the process described earlier. You can take a look at the Orchestration view and see a new port type and two new message types.

Schemas and Maps for the Orchestration Now add a new message schema item to the project, naming it RFPOrchestration.xsd. This is to represent the RFP as it is presented by and returned to the customer. It should mirror the RFP class we created for the Web service. Create a root named `RFP` and then add child element fields named `ID`, `ServiceName`, `Hours`, and `Cost`. Give them the same types as their namesakes in the Web service.

Now add two maps—one to convert a customer RFP into an RFP SOAP request and one to transform a SOAP response from the service into a customer RFP. Add a new map item to the project and name it `RFPODX2RFPWS.btm`. Click the link to designate a Source Schema. Navigate to the Schema node in the BizTalk type picker and select the schema you just created. Now click the Destination Schema link. This time, navigate to the Schema node, but locate the schema created by the Web reference. If you have installed the Web service to the localhost as I have, this will be `RFPConsumeWS.localhost.Reference`. Note how Visual Studio .NET is referring to the namespace of the BizTalk project, but putting all resources created by the Web reference under a namespace that designates the Web service host.

The schema tree for the Web service RFP will look just like the tree for the schema you created. Visual Studio .NET has suppressed all the SOAP envelope information in creating the schema tree you see. Establish direct links between the like-named fields in the source and destination schemas.

Repeat the process to create the complementary map for converting a SOAP response to the customer RFP message. This map should be named `RFPWS2RFPODX.btm`.

Creating the Orchestration Flow Now we are finally ready to create the orchestration depicted in Figure 10.3. Most of what you see there should be familiar to you by now, so we will focus on the tasks specific to consuming a Web service.

Go to the Orchestration view and add four new messages. Two, `RFP` and `RFPOut`, should be typed as belonging to the customer schema you created. One, `WSReq`, represents the SOAP request. Find the multipart message type created by the Web reference for this. If you installed the Web service locally, the type is `RFPCosumeWS.localhost.EstimateSvc_.CostRFP_request`. The final message, `WSResp`, is typed as the SOAP response type. This gives us variables for the incoming customer RFP and our response, as well as the SOAP request-response pair.

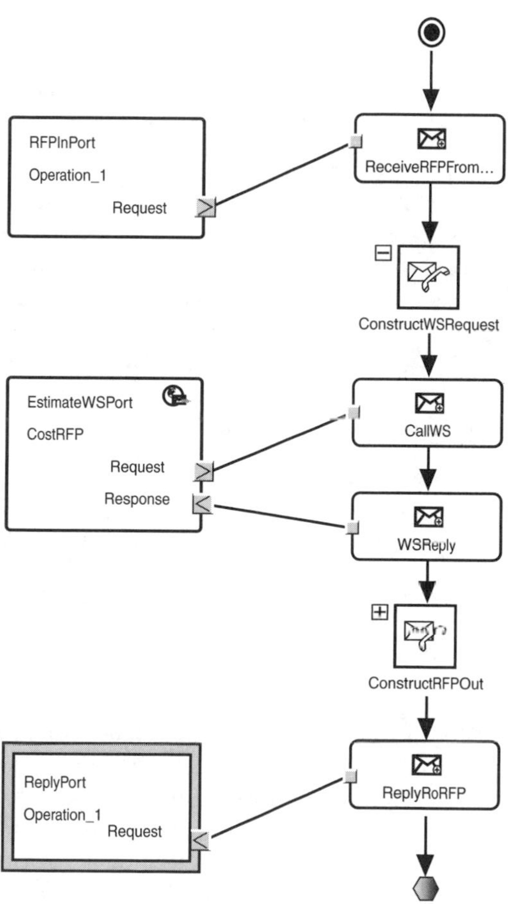

FIGURE 10.3 Orchestration for the Reply to RFP business process.

> **NOTE**
>
> The initial Receive shape and its associated port are a file transport receive operation such as we have created several times before. I'm using a folder named `RFPIn` off the local drive of my machine. Use the default XMLReceive pipeline. Configure the Receive shape by setting Activate to `true` and specifying the Message property as `RFP`.

Now the orchestration has to prepare for the SOAP request by mapping the arriving document into the SOAP request format. To accomplish this, add a Construct Message shape, ConstructWSRequest, in Figure 10.3, and drag a Transform shape into it.

NOTE

This Construct Message shape has been collapsed in the figure for reasons of space.

Select `RFPConsumeWS.RFPODX2RFPWS` as the map for the transformation, `RFP` as the input message, and `WSReq.RFPDocument` as the output message.

Now you are ready to add the Web service call to the orchestration. Drag a Send shape (`CallWS`) and a Receive shape (`WSReply`) to the orchestration surface. Now add a port to the port surface and name it `EstimateWSPort`. On the Select a Port Type page of the Port Configuration Wizard, select Use an Existing Port Type and expand the Web Port Types node in the type tree. You should see `RFPConsumeWS.localhost.EstimateSvc_.EstimateSvc`, which is the port type created by the Web reference. Select that as your type. All the choices on the next page, Port Binding, will be made for you. You will see SOAP as the transport, the URL of your Web service as the URI, and the default pass-through send and receive pipelines will be specified.

Drag a connection from `CallWS` to the Request connector on the port, and then drag a connection from the Response connector to `WSReply`. Configure `CallWS` with `WSReq` as the Message property value, and `WSReply` with `WSResp` as the value for Message.

Complete the orchestration design by adding a Construct Message shape that uses a map to convert the SOAP response to a customer RFP. `WSResp` is the input message, and `RFPOut` is the output message. Now add a Send shape and a one-way file transport port to send `RFPOut` to a file folder of your choice.

Create a keyfile and point to it in the project properties, and then build the BizTalk solution. If there are no errors, go ahead and deploy it. Enlist and start the orchestration as we've done before and be sure the BizTalk host is running. Now you can take a message that conforms to the schema you created (`RFPSample.xml` in the chapter download is one such) and drop it into your input location. The orchestration consumes it and drops a response into the output folder. When you inspect the output message, you will find that the orchestration has added a value for the Cost field courtesy of the Web service.

Exposing an Orchestration as a Web Service

The complementary process, exposing an entire orchestration as a Web service, is also useful to solution architects. Many organizations are now set up to consume Web services, so even if your partners or internal applications are not enabled for BizTalk, they can make use of your business process just as if it was a Web service.

The support is not native to orchestration, however. After you have developed an orchestration, you run a separate tool, the BizTalk Web Services Publishing Wizard. This tool examines the orchestrations and other BizTalk artifacts in an assembly. The wizard then exposes each port in the orchestration as a Web service method by creating an ASP.NET page and an associated site for the page or pages generated.

Figure 10.4 shows the wizard after a programmer has designated an assembly. The assembly has been examined and found to contain a single orchestration and a single port. Based on this, the wizard will generate a Web folder named for the orchestration, followed by an underscore and the word proxy—in this case, `ExposeRFP_proxy`. Now, because this example has a single orchestration and a single port, the generated page will be named for the orchestration: `RFPCost.asmx`. If there are multiple ports in the orchestration, multiple pages will be created using the naming scheme *`orchestration_port`*`.asmx`. Each page is callable from a Web service client. Internally, the page uses the BizTalk APIs to invoke the orchestration.

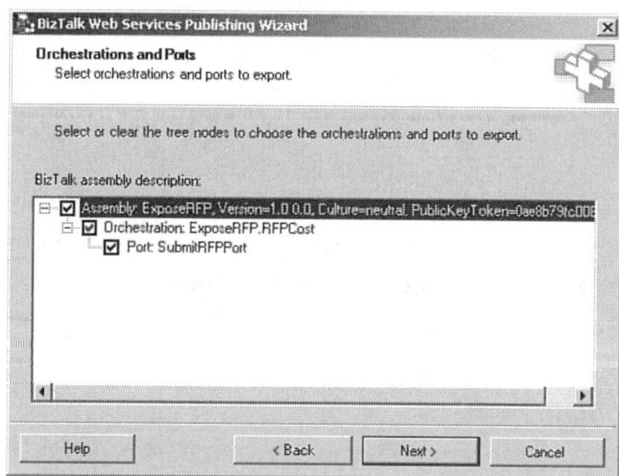

FIGURE 10.4 BizTalk assemblies are examined for orchestrations and ports that may be exposed as Web services.

There are a few more considerations embraced by the publishing wizard. Figure 10.5 shows a page of the wizard with a few of these. You are able to supply a namespace independent of your orchestration's namespace for use as the Web service namespace. This affords you some flexibility if you are publishing an orchestration designed and developed by someone else for use in your particular environment.

A powerful feature of SOAP is the open and extensible nature of the SOAP envelope. Developers are able to extend the header with elements of their specification. SOAP agents are instructed as to whether they must understand each element to process the message. The Web Services Publishing Wizard gives you the opportunity to explicitly specify header elements. You may also instruct your Web service that there may be additional headers that will not be specified. These unknown headers should be ignored when received.

Finally, you may include support for Microsoft SharePoint Portal Server single sign-on. This is particularly useful because SharePoint Web parts make excellent Web service clients and SharePoint may be used with BizTalk Human Workflow Services. By supporting single sign-on, you make your orchestration compatible with these uses.

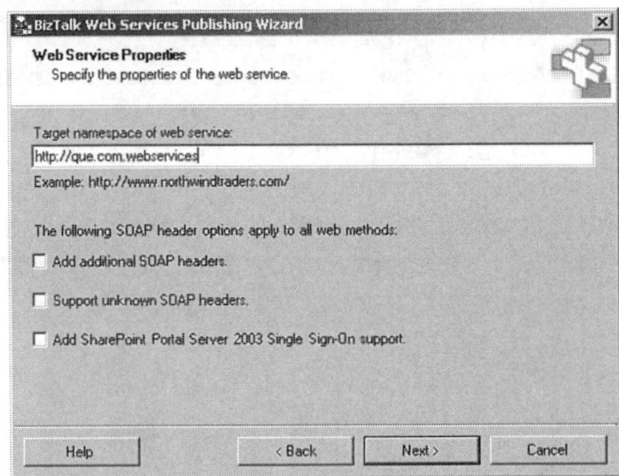

FIGURE 10.5 The wizard supports the use of additional SOAP header elements.

After you make a few more decisions about whether to support anonymous access to the Web service files and whether to allow the wizard to create receive locations, the wizard proceeds to create your pages. Your orchestration will execute as always, and the Web service client will be unaware that the service is implemented using BizTalk.

Orchestration Facade Sample

Imagine a simplified request for proposal message such as is given in Listing 10.3. This is a minor variation on the .NET class-based RFP we saw earlier in the chapter. We'll write a simple orchestration that performs a cost calculation for the RFP and expose the orchestration as a Web service method. A client application could view the orchestration like a remote function, but we have the flexibility and features of orchestration in creating the process implementation.

LISTING 10.3 Sample RFP message for the Web Service Façade

```
<ns0:RFP xmlns:ns0="http://ExposeRFP.RFP">
  <Service>Consulting</Service>
  <Hours>9.0</Hours>
  <Cost>340.0</Cost>
  <ID>12345</ID>
  <Status>Proposed</Status>
</ns0:RFP>
```

Creating the Message Schema

Start the project by creating a new BizTalk solution named `ExposeRFP` and adding a schema item named RFP.xsd. The `Hours` and `Cost` fields are decimal types, and the rest are strings. Most important, all fields are required. During the mapping between the .NET Web service wrapper and the orchestration engine, XML elements are mapped to and from .NET types. The process cannot handle a null or missing field, so it is imperative that your messages have all fields present in all instances. After creating the schema, create a property schema and promote all the fields so that we can work with them in a Message Assignment shape.

Creating the Business Process

The point of this sample is to illustrate the process of publishing an orchestration, so we'll keep the business process simple. The schedule depicted in Figure 10.6 shows the process. Note how the port's request and response functions are connected to Send and Receive shapes at either end of the process.

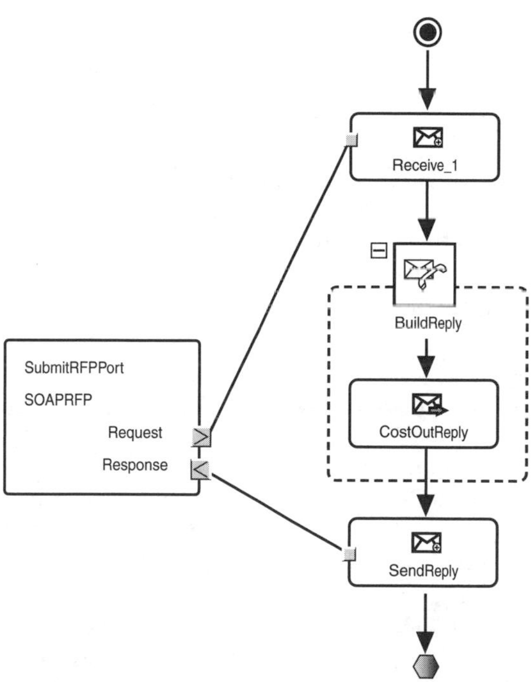

FIGURE 10.6 The SOAP request starts the orchestration, and the response is the end result of the business process.

The orchestration contains two message variables, `RFPIn` and `RFPOut`, which correspond to the request and response and are both typed as conforming to the RFP schema. The Receive shape will initiate the orchestration and cause the runtime engine to load a new instance, so set the Activate property to `True`. The shape uses `RFPIn` as its message. This gets the prospective customer's RFP into the orchestration and gives us data on which to operate.

The BuildReply Message Construction shape builds the output RFP message. All the fields are mapped from the input message, but we need to calculate a value for the Cost field and set a value of Estimated for the Status field to indicate that the RFP has been examined and an estimate provided for the customer's consideration. We accomplish this with a Message Assignment shape that has the expression given in Listing 10.4. Note the syntax of selecting the fields in the `RFPOut` message. This differs from the syntax seen in Chapter 9 because we are using a property schema rather than distinguished properties.

LISTING 10.4 Message Assignment Expressions for Estimating the Cost of the RFP

```
RFPOut = RFPIn;
RFPOut(ExposeRFP.Cost) = RFPIn(ExposeRFP.Hours) * 100;
RFPOut(ExposeRFP.Status) = "Estimated";
```

The Send shape uses `RFPOut` as its message. It serves to return a value that will be the SOAP response. All of this requires a SOAP port, so turn your attention to the port named `SubmitRFPPort` on the Port Surface in Figure 10.6.

The port uses the Request-Response communications pattern to comply with the nature of the SOAP protocol and the Receive-Send communication direction to indicate that this is an incoming message. Other than this, we have to defer specification until deployment time. Although we know the transport will be SOAP, we cannot provide a URL. The Web Services Publishing Wizard will generate a name conforming to the pattern based on the name of the orchestration as discussed previously, and the location of the generated wrapper will also be specified by the wizard. Having specified the orchestration, we can build the solution and create an assembly.

Publishing the Orchestration as a Web Service

Now start the Web Services Publishing Wizard from the Visual Studio Tools menu. On the Create Web Service page, ensure that the first option, Publish BizTalk orchestrations as Web services, is selected and click Next. The next page, BizTalk Assembly, should be filled in for you with the fully qualified file path and filename of the assembly. If you were to launch the wizard from the Windows Start menu, you would have to provide this information yourself. When you click Next, there will be a delay as the wizard inspects the assembly for artifacts it can publish.

The Orchestrations and Ports page is dominated by a tree view anchored by the assembly name. The immediate child is the orchestration in the assembly, and it has the `SOAPRFPPort` as a child. Ensure all three nodes are checked so that they will be published. Click Next.

The next page is named Web Service Properties. The only thing you must do on this page is provide a namespace for the generated Web service. We will use `http://que.orchestrations.webservices` for this example. We are not using SOAP header extensions, nor are we anticipating use with Microsoft SharePoint, so ensure that the three check boxes on this page are cleared. Click the Next button to proceed.

The next page is where you have to start taking notes. The Web Service Project page proposes a project name and location. We will need this information at deployment time to configure the port. Accept the defaults for this project of `ExposeRFP_Proxy` for the project name and location. The wizard indicates that the project will be created at `http://localhost/ExposeRFP_Proxy`. Check the box labeled Allow Anonymous Access to Web Service to simplify testing.

The final page you see before the wizard generates the proxy is named Web Service Summary and it displays the rest of the information you will need to configure the port. Also, be careful to note the name of the proxy page. The service you are going to call from the client application is named using the form *`projectname_orchestrationname_soapportname`*. If you are publishing an orchestration with more than one SOAP-callable port, you will get one wrapper for each such port. The name of the SOAP port becomes the service's Web method name, as well. When developing a Web service client for your orchestration, you will point your client-generating tool to the wrapper implementation to obtain a WSDL document.

Orchestration Debugging

By now, we've worked with enough orchestrations that you may be wondering how to debug an orchestration. Unlike most other development tasks, debugging has very little to do with Visual Studio. NET. Debugging is an extension of message and orchestration tracking, so the debugging features of BizTalk are found in the Health and Activity Tracking tool. This tool is covered in depth in Chapter 16, "BizTalk Health and Activity Tracking," but we'll hit the highlights for debugging here, in case you need to debug your sample orchestrations now. The first thing to look at is configuring Health and Activity Tracking so that the system records the information you need.

When you have the Health and Activity Tracking application open, you should select the Orchestration menu item from the Configuration menu on the main menu bar. You will see a grid listing all the orchestrations deployed on the server and a series of check boxes underneath the grid reflecting the event and data recording options for the Health and Activity Tracking application. These let you configure what events and data will be recorded on a per orchestration basis. You have the option of recording start and end events for any instance of the selected orchestration, message send and receive events, and orchestration events. Within message events, you may record inbound and outbound message bodies, which is useful if you need to see the details of how data is being manipulated in your orchestration. You must record orchestration events to use the debugger.

Orchestration debugging begins with an instance of an orchestration. You can use the Operations menu to configure and execute a query for service instances, selecting Orchestration for the class. Alternatively, if you are debugging a suspended orchestration, you can use the Queries menu to execute the preplanned query for suspended orchestrations. You may also inspect the execution history of recent service instances. Regardless of how you find a record of an orchestration, you can initiate debugging. Locate the Service Instance ID column (typically on the far right of the row) and right-click the cell. The Orchestration Debugger view appears when you click the Orchestration Debugger menu item on the context menu. This view is depicted in Figure 10.7. This is the view you have initially, regardless of whether the orchestration instance completed is in a breakpoint, or is suspended.

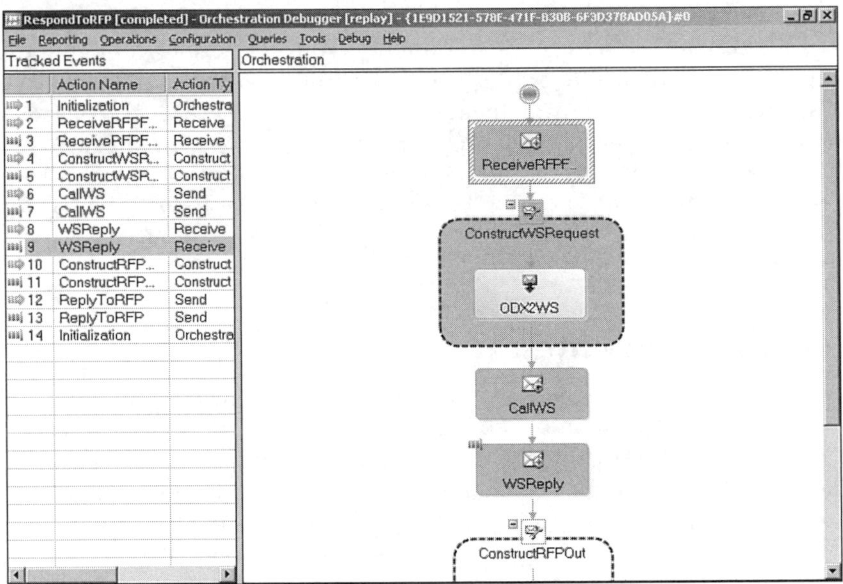

FIGURE 10.7 The process view of the Orchestration Debugger allows you to set breakpoints and inspect variables.

If you are inspecting a completed instance, you will be limited to inspecting the list of actions in a grid on the left and the flow chart view of the orchestration. If the orchestration is in breakpoint or suspended, you can attach to the BizTalk host process using the Attach item off the Debug menu. After you are attached to a running instance, you can resume the execution or inspect variables and their values the same as you would in a conventional IDE such as Visual Studio.

There is one other use for the Process view of an orchestration when you are inspecting a completed instance. We are accustomed to setting a breakpoint in source code, launching the application, and seeing the flow of control halted at the breakpoint. There is no way in the Orchestration Debugger to launch an arbitrary orchestration instance as there was in an unsupported tool in earlier versions of BizTalk. This is a problem if you want to inspect the inner workings of an orchestration that runs to completion but may not be producing the results you expect. After you've located any instance of an orchestration class, you may set a breakpoint by clicking on a step of the process flowchart and pressing F9 or by right-clicking and selecting Set Breakpoint on Class from the context menu. Whenever any instance of that class launches, the orchestration will halt at the breakpoint.

CAUTION

This action will not automatically launch the Orchestration Debugger. You will need to execute a query and open the service instance. To attach to the host, the user ID under which you are running must be a member of BizTalk Server Administrators Group. Be sure to clear all breakpoints on an orchestration class when you are finished or you will be unable to run any instances of that class to completion. The cause of this problem will not be readily apparent.

After you attach to an orchestration instance in breakpoint, the process flowchart will show what action is currently on hold and show the variables and their value. There is no way to single step through the process, but you may resume or terminate the instance, or set as many additional breakpoints as you may need. If you choose to continue an instance to proceed to another breakpoint, you will need to reattach to the host to see the breakpoint activity.

You can also use the debugging tools in Visual Studio .NET when debugging orchestrations. If your orchestration is calling your own custom .NET components, you may want to debug them while in an orchestration. To do this, set a breakpoint in the orchestration process flow prior to the point at which the component is invoked. Also set a breakpoint in your .NET code in Visual Studio. Start an instance of the orchestration in question. When the orchestration reaches its breakpoint, switch to Visual Studio .NET and attach to the `btsntsvc.exe` process, which is the orchestration engine. This is done through the Visual Studio Processes dialog box, which is invoked with the Debug Processes menu item. When you have done so, you may resume orchestration processing. The Visual Studio breakpoint will be triggered when the component is invoked and the code breakpoint is reached.

Summary

Web services and service-oriented architectures are quickly becoming important fixtures in the enterprise programming landscape. BizTalk Server 2004 offers Web service features to orchestration programmers for the first time. The capability to call a Web service in the course of an orchestration is essential when integrating with service-oriented architectures, but the capability to turn around and encapsulate an orchestration as a Web service makes BizTalk orchestrations widely available throughout the enterprise, even in groups and applications that are not conversant with BizTalk. The Web service becomes a façade for an entire business process. An organization with the business expertise represented by the orchestration has the full resources of BizTalk to implement its process, whereas organizations that merely interact with the implementing organization are shielded from both the complexities of the process and the details of orchestration. This encapsulation is implemented through the simple means of generating some ASP.NET wrapper code. To the outside world, the orchestration becomes just another Web service, and all the familiar Web service client programming tools come into play.

11 Developing Rules

IN THIS CHAPTER

- Rules Architecture
- Rules Development
- Authoring Policies and Vocabularies
- Rule Development APIs
- Business Rule Composer
- Standalone Rules Sample

Programmers are most at home with procedural code, but we've seen that such code is inflexible. Procedural code requires recompiling whenever something changes in the business it seeks to enable. Orchestration gave us a measure of flexibility for process modeling. When the steps and flow of a process change, an analyst can reorganize the process and deploy a new version of the orchestration. That isn't even required when the flow is the same but bindings change. But the rules and policies of the process are still hidden in what is essentially procedural code—the expressions in message assignments and other shapes. A business analyst working with changing rules in an orchestration can quickly find himself looking for a .NET programmer.

BizTalk Server 2004 introduces a new approach to this problem. Just as orchestration abstracts process from code, BizTalk rules abstract business rules from procedural code. The rules implementation in BizTalk is a full-featured inference engine. It is conveniently exposed as a separate architectural component within BizTalk, so you can write rule-based applications outside of messaging and orchestration. Of course, it is also well-integrated with orchestration, so you can call on your business rules to manage business knowledge within an orchestration. The facts on which the rules are based can be drawn from XML documents, relational databases, and .NET components. The rules themselves are usually composed in a tool for analysts called the Business Rule Composer, but they can also be constructed through a series of .NET APIs or even XML documents written according to a specific pair of Microsoft schemas.

This chapter explores the architecture of the BizTalk rules engine, the process of developing rules through the various means available, and how to deploy and use rules outside of orchestration. We'll build a sample console application that loads an existing set of rules and applies it to an XML document. In Chapter 12, "Orchestrating—Advanced Concepts," we'll integrate the rules we built with an orchestration to improve the RFP estimating process we've worked with off and on throughout this book.

Rules Architecture

Before we can do anything useful, we have to understand how BizTalk organizes rules. The elemental components in the rules architecture are *facts*. A fact is some specific data item brought into memory. A fact can be a field in an XML document, a property in a .NET object, or the value of a column in a row of relational data. Actions are a similarly low-level component. They are the data assignments or operations executed as part of a rule. In addition to assigning XML fields, relational columns, or .NET properties, an action can invoke a method on a .NET object.

Conditions

The next step up is the condition. This is the "If" portion of a rule. The expression cost > 500 is an example of a condition. We have two facts: cost and the constant 500, and a predicate: >. The curious term predicate comes from the branch of mathematics used to power rule-based systems, the first order predicate calculus. That field is the theory that tells us how to reason logically and what may be inferred in a rigorous manner. This is the last time we shall mention the predicate calculus, so you can relax.

Building Rules from Conditions and Actions

Now that we have the "If" portion, we can build rules. A BizTalk *rule* consists of one or more conditions that collectively evaluate to a Boolean value. The logical operators `AND`, `OR`, and `NOT` are available to combine conditions.

As any programmer knows, "If" is useless without "Then." The "Then" portion of a BizTalk rule is called an *action*. Actually, BizTalk performs a series of actions for any given rule. A typical action would be to set the value of an XML message, set a value in a relational database, or call a .NET method to perform some action outside the rule engine.

Policies—Collections of Rules

Rules are collected to form policies. A *policy* in BizTalk is a set of related rules that share a body of business knowledge. In our sample, the body of knowledge is how to estimate the cost of the services requested in an RFP. You load and execute a policy to perform some reasoning about a particular problem. Policies are saved in the BizTalk rules database and are subject to versioning, allowing us to manage the evolution of business knowledge and control what rules are applied in our applications.

Rule Execution

The process by which rules are executed is radically different from what you are used to in procedural code. When a policy is executed, the facts are brought into memory, a process called *assertion*. Facts may be loaded into memory prior to execution, or new instances of facts may be asserted as an action in a rule. Rule-based systems come in several forms. The one most commonly used, which is also the one BizTalk implements, is a forward chaining inference engine. That mouthful means that facts are used to evaluate rule conditions. When the available facts exist to evaluate a rule's condition and it evaluates to true, the rule is fired. As rules fire, new facts are asserted into memory. For example, firing a rule might cause a field to be set in a message. This becomes a new fact in memory, which may cause another rule to fire. This continues until no more rules can fire or a specific number of passes through the rule base have occurred. The latter restriction avoids endless execution of the rules engine.

There is a bit more to rule firing than that. The rule engine does not work its way through the list of rules sequentially. A rule developer can assign priorities to rules. For each pass through the policy, the rule engine assembles an agenda of matched rules for firing. Within that agenda, the priorities determine which rules fire in which order, from highest priority to lowest. The new facts asserted into memory are applied to the next pass through the policy. Newly asserted facts are never used in the pass during which they were asserted.

As you might imagine, the binding of facts to XML documents, relational databases, or .NET objects can involve names only a programmer could love. They deal with XPath expressions, database names, and .NET qualified names. If Microsoft had left things like that, no business analyst would touch rule development. Policies are therefore complemented by *vocabularies*. A vocabulary is a set of associated name pairs. Each pair consists of a friendly name a business analyst might use, such as Cost or Age, and the technical names the rule engine needs to integrate rules with the sources of facts. Analysts and programmers can work together to create vocabularies. Rules can then be built using the friendly names in vocabularies. Not only does this allow analysts to work on the rules without the need to have a programmer hovering nearby, but it simplifies rules and makes them much more readable. Without vocabularies, a typical condition could read

```
Consulting.Rates.rate_name is equal to RFPEstimateXML.RulesRFP:/RFP/Service
```

This compares a database value, the concatenation of the database, table, and column, and a field in an XML document, which is the concatenation of the .NET-style qualified name for the document schema and the XPath expression needed to locate the field within a document instance. With vocabularies, the condition can become

```
SvcName is equal to Service
```

That's somewhat easier, isn't it? The design-time side of the BizTalk rules architecture is shown in Figure 11.1.

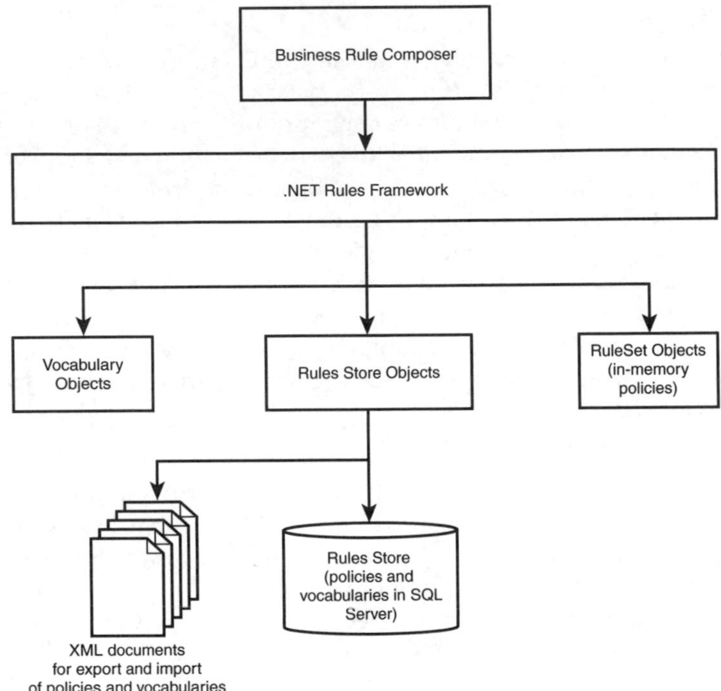

FIGURE 11.1 Tools, .NET object models, and a SQL Server database combine to create and store BizTalk policies and vocabularies.

Using Policies in Applications

Actually making use of policies requires a host application, the .NET Rules Framework APIs, and the Rule Engine Update Service. The latter monitors the rules store to detect changes to published policies. This service ensures that the latest version is always loaded into memory for execution unless the host application explicitly specifies otherwise. The host application uses .NET objects from the Rules Framework to load and execute policies. Rules and facts are cached using some strategies we'll get into in the "Fact-base" and "Policy Caching" sections later in this chapter. The runtime side of the BizTalk Rules architecture is depicted in Figure 11.2.

Host applications can be any executable or assembly that can load and execute .NET classes. We'll see a standalone console application later in this chapter. Orchestrations are also hosts for policies. The Business Rule Composer application also acts as a host application when you test a policy you are designing. Before we get into building applications, let's look at the details of rules development.

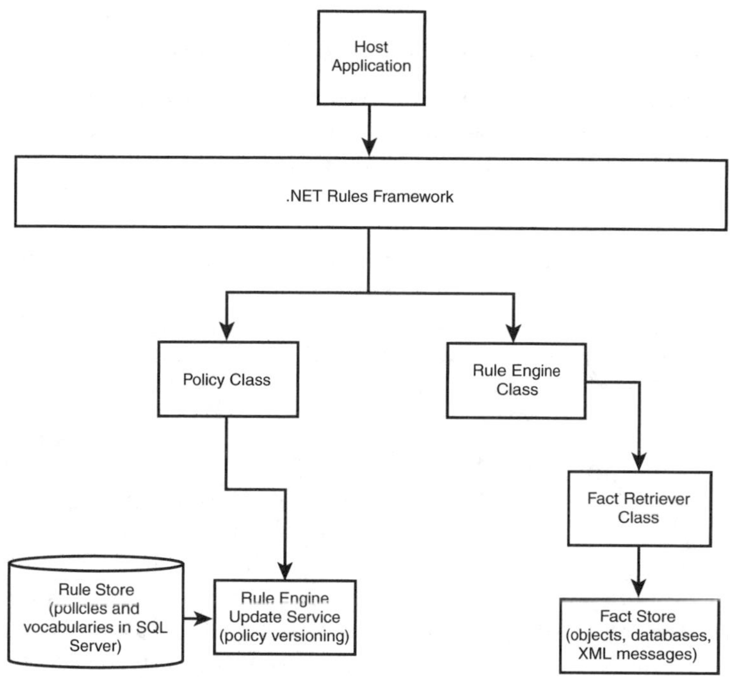

FIGURE 11.2 Applications use the .NET Rules Framework to load and execute policies.

Rules Development

Rules development is concerned with the integration of external facts, vocabularies, and policies to create a store of rules that can be used to create rule-based applications. In some respects, rules development is conceptually similar to designing an XML Schema or an object model for an application.

The first step is to consider the facts in the domain under discussion. Look for objects and properties that relate information about the business topic. Along the way, you should identify common concepts, such as customers and orders. You'll have to relate these to specific fact representations, but these concepts form your vocabulary for thinking about the problem.

TIP

It is easier to find problems if you are thinking about the problem in terms of high-level concepts than if you are thinking about specific columns in a database or fields in a document.

After you have your facts and vocabulary, you can start to relate the two. Besides thinking about the mechanics of integrating various fact sources into a rule-based application, you'll want to think about how often the facts and rules change. This dictates how you tell the rule engine to cache your facts and the policy you are executing.

Let's begin with facts. As we stated earlier, there are three types of sources for facts: .NET objects, database tables, and XML documents. Not only can these facts appear in the conditions of rules, but they also appear in the actions. The permanent effects of executing a policy consist of the side effects on your facts. After the policy terminates, you examine your objects, tables, and documents to use the effects of applying business rules in your application. When used with orchestration, as we shall see in Chapter 12, the effect of rule processing usually consists of changing fields in messages or changing objects that are used to change messages or control the flow of execution in an orchestration. If you are using the BizTalk rule engine with your own application, exclusive of BizTalk and orchestration, the effects can be used however you want.

.NET Objects Fact Sources

Any .NET class can be a source for facts. There is no need for the class to support serialization or implement any special interfaces. How you get them into memory, however, depends on how often the facts change. We'll defer that discussion for a moment, coming back to it in the "Fact-base" section. The same issues also apply to other sorts of facts. .NET objects are perhaps the simplest form of facts to use. The least amount of work you need to do to use .NET objects as fact sources is to instantiate your object and pass it as an instance of the basic `Object` class.

Database Fact Sources

Relational databases are only slightly harder to use. As long as you can access the database through the .NET ADO classes, you can use it with the rule engine. You simply identify one column of a table as a fact in the condition part of your rules. As with .NET objects, there are some issues relating to how you want to load tables into memory.

NOTE

There is one conceptual issue you have to understand right now, however. If you do much database work, you may be accustomed to thinking of a table as a set. You can readily issue SQL queries to see if some value appears in a specified column anywhere in the table, to get a count of all rows that meet a certain criteria, or get some other global information about the table.

The rule engine, however, views a table, or, more precisely, a specific column, as a collection of facts. When you specify a column in a rule condition, the rule engine will iterate through all the rows and consider each value as a separate fact. When you write your rules, therefore, think in terms of values appearing rather than not appearing. The thing you want to avoid is similar to the else part of an `if-then-else` statement or the `otherwise` part of a `switch` statement. It is very difficult to say "You've gotten here without triggering anything, so..."; instead, you have to say, "I see this fact, therefore I will do this..."

For example, if you are writing rules that relate to the color of something, you can write rules that govern what will happen based on a specific color being observed. You might easily have rules for red, green, brown, and yellow, for example. You cannot easily write a rule that says "For all other colors do this." A rule will match for firing only if the value appears. Each row is considered in isolation. If one value fires one rule with a certain effect and another fires a different rule with a contradictory effect, the state of the fact-base will depend on which rule fires last.

When you are dealing with database facts, you designate a specific database and table, and then point to a column within that table. The rule engine is able to get all the type information it needs by querying the database. At runtime, the values of the column are loaded into memory and used.

XML Document Fact Sources

Because BizTalk is about messages, and messages are frequently XML documents, XML documents are a crucial source of facts in a rule-based application. Such messages are the best way for you to get facts in and out of legacy applications. They are also an easy and durable way for you to record the effects of rule processing.

Just as you point to a relational table's column for database facts, you follow a similar procedure for using XML facts. Instead of a database, you point to a schema. Then you locate the field you desire using an XPath expression. If you are using the Business Rule Composer, this is as simple as navigating through a tree, just as you would find a field for property promotion. The composer creates the XPath syntax for you. If you are using the .NET APIs and creating rules through procedural code, you provide the XPath expression yourself. At runtime, you provide an instance of the document to the rule engine.

When a document field is used as part of a rule condition, the value of that field is read. If the field is the target of an action in a fired rule, the new value is written to the field. The document is changed in memory. If you want to preserve the original message, you must be careful to write the changed document out to a different file. In an orchestration, you would make a copy of the message, and then submit the copy to the fact-base.

Now that we know something about rule construction, we need to put rules together into useful collections that can be used in applications. First we'll look at cleaning up the names in rules and collections of rules, then we'll group rules into collections called *policies*, and finally we'll look at how the rule engine caches policies.

Vocabularies

It doesn't take long for an analyst to appreciate the value of and the need for vocabularies when building rules for policies. Without them, conditions and actions are verbose expressions stuffed with XPath expressions, .NET property names, and qualified database names. Worse, when the underlying schemas, classes, and relational schemas change, the rules are broken.

With vocabularies, you can write rules using compact names that are meaningful to the domain of business knowledge under discussion. When the sources of facts change, you edit the vocabulary to point to the new source of the facts. The policy remains unchanged because it is expressed purely in the language of the vocabulary. Because policies and vocabularies are immutable after they are published, you will have to change the link and republish new versions of each, but this is a simple matter in the Business Rule Composer. It is easier to do this than to edit rules and test the policy all over again. This scheme maintains the integrity of policies by ensuring that a vocabulary can never change the facts underlying a policy.

Each version of a vocabulary is given a GUID internally to uniquely identify it. Each name within the policy also gets a GUID. A policy, in turn, links to the vocabulary on which it is built by specifying the GUID of the vocabulary. The policy also contains links to the names it draws on from the vocabulary by specifying the GUID of the names. Although the .NET APIs enable you to specify and load particular vocabularies and manage links between policies and vocabularies, you will usually let the rule engine trace links and retrieve names and the physical facts to which they point based on the information in the linked vocabulary.

Fact-base

We've been coy regarding how facts are moved into memory. This relates to the nature of the volatile store of facts for execution, called the *fact-base*. The currency of the fact-base depends on how often facts change. Left to itself, the rule engine will not refresh the fact-base. Consequently, facts loaded into it will remain unchanged by the outside world for the duration of the policy execution cycle. If you don't expect facts to change while the policy is running, your programming task is simplified. You merely instantiate the objects you need—loading XML documents into instance of `System.Xml.XmlDocument`, using ADO datasets for tables, or simply instantiating your own .NET objects—and pass them into the rule engine as an array of objects. This technique is called a *short-term fact-base* because the facts are instantiated and used without regard to any outside source.

Suppose your facts change frequently. In that case, you need a long-term fact-base. The terms long-term and short-term refer to the durability and life span of facts. A long-term fact-base has to worry about the long-term physical fact store. This is important in BizTalk, as you may be dealing with messages flowing through the system or a database that is constantly changed. You cannot simply instantiate some facts and ignore the effects of the outside world while you are processing the rules.

Long-term fact-bases are managed for the rule engine by creating fact retrievers. These are custom components that implement the `IFactRetriever` interface. When you configure the rule engine to use a fact retriever for your policy, the rule engine will resort to the fact retriever whenever it needs to examine or change facts. Because fact retrievers are custom components, they can implement any caching strategy that makes sense for your application. `IFactRetriever` is a very simple interface, consisting of exactly one method,

UpdateFacts. Virtually all the implementation effort that goes into writing a fact retriever relates to your caching strategy.

Policy Caching

It is important to understand the life cycle of a policy as it moves through development into use if we want to understand how the rule engine works with the Rule Update Service to obtain the latest version of a policy. Because the outcome of applying business rules depends on the rules used and the vocabulary (if any) those rules depend on, the rules architecture renders a finished policy immutable. This is version control for rules and policies.

While you are working on a policy, you are able to save and edit the policy as much as you like. The policy's rules are saved to the rule store, but the policy is not available for use by most host applications. Only those hosts using a class specially designed for the task, PolicyTester, can see the policy. When you are ready to put it into use, you publish the policy. At this time, the rule store makes the policy immutable but does not put it into effect. You can no longer edit the policy. If you want to continue work, you must copy the policy to a new version. You can think of the policy's status at this point as being staged for deployment.

When you are ready to put the policy into service with nontest applications, you deploy the policy. At this time the local rule store publishes information on the policy to the Rule Update Service. This is a Windows service that monitors the rule store. Nontest applications access the current version of the policy by referencing the service. As you will see in our sample host application, the code needed to find and execute a deployed policy is a good deal simpler than that needed to work with a policy that is under development.

If you need to deploy the policy to other servers, you can export the policy and its associated vocabulary as a pair of XML documents written according to a pair of unpublished Microsoft schemas that together constitute the Business Rules Language (BRL). You may then take the documents to another server and import them into that machine's local rule store.

Authoring Policies and Vocabularies

There are several ways to author policies and vocabularies. The most common way, and the one used exclusively by the business analysts who are the main target of rule-based processing, is to use the Business Rule Composer tool. We'll go into that later, in the "Business Rule Composer" section, right before we get into the sample. Right now we're going to discuss authoring for programmers. These techniques let you write applications that create rules dynamically and let you create tools for application development, as well.

You can author rulesets outside the composer in two ways. These approaches are primarily for tools development and system administration. The first uses XML documents. This is the approach BizTalk uses to export and import policies and vocabularies. The other is through .NET APIs and programming.

BRL-Syntax XML Documents

Those of you with experience with database administration may have conducted bulk data dumps of a relational database to a text file. These have usually been flat files in formats such as CSV. XML offers more structure, so it should not be surprising that that is how BizTalk gets rules data in and out of SQL Server stores. It is also used to save policies and vocabularies in file stores outside SQL Server. Although it is not common, it is possible to run a rules-based application entirely with file stores.

The XML syntax Microsoft devised for this task is known as the Business Rules Language, or BRL. This syntax is not presently described in the BizTalk documentation.

> **NOTE**
>
> The namespace for BRL is declared as `http://schemas.microsoft.com/businessruleslanguage/2002`. This is a namespace proprietary to Microsoft.

Although policies and vocabularies are exported to separate documents from the Business Rule Composer, both documents have the same document element, `brl`. Listing 11.1 shows the beginning of a policy file, known here as a ruleset.

LISTING 11.1 Partial Ruleset Document Showing Version, Configuration, and Binding Information

```
<brl xmlns="http://schemas.microsoft.com/businessruleslanguage/2002">
  <ruleset name="RFP">
    <version major="1" minor="4" description=""
         modifiedby="myserver\user"
         date="2004-02-15T00:29:02.6381024-05:00" />
    <configuration>
      <factretriever>
        <assembly>DbFactRetriever, Version=1.0.1505.34508,
        Culture=neutral, PublicKeyToken=d4e488d64aff1da4</assembly>
        <class>
          Que.BizTalk.RFP.myFactRetriever.RFPDbFactRetriever
        </class>
      </factretriever>
    </configuration>
    <bindings>
      <xmldocument ref="xml_0" doctype="RFPEstimateXML.RulesRFP"
          instances="16" selectivity="1" instance="0">
        <selector>/*[local-name()='RFP' and
➥namespace-uri()='http://RFPEstimateXML.RulesRFP']</selector>
        <schema>C:\RulesRFP.xsd</schema>
```

LISTING 11.1 Continued

```
        </xmldocument>
        <datarow ref="db_1" server="myserver\Consulting"
                 dataset="Consulting" table="Rates" instances="16"
                 selectivity="1" isdataconnection="true"
                 instance="0" />
    </bindings>
```

The first thing to notice is how the version element declares the major and minor version of the policy, as well as who modified the policy and when. Version control is very important in rules development. Moving down to the configuration element, we see that the policy is configured to use a database fact retriever. The assembly and class information is specified. The last area to look at is the bindings section. The first child of the bindings element binds an XML document to the policy as a fact source by specifying the .NET-style qualified class name, the XPath expression that selects the root of the document based on local name and namespace, and the physical file that specifies the schema. Note that this last item is a file path, so be sure to transfer the file to the new server when exporting a ruleset.

The document in question goes on to specify rules using an XML structure that allows us to express conditions and actions in prefix notation. Listing 11.2 depicts a rule with one compound condition and three actions. The last two actions have been edited for space. The rule in friendly form is in Listing 11.2.

LISTING 11.2 Business Rule in Friendly Form

```
if Hours is greater than 160 AND SvcName equals Service
then
   Approved True
   Comments Discount Approved
   Cost (0.9*(Hours * HourlyRate))
```

Note how the rule is anchored by the rule element. The name, priority, and status of the rule are given there using attributes. Everything below the rule expresses the structure of the rule.

The condition is contained within the `if` element. True to the prefix notation, the `AND` element (which is the logical operator combining the two conditions) comes first. The greater than operator for the first predicate comes next. The `vocabularylink` element identifies this operator in the built-in predicates vocabulary. From there, we bind to a fact—in this case, the `Hours` field in our XML document. This forms the left hand side (`lhs`) of the predicate. The right hand side (`rhs`) is a constant; the decimal value `160`. See Listing 11.3.

LISTING 11.3 Rule Definition Fragment from the Ruleset Document

```
<rule name="DiscountRate" priority="0" active="true">
  <if>
    <and>
      <compare operator="greater than">
        <vocabularylink uri="3f0e9bcc-6212-4e6a-853c-e517f157a626"
➥element="b276a0f4-12d9-4380-b242-135bbfc5e287" />
        <lhs>
           <function>
             <vocabularylink
➥uri="8a4906c8-3797-4ae6-a9b6-864c23c81438"
➥element="728b3a0b-b270-4cfa-aac6-b24e3aaad8dd" />
             <xmldocumentmember xmldocumentref="xml_0" type="decimal"
➥sideeffects="false">
               <field>*[local-name()='Hours' and
➥namespace-uri()='']</field>
               <fieldalias>Hours</fieldalias>
             </xmldocumentmember>
           </function>
         </lhs>
         <rhs>
           <constant>
             <decimal>160</decimal>
           </constant>
         </rhs>
       </compare>
       <compare operator="equal">
         … <!-- details omitted for space -->
       </compare>
     </and>
   </if>
   <then>
     <function>
       <vocabularylink uri="8a4906c8-3797-4ae6-a9b6-864c23c81438"
➥element="89745202-17d8-412f-bfa3-382d67111a91" />
          <xmldocumentmember xmldocumentref="xml_0" type="boolean"
➥sideeffects="true">
            <field>*[local-name()='Approved' and
➥namespace-uri()='']</field>
            <fieldalias>Approved</fieldalias>
            <argument>
              <constant>
                <boolean>true</boolean>
              </constant>
```

LISTING 11.3 Continued

```
          </argument>
        </xmldocumentmember>
      </function>
      <function>
       … <!-- details omitted for space -->
      </function>
      <function>
       … <!-- omitted for space -->
      </function>
    </then>
  </rule>
```

We continue in this fashion until we reach the `then` element, which anchors the actions section of the rule. The first action, from Listing 11.2, is to assign the `Approved` field of an XML document to the Boolean value `true`. The assignment function takes an XML document binding and a single argument, the value.

The vocabulary links in Listings 11.1 and 11.3 associate the ruleset document with the two built-in vocabularies (functions and predicates) and a vocabulary of our own devising. Listing 11.4 shows a portion of our vocabulary.

As with the ruleset document, we begin with a `brl` element. This is followed by the `vocabulary` element with its version control information. From there, we have a series of `vocabularydefinition` elements. Each one binds a friendly name to a database column or XML document field.

LISTING 11.4 Vocabulary BRL Document

```
<brl xmlns="http://schemas.microsoft.com/businessruleslanguage/2002">
  <vocabulary id="8a4906c8-3797-4ae6-a9b6-864c23c81438" name="RFP"
            uri="" description="">
    <version major="1" minor="1" description=""
        modifiedby="myserver\user"
        date="2004-02-14T21:57:55.6504144-05:00" />
    <vocabularydefinition id="693a705f-a6a4-4e37-92b9-06a52a2553c7"
        name="SvcName" description="">
      <bindingdefinition>
        <databasecolumnbindingdefinition column="rate_name"
               type="string">
          <databaseinfo server="myserver\Consulting"
               database="Consulting" table="Rates"
               connection="true" instance="0" />
        </databasecolumnbindingdefinition>
      </bindingdefinition>
```

LISTING 11.4 Continued

```
      <formatstring language="en-US" string="SvcName" />
    </vocabularydefinition>
    <vocabularydefinition id="0c2f3a3a-e598-4c96-9bb2-0b0797e9ef3e"
         name="Cost" description="">
      <bindingdefinition>
        <documentelementbindingdefinition
            field="*[local-name()='Estimate' and namespace-uri()='']"
            fieldalias="Estimate" type="decimal">
          <documentinfo schema="C:\RulesRFP.xsd"
                        documenttype="RFPEstimateXML.RulesRFP"
                        selector="/*[local-name()='RFP' and
                          namespace-uri()='http://RFPEstimateXML.RulesRFP']"
                        selectoralias="/*[local-name()='RFP' and
                        namespace-uri()='http://RFPEstimateXML.RulesRFP']"
                        instance="0" />
          <argument position="0">
            <valuedefinitionliteral type="decimal">
              <decimal>0</decimal>
            </valuedefinitionliteral>
          </argument>
        </documentelementbindingdefinition>
      </bindingdefinition>
      <formatstring language="en-US" string="Cost {0}"
                    delimiter="{[0-9]+}">
        <argument position="0">
          <valuedefinitionliteral type="decimal">
            <decimal>0</decimal>
          </valuedefinitionliteral>
        </argument>
      </formatstring>
    </vocabularydefinition>
...
</brl>
```

The first definition is a binding between the name `SvcName` and the column `rate_name` in the `Rates` table of the `Consulting` database. We first name the column in the `databasec-olumnbindingdefinition` element and then provide the database and table information in the `databaseinfo` element.

The second definition shown is an association of the name `Cost` with the `Estimate` field in an XML document. The `documentelementbindingdefinition` element denotes a binding to an element in an XML document, not a binding to the XML document element. After providing a suitable XPath expression in that element to select the field, the `documentinfo` element provides the .NET-style type of the document, the physical schema file, and the XPath explicitly locating the document element of this particular document class.

As you can see, authoring rulesets and vocabularies in BRL is an exacting task. You would never want to do this by hand, but the schema exists. It could conceivably be used to modify an existing export file. For example, you might use XPath to locate and fix up schema file paths to reflect the target server environment. You could also use XSLT to display rulesets as HTML by way of providing formal documentation.

.NET APIs for Rule-Based Application Development

The other way to author rules is programmatically, using the classes of the .NET APIs for rules development. The classes you will need are found in the `Microsoft.RuleEngine` package. This is implemented in the `Microsoft.RuleEngine.dll` assembly found in the BizTalk Server 2004 installation folder.

The basic approach is to create instances of the `LogicalExpression` class, representing the condition portion of a rule, an instance of `ActionCollection` to hold the actions for the rule. When both objects are properly set, you add them to an instance of the Rule class. The rule is then added to a `RuleSet` object.

When you want to persist your rules, you use one of the `FileRuleStore` or `SqlRuleStore` classes. To run a ruleset under development, you will need a `PolicyTester` object. After the ruleset is in production, you can use the simpler `Policy` class.

These classes are just a few of the many classes in the rule development APIs, but they are the principal classes used for authoring. If you expect to create authoring tools and work with the .NET classes extensively, you will need to study the product documentation in detail. However, it is worth our while right now to consider the major classes used in rule-based application development.

Rule Development APIs

The rules APIs belong to two packages. The main package is `Microsoft.RuleEngine`, implemented in `Microsoft.RuleEngine.dll`. The other, `Microsoft.BizTalk.RuleEngineExtensions`, adds three classes to extend the rule-based system. Both assemblies are located in the BizTalk Server installation folder. These packages contain literally dozens of classes, but there are a few that are essential. We shall consider these core classes in this section.

Figure 11.3 depicts the using and inheritance relationships that will be of interest to beginning rule engine developers. At the top of things is `Policy`. Another class, `PolicyTester`, may take its place during development, but `Policy` represents a completed, production knowledge-based system available for execution. To execute, it must be configured, and it must load a ruleset. The `RuleSet` class, in turn, loads and uses one or more instances of the `Rule` class. `Rule` objects, as we have seen, contain `LogicalExpression` objects and `Action` objects.

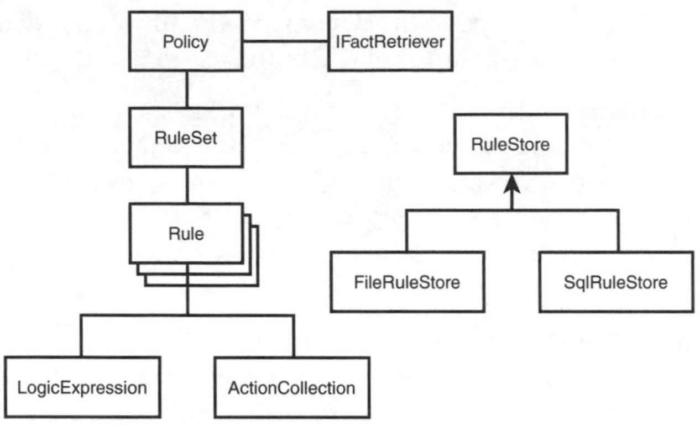

FIGURE 11.3 Using and inheritance relationships among the major rules-development classes.

As important as rules are, though, we cannot have a knowledge-based system without facts. Instances of `Policy` use classes you develop that implement the `IFactRetriever` interface. This is the interface that manages long-term facts and the fact-base. When a policy has loaded rules and facts, it is ready for execution by the rule engine.

A rule engine that could hold policies only in memory would be an interesting lab tool, but would not be suitable for enterprise applications. The abstract class `RuleStore` develops the semantics of a durable store for policies and vocabularies. It is implemented by two derived classes, `FileRuleStore` and `SqlRuleStore`. As the names imply, `FileRuleStore` uses disk files for storage and `SqlRuleStore` uses a SQL Server relational engine.

As we take up these classes for closer examination, we will look only at the more commonly used methods and properties. The complete documentation for these classes can be overwhelming. You are urged to study the documentation in greater depth as you work with knowledge-based programming. The intent here is to help point you in the right direction and identify the more useful aspects of the .NET APIs.

`Policy`

You might wonder why `Policy` and `RuleSet` both appear in Figure 11.3. Isn't a policy a ruleset? Where is the rule engine class? A BizTalk policy is indeed a ruleset, and there is a class corresponding to the BizTalk rule engine, but the `Policy` class is a useful encapsulation of a number of things. It shields programmers from the nuts and bolts of working with rule stores and the rule engine. As such, you will configure a Policy instance and work with it as if it were the rule engine itself. It loads an instance of `RuleSet`, so you do have a distinction between the `Policy` class and the generalized concept of a BizTalk policy.

The `Policy` class has two constructors. One takes a string whose value names the policy you want to work with. The other takes the same parameter and adds two `System.Int32` parameters for the major and minor policy version numbers. Any policy loaded through the Policy constructor must be deployed in the rule store. Another class, PolicyTester, is very similar in its interface to Policy, but it has additional constructors that let you load published policies and policies from other servers. Policy, in contrast, works with the local store and is concerned with production-ready rulesets.

Policy has four public properties. MinorRevision and MajorRevision collectively define the version number of the Policy instance. PolicyName is the name of the policy. RuleSetInfo is a class that repeats the preceding information and adds data regarding who saved the policy and when. All four properties are read-only.

The Policy class has one major public method: Execute. This method has four overloaded forms. The purpose of this method is to load facts into the policy and apply the ruleset to them. The first form takes a System.Object parameter, which is some instance of a class representing a fact in the system. The second form takes an array of such parameters. The remaining forms repeat this pattern (single object and array of objects), but add a second parameter, an instance of an object implementing the IRuleSetTrackingInterceptor. This interface is used to implement a debugging system for the rule engine.

RuleSet

This class has an imposing eight versions of its constructor. The first takes a string parameter that names the ruleset. Unlike Policy, though, this does not mean that the class loads the named ruleset from the store. It merely initializes a new instance of the class and gives it the specified name. There is another constructor that takes a name and a version number and performs the same initialization.

There are two more versions of the constructor that take the same parameters and add an object of the type System.Collections.ICollection. This is a collection of rules to compose the ruleset.

That takes us through half the constructor versions. The remaining versions repeat all that we have seen, but also add a final parameter of the type VocabularyLink. This parameter draws in the vocabulary that provides the ruleset with its friendly names and specific fact bindings.

The class has six properties, of which three are of particular importance to programmers. These are explained in Table 11.1.

TABLE 11.1 Important Properties of the RuleSet Class

Property	Meaning
ExecutionConfiguration	Read/write property for an instance of a class, RuleSetExecutionConfiguration, that manages fact retrievers, other objects controlling rules execution, and parameters for memory and loop size. These factors govern the execution of rules in the rule engine.
Rules	Read-only RulesDictionary object. This class collects the rules in the ruleset.
VocabularyLink	Read/write instance of the class of the same name. This property associates the ruleset with the names and bindings to facts.

Rule

This is the class you will use if you are building rulesets dynamically in an application. You might do this to build tools, or you might use it to automatically generate rulesets in which you have a known set of basic rules that include values that change regularly. In that case, you could regenerate the ruleset by drawing the values from an application or database and creating the rules programmatically.

There are six constructors for this class. The first takes a `System.String` naming the new rule. This does not load a rule from any store. It merely creates an empty rule object and gives it a name. The next takes a name parameter and adds a `VocabularyLink` object as the second parameter. This constructor also gives you an empty object, but now you have a link to a name you might use in the rule you will construct.

The remaining constructors build complete rules based on the parameters passed to the constructor. The first constructor of this group takes a `System.String` for the name, a `LogicalExpression` object for the rule condition, and an `ActionCollection` object for the actions. The next form takes the name parameter, a `System.Int32` representing the priority for the rule, and then the `LogicalExpression` and the `ActionCollection` objects.

The last two constructors repeat the two forms we just discussed and add a `VocabularyLink` object at the end. The first of these two takes a name, condition, actions, and the link. The final form takes a name, priority, condition, actions, and the link.

The `Rule` class has six properties, all of which are read/write. The properties describe the parts and status of the rule object. `Actions` is an `ActionCollection` containing the rule's actions. `Active` is a Boolean which indicates whether the rule is active or dormant. `Conditions` is a `LogicalExpression`. Despite the name, a rule has only one condition, but it may be a compound expression. `Name` is a `String` that must be unique within the ruleset. `Priority` is an `Int32` and it has an interesting range of values. The larger the value, the higher the priority. Zero (`0`), though, is both the default and the middle value. `VocabularyLink` is both the name of the final property and its type. It establishes a link between the rule and a domain-specific definition.

The class has just one method, `Clone`. It produces a deep copy of the rule. It is a quick and convenient way to generate a large number of similar rules. After calling `Clone`, you can modify those parts of the rule that differ from the original.

LogicalExpression

Now we proceed into the internal workings and components of a rule. `LogicalExpression` represents the rule condition. It has a single constructor that takes no parameters and creates an empty condition object.

This class has two properties. The first, `Type`, is a read-only property of the `System.Type` class. `VocabularyLink` is a read/write property that is typed as an object of the class with that name.

This class, like `Rule`, has a single method, `Clone`, that makes a deep copy of the condition.

These are all the properties and methods of the class. Conspicuously absent is any sort of method for building the logical expression itself. It turns out there are classes representing all the predicates, such as `NotEqual`, and classes for the three logical operators to make compound expressions or their negation: `LogicalAnd`, `LogicalOr`, and `LogicalNot`. Using these in combination with your own classes or vocabulary links gives you the flexibility to build conditions for rules.

ActionCollection

This class, as we have seen in previous sections, is a collection of actions executed in sequence when the rule's condition evaluates to `true`.

The class has two constructors. One takes no parameters and produces an empty collection. The other takes an instance of `ICollection` and creates an object based on an existing collection of actions.

This class has a single property, `Item`, which functions as the class indexer in C#. It is a read/write property that takes an integer index and gets or sets an instance of the `Function` class. `Function` comes from the `RuleEngine` namespace. It is an abstract class that serves as the ancestor for any class implementing an action. This abstraction allows `ActionCollection` to handle all sorts of actions without special-purpose code.

This class has eight methods, and several of them have overloaded forms. These methods are listed in Table 11.2.

TABLE 11.2 `ActionCollection` Class Methods

Method	Forms	Meaning
`Add`	`int Add(Function action)` `int Add(System.Object action)`	Adds the `Function` or `Object` to the end of collection. The `Object` form permits use with existing components. The return value is the index of the location where the item resides.
`AddRange`	`void AddRange(ICollection actions)`	Adds the collection of actions to the end of the existing collection of actions.
`Clone`	`object Clone( )`	Makes a deep copy of the object.
`Contains`	`bool Contains(Function item)` `bool Contains(System.Object item)`	Returns `true` if the item is found in the collection.
`CopyTo`	`void CopyTo(Function[] receiver, System.Int32 index)` `void CopyTo(System.Array receiver, System.Int32 index)`	Copies the entire collection to receiver beginning at the location denoted by `index`.
`IndexOf`	`int IndexOf(Function item)` `virtual int IndexOf(System.Object item)`	Returns the index of item in the actions collection, or –1 if not found.

TABLE 11.2 Continued

Method	Forms	Meaning
`Insert`	`void Insert(System.Int32 index, Function action)` `virtual void Insert(System.Int32 index, System.Object action)`	Inserts action into the collection at the location specified by `index`.
`Remove`	`void Remove(Function action)` `virtual void Remove(System.Object action)`	Removes action from the collection.

`FileRuleStore`

If you refer back to Figure 11.3, you'll notice the inheritance tree with the `RuleStore` class at its head and the classes `FileRuleStore` and `SqlRuleStore` derived from it. The other classes formed an interrelated set of classes needed to make rules work as something we can execute. The storage classes are needed to give us a place to store vocabularies and rulesets.

Most programmers will not be implementing their own rule store classes, so there is no great need to cover the abstract base class. When you are dealing with the SQL Server rule store, you can load rulesets using the methods of `Policy` and `PolicyTester`. For brevity's sake, then, let's look at the details of `FileRuleStore` as our means of orienting to the whole topic of rule storage.

`FileRuleStore` has four constructors, covered in Table 11.3. Basically, all initialize the newly created object by locating the file store. The last three constructors add parameters for security and loading convenience.

TABLE 11.3 `FileRuleStore` Constructors

Constructor	Usage
`FileRuleStore(System.String)`	Initializes the object using a URI locating the file-based rule store.
`FileRuleStore(System.String uri, IRuleLanguageConverter converter)`	Initializes the object using the store at uri in conjunction with convert. `IRuleLanguageConverter` is a class permitting loading and saving of rulesets and vocabularies to and from a stream object.
`FileRuleStore(System.String uri, System.Security.Principal.WindowsIdentity credentials)`	Initializes the object at `uri` using credentials for authorization.
`FileRuleStore(System.String uri, System.Security.Principal.WindowsIdentity credentials, IRuleLanguageConverter converter)`	Performs initialization of the store at `uri`, with security provided by credentials, and rules and vocabularies in converter.

FileRuleStore has no properties, but it does have six methods listed in Table 11.4. There is nothing remarkable about these methods. A file rule store is a simple collection of rulesets and vocabularies. These methods implement the common collection operations of adding, removing, and reading items in a collection.

TABLE 11.4 FileRuleStore Methods

Method	Usage
override void Add(RuleSet rules, System.Boolean publish) override void Add(RuleSetDictionary rulesets, System.Boolean publish) override void Add(Vocabulary names, System. Boolean publish) override void Add(VocabularyDictionary nameCollection, System.Boolean publish) override void Add(RuleSetDictionary rulesets, VocabularyDictionary nameCollection, System. Boolean publish)	Adds the ruleset(s), vocabulary(ies), or both to the rule store. If publish is true, the items are published.
override RuleSet GetRuleSet(RuleSetInfo rsInfo)	Retrieves the ruleset described in rsInfo.
override RuleSetInfoCollection . GetRuleSets(RuleStore.Filter filter)	
override RuleSetInfoCollection . GetRuleSets(System.String name, RuleStore.. Filter filter)	Retrieves information about rulesets in the store that meet the criteria in filter and, if included, name, where name is the name of the ruleset. RuleSet.Filter is an enumeration whose values are All, Published, Latest, and LatestPublished.
override VocabularyInfoCollection GetVocabularies(RuleStore.Filter filter) override GetVocabularyInfoCollection GetVocabularies(System.String name, RuleStore.Filter filter)	Retrieves a list of objects describing the vocabularies that match filter and name.
override Vocabulary GetVocabulary (VocabularyInfo vInfo)	Retrieves a vocabulary described in vInfo.
override void Remove(RuleSetInfo rsInfo) override void Remove(RuleSetInfoCollection rsInfos) override void Remove(VocabularyInfo vInfo) override void Remove(VocabularyInfoCollection vInfos)	Removes one or more rulesets or voc abularies described by the objects that describe them.

Note that GetRuleSets and GetVocabularies do not retrieve rulesets and vocabularies directly. Rather, they represent queries on the rulestore to find all the rulesets or vocabularies that match certain criteria specified in the parameters of those methods. You will need to use `GetRuleSet` or `GetVocabulary` to retrieve the actual ruleset or vocabulary you are interested in.

`IFactRetriever` Interface

You will find yourself writing a class that implements this interface whenever you need to manage long-term fact-bases. The interface consists of a single method, so the complexity of this implementation is determined solely by the sophistication of your caching scheme. You need to have a good estimate of how often the fact-base is likely to change and balance that information against the benefits to be gained from caching facts in memory.

The method you need to implement is `UpdateFacts`. This method returns an instance of `System.Object`, which is taken by the rule engine to be a handle to your updated facts. The system will inspect the actual object you return in determining how to deal with it. For example, when it encounters an ADO database connection, it understands that it should use ADO objects and methods to retrieve facts from the database in question. `UpdateFacts` takes three parameters.

The first parameter is a `RuleSetInfo` object describing the ruleset in use. The second is a reference to the `RuleEngine` object executing the ruleset. You use the methods of these classes to get clues as to what facts are needed. The third parameter is a `System.Object` instance. The first time your class is called, this parameter will be null. Thereafter, this parameter is the return value of the previous invocation of `UpdateFacts`, thereby giving you even more information about the state of the fact-base. We'll see an example of a simple `IFactRetriever` implementation in the chapter sample solution.

Business Rule Composer

The Business Rule Composer, depicted in Figure 11.4, is the tool used by analysts and programmers to specify rulesets and vocabularies. It consists of four principal regions. At the top left is the Policy Explorer. It depicts the policies stored in the local rulebase in SQL Server. Below that is the Facts Explorer, which performs the same function for vocabularies, but also lets you find facts in your schemas, databases, and .NET classes. Below that is the Properties view.

The right side of the window is used for a number of purposes. As shown in Figure 11.4, the window is displaying the Rule Editor, with panes for conditions and actions. When testing policies, these panes are replaced by an output window that gives a textual representation of the state of ruleset execution.

The Business Rule Composer lets you build vocabularies, develop rules and policies, and test policies.

Building Vocabularies

Evenv if you do not immediately build a vocabulary, you need to know how to work with the Facts Explorer because some of the tasks apply to rule development. You can use the

XML Schemas, Databases, and .NET Classes tabs to construct names and drag them into conditions and actions in the Rule Editor.

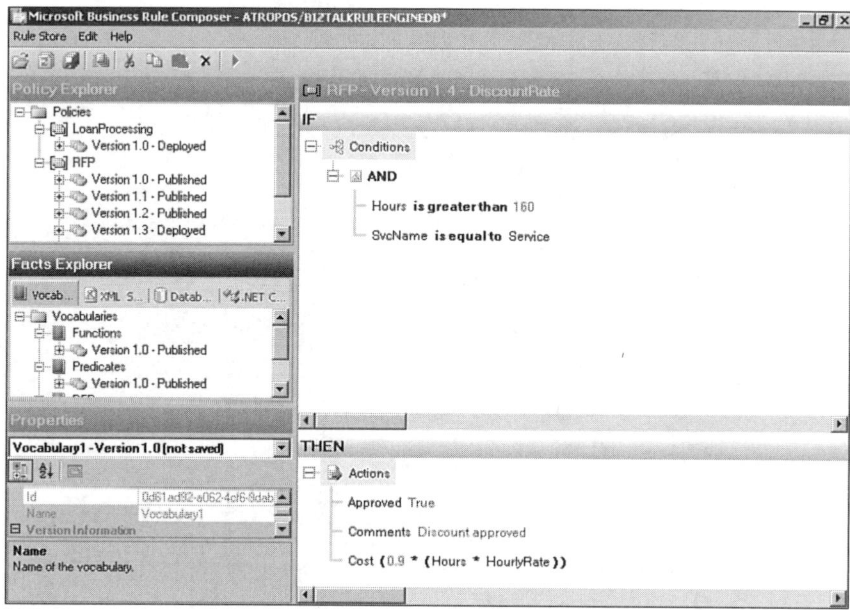

FIGURE 11.4 Typical view of the Business Rule Composer, showing a rule under construction.

Let's look at how to construct a new vocabulary, because this will cover all the tasks you will need. Go to the Facts Explorer and select the Vocabularies tab. Right-click the root node, labeled Vocabularies. The context menu consists of a single entry, Add New Vocabulary. When you select it, you get a new Vocabulary with a child node labeled Version 1.0 (not saved). The Vocabulary node will be highlighted, allowing you to enter a new name. You may also change the name in the Properties view.

If you right-click the child version node, the first item on the context menu is Add New Definition. Selecting this brings up the Vocabulary Definition Wizard. The opening screen of this wizard is shown in Figure 11.5.

This page offers you the choice of the four types of definitions. The first involves constants: single values, ranges, or sets of values. We'll consider the other three in turn, but because the remaining pages depend on which type of definition you select, let's press ahead with constants. If you select this, the next page asks you to pick between these choices and give the definition a name. Picking a single constant value leads to another page, Define a Constant Value, which is straightforward. You select a data type from a drop-down list of .NET types, enter a display name for the constant, and enter a value for your constant.

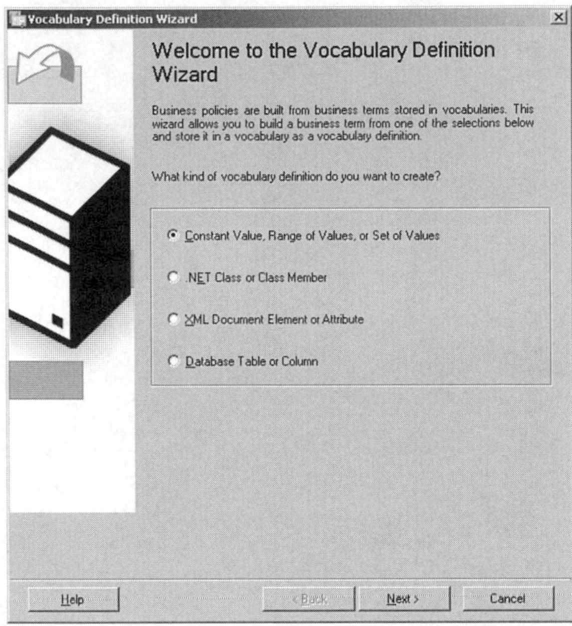

FIGURE 11.5 The opening page of the Vocabulary Definition Wizard offers a choice of definition types.

Ranges are a little more complicated. Figure 11.6 depicts the Define a Range of Values page. A range is defined by a low value and a high value. As with constants, you select a data type and provide a value. To provide that value, select either the low or high value and click Edit. The Parameter Definition dialog box comes up. You will usually provide a number directly, but you may also select from pre-existing vocabulary definitions.

The remainder of this page is devoted to how the definition will be displayed in rules and conditions. When a definition is dragged into a rule, the Rule Composer inserts a placeholder with display cues for the analyst. The display format string guides how the placeholder is built. Digits in braces denote placeholders for your constant values. Moving them around in the string alters the look of the display string. The Rule Composer shows an example of the finished placeholder with its cues under the edit field where the formatting string is entered. In the example shown in Figure 11.6, the display string Liquid Range {0} {1} is turned into the placeholder shown below it by replacing the {0} placeholder with the low value, 0, and {1} with the high value, 100.

The Define a Set of Values page is shown in Figure 11.7. As with ranges, you may select from values you enter yourself or pick from a pre-existing definition. Unlike a range, each item in the set must be specified. This is done by selecting a data type for the set from the drop-down list, and then entering values and clicking Add. If you make a mistake, select the mistaken value in the Values list and click Remove.

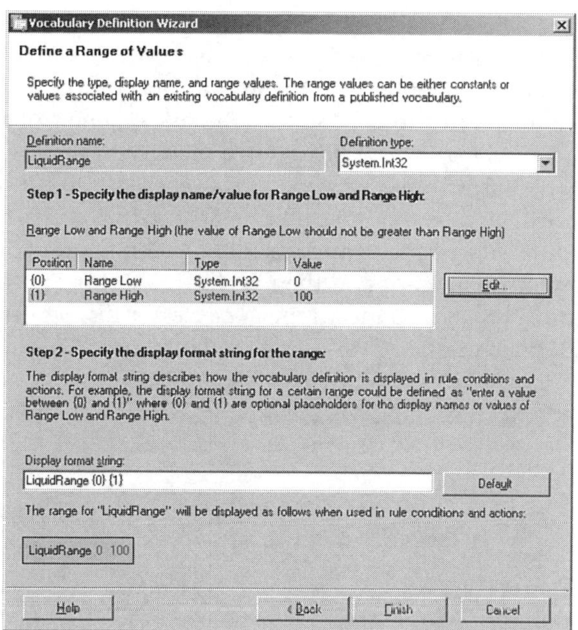

FIGURE 11.6 Defining a range on the Define a Range of Values page.

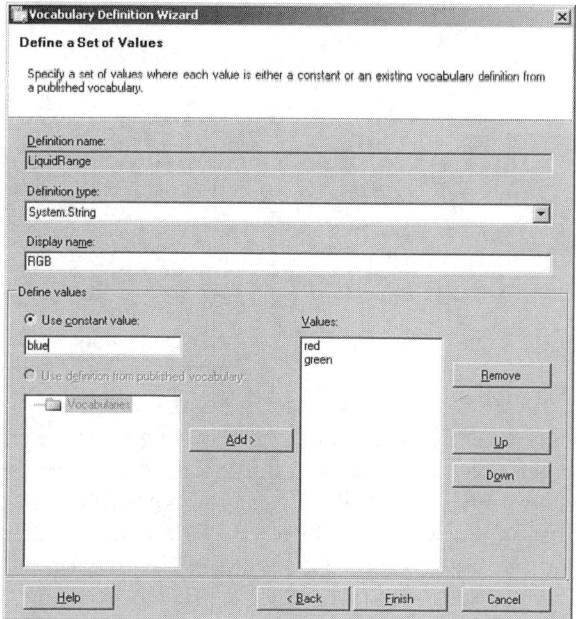

FIGURE 11.7 Specifying a set of values.

Selecting a .NET class is where things get a little more interesting. Figure 11.8 shows the wizard page for this option. The idea here is to locate a .NET class deployed to the global assembly cache (GAC) and bind to the whole class or a specific property of that class to use as a fact. You need a class in the GAC so that the rule engine will always be able to get at the class at runtime. Clicking Browse brings up a pick list of the assemblies in the GAC. After you select one, the Rule Composer inspects the assembly and shows you the Select Binding dialog box, which is a tree view of all the information about the class that the composer gained through inspection of the assembly. You navigate down through the tree until you find the property you want and then click OK to return to the .NET Class page in the wizard. In Figure 11.8, I've bound to the get accessor for the Reason property in the Claims class, a class defined in one of the SDK samples.

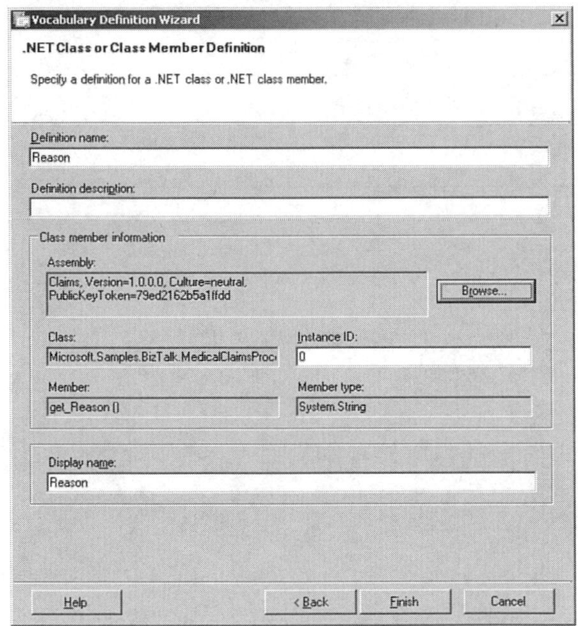

FIGURE 11.8 Binding to a .NET Class or Class Member Definition.

Binding to a field in an XML Schema is similar, but with one exception. Instead of looking for schemas in a globally deployed assembly, you browse for a schema file on disk. When you click Browse, you get a file dialog box that prompts you to select an XML Schema file. After you select one, you see the Select Binding dialog box, which is little more than a tree view of the schema, just as you would see in the BizTalk Schema Editor. The result of selecting a node in the tree, however, is to generate an XPath expression locating the node. In Figure 11.9, we see the result of binding to the Hours element of a schema we will develop in the chapter sample. Note how we've selected the Perform "Get" Operation option button at the bottom. If we had selected Perform "Set" Operation, the Display name field would not appear. Now, whenever a rule refers to Hours, the rule engine will look in the runtime fact-base for a document conforming to this schema, and, if found, locate the Hours element and use its value.

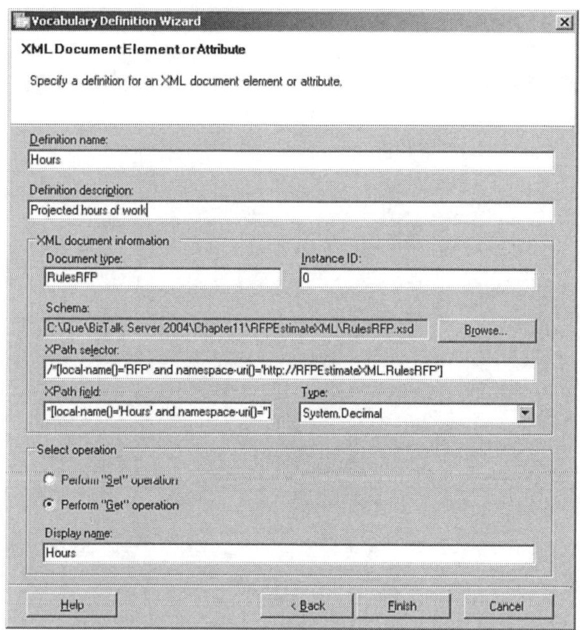

FIGURE 11.9 Binding to a field in an XML document.

CAUTION

Be sure that you put the schema file in a location that will be accessible when you deploy a ruleset or vocabulary. If you will be exporting to another server, or if you are developing on a machine other than the BizTalk Server that will make use of your definitions, you must put the schema on a disk that is accessible under the file path given.

Binding to a relational database is a little more work. You have the option of binding either to a data connection or to a specific table or data row. This applies to how the rule engine will work with your data and not how you specify something for binding. When you click Browse in the Database Table or Database Table Column Definition page of the wizard, depicted in Figure 11.10, you must select at a minimum a table within a database. You cannot select the database alone.

When you click Browse, you will see a simple dialog box titled Connect to SQL Server. You select a server from a drop-down list to begin. You have the option of starting SQL Server if it is not running. The most important option you have to specify is whether to use

Windows authentication or SQL Server authentication. Ensure that the option selected will provide sufficient runtime privileges to access the information. If you are using Windows authentication, you must make sure the runtime engine is running under an account that has appropriate privileges. If you select SQL Server authentication, you must supply login credentials in the dialog box.

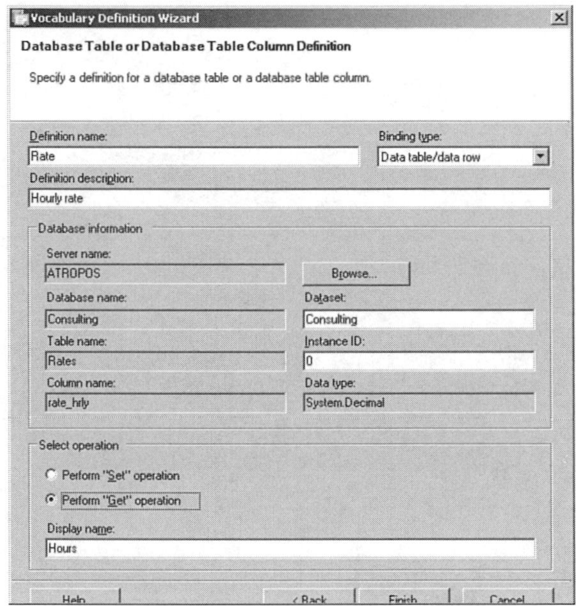

FIGURE 11.10 Binding to a column in a relational table.

After you select a server and log in to it, you will see a Select Binding dialog box. This dialog box is dominated by a tree view of all databases on the selected server. You drill down to the desired database, then the table, and optionally, on to the desired table column. A limited property page at the bottom of the dialog box displays the column information. After you select a table or column to bind to, the information is displayed in the Vocabulary Definition Wizard. Note that just as with XML binding, you must decide between a Get or a Set operation.

We've spent a lot of time discussing how to bind a field in a class, XML document, or database table to a name, yet we've looked at only one tab of the Fact Explorer. The remaining three tabs serve as shortcuts to the tasks previously discussed. Take the XML Schema tab, for example. If you right-click the root Schema node and select Browse, you will have the opportunity to select an XML Schema file from disk. After it is selected, the schema tree view we saw in the wizard appears under the Schema node in the XML Schema tab. If you drag a field in the schema tree over the Vocabulary tab, that tab becomes active. When you drop the field onto a writable Vocabulary (not published), a definition is added and the appropriate page of the Vocabulary Definition Wizard is filled out with the information selected. Similar things happen with the Databases and .NET Classes tabs.

There is one more way to use the Fact Explorer. If you make a selection in any of the tabs, the selected definition may be dragged to the Policy Explorer and dropped into the condition or action of a rule. If you drag a vocabulary name, the friendly name is used. If you drag a selection from one of the other tabs, the qualified name is used directly.

Building Policies

The first thing to do when composing rules is to create a policy to contain them. Rules do not exist in a vacuum. They are a related set of rules built around a body of business knowledge, and they are meant to be executed as a whole. That whole is the policy.

Initially, you will have no policies. Right-click the Policies node in the Policy Explorer and select Add New Policy from the context menu. A new named child node appears to represent all versions of a given policy. Underneath that node will be a child labeled Version 1.0 (not saved). If you are building a new version of an existing policy, you right-click the parent node for a related set of policy versions and select Add New Version.

Either way, you end up with a version node. Now you are ready to build rules.

Building Rules

Right-click the node for the version you are working with and select Add New Rule. The focus now shifts to the right pane of the Rule Composer as two panes appear within it. The outer pane is titled with the name of the policy and the version number. The upper pane that appears within it is titled IF, and the lower child pane is labeled THEN. The IF pane is the Condition Editor, and the THEN pane is the Action Editor.

The Condition Editor has a root node labeled `Conditions`. Right-clicking that node gives you four menu items. There is one each for adding the logical operators `AND`, `OR`, and `NOT`. Below those items is a rule mark, and then a submenu titled `predicates`. Clicking that displays a list of 12 predefined predicates, such as `GreaterThan` and `NotEqual`.

This is where a little bit of planning will help you. Right-clicking any node and selecting a logical operator adds that operator as a child of the clicked node. The first time you do this, you have only the `Conditions` node. Add an operator, and the next time you want to add something, you can click either Conditions or the operator. It's a bit like adding parentheses, where each node is a level of nesting and adding anything to that node is adding something within the parentheses. Let's build a simple condition to illustrate this. When we were discussing how to build a definition based on an XML field, we defined Hours. If you didn't follow along with our discussion, it doesn't matter. Any name will do, even a name you create directly from one of the tabs without a friendly vocabulary name. Imagine that we want to build a condition to test and see if Hours is greater than 20 and less than 40.

Right-click Conditions and select Add AND. An AND node appears under Conditions. Now right-click the AND node and select Predicates GreaterThan. The Condition Editor adds a node `argument1` is greater than `argument2` immediately under AND, where `argument1` and `argument2` are placeholders. If you created Hours in a vocabulary, saved the vocabulary, and published it (more on this in the section "Rules Deployment and Versioning"), you can drag `Hours` from the Fact Explorer's vocabulary and drop it on the `argument1` placeholder. Otherwise, you can browse through the schema in the XML Schemas tab and drag the field to `argument1` directly. In the first case, `argument1` is replaced with Hours, the friendly name defined in the vocabulary. In the second case, you'll be stuck with the elaborate, qualified name that includes the XPath expression that locates the `Hours` field.

Click `argument2` and type **20**. Now you have the first half of the compound condition. Return to the AND node and select Predicates LessThan. A condition expression appears beneath the one we just defined, this time with the predicate `is less than`. Repeat the process you followed earlier to replace the first placeholder (`argument1`) with `Hours`, and type **40** for `argument2`. You've completely defined a compound condition that performs the evaluation we desire.

If you add something by mistake, you can right-click that node and select Delete Predicate or Delete Logical Operator, as the case may be. If you created the node you desire but put it in the wrong place, there are menu items Move Up and Move Down. Use these to attain the expression you want. If you replaced a placeholder with the wrong argument, you can select Reset Argument to restore the placeholder and try again.

Building actions is even simpler because you are building a sequential list rather than a potentially nested series of expressions as in the Condition Editor. Go to the Action Editor. Right-clicking the Actions node displays a context menu with six functions as shown in Table 11.5.

TABLE 11.5 Predefined Action Functions

Function	Meaning
`Assert`	Add a new fact or fact value into the fact-base.
`Clear`	Reset working memory and the rule firing agenda.
`Halt`	Terminate rule processing.
`Retract`	Remove a fact or fact value from the fact-base.
`RetractByType`	Retract a fact type from the fact-base.
`Update`	Update a fact in working memory.

Retract works on a specific fact. This would be a particular field in an XML document or a .NET class or a column in a database table. `RetractByType`, in contrast, applies to a fact type: a schema type, .NET class, or database table. The Action Editor will help you keep this straight. If you attempt to drag the wrong type of item onto an argument, you will get a clear error message.

Assigning a value to a fact is even simpler. Drag a name from the Fact Explorer to the Actions node. The new node that appears is the name of the fact followed by the equal sign, followed by a placeholder. Replace the placeholder with the value you want.

As with the Condition Editor, you can delete, move up, or move down an action within the Actions list with appropriately named items on the context menu. You can also clear, set to null, or set to an empty string any argument from the context menu.

Rules Deployment and Versioning

I've made some statements along the way regarding "publishing" policies and vocabularies. In fact, before we can test either entity or use one in an application, we have to at least publish it. It is now time to take a moment and discuss publishing, deployment, and versioning as they apply to policies and vocabularies.

While you work with a vocabulary or policy, you will, one hopes, save your work frequently. In the Business Rule Composer, this means that items will be saved to the BizTalk rules database. At this point, the item—a policy or vocabulary—is a work in progress, not something that can be submitted to the runtime rule engine.

After you have a policy or vocabulary in a finished state, you will want to publish it. Right-click the node for the version you want to publish and select Publish. This renders the version immutable; no further changes are possible. If changes are required, you will have to create a new version and make the changes there. This allows applications and orchestrations to use policies and vocabularies without concern that the behavior of the application will change because of a shift in the underlying business knowledge.

At this point, you can test a policy (and any associated vocabulary) in the Business Rule Composer, but it will not be available for use from an application until you deploy it. You can use definitions from a vocabulary in a policy after it has been published. They are considered finished but not in production. To deploy a policy or vocabulary, you right-click a published version's node and select Deploy.

Occasionally, you might discover a problem and need to pull a policy out of production. The Undeploy menu item exists for this purpose. Although you could create a new version and use it in applications, an administrator cannot guarantee that some application or orchestration somewhere is not using the faulty version. By undeploying, you ensure that a bad policy cannot be used.

Creating a new version of a policy or vocabulary does not require that you re-create all the rules and definitions. You can drag individual entities to a new version from an old one, saving considerable time. If your changes are minor, you can select the root policy node, the one containing all the versions, right-click, and then select Paste Policy Version. This causes the creation of a new version that is a copy of the previous one. You can then go in and modify those items requiring change.

Policy Testing

The Business Rule Composer provides a facility for testing rulesets. To do this, the runtime engine needs instances of the facts you want to work with. Policy testing begins by right-clicking a published policy node and selecting Test Policy.

When you do this, the Select Facts dialog box, depicted in Figure 11.11, appears. Based on the rules in the policy selected, the rule engine knows what types of facts are needed, but does not have any instances of documents, tables, or objects. The Select Facts dialog box has two windows. The top one displays the types the rule engine knows that it needs. There are entries for all three types, regardless of whether they exist in the specified policy. If one of the entries—XML documents, relational tables, or .NET classes—appears in the policy, an entry is made showing the specific type needed. In Figure 11.11, the policy being tested needs one kind of XML document and one relational table, but no .NET class instances.

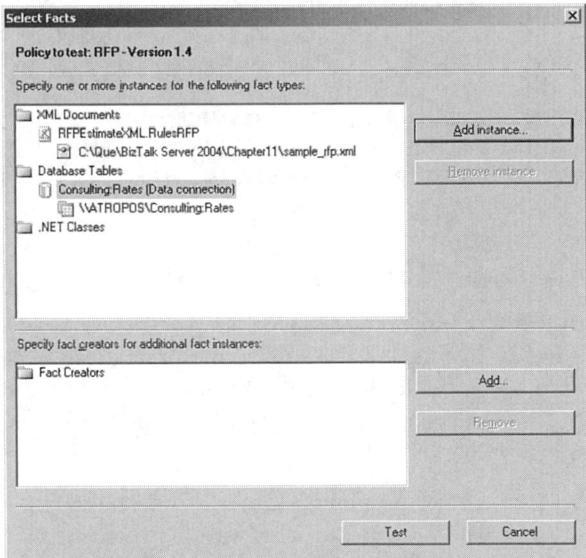

FIGURE 11.11 The Select Facts dialog box lets you specify facts when testing policies.

You can directly specify existing tables and XML documents for use in the top pane by clicking Add Instance and browsing to a document or table. The Business Rule Composer will furnish default fact retrievers for these known types. You cannot browse to a .NET class unless the assembly contains a class implementing the `Microsoft.RuleEngine.IFactCreator` interface.

If you need to create additional facts as the engine runs, you need to specify `IFactCreator` classes for each fact type. This is done in the lower pane by using the Add button and browsing to a deployed assembly.

After you have specified facts on which to operate, click Test. The Select Facts dialog box disappears, and the right pane of the Business Rule Composer is given over to the Output view. The name and version of the policy under test appears in the title of this view, and the top of the view displays the word `Output`. The rule engine will prepare an agenda, fire rules, assert facts, and perform all the other tasks involved in executing the policy. Text messages appear in the Output window in a scrolling view. Each message records a specific action in the rule engine.

NOTE

Policy execution is not like debugging a conventional application. The side effects of execution are visible only by inspecting the fact artifacts—for example, table column values and XML document fields. The Output window is merely a trace of the rule engine in operation. If your artifacts are unchanged or you see fewer then expected operations, it is probably because you have forgotten to specify the proper facts, or any facts at all. The rule engine executes, but finds nothing to match and takes no action.

Standalone Rules Sample

Various samples in this book have worked with the idea of a prospective customer submitting a Request for Proposal (RFP) and getting an estimate back from a vendor for the requested services. Such estimation necessarily involves some business rules. This sample will take a simplified RFP and perform the estimation process as a rule-based application. It will develop a vocabulary and a policy and will be executed from a console application to illustrate the fact that the rule engine can be hosted outside of BizTalk orchestration.

Listing 11.5 shows a sample RFP document such as we might expect to exchange between business partners. It identifies the requesting company by name, names a desired service and the estimated hours of professional services required, and has fields to receive an estimate for the cost of the services, approval status, and comments.

LISTING 11.5 Sample RFP Document Requesting an Estimate for Services

```
<ns0:RFP xmlns:ns0="http://RFPEstimateXML.RulesRFP">
   <Company>General Chaos</Company>
   <Service>Programming</Service>
   <Hours>100</Hours>
   <Estimate>0.0</Estimate>
   <Approved>false</Approved>
   <Notes>request</Notes>
</ns0:RFP>
```

We might well receive such a document through messaging or as part of a business process. In fact, we'll make use of the policy we develop in this chapter in an orchestration in Chapter 12. For the purpose of the current sample, however, we'll assume that the document exists in isolation. We are merely interested in applying business rules to it. This sample embraces the following tasks:

- Building a vocabulary to describe the concepts involved
- Devising rules to estimate services
- Developing a fact retriever for hourly rates in a database table
- Programming rule engine host applications using the `PolicyTester` and `Policy` classes

RFP Vocabulary

The sample document in Listing 11.5 suggests several important concepts. There is the idea of a `Service`, which is the particular professional service desired. In the sample, the requesting company is asking for programming services. This should imply certain rates or fees to the receiving company. Next is the idea of `Cost`. The requesting company wants an estimate of the cost of the requested services. The document does not initially provide this, but the ruleset should be able to determine this for us and insert it into the document.

The cost is derived from the nature of the services provided and the hours involved. Consequently, we need to define a concept, Hours, to pick up the estimated hours from the document.

In addition to updating the `Estimate` field with the value of Cost determined from the rules, we want our policy to update the `Approved` and `Notes` fields in the document. I've chosen to call these `Approved` and `Comments` in the vocabulary. Even though we don't care what those fields contain initially, we need to have them as defined facts in the vocabulary if we expect the policy to deal with them in concise form.

The document does not contain everything. Cost will be calculated based on the hourly rate for the desired services and a discounting rule. The rates are slow to change, so it makes sense to put them into a database. I've created a SQL Server database called Consulting, which consists of a single table, Rates. That table has two columns, `rate_name` for the name of the service, and `rate_hrly` for the hourly rate. In the course of applying the policy, we want the rule engine to consult this table to get the appropriate hourly rate for the requested service. We'll call the service name in the database `SvcName` and the hourly rate `HourlyRate`.

NOTE

The folder `RFPRuleHost` in the sample download contains a SQL script in the file `consulting.sql` that will create a new copy of the database as well as the Rates table. You can execute this script through the SQL Server Query Analyzer by connecting to your database server and clicking the Load Sql Script button. You will need to enter data. The data is arbitrary, but you should make sure the name of the service in the XML document matches some value in the `rate_name` column.

To start, open the Business Rule Composer and select the Vocabularies node in the Fact Explorer's Vocabularies tab. Right-click and select Add New Vocabulary. When the new vocabulary node is created, type **RFP** for the name of the vocabulary.

Let's start with the XML definitions. The download contains an XML Schema file in the `RFPRuleHost` folder named `RulesRFP.xsd`. Right-click the Version 1.0 node and select Add New Definition. When the Vocabulary Definition Wizard opens, select the XML Document Element or Attribute option button and click Next.

In the XML Document Element or Attribute page, type **Service** for the Definition name. Click Browse and find the schema file. When the Select Binding dialog box opens, navigate to the Service node and click OK. Accept the defaults that the wizard creates, but click the Perform "Get" Operation option. Click Finish.

Now repeat this process four more times. You want to create a definition, `Hours`, that is associated with the `Hours` field in the document. Then associate a definition `Cost` with `Estimate` in the document, `Approved` with `Approved`, and `Comments` with `Notes`. `Hours` should perform a Get operation, while `Cost`, `Approved`, and `Comments` require a Set operation.

Now we move on to the database. We're going to create two definitions here, `SvcName` and `HourlyRate`. Right-click the Version 1.0 node and select Add New Definition. Check Database Table or Column and click Next in the wizard. Type **SvcName** as the name of the definition, and ensure that Database Connection is selected in the Binding type list on the Database page. Click Browse, find your server, and navigate to the Consulting database, Rates table, `rate_name` column, and click OK. Ensure Perform "Get" Operation is selected and click Finish to create this definition. Repeat this process to create a definition `HourlyRate` that is associated with the `rate_hrly` column.

When you are finished, you will have all the definitions you need. Right-click the Version 1.0 node and select Save. Right-click again and click Publish.

RFP Policy

Our business policy consists of a few basic items that can be expressed as two rules. First, the base cost of the services to be rendered is the product of `HourlyRate` and `Hours`. We do, however, offer a discount of 10% if the requested hours exceed 160.

Let's start with the discounted case. Right-click the Policies node in the Policy Explorer and select Add New Policy. Type **RFP** for the name. Find the Version 1.0 node, right-click, and select Add New Rule. Type the name **DiscountRate**. Now move to the Condition Editor.

There are two parts to this condition. First, we have to match Service from the document with `SvcName` from the database. The rule engine will iterate over the entire Rates table when considering facts, and we want only this rule to fire when the row we are examining pertains to the service requested in the document. This is how you perform a database look-up in the rule engine. The other half of the condition is to see if `Hours` is greater than 160.

Right-click Conditions and select Add Logical AND. Now right click the AND and select Predicates GreaterThan. When the predicate appears, drag `Hours` from the Vocabulary Explorer to the first placeholder, and then select the second placeholder and type **`160`**.

Add the second half of the condition by right clicking AND and selecting Predicates Equal. Drag `SvcName` from the vocabulary to the first placeholder and Service to the second placeholder.

Now we need three actions. Because we found a match for the service, we'll approve the RFP. We'll also calculate `Cost` using the 10% formula and enter the string **`Discount approved`** into the `Comments` field, which is defined as the `Notes` element in the schema.

Drag `Approved` from the vocabulary to the Action Editor and drop it. `Approved` appears with the default `false` based on the data type of Boolean in the schema. Click the placeholder and select `True` from the list. Now drag `Comments` from the vocabulary, drop it, and type **`Discount approved`** for the placeholder.

Now we have to create an action that involves a calculation. Drag `Cost` from the vocabulary to the Action Editor and drop it. `Cost` appears with a single placeholder. Right-click that placeholder and select Functions Multiply from the context menu. Click the first placeholder and type **`0.9`** (for 90%). Right-click the second placeholder and select Functions Multiply again. Use `Hours` from the vocabulary to replace the first placeholder, and replace the second placeholder with `HourlyRate`. The expression for the action should read `Cost (0.9 * (Hours * HourlyRate))`.

If you've followed the process, you have a rule named DiscountRate with a compound condition and three actions. Now return to the Policy Explorer to create another rule.

Right-click the Version 1.0 node and select Add New Rule. Type **`NormalRate`** for the name of the rule. Create a compound condition like the one for **`DiscountRate`**, except that `Hours` should use the `LessThanEqual` predicate. Create three conditions like you did for DiscountRate. The first sets `Approved` to `True`, the second sets `Comments` to `Normal rate`, and the third is a calculation that looks like `Cost (Hours * HourlyRate)`.

That completes our policy. Save it and publish it. You can test the policy using the sample file `sample_rfp.xml` in the `RFPEstimateXML` folder of the download. When you are sure you have a valid policy, deploy it so that we can use it with the host we will be developing.

Database Fact Retriever

Because we are going to use a database for the source of some facts, and we are writing our own host and not just using the Rule Composer, we need a fact retriever component. Our host application can hand this to the `PolicyTester` object before execution. Create a C# class library project in Visual Studio and name it **`DbFactRetriever`**.

Because our table of service names and hourly rates seldom changes, our fact retriever can consist of creating a `DataConnection` object once and using it throughout the execution cycle. In other words, we are loading the connection the first time the rule engine requires a database value and we are retaining it for the life of the policy execution cycle. It's a small table and a small policy, so reading from the database instead of memory whenever we need a value imposes low overhead. For a larger table, we might want to cache a DataSet, but then we would have to manage the process of keeping the cache fresh. Listing 11.6 shows the source code for the fact retriever class.

LISTING 11.6 Simple Database Fact Retriever Class

```
using System;
using System.Collections;
using Microsoft.RuleEngine;
using System.IO;
using System.Data;
using System.Data.SqlClient;

namespace Que.BizTalk.RFP.myFactRetriever
{
   public class RFPDbFactRetriever:IFactRetriever
   {
      public object UpdateFacts(RuleSetInfo rulesetInfo,
➥Microsoft.RuleEngine.RuleEngine engine, object factsHandleIn)
      {
         object factsHandleOut;

         if (factsHandleIn == null)
         {
            SqlConnection con1 = new SqlConnection("Initial
➥Catalog=Consulting;
➥Data Source=(local);Integrated Security=SSPI;");
            DataConnection dc1 = new DataConnection("Consulting",
➥"Rates",
➥con1);
            engine.Assert(dc1);
            factsHandleOut = dc1;
         }
         else
            factsHandleOut = factsHandleIn;
         return factsHandleOut;
      }
   }
}
```

This implementation relies on the fact that the third parameter to `UpdateFacts`, the facts handle, will be null on the first invocation to tell us when we need to create a database connection. If it is, we use typical ADO methods to establish a database connection. The connection string is hard-coded for this sample, which limits this class's use to this sample, but we are using integrated Windows security, so the embedded string isn't a security risk.

We do two things with the database connection object. First, we pass it as a parameter to the `Assert` method of the rule engine. Asserting facts into the fact-base is the rule engine equivalent of a fact coming to light in the real world. A newly asserted fact causes the rule engine to reevaluate the ruleset to see if any rule conditions match the new state of the fact-base. The second thing we do is return the connection object as the return value of this method.

If `factsHandleIn` is not null, we merely pass it back as the method return value. We can do this because the `Rates` table is not going to change over the life of this example. We would need to maintain some state information or determine the state of our facts from the passed-in handle in a more complicated example. This method gets called whenever the engine determines that it needs facts from the fact-base, so we need to determine if the fact-base is stale before passing back a handle.

Rules Host Application

We're down to the last task in our sample: creating a host application to run the policy. In fact, I'm going to show you two versions to highlight the difference between the `PolicyTester` and `Policy` classes.

`PolicyTester` is somewhat more flexible and can deal with policies on different servers. I'm going to restrict this sample to a console application that looks at a specific XML document.

In Visual Studio .NET, create a new Console Application project and name it `RFPRuleHost`. Listing 11.7 provides the source code for this application.

LISTING 11.7 PolicyTester-based Version of the Rules Host

```
using System;
using System.Xml;
using System.Collections;
using Microsoft.RuleEngine;
using Microsoft.BizTalk.RuleEngineExtensions;
using System.IO;

namespace Que.BizTalk.Rules
{
   class RFPHost
   {
```

LISTING 11.7 Continued

```
        [STAThread]
        static void Main(string[] args)
        {
            try
            {
                RuleSetInfo rsInfo = new RuleSetInfo("RFP", 1, 1);
                Microsoft.BizTalk.RuleEngineExtensions.
➥RuleSetDeploymentDriver
➥dd = new Microsoft.BizTalk.RuleEngineExtensions.
➥RuleSetDeploymentDriver();
                RuleStore sqlrs;

                sqlrs = dd.GetRuleStore();
                RuleSet rfpRules = sqlrs.GetRuleSet(rsInfo);
                RuleSetExecutionConfiguration exConfig =
➥new RuleSetExecutionConfiguration();
                RuleEngineComponentConfiguration dbconfig= new ➥RuleEngineComponentCon-
figuration("DbFactRetriever",
➥"Que.BizTalk.RFP.myFactRetriever.RFPDbFactRetriever");
                exConfig.FactRetriever = dbconfig;
                rfpRules.ExecutionConfiguration = exConfig;

                XmlDocument doc = new XmlDocument();
                doc.Load("sample_rfp.xml");
                TypedXmlDocument RFPDoc = new
➥TypedXmlDocument("RFPEstimateXML.RulesRFP", doc);
                PolicyTester host = new PolicyTester(rfpRules);
                host.Execute(RFPDoc);

                FileInfo finfo = new FileInfo("ProcessedRFP.xml");
                StreamWriter writer = finfo.CreateText();
                writer.Write(RFPDoc.Document.OuterXml);
                writer.Close();
            }
            catch (Exception e)
            {
                System.Console.WriteLine(e.ToString());
            }
        }
    }
}
```

The first task is to locate the local rule store and load the desired policy. The `SqlRuleStore` class can be instantiated with a number of options based on which physical server we want. Because we are dealing with the local server, we can take a shortcut through the `DeploymentDriver` class. This class is intended to deploy policies from the local store to some other server. It therefore implicitly knows how to connect to the local rule store. That is what the `GetRuleStore` method does for us. After we have that store, we pass it a `RuleSetInfo` object initialized with the name, `RFP`, of the policy we want. This policy will drag in the vocabulary through its internal links.

With the proper ruleset in hand, we need to set up the rule engine to use the fact retriever we built. That is the purpose of `exConfig` and `dbConfig`. The `dbConfig` object is initialized by passing the class name and qualified .NET assembly name of the fact retriever to a `RuleEngineComponentConfiguration` object. This takes care of locating the assembly and creating an instance of the fact retriever. We then assign that object, `dbConfig`, to the `FactRetriever` property of `exConfig` and pass `exConfig` to the `ExecutionConfiguration` property of the ruleset object `rfpRules`. The ruleset object is now configured with a fact retriever for the database and the policy we want to execute. All that remains is to point it toward the XML document with the rest of our facts and commence execution.

We load the sample XML file into an `XmlDocument` instance. This is standard XML processing with the `System.Xml` namespace. The `Microsoft.RuleEngine` namespace, however, needs its own class, `TypedXmlDocument`, to check the type of the document and assert it properly into the fact-base. We create an object of this class by passing it the .NET qualified form of the document and the `XmlDocument` instance.

All our facts are in order at this time, so we create a `PolicyTester` object by passing the ruleset into the constructor and calling `Execute`. When the method returns, the typed XML document reflects the side effects of executing the policy, so we write it out to a disk file. If the `Service` in the XML document matches a service name in the rates table, the document should be approved and have a `Cost` calculated and inserted into the `Estimate` field. You can check this by opening the file `ProcessedRFP.xml`.

Notice how much code was required just to find the local rule store and load the current version of the policy. This code is useful if you are testing an unpublished policy or a policy on another server. Now let's see a version of the same application that is designed expressly to use the current, deployed version. This relies on the Rule Update Service to find the correct version of the policy. Notice how the code, shown in Listing 11.8, is simplified.

NOTE

The source file `RFPRuleHost.cs` contains both forms of the application. The lines specific to the `PolicyTester` version are commented out, leaving the `Policy` version that follows.

LISTING 11.8 Policy-based Version of the Rule Host

```
static void Main(string[] args)
{
   try
   {
      XmlDocument doc = new XmlDocument();
      doc.Load("sample_rfp.xml");

      TypedXmlDocument RFPDoc = new
➥TypedXmlDocument("RFPEstimateXML.RulesRFP", doc);

      Policy host = new Policy("RFP");
      host.Execute(RFPDoc);

      FileInfo finfo = new FileInfo("ProcessedRFP.xml");
      StreamWriter writer = finfo.CreateText();
      writer.Write(RFPDoc.Document.OuterXml);
      writer.Close();
   }
   catch (Exception e)
   {
      System.Console.WriteLine(e.ToString());
   }
}
```

All that is required in this case is to create the XML fact document and instantiate a new `Policy` instance, passing it the name of the policy we want to run. `Policy` locates the local rule store and retrieves the most current deployed version of the policy. The `Policy` class version of `Execute` takes the XML document as a parameter. Because the policy uses a vocabulary that locates the specific database instance we are using, the rule engine is able to supply a default fact retriever for us.

Summary

Rule-based development is substantially different from procedural programming, but it offers a flexible way to inject business knowledge into a BizTalk Server application. It is a new feature of this release of BizTalk Server and may easily become as important as orchestration proved to be in earlier versions. Business analysts are able to work with the Business Rule Composer to capture their expertise, and the policies they specify may be used with compiled code or orchestrations without requiring a programmer's intervention whenever the rules change.

We saw how to work with the Business Rule Composer to create vocabularies and policies and even test those entities with sample data. Complex rules and definitions involving entities as diverse as XML documents, databases, and .NET objects can be created without programming.

BizTalk offers a complex framework of .NET classes for rule-based applications. Hopefully, the introduction to this framework you received in this chapter will guide you in the creation of tools and utilities. The sample code proved that the rule engine may be utilized entirely independently of the rest of BizTalk Server 2004. This opens the way to the creation of rule-based and rule-using applications that do not necessarily involve messaging and orchestration.

CHAPTER 12

Orchestrating—Advanced Concepts

IN THIS CHAPTER

- Advanced Transactions
- Orchestration Hydration
- Orchestration and Rules
- Direct Port Binding Between Orchestrations
- Parties, Roles, and Role Links: Indirection for Enterprise Deployments

Orchestrations are one of the most important and powerful tools in BizTalk Server. With the current edition of the product, orchestrations take an even more prominent role. You've seen how to design and develop an orchestration, how to send and receive messages, how to control the flow of execution in an orchestration, and other fundamental concepts of orchestration. There are a few more concepts to cover—advanced concepts that bring additional logical mechanisms to bear on the problem of implementing business processes in orchestrations. Foremost among these transactions is the extension of database style transactional processing to processes that involve messaging and may span periods of time much longer than those to which we are accustomed in database processing.

In this chapter we cover the details of transactions in BizTalk orchestration. You will learn about the two types of transactions, how to implement them in an orchestration, and what their limitations are. You will learn about backing out of a failed transaction when conventional database-style rollback is unavailable. We'll also look at a closely related topic, orchestration life cycles. The two are related because BizTalk uses the mechanism for guaranteeing the durability of a long-running orchestration to provide a baseline for the state of transactions at important checkpoints.

Beyond transactions, we need to cover a few other advanced concepts. First, we build on our discussion of rule-based applications to demonstrate the use of the Call Rules shape. This shape enables us to use a rulebase in an orchestration without having to write a separate application to host the rule engine. Next, you'll learn how to use direct port binding to pass messages between orchestrations, a measure that simplifies messaging between orchestrations. The last topic beyond transactions is role links, a mechanism that extends message routing at ports by providing a role-based layer of indirection between your orchestration and messaging port locations for specific business partners.

Advanced Transactions

If you've done any sort of extended work with databases, you know that transactions are a very useful tool for ensuring the integrity of data in the face of multiple, interrelated actions. The classic example is a bank funds transfer. You withdraw money from one account and deposit it into another. The two operations are complementary. If both complete successfully, the bank's books will balance. If either operation fails for some reason and the other completes, the books will show too much or too little money. Transactions were developed to prevent this. A transaction coordinator is given a scope. Within this scope, all actions must complete for the transaction to be committed. If committed, the effects of all actions within the scope of the transaction are applied to the database by the transaction coordinator. If any fail, the effects of the successfully completed operations are rolled back so that the database is restored to its condition before the start of the transaction. In short, all operations take effect, or none do.

Transactions are comparatively simple to implement within a single database manager like SQL Server. The database manager acts as the transaction coordinator, and it can perform commits and rollbacks because it controls all the operations in the system. When developers wanted to implement transactions spanning different applications, the problem became harder. The Windows DTC, or Distributed Transaction Coordinator, was introduced to act as the overarching transaction coordinator. So long as all the operations participating in a transaction use the interfaces of .NET serviced components (or the related COM+ interfaces, which preceded .NET), the familiar mechanisms of transactions can be used.

BizTalk orchestration introduces new difficulties. Most messaging operations, for example, do not have transactional capabilities. SOAP is in the process of adding them, but they are not yet a standard feature of Web services. Business processes, moreover, can take place over periods of time much longer than those typical of database transactions. It is feasible to lock resources, like database handles, for the seconds and fractions of a second typical of database transactions, but not over the minutes or hours that might be involved in a process such as a purchasing approval process. BizTalk generalizes the idea of transactions and adds exception handling and a mechanism called compensation to give us the logical effect of transactions, even when we can't have the formal, precise effects of classic database transactions.

BizTalk Orchestrations support two kinds of transactions: atomic and long-running. Atomic transactions are very similar to classic database transactions. In fact, if you follow certain limits, you can make an atomic transaction a DTC-style transaction. Long-running transactions lack the full formalisms of atomic transactions, but allow us to have the general logic of a transaction even when dealing with operations over long periods of time, periods too long to allow BizTalk to effectively lock resources for DTC-style atomic transactions. Freed of those formalisms, we can bring data consistency and durability of state to processes involving messaging and nontransactional components. We do not, however, get isolation. Changes are immediately visible outside the transaction boundary, so we lose something compared to formal transactional mechanisms. Long-running BizTalk transactions are, however, a major improvement over much of what is seen in custom Web applications today because they offer a standard mechanism for providing code for reversing actions that are no longer correct.

Atomic Transactions

An *atomic* transaction is defined as one possessing four attributes known by the acronym ACID:

- Atomic—The transaction forms an atomic unit of work so that all operations in the transaction take effect on the system, or none take effect.
- Consistency—The transaction preserves the internal integrity of the system's state. If the system is internally consistent before the transaction, it remains consistent after the transaction, regardless of whether the transaction was committed or rolled back.
- Isolation—The effects of transactions are isolated from one another, even if they are performed concurrently. Operations within a transaction are unaffected by and isolated from operations occurring outside the scope of the transaction.
- Durability—The effects of a transaction are permanent after a transaction commits, even if the system subsequently crashes.

Atomic transactions are the most powerful form of transactions BizTalk orchestration offers, but they impose the most restrictions. One fairly obvious restriction is that you cannot nest a long-running transaction within an atomic transaction. Because atomic transactions offer the strongest guarantees for correctness, specifically isolation and atomicity, it stands to reason that long-running transactions offer less protection. An atomic transaction containing a long-running transaction would be unable to meet its requirements for rollback if the long-running transaction contained within it cannot meet its standards for isolation. Besides banning long-running transactions, atomic transactions cannot contain other atomic transactions. After you have declared a scope to be an atomic transaction, you have barred the way to any further nesting. Additionally, an atomic transaction cannot have an exception handler. Such transactions do not need exception handlers, though, because a fault will result in either a retry or an automatic rollback.

The high level of isolation imposes a less-obvious restriction, though one with far-reaching effects. The effects of actions within an atomic transaction must not be visible to—must be isolated from—the rest of the orchestration. Messages have a major impact on the state of an orchestration. They represent data flowing into and out of the orchestration. Similarly, the asynchronous launch of an orchestration has effects on the overall state of the orchestration that cannot be undone. This leads to some behavior in atomic transactions that might seem curious to you at first. The actions taken by Send, Receive, and Start Orchestration shapes within an atomic transaction will not take place until the transaction commits.

What does this mean to you as you design an orchestration? You must be aware of what is going on with respect to the MessageBox. When a message is received in an atomic transaction, it is delivered to the orchestration but not removed from the MessageBox until the transaction commits. If you write any components that check the MessageBox, you may get results other than what you expect. In addition, you cannot construct an atomic transaction with a request-response pair of actions, nor can you have Send and Receive shapes that use the same correlation set. Either of these would lead to unrecoverable conditions if they were permitted.

Creating an atomic transaction is simple enough. First, click the design surface so that the properties of the orchestration as a whole appear in the Properties view. Find the `Transaction Type` property and set it to `Long Running`. Now add a Scope shape to the orchestration. Set the `Transaction Type` property for this shape to `Atomic`. Now you have to select a value for the `Isolation Level` property. Your choices are the following:

- `Serializable`—The default, this isolation level is also the most restrictive. It ensures that concurrent transactions are blocked from making changes to data until the currently executing transaction commits its data.
- `Read Committed`—This level prevents the current transaction from reading data modification in concurrently executing transactions until they have committed.
- `Repeatable Read`—Requires read locks on data until the transaction commits. If another transaction needs to write a change to some data, it acquires the lock. Transactions that have previously read the data will not see the change. This level provides the least protection but the best performance.

The value set for this property becomes especially important when you want to go further and make your atomic transaction a full-fledged DTC-style transaction. There are two rules you must satisfy to get this level of transactional support. First, all components used within the transaction must be derived from `System.EnterpriseServices.ServicedComponents`. Second, the isolation levels set for the components must agree and must be compatible with the isolation level of the transaction. ServicedComponents is the .NET base class for writing COM+ components that can participate in transactions managed by the DTC. As such, turning an atomic transaction into a DTC-style transaction is not so much a matter of BizTalk offering a special feature as it is making the orchestration a COM+ transactional application.

TIP

Atomic transactions have another use unrelated to ordinary transactional concerns. If you are using .NET components that are not serializable, you can use them safely only within an atomic transaction. Because of actions the orchestration engine takes with respect to orchestration life cycle and operating efficiency, data from nonserializable components may be lost if they are used outside of atomic transactions. We discuss these actions in the section "Orchestration Hydration" later in this chapter.

Long-Running Transactions

Orchestrations will very often have situations in which the business process could use the general idea of a transaction without the overhead of formal transactional mechanisms. You may execute a series of actions only to encounter some error condition that leads you to want to back out the effects of the actions taken so far and restore the state of the orchestration to a point prior to the start of the sequence. Formal transactional mechanisms such as those offered by the DTC are convenient, but come at a cost in terms of performance and design issues. You have to make sure your components are transactional and are configured with the proper level of isolation. The locks inherent in making isolation work come at a serious performance cost. Maintaining locks ties up system resources and is usually not feasible over the time spans typical of long-running business processes.

You may not need the isolation of atomic transactions. Correlation sets ensure that related messages are processed by the same orchestration instance. If the data in question pertains only to the instance in question, there is no problem with isolation. Moreover, the actions involved may not be compatible with formal transactional rollback. This is a big problem for messaging, which, after all, is at the heart of BizTalk applications. With the notable exception of MSMQ, BizTalk messaging protocols are not inherently transactional. To achieve a capability for undoing or backing out of actions taken previously, then, you'll have to go outside traditional DTC-style mechanism. Because you have to do that, why incur the penalties that come with atomic transactions? Long-running business processes involving messaging, moreover, have an issue that typically does not arise in traditional database processing. Actions in a transaction may go on so long that you want to abandon the effort after some time interval. A prospective customer, for example, may simply have walked away from an online shopping cart. You have no control over the actions of external participants, nor any way of knowing when they are lost to the system. These are the issues long-running transactions were created to address and which frequently arise in BizTalk applications.

Long-running transactions are easy to specify, but it is somewhat harder to get their fault handling and data integrity issues properly implemented. To create a long-running transaction, make the orchestration as a whole transactional, as we described for atomic transactions. Next, add a scope and set its `Transaction Type` property to `Long Running`. Because long-running transactions are less restrictive than their atomic counterparts, you can nest long-running transactions within one another, and you can nest atomic transactions within long-running transactions. Data in a long-running transaction is in scope for any transaction that contains the current transaction, is contained by the current transaction, or is global to the orchestration. The only data that is not in scope is that in transactions that operate at a level parallel to the current transaction.

Setting a timeout in earlier versions of BizTalk Server was simply a matter of specifying the number of seconds to wait. Because BizTalk Server 2004 uses .NET for its scripting and expressions, it can offer a bit more flexibility. If you click the ellipsis button to configure the Timeout property for a long-running transaction, the BizTalk Expression Editor dialog box appears. You then type an expression that evaluates to a UTC time. Although there are a number of ways to do this, you will conventionally use a `TimeSpan` object to specify a duration because you usually have no control over the exact time when your orchestration executes. `TimeSpan` has four versions of its constructor: one for 100-nanosecond time ticks; one for hours, minutes, and seconds; one for days, hours, minutes, and seconds; and the constructor for control freaks, which takes days, hours, minutes, seconds, and milliseconds. The expression entered in the dialog box in Figure 12.1 specifies a timeout interval of 15 minutes and 30 seconds.

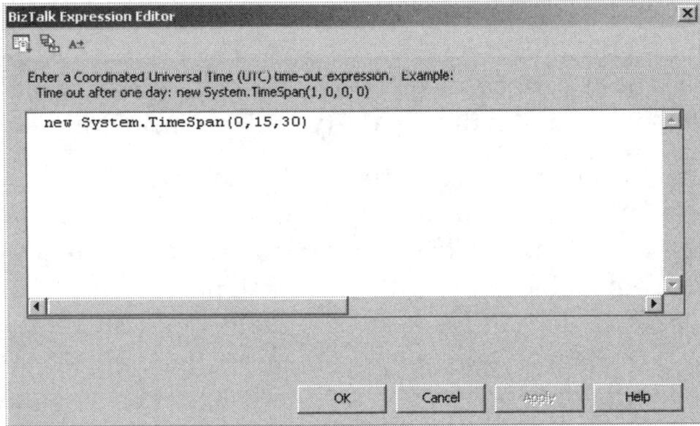

FIGURE 12.1 Using the BizTalk Expression Editor to specify a timeout interval for a long-running transaction.

That's the easy part of specifying long-running transactions. Unlike atomic transactions, the designer of a long-running transaction has to worry about how faults occur and how to recover the state of the orchestration to correct for the fault.

Exception Handling in Transactions

Internal faults are handled as .NET exceptions. The following actions generate an exception in an orchestration:

- Forced termination—A sibling branch in a surrounding scope invokes the Terminate shape for the orchestration, throwing a `Microsoft.XLANGs.BaseTypes.ForcedTerminationException` instance.
- System-generated exception—A fault in .NET or the operating system occurs.

- User code fault—User code in a component or expression throws an exception.
- Transaction failure—A major failure of the transaction, such as a machine crash during the transaction, will generate an exception coming from the orchestration engine upon recovery.
- Timeout expiration—An instance of `Microsoft.XLANGs.BaseTypes.TimeoutException` is thrown by the orchestration engine when the timeout interval expires.
- Throw Exception shape—When this shape is encountered in the course of orchestration processing, an instance of the exception class specified in the shape's Exception Object property will be thrown.
- Receipt of a fault message—A two-way, send-receive pattern port will throw an exception when an instance of the designated fault message is received in response to the outgoing message.

The last fault type requires a bit more explanation. Any two-way port can have a fault message type associated with it. This is done by right-clicking the operation node for the port type in the Orchestration view and selecting New Fault Message from the context message. When an orchestration uses a receive-send pattern port, it can send a fault message instance when it encounters an error in processing an incoming request. This is typically done from the exception handler block that catches the exception thrown inside the orchestration. If, however, the orchestration sent a request through the port and receives a fault message instance in reply, an exception will be thrown in the orchestration in response.

Exceptions are caught and handled in a long-running transaction by adding an exception handler block to the transaction. Right-click the transaction's Scope shape and select New Exception Handler. A new block is added at the end of the scope shape. Each exception handler has two properties that must be configured. The first is `Exception Object Name`, which is simply an identifier for this exception. The other is `Exception Object Type`, which is the .NET type of the exception to be handled.

You process different kinds of exceptions the same as in .NET code, with multiple exception handlers. If you need to throw an exception from within a handler, you can use the Throw Exception shape. Exception handling also works like .NET: an exception, once thrown, will continue outward through scopes until an exception handler is encountered that is configured for the type of the exception. In the worst case, when an orchestration has no explicit exception handlers for a thrown exception, the BizTalk orchestration engine handles the exception and writes an event to the operating system event log.

If you want to throw an exception from within an orchestration—for example, when you've reached an unrecoverable situation in the business process and want to abort to a recovery mechanism—you can use the Throw Exception shape. Configuring this shape consists of giving it a name and setting the value of the `Exception Object` property. The latter property is given a drop-down list in the Visual Studio .NET Properties view. That list will always be populated with `General Exception`. Additionally, any orchestration variables that you may have declared with a type derived from `System.Exception` will also appear. `General Exception` may look like an easy way out, particularly if you want to transfer control to an exception handler without looking at the error exception's properties, but there is a major limitation. You may use `General Exception` only to rethrow an exception from within an exception handler block. You must have an explicit exception variable anywhere else in an orchestration.

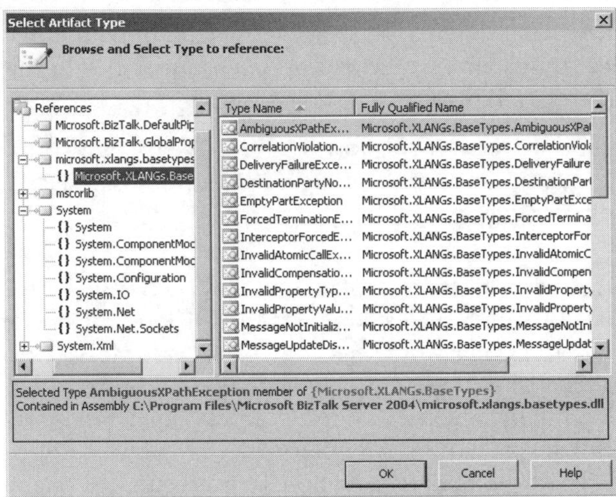

FIGURE 12.2 The Select Artifact Type dialog box is used to specify the type of exception an exception handler block will catch.

Compensation in Transactions

There are occasions when a transaction completes successfully but must have its actions reversed for business reasons. For example, you might complete a transaction to place an order, only to be notified that the product is no longer supported or to have the customer send a notice canceling the order. It is useful to have a block similar in form to an exception handler that can be explicitly invoked to undo the associated transaction. This is the purpose of compensation blocks. These blocks consist of orchestration logic that can be invoked only following completion of the transaction.

Unlike exception handlers, compensation blocks may be created for both atomic and long-running transactions. Indeed, all transactions have a compensation block. If the orchestration designer does not explicitly create one, BizTalk creates an implicit compensation block. If compensation is invoked for a transaction with no explicit compensation block, the implicit block will be called into play. All it does is call the compensation blocks of any nested transactions, calling them in the reverse order of completion. Compensation blocks may also be defined for the orchestration as a whole.

To create a compensation block, right-click the transaction and select New Compensation Block from the context menu. A new area appears at the bottom of the transaction shape. You can then drag and drop action shapes from the toolbox into the block to implement the undo logic. Note that the flow of control does not automatically flow into the compensation block from the transaction. Compensation blocks must be explicitly invoked, typically following a Decide shape or after receiving a message detecting the need to roll back the actions of the transaction.

Exceptions and Compensation Sample

We'll tie this information together with a laboratory-style sample designed to illustrate the key concepts and design patterns rather than a fictional business example. This should make it simple for you to follow the sequence of events and see how BizTalk processes transactions, exceptions, and compensation. With that information in hand, you can go on to apply these mechanisms to your own applications. In particular, this sample will illustrate the following points:

- Nesting transactions
- Generating, throwing, and catching exceptions in an orchestration
- Compensation

The general scenario will work like this: Our orchestration will be activated by receipt of a simple XML message picked up by a file receive location. This message will consist of only one item of information, an indicator of the user's intention as to whether she wants a fault to occur. If the intention field has a numeric value of one, the orchestration will generate a fault requiring compensation. If the value is zero, the orchestration runs to a successful conclusion. Now, to make things a little more interesting, the main body of the orchestration consists of two long-running transactions, one nested inside the other. The inner transaction, cleverly named `NestedTx`, sets a value indicating that the transaction successfully completed. Immediately following the inner transaction, the outer transaction, `OuterTx`, looks at the user's `Intension` field. If the user wants success, the outer transaction sets an appropriate data value, a string, and then creates an outcome message consisting of the strings from the inner and outer transactions. This message is then sent to a file folder for inspection by the user.

If the user's intention is to create a fault, the outer transaction creates an exception object and throws it. The transaction has an exception handler block that catches this particular type of exception. Because the exception occurred following the completion of the inner transaction, we need to invoke the compensation block for that transaction. The inner transaction's compensation block consists of creating a message that indicates that compensation took place. This message has the same format as the success message and goes to the same location, although we will preface the name of the message with `comp_` to help you immediately detect what happened. By inspecting the outcome messages and comparing them to the intention message you sent in, you will be able to compare your expectations based on the theory presented in the preceding sections with what actually happened inside a running orchestration.

Incidentally, sending a message from the compensation is a common design pattern in orchestration transactions, particularly when working with long-running transactions. As stated previously, these transactions have no formal mechanism for rolling back state. Instead, you need to design a messaging scheme in which some messages notify the receiving application that rollback actions are required. Actually implementing these actions is the responsibility of the receiving application. Making sure that the messaging scheme contains sufficient information about the scope of the rollback actions and the instance of the orchestration that was running is your responsibility as an orchestration designer.

The solution is found in the chapter download as `CompensationProject.btproj`. It consists of two projects: `CompensationProject` for the orchestration and related BizTalk artifacts and `Outcome`, a component library project consisting of a serializing class that creates our outcome messages.

Message Schemas

Our user messages are defined in the schema `Intension.xsd`. An instance of this message directing a failure is found in Listing 12.1.

LISTING 12.1 Input Message Directing Fault Generation

```
<ns0:UserIntension xmlns:ns0="http://CompensationProject.Intension">
  <Fail>1</Fail>
</ns0:UserIntension>
```

Change the value of `Fail` to 0, and you are directing the orchestration to run to a successful conclusion. The value of `Fail` needs to be inspected in the orchestration, so we've used Quick Promotion to create a promoted property field in the default properties schema, `PropertySchema.xsd`. `Fail` is derived by restriction from the base type `xs:unsignedInt`, which equates to a `System.UInt32` in .NET. It is restricted with a `minInclusive` value of zero and a `maxInclusive` value of one—the XML Schema way of saying this field should be either a 0 or a 1.

The outcome message should echo the user's failure intention and display the results of the inner and outer transactions. Because the latter two fields are not directly related to any data in the received intention message, a message map is a poor choice for generating the outcome message. Instead, we use a serializable component and attributes from the `Microsoft.XLANGs.BaseTypes` package. We don't require anything fancy here, just three properties we can set. The code for this component is found in Listing 12.2, and a successful outcome message instance is depicted in Listing 12.3.

LISTING 12.2 Serializing Component for Creating Outcome Messages

```
using System;
using Microsoft.XLANGs.BaseTypes;

namespace Outcome
{
   [Serializable]
   public class OutcomeMsg
   {
      public OutcomeMsg()
      {
         FailIntension = 0;
         OuterAction = "Initialized";
         InnerAction = "Initialized";
      }

      [DistinguishedFieldAttribute]
      public System.UInt32 FailIntension;
      [DistinguishedFieldAttribute]
      public String OuterAction;
      [DistinguishedFieldAttribute]
      public String InnerAction;
   }
}
```


LISTING 12.3 Sample of a Successful OutcomeMsg Instance

```
<?xml version="1.0" encoding="utf-8"?>
<OutcomeMsg xmlns:xsd="http://www.w3.org/2001/XMLSchema"
➥xmlns:xsi="http://www.w3.org/2001/XMLSchema-instance">
  <FailIntension>0</FailIntension>
  <OuterAction>Outer Tx Succeeded</OuterAction>
  <InnerAction>Inner Tx Succeeded</InnerAction>
</OutcomeMsg>
```

Outer Transaction: Processing and Exception Handling

The core of the orchestration is shown in Figure 12.3. We've had to collapse some shapes and omit others in the interest of space, but the key items are shown. This figure shows the boundaries of the outer transaction, except for the exception handler block. Omitted are the start and terminal shapes, the messaging ports, and an activating Receive shape that immediately precedes `OuterTx`. Before you begin to create shapes, be sure to set the

`Transaction Type` property of the orchestration as a whole to `Long Running`. If you do not do this, Visual Studio .NET will flag an error when you attempt to create transactional scopes in the orchestration.

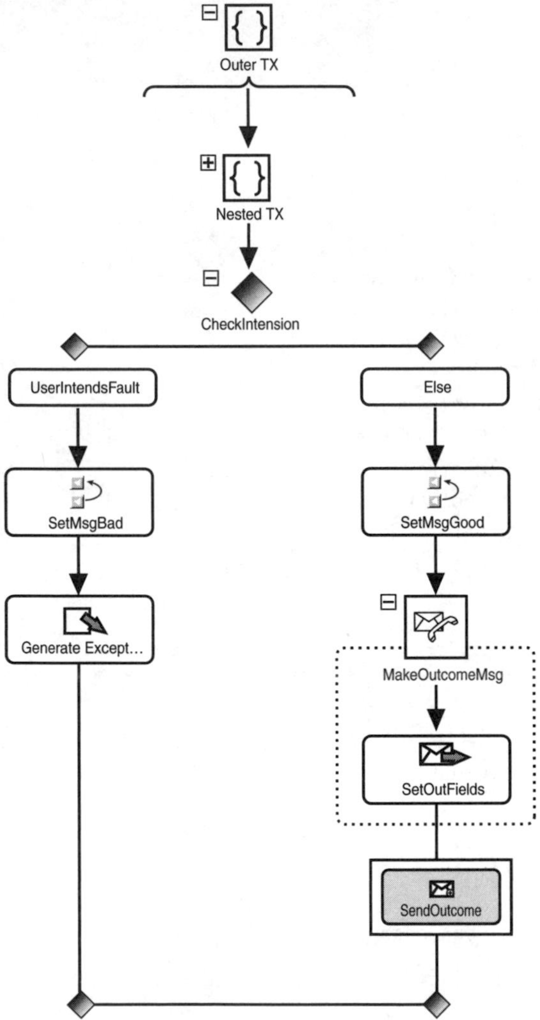

FIGURE 12.3 Major processing in the outer transaction.

Our orchestration has three global variables, AppExc for the exception we will generate, and InnerString and OuterString to capture the results of the inner and outer transactions, respectively. The very first thing that happens in the outer transaction is the inner transaction. An expanded view of this scope is depicted in Figure 12.4. Ignore the Compensation block for a moment and look at the main processing. It consists of a single Expression shape. The scripted expression simply consists of `InnerString = "Inner Tx`

Succeeded"; if we do nothing to compensate, the outcome message will reflect the fact that this transaction concluded successfully. We'll go into greater detail about the compensation block in the next section, but for now, note that it consists of constructing and sending an outcome message reflecting compensated actions.

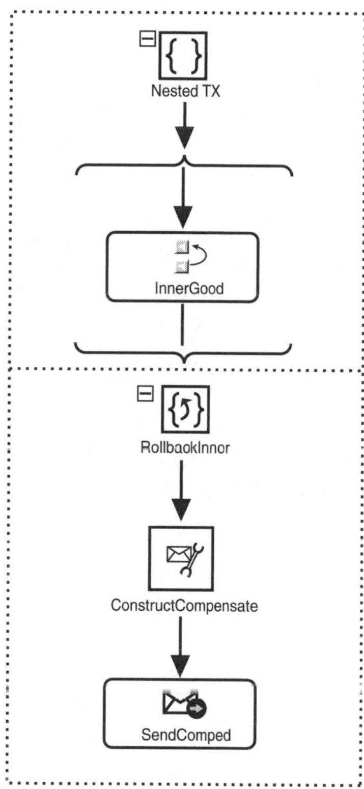

FIGURE 12.4 The inner, nested transaction sets a success value unless compensation is invoked.

After exiting the nested transaction, the outer transaction executes a Decide shape to see if the contrived mischief we've outlined is indicated by the user. The rule to do this is in the UserIntendsFault Rule shape and consists of `IntensionMsg(CompensationProject.PropertySchema.Fail)==1`. We're just looking at the promoted property of the received intention message. Remember that the parenthetical syntax is forced on us by the use of promoted properties. We would need to use distinguished fields to enable the use of dot notation syntax.

Follow the `Else` leg of the Decide shape in Figure 12.3 for a moment. This is what should happen if the user wanted a successful completion. First we set the value of `OuterString` to indicate a successful outcome in the Expression shape named `SetMsgGood`. Then we encounter the Construct Message shape MakeOutcomeMsg. We use a Message Assignment shape to construct an outcome message using the code found in Listing 12.4.

LISTING 12.4 Expression Configuring the Results of a Successful Outcome Message

```
SuccessMsg = new Outcome.OutcomeMsg();
SuccessMsg.FailIntension = IntensionMsg(CompensationProject.PropertySchema.Fail);
SuccessMsg.InnerAction = InnerString;
SuccessMsg.OuterAction = OuterString;
```

After we have the message, we send it. Now turn your attention to the actions under `UserIntendsFault`. This is the leg that generates an exception and invokes compensation. The Expression shape `SetMsgBad` consists of two lines, one setting the `OuterString` variable to a value indicating a fault by user intention and one setting the `AppExc` orchestration variable to a new instance of `System.ApplicationException`. The next shape, Generate Exception, is a Throw Exception shape that is configured to throw `AppExc`.

We need to catch the exception. To do this, we right-clicked `OuterTx` and selected New Exception Handler from the context menu. A dashed rectangle was created at the bottom of the shape, though this is not captured in Figure 12.3. After selecting the new handler, go to the Properties view to configure it to catch the exception we've just thrown. First, give the handler block a name, in our case `CatchOurExc`. Set the `Exception Object Type` property to `System.ApplicationException`. The `Exception Object Name` needs a value, which we've set to the C# programmer's favorite fallback, `e`.

Now drop a Compensate shape into the exception handler block. This shape merely tells BizTalk which completed transaction needs to be compensated. The Compensate shape's `Compensate` property handles this. The list box for this property is populated with the names of any transactional scopes in the orchestration. Select `NestedTx` from the list to invoke the compensation block on the inner transaction. Now let's return to that transaction's processing to see what happens to rollback the successfully completed actions that occurred earlier.

Inner Transaction: Compensation

You add a compensation block to a transaction in much the same way that we added an exception handler to the outer transaction. Right-clicking the inner transaction and selecting New Compensation Block from the context menu causes the Orchestration Designer in Visual Studio .NET to create a block at the bottom of the transaction shape.

> **NOTE**
>
> The basic scheme we outlined at the beginning of this discussion of the sample called for performing compensation by sending a message indicating that compensation had been performed on the inner transaction. In a real-life case, you would send a message canceling an order or reversing some other action, along with enough information to identify the message directing the original action the recipient is supposed to reverse.

For our sample orchestration, the Compensate block consists of a Construct Message shape with a Message Assignment block inside it. The shape constructs an instance of an outcome message using code in the Message Assignment shape that is given in Listing 12.5.

LISTING 12.5 Message Assignment Code Building the Compensation Outcome Message

```
CompMsg = new Outcome.OutcomeMsg();
CompMsg.FailIntension = IntensionMsg(CompensationProject.PropertySchema.Fail);
CompMsg.InnerAction = "Inner Tx Compensated";
CompMsg.OuterAction = OuterString;
```

Because we are interested only in tracing the flow of the orchestration, there is no instance information to include and no original message to reference. We construct a new instance of the serializing component, set the `FailIntension` and `OuterAction` fields to values from the intention message and whatever was set in the outer transaction (in `SetMsgBad`, in this case), and then set an appropriate value for the `InnerAction` field. When the message is constructed, we send it.

The compensation block will then complete, control will revert to the end of the `OuterTx` scope, and the orchestration will proceed to the terminal shape and cease execution.

Orchestration Hydration

One important use of transactional processing is to ensure the correct state of an application following recovery from a catastrophic failure that abnormally terminates the program. Because orchestrations are intended to implement mission-critical business processes, they must be able to support recovery following a failure that takes down the orchestration engine. Because orchestrations involve messaging between parties that may be geographically and organizationally remote, that recovery should be managed in such a way that messages are sent and received once, and once only. The solution to the recovery requirement is known as dehydration and hydration or rehydration. These complementary actions also provide a mechanism for efficient management of system resources during long-running transactions.

Broadly speaking, *dehydration* is simply serialization of the orchestration's state to a SQL Server database. *Rehydration* is the reverse process, restoring an orchestration to its last running state from the database. *State* is a broad term. For rehydration to work as a recovery mechanism, it has to capture every facet of a running orchestration. To understand hydration and dehydration, we have to understand what is dehydrated and when the orchestration engine performs dehydration and rehydration.

The what is simple but far reaching. There are three categories of information that are serialized during the dehydration of an orchestration:

- Internal state of the orchestration engine—This includes what orchestration is running and what checkpoint has been reached.
- Component state—.NET components involved in the orchestration are serialized during dehydration.
- Messages and variables—Message instances and orchestration variables are serialized so that the exact state of the data can be restored.

The first item tells the engine what to dehydrate and rehydrate, so it is the first thing BizTalk looks for during recovery. It is also what provides efficient use of system resources during a long-running orchestration. Rather than leave an orchestration in memory, potentially locking up resources while it waits for an incoming message, the BizTalk orchestration engine can serialize the orchestration and free resources. When the message finally arrives, the engine detects that the orchestration requires rehydration, restores it, and delivers the message.

The next two items in our list of things serialized are the items internal to the orchestration that are required to pick up where the orchestration left off. Components are external code entities, so orchestration asks them to serialize themselves into a stream built on the database. Serialization has become so pervasive in component development that this is not a major burden. This mechanism, however, is the reason for the rule restricting nonserializable components to use in an atomic transaction. Such transactions are the only areas of an orchestration that are guaranteed to execute completely without being interrupted by intermediate dehydration points, so they are the only scope in which such components can be used without fear of compromising the integrity of orchestration state. The last items, messages and orchestration variables, are entities under the direct management of the engine, so it takes care of their hydration. Between components, messages, and variables, we can express the exact and complete internal state of the orchestration.

Perhaps the most interesting aspect of dehydration is that of persistence points, the milestones in an orchestration's life cycle at which hydration is performed. Getting these milestones right is a fine balance between ensuring data integrity and managing performance.

There are several simple and obvious persistence points. When an orchestration completes or is suspended, it will be dehydrated as a means of recording the state of the orchestration. If the orchestration engine is shut down under controlled conditions[md[for example, when the service is shut down manually or in response to a controlled shutdown of the operating system, running orchestrations will be dehydrated.

Transactional boundaries are important persistence points. Not only does this assist with recovery, but it supports compensation, as well. When a transactional scope completes, dehydration is performed. If dehydration should fail, control passes to the first exception handler that is configured to catch the particular exception thrown. If compensation is invoked subsequent to the end of the transaction, the engine can examine the state at the end of the transaction to determine the starting state for the compensation block.

There are several miscellaneous persistence points in dehydration. The asynchronous launch of an orchestration will trigger dehydration, as will encountering a debugging breakpoint. Dehydration is the mechanism that gives the Orchestration Debugger its wealth of data about the internal state of the orchestration at every step of debugging. During a long-running transaction, the orchestration engine will use the state of the orchestration, usually being blocked waiting for an incoming message, and the overall state of orchestrations and system resources to invoke dehydration in the interests of system efficiency.

Messaging activities round out the list of persistence points for dehydration. When a message is sent from an orchestration, dehydration is performed, unless the send is within an atomic transaction. In that case, dehydration will wait until the end of the transaction. However, and this may seem counterintuitive at first, dehydration is not performed on message receipt. The reason for this lies in how the system responds and who is under control of BizTalk. There is no guarantee that a sent message is bound for another orchestration. Many times, in fact, the recipient is an application with no knowledge of BizTalk hosted by a physically remote server. In the interests of respecting the messaging intentions of the orchestration and therefore sending the message precisely once, the engine has to unambiguously know that the message has been sent during recovery operations. An orchestration receiving a message, in contrast, is completely under control of BizTalk. If the system fails after message receipt and a persistence point was encountered after message receipt but before failure, the hydrated state of the orchestration will show the message in the internal state of the orchestration and processing may proceed. If the message was received but no persistence point was reached prior to failure, the orchestration state in the dehydration database will show no record of the message, and the orchestration progress will be seen to be prior to the receive action. The actual message, however, is still in the BizTalk MessageBox, so the rehydrated orchestration can retrieve it and proceed with the receive action as if it has never happened before. In either case, the message is received (from the standpoint of the orchestration) once, as the business process intended.

Orchestration and Rules

Chapter 11, "Developing Rules," showed how to create sophisticated rules-based applications, but it focused on hosting and running the rules engine in a separate application. That's a very interesting capability, but we are chiefly interested in BizTalk applications. Although orchestrations are largely procedural in nature, there will be times when a significant body of business knowledge will be captured in a rulebase, and it would be very useful to be able to tap that knowledge from within an orchestration.

The BizTalk orchestration engine does indeed have the capability to act as a host for rulesets. This is wrapped up for you in the Call Rules shape. This is very easy to configure and use, so the theory portion of this section will be brief. We will then illustrate the process by creating a simple orchestration that calls on the ruleset developed in Chapter 11, in effect replacing the host console application we developed together in that chapter.

Call Rules Shape

The Call Rules shape must be hosted in an atomic transaction. This helps BizTalk dehydrate state to the dehydration database before turning the rule engine loose on the orchestration's data for a while. As always, this means that any orchestration using a Call Rules shape must be configured for a long-running transaction, and you must add an atomic transactional scope to your orchestration. With those preliminaries out of the way, you simply drop a Call Rules shape into the Scope shape, ensure it is selected, and turn your attention to the Properties view in Visual Studio .NET.

A Call Rules shape has two properties you need to worry about. One is the Name and can be anything you want, but the other, Configure Policy, is essential to the success of your orchestration. Clicking the ellipsis button invokes the CallRules Policy Configuration dialog box depicted in Figure 12.5. You have two tasks to perform in this dialog box. One is to select the Rules Policy you want to invoke, and the other is to populate any parameters that policy requires with data from the orchestration.

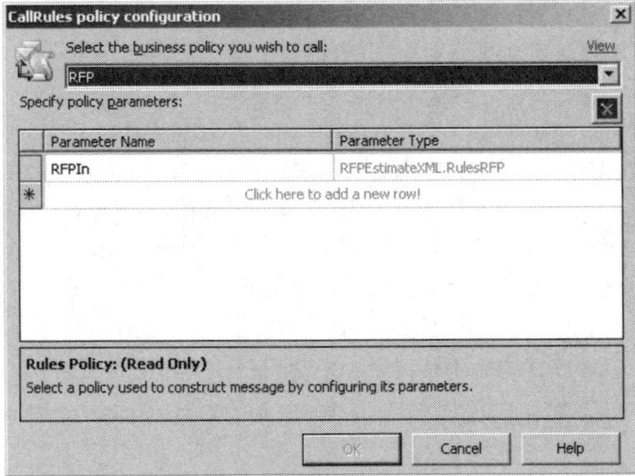

FIGURE 12.5 The CallRules Policy Configuration dialog box establishes the link between your orchestration and a policy in the rulebase.

The drop-down list labeled Select the Business Policy You Wish to Call is populated with the names of all the policies published in the development machine's Rule Store. After you've selected a policy, the dialog box is able to inspect the policy to determine what parameters are available for configuration.

This is when you move on to the Specify Policy Parameters grid. Clicking a row adds a new parameter configuration row to the grid. The right-most cell in each row is a list populated with the types of the parameters in the policy. The left cell is populated with a list of orchestration messages and variables. Select a parameter type and variable of a matching type from the lists. When you are done, click OK to complete configuring the shape's Configure Policy property.

When the orchestration encounters a Call Rules shape during execution, it hosts the rule engine and passes the configured variables or messages as parameters to the policy. As in our standalone example in Chapter 11, the effects of executing the policy are manifested in the parameters passed to the policy. In the case of an orchestration, this means that the variables or messages you passed may be modified when the Call Rules shape completes processing.

Call Rules Sample

If you refer back to the sample program in Chapter 11, you recall that the policy worked on an RFP message document. The business rules decided whether the RFP was approved and indicated this by setting a field in the message to true or false. The sample we are about to present uses an orchestration to receive the RFP message and then turns it over to the RFP policy we developed in Chapter 11. To make things a little more exciting than the previous rules example, and to demonstrate how rules and orchestrations can complement one another, we'll inspect the modified message to determine the approval status. If approved, we want to send the message out to some file location. If rejected, the orchestration will add a comment in the Notes field, indicating that the requested service is not offered, and then send the message to a location where we collect rejected RFPs and the location representing the sender of the RFP. That is, we want to model an internal notification that we're rejecting an RFP as well as notifying the requestor. In the case of approval, we can assume that the RFP will be followed by an order or no action. When rejecting an RFP, we want some internal knowledge of the fact in case the requestor or internal staff want to follow up on the matter.

The orchestration that implements this business process is shown in Figure 12.6. An activating file receive action named `RecvRFP` starts things off by receiving the message `RFPIn`. The orchestration then proceeds to a transaction called `RulesScope`, where the Call Rules shape invokes the previously developed `RFP` policy. You may recall that the policy had a single parameter matching our `RFP` message type. We pass the received message into the policy and wait for the rules engine to complete processing.

After emerging from the transaction, the orchestration inspects the message's Approved field in the Rejected rule shape. If the orchestration rule is true, we copy the `RFPIn` message to `RFPOut`, our output message, and then set the `Notes` field with a rejection message. The `AlertToRejection` Send shape performs the internal notification send. If `Rejected` evaluates to false, the `Else` leg of the Decide shape is executed. `SetApproved` copies `RFPIn` to `RFPOut` and completes the Decide shape's branch.

Regardless of which leg of the Decide shape is executed, we still need to send `RFPOut` to the original requestor. This is accomplished with the `SendRFP` Send shape.

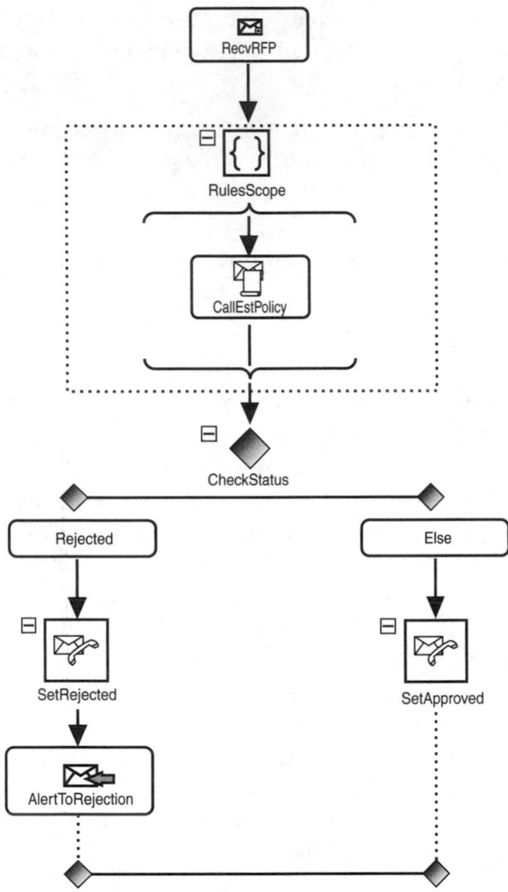

FIGURE 12.6 Orchestration calling a rule-based policy and acting on the results.

Note how the two capabilities, orchestration and the rule engine, complement each other. Orchestration gives us access to the messaging system and procedural flow for the business process. The rule engine gives us access to business knowledge captured in a policy. The policy can act on data received via messaging and modify it in a nonprocedural fashion. When the orchestration regains control, it continues to operate procedurally, but it has the advantage that its data state has (or may have) been modified by the execution of the policy. The Call Rules shape allows an orchestration designer to reuse business knowledge in the performance of a particular business process.

NOTE

The sample code is found in the RFPEstimateXML folder of the chapter download. The solution file is RFPEstimateXML.sln. The project requires you to have completed the project in Chapter 11 because it relies on the rules and vocabulary created by that sample.

Direct Port Binding Between Orchestrations

Passing messages to and from an orchestration imposes a slight performance penalty as control shifts from the orchestration engine's service to the messaging system. This is necessary when communicating with outside applications or partners. A welcome addition to BizTalk Server 2004 is the improved capability for direct port binding when you want to communicate directly with a port on another orchestration. Direct binding bypasses the messaging system. Messages that use this technique remain within the orchestration engine. This simplifies orchestration solutions by avoiding the messaging configuration.

12

In earlier releases of the product, you had to use a convoluted syntax to locate a port on a running instance of an orchestration. This syntax involved a GUID that was a property of the orchestration. It was a very messy process to implement. BizTalk Server 2004 cleans things up considerably. One of the entries in the Port Binding list on the Port Binding page of the Port Configuration Wizard (depicted in Figure 12.7) is Direct. When you select that, the remaining controls on the page change to reflect what you see in Figure 12.7. You have a choice of three options.

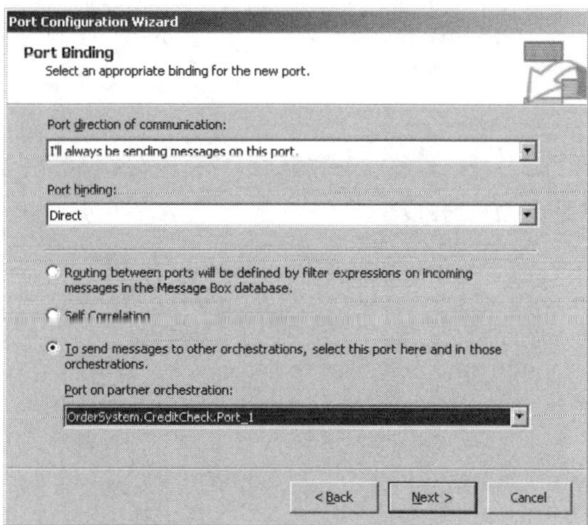

FIGURE 12.7 Direct binding between orchestration ports is configured on the Port Binding page of the Port Configuration Wizard.

The first of these options is routing using filter expressions. This is like dynamic routing except that the process is guaranteed to be between two orchestrations in the same BizTalk Server Group. When you establish a filter expression for the port binding, be sure that the property or properties selected are adequate to identify the receiving port (or ports) on the orchestration. In addition to all the usual message and port properties, you will note that some of the properties in the filter expression list come from the `Microsoft.BizTalk.XLANGs.BTXEngine` package. The properties in this package pertain specifically to orchestration types and instances, which may help you route your messages.

The second option is Self Correlating. This is exactly like using correlation sets built on distinguished fields, except the orchestration engine will generate a correlation token based on the message and the particular instance of the orchestration. You do not need to create the correlation set yourself. This option is used when passing a port reference from one orchestration to another as a parameter, such as when a parent orchestration launches a child with a reference to a callback port. The parent would declare a direct bound receive port, and the child would declare a send port. Both ports would be declared self-correlating.

The third option involves picking a specific port on an orchestration from a list populated with the ports in orchestrations belonging to or referenced in your project. The syntax you will find in the list is the familiar .NET style notation, in this case consisting of `project.orchestration.port_name`. If you need instance resolution, you will need to set up appropriate correlation sets.

NOTE

Because direct binding is a feature specific to BizTalk Server, it is not compliant with BPEL4WS. Direct binding must not be used in orchestrations you plan to export using the Export to BPEL menu option from the context menu in the Solution Explorer window of Visual Studio .NET.

Parties, Roles, and Role Links: Indirection for Enterprise Deployments

When you are working with or creating prepared sample projects for a book, early binding of ports is a great convenience. In real production code, the opposite is true. Deferring port binding until deployment is a great aid to operating a BizTalk Server Group efficiently. BizTalk offers an additional layer of indirection in the form of role links. This feature allows you to model orchestration ports in terms of the roles partners play, the services they offer, and logical links between service producers and consumers. For example, your organization may have a list of suppliers and one or more companies that perform shipping duties for you. If you define roles for suppliers and shippers, you can link your ports with these roles. When the orchestration is in operation, an administrator can change the actual parties that perform these duties without recompiling the orchestration. The roles and their links to your organization remain constant, or nearly so, whereas the actual, physical entities fulfilling these roles can change frequently.

We will look at this feature in stages. The first step is to create parties and roles. Next, we will define role links and show how to use them in an orchestration with the Role Link shape.

Parties and Roles

You can add parties, your physical trading partners through BizTalk Explorer, and you may browse the roles in which they have been enlisted through that tool as well. Creating roles and performing role enlistment, however, is viewed by Microsoft as part of the trading partner management function. These tasks are covered in Part VI of this book, Involving the Information Worker, so we will discuss only the general concepts here.

When you configure a party, you are identifying an organization. Each party has one or more aliases, unique values for identifying the organization. These aliases can be a name, some industry-specific identifier such as a DUNS number, or even a telephone number. A party is a specific, physical entity with which your organization has ties.

Roles, by contrast, are logical entities that refer to a business function. Like Windows user groups, roles can include multiple parties. You might, for example, have a Supplier role, with all the parties that are your company's vendors enlisted in that role. Role links are a representation of the ties between your organization and some role. The orchestration manifestation of role links is the Role Link shape.

Role Links

Role links are exactly what the name implies: a link (for communication) between two roles. One of these roles is the organization—yours—that is hosting the orchestration. The other role in a role link is either a provider of a logical service to you or a consumer of a service you provide. A Supplier role, for example, provides a business service or product to you. A Creditor role, however, receives a payment service from you.

What actual party actually fills the external role is a function of the partner enlistment performed after deployment by the BizTalk administrator. As far as you, the orchestration developer, are concerned, you are dealing with abstract organizations performing a specific role in the business process. You merely want to plug in a communication point and tie some port types to it. We can clarify this by turning to the Role Link shape in orchestrations. A sample Role Link shape is depicted in Figure 12.8.

Role links involve communication, and we will be adding port types to them, so the Role Link shape gets dropped onto the port surface of the Orchestration Designer, not the design surface. By default, it appears with the two roles you see in Figure 12.8, Producer and Consumer. These roles are available to you even if you have not configured any roles.

Role Link shapes have a number of properties to configure. Clicking any of them in the Properties view presents you with an ellipsis button. Clicking this button, or double-clicking the Role Link shape itself, invokes the Role Link Wizard. This wizard will lead you through the process of configuring the role link.

Configuring Role Links with the Role Link Wizard

The first screen of the wizard is a welcome screen. Clicking the Next button brings you to the Role Link Name page. The only item you need to provide is a name for the shape. The shape in Figure 12.8, for example, was named HomeToSupplier on this page. Our intent was to establish an outgoing communications link to our Supplier role from the Home organization, with an acknowledgement message coming back. After you have provided a name, click Next.

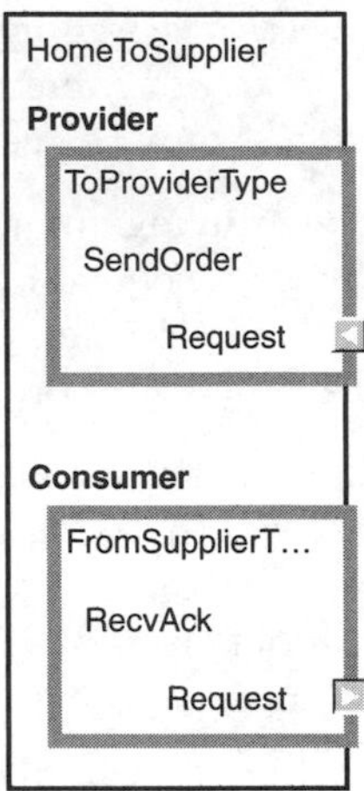

FIGURE 12.8 Role Link shapes are added to the port surface in Orchestration Designer to establish communication between your organization and a logical role.

The Role Link Type page is next. It offers you the choice of defining a new Role Link type or selecting from a list of existing types. This is similar to the choice of port types when configuring a port in an orchestration. If you want an existing type, you check the Use an Existing Role Link Type option button and make a selection from the drop-down list below it. If you want to create a new type, check the top option button, which is labeled Create a New Role Link Type. If you select that option button, the control immediately below the option buttons changes to an edit control in which you provide a name for the new type. Clicking Next in either case brings you to the Role Link Usage page, which you can see in Figure 12.9.

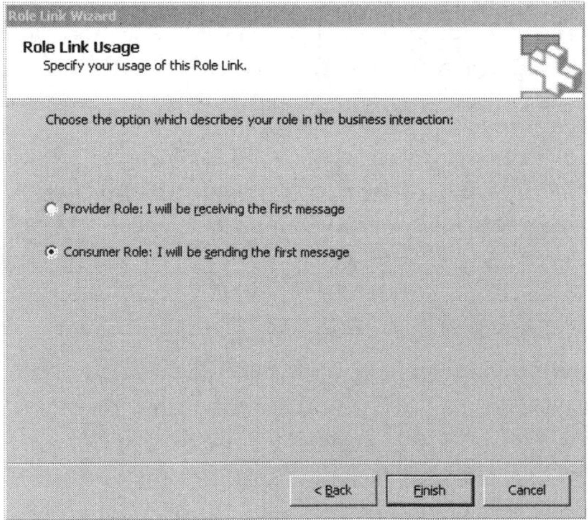

FIGURE 12.9 The Role Link Usage page establishes the initial direction of messaging in a Role Link shape.

In any role link, you need to decide what part your organization will play in the link with respect to the service in question. Are you consuming the outside role's service? In that case, you are a consumer and will be sending the first message to order the service. If your organization is providing the service, you will want to wait for a message from the outside role, the consumer in this case, and then reply to their order. The BizTalk documentation sometimes refers to the provider role as being the "implements role." Provider and Consumer are the only roles available to you in the Role Link Wizard. If you want to involve some other role you have created, you will do this later in the Orchestration view. We'll address that in a moment. When you have completed this page, click Finish to complete the configuration or click Back to review your work.

The Role Link shape you will see at this point differs from Figure 12.8 in that there are no ports. In their place, you have shaded regions reading Insert Receive Ports or Insert Send Ports. Right-clicking either region and selecting Add Port Type invokes our old friend, the Port Type Wizard.

Note that you are adding port types and not actual ports. You will have many ports that could be involved, one for each party in the role. Because party resolution occurs at runtime, the choice of ports will be made then, as well. The shapes that are added to the Role Link shape after you have added your port types behave just like the connectors for physical ports, and you will drag connections to them from Send and Receive shapes just as you would with Port shapes.

Modifying Role Link Types in the Orchestration View

After you've configured your Role Link shape, you may need to modify it. You may want to change the port type selections you made. More important, you might want to bring other roles into the Role Link, roles created by business analysts in describing your business. The tool for all this activity is the Role Link Types node in the Orchestration view.

When you expand this node, you will see child nodes representing each role type you have configured. These further expand to display the pairs of roles that make up each type. Beneath each Role node is a node listing the port type associated with it. You may delete a port type and add a new one, but you must always have a single port type associated with each role in a role link type.

Similarly, you may delete roles in a role link and add new roles, provided the role link type always has two roles. A role link, after all, is a two-way communication link between two parties. This is where you can select other roles that may have been configured by analysts.

Summary

Transactions bring new capabilities and complexities to the business processes you will model in orchestrations. They are your mechanism for bringing integrity to multiple steps in a business process. Atomic transactions act much like traditional database transactions and can even be DTC-style transactions, provided you adhere to some fairly strict conditions. Long-running transactions are much more typical of the business processes you are likely to model in BizTalk orchestrations, but they offer fewer transactional capabilities. Orchestration replaces the loss of DTC-style transactional integrity in long-running transactions with the concept of compensation. Although the implementation of compensation is up to you, the orchestration designer, the semantics are similar. You must ensure that the parties or applications involved in the business process provide appropriate mechanisms to implement your compensation process, however. In addition to compensation, orchestration offers exception handlers analogous to those in traditional programming languages, thereby giving designers additional options for handling fault conditions.

In this chapter, we provided a laboratory-style sample that showed you how to use nested transactions, exception handlers, and compensation. The contrived nature of the sample made it easy for you to trace the flow of control in a fairly typical transaction pattern for orchestrations.

Orchestration hydration and rehydration gave you a theoretical understanding of what is going on behind the scenes with the orchestration engine. More important is that the discussion should help you understand how orchestration uses serialization to provide checkpoints important to orchestration recovery following a major system fault.

Next, we took up the Call Rules shape. This shape is the orchestration's connection to the entire inference system discussed in Chapter 11. It is comparatively simple to configure and offers designers an easy way to make their orchestration a host for the rule engine.

Rounding out our discussion of advanced concepts, we explored direct addressing and role links. Each offers flexibility to orchestration communications. Direct addressing offers a simplifying short cut when communicating strictly between two orchestrations. The syntax of addressing ports under direct binding in BizTalk Server 2004 is a dramatic improvement from that used when BizTalk was first released. Role links offer logical flexibility rather than a performance improvement. By abstracting the actual business entities with which the orchestration is communicated, they offer flexibility and choice in administering your relations with business partners. They allow this function to be passed to business analysts, leaving the orchestration designer free to concentrate on the logical aspects of the business process rather than the implementation details. This means that details can be changed frequently without forcing rework of the orchestrations that use them.

PART IV

Selected Implementation Patterns on BizTalk Server 2004

IN THIS PART

CHAPTER 13

BizTalk Server Messaging Patterns

IN THIS CHAPTER

- Using the SQL Adapter
- Importing a CSV File
- Importing a Positional File
- Uniform Nonsequential Convoy Pattern

By now you should be getting a very good idea of what you can do with BizTalk. You've been introduced to messaging and orchestration and have had an overview of the adapter framework. This chapter focuses on using the BizTalk Server 2004 messaging engine and shows some commonly used patterns.

We will be looking at the following four patterns in this chapter:

- Pattern 1 shows how to use the BizTalk Server 2004 SQL adapter.
- Pattern 2 shows importing a CSV file and converting it to an XML document.
- Pattern 3 builds on Pattern 2, but will use a positional file.
- Pattern 4 shows a uniform sequential convoy pattern (receiving multiple instances of the same message in a single orchestration).

Pattern 1: Using the SQL Adapter

BizTalk Server 2004 includes several default adapters, including an adapter for SQL Server. The SQL adapter allows you to interact with a SQL Server, giving you the capability to add, update, and delete from orchestrations or messaging.

In this pattern we receive an XML document and show how to insert a corresponding row into a SQL table.

Scenario

We will use the common scenario of receiving a business card requisition. We will watch a folder location, and when a document appears in that folder, we will pick it up and insert a row into a SQL table.

Our solution will

- Receive an incoming requisition
- Transmit it through the BizTalk Server 2004 SQL Server adapter

Implementation Steps

To implement this solution, we'll need to follow several steps:

1. Create a destination SQL table.
2. Create an adapter schema.
3. Create a receive port and receive location.
4. Create a send port.
5. Generate an instance document.
6. Test the solution.

To keep the sample as simple as possible, we are using a very stripped-down schema for the requisition. In a real-world application, far more data would likely be required.

Open Visual Studio .NET and create a new project called BTSDG_SQL using the Empty BizTalk Server Project template.

Step 1: Create the Destination Table

Using SQL Server's Query Analyzer or your favorite equivalent tool, create a table with the following structure:

```
CREATE TABLE [dbo].[BusinessCards] (
    [ReceiptNumber] [int] IDENTITY (1, 1) NOT NULL ,
    [Received] [datetime] NULL ,
    [NameOnCard] [varchar] (50) COLLATE SQL_Latin1_General_CP1_CI_AS NOT NULL ,
    [TitleOnCard] [varchar] (50) COLLATE SQL_Latin1_General_CP1_CI_AS NOT NULL ,
    [Quantity] [int] NOT NULL
) ON [PRIMARY]
```

Step 2: Add an Adapter Schema

When working with adapters in BizTalk, you need to add an adapter to your project, which will create a schema describing the data structure and create an orchestration (as a convenience) with predefined port and message types.

To add the SQL adapter, follow these steps:

1. Right-click the `BTSDG_SQL` project in the Solution Explorer, point to Add, and then select Add Generated Items from the context menu.
2. Select the Add Adapter template. On the Add Adapter Wizard screen, choose the SQL Adapter and fill in the relevant data per the example, as shown in Figure 13.1.

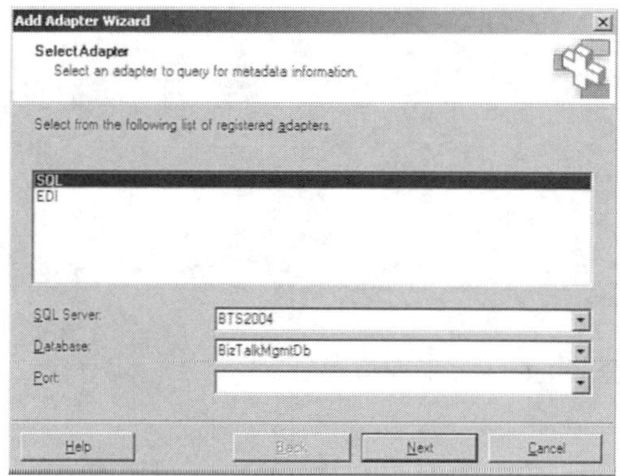

FIGURE 13.1 Specifying the adapter type.

> **NOTE**
>
> You can leave the Port field empty here. If you had any ports set up and configured to use the SQL Adapter, they would be enumerated and listed in this drop-down list. However, we have not yet created the send port we will be using, so we will specify it later using the BizTalk Explorer.

3. Press Next, and on the Database Information screen click the Set button. Specify the server information for the server where you created the test table. Specify appropriate login information. Figure 13.2 shows a sample. Click Next.
4. In the SQL Transport SQL Generation Wizard pane, specify a target namespace of **`http://BTSDG_SQL`** and specify that this is a send port. Next, specify a request document root element of **`BusCard_Request`** and a response document root element of **`BusCard_Response`**, as shown in Figure 13.3. Click Next.
5. On the Statement Type Information screen, specify that you want an Updategram.
6. On the Statement Information screen, specify the BusinessCards table and that you want to insert into the table. Multiselect the NameOnCard, TitleOnCard, and Quantity columns, as shown in Figure 13.4.
7. Click Finish to complete the wizard. Notice in the Solution Explorer that two new items have been added to our project: an orchestration that we will not use (BizTalk Orchestration.odx) and a schema, InsertBusinessCardsService.xsd.

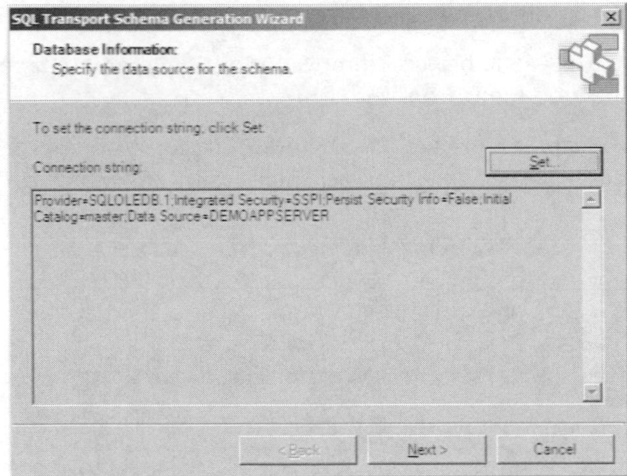

FIGURE 13.2 Specifying database information.

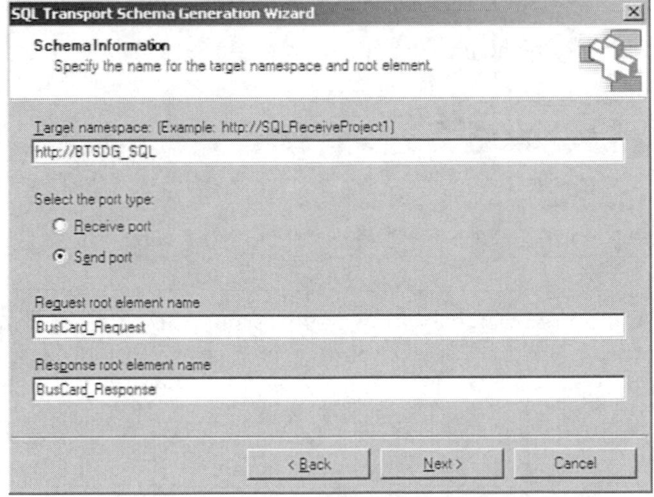

FIGURE 13.3 Specifying schema information.

Step 3: Create the Receive Port and Receive Location

As is the case with most BizTalk demonstration programs, our process will be triggered by a file being dropped into a folder location. This is only one of many possible entry points, chosen here for simplicity.

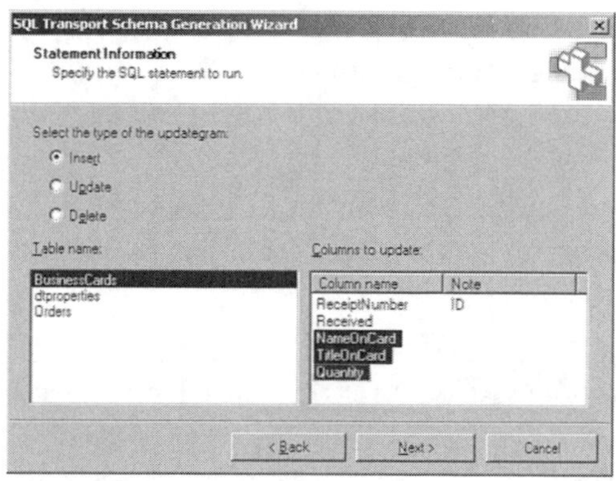

FIGURE 13.4 Specifying SQL statement information.

To create the receive port and receive location, follow these steps:

1. Using Windows Explorer, create a new file folder: C:\FileDrop\BTSDG_SQL\In. This is the folder we will be monitoring for our inbound message.
2. Inside Visual Studio, launch the BizTalk Explorer. Right-click Receive Ports and choose Add Receive Port.
3. Specify One-Way Port as the type of receive port.
4. Name the port **`BTSDG_SQL`** and click OK.
5. In the BizTalk Explorer, right-click the Receive Locations node under the new BTSDG_SQL receive port and choose Add Receive Location. For Transport Type, specify File; for address, specify a Receive Folder of **`C:\FileDrop\BTSDG_SQL\In`** and a file mask of **`*.xml`**. For the Receive Handler, specify BizTalkServerApplication. For the Receive Pipeline, specify Microsoft.BizTalk.DefaultPipelines.PassThruReceive. Name the Receive Location **`BTSDG_SQL`**. The Receive Location dialog box should be as shown in Figure 13.5.
6. In the BizTalk Explorer, right-click the Receive Location and choose Enable from the context menu.

Step 4: Create the Send Port

The send port is where we will send data to the SQL Adapter.

To create the send port, follow these steps:

1. In BizTalk Explorer, right-click Send Ports and choose Add Send Port.
2. For the Port Type, specify Static One-Way Port.

3. Name the port **`BTSDG_SQL`**. For the primary transport type, choose SQL. Click the ellipses beside the Address to bring up the SQL Transport Properties dialog. Fill in appropriate SQL connection information; for an example, see Figure 13.2. Click OK. Specify a Document Target namespace of **`http://BTSDG_SQL`**.

4. Click Configurations, Send node and specify a Send Pipeline of **`Microsoft.BizTalk.DefaultPipelines.PassThruTransmit`**. Click OK to end the wizard and create the port.

5. Click Configurations, Maps and Filters and select Filters. Add a new filter that specifies BTS.ReceivePortName is equal to BTSDG_SQL and click OK to save the port settings.

> **NOTE**
>
> By adding this filter we have added this send port as a subscriber to any messages that are received by the BTSDG_SQL receive port.

6. Right-click the BTSDG_SQL send port and choose Enlist from the context menu.

7. Right-click the BTSDG_SQL send port and choose Start from the context menu.

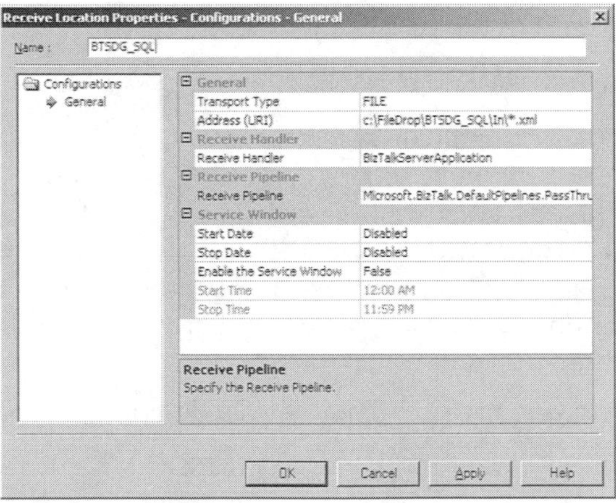

FIGURE 13.5 Specifying the receive location.

Step 5: Create an Instance Document

Next, we will create an instance document that we can use to test the solution.

To create the instance document, follow these steps:

1. In Solution Explorer, right-click the InsertBusinessCardsService.xsd schema and choose Properties.
2. In the Output Instance File Name, browse to the C:\FileDrop\BTSDG_SQL folder, name your instance document **`BTSDG_SQL_Instance`**, and click OK to close the dialog box.
3. In Solution Explorer, right-click the InsertBusinessCardsService.xsd schema again and choose Generate Instance from the context menu.

You should see a message in the Output pane telling you that the instance was successfully created.

The instance document that was generated has triplicate entries for both the `after` and `BusinessCards` nodes. For our example, we want to create only a single entry, so you should edit the instance document to contain the following data:

```
<ns0:BusCard_Request xmlns:ns0="http://BTSDG_SQL">
  <ns0:sync>
    <ns0:after>
      <ns0:BusinessCards NameOnCard="Sam Watkins"
        TitleOnCard="President" Quantity="1000" />
    </ns0:after>
  </ns0:sync>
</ns0:BusCard_Request>
```

Step 6: Testing the Solution

We are now ready to test the solution. Drop an XML instance document into the receive location folder, and a corresponding row will be added to our test table.

To test the solution, follow these steps:

1. In Windows Explorer, browse to the C:\FileDrop\BTSDG_SQL folder.
2. Drag a copy of the file into the C:\FileDrop\BTSDG_SQL\in folder. In a few seconds, you should see some disk activity, and the file should disappear.
3. Open SQL Enterprise Manager and navigate to your test table.
4. Retrieve all rows. Your unique data should be in the last row in the table.

This pattern has shown you how to work with the SQL adapter from within the messaging engine. The SQL adapter, included with BizTalk Server 2004, provides a rich interface into SQL Server, which can be used from messaging or orchestration-based solutions.

Pattern 2: Importing a CSV File

Often, interchanges between applications and partners are done by the exchange of flat files and CSV files. This is fairly common practice, and for many legacy systems, it is the best or the only way for them to communicate with the outside world.

As you have seen in previous chapters, BizTalk Server 2004 has a powerful suite of tools for taking these files and mapping them, or converting them to different formats.

In this pattern, we will cover

- Defining a schema for a CSV file
- Using a pipeline to disassemble a CSV file
- Converting the CSV file to an XML document

Scenario

Again, we will use the common scenario of receiving a business card requisition, only this time it will be a CSV file instead of an XML document. We will watch a folder location, and when a CSV file appears in that folder we will pick it up, convert it to XML, and deposit it into another folder.

Our solution will

- Receive an incoming requisition as a CSV file
- Convert it to an XML document
- Deposit it into a file folder

Implementation Steps

To implement this solution, we'll need to follow several steps:

1. Create a schema to describe the CSV file.
2. Create a receive pipeline to process the CSV file.
3. Deploy the assembly.
4. Create a receive port and receive location.
5. Create a send port.
6. Test the solution.

As with the previous pattern, to keep the sample as simple as possible, we are using a very stripped down schema for the requisition. In a real-world application, far more data would likely be required.

Open Visual Studio .NET and create a new project called **BTSDG_FF** using the Empty BizTalk Server Project template.

Step 1: Create a Schema to Describe the CSV File

Before starting, create the following folder structure:

- C:\FileDrop\BTSDG_FF
- C:\FileDrop\BTSDG_FF\in
- C:\FileDrop\BTSDG_FF\out

13

When you're working with flat files, the first step is to add a schema describing the flat file so the BizTalk Server will be able to disassemble and work with the file properly. To do this, follow these steps:

1. Right-click the BTSDG_FF project in the Solution Explorer, point to Add, and then select Add New Item from the context menu.
2. Select the Schema template and change the name to **FF**. Click OK.
3. With the <Schema> node selected in the left tree view, click Schema Editor Extension in the properties window and select Flat File Extension from the list of available extensions. Note that a new tab has been added at the bottom of the middle window where the schema is displayed.
4. Right-click the Root element and rename it **BusinessCardRequisition**.
5. Right-click the BusinessCardRequisition node, choose New Child Element, and name the new element **NameOnCard**.
6. Right-click the BusinessCardRequisition node, choose New Child Element, and name the new element **TitleOnCard**.
7. Right-click the BusinessCardRequisition node, choose New Child Element, and name the new element **Quantity**. In the property window, change the data type to be xs:int.
8. In the Solution Explorer, right-click the FF schema and choose Properties. Set the Output File Name property to be **C:\FileDrop\BTSDG_FF\BTSDG_Instance.txt**. Set the Generate Instance Output Type to Native (this causes the instance file to be generated as a delimited file instead of an XML document).
9. Right-click the BusinessCardRequisition node and choose Properties. Set the Child Delimiter Type to be character and set the Child Delimiter to be a comma (,).At this point you should be able to right-click the FF.xsd schema in the Solution Explorer and choose Generate Instance. This will create the c:\FileDrop\BTSDG_FF\BTSDG_Instance.txt file, which will contain the following text:

```
NameOnCard,TitleOnCard,1
```

Step 2: Creating the Receive Pipeline

Now that we have a schema defined, the next step is to define a custom pipeline that uses that schema to transform the flat file into something we can work with in BizTalk. To do this, follow these steps:

1. Right-click the BTSDG_FF project in the Solution Explorer, point to Add, and then select Add New Item from the context menu.
2. Select the Receive Pipeline template and change the name to **`ff_recv_pipeline`**. Click OK. A new pipeline will be created and will open in the Visual Studio pipeline designer.
3. From the Visual Studio toolbox, drag the Flat File Disassembler on the Disassemble stage of the pipeline (this is the only place you'll be allowed to drop it).
4. In the document schema drop-down list, select the FF.xsd schema we just created.

Step 3: Deploying the Assembly

We have now created all the pieces we need to be able to work with this flat file. The next step is to strongly name and deploy the assembly. To do this, follow these steps:

1. Run the Visual Studio command prompt and navigate to the BTSDG_FF project folder.
2. Type in **`Sn -k BTSDG_FF.snk`** to generate a key file, and then close the DOS box.
3. In the Solution Explorer, right-click the BTSDG_FF project and choose Properties. Click Assembly and scroll through the properties to Assembly Key File. Navigate to the BTSDG_FF.snk key file you just generated.
4. Right-click the BTSDG_FF project and choose Deploy. Confirm that there were no build or deployment errors.

Now, when a flat file flows through this pipeline, BizTalk will attempt to convert it to an XML document based on the FF.xsd schema.

Step 4: Creating the Receive Port and Receive Location

The next step will be to create the receive port and receive location. To do this, follow these steps:

1. In the BizTalk Explorer, right-click Receive Ports and point at Add New Receive Port.
2. Accept the default port type of Static One-Way.
3. Change the port name to BTSDG_FF.
4. Right-click the Receive Locations folder under the BTSDG_FF receive port and point at Add Receive Location.

5. Set the Transport Type to be File. Set the address to be **`C:\filedrop\BTSDG_FF\in`** and the file mask to be **`*.txt`**.
6. Set the ReceiveHandler to be the BizTalkServerApplication.
7. For the receive pipeline, select the ff_receive_pipeline we just created.

Your receive location should now look as shown in Figure 13.6.

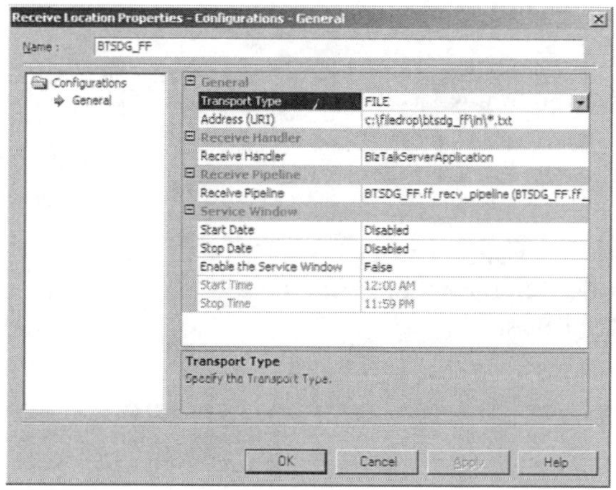

FIGURE 13.6 Receive location properties.

Step 5: Creating the Send Port

The final step will be to create the send port that will deposit the processed file into a folder. To do this, follow these steps:

1. In the BizTalk Explorer, right-click Send Ports and point at Add New Send Port.
2. Accept the default port type of Static One-Way.
3. Change the port name to **`BTSDG_FF`**.
4. For the transport, select FILE. For the address, type in **`C:\filedrop\BTSDG_FF\out`**.
5. Click the Send node. In the properties, choose the Microsoft.BizTalk.DefaultPipelins.XMLTransmit pipeline.
6. Click the Filters and Maps node and expand it. Click the Filters item and add a new Filter. Set the property to be BTS.ReceivePortName, the operation to be ==, and the value to be BTSDG_FF.

Step 6: Testing the Solution

We are now ready to test the solution. To do this, we will drop a CSV instance document into the receive location folder, and a corresponding XML file will be deposited into the output folder.

To test the solution, follow these steps:

1. In the BizTalk Explorer, expand the BTSDG_FF receive port, right-click the BTSDG_FF receive location, and point to Enable.
2. In the BizTalk Explorer, right-click the BTSDG_FF send port and point to Start.
3. In Windows Explorer, browse to the C:\FileDrop\BTSDG_FF folder.
4. Drag a copy of the BTSDG_FF_Instance.txt file into the C:\FileDrop\BTSDG_FF\in folder. In a few seconds, you should see some disk activity and the file should disappear.
5. In Windows Explorer, browse to the C:\FileDrop\BTSDG_FF\out folder. It should contain an XML file that corresponds to the values that were in the CSV file you deposited into the "in" folder.

Many systems exchange messages via flat files. This pattern showed you how the BizTalk Schema Editor can be used to model flat files, and how the BizTalk messaging engine can be used to work with flat files.

Pattern 3: Importing a Positional File

You saw in Pattern 2 how easy it is to work with CSV files. This pattern will build on that project by adding another receive location that takes a positional file as input.

In this pattern we will cover the following:

- Defining a schema for a simple positional file
- Using a pipeline to disassemble a positional file
- Converting the positional file to an XML document

Scenario

In this pattern, we will take an already operational file-processing process (the project defined in Pattern 2) and will add a second entry point into the process.

Implementation Steps

There are several steps we'll need to follow to implement this solution. We will need to

- Create a schema to describe the positional file.
- Create a receive pipeline to process the positional file.
- Deploy the assembly.

- Create a receive location.
- Test the solution.

Step 1: Create a Schema to Describe the Positional File

Before starting, create the following folder:

```
C:\FileDrop\BTSDG_FF\In\Pos
```

To create the positional file schema, follow these steps:

1. Right-click the BTSDG_FFPOS project in the Solution Explorer, point to Add, and then select Add New Item from the context menu.
2. Select the Schema template and change the name to **`FFPOS`**. Click OK.
3. With the `<Schema>` node selected in the left tree view, click Schema Editor Extension in the Properties window, and select Flat File Extension from the list of available extensions. Note that a new tab has been added to the schema window.
4. Right-click the Root element and rename it **`BusinessCardRequisition`**.
5. Right-click the `BusinessCardRequisition` element, and in the property, set the Structure drop-down list to Positional.
6. Right-click the `BusinessCardRequisition` node, choose New Child Element, and name the new element **`NameOnCard`**.
7. Right-click the `BusinessCardRequisition` node, choose New Child Element, and name the new element **`TitleOnCard`**.
8. Right-click the `BusinessCardRequisition` node, choose New Child Element, and name the new element **`Quantity`**. In the property window, change the data type to be xs:int.
9. In the Solution Explorer, right-click the FFPOS schema and choose Properties. Set the Output File Name property to be C:\FileDrop\BTSDG_FF\BTSDG_Instance_Pos.txt. Set the Generate Instance Output Type to Native (this causes the instance file to be generated as a delimited file instead of an XML document).

At this point, you should be able to right-click the FFPOS.xsd schema in the Solution Explorer and choose Generate Instance. This will create the C:\FileDrop\BTSDG_FF\BTSDG_Instance_Pos.txt.

Step 2: Creating the Receive Pipeline

Now that we have a schema defined, the next step is to define a custom pipeline that uses that schema to transform the positional flat file into something we can work with in BizTalk. To do this, follow these steps:

1. Right-click the BTSDG_FFPOS project in the Solution Explorer, point to Add, and then select Add New Item from the context menu.
2. Select the Receive Pipeline template and change the name to **ff_pos_recv_pipeline**. Click OK. A new pipeline will be created and will open in the Visual Studio pipeline designer.
3. From the Visual Studio toolbox, drag the Flat File Disassembler on the Disassemble stage of the pipeline (this is the only place you'll be allowed to drop it).
4. In the document schema drop-down list, select the FFPOS.xsd schema we just created.

Step 3: Deploying the Assembly

We have now created all the pieces we need to be able to work with this flat file. The next step is to strongly name and deploy the assembly. To do this, follow these steps:

1. Run the Visual Studio Command prompt and navigate to the BTSDG_FF project folder.
2. Type in **`Sn -k BTSDG_FFPOS.snk`** to generate a key file, and then close the DOS box.
3. In the Solution Explorer, right-click the BTSDG_FFPOS project and choose Properties. Click Assembly and scroll through the properties to Assembly Key File. Navigate to the BTSDG_FFPOS.snk key file you just generated.
4. Right-click the BTSDG_FFPOS project and choose Deploy. Confirm that there were no build or deployment errors.

Step 4: Creating the Receive Location

The next step will be to create the receive location for positional files. To do this, follow these steps:

1. Right-click the Receive Locations folder under the existing BTSDG_FF receive port and point at Add Receive Location. Name the receive location **`BTSDG_POS`**.
2. Set the Transport Type to be File. Set the address to be C:\filedrop\BTSDG_FF\in_pos and the file mask to be *.txt.
3. Set the ReceiveHandler to be the BizTalkServerApplication.
4. For the receive pipeline, select the `ff_pos_receive_pipeline` we just created.

Your receive location should now look as shown in Figure 13.7.

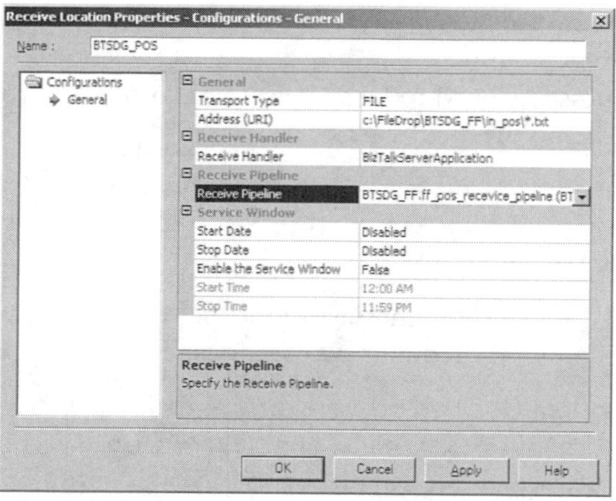

FIGURE 13.7 Receive location properties.

Step 5: Testing the Solution

We are now ready to test the solution.

To do this, we will drop a positional instance document into the receive location folder, and a corresponding XML file will be deposited into the output folder.

To test the solution, follow these steps:

1. In the BizTalk Explorer, expand the BTSDG_POS receive port, right-click the BTSDG_FF receive location, and point to Enable.
2. In the BizTalk Explorer, right-click the BTSDG_FF send port and point to Start (it will be grayed out if the port is already started).
3. In Windows Explorer, browse to the C:\FileDrop\BTSDG_FF folder.
4. Drag a copy of the BTSDG_FF_Pos_Instance.txt file into the C:\FileDrop\BTSDG_FF\in_pos folder. In a few seconds, you should see some disk activity and the file should disappear.
5. In Windows Explorer, browse to the C:\FileDrop\BTSDG_FF\out folder. It should contain an XML file that corresponds to the values that were in the positional file you deposited into the "in" folder.

This pattern built on the previous flat-file example and showed how the BizTalk Schema Editor can be used to model positional flat files.

Pattern 4: Uniform Sequential Convoy Pattern

One of the more confusing issues new BizTalk developers are confronted with is how to implement convoy patterns. A convoy is a situation where messages intended for a specific orchestration instance don't all arrive at once, and data could be spread over several incoming messages. In some convoy patterns, the messages don't necessarily arrive in any definite order. These messages need to be received and correlated properly to create a solution that can work with this messaging pattern.

Fortunately, BizTalk Server 2004 makes it relatively easy to accomplish this by providing mechanisms to accommodate some common convoy patterns. Three types of convoys supported by BizTalk Server 2004 are

- Parallel convoy Two or more messages must be received before processing continues (for example, a process requires two approvals).
- Non-Uniform Sequential Two or more different messages are received in a predefined sequential order (for example, a purchase order needs confirmation of goods received and an invoice before payment process can continue).
- Uniform Sequential Two or more of the same message are received, in any order (for example, a stock sell order may break down into several transactions).

In all convoy cases, something needs to group related messages together. This is done using correlation sets.

To help understand the underlying complexities and to appreciate the work that BizTalk Server is doing for you, consider the case of a parallel convoy where receipt of one of two related messages could create a new instance of an orchestration (for example, shipping notice and invoice; either one could appear first, depending on the vendor). Assuming the correlation has been set up properly, BizTalk will ensure that only one instance of the orchestration will be created for this single business transaction, in contrast to the undesirable case where both messages activate separate orchestration instances.

In this convoy pattern, we will address only the uniform sequential convoy.

In this pattern we will cover

- Creating an orchestration upon receipt of an initial message
- Receiving subsequent related messages
- Exiting the orchestration after all messages have been received

Scenario

For our scenario, we will be dealing with a stock trade. When a buy or sell order is received, it may take multiple transactions to fill the order. In our scenario, we will continue to receive messages until the order has been filled, and then we will send a confirmation message.

Implementation Steps

To implement this solution, we'll need to follow several steps:

1. Create a schema to describe the trade message.
2. Create a schema to describe the confirmation message.
3. Create a map to map from the trade to a confirmation message.
4. Create an orchestration to implement the messaging pattern.
5. Deploy and test the solution.

Create a new empty BizTalk project in Visual Studio .NET. Name it **`BTSDG_UNSConvoy`**.

Step 1: Create a Schema to Describe the Trade Message

To implement this convoy pattern, we need a unique identifier that will tie the various messages together. This identifier needs to be made available to BizTalk so that it can do correlation properly. For our example, we will use an OrderNumber element. Every trade that is part of this transaction will have the same order number. For this to be available to the BizTalk messaging engine, it needs to be promoted as a property. We will promote other fields as distinguished fields to get access to them from orchestration logic.

Because this convoy receives a series of identical messages in no specific order, there is no header message that is sent to start the orchestration. The first message received will be a trade that may or may not be the only one required to meet the order quantity. Because of this, we need to denormalize our data a little bit by including the total number of shares to be sold with each trade. This way, we will know after receipt of the first message (regardless of which one arrives first) how many shares there are in total in the business transaction and how to determine when we've received all the messages.

To create the Trade schema:

1. Right-click the BTSDG_UNSConvoy project in the Solution Explorer, point to Add, and then select Add New Item from the context menu.
2. Select the Schema template, and name the new schema **`Trade`**. Click OK.
3. Right-click the Root element and rename it **`Trade`**.
4. Right-click the Trade node, choose New Child Element, and name the new element **`OrderNumber`**.
5. Right-click the OrderNumber node and choose Promotions and Quick Promote to promote the property (because this is the first promotion, Visual Studio will tell you it will create a new PropertySchema).
6. Right-click the Trade node, choose New Child Element, and name the new element **`Symbol`**.

7. Right-click the Trade node, choose New Child Element, and name the new element **`DateTime`**. In the property window, change the data type to be xs:dateTime.
8. Right-click the Trade node, choose New Child Element, and name the new element **`TotalOrderQuantity`**. In the property window, change the data type to be xs:int.
9. Right-click the Trade node, choose New Child Element, and name the new element **`ThisTradeQuantity`**. In the property window, change the data type to be xs:int.
10. Right-click the Trade node and choose Promotion, Show Promotions. Promote the TotalOrderQuantity and ThisTradeQuantity elements as distinguished fields.
11. Right-click the Trade node, choose `New Child Element`, and name the new element **`UnitPrice`**. In the property window, change the data type to be xs:int.

Your completed schema in the editor should be as shown in Figure 13.8.

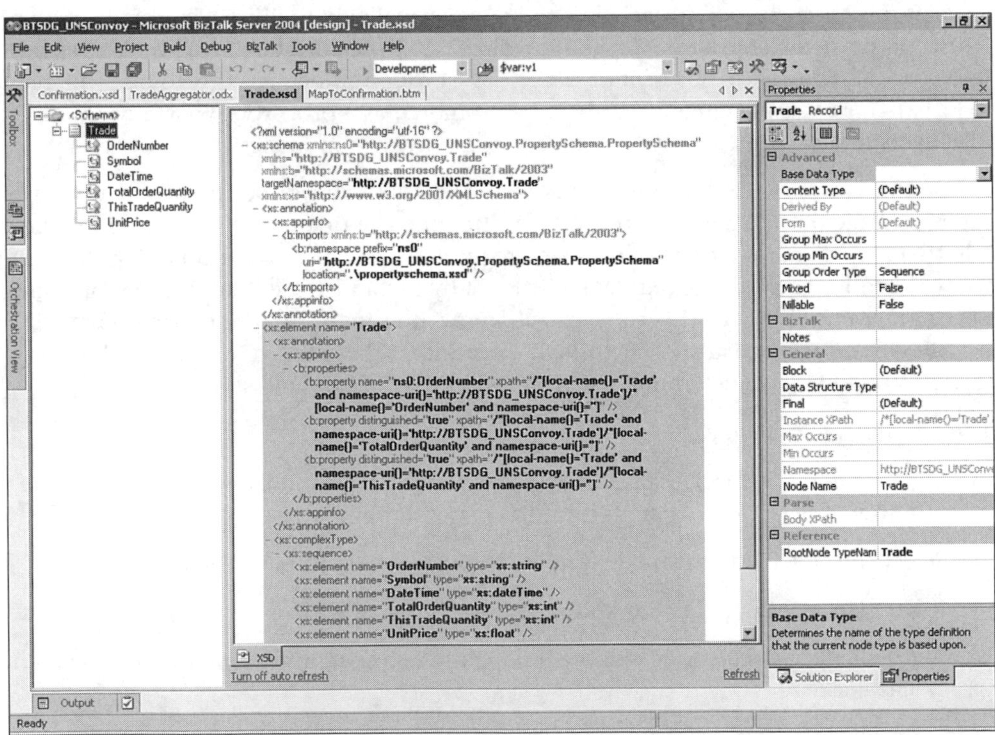

FIGURE 13.8 Trade schema.

Step 2: Create a Schema to Describe the Confirmation Message

In our scenario, after the transaction is complete, we send out a confirmation notice. To create the Confirmation schema, follow these steps:

1. Right-click the BTSDG_UNSConvoy project in the Solution Explorer, point to Add, and then select Add New Item from the context menu.
2. Select the Schema template and name the new schema **`Confirmation`**. Click OK.
3. Right-click the Root element and rename it **`Confirmation`**.
4. Right-click the Trade node, choose New Child Element, and name the new element **`OrderNumber`**.
5. Right-click the Trade node, choose New Child Element, and name the new element **`DateTimeStarted`**. In the property window, change the data type to be xs:dateTime.
6. Right-click the Trade node, choose New Child Element, and name the new element **`DateTimeCompleted`**. In the property window, change the data type to be xs:dateTime. Set the default value to be 2000-01-01T01:00:00.
7. Right-click the Trade node, choose `New Child Element`, and name the new element **`Symbol`**.

Most elements in the confirmation message will be populated from a map; however, we will be directly assigning a value to the DateTimeCompleted element in an Expression shape. For this to work, we need to promote the element. To do this,

1. Right-click DateTimeCompleted and point at Show Promotions.
2. With the Distinguished Fields tab selected, click DateTimeCompleted and click Add. A seal icon should appear on the node to indicate it has been promoted.

Step 3: Create a Map from Trade to Confirmation

Next, we will create a confirmation message based on some of the data in the first trade message by creating a map from the trade message to the confirmation message.

1. Right-click the BTSDG_UNSConvoy project in the Solution Explorer, point to Add, and then select Add New Item from the context menu.
2. Select the Map template and name the new map **`MapToConfirmation`**. Click Open.
3. Click the Open Source Schema link, expand the Schema node, and select the Trade.xsd schema.
4. Click the Open Destination Schema link, expand the Schema node, and select the Confirmation.xsd schema.
5. Connect the OrderNumber elements in each schema by clicking and holding on one and dragging it to the other.
6. Connect the Symbol elements in each schema by clicking and holding on one and dragging it to the other.
7. From the toolbox, drag a DateTime functoid onto the map surface. Connect it to the `DateTimeStarted` element of the Confirmation schema. When the map is applied,

this functoid will provide the current date and time, which will be mapped to the `DateTimeStarted` element of the confirmation message.

Step 4: Create the Orchestration

There are many steps involved in the creation of this orchestration. First, we need to create the empty orchestration, the messages and the orchestration variables we will need.

1. Right-click the BTSDG_UNSConvoy project in the Solution Explorer, point to Add, and then select Add New Item from the context menu.
2. Select the BizTalk Orchestration template and name the orchestration **`TradeAggregator.odx`**.
3. In the Orchestration View window, right-click Messages and point to Add New Message. In the properties of the new message, set the name to be **`TradeMsg`**. Right-click the new message and set the Message Type to be BTSDG_UNSConvoy.Trade.
4. In the Orchestration View window, right-click Messages and point to Add New Message. In the properties of the new message, set the name to be **`ConfirmationMsg`**. Right-click the new message and set the Message Type to be BTSDG_UNSConvoy.Confirmation (this is our interim confirmation message).
5. In the Orchestration View window, right-click Messages and point to Add New Message. In the properties of the new message, set the name to be **`CompletedConfirmation`**. Right-click the new message and set the Message Type to be BTSDG_UNSConvoy.Confirmation (this is our final confirmation message).
6. From the toolbox, drag a Receive shape onto the orchestration surface. Name it **`Receive Initial Message`**.
7. In the properties of the Receive shape, set the Activate property to true.
8. In the properties of the Receive shape, set the Message Type to TradeMsg.

Our orchestration will use a single receive port. Initial and subsequent messages will flow through the same port. To create the port, follow these steps:

1. Right-click the Port Surface area, and point to Add New Configured Port. On the Welcome screen, click Next.
2. In the Port Properties, set the name to `RecvTradesPort`.
3. On the Select a Port Type screen, choose Create a New Port Type, and change the name to **`RecvTradesPortType`**, accepting the other default values.
4. On the Port Binding screen, choose Specify Now. Set the direction to I'll Always Be Receiving Messages on this Port. Set the transport to File, and for a URI, type in **`C:\filedrop\BTSDG_UNSConvoy\in\*.xml`**. For the Receive Pipeline, choose Microsoft.BizTalk.DefaultPipelines.XMLReceive.

5. Click Next and Finish to save the port.
6. Click and hold the green connector of the new port and drag a connection line to the green connector of the Receive shape.

The orchestration will keep looping until the total number of shares traded (based on the trade confirmations received) equals the quantity in the order. For this to work, we need to keep a running total of the number of shares traded, which we do by setting an orchestration variable and basing our looping logic on its value. To do this, follow these steps:

1. In the Orchestration view, expand the Variables tab. Add a new variable called `CurrentUnits` and set the type to System.Int32.
2. In the Orchestration view, add a new variable called `TotalUnits` and set the type to System.Int32.
3. From the toolbox, drag a new Expression shape and place it after the Receive shape. Change the name to **`Set Orchestration Variables`**.
4. Double-click the Expression shape to launch the Expression Editor, and enter the following:

```
TotalUnits = TradeMsg.TotalOrderQuantity
CurrentUnits = TradeMsg.ThisTradeQuantity
```

Next, we will create the confirmation message. To do this, follow these steps:

1. From the toolbox, drag a Transform shape onto the orchestration and place it under the Expression shape. A Construct Message shape will automatically be created to contain it.
2. In the properties of the Construct Message shape, set the name to be **`Construct Confirmation`**.
3. In the properties of the Construct Message shape, set the Messages Constructed to be `ConfirmationMsg`.
4. Double-click the Transform shape to launch the Transform Configuration screen.
5. Click the Existing Map option button and select the BTSDG_UNSConvoy.MapToConfirmation map.
6. Under the Transform node, set the Source to be TradeMsg and the destination to be `ConfirmationMsg`. Click OK to save your changes.

The next part of the orchestration is the actual looping process. We will stay in this loop and continue receiving messages until the trade quantity is met. In a real-world situation, you may also want to add a timeout at this point (in case your loop-exit criteria is never met or is not met in a timely manner), which you could easily do by having the loop inside a Scope shape that has a timeout set.

To create the loop, follow these steps:

1. From the toolbox, drag a Loop shape onto the orchestration and place it under the Message Construction shape.
2. Double-click the Loop shape to launch the Expression Editor, and type in the following expression:

   ```
   CurrentUnits < TotalUnits
   ```

3. From the toolbox, drag a Receive shape onto the orchestration and place it under the loop.
4. Set the name of this Receive shape to Receive Subsequent Trades, and set the Message Type to `TradeMsg`.
5. Click and hold the green connector of the new Receive shape and drag a connection line to the existing receive port (there should be two connection lines from the receive port, one to each Receive shape).
6. Next, we need to increment the number of units traded. To do this, from the toolbox, drag an Expression shape onto the orchestration and place it under the Receive shape.
7. Double-click the Expression shape to launch the Expression Editor, and type in the following expression:

   ```
   CurrentUnits = CurrentUnits + TradeMsg.ThisTradeQuantity;
   ```

Next, we will create a final confirmation message that will be sent when the order has been filled:

1. From the toolbox, drag a Message Assignment shape onto the orchestration and place it below the loop (outside of the loop). A Message Construction shape will be created for you automatically.
2. In the properties of the Message Construction shape, set the Messages Constructed property to `CompletedConfirmation`, and change the name to **`Construct Completed Confirmation`**.
3. Double-click the Message Assignment shape to launch the Expression Editor and enter the following code:

   ```
   CompletedConfirmation = ConfirmationMsg;
   CompletedConfirmation.DateTimeCompleted = System.DateTime.Now;
   ```

Next, we will send the confirmation message:

1. From the toolbox, drag a Send shape onto the orchestration and place it below the Construct Completed Confirmation message construction shape.
2. In the properties of the new Send shape, set the name to **`Send Confirmation`**, and set the Message property to CompletedConfirmation.

3. Right-click the Port Surface area and point at New Configured Port. Click Next on the Welcome screen.
4. In the Port Properties screen, change the name to **`SendConfirmationPort`** and click Next.
5. In the Select a Port Type screen, choose Create a Port Type and name your port **`SendConfirmationPortType`**. Set the direction to I'll Always Be Sending Messages on This Port. Leave the default values of One-way Communication Pattern and Internal Access. Click Next.
6. In the Port Binding screen, specify I Will Always Be Sending Messages on This Port. Choose Specify Now for the port binding.
7. Choose File as a transport. For the URI, type in **`C:\filedrop\BTSDG_UNSConvoy\out\Confirmation %MessageID%.xml`**.
8. For the Send Pipeline, choose Microsoft.BizTalk.DefaultPipelines.XMLTransmit.
9. Click Next and Finish to save the new port.
10. Connect the new port to the Send Confirmation Send shape by clicking and dragging the green connector.

From a visual and process perspective, our orchestration is now complete. We are, however, missing one important—and key—facet.

To associate the messages we receive with their related messages, we need something that uniquely identifies them as belonging to a set. We would then use this unique identifier to route an incoming message to an existing orchestration instance, if one has already been started for that identifier, or if this is the first message in the convoy, to create a new orchestration.

This can be done easily using correlation sets. To create the correlation set, follow these steps:

1. In the Orchestration view, expand the Variables tab. Right-click Correlation Sets and choose New Correlation Set.
2. In the properties of the new correlation set, change the name to **`OrderCorrelationSet`**.
3. Click the Correlation Type property and from the drop-down list, point at `<Create new Correlation Type>`.
4. In the Correlation Type property window, click the ellipses beside Correlation Properties.
5. In the Available Properties tree, expand the BTSDG_UNSConvoy.PropertySchema node.
6. Click the `OrderNumber` node and click Add, and then click OK to save your changes.

Now that we have our correlation set, we need to initialize and use it inside our orchestration. To do this, follow these steps:

1. In the properties of the Receive Initial Trade shape, click the Initializing Correlation Sets property and select `OrderCorrelationSet` in the drop-down list. The arrival of this message sets the value of the correlation set for the started orchestration instance.
2. In the properties of the Receive Subsequent Trades shape, click the Following Correlation Sets property and select `OrderCorrelationSet` in the drop-down list. By "following" the already initialized correlation set, we are indicating that messages routed to this orchestration instance must have the proper value for the `OrderNumber` field; that is, it must match that of the other messages delivered to this orchestration instance. BizTalk will use the `OrderNumber` element to ensure that messages are correlated with the correct running orchestration instance.

Your completed orchestration should look as shown in Figure 13.9.

Step 5: Deploy and Test the Orchestration

As usual, we will be using the file system as a means of getting messages into and out of BizTalk. You could use any transport or endpoint, but the file system is the easiest for testing and demonstration purposes.

Create the following folder structure on the BizTalk machine:

```
C:\filedrop\BTSDG_UNSConvoy\in
C:\filedrop\BTSDG_UNSConvoy\out
```

Next, we will need to create a Trade instance document that will trigger this entire process. To create an instance document, follow these steps:

1. In the Solution Explorer, right-click the Trade.xsd and choose Properties. Set the output instance filename to

   ```
   c:\filedrop\BTSDG_UNSConvoy\trade.xml
   ```

2. Right-click the schema again and choose Generate Instance.
3. Browse to the C:\filedrop\BTSDG_UNSConvoy\trade.xml folder, and using Notepad, edit the trade.xml file.
4. Set the TotalOrderQuantity amount to 100. Set the ThisTradeQuantity to 40. Save the file.
5. Make a copy of trade.xml, and call it trade_2.xml. Edit the file in Notepad, set the TotalOrderQuantity amount to 100. Set the ThisTradeQuantity to 30. Save the file.
6. Repeat the preceding step, creating a trade_3 file.

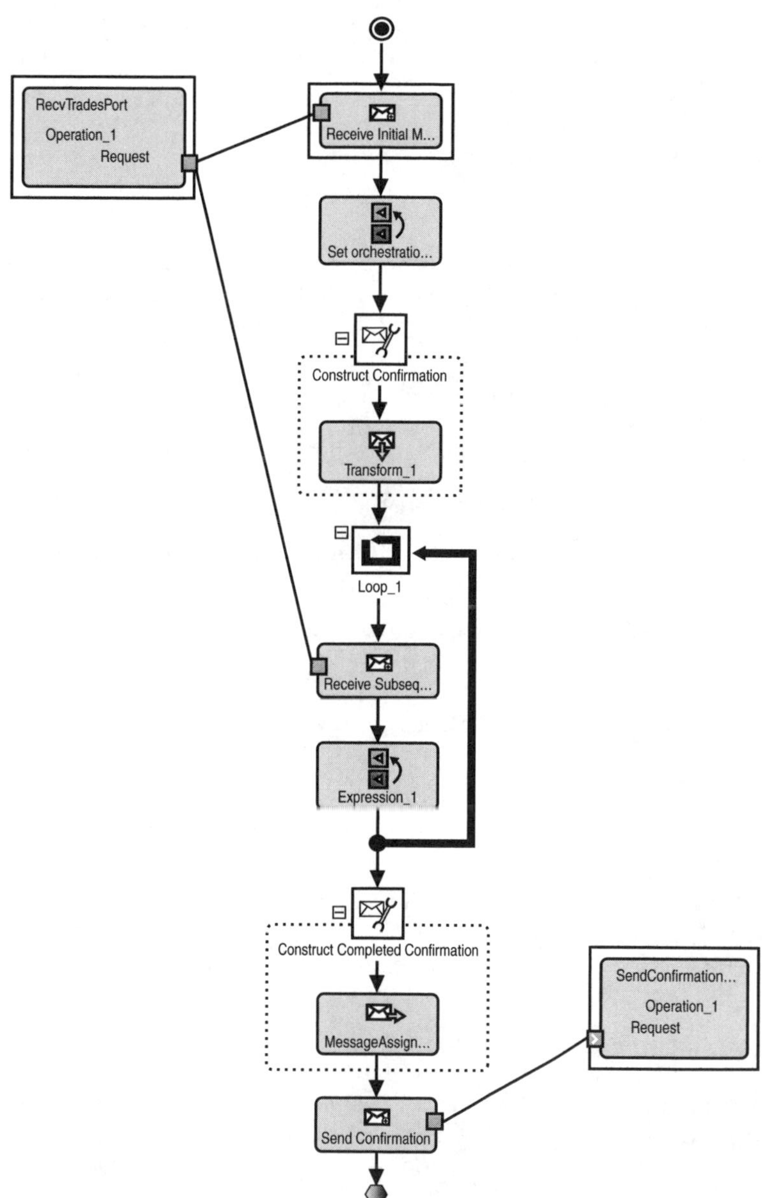

FIGURE 13.9 Trade aggregator orchestration.

We now have three instance documents representing a total order of 100 shares, with the order split into three separate transactions.

For the assembly to be registered in the GAC, we must strongly name it. If you do not do this, you'll receive a deployment error. To strongly name it, follow these steps:

1. Run the Visual Studio command prompt and navigate to the BTSDG_UNSConvoyUNSConvoy project folder.
2. Type in

   ```
   Sn -k BTSDG_UNSConvoy.snk
   ```

   Close the DOS box.
3. In the Solution Explorer, right-click the BTSDG_UNSConvoy project and choose Properties. Click Assembly and scroll through the properties to Assembly Key File. Navigate to the BTSDG_UNSConvoy.snk key file you just generated.

Finally, we're ready to deploy. Right-click the BTSDG_UNSConvoy project and choose Deploy. You should not receive any deployment errors. If you do, retrace the deployment steps and ensure that you followed them all.

Follow these steps to start the orchestration:

1. Bring up the BizTalk Server Explorer (Ctrl+Alt+Z) and expand the Orchestrations node.
2. Right-click the BTSDG_UNSConvoy orchestration and point at Start.
3. Ensure that everything is checked on the Express Start screen and then click OK.
4. The icon beside the BTSDG_UNSConvoy orchestration should no longer be dimmed.

To test the application, drag a copy of the trade.xml file into the C:\filedrop\BTSDG_UNSConvoy\in folder. It should disappear as it is picked up by BizTalk. Check the C:\filedrop\BTSDG_UNSConvoy\out folder; there will be nothing in it.

Drag copies of the trade_2.xml and trade_3.xml files into the C:\filedrop\BTSDG_UNSConvoy\in folder. Check the C:\filedrop\BTSDG_UNSConvoy\out folder and you should see a trade confirmation message.

Convoys are an important messaging pattern, as business transactions are often broken down into a series of grouped messages. In this pattern, we showed how to implement a uniform sequential convoy that receives a variable number of messages of the same type and ensures that the entire set of messages is processed by the same orchestration instance.

Summary

The BizTalk messaging engine is extremely flexible and powerful. This chapter has shown you some common patterns that you can use with the BizTalk messaging engine. We have stepped through importing text files, using an adapter to insert received messages into SQL Server, and examined one example of a convoy pattern. The patterns presented in this chapter are a small subset of what is possible, but provide a good cross-sectional view into some common application requirements and how to meet those requirements.

CHAPTER 14

Orchestration Patterns

IN THIS CHAPTER

- BizTalk Server 2004 and InfoPath
- Introducing the Patterns
- Pattern 1: File-Drop Orchestration Activation
- Pattern 2: Consuming a Web Service
- Pattern 3: Using InfoPath with Orchestration
- Pattern 4: Multiple Entry Points for Orchestration Activation

Up to this point we have explored most of the new exciting features in BizTalk Server 2004. Chapter 15, "Deployment," and Chapter 16, "BizTalk Health and Activity Tracking," will take a pragmatic attempt at meeting real-world requirements with BizTalk Server 2004. We will start by introducing common business scenarios and will show, step-by-step, how to solve those requirements with BizTalk Server 2004.

Complex business problems can be solved with BizTalk Server 2004. Rather than attempt to re-create such a complex and business-specific solution here, we will instead focus on common requirements and patterns that can meet those requirements.

BizTalk Server 2004 and InfoPath

InfoPath is the newest member of the Microsoft Office suite of products.

Conceptually, you can think of InfoPath as a self-contained mobile form with optional intelligence. It is a container for data, presentation layers for the data, and script that can act upon the data.

InfoPath provides powerful form design, validation, and processing options. Built on top of native XML, InfoPath allows multiple views into form data (perhaps context based, or as defined by security settings). But why are we talking about InfoPath in a BizTalk book? Simply put, think of InfoPath as the front end to BizTalk Server 2004 server-side processes. InfoPath is to BizTalk as Outlook is to Exchange: It is a way to enable human interactions with a back-end server.

This patterns chapter will focus on using BizTalk Server 2004 orchestration, so it is natural that we also include InfoPath for the human-facing points in our orchestrations. Where appropriate, we will be using InfoPath for the user interface as we present the patterns in this chapter.

Introducing the Patterns

We will be looking at the following four BizTalk orchestration patterns in this chapter:

- Pattern 1 will show file-drop activation of an orchestration.
- Pattern 2 will show how to consume a Web service in an orchestration.
- Pattern 3 will show how to publish an orchestration as a Web service and use InfoPath to activate the orchestration.
- Pattern 4 will build on Pattern 1 and will show how a single business process can be invoked in multiple ways.

Pattern 1: File-Drop Orchestration Activation

This is perhaps one of the most common BizTalk patterns. Most businesses carry a burden of legacy data and applications—applications that cannot be readily replaced and that you must integrate with. Many of those applications, even ancient ones whose programmers have long since retired and whose source code has vanished, have the capability to produce some form of export file. These export files can be used as integration points into a BizTalk-based business solution. In addition, the same integration points can be used for any mechanism that can copy a file into a folder, such as FTP or automated batch files.

In this pattern we will cover orchestration activation in response to a file arriving at a receive location.

Scenario

We will use the common scenario of a purchase order receipt. Our company, San Diego Sea Foods, receives a purchase order from a customer. When the purchase order arrives, as an XML document, we want to pick it up and trigger our order fulfillment process.

Our solution will do the following:

- Receive an incoming purchase order.
- Modify it to include a timestamp.
- Put the modified purchase order in an outbound folder for further processing.

Implementation Steps

The purchase order was received by FTP in a specific folder and we are monitoring that folder for inbound purchase orders. We will need to do the following:

- Define a document schema.
- Create a new orchestration schedule.
- Deploy and test the solution.

This is a rather simplistic example, but fear not, we will be building on it later.

Open Visual Studio .NET and create a new project called **BTSDG_Activation** using the Empty BizTalk Server Project template.

Step 1: Define an Inbound Document Schema

First, we will create the inbound document schema:

1. Right-click the `BTSDG_Activation` project in the Solution Explorer, point to Add, and then select Add New Item from the context menu.
2. Select the Schema template and name the new item **PurchaseOrderSchema.xsd**. Click Open to launch the BizTalk Schema Editor.
3. Right-click the `Root` node and rename it **PurchaseOrder**. This sets the name of the document element. (Note: The BizTalk Editor allows for multiple root elements, which is not valid XML, to accommodate diverse flat-file structures.)
4. Right-click the `PurchaseOrder` node, point to Insert Schema Node, and then click Child Field Attribute.
5. Type **PONumber** as the field name and then press Enter.
6. Right-click `PurchaseOrder`, point to Insert Schema Node, and click Child Field Attribute.
7. Type **PODate** for the name of the new attribute and then press Enter.
8. Ensure `PODate` is selected, and then go to the Properties view. Scroll until you find Data Type and select `xs:dateTime` from the list of data types.
9. Right-click the `PurchaseOrder` node, point to Insert Schema Node, and then click Child Field Attribute. Name this attribute **CustomerNumber**.
10. Right-click the `PurchaseOrder` node, point to Insert Schema Node, and then click Child Field Attribute. Name this attribute **AcceptedDatetime** and set its data type to be xs:dateTime.
11. Right-click `PurchaseOrder`, point to Insert Schema Node, and click Child Record. Name the element **OrderItems**.
12. Right-click `OrderItems` and insert a Child Record. Name it **OrderItem**.
13. Right-click `OrderItem` and select Properties. In the property window, select the MaxOccurs property and set it to "*". (Note: This is an abbreviation that the BizTalk Editor will change to "unbounded," meaning multiple occurrences of this element are allowed.)
14. Right-click `OrderItem`, point to Insert Schema Node, and click Child Field Element. Name the element **Quantity**, and set its data type (in the property window) to be xs:int.

15. Right-click `OrderItem`, point to Insert Schema Node, and click Child Field Element. Name the element **`PartNumber`**, and set its data type (in the property window) to be xs:string.

16. Right-click `OrderItem`, point to Insert Schema Node, and click Child Field Element. Name the element **`UnitPrice`**, and set its data type (in the property window) to be xs:float.

We have now created a schema that will be our inbound purchase order. For demonstration purposes, we have kept the schema very simple; a real-world schema would be more complex.

By default, as a message flows through an orchestration schedule, it is a monolithic black box that we are passing around. However, in this pattern we will be changing part of the message content and, as such, need visibility into the message itself. We will make the required data visible to the orchestration by "promoting" the field in the schema definition.

BizTalk has two mechanisms for promoting fields: as distinguished fields and as properties. Distinguished fields are visible only in orchestrations; they cannot be used for routing by the messaging engine. Message properties, on the other hand, can be used both by the messaging engine and in orchestration schedules.

As part of this pattern sample, we will be filling in the `AcceptedDatetime` attribute with the current date and time. To gain access to it from the orchestration, we will need to promote it as a distinguished field. To do this, follow these steps:

1. In the Schema Editor, right-click the `AcceptedDatetime` node and select Promotions.
2. From the submenu, choose Show Promotions.
3. Select the `AcceptedDatetime` node and then click the Add button. Click OK.
4. A little seal will appear on top of the `AcceptedDatetime` node to indicate that it is a promoted field.

Your schema should now look like Figure 14.1.

Step 2: Creating the Orchestration

Next, we will create the orchestration schedule we would like to activate on the appearance of the input document.

Right-click the BTSDG_Activation project and add a new BizTalk Orchestration. Name it **`Activation`**.

1. Right-click the port surface and select New Configured Port from the context menu.
2. Name your port **`ReceiveOrder`**.
3. On the Select a Port Type screen, name your port type **`ReceiveOrderPortType`**. Specify that this is a one-way communication pattern and give it public access.

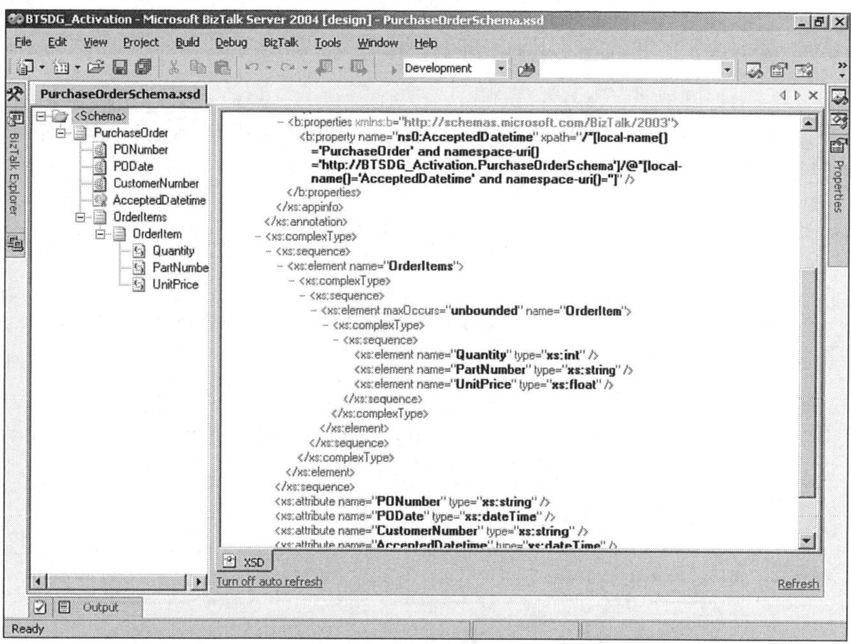

FIGURE 14.1 Purchase Order schema.

> **NOTE**
>
> Normally, you would leave the access at the default setting of Internal. However, we will be building on this sample later in this chapter and will need public access at that time.

4. On the Port Binding screen, choose I'll Be Receiving Messages on This Port for the port direction, and choose Specify Later for the port binding.

5. Right-click the Operation in the new port, and in the Properties window change the identifier to **`AcceptOrder`**.

6. Right-click the Request message in the new port and choose Properties. In the Properties window of the message, select Message Type and expand the Schemas node. Choose the `BTSDG_Activation.PurchaseOrderSchema` schema.

7. To create the inbound message, click the Orchestration tab in the Solution Explorer, right-click the Messages node, add a new message called **`Order`**, and specify a schema of `BTSDG_Activation.PurchaseOrderSchema`.

8. To create the outbound message, in the Orchestration tab right-click the Messages node, add a new message called **`OrderWithTimestamp`**, and specify a schema of `BTSDG_Activation.PurchaseOrderSchema`.

9. Drag a Receive shape from the toolbox into your orchestration. Name it **`ReceiveOrder`**. In the Properties window of this Receive shape, choose Order as the

14

message you will be receiving. You should now be able to drag the green connector on your port to the green connector on the Receive shape.

10. Right-click the Receive shape and change the Activate property to True to specify that messages arriving at the bound receive location will activate new instances of the orchestration.

Next, we will create the outbound message and fill in the timestamp field. To do this, follow these steps:

1. Drag a Message Assignment shape from the toolbox to just below the Receive shape in the orchestration. A Message Construction shape will be created for you automatically, which will contain your Message Assignment shape.
2. To specify which message we are creating, right-click the Message Construction shape and choose `OrderWithTimestamp` from the Messages Constructed drop-down list.
3. Double-click the Message Assignment shape to bring up the Expression Editor and enter the code shown in Figure 14.2.

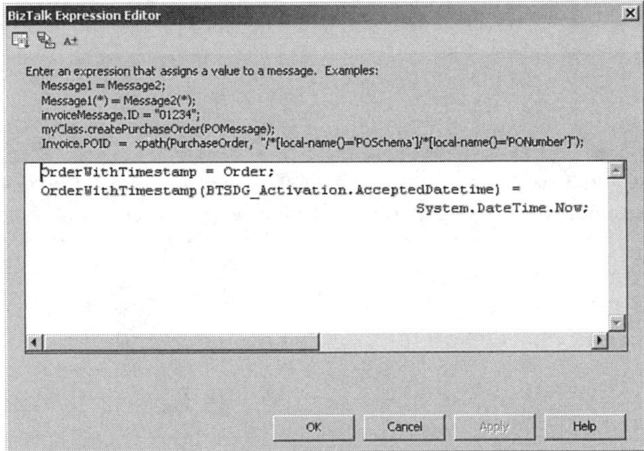

FIGURE 14.2 Assigning a value to the AcceptedDateTime distinguished field.

Finally, we need to deposit the processed message in the outbound file folder. To do this, follow these steps:

1. Right-click the port surface and select New Configured Port from the context menu.
2. Name your port **SendOrder**.
3. On the Select a Port Type screen, name your port type **SendOrderPortType**. Specify that this is a one-way communication pattern and give it public access.

4. On the Port Binding screen, choose I'll Always Be Sending Messages on This Port for the port direction, and choose Specify Later for the port binding.
5. Right-click the Request message in the new port and choose Properties. In the Properties window of the message, select Message Type and expand the Schemas node. Choose the `BTSDG_Activation.PurchaseOrderSchema` schema.
6. From the toolbox, drag a Send shape onto your orchestration surface, placing it below the Message Construction shape.
7. In the Properties window of the Send shape, set the Message property to `OrderWithTimestamp`.
8. You should now be able to drag the green connector on your Send port to the green connector on the Send shape.

Our orchestration is now complete. It should look like Figure 14.3.

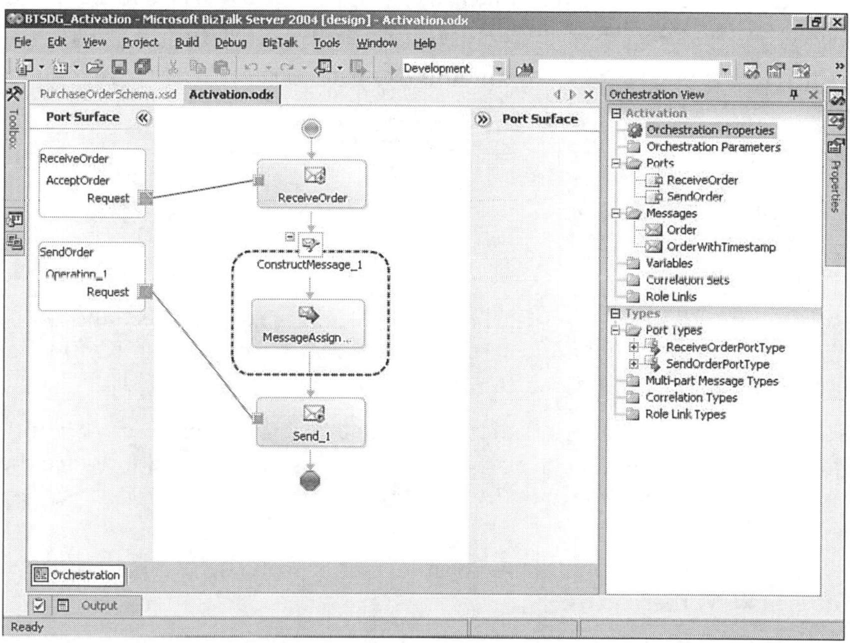

FIGURE 14.3 A completed orchestration.

Step 3: Deploying and Testing the Sample

As is so often the case with BizTalk demos, we will be using the file system as a means of getting messages into and out of BizTalk. You could use any transport or endpoint, but the file system is the easiest for demonstration purposes.

Create the following folder structure on the BizTalk machine:

```
C:\BTS2004DevGuide\Activation\in
C:\BTS2004DevGuide\Activation\out
```

Next we will need to create a `PurchaseOrderSchema` instance document that will trigger this entire process. To create an instance document, follow these steps:

1. In the Solution Explorer, right-click the `PurchaseOrderSchema.xsd` and choose Properties. Set the output instance filename to be

   ```
   c:\BTS2004DevGuide\Activation\PurchaseOrderInstance.xml
   ```

2. Right-click the schema again and choose Generate Instance. Note that after you have set the instance document name, it is persisted with your project; you need to specify it only once.

For the assembly to be registered in the GAC, we must strongly name it. If you do not do this, you'll receive a deployment error. To strongly name it, follow these steps:

1. Run the Visual Studio DOS prompt and navigate to the `BTSDG_Activation` project folder.
2. Type in

   ```
   Sn -k BTSDG_Activation.snk
   ```

   Close the DOS box.
3. In the Solution Explorer, right-click the `BTSDG_Activation` project and choose Properties. Click Assembly and scroll through the properties to Assembly Key File. Navigate to the `BTSDG_Activation.snk` key file you just generated.
4. Finally, we're ready to deploy. Right-click the `BTSDG_Activation` project and choose Deploy. You should not receive any deployment errors. If you do, retrace the deployment steps and ensure that you followed them all.

Deploying will only get your project onto the server, it won't activate it. To start the orchestration, follow these steps:

1. Bring up the BizTalk Server Explorer (Ctrl+Alt+Z) and expand the Orchestrations node.
2. Next we need to create the receive ports that BizTalk will watch for inbound purchase orders. In the BizTalk Explorer, right-click Receive Ports and choose New Receive Location. Specify that this is a one-way port. Name the port **`BTSDG_Activation_Receive`**.
3. For our sample to work, we must specify which folder to watch, which is done by specifying a receive location. Right-click the Receive Locations folder and choose

Add Receive Location. For the transport choose File; for the address, specify the following:

```
c:\BTS2004DevGuide\Activation\In
```

4. For the file mask, specify "*.xml". For the Receive Handler, specify BizTalk Server Application. For the pipeline, choose the XMLReceive pipeline.
5. To create the send port that BizTalk will use to place the output file into our specified folder, right-click Send Ports and choose Add New Send Port. Specify Static One-Way. For the Transport Type, choose File. For the address, specify the following:

```
c:\BTS2004DevGuide\Activation\Out\%Message_ID%.XML
```

For the send pipeline, choose XMLTransmit. Rename the port to `BTSDG_Activation_Send`.

14

NOTE

`%Message_ID%` is a special macro that will be replaced at runtime by the instance ID of this message. This approach ensures unique filenames.

Next we will bind the ports, which links the abstract ports specified in the orchestration with the physical ports, by following these steps:

1. To bind the ports in the orchestration to the physical ports, in BizTalk Explorer, right-click the `BTSDG_Activation` and choose Bind. For the `ReceiveOrder` inbound port, choose `BTSDG_Activation_Receive`. For the `SendOrder` outbound port, choose `BTSDG_Activation_Send`. For the host, choose BizTalk Server Application.
2. Right-click the `BTSDG_Activation` orchestration again, and this time choose Start. On the next screen, make sure all items are checked (which is the default) in order to also start any dependencies.
3. The icon beside the `BTSDG_Activation` orchestration should no longer be dimmed.

To test the application, drag a copy of the instance file `PurchaseOrderInstance.xml` into the C:\BTS2004DevGuide\Activation\in folder. A few seconds later, a file should appear in the C:\BTS2004DevGuide\Activation\out folder. The filename will look like a GUID, which is the message ID, plus an .xml extension. The contents of the file will be the same as the input document, except that `AcceptedDatetime` will be the date and time the file was processed.

In this first pattern, we have covered a very simple, yet very common, business requirement.

Without writing any significant code, we achieved the following:

- Created a business process to pick up a file, modify it, and place it somewhere else.
- Defined a receive location that would trigger creation of a new orchestration instance when a file appears in a specified location.

Pattern 2: Consuming a Web Service

Web services have gone from being just another interesting idea to fundamentally changing the way software is architected. The evolution of the standards has been blindingly fast, vendor support and cooperation has been unprecedented, and adoption is coming fast and furious.

As we will see in the next three patterns, BizTalk plays very well in the Web services space. This is not surprising, because both technologies are XML to the core. In a services-oriented world, BizTalk can play the role of a universal messaging bus, as well as the orchestration layer that aggregates services into larger units of functionality.

In this pattern we will cover

- Consuming a Web service from an orchestration.
- Promoting message fields, making them visible to an orchestration.
- Basing an orchestration control flow decision on a Web service result.

Scenario

For this pattern, we will build on the previous scenario. San Diego Sea Foods, being a technology-savvy company, has opted for an application integration strategy built with Web services. They have built a Web service that performs a credit check by checking a customer's current accounting record and returns a Boolean indicating whether they are approved for a given amount of credit.

Our solution will accomplish the following:

- Receive an incoming credit check request message.
- Call the credit check Web service.
- Deposit the credit check request message into either an "approved" or "denied" folder.

Implementation Steps

The purchase order was received by FTP in a specific folder, and we are monitoring that folder for inbound credit check requests. We will need to

1. Set up.
2. Create the `CreditCheckRequest` schema.

3. Create the Web service.
4. Create the messages.
5. Create the orchestration, receive port, and receive action.
6. Prepare to call the Web service.
7. Call the Web service and receive the result.
8. Make a decision based on the Web service result.
9. Deploy and test the sample.

Step 1: Setting Up

To set up for this pattern implementation, create a new empty BizTalk project and call it **CreditCheck**.

Right-click the new BTSDG_CreditCheck project, click Add New Item, and choose the BizTalk Orchestration template. Call your orchestration **CreditCheck**.

Step 2: Creating the CreditCheckRequest Schema

We will create a special schema for the credit check request, using the schema editor as we have before. As part of this process, we will also be promoting fields that we will need access to during the execution of our orchestration.

To create the CreditCheckRequest schema, follow these steps:

1. In the Solution Explorer, create a new empty BizTalk project called BTSDG_**CreditCheck**. Right-click this project, point to Add, and then select Add New Item from the context menu.
2. Select the Schema template and name the new item **CreditCheckRequest.xsd**. Click Open to launch the BizTalk Schema Editor.
3. Right-click the Root node and rename it **CreditRequest**.
4. Right-click the CreditRequest node, point to Insert schema node, and then click Child Field Element.
5. Type **RequestDate** as the field name and then press Enter.
6. Ensure RequestDate is selected, and then go to the Properties view. Scroll until you find Data Type and select xs:dateTime from the list of data types.
7. Repeat the process for the following child field elements: Company (xs:string), Amount (xs:int), and Disposition (xs:string).
8. Right-click the CreditRequest node and choose Promote, Quick Promotions. You will see a dialog box that informs you that a property schema will be created to contain your quick promotions. Click OK. You'll notice that a small seal icon has appeared in the Company node.

9. Right-click the `Amount` node and choose Promote, Quick Promotion. Repeat this with the `Disposition` field.
10. To verify your promotions, right-click the `CreditRequest` node and choose Promote, Show Promotions. Notice in the first grid that a reference has been created to the `propertyschema.xsd`. This is the schema that was just created for us to track promotions. Notice that the property fields list contains a reference to each of the fields you promoted.

Step 3: Creating the Web Service

For illustration purposes, our Web service will be extremely simplistic. We will not do any actual database access; we'll just accept a customer ID (which we'll proceed to ignore) and an amount. If the amount is less than $5,000, we will approve the request; if not, we will deny it.

Add a new ASP.NET Web service project to your solution.

All the code (in C#) for our simplistic Web service is shown next:

```
[WebService(Namespace="http://BTSDevGuide/webservices/")]
public class CreditChecker : System.Web.Services.WebService
{
     public CreditChecker()
     {
          //CODEGEN: This call is required by the ASP.NET Web Services Designer
          InitializeComponent();
     }

     [WebMethod]
     public bool Check(string name, int amount)
     {
          return (amount<5000);
     }
}
```

Save and build this project. Now let's add a Web reference to this service from the orchestration project, just as you would add a Web reference to any .NET project:

1. Right-click the References node of the `BTSDG_CreditCheck` project and choose Add Web Reference. Choose Web Service on the Local Machine (if running Windows 2003), and then click the `CreditChecker` service.
2. If the Web service was located, you will see a reference to the WSDL file. Name the service **`CreditChecker`** in the Web reference Name text box and click Add Reference.

Step 4: Creating the Messages

This pattern will use a total of four messages: an inbound text message, an outbound XML message, and both a request and a response message for our Web service. Follow these steps:

1. To create the inbound message, in the Orchestration view (this tab becomes visible whenever you have an ODX as the current file in the editor), right-click Messages and choose New Message. In the Properties window of the new message Message_1, select Message Type and expand the Schemas node. Choose the `BTSDG_CreditCheck.CreditCheckRequest` schema. Change the message Identifier to **`InboundCreditCheckRequest`**.
2. To create the outbound message, repeat the first step, changing the message Identifier to **`OutboundCreditCheckResult`**.
3. To create the Web service request message, right-click Messages and choose New Message. In the Properties window of the new message Message_1, select Message Type and expand the Web Message Types node. Choose the `BTSDG_CreditCheck.CreditChecker.CreditChecker_.Check_request` schema. Change the message Identifier to **`CreditCheckWSRequest`**.
4. To create the outbound message, repeat the first step, changing the message Identifier to **`CreditCheckWSResult`**.

Step 5: Creating the Orchestration, Receive Port, and Receive Action

Next, we will create the orchestration that will invoke the Web service. For simplicity, we will specify all port bindings at design time.

Right-click the `BTSDG_CreditCheck` project and add a new BizTalk Orchestration. Name it **`CreditCheck`**. Then do the following steps:

1. Right-click the port surface and select New Port from the context menu.
2. Double-click the new port to run the Port Configuration Wizard. On the Port Properties screen, name your port ReceiveInboundCreditRequest.
3. On the Select a Port Type screen, name your port type **`ReceiveInboundCreditRequestPortType`**.
4. On the Port Binding screen, choose Specify Now, choose File as a Transport, specify a URI of C:\BTS2004DevGuide\CreditCheck\In*.xml, and be sure that the receive pipeline is set to Microsoft.BizTalk.DefaultPipelines.XMLReceive. Click Next, and then click Finish.
5. Right-click the Request message in the new port and choose Properties. In the Properties window of the message, select Message Type and expand the Schemas node. Choose the `BTSDG_CreditCheck.CreditCheckRequest` schema.
6. Drag a Receive shape from the toolbox into your orchestration. In the properties of this Receive shape, choose `InboundCreditCheckRequest` as the message you will be

receiving. You should now be able to drag the green connector on your port to the green connector on the receive shape.

7. Right-click the Receive shape and change the Activate property to true to specify that messages arriving at the bound receive location will activate new instances of the orchestration.

Note that if you are unable to connect the port to the Receive shape, this is because the message referred to by the Receive shape is not of the schema type specified in the receive port. This is an example of how the Orchestration Designer enforces "correct by construction" so that errors are caught at design time, not at runtime.

Step 6: Preparing to Call the Web Service

Before we can call our Web service, we need to prepare the request message the service expects and map values to the parameters.

To do this, we will use a Message Assignment shape, as described in the following steps:

1. Drag a Message Assignment shape from the toolbox to just below the Receive shape in the orchestration. A Message Construction shape will be created for you automatically, which will contain your Message Assignment shape.
2. To specify which message we are creating, right-click the Message Construction shape and choose `CreditCheckWSRequest` from the Messages Constructed drop-down list.
3. Double-click the Message Assignment shape to bring up the expression editor, and enter the following:

```
CreditCheckWSRequest.amount =
InboundCreditCheckRequest(BTSDG_CreditCheck.Amount);
CreditCheckWSRequest.name =
      InboundCreditCheckRequest(BTSDG_CreditCheck.Company);
```

Step 7: Calling the Web Service and Receiving the Result

Next, we will add the Web service call:

1. Right-click the port surface and select New Configured Port from the context menu.
2. Name your port **`CallCreditCheckWS`**.
3. On the Select a Port Type screen, choose Existing Port Type. Expand the Web Port Types and select the Web port type that was created for you when you added the Web reference.
4. On the Port Binding screen, notice that all information has been filled in for you (transport, URI, pipelines). Choose Next and click Finish to end the wizard.

5. From the toolbox, drag a Send shape onto the orchestration surface, placing it right after the Message Assignment shape. In the properties of the new Send shape, set the Message to be `CreditCheckWSRequest`. Name the Send shape **`CreditCheckRequest`**.
6. From the toolbox, drag a Receive shape and place it immediately after the Send shape. In the Properties window of the new Receive shape, set the message to be `CreditCheckWSResult`. Name the Receive shape **`CreditCheckResult`**.
7. Click and hold the green Request connector of the Web service port and drag it to the connector in the Send shape. When you release the mouse button, there should be a linking line between the two connection points.
8. Click and hold the green Response connector of the Web service port and drag it to the connector in the Receive shape. When you release the mouse button, there should be a linking line between the two connection points.

When completed, the first part of your orchestration, from receipt of the request through receiving a response from the Web service, should look like Figure 14.4.

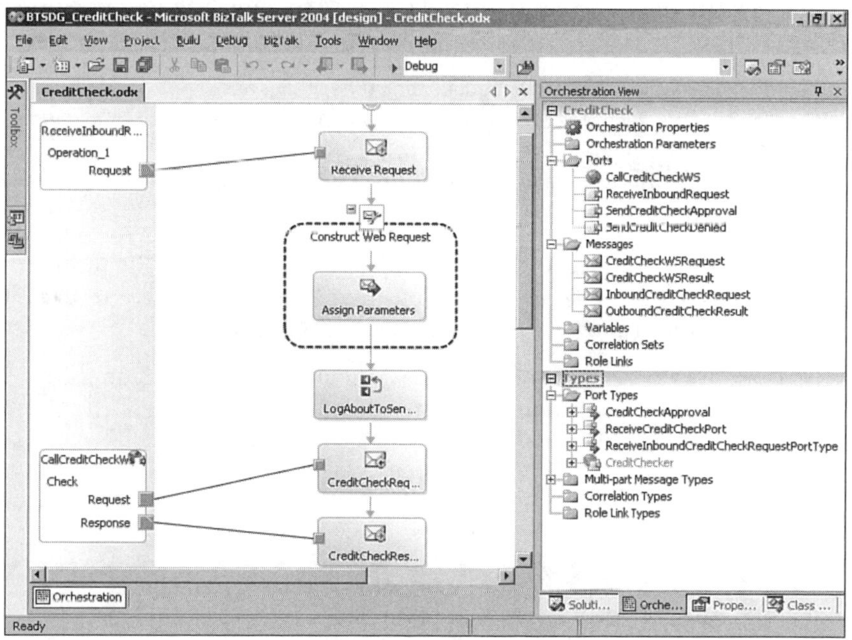

FIGURE 14.4 Activation and Web service call.

Step 8: Making a Decision Based on the Web Service Result

Now we will make a decision based on the Web service result. We will take the Boolean result of the Web service call and put a textual annotation reflecting that result in an output XML file. If the credit check was approved, we will deposit the output file in an Approved folder, and if not, it will go to a Denied folder. Follow these steps:

1. From the toolbox, drag a Decide shape into the orchestration, placing it after the `CreditCheckResult` shape.
2. Right-click Rule_1 of the Decide shape, and in the properties change the name to **`IsApproved`**.
3. To enter our Boolean rule, double-click `IsApproved` to launch the script editor and type in the following:

   ```
   CreditCheckWSResult.CheckResult==true
   ```

4. From the toolbox, drag a Message Assignment shape to the orchestration and place it under the `IsApproved` rule. A Message Construction shape will be created for you. In the properties of the Message Construction shape, set the Messages Constructed property to `OutboundCreditCheckResult`. Repeat this step under the Else branch of the decision fork.
5. Double-click the new Message Assignment shape to launch the script editor and type in the following:

   ```
   OutboundCreditCheckResult = InboundCreditCheckRequest;
   OutboundCreditCheckResult(BTSDG_CreditCheck.Disposition) = "Approved";
   ```

   Repeat this step under the `Else` branch of the decision fork, but replace the word "`Approved`" with the word "`Denied`."
6. Right-click the port surface and choose New Port. Double-click the new port to start the Port Configuration Wizard. Name your port **`SendCreditCheckApproval`**. Create a new Port Type and name it **`CreditCheckApprovalPortType`**.
7. On the Port Binding screen, specify that you'll always be sending messages. Choose Specify Now for the port binding. Specify File as the transport. For the URI, specify the following:

   ```
   c:\bts2004devguide\creditcheck\out\approved\%MessageID%.xml
   ```

> **NOTE**
>
> Note that at runtime the `%MessageID%` macro will be replaced with the GUID message identifier, so the filename in the folder will be the message identifier with an .xml file extension added on.

8. From the toolbox, drag a Send shape and place it below the Message Construction shape in the `IsApproved` branch. Name it **`SendApproval`**, and in the properties, set the Message to be `OutboundCreditCheckResult`. Connect this Send shape to the

`SendApproval` port by dragging from the green connector on the port to the green connector on the Send shape.

9. To do the credit check denial branch, right-click the port surface and choose New Port. Double-click the new port to start the Port Configuration Wizard. Name your port **`SendCreditCheckDenial`**. Create a new Port Type and name it **`SendCreditCheckDenialPortType`**.

10. On the Port Binding screen, specify that you'll always be sending messages. Choose Specify Now for the port binding. Specify File as the transport. For the URI, specify the following:

```
c:\bts2004devguide\creditcheck\out\denied\%MessageID%.xml
```

11. From the toolbox, drag a Send shape and place it below the Message Construction shape in the `Else` branch. Name it **`SendDenial`**, and in the properties set the Message to be `OutboundCreditCheckResult`. Connect this Send shape to the `SendDenial` port by dragging it from the green connector on the port to the green connector on the Send shape.

The second part of your orchestration, acting on the results of the Web service invocation, should look like Figure 14.5.

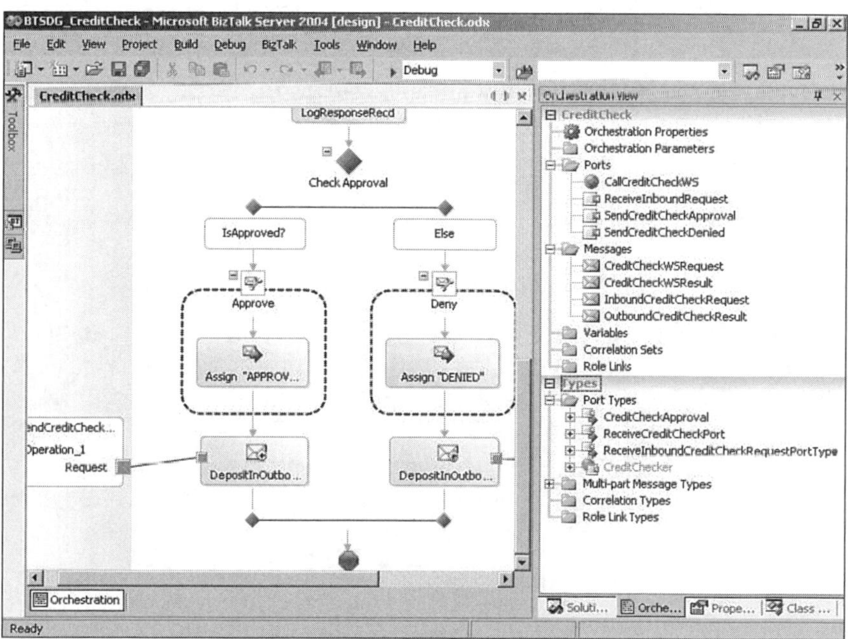

FIGURE 14.5 Flow Control based on Web service result.

Step 9: Deploying and Testing the Sample

Again, we will be using the file system as a means of getting messages in and out of BizTalk because that is the easiest way to create solutions with BizTalk.

Create the following folder structure on the BizTalk machine:

- C:\BTS2004DevGuide\CreditCheck\in
- C:\BTS2004DevGuide\CreditCheck\out\approved
- C:\BTS2004DevGuide\CreditCheck\out\denied

Next we need to create the `CreditCheckRequest` document that will trigger this entire process. To create an instance documenst, follow these steps:

1. In the Solution Explorer, right-click the `CreditCheckRequest.xsd` and choose Properties. Set the output instance file name to be

   ```
   c:\BTS2004DevGuide\CreditCheck\CreditRequestInstance.xml
   ```

2. Right-click the schema again and choose Generate Instance. Note that after you have set the instance document name, it is persisted with your project; you need to specify it only once.

For the assembly to be registered in the GAC, we must strongly name it. If you do not do this, you'll receive a deployment error. To strongly name it, follow these steps:

1. Run the Visual Studio DOS prompt and navigate to the `BTSDG_CreditCheck` project folder.

2. Type in

   ```
   sn -k BTSDG_CreditCheck.snk
   ```

   Close the DOS box.

3. In the Solution Explorer, right-click the `BTSDG_CreditCheck` project and choose Properties. Click Assembly and scroll through the properties to Assembly Key File. Navigate to the `BTSDG_CreditCheck.snk` key file you just generated.

Finally, we're ready to deploy. Right-click the `BTSDG_CreditCheck` project and choose Deploy. You should not receive any deployment errors. If you do, retrace the deployment steps and ensure that you followed them all.

To start the orchestration, follow these steps:

1. Bring up the BizTalk Server Explorer (Ctrl+Alt+Z), and expand the Orchestrations node.

2. Right-click the `BTSDG_CreditCheck` orchestration. We do not need to bind, because we did it all in design mode. Choose Enlist to enlist your orchestration with BizTalk.

3. Right-click the `BTSDG_CreditCheck` orchestration again and this time choose Start. On the next screen, make sure all items are checked (which is the default) to also start any dependencies.

4. The icon beside the `BTSDG_CreditCheck` orchestration should no longer be dimmed.

   To test the application, drag a copy of the instance file into the C:\BTS2004DevGuide\CreditCheck\in folder. If the amount value is less than 5000, it should appear in the C:\BTS2004DevGuide\CreditCheck\out\approved folder; if it is greater than 5000 it will appear in the C:\BTS2004DevGuide\CreditCheck\out\denied folder.

If the implementation steps listed here seem very lengthy, it is because we have gone into explicit detail on each of the steps. As you continue to use BizTalk, you will go through steps much like the ones shown here to develop and deploy your orchestrations, and the steps shown here in explicit detail will seem like second nature.

This pattern has shown how BizTalk 2004 can interact with a simple Web service. In the services-oriented architecture world that we are heading for, this is a very important facet of the product.

Visual Studio makes it extremely simple to create Web services, but if you want to aggregate them, you still need to create your own glue. BizTalk 2004 brings the capability to not only orchestrate Web services, but also to dynamically perform workflow branching based on Web service results.

Pattern 3: Using InfoPath with Orchestration

We said at the start of this chapter that InfoPath and BizTalk play very well together. InfoPath provides a rich environment for rapid forms construction, and BizTalk Orchestration provides a powerful business process automation engine. This pattern will show how the two can work together. Before we drill into the pattern, we will do a quick overview of InfoPath.

InfoPath is the latest member of the Microsoft Office family. As with BizTalk, everything in InfoPath is built on XML, which is the main reason why the two can work so well together. InfoPath operates in two modes: form-filling mode and template design mode. Menu options will change based on the operation mode. In form-filling mode, after data entry in a form has been completed, the user has three options: save the form, export it, or submit it.

When you save an InfoPath form, you save it as an XML document. The following is a simple example of a saved form:

```
<?xml version="1.0" encoding="UTF-8"?>
<?mso-infoPathSolution solutionVersion="1.0.0.1" productVersion="11.0.5531"
➥PIVersion="1.0.0.0" href="file:///C:\Temp\test.xsn" ?>
<?mso-application progid="InfoPath.Document"?><my:myFields
```

```
xmlns:my="http://schemas.microsoft.com/office/infopath/2003/
➥myXSD/2003-10-21T16:14:32"
xml:lang="en-us">
    <my:custname>San Diego Sea Foods</my:custname>
➥<my:custid>123</my:custid>
</my:myFields>
```

You'll note the two processing instructions shown previously (the "`?mso-`" elements). This is what identifies InfoPath forms. After InfoPath is installed, the system knows to launch InfoPath when you attempt to open an XML file that contains these processing instructions. For this reason, even if you specify that you explicitly want to open a form with Internet Explorer, the form will still be opened in InfoPath.

When you design a form (or "template" in InfoPath), InfoPath bundles all the discrete files it needs into a .XSN file. You can think of this as analogous to a CAB file or a .NET assembly.

The current (initial) version of InfoPath does not lend itself well to the concept of schema changes. The assumption is that the schema will be locked down by the time you get to form design. There is no "refresh schema" or "replace schema" capability in the user interface.

However, you can make changes after the fact by directly editing the source files inside the .XSN template.

Both InfoPath and BizTalk support XSD schemas. This makes it possible to construct a schema in BizTalk and then use that schema as a data source when designing an InfoPath form. This is the approach we will take. It is also possible to go the other way, to create a form in InfoPath and then import the schema into BizTalk.

Where BizTalk and InfoPath meet is in the form submission process. InfoPath can submit a form to a Web service, and BizTalk can expose an orchestration as a Web service. This pattern will look at how to bring the two together.

Also in this pattern we will introduce a very handy productivity tip—using a debugger to monitor and help debug an orchestration.

Scenario

For this pattern, we will build a simple business process to automate perhaps one of the most common global business requirements: ordering business cards.

In our scenario, a user completes and submits a requisition form that will be submitted to a BizTalk orchestration that has been exposed as a Web service.

Our solution will do the following:

- Use an InfoPath form to specify the name and title to put on the cards, as well as how many to order.
- Submit the form to a BizTalk orchestration for processing.

Implementation Steps

To build this solution, we will need to do the following:

- Create the Requisition schema.
- Create the Confirmation schema.
- Create a map.
- Create the orchestration.
- Deploy the orchestration.
- Expose the orchestration as a Web service.
- Create the form in InfoPath.
- Test the solution.

Step 1: Creating the Requisition Schema

To create the Requisition schema, follow these steps:

1. In the Solution Explorer, create a new empty BizTalk project called **`BTSDG_BusCards`**. Right-click this project, point to Add, and then select Add New Item from the context menu.
2. Select the Schema template and name the new item **`Requisition.xsd`**. Click Open to launch the BizTalk Schema Editor.
3. Right-click the `Root` node and rename it **`Requisition`**.
4. Right-click the `Requisition` node, point to Insert schema node, and then click Child Field Element.
5. Type **`NameOnCard`** as the field name and press Enter.
6. Repeat the process for the following Child Field Elements: `TitleOnCard` and `Quantity`. In the properties of the `Quantity` field, set the data type to `xs:positiveInteger`.
7. Right-click the `NameOnCard` node and choose Promote, Quick Promotions. A dialog box informs you that a property schema will be created to contain your quick promotions. Click OK. You'll notice that a small seal icon has appeared in the `NameOnCard` node.

NOTE

BizTalk has a list of reserved words. If you use the word "Name" for a child field element, for example, it will accept it. However, if you promote this field as a property field, you will get an error. For a complete list of reserved words that should be avoided, see the product documentation.

Step 2: Creating the Confirmation Schema

Our Web service will follow a request-response pattern. It will receive a request and return a confirmation that includes a confirmation number as well as the person's name that will go on a card.

To create the Confirmation schema, follow these steps:

1. In the Solution Explorer, right-click the `BTSDG_BusCards` project, point to Add, and then select Add New Item from the context menu.
2. Select the Schema template and name the new item **`Confirmation.xsd`**. Click Open to launch the BizTalk Schema Editor.
3. Right-click the `Root` node and rename it **`Confirmation`**.
4. Right-click the `Confirmation` node, point to Insert schema node, and then click Child Field Element.
5. Type **`ConfirmationNumber`** as the field name and press Enter. In the properties, the default data type will be xs:string.
6. Right-click the `Confirmation` node, point to Insert schema node, and then click Child Field Element.
7. Type **`NameOnCard`** as the field name and press Enter. In the properties, the default data type will be `xs:string`.

Step 3: Creating the Requisition-to-Confirmation Map

The confirmation we return will be based on the requisition we receive. To provide our users with a sense that something has really happened with their requisition, we will generate a random number (using a script functoid), call it a confirmation number, and return that number to them along with the name on the card.

There are two ways to create new maps in BizTalk 2004: directly as a project item or as a result of configuring a transform shape. To keep this implementation sequence granular, we will create the map as a discrete step.

To create the map, follow these steps:

1. In the Solution Explorer, right-click the `BTSDG_BusCards` project, point to Add, and then select Add New Item from the context menu.
2. Select the Map template and name the new item **`RequisitionToConfirmation.BTM`**. Click Open to launch the BizTalk Mapper.

3. Click the Open Source Schema link (left pane), expand the Schemas node, and select the `BTSDG_BusCards.Requisition` schema.

4. Click the Open Destination Schema link (right pane) expand the Schemas node, and select the `BTSDG_BusCards.Confirmation` schema.

5. Click both root nodes to expand them. Click and hold the `NameOnCard` node in the source schema and drag it to the `NameOnCard` node in the destination schema. When you release the mouse, a linking line should snap into place showing the mapping.

6. Open the toolbox. If the current file is a BizTalk map, the toolbox will show a series of functoids, small pieces of functionality that can be injected into the mapping process. From the `Advanced` section, drag a Script functoid onto the middle mapping surface.

7. In the properties of the Script functoid, click the ellipses beside Configure Functoid Script.

8. In the Script Type drop-down list, choose Inline C#.

9. In the properties of the Script functoid, click the ellipses beside Configure Functoid Script and type in the following C# code snippet:

```
public string CreateConf()
{
     int num = new Random().Next(1000000);
                    return num.ToString();
}
```

10. Click and hold `ConfigurationNumber` in the destination schema and drag the line on top of the functoid you just inserted. When you let go, the connection line should remain showing the mapping.

11. Save the map.

Step 4: Creating the Orchestration

An effective way to send diagnostic messages to the outside world as you are developing an orchestration is by use of a debugger. A freeware debugger I have used is DebugView, from Sysinternals, which is available at http://www.sysinternals.com/ntw2k/freeware/debugview.shtml. After you have a debugger running, you can send it messages to display using System.Diagnostics.Debug.WriteLine, as you will see later.

Right-click the `BTSDG_BusCards` project and add a new BizTalk Orchestration. Name it **`BusinessCardRequisition`**. Then do the following:

1. Right-click the port surface and select New Configured Port from the context menu.

2. On the Port Properties screen, name your port **`BusinessCardRequisitionPort`**.

3. On the Select a Port Type screen, name your port type **BusinessCardRequisitionPortType**. Specify that this is a request-response communication pattern and give it public access.

4. On the Port Binding screen, choose I'll Be Receiving a Request and Sending a Response for the port direction, and choose Specify Later for the port binding.

5. Right-click the Operation in the new port, and in the Properties window change the identifier to `ReceiveRequisition`.

6. Right-click the Request message in the new port and choose Properties. In the Properties window of the message, select Message Type and expand the Schemas node. Choose the `BTSDG_BusCards.Requisition` schema.

7. Right-click the Response message in the new port and choose Properties. In the Properties window of the message, select Message Type and expand the Schemas node. Choose the `BTSDG_BusCards.Confirmation` schema.

8. To create the inbound message, in the Orchestration tab, right-click the Messages node and add a new message called **Order**, and then specify a schema of `BTSDG_BusCards.Requisition`.

9. To create the outbound message, in the Orchestration tab, right-click the Messages node and add a new message called **OrderConfirmation**, and then specify a schema of `BTSDG_BusCards.Confirmation`.

10. Drag a Receive shape from the toolbox into your orchestration. Name it **ReceiveRequest**. In the properties of this Receive shape, choose `Order` as the message you will be receiving. You should now be able to drag the green connector on your port to the green connector on the Receive shape.

11. Right-click the Receive shape and change the Activate property to true to specify that messages arriving at the bound receive location will activate new instances of the orchestration.

Next, we will add an Expression shape and put in an expression that will echo out a meaningful trace message to a debugger. To do this, follow these steps:

1. Drag an Expression shape from the toolbox into your orchestration.

2. Double-click the Expression shape to launch the Script Editor. Type in the following line:

```
System.Diagnostics.Debug.WriteLine("Business card request for " +
Order(BTSDG_BusCards.NameOnCard) + " processed at "
+ System.DateTime.Now.ToShortTimeString());
```

Next, we will create the confirmation message that we will return to the caller. To do this, follow these steps:

1. Drag a Transformation shape from the toolbox into your orchestration (a Message Construction shape will be automatically created to host your Transformation).
2. In the properties of the Message Construction shape, choose `OrderConfirmation` as the message.
3. Double-click the Transformation shape to launch the Transformation Configuration Wizard.
4. Click Existing Map and select the `RequisitionToConfirmation` map from the drop-down list.
5. Click the Source link and in the Variable Name cell select the `Order` message.
6. Click the Destination link and in the Variable Name cell select the `OrderConfirmation` message.

Last, we will return the message we just created to the request-response port. To do this

1. Drag a Send shape from the toolbox into your orchestration right above the Stop shape.
2. In the Properties window of the Send shape choose `OrderConfirmation` as the message.
3. Click and drag from the green connector of the Send shape to the Response connector of the request-response port.

Your completed orchestration should look like Figure 14.6.

Step 5: Exposing the Orchestration as a Web Service

BizTalk Server 2004 includes a wizard that will quickly generate a standard .NET ASMX project, which will create a proxy to expose your orchestration as a Web service. The wizard makes it painless to put a thin Web services layer between your orchestration and the outside world.

To run the wizard, in the Solution Explorer select the `BTSDG_BusCards` project. From the Visual Studio Tools menu, choose BizTalk Web Services Publishing Wizard. Complete the following steps:

1. In the Create Web Service dialog box choose Publish Orchestrations as Web Services.
2. In the BizTalk assembly dialog box, navigate to the DLL (it should be the default value).

   The wizard will examine your DLL and show you all ports that allow public access. You should see something like what is shown in Figure 14.7.

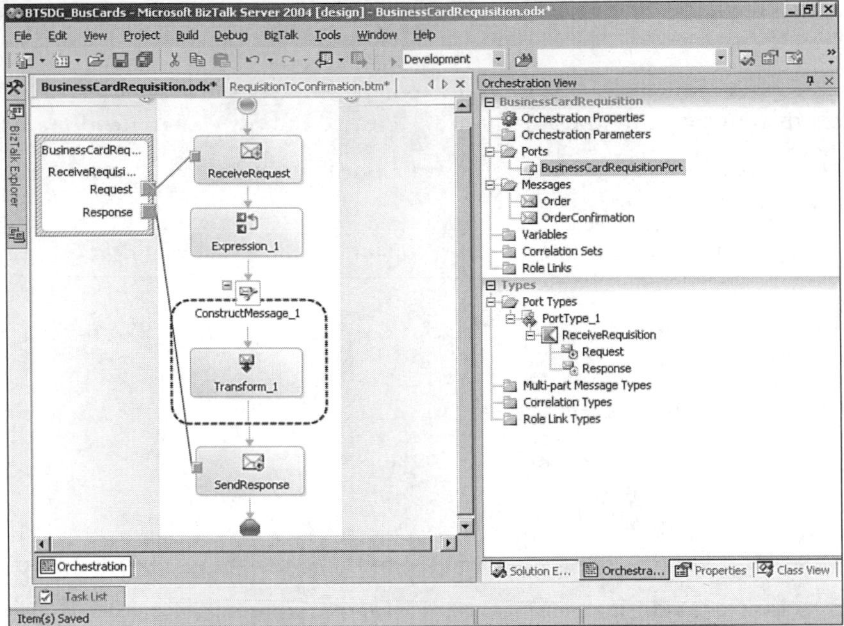

FIGURE 14.6 Business card requisition orchestration.

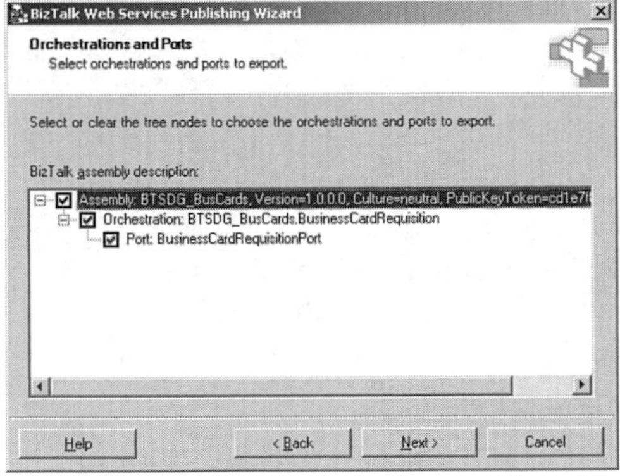

FIGURE 14.7 Web service publishing wizard: Orchestrations and Ports.

3. Click Next.
4. In the Web Services Properties dialog box, put in **`http://BTSDG`** as the namespace; leave the other check boxes unchecked.

5. In the Web Service Project dialog box, check Allow Anonymous Access and Create BizTalk Receive Locations. If you've already run this wizard and it has already created the project, you'll need to choose Overwrite Existing Project.
6. On the Summary screen, click Next.

The wizard will now generate a standard Visual Studio .NET project for you. You can navigate to the project and see the code that was generated.

Step 6: Deploying the Orchestration

For the assembly to be registered in the GAC, we must strongly name it. If you do not do this, you'll receive a deployment error. To strongly name it, follow these steps:

1. Run the Visual Studio DOS prompt and navigate to the `BTSDG_CreditCheck` project folder.
2. Type in

   ```
   sn -k BTSDG_BusCards.snk
   ```

   Close the DOS box.
3. In the Solution Explorer, right-click the `BTSDG_BusCards` project and choose Properties. Click Assembly and scroll through the properties to Assembly Key File. Navigate to the `BTSDG_BusCards.snk` key file you just generated.
4. Finally, we're ready to deploy. In the Solution Explorer, right-click the `BTSDG_BusCards` project and choose Deploy. You should not receive any deployment errors. If you do, retrace the deployment steps and ensure that you followed them all.

To start the orchestration, do the following:

1. Bring up the BizTalk Server Explorer (Ctrl+Alt+Z) and expand the Orchestrations node.
2. Right-click the `BTSDG_BusCards` orchestration and choose Bind. In the Port Binding dialog box, bind the `BusinessCardRequisition` port to

   ```
   WebPort_BTSDG_BusCards_Proxy/BTSDG_BusCards_BusinessCardRequisition_
   ➥BusinessCardRequisitionPort
   ```

3. Still in the binding wizard, click the Host node and specify `BizTalkServerApplication` as the host.
4. Right-click the `BTSDG_BusCards` orchestration. Choose Enlist to enlist your orchestration with BizTalk.

14

5. Right-click the `BTSDG_BusCards` orchestration again and this time choose Start. On the next screen, make sure all items are checked (which is the default) to also start any dependencies.
6. The icon beside the `BTSDG_BusCards` orchestration should no longer be dimmed.

Step 7: Creating the InfoPath Form and Calling the Orchestration

BizTalk Server 2004 and InfoPath both support XSD schemas. If you are working on a project requiring integration of the two products, you could start with whichever product you like. You could design the schema in InfoPath and import it into BizTalk, or you could design a schema in BizTalk and use that as a data source for an InfoPath form.

If you are exposing an orchestration as a Web service, as we have done in this pattern, you have an even easier option: you can tell InfoPath to use a schema as specified in the WSDL generated for the proxy.

The first thing you will need to do is create a new form and assign the Web service proxy input document as a data source. To do this, follow these steps:

1. Start InfoPath.
2. Choose Design a Form from the task pane.
3. Choose New From Data Source in the task pane.
4. In the first screen of the Data Source Setup Wizard, choose Web service and click Next.
5. In the second screen of the Data Source Setup Wizard, choose Receive Data and click Next.
6. In the Web Service Details window, specify the URI of the proxy we just generated when we ran the BizTalk Web Services Wizard:

   ```
   http://localhost/BTSDG_BusCards_Proxy/
       BTSDG_BusCards_BusinessCardRequisition_BusinessCardRequisitionPort.asmx
   ```

7. When you specified the URI to the Web service in the preceding step, the wizard read the WSDL file. On the next screen, you will see a listing of all the Web methods exposed by the service (which in our case will be only `ReceiveRequisition`), which maps directly back to the public access ports we defined in our orchestration schedule. So, choose `ReceiveRequisition` and click Next.
8. On the next screen, specify Design Query View First and click Finish to complete the data source definition process and close the wizard.

You have now defined both the request and response portions of the data source that we will be working with, as specified by the WSDL for the Web service. If you expand the

Data Source in the task pane, you should see the hierarchies shown in Figure 14.8. If you see a different structure, rerun the wizard, ensuring that you have Receive Data selected on the second screen.

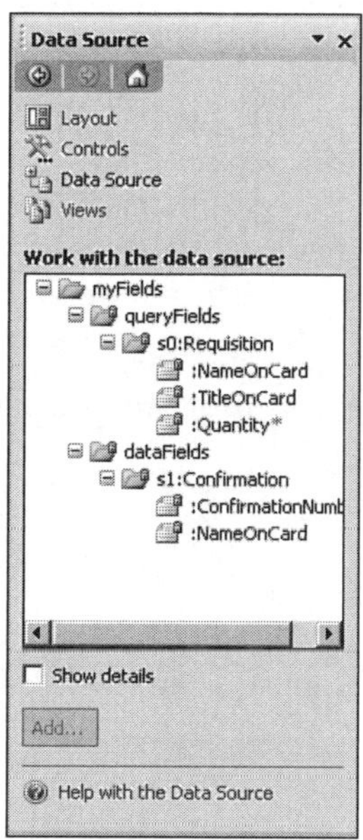

FIGURE 14.8 Schema created by InfoPath from the Web service WSDL.

The queryFields node shows the request portion of our Web service call, and the dataFields shows the response.

These two nodes contain the elements we specified when we created the Order and Confirmation schemas in BizTalk, which we specified as the input and output documents on our public access request-response port. The port was turned into a Web method by the Web publishing wizard. Last, we read the WSDL into InfoPath to create the data source. It's a long path, but there isn't much effort, and we did not write a single line of code along the way.

Now that we have the data source defined, we can go ahead and design the InfoPath forms. When we create the new form template specifying that we wanted to receive data, we set up two views: a request (queryFields) and a response (dataFields).

InfoPath includes a very rich form design environment, but for simplicity's sake we will use the handy auto-layout mode. To do this

1. Click and hold the `s0:Requisition` node in the Data Source view in the task pane.
2. Drag the node onto the Query form surface and place it above the Run Query button.

14

3. Release the mouse button. Choose Controls in Layout Table from the context menu. You will see a table inserted with labels and fields that correspond to our Web service request.
4. Click the Views link in the task pane and choose the Data Entry view. The query form will be replaced with a blank form. Click the Data Source view in the task pane.
5. Click and hold the `s1:Confirmation` node in the Data Source view in the task pane.
6. Drag the node onto the form surface.
7. Release the mouse button. Choose Controls in Layout Table from the context menu. You will see a table inserted with labels and fields corresponding to our Web service response.
8. Right-click each of the two text controls and in the Properties window, set them to Read Only.

Step 8: Testing the Solution

Testing this solution is easy. To do so

1. Ensure that the debugger is running so that you will see the diagnostic message you are writing in your orchestration.
2. In InfoPath, switch back to the Query view.
3. Enter some data and click the Run Query button.
4. Look at the debugger. You should see the message from the script expression in the orchestration.
5. After the Web service returns, InfoPath should switch to the Data Entry view, showing you the name that you had on your request as well as a confirmation number.

In this pattern we have seen a simple example of an incredibly powerful set of technologies working together to solve a business process automation need.

Without writing any significant code (we wrote a few lines for the functoid and one line for the debugger message) we accomplished the following:

- Created a business process.
- Exposed the business process as a Web service.
- Created a user interface to invoke the Web service and communicate a response.

If you think about this, the possible applications are virtually limitless. This is, in my opinion, one of the most powerful capabilities provided by BizTalk Server 2004.

Pattern 4: Multiple Entry Points for Orchestration Activation

Now that we've seen how BizTalk Orchestrations can be exposed as Web services and how InfoPath can invoke those Web services, let's revisit the first pattern we presented and build on it.

Often, a common business process may have multiple entry points. Our first pattern used files appearing in a folder as an activation process; we will now add a Web service and InfoPath layer to it.

In this pattern we will cover

- Orchestration activation in response to a file arriving at a receive location
- The same orchestration being activated in response to a Web service call

Scenario

In our scenario for Pattern 1, we had an XML order file arriving in a monitored folder, perhaps arriving via FTP. In this extension of that scenario, we will allow our fictitious company to also receive orders by Web service invocation.

Our solution will do the following:

- Receive an incoming purchase either by monitoring a folder or from a Web service request.
- Modify it to include a timestamp.
- Put the modified purchase order into an outbound folder for further processing.

Implementation Steps

The purchase order was received by FTP in a specific folder, and we are monitoring that folder for inbound purchase orders. We will need to

- Publish our orchestration schedule as a Web service.
- Create an InfoPath form to submit data to the Web service.
- Use the BizTalk Explorer to bind the ports to physical send and receive locations.
- Test the pattern.

Open the existing `BTSDG_Activation` project we created in Pattern 1.

Step 1: Publishing the Orchestration

To run the wizard, in the Solution Explorer select the `BTSDG_BusCards` project. From the Visual Studio Tools menu, choose BizTalk Web Services Publishing Wizard.

1. In the Create Web Service dialog box, choose Publish Orchestrations as Web Services.
2. In the BizTalk assembly dialog box, navigate to the DLL (it should be the default value).
3. The wizard will examine your DLL and show you all ports that allow public access. You should see something similar to Figure 14.9. Then click Next.

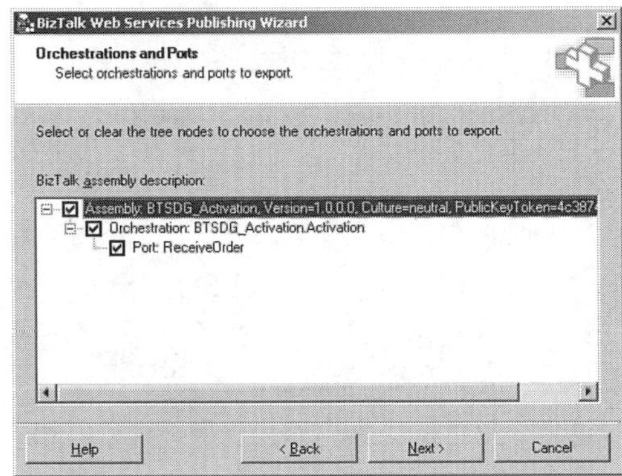

FIGURE 14.9 Web service publishing wizard: Orchestrations and Ports.

4. In the Web Services Properties dialog box, put in **`http://BTSDG`** as the namespace; leave the other check boxes unchecked.
5. In the Web Service Project dialog box, check Allow Anonymous Access and Create BizTalk Receive Locations. If you've already run this wizard and it has already created the project, you'll need to choose Overwrite Existing Project.
6. On the Summary screen, click Next.

The wizard will now generate a standard Visual Studio .NET project for you. If you would like to see the project, you can click the link provided in the final screen of the wizard.

Step 2: Creating the InfoPath Form

The next step will be to create the InfoPath form that will post data to our Web service proxy. To do this, follow these steps:

1. From the InfoPath task pane, choose Design a Form, New from Data Source, and choose Web Service as the data source. Specify that you want to Submit Data.
2. Navigate to the Web service proxy we just created:

   `http://localhost/BTSDG_Activation_Proxy/BTSDG_Activation_Activation.asmx`

3. You should see a screen showing all the public access ports in the orchestration, which in this case is just the `AcceptOrder` port. Select this as the port you want to submit the form data to.

4. In the Data Source view of the task pane, expand the Data Fields node. Drag the `s0:PurchaseOrder` node onto the form surface and specify that you want Controls in a Layout Table.

5. In the Data Source view of the task pane, drag the `OrderItems` node onto the form surface and specify that you want Section with Controls. Your form should now look like Figure 14.10.

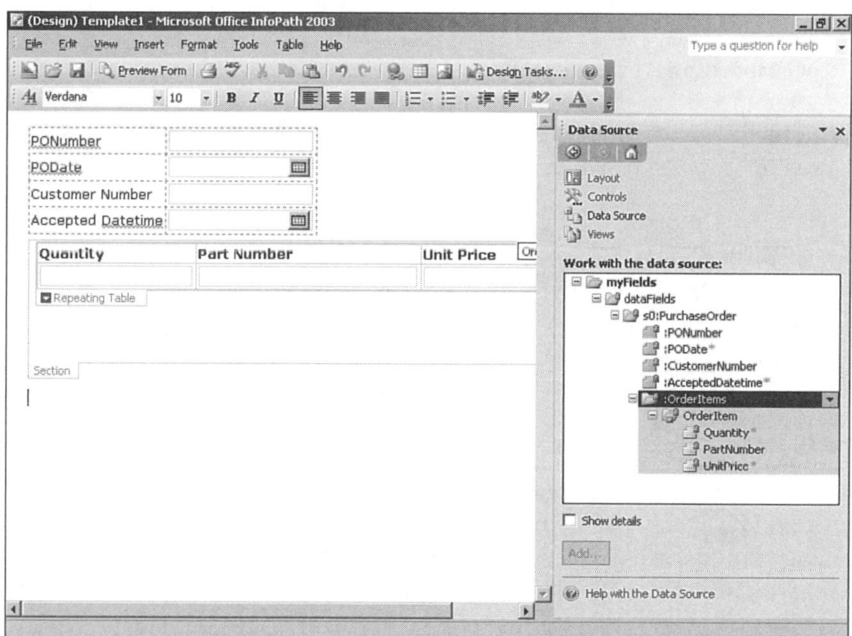

FIGURE 14.10 Data view in InfoPath form.

We do not need to specify where we want to post to, because this was done automatically for us when we specified the form data source. You can confirm this by looking at Submit details in the Tools menu.

Step 3: Binding the Ports

Next, we will need to configure the receive locations. We currently have two ports and two receive locations set up related to the Activation orchestration: the original `BTSDG_Activation_Receive` port and the new `WebPort_BTSDG_Activation_Proxy/BTSDG_Activation_Activation_ReceiveOrder` that was created for us by the publishing wizard. However, because there is a one-to-one relationship between an orchestration port and a physical port, for this pattern to achieve its goal we need a single port with two receive locations. We will do this by creating a new file receive location under the WebPort, but you can't have multiple receive locations monitoring the same physical receive location and pattern.

1. To avoid a configuration conflict previously explained, in the BizTalk Explorer, double-click the `Receive Location1` of the `BTSDG_Activation_Receive` port, and in the Address Properties, change the file mask to be `*.txt`.

2. Expand the `WebPort_BTSDG_Activation_Proxy/BTSDG_Activation_Activation` node. Right-click Receive Locations and specify that you want to create a new receive location. For the transport choose File; for the address, specify the following:

   ```
   c:\BTS2004DevGuide\Activation\In
   ```

   For the file mask, specify `*.xml`. For the Receive Handler, specify BizTalk Server Application. For the pipeline, choose the `XMLReceive` pipeline.

Step 4: Testing the Pattern

To test the InfoPath side of this pattern:

> Go to Form Preview, fill in some form data, and from the File menu choose Submit. You should see a file appear in the C:\BTS2004DevGuide\Activation\Out folder that contains your data as well as a current time stamp.

To test the file drop receive location

> Copy the instance file we created in Pattern 1 from C:\BTS2004DevGuide\Activation\ to C:\BTS2004DevGuide\Activation\In. Here, too, you should see a new file appear in the C:\BTS2004DevGuide\Activation\Out folder, which includes the data in the instance document.

In this pattern we have seen how to have a common business process with multiple points of entry. It's not hard to see how this technique could be used to streamline and standardize operations across an enterprise. Imagine an order-processing orchestration that can be invoked by file drop, InfoPath submission, or invocation from a CRM system. Having a single process greatly simplifies accommodating inevitable change and promotes cross-enterprise standardization of business processes.

Summary

As you develop more and more diverse BizTalk Server 2004 solutions, you will notice that certain patterns reoccur and are often common between solutions. This chapter has introduced some common design patterns that can be used for BizTalk Server 2004 solutions.

PART V

Managing, Monitoring, and Deploying BizTalk Server 2004

IN THIS PART

CHAPTER 15
Deployment

IN THIS CHAPTER

- Distributed Deployment
- Deploying for Scalability
- Deploying the Various BizTalk Server Services
- Deploying for High Availability

BizTalk Server 2004 is designed to provide convenience and flexibility for management of multiple servers that are part of a BizTalk Server Group from a centralized location. Management and maintenance of multiple BizTalk servers is simplified by abstracting away the physical servers from the roles the servers play using the concept of *hosts*, which are logical containers. Because of this level of indirection, the servers are not tightly bound to the roles they are designated to perform.

By adding servers, called *host instances*, into hosts, the servers take on the responsibility of performing the tasks that the hosts are designated to play. This design simplifies the process of adding, removing, starting, and stopping specific BizTalk host instances without impacting other running BizTalk host instances. Thus, servers are updated in real-time without impacting availability. The design is also flexible enough to have one server perform multiple tasks, such as Receiving, Processing, and Transmitting. These tasks can further be configured to run in separate address spaces by defining multiple hosts and adding the same server to each of the hosts. Hosts can be configured with different security credentials, thereby restricting access to certain functionality.

This chapter is not about defining the setup and configuration of BizTalk. It focuses on the various deployment topology permutations possible within BizTalk. It also touches on the different deployment configurations required to achieve optimal sustained throughput. The chapter helps provide general guidance on how best to plan for and configure your topology for future growth, taking into account stress, performance, latency, and ways to avoid potential bottlenecks.

There is no optimal deployment configuration. Performance depends on the type of scenario, the complexity of the workflow, the volume of tracking enabled, the nature of the transports, custom components, and the type of hardware used. However, following the best practices when defining a deployment topology will help you achieve optimal performance now and budget for growth in the future. When defining a deployment topology, it is important to measure performance characterization in a staging environment that closely resembles the production environment.

Distributed Deployment

After the BizTalk software has been installed and configured on the BizTalk servers, the servers can be logically grouped by creating hosts. These hosts can then be configured to perform specific tasks, such as Receiving, Processing, Transmitting, Tracking, and so on. Distributed deployment can be configured as follows:

- Modify the Receive Handlers for a particular adapter to map to a specific host, such as RxHost.
- Modify the Send Handlers for a particular adapter to map to a specific host, such as TxHost.
- Enlist the orchestration to a specific host, such as PxHost.
- Configure a dedicated host to handle the task of moving Tracking data from the Message Box to the DTADb, such as TrkHost. Ensure that the Host Tracking check box is selected for this host and disabled for other hosts.
- In addition, a separate host can be created for each receiving and/or sending adapter, such as RxHostHTTP or TxHostSMTP.

Figure 15.1 shows a sample distributed deployment topology, separating Receiving, Processing, Transmitting, and Tracking.

The deployment topology you adopt may be driven by one or a combination of the following objectives:

- Scalability (Scale-Out and Scale-Up)
- High Availability
- Security

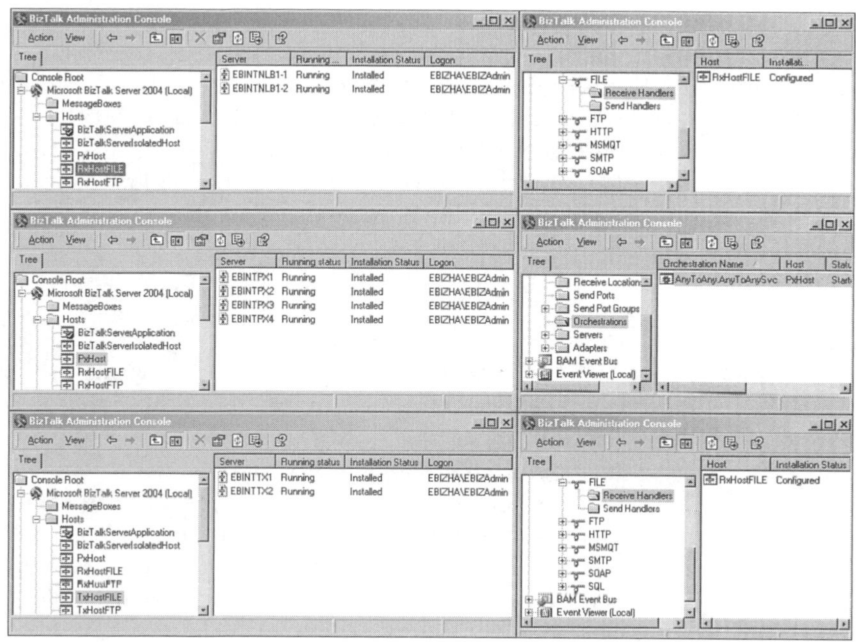

FIGURE 15.1 Multiple hosts and host instances.

Deploying for Scalability

Scaling out involves adding multiple BizTalk servers until the SQL Server Message Box database becomes the bottleneck because of severe contention. Thereafter, it is recommended to scale out the database tier, adding Message Box databases. This will help support more BizTalk servers. When the SQL tier again becomes the bottleneck, adding more Message Box databases will help scale out adding more BizTalk servers. However, this design does not scale ad infinitum. Ultimately, the Master Message Box will get saturated supporting, or routing data to, multiple Message Box databases. When this happens, it is recommended to scale up the Master Message Box database, adding more CPUs and/or faster disks.

Scaling Out BizTalk Servers

BizTalk Server 2004 is a persistent messaging system whereby all data is persisted to disk. However, no data is persisted locally on the BizTalk servers; all data is persisted within multiple SQL Server database tables. All orchestration and adapter code, with the exception of the HTTP and SOAP receive adapters, is hosted within the BizTalk Server service. The HTTP and SOAP adapters are hosted within an ISAPI extension (BTSHTTPReceive.dll) shipped with the product. After the product is installed and configured, either by creating or joining the BizTalk Group on the BizTalk servers to reference the SQL Server databases, what needs to be done next is to logically group machines using hosts. Further, it is necessary to add the compiled scenario/assembly to the GAC locally on all the BizTalk server machines. In addition to deploying the assemblies, any resources, such as SOAP Web services, HTTP Vroots, File Receive locations, and so on required to support the scenarios must be set up. The Scenario (assemblies) also needs to be deployed—that is, artifacts added into the BizTalkMgmtDb database—from at least one of the BizTalk servers. Although BizTalk can be configured to run on a single machine, when scaling out it is recommended to first separate the SQL databases onto a dedicated server, preferably with high-speed disks.

BizTalk Hosts

Scaling out is achieved by configuring multiple BizTalk servers within a single BizTalk group. BizTalk functionality can be logically fragmented into four horizontal tiers: receiving, processing, transmitting, and database. The process by which functionality is isolated in the BizTalk System is achieved by using BizTalk hosts. Hosts are logical containers into which host instances (BizTalk servers) are added. Creating multiple hosts, or Logical Groups, and adding multiple BizTalk servers (host instances) into these groups helps isolate functionality. Thus, adding multiple BizTalk servers to a host helps scale-out by having multiple machines perform the role designated to the host—for example, receiving.

BizTalk Host Instances

A host instance is effectively an instance of a Windows Service (BTSNTSvc.exe) running on a BizTalk server. It is possible to have multiple BizTalk host instances running on a single BizTalk server. This is achieved by creating multiple hosts and adding the same BizTalk server into the multiple hosts. This feature is useful if the server is underutilized—for example, if the receiving server is utilizing less than 25% CPU, this server can be added as another host instance to the Tracking host, thereby taking on the added responsibility of moving tracking data from the Message Box database to the Tracking databases.

BizTalk Host Security

Each host can be configured to run with different security credentials. All host instances within that host run under the same credentials assigned to a particular host. Using this design, it is possible to have the receiving host instances (for example, RxHost) run with different security credentials than those of the processing and transmitting host instances (for example, PxHost and TxHost, respectively).

The four tiers can be broadly viewed as follows:

- Receiving Servers (RxHost)

  FILE: Either local or UNC path

  HTTP/SOAP: Multiple NLB servers (for example, Port: 80)

  MSMQT: Multiple NLB servers (for example, {Port: 1801/3527)

  FTP/SQL: Multiple Receiving servers

- Processing Servers (PxHost)

  Multiple orchestration servers

- Transmitting Servers (TxHost)

  Multiple sending servers

- Tracking Servers (TrkHost)

  One or more Tracking servers

Scaling Out SQL Servers

BizTalk servers are by design stateless with no data persisted locally. All data is stored in a central location within the SQL Server databases. It is the SQL Server databases, specifically the BizTalk Management database, which brings multiple BizTalk servers together as a single group. BizTalk has a hard dependency on SQL Server being installed. Because SQL Server is essential to the running of the BizTalk service, it is strongly recommended that SQL be installed in a highly available manner on an MSCS cluster, using either RAID5 or SAN disks with a backup power supply. These databases should be backed up regularly using SQL Server best practices. The BizTalk service is designed to automatically recover from a SQL Server connection failure. Depending on the features configured, multiple databases are created, the most important of which are explained in the following section.

Following is a list of databases created by the BizTalk System:

- BizTalk Management and Other Databases

  BizTalkMgmtDb

  BizTalkRuleEngineDb

  BizTalkEDIDb

  BizTalkHWSDb

  TPM

- Message Box Databases

  BizTalkMsgBoxDb

  BizTalkMsgBoxDb2

  BizTalkMsgBoxDb3

  BizTalkMsgBoxDbN

- Tracking/Analysis Databases

  BizTalkDTADb

  BAMStarSchema

  BAMPrimaryImport

  BAMArchive

  BizTalkAnalysisDb (Analysis)

  BAMAnalysis (Analysis)

- SSO Database

  SSODB

Message Box Database

Because the Message Box database tables are the most contended on, the manner in which these databases are deployed has a major impact on scalability. If the CPU is saturated on the SQL Server machine, moving the Message Box to a dedicated SQL Server will help alleviate the CPU problem. If disk IO latency is the problem (high Disk Transfers/Sec and higher SQL Lock Wait Time and SQL Lock Timeouts), deploying the Message Box database on a dedicated high-speed disk will help alleviate the disk contention and latency problem. In addition, it is recommended to deploy the DBF and LOG files onto separate physical disks.

Despite following all the best practices at some point—that is, after adding multiple BizTalk servers—the Message Box database will become the bottleneck. At this stage it is recommended to scale out by deploying the Message Box database onto a dedicated server. Further it is possible to scale out to multiple Message Box databases. This can be accomplished by using the BizTalk MMC. To do this, right-click the Message Boxes node in the left pane and select New Message Box; provide the SQL Server Name and Message Box Name. If the CPU and/or disk IO on the existing server were reaching saturation points, it is highly recommended to deploy the new Message Box database on another dedicated SQL Server, again deploying the database and log files on separate high-speed disks.

Master Message Box Database

Every BizTalk Group must have one, and only one, Master Message Box. This is the first (default) Message Box created when the BizTalk Group is initially configured. This is where routing is performed and the central point where all subscriptions are held. Instance subscriptions live only on the master and the instance's Message Box. The Master Message Box database is also responsible for performing enqueueing and dequeueing of messages.

NOTE

Instance subscriptions route messages to already running instances and so require those messages to be delivered to the specific Message Box on which the instance exists.

Multiple Message Box Databases

When the Master Message Box database becomes the bottleneck and negatively impacts performance, it is recommended to scale out by adding multiple Message Boxes. In addition to tracking data, message body data is also written to the Message Box database. The Master Message Box database can become the bottleneck if multiple BizTalk servers are subjected to extreme load. All tracking data and message data are written to the Message Box database, making this database the point of contention. This can be detected by analyzing the SQL Lock counters (SQLServer:Locks:, SQL Lock Wait Time, SQL Lock Timeouts (ms)). This contention impacts system performance either because of CPU saturation or Disk IO latency (PhysicalDisk: Current Disk Queue Length).

- If the CPU is saturated, it is possible to scale up by adding more CPUs.
- If the disk is the cause of the bottleneck, moving the DTADb (which contains all the tracking data) database to a dedicated server or disk will help alleviate some contention on the disks on which the Message Box database is deployed.

TIP

It is also recommended to separate the DBF file and the LOG file onto separate disks.

- If it is not possible to use high-speed SAN disks, at least ensure that the disks have multiple spindles and are of a high RPM. This will help provide higher Disk Transfers/Sec.
- If all the best practices are followed and the contention still persists, it is recommended to scale out to multiple Message Box databases.
- If the CPU and/or disk on the SQL Server hosting the Master Message Box database are not saturated, it is possible to create the new Message Box databases on the same SQL Server.

Scaling out to multiple message boxes is seamless as far as the BizTalk servers are concerned. None of the BizTalk Server service instances (Windows processes) have any affinity to any particular Message Box. The Messaging Agent abstracts away this round-robin load-balancing mechanism, thus the BizTalk service instances have no knowledge as to the physical location of the data. Adding a new Message Box does not require stopping any of the running BizTalk service instances. It takes approximately 60 seconds before the new message box will be utilized.

SCALING OUT TO TWO MESSAGE BOX DATABASES MAY NOT IMPROVE THROUGHPUT

When scaling out the Message Boxes, it is recommended to disable publishing on the Master Message Box so that all its resources can be allocated toward subscription creation, subscription deletion, and routing. This relieves contention on the Master Message Box, which is used to route data to the other Message Box databases. In a two Message Box database configuration, because only one Message Box handles all publishing, scaling out from one Message Box, which also happens to be the Master with publishing disabled, to two Message Boxes, where publishing is enabled, not much throughput improvement is realized. Scaling out to three or more Message Boxes helps provide a more linear throughput scale curve.

SCALING OUT TO THREE OR MORE MESSAGE BOX DATABASES MAY NOT IMPROVE THROUGHPUT

Throughput using one Message Box may be better than when using three Message Boxes. This can happen if fewer BizTalk servers are used. For example, one Receive server plus one Processing server plus one Transmit server are unable to saturate one Message Box database. In this situation, scaling out to three Message Box databases does not help improve throughput. One of the reasons for this may be because the BizTalk machines are themselves saturated; that is, CPU bound. In this case (when only few BizTalk servers are configured), it is preferable to use one Message Box database. The reason why throughput may drop rather than stay the same is because multiple Message Box databases have to maintain the data related to a single transaction. There is the additional overhead on the Master Message Box database having to perform the routing of data to the other Message Box databases. There is also the additional overhead of network traffic and distributed transactions. Thus, it is recommended to scale out the database tier, deploying multiple Message Box databases, only when the SQL Server machines hosting the Message Box database become the point of contention.

Tracking the DTADb Database

It is not possible to infinitely scale out the database tier by adding multiple Message Box databases. This is because larger volumes of data need to be moved by the Tracking subservice from the multiple Message Box databases to the single DTADb database. However, the DTADb cannot be scaled out by adding multiple DTADb databases. Thus, ultimately the DTADb database becomes the single point of contention. When the DTADb becomes saturated, it is recommended to scale up the DTADb by adding more memory, CPUs and higher-speed dedicated disks as required. The reason the DTADb database cannot be scaled out is because HAT and BAM are designed to query a central database.

Backlog Queue Buildup in the Message Box Database At some point, under persistent load, the Tracking subservice cannot keep up with moving the large volume of data to the DTADb database and deleting the same from the Message Box database. The process of moving data to the DTADb and deleting data from the Message Box database is synchronous. Under severe persistent load for long durations, a queue can build up in the Message Box database. This results in the Message Box database growing, impacting the runtime performance. The reason this can happen is that the DTADb database grows too large and this impacts the process of inserting data into the DTADb database. This, in turn, slows down the process of deleting Tracking data from the Message Box database. Thus, it is recommended to periodically archive and clean up the DTADb database, based on the volume of data passing through the system. This is not a problem if Tracking is disabled. This problem can also be addressed by scaling up the server on which the DTADb database is installed.

DIFFERENT DEPLOYMENT CONFIGURATIONS CAN HELP IMPROVE THROUGHPUT

Depending on the scenario it is possible that additional Receiving and/or Transmitting servers may not help improve throughput. These additional servers may simply serve to add contention on the Message Box databases. Although the receiving rate may improve end-to-end, throughput may drop. The reason that this is possible is because the processing/orchestration tier servers could be the bottleneck. Thus, flooding the system with additional incoming documents causes a queue to build up in the Message Box database, having a detrimental effect on performance. In this situation, adding additional processing servers will help improve throughput. This is not clear-cut and requires performance characterization profiling on your particular scenario to discover the best deployment topology and configuration. It is also possible to overload servers that are underutilized and configure them to do additional work. For example, if the receiving server is using less than 30% CPU, it is possible to add this server as a host instance in the Transmitting host. This server can also perform the role of sending, thereby maximizing resource utilization and improving throughput without additional hardware.

Figure 15.2 depicts the four tiers of a sample scale-out topology.

Scaling Up BizTalk Servers

After the BizTalk servers are saturated because of excessive load, it is possible to scale up the BizTalk servers by adding more memory, more CPUs, and/or higher-speed disks. However, it is important to note that if the SQL tier is the bottleneck, that tier will have to be scaled up and/or out before any benefit is realized by scaling up the BizTalk tier. If the BizTalk server is CPU bound (for example, excessive load receiving HTTP requests or processing multiple concurrent orchestration instances), adding more CPUs will help alleviate the problem. However, if the BizTalk server is disk IO bound [high Disk Queue Length] because of excessive disk IO (for example, receiving or sending files to local drives), upgrading to higher-speed disks with multiple spindles will help alleviate the problem. Low memory conditions can also manifest as a high disk latency problem. This can be caused by the swapping [high Hard Page Faults/Sec.] of data in or out of memory to the disk, causing disk thrashing.

Scaling Up SQL Servers

SQL Server performs best when a large amount of memory is made available. However, under severe stress, SQL Server can become CPU bound. When this occurs, it is recommended to scale up adding multiple CPUs. Under severe stress, the SQL Server can slow down the BizTalk servers because of high disk latency. When this happens, the CPU usage on the SQL Server is not maxed out. The counters such as [PhysicalDisk: Disk Transfers/Sec.] drops and inversely [PhysicalDisk:Current Disk Queue Length] increases. This indirectly has a detrimental effect on the SQL Server databases and manifests itself as high [SQLServer:Locks: Lock Timeouts/Sec.] and high [SQLServer:Locks: Lock Waittime (ms)]. When this occurs, it is recommended to upgrade the disks to either high-speed RAID5 disks with multiple spindles or, if possible, to a SAN drive using fiber optic channels. In addition, separating the DBF and LOG files onto dedicated disks helps reduce disk IO contention. Pre-allocating space for both the DBF and LOG files also helps avoid having SQL to dynamically auto-grow the databases at runtime.

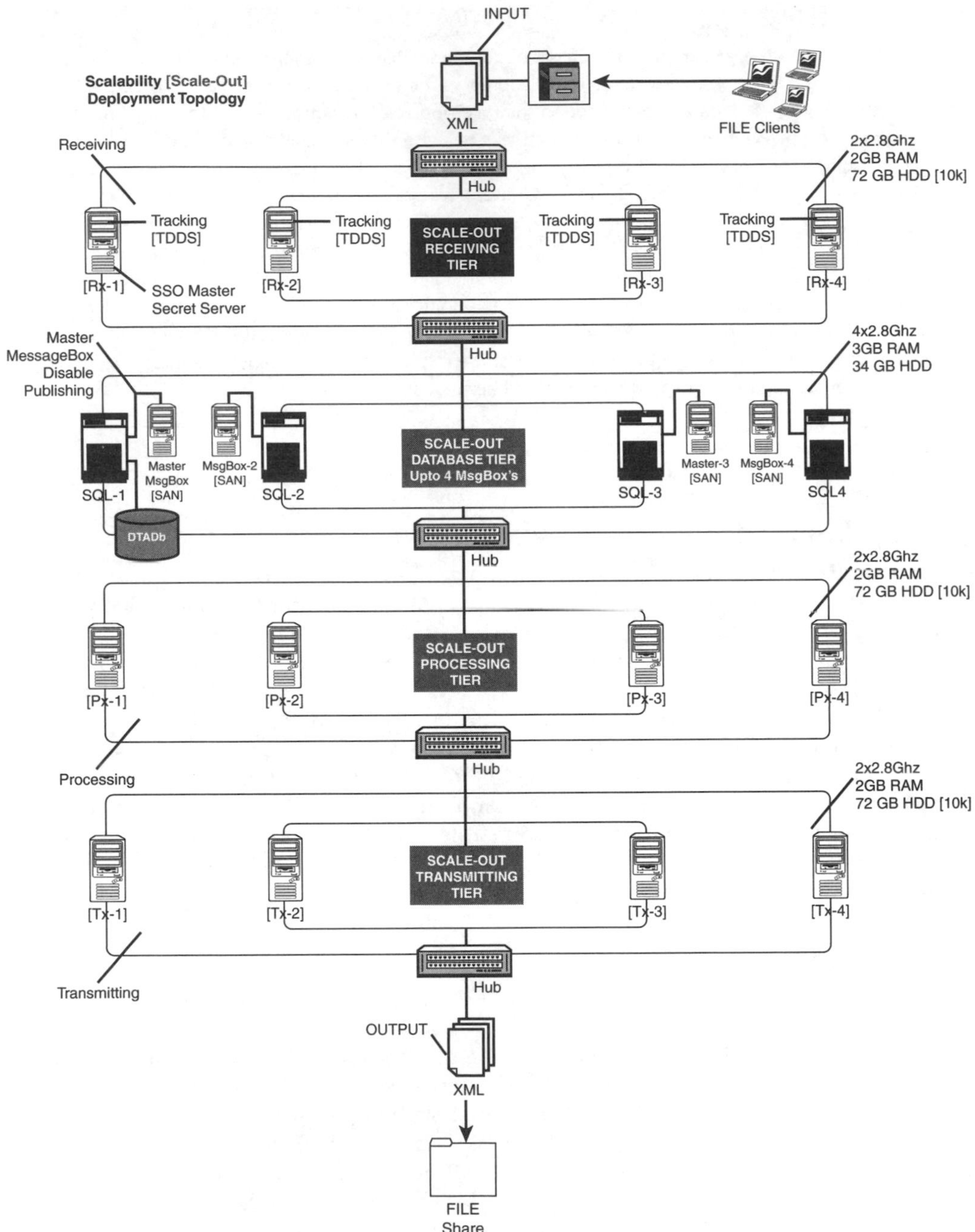

FIGURE 15.2 Scale-out deployment topology.

Figure 15.3 depicts a sample scale up of the database tier.

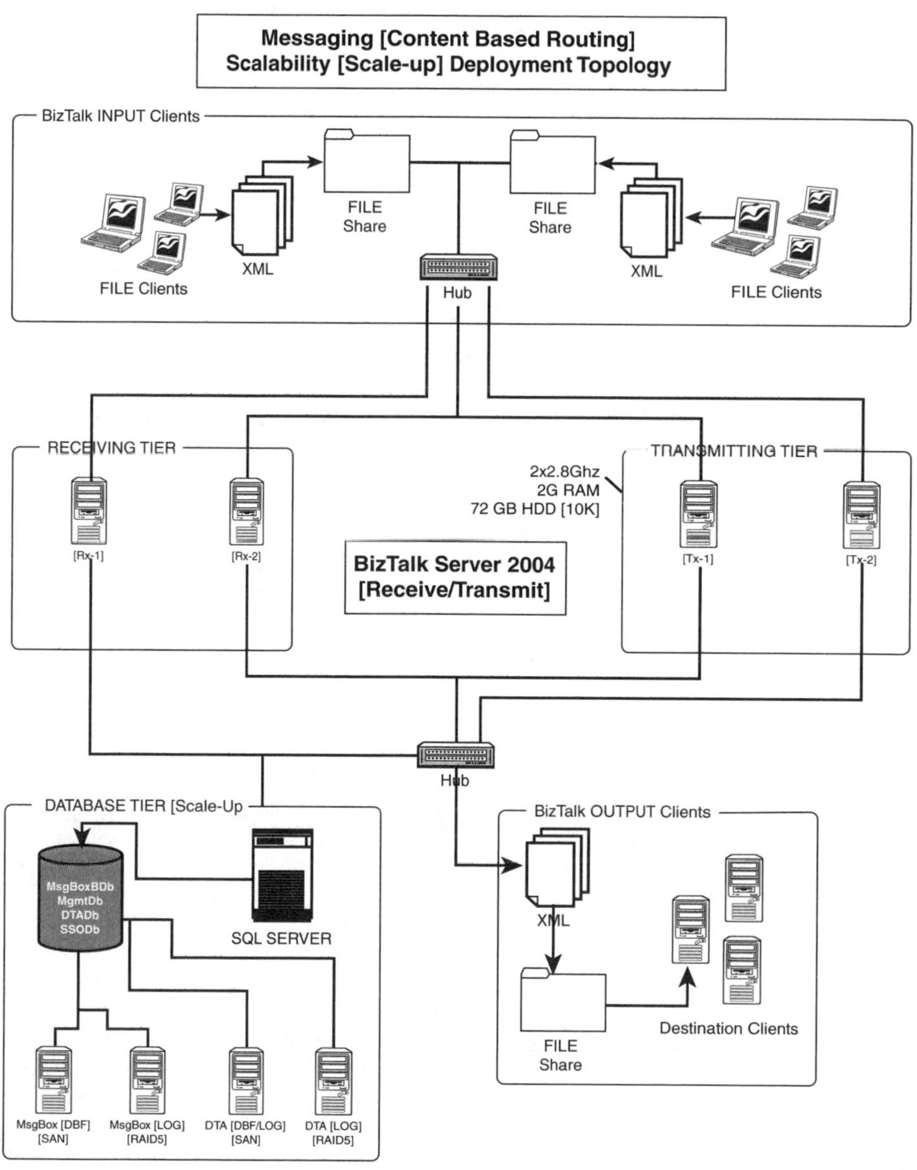

FIGURE 15.3 Scale-up deployment topology.

Deploying the Various BizTalk Server Services

The following section describes the key BizTalk Server services:

- Enterprise Single Sign-on Service
- The BizTalk Service
- The Tracking Sub-Service
- The MSMQT Sub-Service
- The Rules Engine Update Service

Enterprise Single Sign-on Service (ENTSSO.exe)

BizTalk Server 2004 has a hard dependency on the Enterprise Single Sign-on Service (ENTSSO.exe) running on the local machine. This service can be set up to run either in normal mode or in the Master Secret Server mode. This service is used by BizTalk to encrypt all metadata related to the configuration of the BizTalk group. In addition, the SSO service can be used to seamlessly integrate BizTalk with other disparate systems.

Currently, SSO supports end-to-end integration of BizTalk with other systems using the HTTP and SOAP transports. To take advantage of this feature, User/Group to Application mappings need to be set up in the SSO database. The SSO service can then pass the appropriate credentials on to the back-end system by retrieving the current users' mapped credentials to the relevant application from the SSODb database. The SSO service depends on the SSODb database being available. This database can be installed on the same cluster on which all the other BizTalk databases are installed.

SSO MASTER SECRET SERVER

The locally running SSO service instances depend on a central SSO Service, running in Master Secret Server mode, being highly available. Every BizTalk Server Group must have one and only one instance of the SSO service running in Master Secret Server mode. All other instances of the SSO service communicate with the Master Secret Server via RCP. By design, all SSO service instances cache the secret retrieved from the Master Secret Server. Thus, already running SSO service instances will continue to perform all runtime operations even if the Master Secret Server becomes unavailable. However, it is recommended to install this instance of the SSO service (Master Secret Server) on an MSCS cluster, making it highly available for all operations. The SSO service is a cluster-aware service and it is recommended that the SSO-Master Secret Server be clustered as a Resource Generic Service. This Master Secret Server (SSO service) holds and propagates the secret key (which is a unique guid generated to encrypt/decrypt data) that is used by all the SSO service instances in the BizTalk Group to encrypt and decrypt data. It is essential that this key not be lost or compromised. Thus it is highly recommended that this key be backed up and stored in a safe location. Without this key it is impossible to decrypt previously encrypted data.

The BizTalk Service (BTSNTSvc.exe)

The BizTalk service is not a cluster-aware service and does not need to be installed on a cluster. High availability is provided by setting up multiple redundant servers at each tier. The BizTalk Server functionality can conceptually be divided into four tiers: receiving, processing, transmitting, and database. At the receiving tier, depending on the transports used to solve the business needs, either NLB (Network Load Balancing) can be used for the following transports HTTP/SOAP/MSMQT or multiple servers can be deployed to provide high availability. At the processing (orchestration) tier where business process workflows are executed, multiple servers can be deployed to share the work and provide high availability. At the transmitting tier for all transports, multiple servers can be deployed to share the work and provide high availability. The BizTalk service makes extensive use of memory and, depending on the transport used, may extensively use system resources. For example, FILE transport needs access to the file IO system. HTTP and SOAP use the HTTP transport and require IIS. The SSO service instances use RPC to communicate with the SSO-Master Secret Server. All BizTalk service instances use MSDTC to commit or roll back transactions. It is not necessary to have SQL installed locally on the BizTalk machines as long as SQL client connectivity tools are installed. This BizTalk service also hosts the Tracking Sub-Service and the MSMQT Sub-Service.

The Tracking Sub-Service [BTSNTSvc.exe]

The Tracking system consists of three components: the Tracking Interceptors, which fire in real-time and write data to the Message Box database; the DTADb database, within which tracked data from all Message Box databases ultimately converge; and the Tracking Sub-Service, which is used to move data from the Message Box databases to the DTADb database.

Tracking data may be written by either Business Activity Monitoring (BAM) or Health Activity Tracking (HAT). Data is initially written to the Message Box database. To avoid bloating of the Message Box database(s), this data is then moved to the DTADb database and deleted from the Message Box database. Ensure that the cleanup jobs are running and the SQL Server Agent service is started. This can be verified by opening SQL Enterprise Manager and expanding the Management node to ensure that the SQL Server Agent service is running and the jobs defined under the Jobs node are started.

The Tracking sub-service runs within the BizTalk service (BTSNTSvc). It is recommended to have at least one BizTalk server, which is running the Tracking sub-service, servicing one Message Box database. Create a host (TrkHost, for example) ensuring that the Enable Host Tracking property is selected. Add a host instance (BizTalk Server) into this host. This will ensure that this host instance will perform the role of moving data from the Message Box database into the DTADb Tracking database. If multiple host instances are added to this host, only one host instance (BizTalk Server) will undertake the task of servicing one Message Box database. If multiple Message Box databases exist, multiple host instances will take on the role of servicing multiple Message Box databases. This process—that is, which server services which Message Box database, is nondeterministic and cannot be explicitly configured. For example, if two BizTalk servers are servicing two Message Box databases and one server (host instance) is stopped, the other BizTalk Server service will determine that the second Message Box is not being serviced and will take on the responsibility of servicing both the Message Box databases. Depending on the load the system is subjected to, the process of tracking can have a cost of up to approximately 15% on the BizTalk system. It is possible to have the servers running the Tracking sub-service also perform other tasks, such as Receiving, Processing, or Transmitting. It is recommended to have this Tracking sub-service functionality isolated from the other processes by creating different hosts and adding the same BizTalk Server machine into these different hosts running under different security credentials.

Figure 15.4 depicts a sample deployment showing the flow of tracking data.

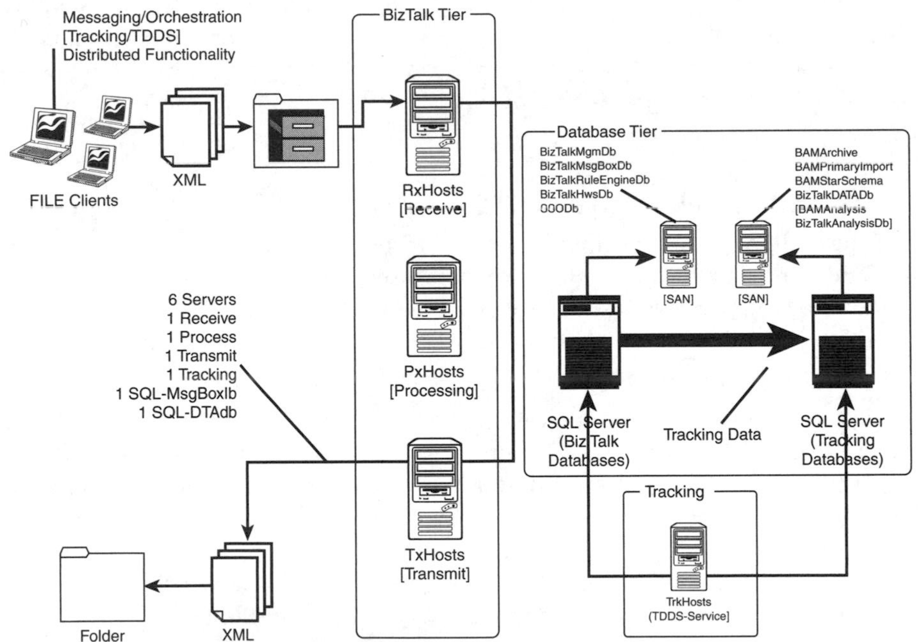

FIGURE 15.4 Tracking Dataflow diagram.

IMPACT OF NOT RUNNING THE TRACKING SUB-SERVICE

If the host responsible for tracking is stopped, the Tracking Sub-Service will not run. The impact of this is as follows:

- HAT tracking data will not be moved from the Message Box database to the DTADb database.

- BAM tracking data will not be moved from the Message Box database to the BAMPrimaryImport database.
- Because data is not moved, it cannot be deleted from the Message Box database.

However, the interceptors will still fire writing data to the Message Box database. If the data is not moved, this will cause bloating of the Message Box database, impacting runtime performance over time. Even if custom properties are not tracked or BAM profiles are not set up, by default some data is tracked, such as Pipelines-Receive/Send. If you do not want to run the Tracking sub-service, turn off all tracking so that no interceptors save data to the database. Use the HAT Configuration tool to disable this default tracking.

IMPACT OF NOT RUNNING THE SQL SERVER AGENT

In addition to the Tracking data, Message Body data is also written to the Message Box database. This data, after it is successfully processed by the BizTalk system, is deleted by SQL jobs running on the SQL Server. To ensure that the cleanup jobs are run periodically, the SQL Server Agent service must be started on the SQL Server. If the SQL Server Agent is not running, this will prevent Message Body data from being cleaned up, causing bloat in the Message Box database and impacting runtime performance over time.

The MSMQT Sub-Service (BTSNTSvc.exe)

The native MSMQT adapter that ships within BizTalk Server 2004 runs within the BizTalk service as a sub-service. There is no physical queue created on the machine. All messages received by BizTalk through its MSMQT receive locations are persisted directly to the Message Box database. Thus it is not necessary to have Windows MSMQ service set up on the BizTalk Server, and it is not possible to use the MSMQ runtime APIs to read or peek messages within this pseudo queue. This helps reduce the additional overhead of having BizTalk indirectly communicate with a native MSMQ queue service.

Rules Engine Update Service (RuleEngineUpdateService.exe)

Rules are stored in the database. The Rule Engine Update Service is used for the notification of deployment or undeployment of policies. This service is utilized if rules are used within the orchestration and it caches these policies in memory. If the policies are changed, the service synchronizes with the database within seconds.

Various Deployment Topologies

The following describes the various deployment topologies that can be configured within the BizTalk system:

- Single-Server Deployment Configuration
- Two-Server Deployment Configuration

- High-Availability Deployment Configuration
- Secure Deployment Configuration
- Multiple Machine Deployment Configuration

Single-Server Deployment Configuration

This is a minimal deployment topology where all the BizTalk functionality and all the SQL Server databases reside on a single machine. Because only one machine handles all the load, including the SQL databases, this machine will have to be capable (HDD, CPU, memory) of running the SQL Server service, SSO-Master Secret Server, Tracking, and one or more BizTalk Server service instance. Because all resources reside and run locally, Local Windows Groups and user accounts can be used. This is not a recommended topology if high volumes of data and stress will be put on the system or if high availability is a requirement.

Figure 15.5 depicts a sample single-server deployment.

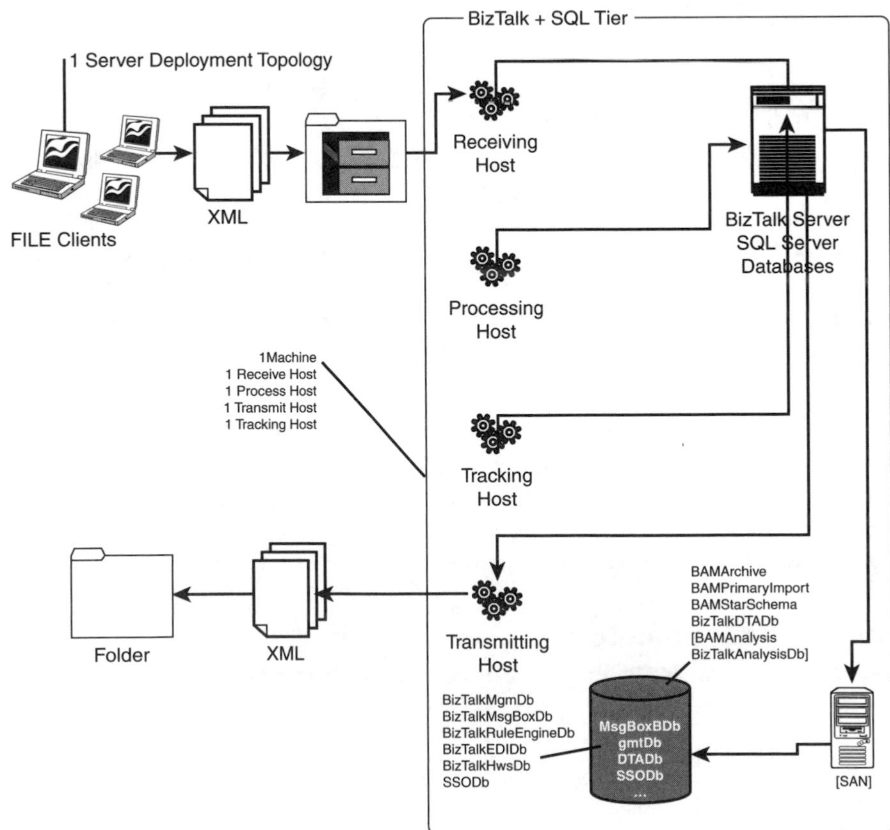

FIGURE 15.5 Single-server deployment configuration.

Two-Server Deployment Configuration

This is a minimal deployment configuration whereby all the databases reside on a dedicated SQL Server and all the BizTalk functionality is executed on a dedicated BizTalk server. For this configuration, it is recommended to install SQL in Mixed Mode Authentication with SSPI security. Although it is possible to use Local Windows Groups, it is recommended to use Domain Global Groups. If Local Windows Groups are used, these groups will have to be manually created on the SQL Server machine that is used to create SQL Server Logins by the configuration tool, ConfigurationFramework.exe. In this configuration, the BizTalk Server performs all the functionality of BizTalk, including tracking, and also hosts the SSO-Master Secret Server service. This topology is an improvement over the single-machine configuration because the contention caused by the SQL databases (which can be CPU and disk intensive) are deployed onto a dedicated server.

Figure 15.6 depicts a sample two-server deployment.

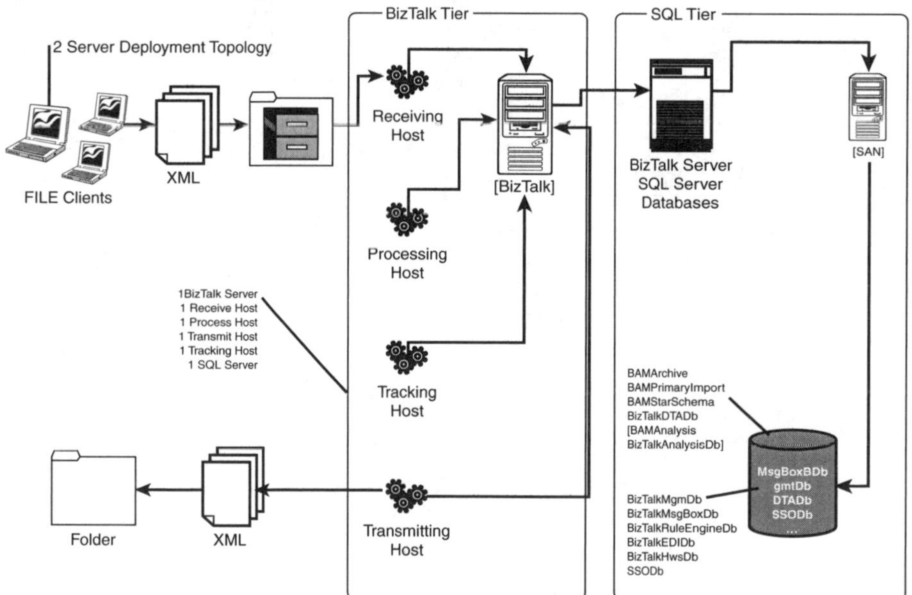

FIGURE 15.6 Two-server deployment topology.

High-Availability Deployment Configuration

This deployment topology provides availability by configuring more than one BizTalk server to perform the functionality of Receiving, Processing, and Transmitting. On the database tier, availability is achieved by clustering the SQL Server service hosting all the BizTalk Server databases. It is also imperative that the SSO-Master Secret Server service is clustered, because this can be the single point of failure. In this topology if one server at any tier fails, the system will still continue to function normally. This is accomplished because multiple redundant servers are deployed at each tier. The other good server will take on the responsibility of performing the work of the failed server. This design is useful to take a server down for maintenance. If a server that partially completed processing a message failed, the lock on the message in the database will be released and SQL will roll back any uncommitted transactions. This message will then be retrieved by the other good server and processed to completion. Figure 15.7 depicts a high-availability deployment topology.

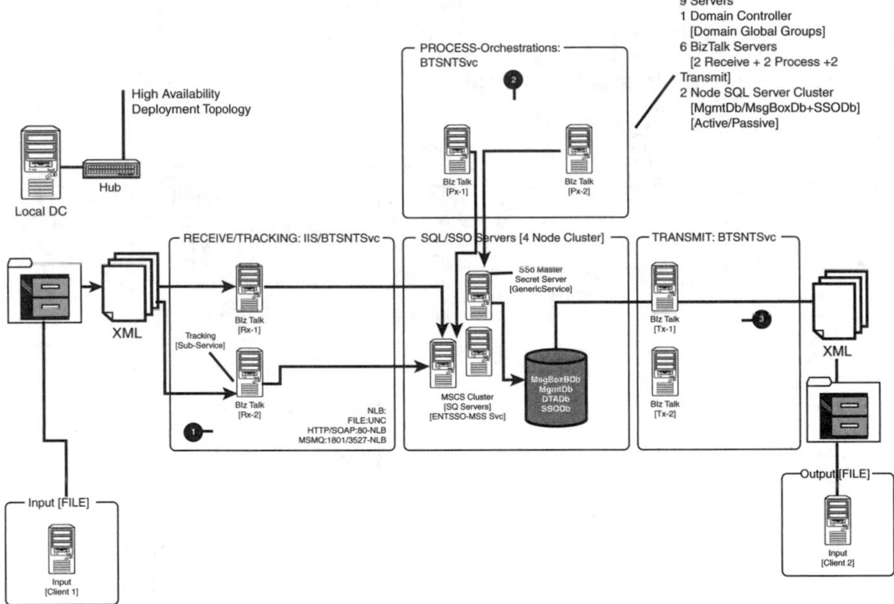

FIGURE 15.7 High-availability deployment topology.

Secure Deployment Configuration

This deployment topology (as shown in Figure 15.8) depends on the specific scenario for which BizTalk is deployed. At a generic level, it is possible to isolate the Receiving functionality into a DMZ sandwiched between two firewalls. The processing, transmitting and database tiers can be deployed behind the second firewall within an INTRANET domain. In addition, management tools such as HAT/BAM and software can be deployed behind a third firewall within the CORPORATE domain. The specific transport used by the scenario will dictate the different ports that need to be opened for the scenario to function.

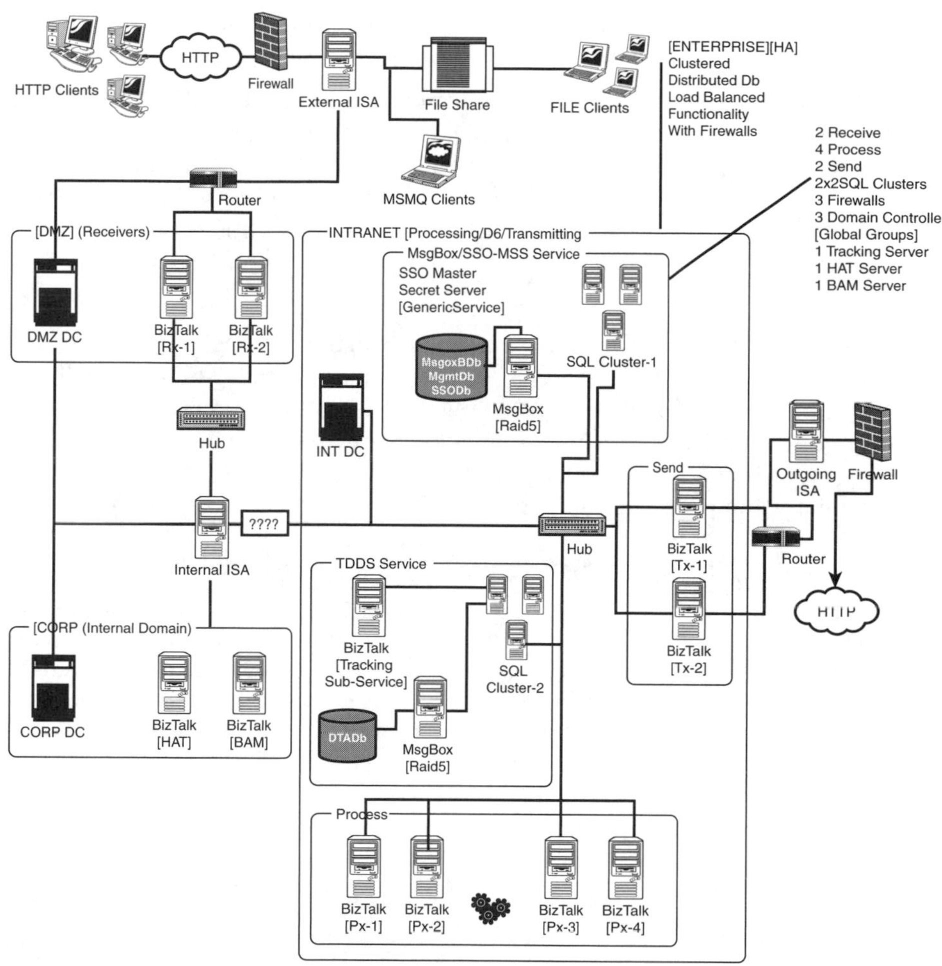

FIGURE 15.8 Secure deployment topology.

Multiple Machine Deployment Configuration

This is an improvement over the two-machine configuration. Depending on the scenario, multiple BizTalk servers and a dedicated SQL Server can be used. The BizTalk functionality can be logically isolated into Receiving, Processing, Transmitting, and Tracking. Thus, a dedicated host can be created for each logical tier and one dedicated server (host instance) can be added to each host. Mapping the Receive and Send adapters to independent hosts and enlisting the orchestration against the third host ensures that only specific functionality is executed on the respective servers. Depending on the complexity of the scenario[md}for example, complex Maps on the receive and send ports or complex orchestration—hosts can be configured such that resource usage can be evenly spread across multiple servers.

- Complex Orchestrations—If the receiving and sending functionality is lightweight and the orchestration workflow is complex, a single server can host both the receiving and sending functionality. Both receiving and sending functionality can run in one host, or they can be deployed into separate dedicated hosts. Thus, two BizTalk service instances will be running on the same machine. In this case, the orchestration functionality can be deployed onto its own dedicated host on a separate machine.
- Messaging Only Scenario—If the scenario is messaging based where no orchestrations are required, two BizTalk servers can be set up to handle all functionality. One server can be set up to handle all receiving, and the other can be set up to handle all sending functionality. Data can be routed based on a promoted property using filters and the input schema can be mapped to an output schema. All this can be accomplished by setting properties on either the receive locations or send ports.

MAXIMUM BIZTALK SERVERS PER MESSAGE BOX

Within one BizTalk Group, under sustained load, one Message Box provides optimal throughput for up to approximately four BizTalk servers. Thereafter, introducing additional BizTalk servers causes throughput to plateau and drop because of severe contention on the Message Box database. After the limit is reached, adding BizTalk servers does not help improve throughput. Additional servers serve only to create more contention on the Message Box and DTADb databases. To get better throughput it is recommended to either scale up the SQL Server (Message Box database) or scale out to at least three Message Boxes. See the section "Multiple Message Box Databases" on why throughput does not improve when scaling out to two Message Boxes. However, these numbers are based on many factors and depend on the type of hardware and scenario-specific complexity.

Scaling Out Receiving Transports

All receiving adapters can be scaled out by adding multiple receiving servers. However, the following sections describe the adapters that can be set up using NLB to scale out the receiving tier.

- Scaling Out MSMQT Transport
- Scaling Out HTTP/SOAP Transport

Scaling Out MSMQT Transport

The MSMQT adapter is Transactional by design and guarantees Ordered Delivery. Thus, messages arriving at the receive location are delivered to the Message Box in the order in which they arrive. However, this design inherently has the following side effects:

- Impact of throughput—To guarantee (Ordered Delivery) only one thread can service one MSMQT Receive Location (Input Queue). This is necessary to avoid receiving multiple messages arriving concurrently at the same MSMQT Receive Location. Using only a single thread for a single MSMQT Receive Location limits the amount of data that can flow through the system. This is because the same blocking thread has to serially service all incoming requests to this input queue. One workaround to this design is to architect a scenario such that multiple MSMQT Receive Locations (Input Queues) are created and data is routed to these multiple input queues so that the system can concurrently receive input documents, thereby improving system throughput. If this workaround is not an option and ordered delivery is not a requirement, the other solution is to create a custom multithreaded adapter (nonordered delivery) for the MSMQ transport that can receive messages concurrently on multiple threads for the same receive location. The BizTalk Adapter Framework can be used to create such a custom MSMQ adapter. However, if multiple clients are used to send messages to the BizTalk receiving queue, BizTalk will create additional threads to manage each client's messages. In this case messages will only be serialized for each client connection.

- Impact on Scalability—By design, to scale out the receiving tier, it is recommended to add multiple host instances (BizTalk Server Service Processes) to a particular host (logical container) and to then map this host to the Handler (for example, Receive Handler) for a particular adapter, such as MSMQT Transport. Thus, it is possible to scale out and improve throughput by having multiple servers concurrently share in the workload servicing the same receive location.

  Specific to the MSMQT adapter, it is necessary to set up the infrastructure so that clients (outgoing queues) can send messages to a single virtual receiving queue. This can be accomplished by setting up WLBS [NLB Ports: 1801/3527] on the Receiving Servers and having the clients send messages directly to this load-balanced static Virtual IP (for example, Format Name: DIRECT=TCP:10.10.10.10\PRIVATE$\QueueName). Alternatively, clients can send messages directly to a virtual DNS name, mapping the VIP to this DNS name on the domain such as Format Name: DIRECT=OS:DNSName\PRIVATE$\QueueName. Because of the Transactional (Ordered Delivery) design of the MSMQT adapter, it is not possible to have more than one BizTalk Server service a single MSMQT Receive Location. Even though a host is mapped to a Receive Handler and multiple host instances are added to this host, only one host instance can ever service the single MSMQT Receive Location. Thus, the other host instances (BizTalk Server Service Processes) are unable to share the workload. The way around this is to have multiple receive locations, thereby having multiple BizTalk servers servicing multiple receive locations. However, if multiple clients are used, the other passive server can service the other clients. In this case, although each client is serialized on its receive locations, the system can concurrently process incoming messages for the same receive location.

- Impact on High Availability—Even if multiple receive locations are created so that multiple BizTalk servers can share the workload, only one BizTalk Server services a single receive location at any given time. After a BizTalk Server services a particular receive location, that server will continue to service the receive location for the lifetime of that BizTalk Server service process. However, this design—only one server having affinity to a particular receive location—does not impact high availability. If this host instance that is servicing a particular receive location is down, either because of hardware or software failure or taken down for maintenance, the other host instances (not servicing this receive location) will detect that this receive location (Input Queue) is not being serviced and will take over servicing this receive location. This process is seamless and should happen within 60 seconds. After this happens, this new host instance locks the receive location and will continue to have affinity to this receive location for the lifetime of this BizTalk Service Process. Although throughput is not improved by balancing load (NLB) across multiple receiving servers; it does provide high availability. The passive server takes over receiving incoming messages when the BizTalk service on the active server is stopped. If multiple queues are used, the load is indeed balanced. Thus by design, only one BizTalk Server can provide service to one receiving queue and only one BizTalk Server can provide service to one sending queue. The queues can be accessed either by using the format [DIRECT=TCP:10.10.10.10\Private$\QueueName] or by using the DNS format [DIRECT=OS:VirtualDNSName\Private$\QueueName].

NONDETERMINISTIC DESIGN

Multiple receive locations (Input Queues) and multiple host instances (BizTalk Servers) can be set up so that the system can handle concurrent load and provide improved throughput. However, based on the above scalability design, BizTalk automatically sets affinity in a nondeterministic manner to a particular receive location. For example, if a host instance servicing a particular receive location fails, another host instance takes over the responsibility of servicing this orphaned receive location. When this happens, this new host instance has affinity to the receive location and the original host instance, which relinquished affinity to the receive location, is unable to reacquire affinity to the receive location. However, if the receive location is inactive for a period of five or more minutes, this lock is released and any of the receiving servers may reacquire affinity when the next message arrives.

STATIC MSMQT HOSTS

Unlike other native transport adapters, it is not possible to change the Receive and Send Handlers [Default: BizTalkServerApplication] for the MSMQT adapter. Thus, all functionality [Receive/Send] runs on one host. Adding multiple servers to this host does provide failover and high availability. However, it is not possible to split functionality across isolated machines dedicated for Receiving and/or Transmitting. Because of this design, it is not possible to set up the Receiving Host and Transmitting Host to run under different user credentials. Because MSMQT exclusively needs the well-known port, there cannot be more than one host with MSMQT. Otherwise, more than one instance with MSMQT may be directed to the single server, and the second one will fail. The administration solution for avoiding this situation was to allow MSMQT only on one host, although you can configure as many instances (BizTalk Server Processes) as required.

SIDE-BY-SIDE MSMQ AND MSMQT INSTALLATION

By default when a BizTalk Group is configured, the MSMQT adapter, unlike the other native adapters, is not automatically set up. The MSMQT adapter has to be manually added, or configured. This is so that the MSMQT adapter does not conflict with the native Windows MSMQ Service if it is already installed and configured. However, it is possible to have both the native Windows MSMQ Service and the BizTalk MSMQT subservice run side-by-side. This is accomplished by setting up at least two IP addresses for the same machine, binding the native MSMQ Service to the first IP and binding the BizTalk MSMQT subservice to the second IP. All format names can then be used to send messages to queues on remote machines. However, there is a limitation; it is not possible to use the DIRECT format name to send messages to the local MSMQ queues (native MSMQ queues) on the same server.

Scaling Out HTTP/SOAP Transport

The HTTP and SOAP receiving adapters can be scaled using the WLBS service. This process is similar to the way load is balanced for any HTTP Web site or SOAP Web service. This can be accomplished by setting up WLBS [NLB Ports: 80/443] on the Receiving Servers and having the clients send messages directly to this load-balanced static Virtual IP, such as `http://10.10.10.10/MyWebSite/BTSHTTPReceive.dll`. Alternatively, clients can send messages directly to a virtual (mapping the VIP to this DNS name on the domain) DNS name, such as `http://www.MyDNSSite/MyWebSite/BTSHTTPReceive.dll`. Simply adding more BizTalk servers to the host (default BizTalkServerIsolatedHost) within which the Receive adapter is mapped to enables the server to share in the workload.

CAUTION

WARNING [W2K3]—To avoid SQL security access errors, on Windows 2003 machines, assuming your VROOT is running under the Default Application Pool, change the identity for the DefaultAppPool under Application Pools from IWAM_MACHINENAME to a valid domain user account.

WARNING [W2K3]—Add the BTSHTTPReceive.dll to the Web Service Extensions. This will help avoid the `HTTP: 404 Not Found` error.

WARNING—If both HTTP and SOAP transports are used, they should be set up so that they both run within different isolated hosts.

Deploying for High Availability

BizTalk functionality can be distributed across two physical tiers:

- The BizTalk Server tier
- The SQL Server tier

Configuring the BizTalk Server Tier for High Availability

High availability is accomplished by configuring multiple redundant servers servicing each BizTalk tier. This design can be viewed as an Active-Active configuration where all servers in each tier share the load. In the event of a failure condition experienced at any tier, the BizTalk system is designed so that the other redundant server(s) will take on the responsibility of servicing the additional load.

The BizTalk tier can be further subdivided into three logical tiers, which are discussed in the sections that follow.

Redundant Receiving Servers

Adding two or more receiving servers provides availability at this tier. The mechanism used to balance the load differs depending on the type of transport adopted. For example, using the HTTP/SOAP transport requires the balancing of load using some form of load balancing, such as WLBS. This is accomplished by enabling NLB on two or more servers and balancing the load on port 80. Balancing the load for the MSMQT transport can also be accomplished by using the WLBS service and balancing the load on port 1801 and 3527. Other transports such as FILE/FTP and SQL do not require any form of load balancing mechanism. To set up NLB, add a shared virtual IP to each of the receiving machines (MACHINE1: 10.10.10.1 MACHINE2: 10.10.10.2 VIP: 10.10.10.10). To provide seamless access to the receiving servers, you can also map a DNS entry on the domain controller to the static VIP.

Redundant Processing Servers

These are servers that instantiate the orchestration instances and process the business workflow. All servers subscribe to work, and on a first-to-succeed basis, lock, process, and commit orchestration instances. In the event that the server currently processing an orchestration instance suffers a catastrophic failure, the lock on the data is automatically released by SQL, any uncommitted data is rolled-back, and the other redundant server is free to process this incomplete orchestration instance.

Redundant Transmitting Servers

Similar to the processing tier, multiple transmitting servers help provide high availability at this tier regardless of the send transport type used. In case of a failure condition encountered sending data to a remote destination, the send adapter will retry (Number of Retries and Retry Interval) depending on how the send port is configured. If one of the servers encounters a catastrophic failure transmitting data, the lock on the publishing data is released by the SQL Server service; thus, other redundant servers can acquire the lock and attempt to transmit the same message.

Configuring the SQL Server Tier for High Availability

The BizTalk databases on SQL Server can be the single point of failure. To provide availability, it is highly recommended to cluster the SQL Servers using the MSCS service in Active/Passive mode using two or more redundant servers with data stored on a shared disk array or SAN.

The BizTalk service is designed such that when the SQL Server service is unavailable the BizTalk servers require no manual intervention. The SQL service can become unavailable either because the active node in the cluster group is intentionally failed over (for maintenance, for example) to the passive node, or because of the normal failure conditions. When this occurs the BizTalk service instances experience database connection failures. The BizTalk service instances then automatically shut down and restart 60 seconds later, attempting to reconnect to the databases. When this problem is encountered, a message is logged to the Application Event Log. This process will be repeated until BizTalk successfully reconnects to the databases.

CAUTION

Because data is spread across all the Message Box databases, adding multiple Message Boxes does not provide high availability. It is still necessary to cluster every Message Box database. However, it is possible to have multiple Message Box databases installed on the same SQL Server cluster. Multiple Message Box databases do indeed help in providing scalability.

TIP

MSMQT, the Reliable Transport: During failure situations, it is possible that the same document can be retried and retransmitted more than once. For example, this can happen when using an unreliable high-performance adapter such as the FILE transport adapter. If it is absolutely necessary that this not occur, using the MSMQT (ordered delivery) adapter can help avoid this situation.

Clustering the SSO Master Secret Server

In addition to the SQL Servers being the single point of failure, the SSO Master Secret Server also needs to be configured as a highly available resource. This is accomplished by clustering the SSO Master Secret Server service.

It is recommended to set up the SSO-Master Secret Server on an MSCS cluster in Active-Passive mode. Thus, only one node in the MSCS cluster will be active at any given time.

This can be set up on the same cluster on which the SQL Server databases are installed. The SSO-Master Secret Server uses little or no resources, because the main role of this service is to load and cache the secret key at startup and replicate this key to the other SSO services running on each BizTalk server.

Installing the BizTalk Server Service on an MSCS Cluster

The BizTalk Server service is not designed to be cluster aware. However, it is possible to have BizTalk installed independently on each node of an MSCS cluster running nonclustered. Because of the hard dependency BizTalk has on SSO, SSO is required to be installed locally. In this case, neither of the services are set up as clustered resources. Thus, installing BizTalk (one node as the Master Secret Server) on a cluster does not provide high availability. It does, however, provide scalability. Both nodes are active and performing work. In such a situation, if the BizTalk service running on NODE1 (SSO as Master Secret Server) failed, the other node will not take over as the Master Secret Server. This problem will have to be manually resolved.

Table 15.1 lists the possible combinations of installing SQL databases, SSO-Master Secret Server, and the BizTalk service on an MSCS cluster. For example, it is possible to install the BizTalk service (nonclustered) on the cluster if the SSO-Master Secret Server service is not clustered. If the SSO-Master Secret Server service is clustered, it is not possible to install the BizTalk service on the cluster nodes.

TABLE 15.1 SSO-BizTalk MSCS Cluster Installation Permutations

Windows	Clustering			Status
Groups	SQL	SSO-MSS	BTS	
Global	YES	NO	NO	PASS
Global	YES	NO	YES	PASS
Global	YES	YES	NO	PASS
Global	YES	YES	YES	FAIL
Global	NO	YES	NO	PASS
Global	NO	YES	YES	FAIL
Local	NO	NO	YES	FAIL

As can be seen from Table 15.1, if SSO (Master Secret Server) is clustered, BizTalk should not be set up on the same cluster. It is possible to configure BizTalk on a cluster if the SSO-MSS is not clustered. However, BizTalk Server will be set up as a standalone service. To provide high availability, the SSO Service (Master Secret Server) resource must be clustered. When this is done, BizTalk cannot run on either node in the cluster. Thus, it is not recommended to have both BTS and SSO-Master Secret Server (Clustered) on the same MSCS cluster. In addition, installing the BizTalk databases on a clustered SQL Server with Local Groups is not supported.

WHY BIZTALK SHOULD NOT BE INSTALLED ON AN MSCS CLUSTER WHEN SSO IS CLUSTERED

Assume that BizTalk is installed on both nodes in the cluster.

Node1: The BizTalk service successfully starts up after contacting the locally running SSO service.

Other BTS Instances: All other remote (nonclustered) BizTalk service instances successfully contact the clustered SSO-Master Secret Server, using their locally running SSO service instances.

Node2: This node fails to start the BizTalk service because the local SSO service, which is also configured a Master Secret Server, fails to start and connect to the currently running SSO-Master Secret Server (Node1).

Thus, the BizTalk service fails to start SSO locally because it is already running on the other node (Node1). If this BizTalk service starts up, it will force SSO to start up as the Master Secret Server, causing the SSO service running on Node1 to shut down, indirectly shutting down BizTalk service running on Node1.

Summary

In this chapter, you examined the flexible deployment configurations of the BizTalk Server 2004 system with relation to the concept of hosts and host instances. You started with the deployment of BizTalk in a scalable environment covering scale out and scale up. We then covered the various services within BizTalk and the roles they play within a large deployment topology. Thereafter, we covered various deployment topologies. We touched on the balancing of load on the receiving servers with relation to HTTP, SOAP, and the MSMQT adapters. Finally, we went on to analyze the deployment of BizTalk in a robust highly available environment.

CHAPTER 16

Health and Activity Tracking

IN THIS CHAPTER

- Debugging a BizTalk Application
- Tracking BizTalk Applications

Health and Activity Tracking serves the needs of developers and operations administrators. In a running BizTalk application, developers want to debug the BizTalk application that is still under development or diagnose any issues with the application on the production system. The purpose of debugging is to aid in the development of orchestration and messaging solutions by allowing the developers to set breakpoints at class level and instance level. I will explain the difference between each type of breakpoint later in this chapter.

BizTalk Health and Activity Tracking can even be used post deployment to track a specific message and to get information about parts of a live solution. Hence, Health and Activity Tracking (HAT) can be broadly divided into two sub features: debugging and tracking. Tracking messages allows businesses to satisfactorily answer customer inquiries about the status of their orders or answer business partner queries about their shipments. Tracking is also useful for auditing purposes.

This chapter covers techniques on debugging aspects such as Replay mode, Live mode, remote debugging, setting class levels and instance level breakpoints. Later in the chapter you will learn how to configure a BizTalk application for tracking purposes and how to display tracking information along with the various views the user interface provides, such as Operations view and Reporting view. At the end of the chapter, topics such as using the tracking user interface for viewing archived data and creating and saving custom queries are covered.

We'll also cover the advanced features and finer points of this tool. Finally, we'll tie everything together with a simple integration project.

Debugging a BizTalk Application

Health and Activity Tracking facilitates the debugging of orchestrations, because standard .NET language debuggers are not sufficient to debug them. BizTalk application debugging is slightly different from normal debugging in the sense that when you are developing an application, developers tend to debug in their favorite development environment; however, an orchestration can be debugged only after it is deployed and executed on the BizTalk Server machine using the Health and Activity Tracking tool. BizTalk Server Orchestration debugging can be done in two modes:

- Replay mode
- Live mode

When a BizTalk orchestration gets executed, all the actions are tracked. Let's begin with Replay mode debugging.

Replay Mode Debugging

Replay mode debugging can be thought of as reporting data. This is primarily used on orchestrations to understand how a message flowed through the business process. The Replay mode debugging enables you to track the activity of an orchestration instance on a shape-by-shape basis. By default, all the orchestration events are configured to be tracked, which allows you to view an orchestration activity inside the orchestration debugger. Please refer to the section "Configuring BizTalk Application for Tracking" for details on how to configure orchestration tracking.

Executing an Orchestration Instance

Let's begin by actually executing a BizTalk orchestration. This is a simple orchestration that automates approval of the purchase orders business process. If you already have an orchestration that has been executed at least once, skip the following steps and proceed to the "Replaying an Orchestration Instance in the Debugger" section. The complete sample BizTalk application in this example can be found at the download for this chapter. This sample is used extensively in this chapter to explain various concepts. Copy the `DebugExample` folder and its subfolder from `chapter16` download to your local hard drive on C:\.

1. At the Visual Studio command prompt, switch to the `DebugExample` folder (this is the parent of the folder `POApprove`, where your source code files for this project reside).
2. At the command prompt, type **`sn -k POApprove.snk`**. You will receive a message that a key pair was written to `POApprove.snk`.
3. In Visual Studio, open the solution POApprove.sln. Right-click the `POApproveSchema` project in the Solution Explorer and click Properties.

4. In the project properties dialog box, select Assembly from the Common Properties folder.
5. Scroll down in the right pane. The last category should be Strong name. Select the Assembly key file property and click the ellipsis to its right.
6. Browse to the key/pair file you created in step 2 and click Open to select it as the value of the project's Assembly key file property.
7. In the project properties dialog box, select Deployment from the Configuration Properties folder. If you do not have BizTalkMgmtDb on the local machine, type the name of the server where that database exists.
8. Click OK to apply the property selection and close the project properties dialog box.
9. Right-click the POApproveSchema project node in the Solution Explorer and click Build. The Output view should indicate successful completion with 1 succeeded, 0 failed, 0 skipped.
10. Repeat steps 3–9 for the projects `POApprove_Transforms` and `POApproveBusinessProcess`.
11. Right-click the `POApproveSchema` project node in the Solution Explorer and click Deploy. The Output view should indicate successful completion with 1 succeeded, 0 failed, 0 skipped.
12. Repeat step 11 for the projects `POApprove_Transforms` and `POApproveBusinessProcess`.

16

13. Create a Receive Port to receive the purchase order. Open BizTalk Explorer from within Visual Studio .NET by choosing BizTalk Explorer from the View menu. Expand the Configuration Databases node and expand on the database where your BizTalk Management exists. Right-click the ReceivePorts node and choose Add Receive Port. Choose One-Way Port and click OK on the Create New Receive Port dialog box. In the One-Way Receive Port property dialog box, change the receive port name to **`POReceivePort`** and click OK. Right-click the Receive Locations node and add a new receive location; change the name to **`PO Receive Location`**. Choose FILE transport from the Transport Type drop–down menu, click the Address (URI) field, and click the ellipses. The File Transport Properties dialog box is presented. Enter **`C:\DebugExample\Input`** in the receive folder and leave the file mask as *.xml. Click OK. Under Receive Handler, choose BizTalkServerApplication (available in the default installation). Choose Microsoft.BizTalk.DefaultPipelines.XMLReceive from the Receive Pipeline drop–down menu and click OK.

14. In BizTalk Explorer, right-click the SendPorts node and choose Add Send Port. Choose Static One-Way Port and click OK in the Create New Send Port dialog box. In the Static One-Way Send Port property dialog box, change the send port name to **`PODenySendPort`** and click OK. Choose FILE transport from the Transport Type drop–down menu, click the Address (URI) field, and click the ellipses. The File Transport Properties dialog box is presented. Enter **`C:\DebugExample\Denials`** in the Destination folder and type the filename **`Deny%MessageID%.xml`**. Click OK. Click the Send folder under configurations and choose Microsoft.BizTalk.DefaultPipelines.XMLTransmit from the Send Pipeline drop-down menu.

15. Use the guidance from step 14 and create a Send Port PO-InvoiceSendPort to Send Invoices from the orchestration. Use FILE transport and configure the port to write to the `Invoice%MessageID%.xml` file to location `C:\DebugExample\Invoices` folder; use the default XML Transmit pipeline.

16. Now we can bind the logical orchestration ports to the physical ports we have created in steps 13, 14 and 15. In BizTalk Explorer, expand the Orchestrations node and right-click on the POApproveBusinessProcess.POApproveProcess and choose Bind. Under the Port Binding properties dialog box, for binding choose the Physical receive port POReceivePort from the drop–down list for Port_To_RecvPO Logical port. Similarly, choose PODenySendPort for SendDenialPort and PO-InvoiceSendPort for the SendInvoicePort. For Host, choose the default BizTalkServerApplication host. Then click OK.

17. The orchestration is now completely bound. We now have to enlist and start the orchestration; this can be achieved by right-clicking the POApproveBusinessProcess.POApproveProcess orchestration and choosing Start. Leave all options selected and click OK on the BizTalk Explorer—Express Start dialog box.

18. Now that we have a running BizTalk Orchestration, let's execute it by copying the file PO100000.xml from the `C:\DebugExample` folder to the `C:\DebugExample\Input` folder.

19. Notice that the file is picked up for processing by BizTalk Server. (If the file is not picked up, be sure that your default BizTalkServerApplication host is running from the BizTalk Server Administration tool.)

20. This will create an instance of the POApproveProcess orchestration and open the orchestration in Visual Studio. Notice that if the POAmount is greater than 10000 the order will be denied automatically. Because in our message the POAmount is greater than 10000, a Denial message is generated by the orchestration, which will be sent to the C:\DebugExample\Denials folder.

We are now ready to replay the orchestration instance that was just executed.

Replaying an Orchestration Instance in the Debugger

When you have an executed orchestration instance on the server, open the Health and Activity Tracking UI from Microsoft BizTalk Server 2004 menu options under Start, All Programs. This launches the Health and Activity Tracking UI. From the Queries menu, choose the Most Recent 100 Service Instances option; this will display the 100 most recently executed services on the system that the UI is connected to. If you are opening the Health and Activity Tracking UI for the first time, you will encounter the security warning dialog box depicted in Figure 16.1. If you trust your local site, choose Yes to indicate that you trust your local BizTalk Installation. If you choose No, you will be unable to continue. Click the Run Query button in the Query Builder view.

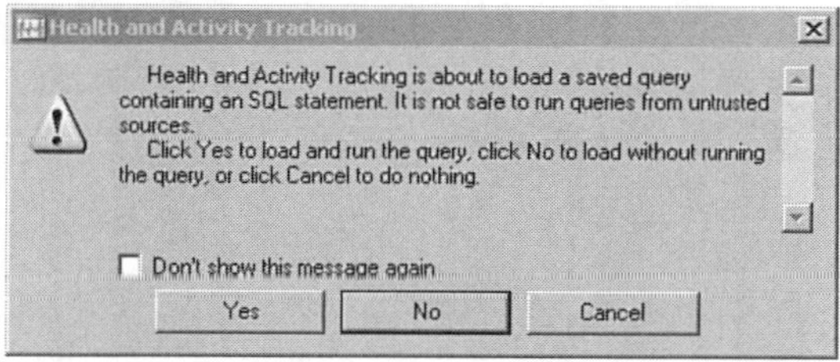

FIGURE 16.1 Health and Activity Tracking security warning.

Notice that the most recent service instances, such as orchestration and pipelines, that were executed on the system are presented. Choose the orchestration instance that was executed in the previous steps and select Orchestration Debugger from the right-click menu as shown in Figure 16.2. This invokes the Orchestration Debugger and displays the orchestration that was executed along with its tracked events on the left pane.

NOTE

Users should be part of the BizTalk Server Administrators NT group on the BizTalkMsgBoxDb machine to be able to attach an orchestration instance to the debugger.

Notice that the tracked events pane displays the Action name, Action type, and the execution date and time. Action name corresponds to the name given to an orchestration shape inside your orchestration. Action type represents the orchestration shape used. There are two entries per shape: one when the action is entered and the second when that particular action is completed. Clicking the first Action turns the orchestration shape color to green, indicating when the shape has started. Clicking the corresponding second action turns the shape to blue, indicating when that particular shape execution was completed. The initialization Action name in the beginning indicates when the orchestration instance started the execution, and the initialization at the end indicates when the orchestration instance has completed its execution. By clicking the last initialization action, you can see what particular path a message has taken during the execution of the orchestration instance. In our example, you will note that the Denial message was created and sent (see Figure 16.3).

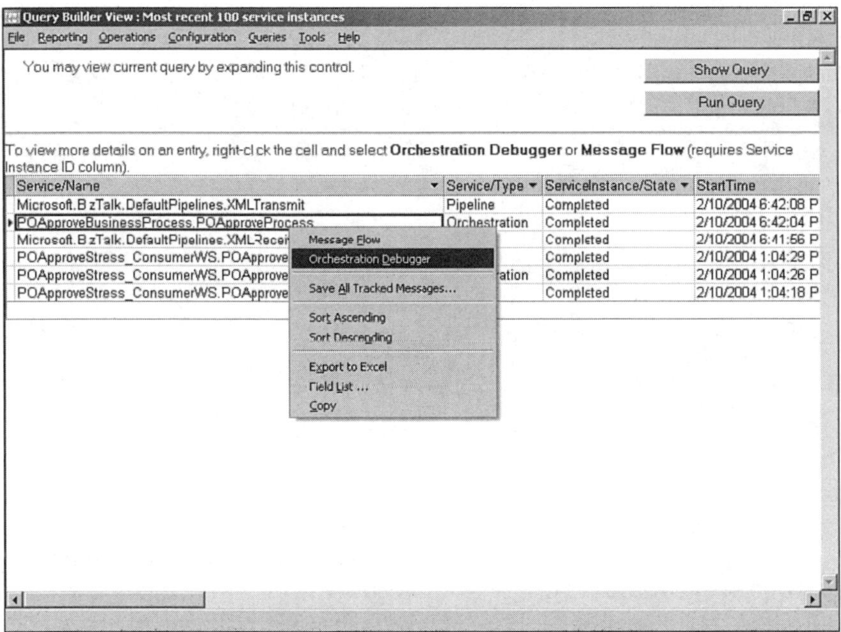

FIGURE 16.2 Opening an instance of orchestration in Debugger.

Live Mode Debugging

Whereas Replay mode debugging gives insight into the execution of a particular orchestration instance, debugging live is much more interesting during the development phase. Live mode debugging is also known as Interactive mode debugging. The Live mode debugging allows users to debug an orchestration instance via usage of breakpoints. Breakpoints can be set at class level and instance level. Setting a class-level breakpoint causes every orchestration instance of that class to break at the breakpoint. Hence, it is not recommended to use class-level breakpoints in the live production environment.

CAUTION

If an instance of orchestration is attached to the debugger, the same instance cannot be attached to the debugger from a different machine.

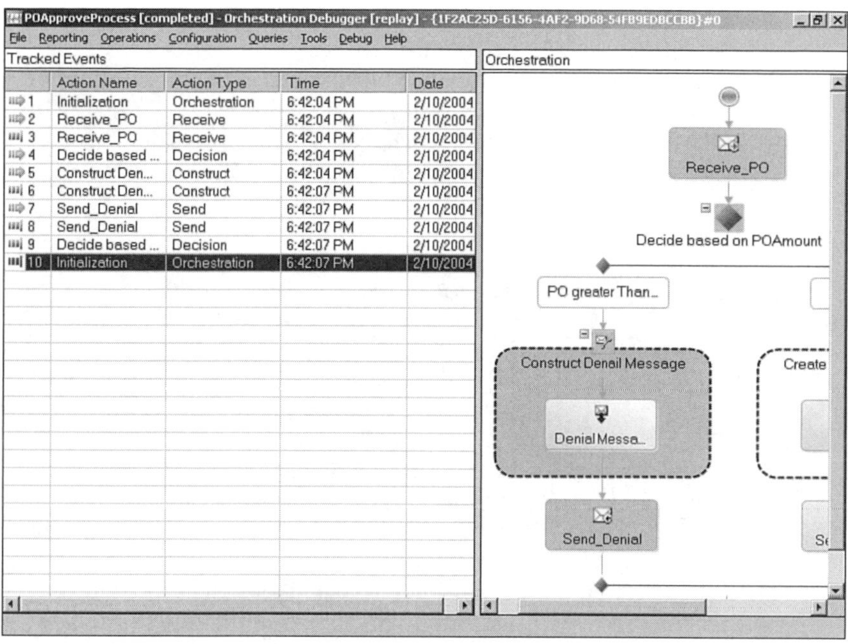

FIGURE 16.3 Orchestration Debugger in Replay mode.

Setting a Class-Level Breakpoint to Debug in Live Mode

To set a class-level breakpoint on an orchestration, you need to execute at least one instance of the orchestration. After you have an executed orchestration instance on the server, open the Health and Activity Tracking UI from the Microsoft BizTalk Server 2004 menu options under All Programs. This action will display the Health and Activity Tracking UI. From the Queries menu choose the Most Recent 100 Service Instances option. This will display the most recent executed service instances. Choose the orchestration that you are interested in putting a class-level breakpoint on. (Follow steps 1-19 described in the Replay mode section and run the example if you do not already have an orchestration instance.) Right-click and choose to open the orchestration instance in the debugger. Inside the orchestration pane, choose the shape at which you would like the breakpoint, right-click the shape, and choose Set Breakpoint in Class or select the shape on the orchestration pane and choose F9 (see Figure 16.4).

When a class-level breakpoint is set, all the future instances of this orchestration will break at that orchestration shape ready to be debugged. You can place one or more class-level breakpoints by setting breakpoints on different orchestration shapes. After a class-level breakpoint is set, you can then debug new instances of the orchestration in Live mode.

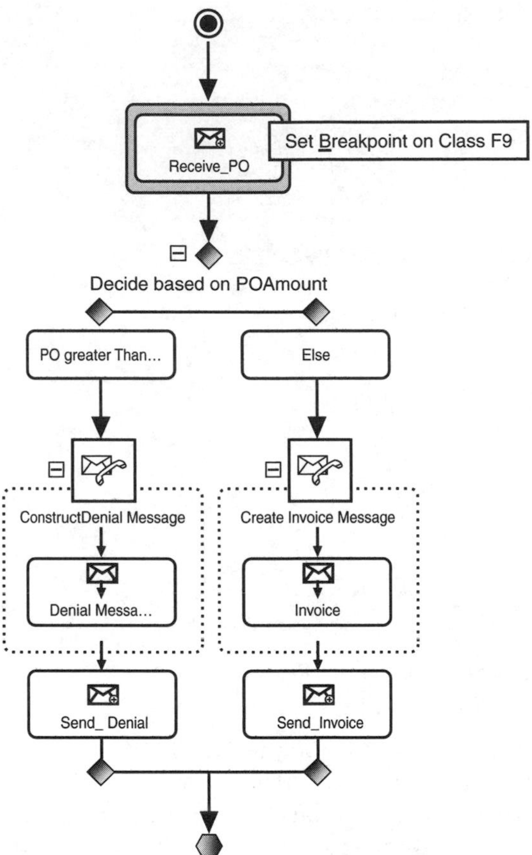

FIGURE 16.4 Setting a class-level breakpoint in Orchestration Debugger.

Attaching to an Orchestration Instance from Orchestration Debugger

After a class-level breakpoint is set on an orchestration, all the future instances of the orchestrations go into "In Breakpoint" state when the instance execution reaches the breakpoint. To debug, you will need to attach debugger to the orchestration instance in that state, as shown in the following steps:

1. Open the Health and Activity Tracking UI.
2. From the Operations menu, choose Service Instances and run the query to display all the orchestration instances that are currently running.
3. Choose the orchestration on which you have previously set a class-level breakpoint. The status of this instance will be "In Breakpoint." Right-click this orchestration instance and choose Orchestration Debugger.

4. Orchestration Debugger displays the orchestration instance. From the debugger window, choose Attach from the Debug menu. The debugger is then attached to the orchestration instance.

The variable list section in the debugger window displays all the variables and their current values at the breakpoint, with the exception of user-created .NET classes. The information shown in the debugger (messages, context, variables, and so on) is read-only. To save messages from the variable list pane, right-click the message and choose Save Message. It should be noted that saving from the variable list window has a limitation of 20MB message size; however, this limitation does not exist when a message is saved from any other view. To view the message details, select the available message that is in scope from the variable list pane, and under the variable properties pane expand the message part name you are interested in. Expanding the collection object of the part properties makes the debugger show all the promoted properties and their values associated with the message part (when present). Interesting message context properties associated with the message can also be seen under Message Context collection.

Choosing the Show Action in Breakpoint option from the Debug menu will lead you to the next action shape to be executed. The shape will be highlighted in yellow.

Removing a Class-Level Breakpoint

To remove a class-level breakpoint on an orchestration, you need to open an instance of the orchestration in Orchestration Debugger on which there was one or more class-level breakpoints previously set. Select the shape on which there was a breakpoint, right-click the shape, and choose Remove Breakpoint on Class, or select the shape on the orchestration pane and choose F9. This ensures that all the future instances of this orchestration will not break at that orchestration shape. To remove all breakpoints, choose Clear All Breakpoints on Class from the Debug menu option.

All the shortcut keys related to the debugger are listed in Table 16.1, which can serve as a "cheat sheet" during your development of orchestrations.

TABLE 16.1 Orchestration Debugger Shortcut Keys

Menu Option	Shortcut Key	Alternative Shortcut Key
Clear All Breakpoints on Class	Ctrl+Shift+F9	Alt+D+K
Set a Breakpoint	F9	-
Attach	Ctrl+A	Alt+D+A
Detach	Shift+F5	Alt+D+D
Continue	Ctrl+G	-
Resume in Debug Mode	-	Alt+D+I
Terminate	-	Alt+D+T
Show Action in Breakpoint	Ctrl+S	Alt+D+S
Show Tracked Exceptions	-	Alt+D+X
View Calling Orchestration	-	Alt+D+V
Switch to Message Flow	-	Alt+D+F

Detaching an Orchestration Instance from Debugger

When an orchestration that was previously in "In Breakpoint" state is being debugged, the orchestration instance gets automatically detached when the orchestration state changes to Suspend, Terminate, or completed. However, at times, you might specifically want to detach the orchestration instance manually from the debugger. In such cases, you can choose the Detach option from the Debug menu in the Orchestration Debugger window.

Resuming an Orchestration Instance on Debugger

After an orchestration instance is attached to the debugger, to resume the execution of that particular instance, you can choose Continue from the Debug menu from within the Orchestration Debugger. The Orchestration instance will continue execution until it hits another breakpoint, and if there is no other breakpoint, the instance completes. Tracked events won't be refreshed until you choose Refresh from the File menu.

Debugging a Start Orchestration Shape

If the orchestration is executing another orchestration using a Start Orchestration shape, the orchestration instances that are generated by the Start orchestration shape can be debugged like any other orchestration because it has its own Instance ID and shows as a separate instance.

Debugging a Called Orchestration

If your orchestration is calling another orchestration using a Call shape, the called orchestration can be debugged by right-clicking the Action for Call shape under the tracked events pane and choosing View Called Orchestration. The called orchestration will be rendered in the same Orchestration Debugger window. After the called orchestration is rendered in the debugger, the user experience is similar to debugging any other orchestration instance. To navigate back to the Caller (parent orchestration) when your orchestration debugger is rendering the called orchestration, choose View Calling Orchestration from the Debug menu. This option is not available when the orchestration being debugged is not a called orchestration. Called orchestrations do not have an Instance ID of their own.

> **NOTE**
>
> Unlike the started orchestration, the called orchestrations do not have a separate GUID. If you have call orchestration in a loop or are calling many orchestrations from a single orchestration, the Debugger window will show the parent GUID concatenated with #<x>, where x is the number representing the orchestration called.

Debugging an Orchestration Instance That Is in Suspended (Resumable) State

To debug an instance in Suspended (resumable) state, open the orchestration instance in the Orchestration Debugger and choose the Resume in Debug Mode option under the Debug menu, which will cause the orchestration instance to go into "In Breakpoint" state. You can then debug the orchestration instance as you would normally do.

Setting an Instance-Level Breakpoint

Any breakpoint that is set while debugging an instance is considered an instance-level breakpoint. Setting an instance-level breakpoint will not affect the future instances of a given orchestration class. During a debugging session, that is, after you have attached an orchestration instance to the debugger, you can set a breakpoint on any shape. Setting a breakpoint using this approach will set the instance-level breakpoint. This breakpoint is for the life of the specific orchestration instance.

> **NOTE**
>
> Instance-level breakpoints will not be affected by attaching and detaching to a particular orchestration instance.

1. If you haven't already, run the example mentioned in the "Replay Mode Debugging" section by following steps 1–19.
2. Set a class breakpoint on the orchestration instance (refer to the section titled "Setting a Class-Level Breakpoint to Debug in Live Mode").
3. Execute an orchestration instance by copying the file PO100000.xml from the `C:\DebugExample` folder to the `C:\DebugExample\Input` folder.
4. Open HAT and choose Service Instances from the Operations menu and run the query. This will display all the orchestration instances that are currently running.
5. Choose the orchestration instance on which you have previously set a class level breakpoint; the status of this instance will be "In Breakpoint." Right-click this orchestration instance and choose Open in Orchestration Debugger.
6. Orchestration debugger displays the orchestration instance. From the debugger window, choose Attach from the Debug menu. The orchestration instance is then attached to the debugger.
7. Right-click any shape in the orchestration where you would like to set an instance level breakpoint (see Figure 16.5).

You can choose to set as many instance-level breakpoints as the number of shapes in the orchestration. After setting the breakpoints, you can resume debugging after inspecting the values of the messages and ports.

What Cannot Be Debugged?

Following are the restrictions to keep in mind while using the orchestration debugger:

- You will not have the capability to debug inside the message construction; however, the message construction block itself can have a breakpoint.
- You will not have the capability to debug inside the atomic orchestrations.

- You will not have the capability to set a breakpoint inside the atomic scope.
- You will not have the capability to set a breakpoint on the Group shape; however, it is allowed to have breakpoints on orchestration shapes inside the Group shape.
- You will not have the capability to set a breakpoint on the compensation block; however, the actions inside the compensation block can have a breakpoint set.
- You will not have the capability to set a breakpoint on the catch block; however, the actions inside the catch block can have a breakpoint set.

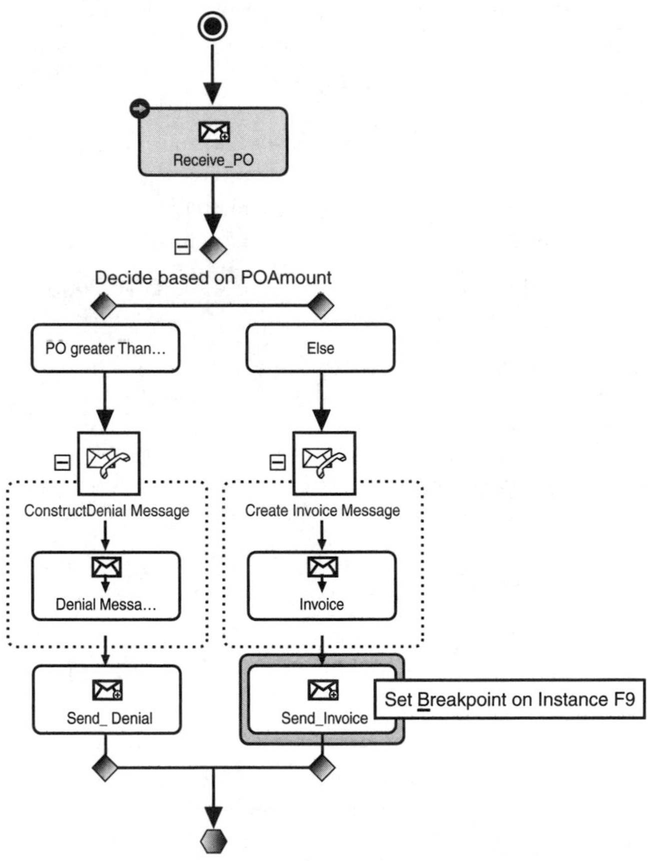

FIGURE 16.5 Setting an instance-level breakpoint in Orchestration Debugger.

Remote Debugging

You can debug orchestration on a remote server from a machine that has Administration tools installed. You should also be part of BizTalk Server Administrators NT group on the machine where BizTalkMsgBoxDb exists.

For error propagation from the remote machine to the client debugger machine, you need to modify the BTSNTSvc.exe.config file located in the INSTALLDIR of the BizTalk Server. You need to add an XML element under system.runtime.remoting, as depicted in Listing 16.1.

LISTING 16.1 Propagating Errors During Remote Debugging

```
<system.runtime.remoting>
<CustomErrors Mode ="off"/>
```

Tracking BizTalk Applications

Tracking an application is an important aspect of any business. Tracking the systems help the businesses to resolve issues that can arise when dealing with trading partners. Tracking helps address important customer queries, such as When will an order be fulfilled? Have you received a certain order yet? Tracking provides a capability to understand and troubleshoot when an error occurs and save messages for further analysis by the programmers when a problem occurs. You can also measure performance and usage trends. This tool will help you find the messages based on the schemas, ports, parties, and promoted properties.

A default level of tracking is turned on for any developed orchestration. However, the message body tracking is not turned on by default for performance reasons. Developers and administrators also have the capability to configure how much they would like to enable tracking per BizTalk application. Tracking information is saved in a SQL Server database called BizTalkDTADb (in a custom configuration, the name of the database may vary).

Whenever a message is received by BizTalk server, a corresponding pipeline gets executed based on the subscription. This message will then be properly routed either to a pipeline or to an orchestration, based on the user configuration for the BizTalk application. When a Service (pipeline or an orchestration) is executed, a GUID is created for each Service.

Although most of the events are tracked by default, inbound and outbound message bodies are not tracked by default. However, message tracking can be turned on in the live environment without taking down the running application. Following are the events that are tracked by default.

- Service start and stop events
- Orchestration events required by the debugger
- Message send and receive events

There are two types of services: orchestrations and pipelines. To get a better understanding of the inner workings, let us examine a simple scenario. In this scenario, a message is received by an orchestration through a receive pipeline and then the message is processed and sent through a send pipeline. Three service instances and four message instances are created. A service instance is created when the receive pipeline is executed; an orchestration instance is then invoked, which processes the message that was parsed and submitted to the BizTalk message box database by the receive pipeline. On completion of the processing, the orchestration generates a message that will be subscribed by the send pipeline. A service instance consumes a message instance and generates the processed message instance to be consumed by the next subscriber. Refer to Figure 16.6 to get an understanding of how the processing occurs and when a service instance and message instance are created.

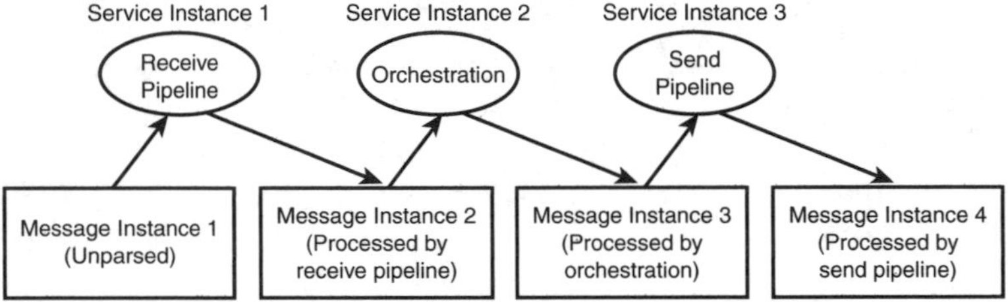

FIGURE 16.6 Understanding the service instances and message instances.

Both service instances and message instances will acquire various states during the processing phase. See Table 16.2 for the various states and the description of each state.

TABLE 16.2 Instance States

Instance State	Description
Active	Instance is running.
Suspended (Resumable)	Instance is suspended but can be resumed.
Suspended (Not Resumable)	Instance is suspended and cannot be resumed.
In Breakpoint	Service instance has hit a breakpoint and is still active, ready to be attached to the debugger.
Dehydrated	Instance is persisted to the database.
Completed with discarded messages	Instance completed but there are messages that are routed to the instance after instance completion.
Ready to run	Service instance that has not yet started but is ready to run.

Because HAT allows access to business data and information, for security purposes you should grant permissions to view the information that a specific user needs to perform a specific task. For most of the tasks, you must be a BizTalk Server administrator to access data through the HAT views. Table 16.3 consolidates the permission requirements for the various views provided in the HAT.

TABLE 16.3 Security Requirements for HAT

HAT Views/Actions	Security Requirements
Instance Activity view	Member of BizTalk Server Administrator NT group
Results view	Member of BizTalk Server Administrator NT group
Tracking Options view	Member of BizTalk Server Administrator NT group
Browse health monitoring cube	Member of BizTalk Server Administrator NT group
Suspend/Terminate instances	Member of BizTalk Server Administrator NT group
Save message bodies	Member of BizTalk Server Administrator NT group
Archiving/purging messages from the MessageBox database	Member of the db_owner role in the MessageBox database
Archiving/purging messages from the Tracking database	Member of the db_owner role in the Tracking database
Always track all properties	Member of the BTS_Admin_User SQL role in the Configuration database. BTS_Admin_User SQL role must have SELECT and UPDATE permissions to the bt_Properties and bt_DocumentSpec tables in the Configuration database.

Configuring BizTalk Application for Tracking

You can configure tracking options on pipelines, orchestrations, and policies for rules along with Message properties. Because tracking involves processing overhead, choosing the amount of data to be tracked should be weighed against the performance requirements of your BizTalk application.

16

> **TIP**
>
> You can sort the results list by clicking the header of the column you want to sort on in all the Configuration view options.

Configuring Tracking Options for Pipelines

Pipelines are the means for processing the messages that are received and sent through a BizTalk application via receive and send ports. To configure pipelines for tracking, open the BizTalk Server Health and Activity Tracking UI and from the Configuration menu choose Pipelines.

All deployed pipelines will be displayed in this view, which includes the default BizTalk pipelines as well as custom pipelines. For each pipeline there are events and data to be tracked. Service start and end events and message start and end events are tracked by default. You can track the message bodies for inbound or outbound messages or both by choosing the appropriate check boxes. You can choose multiple pipelines by Ctrl-clicking or Shift-clicking more than one pipeline. You also can deselect the defaults for performance reasons; however, no information will be tracked for those pipelines.

Configuring Tracking Options for Ports

Very often, a pipeline is used in one or more applications across one or more ports. When you configure the tracking on the pipeline, all ports using the pipeline will be tracked. However, it may not be a business requirement to track all such pipelines; in such cases, you can set tracking options on specific ports without configuring the pipelines. If a single pipeline is used in many ports, setting tracking options at the port level enables you to track messages for specific flow.

In our example in the Replay mode debugging, we used default BizTalk pipeline Microsoft.BizTalk.DefaultPipelines.XMLTransmit for both the send ports (`PODenySendPort`, `PO-InvoiceSendPort`). You also can track the message body on only one of the ports (`PODenySendPort`). To do so, follow these steps.

1. If you haven't already, run the sample described in the "Replay Mode Debugging" section earlier in this chapter.
2. Open Visual Studio; choose BizTalk Explorer from the View menu. Browse to your BizTalkMgmtDb node and expand Send Ports node.
3. Right-click `PODenySendPort` and choose Edit from the context menu.
4. In the configurations pane, click Send, as shown in Figure 16.7.
5. Under General, check the Before Send and After Send check boxes for Tracking Type. Then click OK.

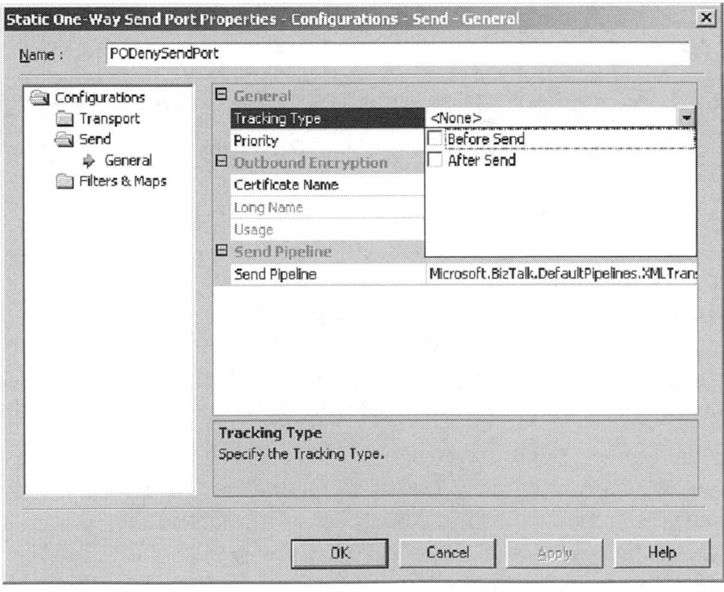

FIGURE 16.7 Configuring tracking options on the send port.

The preceding steps will ensure that all the message bodies are tracked before they reach the send port (`PODenySendPort`) and after they are processed by the send port (`PODenySendPort`). Note that the message bodies processed by `PO-InvoiceSendPort` are not tracked. You can similarly set the tracking options on the receive port. You can save the message bodies to troubleshoot issues or to resubmit the message. Refer to "Saving the Message Body" section for saving the message bodies.

When a message is suspended because it is invalid, or if no host is expecting the message, the message may be placed in the suspended queue without being tracked. If you terminate this message, there will be no record of it. Message-body tracking is not equivalent to legal tracking and does not support nonrepudiation. Message bodies remain in the `BizTalkMsgBoxDb` database, and the database is automatically purged periodically via scheduled SQL jobs. If you have a need to save any of the data, you must archive it before the database is purged.

Configuring Tracking Options on Orchestrations

To configure orchestrations for tracking, open BizTalk Server Health and Activity Tracking UI and choose Orchestrations from the Configuration menu.

All deployed orchestrations will be displayed in this view. For each orchestration there are events and data to be tracked. Service start and end events and Message start and end events are tracked by default along with the orchestration events required by the orchestration debugger. You can choose to track the message bodies for inbound or outbound messages, or both, by choosing the appropriate check boxes. You can choose multiple orchestrations by Ctrl-clicking or Shift-clicking more than one deployed orchestration. You also can deselect the defaults for performance reasons; however, no information will be tracked for those orchestrations. If the orchestration events (required by Orchestration Debugger) option is unchecked, and no breakpoint on class is set for that orchestration (see the "Debugging a BizTalk Application" section), no events will be tracked and the debugger renders orchestration with no action information.

16

Configuring Tracking Options on Rules Policies

To configure tracking on business rules policies, open the BizTalk Server Health and Activity Tracking UI and from the Configuration menu choose Policies. The UI presents you with all the deployed policies that can be configured for tracking. By default, nothing is tracked. Refer to Chapter 11, "Developing Rules" to get a good understanding of business rules. You will be able to track the fact activity, the rules that are fired, conditions that were evaluated, and the agenda updates. Figure 16.8 shows how to set tracking options on business rules policies.

Configuring Tracking Options on Message Properties

Tracking message properties enables you to quickly narrow the search for a specific message based on the message property. For example, you can promote a POID field and search for a specific purchase order number. To configure tracking on message properties, open the BizTalk Server Health and Activity Tracking UI and from the Configuration menu choose Message Properties. All the deployed schemas, including global promoted properties used by BizTalk, can be seen in this view. All the message properties for a given schema that can be tracked are displayed in the lower pane. Tracking can be configured on the Document schema or a Property schema; if a message property is selected to be tracked on a Property schema, the message property of all Document schemas referring to the Property schema will be tracked.

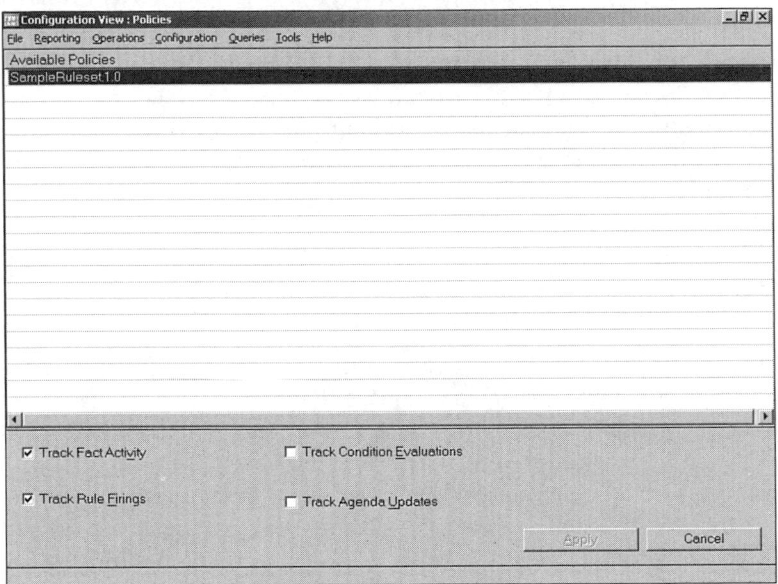

FIGURE 16.8 Configuring tracking on business rules policies.

NOTE

A promoted property may contain sensitive data, and if the property is tracked, this data can be viewed by any user with permissions to run HAT. If you apply the `isSensitive` attribute to any sensitive properties in a Property schema, that property is no longer visible in the Message Property tracking configuration selections.

Tracking the Path of a Message

It is important for businesses to find out what processing steps were taken on a given message. HAT provides an easy way to navigate the path taken by the message inside the BizTalk application. Message Flow view in HAT helps you navigate through the path that was taken by the message. Message Flow view is available by right-clicking the context menu of any service or message instance via Operations or Reporting views that are available in the HAT main menu.

To view the processing steps taken by a message, choose any service instance from the results pane of the Queries, Most Recent 100 Services from the Main menu. Right-click the instance and choose Message Flow from the context menu and navigate through the links.

To understand how the message flow helps navigate the message path, take a look at the following example:

1. If you haven't already, run the sample described in the "Replay Mode Debugging" section.
2. Open HAT; from the Queries menu, choose Most Recent 100 Services.
3. Our example generates three service instances, one each for the receivepipeline, orchestration, and send pipeline. Locate the receive pipeline, right-click it, and choose Message Flow.
4. You will see the Message Flow window (see Figure 16.9). In this window note that you can view important information regarding this service instance along with the message activity for the service instance. You will notice where the message was coming in from and where it is destined to (URL and Port) and the related details.

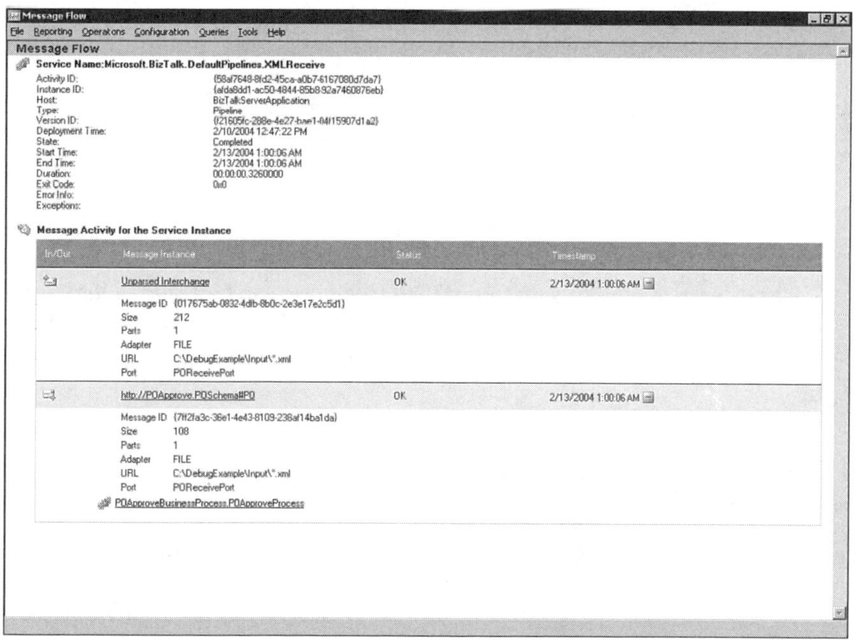

FIGURE 16.9 Message flow of an instance.

5. Click the `PoApproveBusinessProcess.POApproveProcess` link in the outgoing message activity section.

6. Because an orchestration was involved in this processing step, there is a Switch to Orchestration Debugger option available in this window (see Figure 16.10).

7. Switch to Orchestration Debugger by clicking the Orchestration Debugger link located under main menu of the window. Here you can debug the orchestration instance in the Replay mode.

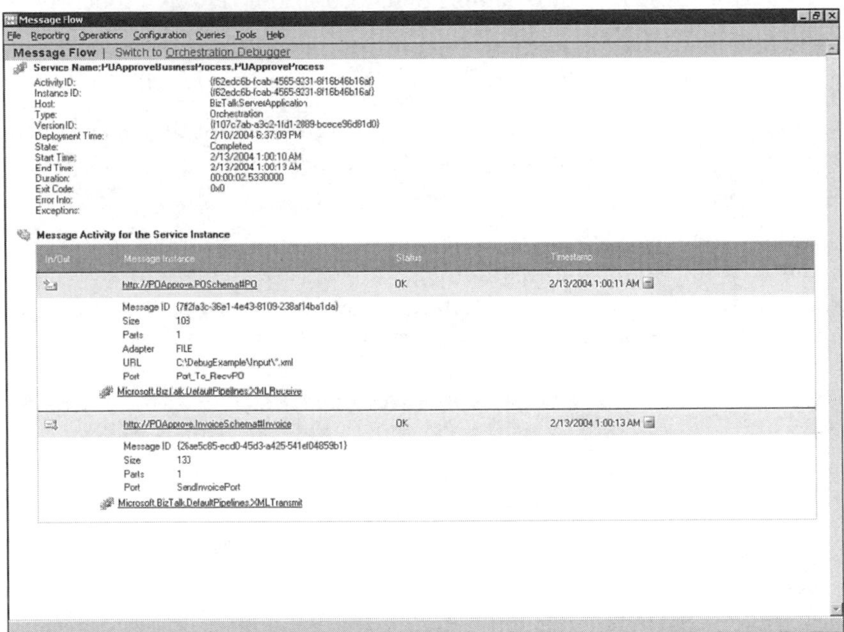

FIGURE 16.10 Message flow of service instance (switch to Orchestration Debugger).

8. To switch back to message flow, choose Switch to Message Flow from the Debug menu.

9. You will see the Message Flow window. Click the `Microsoft.BizTalk.DefaultPipelines.XMLTransmit` link in the outgoing message activity section.

10. Because that is the last step in this message activity, there is no link in the outgoing message activity section.

In the preceding steps, you have learned how to navigate the path taken by the message inside a BizTalk user application.

Tracking EDI Data

To view the properties of Electronic Data Interchange (EDI) documents and their processing information, open HAT and choose EDI Reports from the Reporting menu option. You can view the details of all the EDI documents that were processed on your system. The information of EDI documents is stored in BizTalk EDI Adapter database. You can choose to filter based on the direction of the message (send or receive), time, status, and the EDI schema. You can also view details of the message by choosing the EDI Details right-click context menu; this will present you with the EDI Details view (see Figure 16.11). In the Details view are four tabs. When an error occurs, the error details are presented in this view. There is also a Show EDI Message button in this view, which when chosen opens and displays the message in Microsoft Notepad.

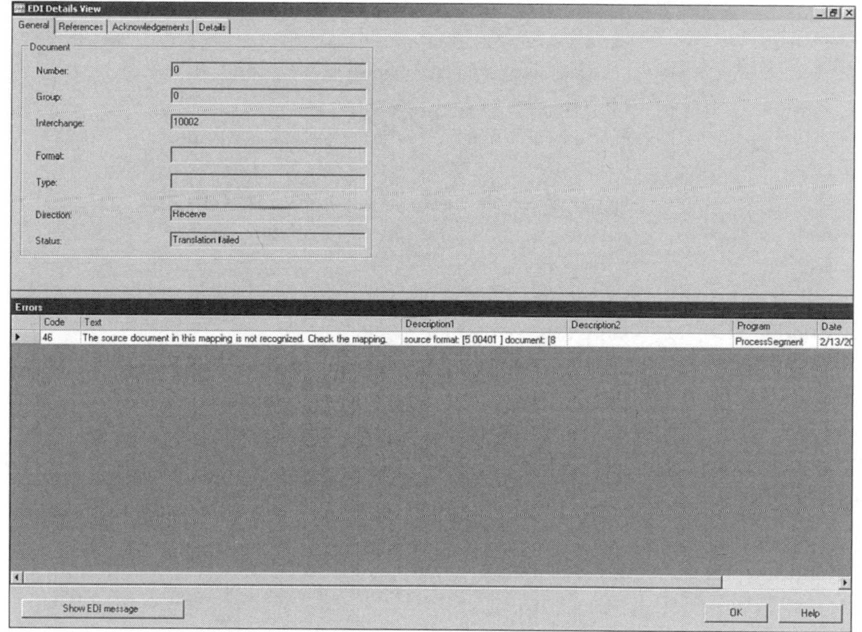

FIGURE 16.11 EDI Details view.

Troubleshooting the Problems with BizTalk Application

When a BizTalk user application doesn't work as expected, you can diagnose the problems using Operations view. Operations view presents you with the real-time data that is being processed by BizTalk. The Operations: Service Instances window displays all the orchestrations that are not yet completed; the state of the orchestration instances can be any of the states described in the Instance States table. (Refer to Table 16.2). The Operations: Messages window displays all the messages that are under processing in the message box.

When services instances get suspended, to diagnose the reason for failure, you can choose the Message Details or Service Details from the right-click context menu option on a given instance.

You can narrow the search in the Operations view by choosing the appropriate header column drop-down menu.

The Service Instances option from the Operations menu option presents a pivot table, and you can use standard pivot table drag-and-drop features to add or remove the columns from the view. The default fields presented are explained in Table 16.4.

TABLE 16.4 Operations: Service Instances View

Column Name	Description
Service Name	Name of the orchestration service
Assembly Name	BizTalk Assembly that contains the orchestration service
Service Class	Orchestration or a messaging service
Status	Current state of the service
MsgBox Server	Name of the machine where the BizTalk MsgBox is located
MsgBox DB	Name of the BizTalk Message Box database
Host	Name of BizTalk Host that is currently processing the service
Activation Time	Activation time of the service (local time)
Error Code	Error code (if any)
Error Category	Error category (if any)
Error Description	Error description (if any)
Last Processing Server	Which particular BizTalk Server was processing when an error was encountered
Pending Job	Any pending job
Pending Job Submit Time	Time the pending job was submitted (local time)
Service Instance ID	GUID representing the Service Instance

During processing of messages by BizTalk Server, orchestrations and messages attain various states. Table 16.5 depicts various states attained by the services and their transitions upon applying a certain operation.

When a service attains Suspended (resumable) state either because of a transport failure or for some other reason, you can either terminate, resume, or attach to a debugger by choosing Terminate Service, Resume Service, or Orchestration Debugger, respectively, from the context menu. If the issue is because of the transport failure, you can correct the transport issues or change the send port to a different transport and resume the service. The message will than be successfully processed.

TABLE 16.5 State Transitions shows the state attained by the service after a specific operation is performed.

Starting State of the of the Service	State Attained After the Operation Is Applied						
	Active	**In Breakpoint**	**Dehydrated**	**Suspended**	**Terminated**	**Pending Terminate**	**Pending Suspend**
In Breakpoint	Choose to Continue from debugger		Stop BizTalk NT Service (Btsntsvc)			Choose to Terminate from context menu	Choose to Suspend from context menu
Ready to Run				Choose to Suspend from context menu	Choose to Terminate from context menu		
Active			Stop BizTalk NT Service (Btsntsvc)			Choose to Terminate from context menu	Choose to Suspend from context menu
Dehydrated				Choose to Suspend from context menu	Choose to Terminate from context menu		
Suspended (resumable)	Resume service from context menu	Resume in breakpoint from debugger			Choose to Terminate from context menu		
Suspended (Not resumable)						Choose to Terminate f rom context menu	
Completed with discarded messages						Choose to Terminate from context menu	
Pending Suspend		Attach can be attempted but should eventually fail	Stop BizTalk NT Service (Btsntsvc)	Request processed	Terminate will work only when instance is dehydrated		
Pending terminate		Attach can be attempted but should eventually fail	tSop BizTalk NT Service (Btsntsvc)		Request processed or nstance dehydrated		

16

Saving the Message Body

HAT lets you save the tracked message bodies. (See the "Configuring BizTalk Application for Tracking" section earlier in this chapter to set the tracking options). Saving the message body can be done in various views. In Reporting view, you can save a message by right-clicking a service instance or a message instance and selecting Save All Messages from the context menu. In Operations view, you can save a single message when it is still available in the BizTalkMsgBoxDb; that is, before all referencing service instances have finished. When an instance goes to Suspended (not resumable) state, you have the capability to save and resubmit the message.

When you save messages, to distinguish which messages are grouped together, it will be helpful to specify different folders for messages from different orchestrations or pipelines. HAT saves the message parts and message context separately in a different file. If your message contains multiple parts, each part is stored in a separate file. However, all the messages are saved prefixed with the message ID, making it easy to group them together. In our example described in the "Configuring Tracking Options for Ports" section, after configuring the send port (PODenySendPort) tracking settings on, follow these steps to understand how the message body can be saved:

1. Execute an orchestration instance by copying the file PO100000.xml from the C:\DebugExample folder to the C:\DebugExample\Input folder.
2. Open HAT; choose Most Recent 100 Service Instances from the Queries menu option.
3. Locate the most recent service with the service name Microsoft.BizTalk.DefaultPipelines.XMLTransmit, right–click, and choose Save All Tracked Messages from the context menu.
4. Notice the warning dialog box about saving to a secure destination. Choose OK.
5. Browse to a secure folder, or create one in the dialog box presented and choose OK.

You will notice there are four files saved (message and its associated context before and after the send port). The file with _part.out extension is the actual message and the file with _context.xml contains the message context information. See the following code:

```
{MsgID}_<MessagePartID>_part.out
{MsgID}_context.xml
```

CAUTION

If you track outbound on-the-wire message bodies, all the transport properties are removed from the context of the tracked message body. In addition, properties from inbound transports will be removed from the context of the tracked message body.

If you try to save message on the messages that are not tracked, you will see a Web page error dialog box.

Finding the Messages

It is very useful for businesses to be able to find a message quickly in a complex deployment. To retrieve messages either by tracked message properties or BizTalk application information, you can use Find Message view. In this view, you can find messages based on the document schema and then further filter the messages based on routing properties and/or message properties. Routing properties consist of port and party information. Filtering is available by date range of the processed message. You can also narrow down the search to a specific message property; however, that property must have been previously configured for tracking. You can use up to five promoted property conditions to filter the results. There is an implicit AND clause between multiple conditions, so the data returned matches all the conditions. Promoted properties from the schema are used to populate list fields. To specify a bounding range, you can query the same property in multiple fields. For example, you can perform the following query:

```
POAmount < 1000
POAmount > 200
```

The resultant list is a dynamic set that displays the tracked message properties as separate columns. The value for these columns will be blank for untracked data, if the tracking is turned on in a later stage (see Figure 16.12).

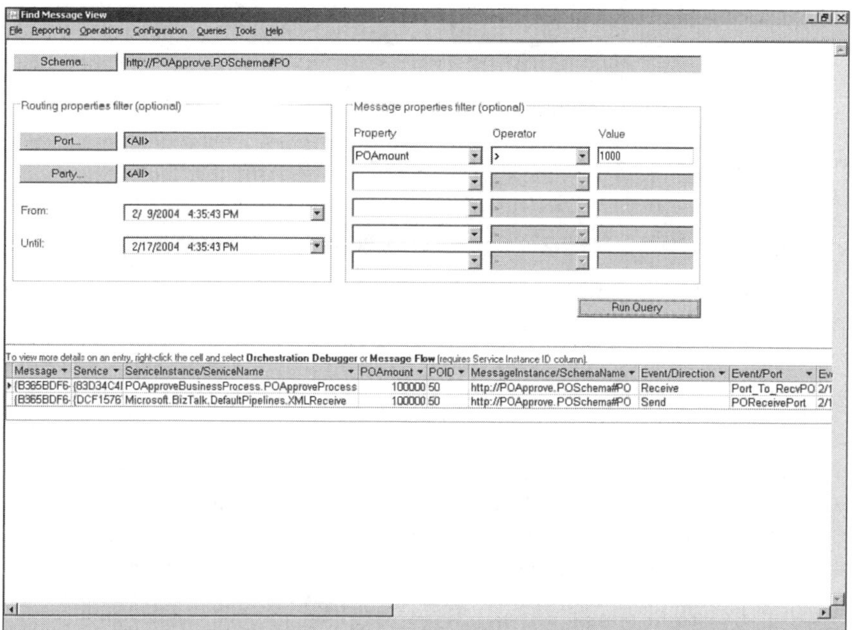

FIGURE 16.12 Find Messages view.

Setting Tracking Options at Host Level

If you have multiple hosts and would like to set tracking settings on or off, open the BizTalk Server Administration tool from Start, All Programs. Browse to the host you would like to set the tracking options on, choose Properties from the context menu, and set the Host Tracking check box (see Figure 16.13).

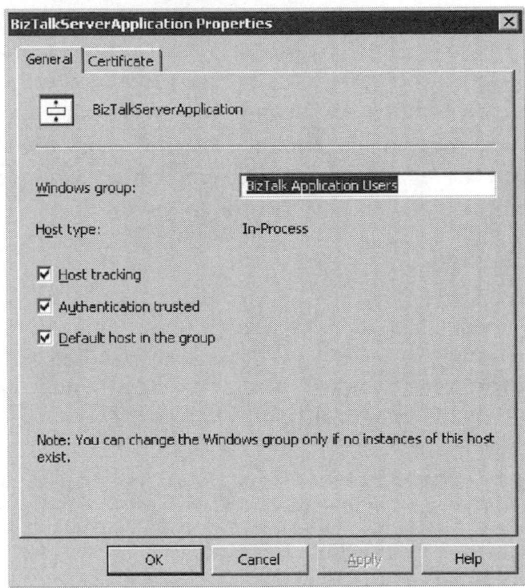

FIGURE 16.13 Set Tracking options on BizTalk Server Host Application.

> **NOTE**
>
> You must have db_securityadmin privilege on BizTalkDTADb to be able to set the Host Tracking option.

Service and Message Metrics

You can create the service and message metrics to have an aggregated view on the service events or messages; however, BizTalk Analysis database must have been configured during the configuration phase of the BizTalk product setup. After you have running BizTalk applications, follow these steps to get a snapshot of service and message metrics:

1. From the Start menu, open SQL Analysis Manager located under All Programs/Microsoft SQL Server/Analysis Services.
2. Navigate to the analysis database on the server configured during the installation of the BizTalk Server.

3. Expand the Cubes and process Message Metrics or Service Metrics by right-clicking the cube and choosing to process.

4. Open HAT; Choose Service or Message Metrics from the Reporting menu. See Figure 16.14 displaying the Aggregation view with Message Metrics.

NOTE

The Service and Message Metrics views access the current contents of the cubes. If you want to look at the latest data, these cubes need to be processed each time you use them. You can either manually process the cubes or create a Data Transformation Services (DTS) package and schedule it to run regularly.

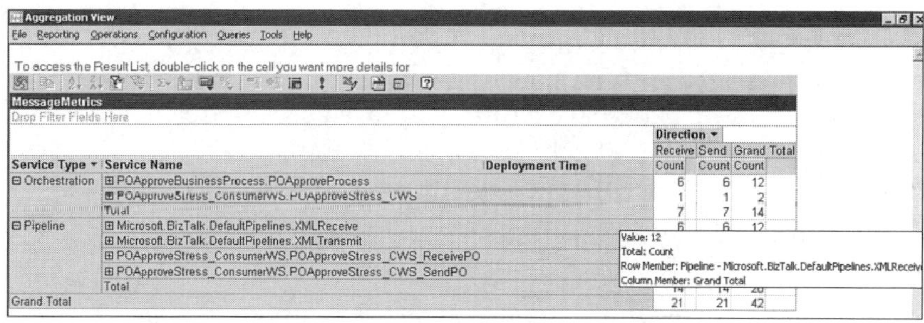

FIGURE 16.14 Aggregation view showing Message Metrics.

Archiving Tracking Database

Because the tracking data grows along with the business, typical enterprises archive their tracking data just like any other SQL database. Tracking information is stored in `BizTalkDTADb`; however, the message bodies are stored in the `BizTalkMsgBoxDb`. There are references in `BizTalkDTADb` that point to the actual message bodies in the `BizTalkMsgBoxDb`. If you want to purge the `BizTalkDTADb`, you can refer to the Purge tool located at `[INSTALLDIR]\SDK\Samples\Admin\Database Maintenance\` and develop appropriate script to run against your implementation.

Viewing the Archived Data

By default, the Health and Activity Tracking UI is configured to view the live data, the data available in BizTalkDTADb. Although live data helps you in monitoring the services and troubleshooting the issues, it may be necessary at times to view the archived data. To view the archived data, you can point HAT to the appropriate tracking archive database by setting the archived database in the Preferences dialog box available under the Tools menu. Analyzing archived data enables businesses to examine the trends and formulate business strategies based on the trends.

Creating and Saving Custom Tracking Queries

There are about 10 queries that come out-of-the-box when you install BizTalk Server; however, programmers and business analysts might want to create their own queries to analyze the tracked data. Fortunately, it is very easy to build a custom query and save it for later use.

Launch the Health and Activity tool and choose any query from the Queries menu. Click the Show Query button. You will notice the SQL code for the query you have chosen. To create custom queries, choose the Query Builder option on the Reporting menu. In this window you can form a SQL query with a combination of SQL code and dragging and dropping the appropriate SQL views from SQL views pane to the SQL query pane. You can also save the custom queries to the default location at `[INSTALLDIR]\Tracking\Queries` directory. `[INSTALLDIR]` refers to `C:\Program files\Biztalk 2004` in a default installation. To expand and/or customize the Queries menu; you can also point to more than one directory to search for queries by setting the directories to be searched with a comma delimiter. Setting the search path for queries is available on the Preferences dialog box under the Tools menu. After you have created and saved custom queries, by making changes to the search path, the UI will add the new entries and display all the custom queries you have created along with the default queries.

Summary

In this chapter you have learned how to debug orchestrations in two modes: Live mode and Replay mode. You have also learned how to configure and track BizTalk Messages, Pipelines, Orchestrations, and Policies. Finally, you learned how to write your own queries and how to add them to the Tracking User Interface.

CHAPTER 17

Management

IN THIS CHAPTER

- Understanding BizTalk Entities
- Design Factors for Multiserver Topology
- Creating and Configuring BizTalk Entities
- WMI Programming for BizTalk Object Model
- BizTalk Server 2004 Enterprise Edition Management Pack

In many real-world scenarios, multiple BizTalk servers will be deployed in a multinode topology for high availability and performance reasons. Suppose we have deployed three BizTalk servers—one server is just receiving messages and the other two servers are processing orchestrations and sending messages. To keep this system up and running, someone needs to monitor the health of the system for failures. These failures might be due to problems with BizTalk server databases, receive locations, send ports, or hosts. One of the jobs of an administrator is to monitor these and other entities.

BizTalk administrative tasks are mainly composed of the following:

- Creating and configuring BizTalk entities
- Monitoring the health of a BizTalk server topology

Before you start learning about different tasks, let's talk about the different BizTalk entities that may need to be monitored. Many of these entities are described in greater detail elsewhere in this book in a developer-centric way. In this chapter we adopt the point of view of the administrator.

Understanding BizTalk Entities

From an administrator's perspective, a BizTalk Server solution has several kinds of manageable entities, each with its own properties and capabilities. To manage them properly, it is important for an administrator to understand how these different entities are related.

A *BizTalk Server* is a physical computer on which the BizTalk Server 2004 software is installed. It is also the entity on which host and host instances are created and configured.

A *BizTalk Server Group* acts as a container for multiple BizTalk servers. Each BizTalk server group has a single BizTalk Management database that is shared by the servers in that group.

During the creation of a new BizTalk server, you can either join an existing BizTalk server group or create a new one. If you create a new BizTalk server group, a new Management database will always be created. All the BizTalk servers grouped in a BizTalk server group share the following databases:

- BizTalk Management database
- Master MessageBox database
- Tracking database
- Tracking Analysis (OLAP) database
- BAM (Business Activity Monitoring) database
- Rule Engine database

A *host* is a container for other BizTalk entities, including orchestrations and receive and send handlers. Thus, a host can be configured to perform activities such as receiving, processing, and sending messages. There are two types of hosts:

- In-Process host—This kind of host runs within the memory space of the BizTalk service. The File, SMTP, FTP, and SQL adapters all run in this kind of host. An In-Process host can be used for receiving messages, sending messages, and processing orchestrations.
- Isolated host—As the name suggests, this type of host runs within its own memory space, which means that a separate process will be created to run such a host. Good examples are the SOAP and HTTP adapters. These adapters run under a worker process (W3P.exe) created by IIS. The BizTalk Service does not control this type of host. An isolated host can be used for receiving and sending messages, but not for processing messages in orchestrations.

If a scenario demands high performance, it is usually helpful to create different hosts for receiving, processing, and sending messages. Dedicating a host for each of these three activities essentially decouples their work queues, which helps BizTalk efficiently partition the work. This topic is explored in more detail later in the chapter.

Additionally, it can be useful to create multiple hosts for the purpose of setting up security boundaries. Different hosts can be run under different security contexts, which can be very useful when a BizTalk solution demands messaging interactions with external trading partners.

A *host instance* is the actual BizTalk Service that runs on a physical BizTalk server machine. This service comprises XLANG, MSMQT, TDDS, and BizTalk Messaging Service. These subservices are not visible to the administrator. The default installation of BizTalk Server 2004 creates one BizTalk Service (BizTalk Server Application BTSNTSvcs.exe).

You need to consider the following guidelines when you create hosts and host instances.

- A BizTalk Server can hold multiple hosts.
- A host can hold multiple host instances.
- The act of mapping a host to a BizTalk Server creates a host instance.
- A host can be mapped to one or more BizTalk Servers.
- A host can register only one host instance of a specific server.

A *receive location* is a communications endpoint that is used as an address for incoming messages. If a receive location is disabled, BizTalk Server will not be able to receive any incoming messages at that location, which will cause a server down situation. There are various reasons for disabling a receive location, such as an invalid address URI, a network connection failure, an invalid username/password, and so on.

A *send port* is a communications endpoint that is used to transmit outgoing messages. The send location is used as the address for all outgoing messages from different transports, such as File, MSMQT, SQL, SMTP, FTP, or any custom adapter.

A *send port group* is a collection of send ports used to send a message to multiple destinations.

An *adapter* is a piece of messaging middleware that exchanges messages with a system external to BizTalk. Adapters can be broadly categorized into three types:

- Transport adapters—These adapters implement transport protocols for receiving and sending messages. BizTalk Server 2004 provides out-of-the-box adapters for six transport protocols: FILE, SMTP, HTTP, SOAP, FTP, and BizTalk Server Message Queuing.

  These adapters are known as *native adapters* because they come as part of the BizTalk Server 2004 installation.
- Application adapters—These adapters are used for exchanging messages with systems or applications such as SAP and Siebel.
- Database adapters—These adapters are used for connecting to various databases such as SQL Server, Oracle, or DB2 as a source or destination for messages. BizTalk Server 2004 comes with an adapter for SQL Server.

A *receive handler* manages inbound messages and is essentially a mapping between hosts and receive locations. A receive handler is also used to configure global properties for all receive locations under that handler. These global properties can be overridden for a specific receive location.

One example is setting up firewall properties for the FTP receive handler which, by default, are the same properties for all FTP receive locations. The properties could be overridden when you create a specific FTP receive location.

You can add more than one receive handler per BizTalk server group for each adapter. Multiple receive handlers per adapter are useful to achieve the following goals:

- Security boundary—You might decide to have more stringent security requirements for the receipt of messages from the outside world. This can be achieved in part by adding a separate receive handler for the required adapter. This receive handler can then be mapped to a host with tighter security.
- High-performance requirement—In some situations, you may have to meet a binding SLA (Service Level Agreement) in the processing of all messages. In such a situation you can create receive handlers with dedicated hosts.

A *send handler* manages outbound messages and is essentially a mapping between hosts and send ports. Like a receive handler, a send handler can be used to configure global properties for all send ports under that handler. These global properties can be overridden for a specific send port.

You cannot add more than one send handler per BizTalk server group for each adapter. Scalability on the send side can be achieved by adding more BizTalk servers.

An example is setting up proxy properties for the HTTP send handler level, which by default are the same properties for all HTTP send ports. The properties could be overridden when you create a specific HTTP send port.

An *orchestration* is an executable business process that usually includes the exchange of messages with entities outside of BizTalk server. Thus, orchestration is often called *message processing* from the administrator's point of view.

Several BizTalk Server databases are installed during a complete installation of BizTalk Server 2004:

- BizTalk Management database—This database stores information about different artifacts, such as orchestrations, receive locations, send ports, party, and so on.
- BizTalk Tracking database—This database stores all business and health-related information about messages that flow through BizTalk.
- Tracking Analysis database—This database contains Health and Business monitoring OLAP cubes for monitoring.
- Enterprise Single-Sign On database—This is a credential server that stores all information about receive and send locations securely using a master-secret key.
- Business Rule Engine database—This database acts as a repository for vocabulary, rules, and policies.

- BAM Primary database—This database collects all tracking data required by Business Activity Monitoring.
- BAM StarSchema database—This database contains staging, measure, and dimension tables.
- BAM Analysis database—This database contains OLAP cubes for online and offline analysis. This database is created under Analysis Services.
- BizTalk HWS Administration database—This database contains all administration related to Human WorkFlow Services.
- BizTalk EDI database—This database stores EDI tracking and processing data.
- Trading Partner Management database—This stores meta information for Business Activity Services.

The MessageBox is the heart of BizTalk. It stores all messages and subscriptions for those messages. MessageBox also persists information about running orchestrations during the dehydration process.

During installation of BizTalk Server 2004, a MessageBox is created that is known as the Master MessageBox. This holds all subscriptions for all messages. Each BizTalk server group can have only one Master MessageBox, but can have zero or more additional MessageBoxes for improved throughput. BizTalk supports up to five MessageBoxes (including the Master MessageBox) for a given BizTalk server group.

TIP

In very high-performance scenarios, it can be advantageous to have a dedicated Master MessageBox that does not do any message processing; this can be achieved by disabling message publishing on the Master MessageBox. In this case, the Master MessageBox will hold only subscriptions and will not participate in the processing of messages.

The MessageBox holds different message queues:

- Work Queue—This queue is where work items (messages) wait to be processed. During installation, BizTalk Server creates two work queues, one for each host, namely `BiztalkServerApplicationQ` and `BizTalkServerIsolationQ`. If you add a new Host, BizTalk creates a new work queue. All work items will be enqueued/dequeued in the MessageBox by all HostInstances of host, which is configured in receive port/send port.
- Suspended Queue—This queue holds work items (messages) that did not get processed by BizTalk Server. Messages may end up in the suspended queue for various reasons such as pipeline failures or send port problems. This queue stores these work items until they have been resubmitted or deleted manually using the Health Activity Tracking tool.

So far we have discussed the different manageable entities of BizTalk Server. Now we will talk about different administrative tasks that are performed on these entities.

Design Factors for Multiserver Topology

Designing a topology for a BizTalk solution is a very broad topic. Topology will always depend heavily on the requirements of the scenario.

This section discusses general deciding factors that can affect the design of a topology, but it should not be considered a comprehensive treatment of topology design. We take a simple scenario as motivation for the topics discussed.

Scenario**:** A bank wants to process a peak load of 40 transactions per second. Further, the bank requires a highly available solution. These are very generic requirements that can be mapped to almost any enterprise solution. We will design a BizTalk Server topology based on the preceding requirements. Following are some of the important factors:

- The rate of message processing—This is one of the first things to consider before beginning topology design. In our scenario, the bank wants to process 40 transactions per second end-to-end. Some scenarios may actually require different peak rates of message receipt and processing.

  Let's assume in our simple scenario that each incoming message is processed by an orchestration that then sends out a new message. This actually requires two MessageBox hops: one between the receive location and the orchestration and a second between the orchestration and the send port. Thus, two messages will go through the MessageBox for a single transaction. We can say that the MessageBox needs to process 80 messages per second to achieve 40 transactions per second. Now based on 80 messages per second, we can start to decide the following:

  - Number of physical BizTalk Servers—This largely depends on the required rate of message processing. Adding more servers will allow a higher rate of processing, although there is less than a linear return on this investment. No mathematical rule can be applied to find out how many BizTalk servers are required to achieve your goal. Be sure to consider peak loads in addition to the normal rate of processing.

  - Number of MessageBoxes—This also largely depends on the required rate of message processing. As we add MessageBoxes, messages will be spread across multiple MessageBoxes, allowing for more efficient handling. Again, there is less than a linear return on the addition of MessageBoxes.

  - Number of Hosts—We could use a single host for receiving, processing, and sending messages. But dedicating a host for each of these tasks can help boost throughput by decoupling the work queues for each.

TIP

If a BizTalk solution has certain orchestrations that demand a higher priority than others, we can create a dedicated host for those orchestrations to ensure that they are given the computing resources they need. In general, create different hosts so that orchestrations can be spread across multiple hosts, which will help to balance the load.

- High availability—Availability is an important characteristic of all enterprise solutions. Generally, we need to have a minimum of two physical BizTalk servers in a topology so that if one server goes down, the other server can pick up the additional load.

  It is also recommended to have a SQL Server cluster for BizTalk databases. If performance requirements are high, it is recommended to have dedicated disks for the MessageBox and Tracking databases. This helps to reduce disk I/O.

Creating and Configuring BizTalk Entities

After a topology has been defined, the next job of an administrator is to create and configure the BizTalk entities that fulfill that topology.

The tasks described here are generally performed in the BizTalk Administration Console. To open this tool, click your Start menu and select All Programs, Microsoft BizTalk Server 2004. Then select BizTalk Server Administration to open the BizTalk Administration Console.

Viewing the Microsoft BizTalk Server 2004 Properties Dialog Box

Open the BizTalk Administration Console, right-click the Microsoft BizTalk Server 2004 node, and select Properties. Be sure the General tab is active, as shown in Figure 17.1.

You can modify the following properties on this tab.

- Cache Refresh—Each host instance retrieves a cache from the BizTalk Management database as BizTalk Service starts at regular cache refresh intervals. This cache interval is in seconds. The default value for the cache interval is 60 seconds.
- Enterprise SSO Server Name—This is a Master Secret SSO Server and is configured during BizTalk Server installation.
- Signing Certificate—The signing certificate has two input boxes:
  - Thumbprint—This box is used for entering the thumbprint of the signing certificate, which will be used for signing outbound documents going to trading partners. Thumbprint is a digest of the certificate and can be found in certificate details.
  - Comment—This box is used for entering comments about the certificate.

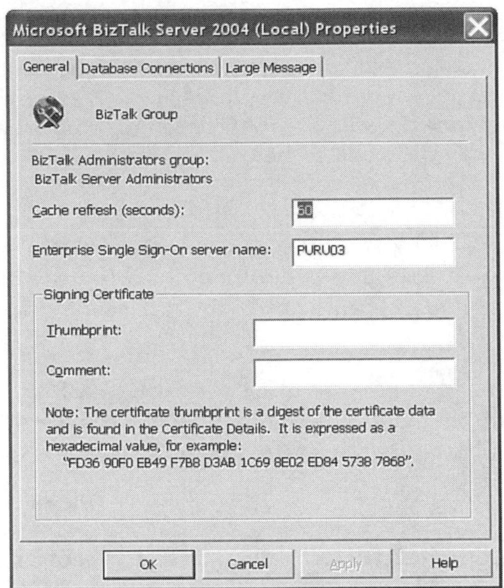

FIGURE 17.1 Microsoft BizTalk Server 2004 Properties, General tab.

> **NOTE**
>
> You must ensure that the Private key for the signing certificate has been imported in the certificate store using the BizTalk Service account.

The second tab is the Database Connections tab. On this tab you cannot modify properties. These properties are configured during installation.

Next is the Large Message tab. Messages bigger than a threshold size are considered *large messages* and handled specially. On the inbound side, large messages are broken into fragments and stored in the MessageBox as such. The size of the fragment is determined by the fragment size parameter. Large messages will always be sent to the MessageBox in a one-message-per-batch fashion—that is, batching of multiple messages does not occur. By setting the threshold too high, you may end up holding too many large messages in memory, which can limit the number of messages that you can process concurrently. On the other hand, setting the threshold too low can significantly slow down message processing because messages are not batched. The fragment size also determines how a message is stored in the database. If you set the size too high, SQL Server may need to work harder to find suitable spots for messages. On the other hand, setting it too low makes the storing and retrieval process slower because it must deal with multiple fragments. When you adjust the threshold, you should consider the following:

- What is the average size of your individual disassembled messages?
- How big are your machines, in terms of memory and processing power?
- What are throughput and latency requirements?

Creating, Deleting, and Managing MessageBox

This section covers how to create, delete, and manage MessageBox.

Create a New MessageBox

Open the BizTalk Administration Console and select the MessageBoxes node. Right-click it to select the New, MessageBox menu options as shown in Figure 17.2.

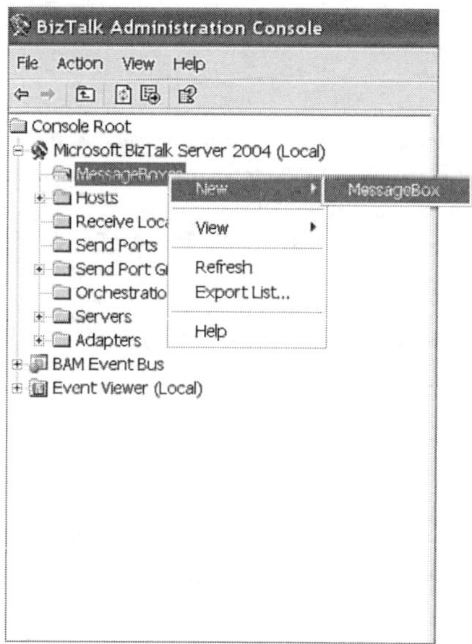

FIGURE 17.2 Create a New MessageBox.

You need to specify the database name for the MessageBox and SQL Server Name. You must also have system administration rights on SQL Server to create the database. This is required because SQL logins for the NT groups representing each host in the associated group must be created in SQL Server. If you select Disable New Message Publication, MessageBox will not be notified for arrival of new activation messages. This means messages required to create new service instances for messaging and orchestration will not be published to MessageBox. This is useful under high-performance requirements. Because of this setting, only correlated messages will be sent to that particular MessageBox.

Delete a MessageBox

On production server topology, it is generally not recommended that you delete a MessageBox, but under some situations you may need to delete one anyway. Usually, adding or deleting a MessageBox happens during the development phase to tune performance by experimenting with fewer or more MessageBoxes. After a MessageBox has been created and starts processing messages, deleting that MessageBox without first choosing the Disable New Message Publication property of the MessageBox may cause the system to lose messages. To avoid such a situation, you must ensure that no work items are left in that MessageBox, that no dehydrated orchestrations are sitting in that MessageBox, and that it has stopped accepting new messages.

NOTE

Work items in MessageBox are composed of the following:

- Activation messages that are not being picked by subscribed services such as Messaging and Orchestration.
- Dehydrated orchestrations.
- All the messages that are not picked by TDDS service and transferred to the tracking database. TDDS is a tracking service that moves messages from MessageBox to tracking service. It is important to note that the body of a message is always stored in MessageBox. You need to run TrackedMessages_Copy_BizTalkMsgBoxDb SQL job to move the body of messages from MessageBox to the Tracking database. It is important to note that moving the body of a message to the Tracking database is a CPU-intensive job that should be performed when there is low stress on the system.

To delete a MessageBox, follow these steps:

1. Enable the Disable New Message Publication check box.
2. Make sure the MessageBox is not Master MessageBox. Master MessageBox cannot be deleted.
3. Ensure that no work items are left in the MessageBox.
4. Select the MessageBox that needs to be deleted using BizTalk Administration Console and select Delete to delete it.

Manage MessageBox

One of the important tasks of an administrator is to manage MessageBox—that is, to make sure all SQL jobs related to MessageBox are up and running. If these SQL jobs are not running, MessageBox will keep on growing, which will eventually slow down the whole BizTalk Server. To monitor the size of the database file and the log file, Microsoft Operation Management Pack for BizTalk 2004 (MOM) can be used. We will discuss later how to use MOM for monitoring BizTalk Server.

To manage MessageBox, first allocate appropriate space to the data file based on the maximum amount of data you expect in MessageBox. Permit the data file to grow automatically, but place limits on the growth by specifying a maximum data file growth size file. This can be done using SQL Server Enterprise Manager MMC. Right-click the database under the Databases node and select Properties. Using DataFile, Transaction Log, and Filegroups tab, you can restrict file size growth. Allowing files to grow automatically can cause fragmentation of files. Therefore, files and filegroups should be created on available local disks, if possible. It is important to know that the log file for BizTalk MessageBox grows very fast; usually the size of the log file is three to four times the size of the database.

Creating and Deleting Host

Creating Host is the process of creating logical container for Host Instances. This section covers how to create and delete Host.

Create New Host

Open BizTalk Administration Console, select Hosts node, and then right-click to select Host, New as shown in Figure 17.3.

FIGURE 17.3 Add Host.

Enter a host name, and then enter the name of the Windows Group. The Windows Group needs to be either a local or domain group and should be created beforehand. Local groups can be created using the Computer Management Console. Open the Computer

Management Console and under Local Users and Groups, select the Groups folder. Right-click Groups and select New Group to create a new group. To create a domain group, you either have to ask the domain administrator or you need to have domain administrator privileges. The account under which BizTalk service is running should be part of this group. Select the Host type from the drop-down box, which can be either In-Process or Isolated. Then select the Host Tracking option. When this option is enabled, BizTalk loads BizTalk tracking components for processing Health Activity Monitoring and Business information for this host. Therefore, all the BizTalk entities running under this host must have read and write access to Tracking and MessageBox databases. But if Host Tracking is not enabled, it needs only write access to MessageBox. When BizTalk Server is installed, Host Tracking is enabled on the default host. BizTalk Server needs at least one host with Host Tracking enabled per BizTalk Server Group, but keep in mind the Host Tracking option is not available for Isolated Host. Host Tracking has an impact on performance when it is enabled, so it is highly recommended to have a dedicated Host for Tracking. Host can be marked as Authentication Trusted, which allows Host to put the Security ID of sender (SSID) on the context of the message. It also allows Host to submit a message with Party ID (PID) other than identity of trusted host itself.

TIP

The primary purpose of authentication trust is

- To allow the receive pipeline to resolve PID and pass that PID for authorization and Outbound Party Resolution.
- To pass Windows SID for authorization of Orchestration actions.

Last, check box it to mark Default host in the group. During installation of BizTalk Server, the Configuration Wizard creates Host, which is marked as the default host in the group. For Orchestration enlistment, the default host is used, unless the user explicitly specifies In-Process host.

After Host creation, right-click Host, go to Properties, and select the Certificate tab for the decryption certificate.

When a trading partner sends an encrypted message, Host needs to be authorized to receive encrypted messages. It must have the private key of the certificate so that it can be used to decrypt the inbound message. The Decryption Certificate tab has two input boxes:

- Thumbprint—This box is used for entering the thumbprint of the decryption certificate that will be used for decrypting inbound documents coming from trading partners. Thumbprint is a digest of the certificate and can be found in the certificate details.
- Comments—This box is used for entering the comments about the certificate.

CAUTION

The user must ensure that the private key for the certificate has been imported into the certificate store using the BizTalk Service account.

Delete Host

Open BizTalk Administration Console. Then select the host that needs to be deleted. Right-click the selected host under the Hosts node and choose Delete to delete the host.

When you select the Delete option, a message box pops up to ensure that you want to delete the host.

CAUTION

You cannot delete a host under the following circumstances:

- If Host is the default host.
- If Orchestration is enlisted for that host.
- If Host has the Tracking Host option enabled.
- If Host is configured for adapter.

Installing, Starting, Stopping, Deleting, and Configuring Host Instance

After Host is added, you can install Host Instance in Host. This section describes different operations that can be performed on Host Instance.

Install Host Instance

Open BizTalk Administration Console. Then select the appropriate Host node. Right-click Host and choose New, Instance menu options. Then select the BizTalk Server on which Host Instance needs to be run.

Click the Set Credentials button to set appropriate Windows credentials. These Windows credentials will be used to run Host Instance. The username specified for the credentials must be part of the Windows group for Host; otherwise, Host Instance might run into permission or authentication issues. The specified user account will be given Log On As Service Account rights automatically. After successfully installing Host Instance "Installation Status" of HostInstance, in the right pane of BizTalk Administration Console will be Installed. If installation fails, the status becomes Unknown. The user also must have SQL permissions on the following databases: BAM Primary Import, Management, MessageBox, Rule Engine, and Tracking.

The user needs to have the following permissions of SQL Server:

- The user must be a member of the sysadmin SQL Server role.
- The user must be a member of the securityadmin SQL Server role and a member of the db_owner SQL database role.
- The user must be a member of the securityadmin SQL Server role and a member of the db_accessadmin and db_securityadmin SQL database roles.

Start Host Instance

After Host Instance has been installed successfully, right-click Host Instance and select Start to start Host Instance; the running status becomes Running Pending. If you click the Refresh button to refresh the status, it becomes Running. There is always a delay in starting Host Instance and a delay to changes in Running Status in the Administration Console. After Host Instance is started successfully, Host can process documents.

Stop Host Instance

Host Instance can be stopped by right-clicking Host Instance when it is in Running state.

Delete Host Instance

To delete Host Instance, right-click Host Instance and select Delete. The deletion of Host Instance results in the removal of BizTalk Service (NT Service). During the deletion process a message box pops up to ensure that the user wants to delete the Host Instance.

Configure Host Instance

To configure Host Instance Properties after Host Instance is installed successfully, right-click the Host Instance and select the Properties option. The user can select the disable check box to disable the Host Instance. Also you can change the identity of Host Instance by clicking the Change button.

Enabling, Disabling, and Configuring Receive Location

This section covers how to enable, disable, and configure a receive location.

Enable and Disable Receive Location

A receive location can be in one of two states: enabled or disabled. An enabled receive location accepts inbound messages at the specified address and submits them to the MessageBox.

To enable a receive location, open the BizTalk Administration Console. Then select the receive location that needs to be enabled. Right-click the selected receive location and choose Enable.

> **NOTE**
>
> When a receive location is disabled, messages cannot be received at the corresponding address. To disable a receive location, open the BizTalk Administration Console, select a receive location, right-click and choose Disable.

Configure Receive Location

To configure the properties of the receive location, open the BizTalk Administration Console. Select the receive location that needs to be configured. Right-click the receive location and choose the properties option.

You can select the receive handler from the drop-down box on the General tab. The Schedule tab as shown in Figure 17.4 is used to configure an optional service window for the receive location. This is useful if you need to enable the receive location only during a certain time window.

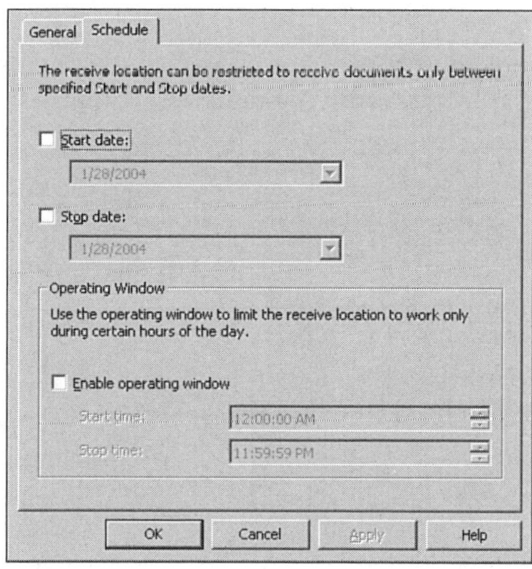

FIGURE 17.4 The Schedule tab.

Enlist, Start, Stop, and Unenlist Send Port

Send ports are fundamentally different from receive locations and carry more sophisticated administrative settings than just enable/disable. The reason is that a send port, unlike a receive location, has a subscription for messages that come through the MessageBox.

The act of enlistment creates the subscription for a send port. Then, when a send port is started, the subscription becomes active and the send port will start sending messages. If a send port remains in the enlisted (but not started) state, or is stopped (sometime after it has been started), all messages destined for it will be queued in MessageBox until that send port is started. This is very useful for administrators because it allows you to stop sending messages from BizTalk to some external system or trading partner that is (temporarily) not functioning and instead queue up those messages without losing them. This makes the solution more efficient because BizTalk would otherwise keep retrying to send the messages and eventually put the messages into the suspended queue. After the system or trading partner is back up, you can start the send port.

Enlist Send Port

To enlist the send port, open BizTalk Administration Console. Select the send port that needs to be enlisted, right-click the send port, and select Enlist.

Start and Stop Send Port

Open BizTalk Administration Console. Select the send port that needs to be started, right-click the send port, and select Start. If the send port is bound—that is, not yet enlisted—and you select the Start option (skipping the Enlist option) enlistment will happen automatically.

To stop the send port, open BizTalk Administration Console, then select the send port that needs to be stopped. Right-click the send port and select Stop.

Unenlist Send Port

The unenlistment process removes the subscription for the send port. So if any Orchestration is bound to that send port and orchestration is running, all the messages sent to that send port will end up in the suspended queue. To unenlist a send port, open BizTalk Administration Console. Then select the send port that needs to be unenlisted. Right-click that send port and select Unenlist.

Enlist, Start, Stop and Unenlist Orchestrations

This section covers how to enlist, start, stop, and unenlist orchestrations.

Enlist Orchestration

Orchestrations are similar to send ports in that they, too, have subscriptions for messages that come through the MessageBox.

After an orchestration is bound to receive locations and send ports, enlistment of orchestration can be done using BizTalk Administration Console. After enlistment is done, BizTalk creates a subscription that is configured during the binding process.

To enlist orchestration, open BizTalk Administration Console. Then select the orchestration that needs to be enlisted. Right-click the orchestration and select Enlist.

NOTE

Another important point to note is the order in which orchestration must be enlisted. One orchestration can be called by another orchestration, or one orchestration can be executed by another orchestration. In that case, all dependent (Start/Call Orchestrations) orchestrations must be enlisted first; otherwise, you will get an error if you try to enlist an orchestration that has a dependent orchestration that is not yet enlisted.

This will pop up the Enlistment Wizard Welcome screen. Click Next.

On the second screen of the wizard, you can configure Host for the receive locations by clicking the Configure button, as shown in Figure 17.5.

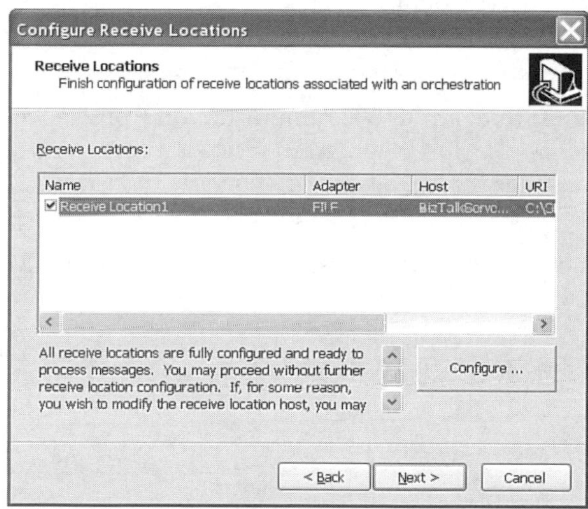

FIGURE 17.5 Configure Host for the receive location.

This will open another window where you can select the appropriate host from the drop-down box. Then click Next to finish the enlistment process.

Start Orchestration

To start the actual processing, you need to start orchestration. After orchestration is enlisted, orchestration can be started to process messages. The Start Orchestration operation will fail if the receive location is not configured correctly or the send port/send port groups are not enlisted.

To start orchestration, open BizTalk Administration Console. Select the orchestration that needs to be started, right-click the orchestration, and select Start. This will pop up a dialog box to enable all receive locations associated with orchestration. Click Yes to enable receive locations. It will open another dialog box for resuming all instances of orchestration.

Stop Orchestration

Stop Orchestration will suspend all the activation messages. Only started orchestrations can be stopped. To stop an orchestration, open BizTalk Administration Console, then select the orchestration that needs to stopped. Right-click the orchestration and choose Stop. This will pop up a dialog box to disable the receive location. Click Yes to disable the receive location. Another dialog box pops up to terminate running orchestration instances. You can select Yes to terminate a running instance of an orchestration.

Unenlist Orchestration

After an orchestration is stopped, you can unenlist the orchestration. The process of unenlistment removes the subscription from the MessageBox. To unenlist an orchestration, open BizTalk Administration Console. Then select the orchestration that needs to be unenlisted. Right-click it and select Unenlist.

Installing an Adapter

Before adding an adapter through BizTalk Administration Console, you must first register the adapter. To register an adapter, you need to create a .reg file. A sample .reg file is available in the installation folder of BizTalk Server at <*drive*>:\Program Files\Microsoft BizTalk Server 2004\SDK\Samples\Adapters\File Adapter.

To install an adapter, open BizTalk Administration Console. Then select and right-click the Adapters node as shown in Figure 17.6.

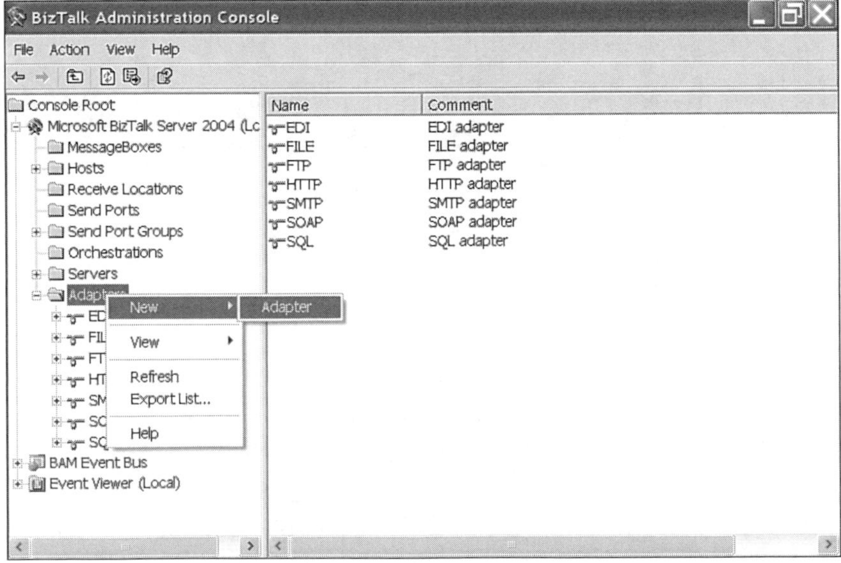

FIGURE 17.6 Select the New, Adapter options, which will open the Add Adapter Wizard.

Enter a name into the Name input box in the Add Adapter screen. Then select the appropriate adapter from the drop-down box. After the adapter is added, a receive and/or send handler will be created automatically for that adapter. Depending on the type of adapter, Host will be selected for the send and receive handler.

CAUTION

The default installation of BizTalk Server will not install MSMQT Adapter. You need to install MSMQT Adapter using the preceding steps. After MSMQT Adapter is installed, it cannot be removed because it requires a static handler.

Creating and Deleting Receive Handler

Creating a new receive handler is nothing more than associating a Host with an adapter. You can associate only one receive handler to a Host, meaning that you cannot associate the same Host with multiple receive handlers for the same adapter.

Deleting the receive handler removes the association between Host and adapter. It also removes mapping between Host and receive locations. The receive handler will not be deleted if the receive location is being configured to use that receive handler or it is the only receive handler in that group.

Create Receive Handler

Open BizTalk Administration Console. Then select the Receive Handler node of the adapter that needs to be configured, as shown in Figure 17.7.

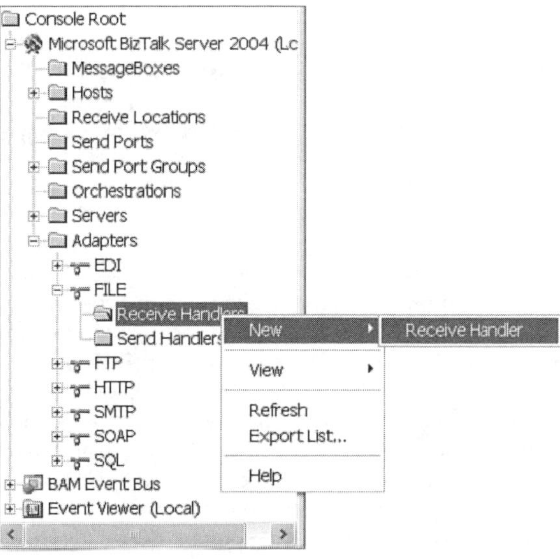

FIGURE 17.7 Right-click the receive handler and choose New, Receive Handler. This will start the Receive Handler Wizard.

17

Click Next from the Welcome to the Receive Handler Wizard screen to select the appropriate receive handler from the drop-down box. Click Next to finish the wizard.

Delete Receive Handler

To delete a receive handler, open the BizTalk Administration Console. Then select the appropriate receive handler and select Host from the right pane.

Right-click Host and select the delete option to delete the receive handler.

Configuring Send Handler

Because there is a restriction of one send handler per BizTalk Server Group, you cannot add or delete a send handler. But you can change the Host associated with a send handler. To configure the properties of a send handler, open BizTalk Administration Console and select the send handler that needs to be configured. Select Host from the right pane.

Right-click Host and select properties to change the host.

CAUTION

Note the following:

- BizTalk Server Message Queuing Adapter's Receive and Send Handler both need to be run in one Host.
- Host cannot be changed for handlers of BizTalk Server Message Queuing Adapter.
- New Receive Handler cannot be created for BizTalk Server Message Queuing.
- BizTalk Message Queuing Adapter cannot be deleted after it has been created.

All the preceding tasks are performed using BizTalk Administration Console. There is another important administrative task to accomplish—backing up BizTalk databases.

BACKING UP BIZTALK DATABASES

A database backup creates a duplicate of the data that is in the database when the backup completes. Database backups are self-contained. You can re-create the entire database from a database backup in one step by restoring the database. The restore process overwrites the existing database or creates the database if it does not exist. The restored database will match the state of the database at the time the backup completed, minus any uncommitted transactions. Uncommitted transactions are rolled back when the database is recovered. BizTalk Server provides SQL job Backup BizTalk Server, which has two steps: Backfull and Mark & Backup log. You can find this SQL job under the Jobs node in SQL Server Enterprise Manager. Also you need to specify the path where you want to take the backup. To specify the backup path, you need to edit the SQL job. To do so, double-click Backup BizTalk Server job and select the Steps tab. On the Steps tab, you will find the preceding steps. Double-click Backfull. If you do not specify a path, it will back up to the default backup location of SQL Server. It is also important to decide how often you want to run this job. One of the important deciding factors is how fast your data file and log files are growing.

Another important task of the administrator is to move solutions from development and testing through staging to a production environment. It would be a very tedious job if the administrator performed those tasks manually. BizTalk Server provides WMI classes that can be used to perform programmatically different tasks, which we will be discussing in the following section.

WMI Programming for BizTalk Object Model

Before we start to discuss WMI classes for BizTalk Object Model, let's talk about WMI. Windows Management Instrumentation (WMI) is a scalable, extensible management infrastructure included as part of Windows 2000. Through a set of object classes, applications and scripts can view and change properties, execute methods, and receive events about modeled objects. For example, WMI exposes a wealth of information about the operating system (how many processes are running, the operational state of a particular service, current processor usage, and so on) and publishes it in a common schema that is accessible locally and remotely through standard script languages. This schema file is know as an MOF file.

BizTalk Server also provides an MOF file that is located in the following directory: `<drive>:Program Files\Microsoft BizTalk Server 2004\BTSWMISchema.mof`. A human workflow services MOF file is located in the following directory location: `<drive>:\Program Files\Microsoft BizTalk Server 2004\Hws\Hws Admin Server\Bin\Microsoft.BizTalk.Hws.AdminWMIProvider.mof`. You can open these files in any editor and can view different classes and methods. Also you can use WBEMTest to enumerate different WMI classes of BizTalk Object Model. Windows Management Instrumentation (WMI) Tester, also called WBEMTest, is a general-purpose tool for viewing and modifying Common Information Model (CIM) classes, instances, and methods during the development of WMI providers and WMI applications. You can also use WBEMTest to troubleshoot WMI and programs that depend on WMI. At the Run command, type **`wbemtest`** and then connect to the root\MicrosoftBizTalkServer namespace to enumerate all classes. Make sure you select the recursive option for enumerating all classes. Another tool available to enumerate WMI classes is CIM studio. You can download this tool from the Microsoft site; the link is `http://www.microsoft.com/downloads/details.aspx?FamilyId=6430F853-1120-48DB-8CC5-F2ABDC3ED314&displaylang=en`.

Classes Provided in the BTSWMISchema.mof File

- MSBTS_AdapterSetting—This WMI class is used to register adapters.
- MSBTS_DeploymentService—This WMI class is used to deploy and undeploy assemblies from the BizTalk Management database. It is also used to export and import binding files.
- MSBTS_GroupSetting—This WMI class is used to represent information about BizTalk Server groups, such as different database names and hosting SQL Server names.

17

- MSBTS_Host—This WMI class is used to start and stop all Host instances in a given BizTalk Host. It is also used to Get/Set properties such as HostTracking, HostType, and so on.
- MSBTS_HostInstance—This WMI class is used to Install, Uninstall, Start, and Stop a specific Host instance in a given BizTalk Host.
- MSBTS_HostInstanceSetting—This WMI class is used to read properties such as Name, NTGroupName, and Configuration state.
- MSBTS_HostQueue—This WMI class is used to resume, suspend, and terminate service instances.
- MSBTS_HostSetting—This WMI class is used to set Host settings such as AuthTrusted, HostTracking, and HostType.
- MSBTS_MessageInstance—This WMI class is used to save message instances and context to files.
- MSBTS_MessageInstanceSuspendedEvent—This WMI class is used to get details about suspended service instances.
- MSBTS_MsgBoxSetting—This WMI class is used to retrieve MessageBox details, such as the MessageBox database name and IsMasterMessageBox.
- MSBTS_Orchestration—This class is used to enlist, start, stop, and unenlist orchestration.
- MSBTS_ReceiveHandler—This WMI class is used to configure receive handlers with the appropriate adapter and Host.
- MSBTS_ReceiveLocation—This WMI class is used to create, enable, and disable the receive location.
- MSBTS_ReceiveLocationOrchestration—This WMI class is used to enumerate all possible combinations on orchestrations and receive locations.
- MSBTS_ReceivePort—This WMI class is used to create and configure receive ports.
- MSBTS_SendHandler—This WMI class is used to configure send handlers with the appropriate adapter and Host.
- MSBTS_SendPort—This WMI class is used to create and configure send ports.
- MSBTS_SendPortGroup—This WMI class is used to start, enlist, stop, and unenlist send port groups.
- MSBTS_SendPortGroup2SendPort—This WMI class represents a many-many relationship between send port groups and send ports.
- MSBTS_Server—This WMI class is used to start and stop all BizTalk Services on a given server.

- MSBTS_ServerHost—This WMI class is used to map and ummap relationships between BizTalk Servers and BizTalk Hosts.
- MSBTS_ServiceInstance—This WMI class is used to resume, suspend, and terminate an instance of service.
- MSBTS_ServiceInstanceSuspendedEvent—This WMI class is used to get details of a suspended service instance, such as error description, eventid, and serviceinstanceid.
- MSBTS_TrackedMessageInstance—This WMI class is used to save message parts and context from a MessageBox or from an archived database to file.

Classes Provided in Microsoft.BizTalk.Hws.AdminWMIProvider.mof

These classes will help the administrator perform various tasks such as register action, delete activity flow, and start/stop Hws service.

- Hws_Action—This WMI class is used to register and unregister orchestration as an action.
- Hws_ActivityFlow—This WMI class is used to delete activity flow or delete all activity flows before a specified date. It also can be used to retrieve an XML representation of activity flow.
- Hws_ActivityModel—This WMI class is used to load, enumerate, and delete installed activity models.
- Hws_Constraint—This WMI class represents a single constraint in the Human Work Flow system. It also supports basic operations such as load, create, update, and delete constraint.
- Hws_ConstraintFact—This WMI class is used to enumerate and load each property of fact.
- Hws_Core—This WMI class represents global settings for Human Workflow Services such as BizTalk Server name, Tracking database name, BizTalk Server Management database, and so on.
- Hws_FactObject—This WMI class represents an object exposed by fact retriever.
- Hws_ FactRetriever—This class is used to load, create, update, delete, and enumerate a registered Human Workflow Services fact store.
- Hws_Service—This WMI class has two methods, StartService and StopService, which are used to start and stop IIS service.

Now we will program some of the most commonly used administrative tasks using WMI.

Programming Host Example

Earlier in the chapter, we saw how to create a Host using the Administration Console. Now we will use the C# programming language to create a Host programmatically. This type of script reduces the burden of manual work on the administrator and also assists greatly with the repetition of such operations over the life of a BizTalk installation.

The sample in Listing 17.1 shows how to create Host.Download CreateHost solution from Management folder. Make sure you add a reference to the System.Management.dll in your C# project.

LISTING 17.1 CreateHost.cs

```
using System;
using System.IO;
using System.Xml;
using System.Management;

public class CreateHost
{


    public static void Main()
    {


        string bts_WMINameSpace;
        string bts_HostSettingNameSpace;

// WMI NameSpace for BizTalk Server
        bts_WMINameSpace = @"root\MicrosoftBizTalkServer";
// WMI class for HostSetting
        bts_HostSettingNameSpace = "MSBTS_HostSetting";

        try
        {
            PutOptions options = new PutOptions();
            options.Type = PutType.CreateOnly;
            ManagementObject bts_AdminObject = null;
            System.Management.ObjectGetOptions bts_objOptions =
➥new ObjectGetOptions();
            // Creating instance of BizTalk Host.
            ManagementClass bts_AdminObjClass = new ManagementClass(bts_
➥WMINameSpace, bts_HostSettingNameSpace, bts_objOptions);
            bts_AdminObject = bts_AdminObjClass.CreateInstance();
```

LISTING 17.1 Continued

```
            ManagementObject appObject = bts_AdminObject;
            // Assigning Host Properties.
            appObject["Name"] = "TestHost";
            appObject["NTGroupName"] = "BizTalk Application Users";
            appObject["IsDefault"] = false;
            appObject["HostTracking"] = true;
            appObject["AuthTrusted"] = true;
            appObject["HostType"] = 1;
            appObject.Put(options);




        }
        catch(Exception e)
        {

            System.Diagnostics.EventLog.WriteEntry("WMIApplication",
➥e.Message,System.Diagnostics.EventLogEntryType.Error);
        }
    }
}
```

When run successfully, the console application will create a Host "TestHost" of the In-Process type. You can verify this by opening the BizTalk Administration Console and examining the list of hosts.

Mapping HostInstance Example

In the preceding example we saw how to create a Host. The following example (shown in Listing 17.2) shows how to map a HostInstance to a Host and start the HostInstance. This is also a very commonly performed task by an administrator.

Download CreateStartHostInstance solution from the Management folder. Make sure you add a reference to System.Management.dll.

CAUTION

See comments in the code to make appropriate changes before you run this program. Also it is important to run the preceding console application (CreateHost) before you run this application because in this example, we are using the newly created TestHost to map the HostInstance.

You need to make the following changes before running the sample code:

1. Provide the correct server name.

   ```
   bts_AdminObjectServerHost["ServerName"] = "Puru01";
   ```

2. Provide the correct Host and server name. In the following case, TestHost is the Host name and PURU01 is the server name.

   ```
   bts_AdminObjectHostInstance["Name"] = "Microsoft BizTalk Server TestHost
   PURU01";
   ```

3. Provide the correct username and password.

   ```
   user = @"MyUser";
   pwd = "test123";
   ```

LISTING 17.2 CreateHostInstance.cs

```
using System;
using System.Management;


namespace Create_and_Start_HostInstance
{
    /// <summary>
    /// Summary description for Class1.
    /// </summary>
    class AddStartHostInstance
    {
        /// <summary>
        /// The main entry point for the application.
        /// </summary>
        [STAThread]
        static void Main(string[] args)
        {
            string bts_WMINameSpace;
            string bts_ServerAppTypeNameSpace;
            string bts_HostInstanceNameSpace;
            string user;
            string pwd;
            bts_ServerAppTypeNameSpace = "MSBTS_ServerHost";
            bts_HostInstanceNameSpace = "MSBTS_HostInstance";
            // WMI NameSpace for BizTalk Server
            bts_WMINameSpace = @"root\MicrosoftBizTalkServer";
```

LISTING 17.2 Continued

```
            try
            {
                PutOptions options = new PutOptions();
                options.Type = PutType.CreateOnly;
                ManagementObject bts_AdminObjectServerHost = null;
                ManagementObject bts_AdminObjectHostInstance = null;
                System.Management.ObjectGetOptions bts_objOptions =
➥ new ObjectGetOptions();
                // Creating instance of BizTalk Host.
                ManagementClass bts_AdminObjClassServerHost = new
ManagementClass(bts_WMINameSpace, bts_ServerAppTypeNameSpace, bts_objOptions);
                bts_AdminObjectServerHost =
➥bts_AdminObjClassServerHost.CreateInstance();
// Make sure to put correct Server Name,username and // password
                bts_AdminObjectServerHost["ServerName"] = "Puru01";
                bts_AdminObjectServerHost["HostName"] = "TestHost";
                bts_AdminObjectServerHost.InvokeMethod("Map", null);

                ManagementClass bts_AdminObjClassHostInstance = new Management-
Class(bts_WMINameSpace, bts_HostInstanceNameSpace, bts_objOptions);
                bts_AdminObjectHostInstance =
➥bts_AdminObjClassHostInstance.CreateInstance();
// Make Sure you correct HostName and MachineName for HostInstance name,
                //In this case TestHost is Hostname and
➥ PURU01 is MachineName You need to replace Puru01 with correct servername.
                bts_AdminObjectHostInstance["Name"] =
➥"Microsoft BizTalk Server TestHost PURU01";

//Also provide correct user name and password.
                user = @"MyUser";
                pwd = "test123";                object [] objparams = new object[3];
                objparams[0] = user;
                objparams[1] = pwd;
                objparams[2] = true;
                bts_AdminObjectHostInstance.InvokeMethod("Install",objparams);
                bts_AdminObjectHostInstance.InvokeMethod("Start", null);




            }
```

17

LISTING 17.2 Continued

```
            catch(Exception e)
            {

                System.Diagnostics.EventLog.WriteEntry("WMIApplication",e.Message,
➥System.Diagnostics.EventLogEntryType.Error);
            }

        }
    }
}
```

After running the preceding sample code successfully, you will find HostInstance is mapped to TestHost Host. You can verify this by opening the BizTalk Administration Console. You'll find that HostInstance is mapped in TestHost Host.

Adding MSMQT Adapter Example

Sometimes a custom adapter is written for scenarios. The job of the administrator would be to add this adapter so that receive locations and send ports can be configured to use this adapter. Listing 17.3 shows how to add an MSMQT adapter using C#.

> **CAUTION**
>
> This adapter is not added during installation of BizTalk Server. After the MSMQT adapter is added, you will not be able to remove it from the adapters.

LISTING 17.3 AddAdapter.cs

```
using System;
using System.Management;

namespace WMI
{
    /// <summary>
    /// Summary description for Class1.
    /// </summary>
    class AddAdapter
    {
        /// <summary>
        /// The main entry point for the application.
        /// </summary>
        [STAThread]
        static void Main(string[] args)
        {
```

LISTING 17.3 Continued

```
            ManagementObject AddAdapter_objInstance = null;

            try
            {
                ManagementClass AddAdapter_objClass = new
ManagementClass(@"root\MicrosoftBizTalkServer","MSBTS_AdapterSetting",
➥new ObjectGetOptions());
                AddAdapter_objInstance = AddAdapter_objClass.CreateInstance();
                AddAdapter_objInstance.SetPropertyValue("Name",
➥"BizTalkMessageQueue");
                AddAdapter_objInstance.SetPropertyValue("MgmtCLSID","{9A7B0162-2CD5-
4F61-B7EB-C40A3442A5F8}");
                AddAdapter_objInstance.SetPropertyValue("Comment","MSMQTAdapter");
                AddAdapter_objInstance.Put();

            }
            catch(Exception e)
            {
                System.Diagnostics.EventLog.WriteEntry("WMIAddAdapter",e.Message,
➥System.Diagnostics.EventLogEntryType.Error);

            }
        }
    }
}
```


After running the preceding sample code, BizTalkMessageQueue adapter will be added under the Adapters node in BizTalk Administration Console. You can verify this by opening the BizTalk Administration Console.

Example for Resuming Service Instance

Sometimes a service instance may go into a suspended resumable state because either the send port has an invalid address uri or orchestration is not started. In the following example, as shown in Listing 17.4, we use VBScript to resume service instances. You can download ResumeAll.vbs from Management folder.

LISTING 17.4 ResumeAll.vbs

```
On Error Resume Next
Dim obj_BizTalkService,obj_ServiceInstances,obj_HostQueue,int_totalServicesin-
stancescount,
➥str_HostQueueName,int_Index
Dim Service_ClassID()
```

LISTING 17.4 Continued

```
Dim Service_TypeID()
Dim Service_InstanceID()

set obj_BizTalkService = GetObject("winmgmts:\\.\root\MicrosoftBizTalkServer")
set obj_ServiceInstances = obj_BizTalkService.ExecQuery
➥("select * from MSBTS_serviceinstance where servicestatus=4")
int_totalServicesinstancescount = obj_ServiceInstances.count


redim Service_ClassID(int_totalServicesinstancescount-1)
redim Service_TypeID(int_totalServicesinstancescount-1)
reDim Service_InstanceID(int_totalServicesinstancescount-1)

str_HostQueueName = "MSBTS_HostQueue.HostName=""BizTalkServerApplication"""

set obj_HostQueue = obj_BizTalkService.Get(str_HostQueueName)

If Err <> 0 Then
    call ErrHandler
End If


int_index = 0

for each instance in obj_ServiceInstances

    wscript.echo "Found suspended instance """ & instance.Properties_
➥("ServiceName") & """ on Host " & instance.Properties_("HostName")

    Service_ClassID(int_index) = instance.Properties_("ServiceClassId")

    Service_TypeID(int_index) = instance.Properties_("ServiceTypeId")

    Service_InstanceID(int_index) = instance.Properties_("InstanceId")

    int_index = int_index + 1

next

If int_totalServicesinstancescount <> 0 Then
    obj_HostQueue.ResumeServiceInstancesByID Service_ClassID,
➥Service_TypeID, Service_InstanceID, 1
```

LISTING 17.4 Continued

```
Else
    MsgBox "No Instances Resumed"
End If

If Err <> 0 Then

    call ErrHandler

End If


sub ErrHandler()

    MsgBox Err.Description & Err.Number
end sub
```

To see this script working, you need to download CreateReceiveLocationSendPort solution from the Management folder and run CreateReceiveLocationSendPort.exe console application. This application will create and start receive location and send port. Drop any xml message in the receive folder specified in receive location. After all retry counts are exhausted for the send port, the service instance for messaging will be in suspended resumable state. You can verify this by opening HAT. You will find suspended resumable service instance under Operations, ServiceInstances. Make sure you select Messaging class from the drop-down box. If the status of service instance is Delivered, Not Consumed, that means the retry count is not yet exhausted. After service goes into suspended resumable state, you can edit the send port address uri to the correct destination address. Then run the preceding script. After successful completion of the script, the message will be delivered to the destination address. In addition, the Suspended Service instance will be deleted from HAT.

We have seen so far how to use WMI programming to perform different administrative tasks. Now we will talk about another tool—Microsoft Operation Management(MOM) Pack for BizTalk Server 2004, which will assist the administrator in monitoring the health of the system and in reacting to failures in the system. Reaction can include running script and sending email or pager to the administrator to notify failures in system.

BizTalk Server 2004 Enterprise Edition Management Pack

MOM Pack is a set of predefined rules and counters that includes Messaging Engine, XLANG Engine, Enterprise Single Sign On, BizTalk databases, and Windows events.

The BizTalk Server 2004 Management pack has more than 100 rules. The most commonly used rules are as follows:

- Performance threshold rules for performance counters, such as documents received/Sec, documents processed/sec, and so on.
- Performance measurement rules for database file size.
- Windows event-processing rules for BizTalk Messaging an XLANG engine, such as when a message goes into the suspended queue.
- Windows event-processing rules for connectivity with SQL Server and Enterprise Single-Sign On Server.
- WMI event-processing rules for MessageInstance Suspended and ServiceInstance Suspended.

Installing and Configuring MOM for BizTalk 2004

Install MOM 2000 on the computer that will be used to monitor BizTalk servers. MOM can be also installed on BizTalk Server itself, but it is recommended that you install it on a computer that is dedicated to monitoring BizTalk servers.

NOTE

Make sure the user account that is used by Agent Manager Domain has administrative privileges on each BizTalk Server, including the SQL Server that hosts BizTalk Server databases. You also need to add the following local policy settings: Act as part of the OS, Create a token object, Log on as a batch job, Log on as a service. To add these local policy settings, you need to open the local security settings window under Administrative Tools and then select User Rights Assignment under Local Policies to add a user account to different policies. The user account is the account specified during installation of MOM.

Import the BizTalk Server 2004 Management Pack to the computer on which MOM is installed. The following steps can be taken to install the Management Pack:

1. Click the Start menu and select All Programs, Microsoft Operation Manager.
2. Click the MOM Administration Console. This will open the MOM MMC-Snap In.
3. Expand the rules tree and select Processing Rules Group as shown in Figure 17.8.
4. Right-click Processing Rules Group and select Import Management Pack. Click the Browse button to select the MOM pack from the appropriate media/drive. Select the default option as shown in Figure 17.9.

NOTE

If you are importing MOM pack for the first time, select the default option, or you can select the appropriate option that corresponds to the desired behavior.

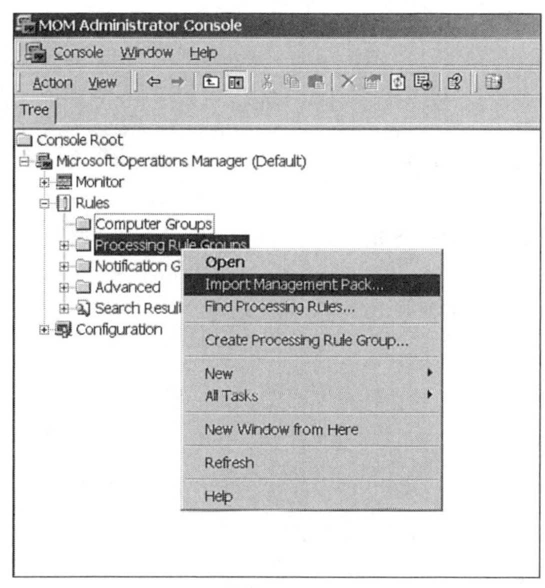

FIGURE 17.8 Import Management Pack.

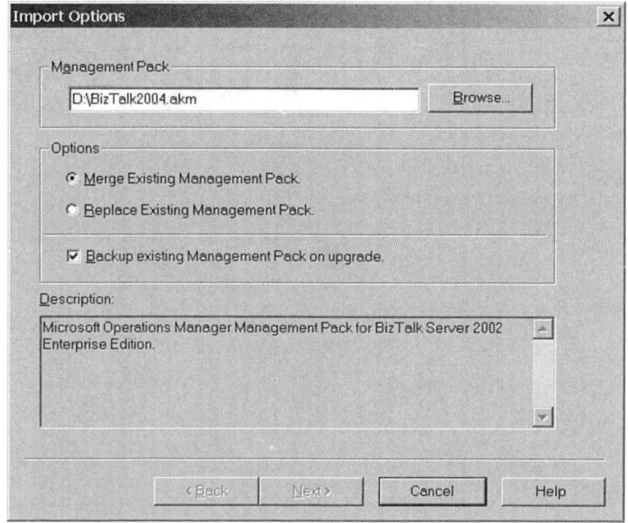

FIGURE 17.9 Import options.

After MOM pack is installed, it will create Microsoft BizTalk Server 2004 Group under Computer Groups. This group will contain all computers managed by MOM that contain the following registry key entry on each BizTalk Server:

- HKEY_LOCAL_MACHINE\SOFTWARE\Microsoft\BizTalk Server\1.0. This registry key will be used as Computer Attribute. It creates public views as well as a Processing Rules Group, such as BizTalk Server 2004 Core and Enterprise Single Sign On.

We will discuss Public Views and Processing Rule Groups later in the chapter.

Installing MOM Agent on Remote BizTalk Servers

Install MOM Agent on remote BizTalk Servers. To monitor BizTalk Servers, we need to install MOM Agent on each BizTalk Server. The function of MOM Agent is to collect monitoring data and send it to the MOM Server. Follow these steps:

1. Click the Start menu and select Programs, Microsoft Operation Manager.
2. Click MOM Administration Console. This opens the MOM MMC-Snap In.
3. Expand the configuration tree and select Agent Managers.
4. Select Consolidator in the right pane.
5. Right-click it and select Properties, as shown in Figure 17.10.

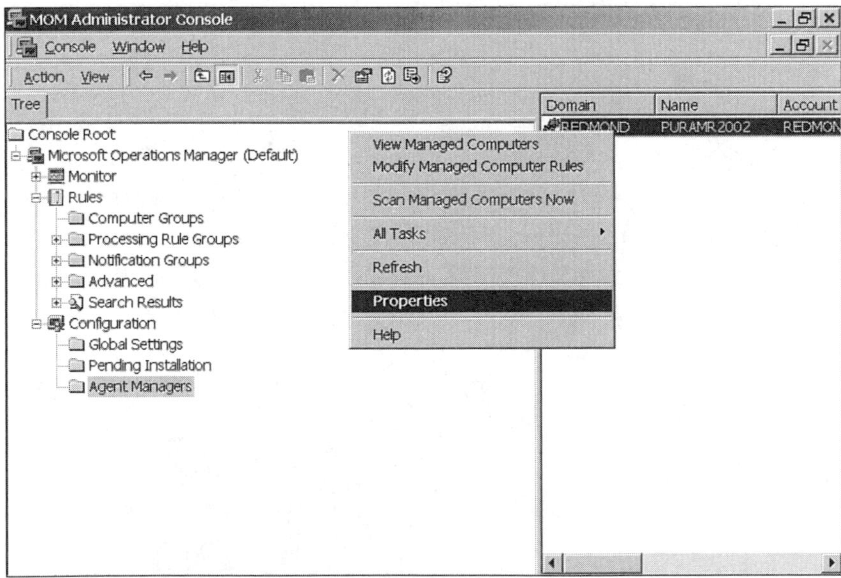

FIGURE 17.10 Consolidator Properties.

6. Select the Managed Computer Rules tab as shown in Figure 17.11.
7. Click the Add button to include the computer (BizTalk Server) that needs to be monitored.

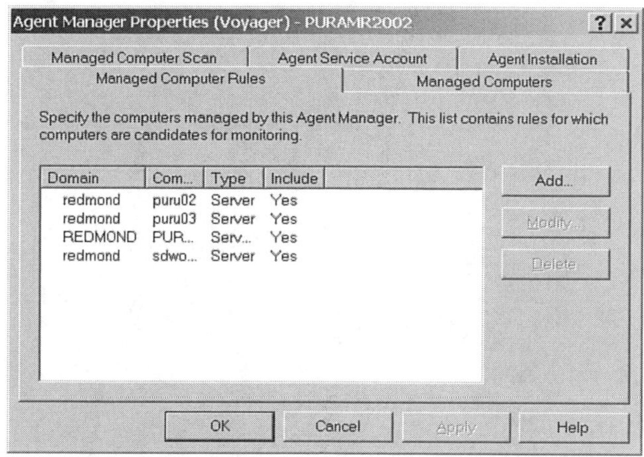

FIGURE 17.11 Agent Manager Properties.

8. Provide the correct computer name and then click Next to finish.
9. After the computer is added, you need to go to the pending installation to approve the installation of MOM Agent on the added computer.

> **TIP**
>
> You can verify if the agent is installed by clicking All Agents under the Monitor.

Public Views

Views display specific content of the MOM database. There are two types of views: public views and private views. Public views are available to anyone and are stored in the Public Views folder. Private views are available only to the user who creates those views. These views are stored in the My Views folder.

These views are updated every 15 minutes. BizTalk Server 2004 MOM pack offers views for performance counters. Some of the views are as follows:

- Orchestrations rehydrated/sec
- Orchestrations rehydrated
- Documents processed/sec
- Orchestrations-Transactional scopes committed/sec
- Orchestrations-% used physical memory
- Orchestrations-Transactional scopes aborted

- Online MessageBox databases
- Orchestrations suspended/sec
- Orchestrations-Transactional scopes compensated
- Documents suspended/sec
- Documents suspended
- Orchestrations completed/sec
- Orchestrations-% allocated private memory
- Running orchestrations
- Orchestrations completed
- Documents received
- Orchestrations suspended
- Orchestrations-Persistence points/sec
- Orchestrations-Transactional scopes compensated/sec
- Orchestrations discarded/sec
- Orchestrations dehydrated
- Orchestrations-Transactional scopes aborted/sec
- MessageBox databases connection failures
- Orchestrations-Database transactions
- Orchestrations discarded
- Runnable orchestrations
- Documents received/sec
- Documents processed

Accessing Public Views

To access views, click Start, All Programs, Microsoft Operations Manager, and then click MOM Administrator Console. Expand the Monitor tree and then the Public Views tree. Click MicrosoftBizTalkServer2004 and then select BizTalk Performance as shown in Figure 17.12.

The graphical view enables you to see the performance of your system for a given performance counter against time.

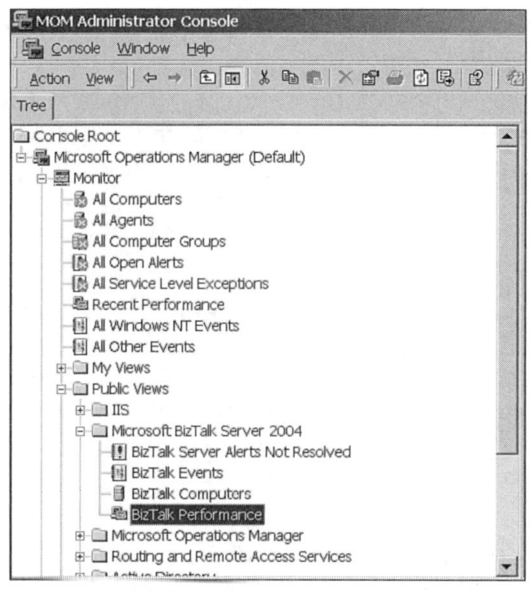

FIGURE 17.12 Access Public Views.

Processing Rules

MOM package for BizTalk Server 2004 provides some basic fully configured views out-of-the-box for Windows NT events, WMI events, and performance counters. These processing rules are categorized into three groups: Event Processing Rules, Alert Processing Rules, and Performance Processing Rules.

Event Processing Rules Usually, each error message that occurs in event log has a unique EventID, but sometimes a series of errors occur due to a failure such as the SQL Server for SSO database is down. This will cause Enterprise SSO service to be down which will throw an error message in the event log. Because of a failure to start an SSO service, BizTalk Service would not be able to start, which will write another error message in the event log. To capture these events and take action, we can set up event processing rules.

To create an event processing rule, follow these steps:

1. In the left pane of the MOM Administrator Console, expand Rules, and then expand Processing Rule Groups. The list of existing processing rule groups is displayed.
2. Expand the item for the processing rule group that will contain the new rule.
3. In the left pane of the MOM Administrator Console, right-click the Event Processing Rules item for the processing rule group that will contain the new rule.
4. On the context menu, click NewEvent Processing Rule.

5. Specify the type of rule (such as Alert on or Respond to Event), and then click Next to proceed through the prompts.
6. Select a data provider to serve as the source of the event. For example, select Application for the data provider to monitor events in the Windows NT application event log. Additional criteria can be specified for the event (such as a specific event ID), as well as a schedule of when the rule should be active. When prompted, you can specify that an alert be generated for the event, as well as specify any responses to the event (such as launching a script).
7. Enter appropriate knowledge-base content during the creation of the rule. It is important to provide key information for the knowledge base because users of the Management Pack depend on the knowledge base when a rule is triggered. However, if you are using MOM in author mode, do not enter knowledge-base content on the Knowledge Base property page. Instead, enter information on the Knowledge Authoring property page and then set the component type to MCS on the Advanced property page.
8. The final property page prompts you for the name of the rule and whether the rule is enabled. You can change the properties of a rule after it is created by opening the property page for the rule in the MOM Administrator Console.

Alert Processing Rules Alert Processing rules are used for responding to alerts. To create an alert processing rule, follow these steps:

1. In the left pane of the MOM Administrator Console, expand Rules, and then expand Processing Rule Groups.
2. Expand the item for the processing rule group that will contain the new rule.
3. In the left pane of the MOM Administrator Console, right-click the Alert Processing Rules item for the processing rule group that will contain the new rule.
4. On the context menu, click NewAlert Processing Rule. The property page allows you to restrict the alert rule to a specific alert source, severity level, or processing rule group.
5. Click Advanced for more options, make any desired changes, and then click Close.

   For example, the Advanced Criteria property page allows you to monitor severity levels using an "is at least" qualifier instead of the "equals" qualifier.
6. After you have specified the alert criteria, click Next.
7. On the Schedule property page, specify when the alert rule is active, and then click Next.
8. On the Response property page, add desired responses (such as launching a script or sending an SNMP trap), and then click Next.

9. The Knowledge Base property page is displayed. It is important to provide key information for the knowledge base; users of the Management Pack depend on the knowledge base when a rule is triggered. However, if you are using MOM in author mode, do not enter knowledge-base content on the Knowledge Base property page. Instead, enter information on the Knowledge Authoring property page and then set the component type to MCS on the Advanced property page.
10. Proceed with the prompts. The final property page prompts you for the name of the rule, as well as whether the rule is enabled.
11. You can change the properties of a rule after it is created by opening the property page for the rule in the MOM Administrator Console.

Performance Processing Rules MOM uses performance processing rules to respond to events related to Windows NT performance counters or WMI numeric events.

For example, you can have performance processing rules for monitoring MessagesReceived/Sec and MessagesProcessed/Sec for BizTalk. To create a performance processing rule,

1. Determine which processing rule group will contain the new performance processing rule.
2. In the left pane of the MOM Administrator Console, expand Rules, and then expand Processing Rule Groups. The list of existing processing rule groups is displayed.
3. Expand the item for the processing rule group that will contain the new rule.
4. Add a new performance processing rule to the processing rule group.
5. In the left pane of the MOM Administrator Console, right-click the Performance Processing Rules item for the processing rule group that will contain the new rule, and then click NewPerformance Processing Rule on the context menu. The Performance Processing Rule Type property page is displayed.
6. Select the Sample Performance Data (Measuring) rule or the Compare Performance Data (Threshold) rule. For purposes of this example, choose a measuring rule, and then click Next. The Data Provider property page is displayed.
7. Select a performance log provider from the list, and then click Next.
8. Specify when the alert rule is active, and then click Next.
9. On the Responses property page, add any desired responses (such as launch a script, execute a command, or update a state variable), and then click Next.
10. Enter appropriate knowledge-base content, and then click Next. It is important to provide key information for the knowledge base because users of the Management Pack depend on the knowledge base when a rule is triggered. However, if you are using MOM in author mode, do not enter knowledge-base content on the

Knowledge Base property page. Instead, enter information on the Knowledge Authoring property page and then set the component type to MCS on the Advanced property page.

11. On the final property page, enter the name of the rule and whether the rule is enabled. You can change the properties of a rule after it is created by opening the property page for the rule in the MOM Administrator Console.

Summary

In this chapter you learned how to perform different BizTalk administrative tasks manually and by using Windows Management Instrumentation (WMI). You also learned how to use Microsoft Operation Management (MOM) pack for BizTalk Server 2004 for monitoring BizTalk Server Group.

PART VI

Involving the Information Worker with BizTalk Server 2004

IN THIS PART

CHAPTER 18

Human-based Workflow

IN THIS CHAPTER

- Workflow Model
- Programming Model
- Building an Action
- Action Deployment and Administration
- HWS Security and Constraints
- Using the HWS Web Service
- Developing Activity Models

Human Workflow Services (HWS) is a set of capabilities within BizTalk Server 2004 that enables ad hoc and semi-structured workflows to be developed and made available to information workers through client applications. HWS has been built around the premise that workflow consists of sets of repeatable actions that users can perform to accomplish a business goal. Workflow evolves at users' discretion as they stitch actions together to construct a workflow that represents their business process.

A document review process, for example, involves a set of people collaborating to sign off on the document's content. To get sign off, however, the initiator of the review needs to get the appropriate users to review the document and submit their comments on the content. After incorporating user feedback into the document, the initiator will want to either resubmit the document for review or request final approval.

Even in simple processes, such as the one previously described, the user has to perform a set of unique actions on the document: review, incorporate feedback, resubmit for review, and request final approval. Imagine if these actions were available to the user as parameterized orchestrations. The user could then perform one or more of these actions by filling out a form, resulting in assigning tasks to the participants. During the course of filling out the form, a user would supply information about the document to be reviewed, the participating users, and the review duration, for example.

The order in which the user performed these actions could be tracked, and the tasks performed by users as a result of these actions can be captured as well. Already, you can see that a workflow is evolving based on a user performing actions. Further, let's say that each of the users assigned a task within this process had a *delegate* action available. Users who do not want to participate in the document review may delegate their work by simply filling out a form corresponding to the *delegate* action.

The preceding example illustrates how a collaborative process, such as document review, can be composed in an ad-hoc manner by a user using a set of repeatable actions. The same process may also have some inherent structure put in place so that the final approval cannot be performed until at least one *review* has been performed on the document. HWS supports both ad-hoc and semi-structured workflow concepts previously described. The main capabilities of HWS are summarized next:

- Allows users to modify workflows on-the-fly.
- Allows users to define a workflow model, which can accommodate dynamic change.
- Monitors what users do as part of a day-to-day workflow.
- Adapts workflows over time to changes in the organization or business.
- Discovers workflow from actions of users rather than from a designed workflow.

The rest of the chapter will explain how you can build on these capabilities as a solution developer and make them available to users through client applications.

Workflow Model

This section defines the basic elements that compose an HWS workflow and presents the workflow model.

HWS defines workflow as a set of activities that take place between people or processes within a given context. Figure 18.1 shows the basic model.

Workflows in HWS are called *Activity Flows*, which in turn are composed of one or more actions. An Action may contain one or more *Tasks*. Tasks define work that needs to be done by the Actor. The participants in the workflow are called *Actors*, which are external entities that either start an Activity Flow or participate in an ongoing Activity Flow.

An *Action* is the fundamental unit of work as seen by the Actor.

An Action is always initiated by an Actor. The *Initiator* of the first Action within an Activity Flow also becomes the *Owner* of the Activity Flow.

> *Example: An employee (Initiator/Owner) starts an Expense Approval (Action) for an expense document (Resource). He names his manager (Target) as approver (Task), his manager's assistant (Target) as reviewer (Task), and a finance person (Target) as controller (Task).*

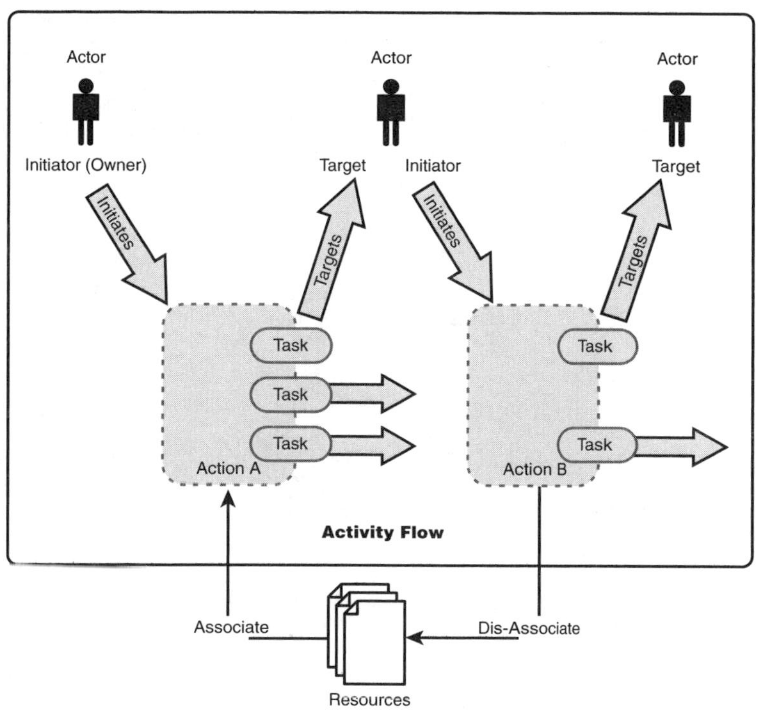

FIGURE 18.1 Activity Flow model.

The Target proceeds to complete the requested task. Optionally, the Target may decide to initiate another Action as part of the Activity Flow.

> *Example: The employee's manager (Target/Initiator) might approve the expense report or might delegate (Action) the report to his substitute (Target). In both cases the expense report will be either approved or not approved after the task items have been completed.*

An HWS Workflow can either be created from a running workflow (Activity Flow) or designed a priori. An Activity Model predefines the routing between the different Actions. Actors are defined by the model and can either initiate an Action or can be a target.

Creating an Activity Flow from multiple Actions is called *composition*. Composition is core to the HWS workflow system. Figure 18.2 shows the composition of Actions into Activity Flows.

Figure 18.2 shows an Actor, who is a target of a Task in an Activity Flow, initiating an Action by submitting parameters using a user interface. This initiated Action is then composed with the previous Action as part of the same Activity Flow. The state of the Activity Flow before and after composition is shown on the left side.

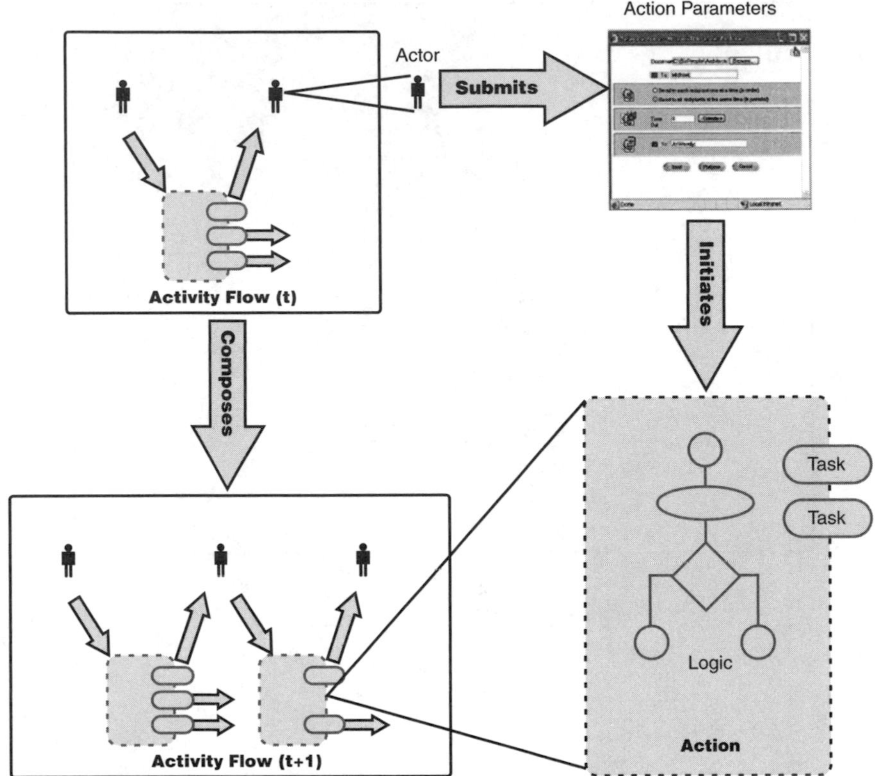

FIGURE 18.2 Composition model.

The composition of an Action into an Activity Flow takes into account Constraints associated with the Action. *Constraints* govern which user is allowed to initiate an Action and which users are allowed to receive tasks from the Action.

Programming Model

HWS provides a flexible and powerful set of APIs to enable workflow design, runtime, and administrative capabilities. These APIs are listed next:

- A Web service interface under `Microsoft.BizTalk.Hws.SoapService` enables clients to compose, query and discover workflows.
- An Activity Model designer API under `Microsoft.BizTalk.Hws.WorkflowDesign` enables construction, deployment, and discovery of Activity Models.
- WMI classes under `\Root\MicrosoftBizTalkServer` provide for workflow-related administrative functions.
- `IFactRetriever` interface under `Microsoft.BizTalk.Hws.Runtime` enables development of custom role providers.

In the next section, we will examine how you can leverage these APIs within a client application and how to design an Activity Model.

Building an Action

Now that you have an understanding of what HWS is and the basic architecture of the system, you are prepared to begin constructing your own workflows in HWS. As you have previously read, actions are the basic building blocks of workflow in HWS, so the first step in creating a workflow solution is to build the actions that will compose the workflow. A number of workflows involve a "contract agreement" step, where a person is required to review and sign a contract, so it would make sense to create a contract agreement action in our system.

> **NOTE**
>
> It will be helpful if you build and deploy the sample actions that are located in the SDK/Samples/Hws/Actions by running the DeployActions.cmd file located in that directory. This will set up the sample actions on your system, and those sample actions are used in some of the code in this chapter.

Creating an Action Project

The first step in creating an action is to create a new Human Workflows Services Action project in Visual Studio (this project template can be found in the BizTalk projects folder). After you have created your project, you will end up with a solution like Figure 18.3. After creation, an action project contains three schema files and an orchestration file.

Modifying the Schemas

In HWS, there are three types of user-modifiable schemas that are used by an action: the Activate schema, the Task schemas, and the Synchronize schema.

Every user-modifiable schema in HWS contains three major sections:

- The HWSSection of the schema contains a number of properties that allow HWS to track and route workflow messages through the system, and as such, should not be modified by the user.
- The ActionSection is the user-modifiable section of an HWS schema. Here we will add any elements that carry data specific to our action.
- The Payloads section of the schema is designed to carry data that is specific to the workflow the action is contained within.

  A workflow often adds an additional layer of context around individual actions, and there may be data specific to that layer that is required throughout the workflow. For example, if our contract agreement action was used in an order-processing workflow, the details of the order may be carried in a document contained in the Payloads section. Because of this design, one rule of action development is that any data that is sent to the action in the Payloads section of the activation message should always be carried through and sent out of the action in the Payloads section of any task and synchronize messages.

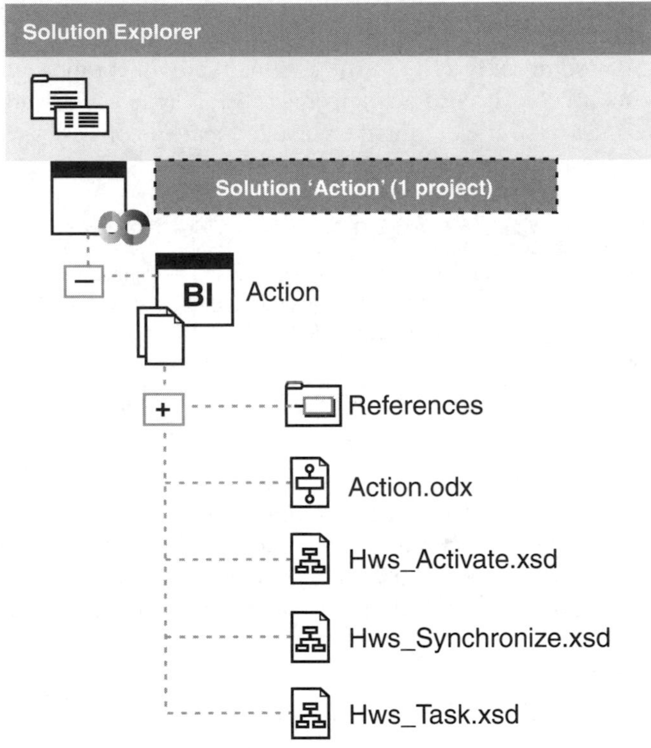

FIGURE 18.3 A newly created HWS project in the Solution Explorer.

The Activate schema specifies the format of the message that will be sent to the action to cause it to begin processing. In the action project, this schema is contained in the HWS_Activate.xsd file. Activation schemas should contain all the data an action will need to perform its logic, including instance data and target users. For the contract agreement step, we'll need the activation message to supply the username of the person who will be signing the contract, and the contract itself. These two string elements should be added to the HWS_Activate schema, creating the schema shown in Listing 18.1.

LISTING 18.1 The New HWS_Activate Schema

```
<xs:element name="ActionSection">
  <xs:complexType>
    <xs:sequence>
```

LISTING 18.1 Continued

```
      <xs:element name="ContractApprover" type="xs:string" />
      <xs:element name="Contract" type="xs:string" />
    </xs:sequence>
  </xs:complexType>
</xs:element>
```

Task schemas specify the formats of messages sent from an action to its targets. An action may have any number of task schemas, as an action may need to send different types of message to some of its targets. For example, imagine an action that conducts an interview. Such an action may want to send one type of message to most of the interviewers, but a special type of message to the managing interviewer, who has the final say.

An important thing to realize about task schemas is that although they are used to convey information to workflow participants, the same message schema is used by the recipient of the task message to communicate back to the action that sent the task. So, when designing the message schema, you must take into account both data going out and coming in. For our contract agreement action, we want to send out the contract to the user, and we want to receive a yes or no approval of the contract; we also want users to be able to supply comments in the event they reject the contract. So, we add string elements for the contract, the approving user, and comments data, and a Boolean element for the approval answer, resulting in the schema in Listing 18.2.

LISTING 18.2 Action Section of the New Task Schema

```
<xs:element name="ActionSection">
  <xs:complexType>
    <xs:sequence>
      <xs:element name="Contract" type="xs:string" />
      <xs:element name="ContractApprover" type="xs:string" />
      <xs:element name="ContractApproved" type="xs:boolean" />
      <xs:element name="Comments" type="xs:string" />
    </xs:sequence>
  </xs:complexType>
</xs:element>
```

18

Synchronize schemas are a slightly more advanced action message type. They do not directly affect what the action does, so for beginning action developers they can be ignored. I will discuss this message type in the section "The Synchronize Message" later in this chapter.

One final important note about action schemas: Every XML Schema has a namespace that uniquely identifies that schema. When the HWS action project template generated the default activation, task, and synchronize schemas, it gave them all default namespaces. It is important that you modify the namespace of each one of your schemas; otherwise, you could run into problems when you use the action in a workflow, because BizTalk does not react well to multiple schemas with the same namespace. This won't be a problem for your first action project, but if you create a second project and deploy that to BizTalk without modifying the schema namespaces, you will run into errors. To modify your schema's namespace, open the schema in the schema editor in Visual Studio and edit the properties of the schema's root node. In the Properties window you will see a property called Target Namespace. Change the value of that property to something unique in your system.

Modifying the Action Logic

Now that we have prepared all the message schema the action will use, we need to modify the orchestration logic of the action so that it does what we want. To do this, we open up the Action.odx file in the action project. Don't be concerned at the complexity of the orchestration. You really don't need to worry about 90% of it. All of the logic already present is there to enable the various features of HWS. It is worth understanding the basic function of each of the major sections of the template action orchestration so that you have an idea of what's happening at runtime. If you examine Figure 18.4, you will see a collapsed version of the action orchestration, with five sections highlighted.

Section 1 contains the `ActivateAndSendInstanceIdBack` scope block. This section contains the logic where the action receives the activation message defined by the activation schema we talked about before and sends some data back to the HWS system. The only time you will need to modify anything in this section is if you change the Namespace or Type Name of your activate message schema. Changing the activate schema's Namespace or Type Name will invalidate the `ActivateMessage` variable defined for the project, and you will need to go into this section to update the Receive shape that receives the ActivateMessage and the receive port it is connected to.

Section 2 contains the `ListenForAbortOrFinishMessage` scope block. Contained in this block is the logic that enables HWS to interrupt an action while it is running. You will see how to do this later when we discuss the HWS Web service. This logic must run in parallel to the main action logic, so that an action can be interrupted at any time. You should never need to make changes to this section of the action.

Section 3 contains the `CheckForDependentComposition` scope block. We'll talk more about dependent composition later when we discuss the synchronize message, but this section is responsible for waiting for the receipt of a synchronize message if the activation message indicates that the action has been dependently composed.

Section 4 is the most important section and contains the `ScopeAllActionSpecificLogic` scope block. This block is initially empty and is a placeholder indicating where all your action-specific logic should be placed. Most orchestration shapes you add to your action, especially those that perform the primary logic in your orchestration, should go here.

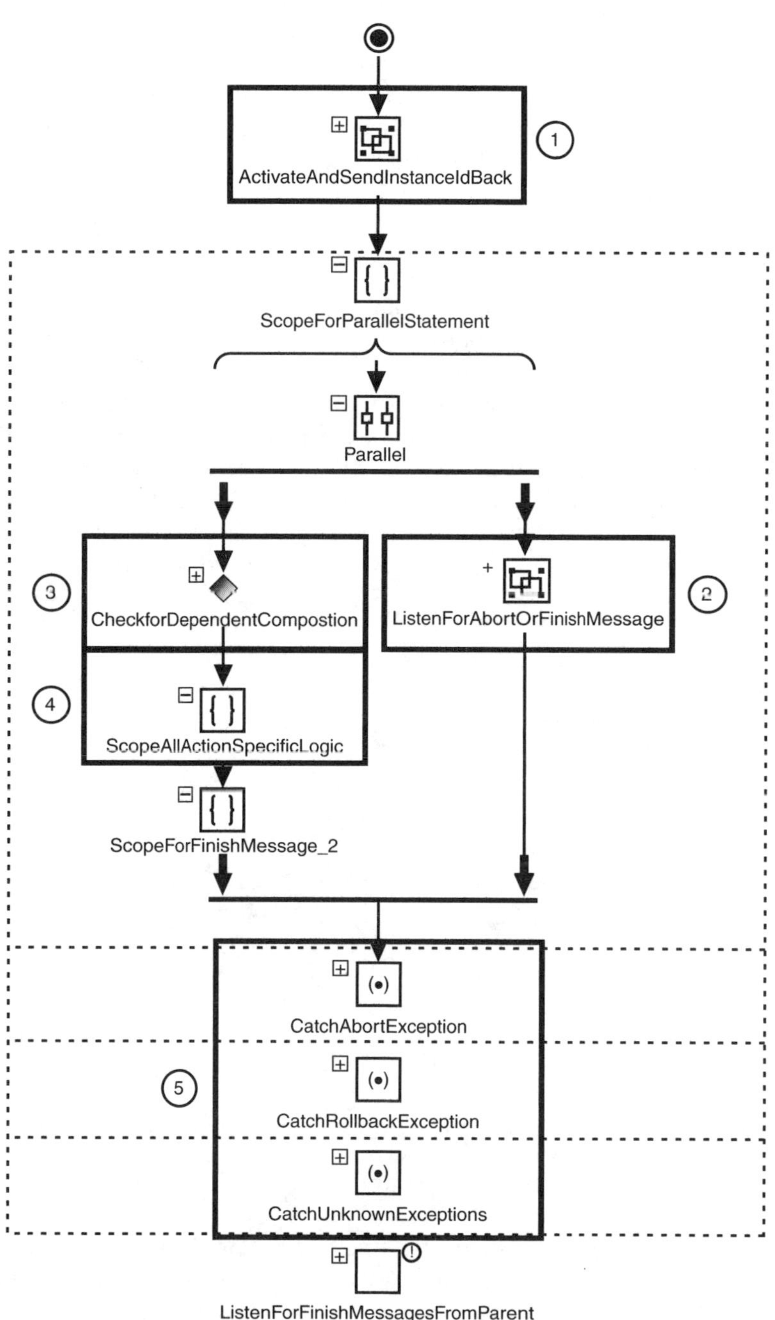

FIGURE 18.4 Collapsed view of the default action orchestration.

Section 5 contains the exception blocks in the orchestration. These exception blocks will execute if the action receives a message from the HWS system to rollback or abort. A *rollback* exception indicates the action should attempt to undo any external changes it has made, whereas an *abort* indicates that the action should terminate. If you need to perform any action-specific rollback or abort logic, you will need to add that logic inside these exception blocks. For instance, if your action logic updates a database entry, it would make sense to roll back that update in the rollback exception and possibly in the abort exception.

The first step is to create a new message variable called `ContractApprovalTask`, which is of type HWS_Task, and a new variable named `TaskId`, which is of type System.Guid. Next, add a message construction block to create the `TaskMessage` variable to the `DoAllActionSpecificLogic` scope. If you examine the full schema of the task message, you will see that a number of message elements need to be assigned data. Most of that data, however, is contained in the activation message that the action received when it started. The easiest way to fill out the required element of the task message is to create a message map that maps the `ActivationMessage` variable to the `TaskMessage` variable. You can refer to Chapter 4, "Mapping Messages," to see how to create a message map. See Figure 18.5 to see how the final map should look.

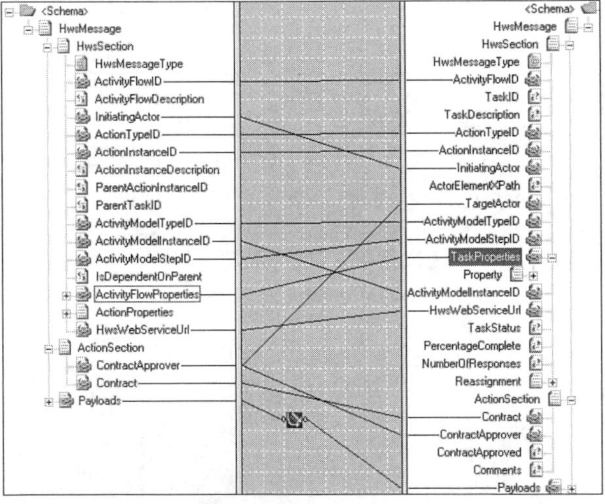

FIGURE 18.5 Message map from activation message to task message.

Although most of the elements of the task message are supplied from the activation message, a few required fields must have default values supplied by the map itself. The `TaskId` field should be initialized to a value of `{00000000-0000-0000-000000000000}` by typing in that value in the Value property (this value will be updated later, but the element must have a value specified for the map to create it), the `TaskStatus` field should be initialized to a value of InProgress, the `PercentageComplete` element should be initialized to 0, and finally, the ActorElementXPath element should be initialized to the XPath of the ContractApprover element in the activation message. Without initialization of these values, the message will cause an error at runtime. Finally, the Payloads element from the activation message should be copied to the Payloads element of the task message by connecting those elements with a mass copy functoid, which will copy all subelements of the activation payloads node.

Now that we've got our map ready, we add a Transform shape to the MessageConstruction block and configure it to use our new map to map data between the activation message and the task message. After that's done, the message is almost ready to be sent; however, you'll remember that the TaskId element was initialized to a dummy value. Each task must be sent out with a unique TaskID value, so we need to add a MessageAssignment shape after the Transform shape. The Expression value for the Message Assignment shape should match Listing 18.3. As you can see, we generate a new guid value for the TaskId variable we created earlier and assign that value to the TaskId of the TaskMessage.

LISTING 18.3 Expression Value to Create a New Task ID

```
taskId = System.Guid.NewGuid();
ContractApprovalTask(Microsoft.BizTalk.Hws.HwsPromotedProperties.TaskID) =
➥taskId.ToString();
```

Now that we have the task message prepared, we need to send it out to the user. This is no different from sending any other message out from an orchestration by creating a Send shape and a new send port. After the action has sent the message out, it must wait for a response. As usual, this is accomplished by adding a Receive shape to the orchestration logic. Again, as you have previously read, you need to create a new message variable, again of the HWS_Task message type, and then add a Receive shape and port for that message variable. One nice thing about HWS action orchestrations is that the template has already set up the correlation you need to use in your Receive shape in the corActionInstanceInterruptCorrelation correlation.

18

After you have completed the preceding steps, your action's DoAllActionSpecificLogic scope should look like Figure 18.6. At this point, your action is ready to be compiled and deployed into your HWS system.

The Synchronize Message

You'll remember when we reviewed the different message schema types involved in the HWS, I said that the synchronize message did not need to be modified during basic action development. So what exactly is it used for? To understand its use case, you have to understand how workflows are formed in HWS. Users create dynamic workflows in HWS by composing actions one at a time using the HWS Web service (users can also follow predefined workflows, know as activity models, which will be discussed later). Normally, a user would compose an action, the action logic would execute, and one of the users who received a task from that action would compose another action into the workflow. Composition where the action starts immediately is called Independent Composition in HWS. There are cases where a user might actually want to preload multiple actions into the workflow and have them execute sequentially. In this case, the user wants to compose one or more actions in a workflow that will wait for the previous action to finish before starting. Composition in which the action waits for a parent action to finish before starting is called Dependent Composition in HWS because the action is dependent on its parent.

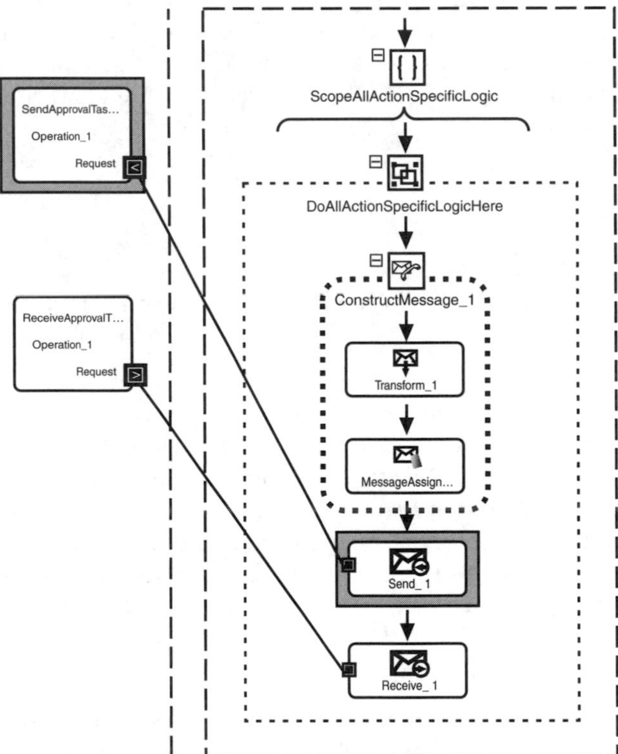

FIGURE 18.6 The completed Contract Agreement action orchestration.

The way the parent action indicates that dependent actions waiting on it should start is by sending out a synchronize message. Although the synchronize message is just another orchestration message, there are certain requirements imposed by HWS in developing an orchestration that sends and receives synchronize messages, which are outlined next.

The most important requirement to understand is that for two actions to be dependently composed as parent and child, the parent must send and the child must receive synchronize messages with the same schema namespace. By default, every HWS action receives a synchronize message that has a type matching the `HWS_Synchronize` schema that is present in each new action project. Although this is a helpful step in understanding synchronize messages, it creates a problem with the first requirement. If two actions are developed and each has its own synchronize message schema, those actions will not be able to be composed dependently. The best way to work around this issue is to create a separate BizTalk project that contains only a synchronize message, and have all your action projects reference the common synchronize schema project. In each project that references the common synchronize schema project, you should delete the HWS_Synchronize.xsd file.

After you have your common synchronize schema, there are two steps to updating your action:

1. If you want your action to be able to be a child of a dependent composition, you will need to update the message type of the `SyncMessage` variable (which will involve updating some of the shapes in the `CheckForDependentComposition` scope block discussed earlier). Because the default action orchestration already has all the shapes required to receive the synchronize message, you will not need to modify your action logic. Finally, and most important, you will need to modify the properties of your activation message to notify HWS that your action can receive your synchronize schema type. Open the properties of the `<Schema>` node of your activation message schema. In the Properties list, you will see an Incoming Sync Messages property. Edit that property and make sure the list contains only your synchronize message schema.

2. If you want your action to be able to be a parent of a dependent composition, you will need to add a new message variable and logic in your orchestration to send out the message variable. Sending a synchronize message is no different than sending any other message, except that you must use a specific port. If you examine the predefined ports for the action orchestration at the top left of the screen in the Action.odx file, you will find a port called `ActionDirectBoundOutPort`; in this port is an operation labeled `SendOrReceiveSyncMessage`. You must connect the Send shape you use to send the synchronize message to this operation in order for the message to work properly. Finally, like step 1, you must edit the properties of the activation schema, this time updating the list of schema namespaces sent out to include your outgoing sync message's namespace in the Outgoing sync messages property of the activation schema.

Action Deployment and Administration

Now that you have an action developed, you need to add that action into the HWS system. The initial steps involved in this are the following:

1. Building and deploying the action orchestration to the BizTalk Server.

2. Binding the logical ports of the action to physical ports on the server.

NOTE

Note that HWS has specific requirements for two of the ports required by all actions: the port that receives the activation message and the port that receives the interrupt message. These definitions can be found in the help files, under SDK, Programming Guide, Programming with Human Workflow Services, Creating Actions, Registering and Deploying an Action. You must bind your activation port to the well-defined activation port, and you must bind your interrupt port and all task response receive ports to the well-defined interrupt port.

3. Enlisting and starting your orchestration on the BizTalk Server.

At this point, the orchestration is ready to be started in BizTalk; however, HWS will not yet allow users to activate the orchestration. To allow HWS to recognize and use the action, two more steps are involved: registering the action with HWS and creating constraints.

Registering the Action with HWS

Click the Start button, navigate to Programs, Microsoft BizTalk Server 2004, HWS Server Administration. This shortcut opens the HWS MMC administration console. After this is open, if you expand the root node you will see an actions node. Click this node. A list of orchestrations deployed in your BizTalk Server that meet the requirements of an HWS action are displayed in the right pane, as shown in Figure 18.7. You should see the contract approval action listed, and its state should be running. Only actions listed with a state of registered can be activated by an HWS user. To register an action, right-click the action and select Register Action: <Action name> from the menu. You should go ahead and register the contract agreement action here.

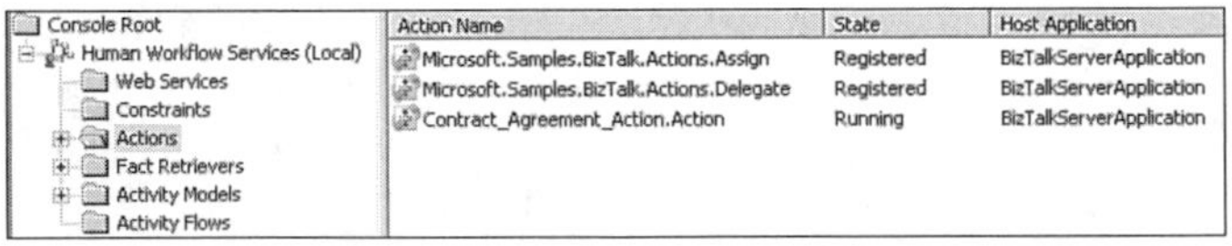

Console Root
Human Workflow Services (Local)
Web Services
Constraints
Actions
Fact Retrievers
Activity Models
Activity Flows

Action Name	State	Host Application
Microsoft.Samples.BizTalk.Actions.Assign	Registered	BizTalkServerApplication
Microsoft.Samples.BizTalk.Actions.Delegate	Registered	BizTalkServerApplication
Contract_Agreement_Action.Action	Running	BizTalkServerApplication

FIGURE 18.7 The actions node of the HWS admin console.

Registering an action in HWS does two things: It makes the action available in the HWS system, and it updates the action dependence information in HWS. What the latter part means is that if you change the synchronize message namespaces used in your action, you must unregister and reregister the action in the MMC console for HWS to recognize the changes you have made.

NOTE

HWS action registration is completely independent from orchestration deployment in the BizTalk Server. If you want to make changes to your action logic, you can simply undeploy and redeploy the action in BizTalk without unregistering the action in HWS.

After an action is registered, the HWS system knows that the action exists; however, users will still not be able to activate it through the HWS Web service. This is because of the HWS security model.

HWS Security and Constraints

HWS security is based on authenticating users via NTLM and then determining what a user can do based on authority rules called *constraints*. The HWS constraint system is a granting security model, which means that unless a user is given authority to perform an action by a constraint, the user will not have the authority to do anything. This makes for a very secure system because it requires action on the part of the administrator before a user is authorized to perform any action in the system. As a result of constraints, the HWS Web service is able to inform users as to what their next action might possibly be. If users are constrained so that they can activate only 2 out of the 10 actions in a system, the HWS Web service will tell them that when they ask the HWS Web service what action they can perform.

NOTE

It is also possible to configure HWS security so that constraints serve only as a guidance mechanism. In this case, the Web service would tell the same users described previously that they could perform those same two actions; however, if a user tried to activate one of the other eight actions, it would succeed where it would have failed in the previous case.

There are three types of constraints in HWS: system constraints, activity model system constraints, and activity model step constraints. The latter two will be discussed later in the section covering activity models. In the context of an action in HWS, a user may fall into one of three roles: Initiator, Target, or Enacted on User. An initiator is the user who is making the call into the Web service to activate an action. A target is a user who may receive a task message from the action during its execution.

To understand the Enacted on User role, you should understand how workflows are composed at runtime. During a workflow, users compose actions into the workflow. Each action is added to the workflow by an initiator, and that action sends tasks to some or all of its target users. Normally, only the initiator of an action or one of the targets of the action could compose a next action in the workflow. There are cases, though, where another user (not an initiator or target) would want to compose a next action. Such a case might exist if the target of an action didn't complete the task in time, and the third user wanted to escalate that task to the target user's manager, using an Escalate action. Because the third user did not initiate the action that sent the task, nor was that user the target of that action, he or she wouldn't be able to compose the Escalate action into the workflow. The enacted on user concept allows this case to succeed. The target user not performing the task becomes the enacted on user when the third user composes the Escalate action.

Creating System Constraints

System constraints are created by using the HWS MMC that we used previously to register an action. If you launch the HWS MMC and expand the root node, you will see a Constraints node. Clicking that node displays all the system and activity model system constraints present in your installation. To add a new constraint, right-click the Constraints node and select the Add Constraint menu option. The Add Constraint dialog box shown in Figure 18.8 should appear.

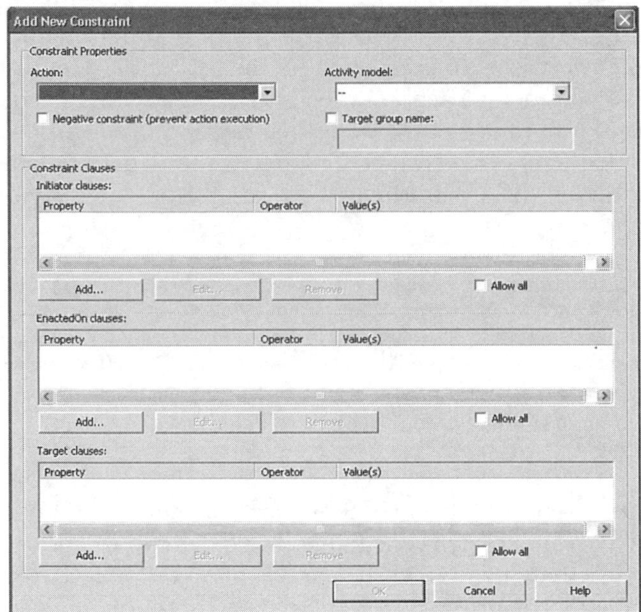

FIGURE 18.8 The Add New Constraint dialog box in the HWS admin console.

As you can see, a constraint relates clauses in each of the three constraint roles to an action type. You can select the action type by selecting an action in the action drop-down list. Because we need to add constraints for our contract agreement action, we'll select that action from the Action drop-down list.

Each of the list boxes in the dialog box contain individual clauses for the role specified at the top left of the list box. At the bottom right of each clause list box is a check box labeled Allow All. Checking that box means that any user can function in the associated role for that action. In a testing environment, it is usually easiest to create constraints for each one of your actions, allowing all users to function in all roles. More restrictive clauses can be added to a constraint by clicking the Add button for the desired role, which launches the Add Clause dialog box. We'll check the Allow All box (shown in Figure 18.8) for our target role, and then add a clause for our initiator role.

In HWS, a clause takes the form of a property, an operator, and a comparison value combination. A property is a user fact supplied by a registered fact retriever, an operator is one of six comparison operators supported (equal, not equal, greater than, less than, includes, and does not include), and a comparison value is the value the operator compares against.

To construct the clause, we first select the User Name property from the property drop–down list; then select the Not Equal operator from the operator drop-down list, and finally, type in a comparison value of `User1` in the Evaluate Against Specific Values combo box. The Add Clause dialog box should now look like that shown in Figure 18.9. Clearly this clause will not perform very differently than if we had chosen the Allow All check box, but you can see how it would be possible to restrict the set of users who could activate or be targets of an action by changing the clause.

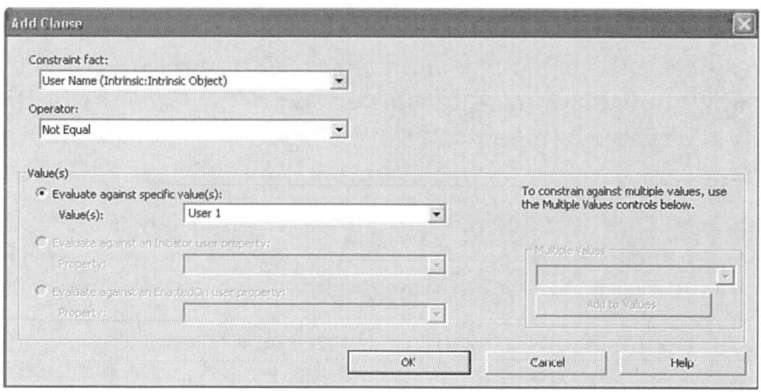

FIGURE 18.9 The Add Clause dialog box from the HWS admin console.

After we click OK in the Add Clause dialog box, the clause is added to the list of clauses for the initiator role, and now that the constraint has at least one initiator and target clause, it can be added to the system by clicking OK in the Add New Constraint dialog box (resulting in Figure 18.10).

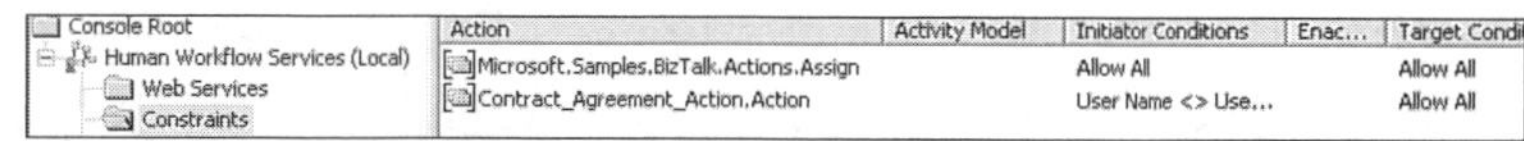

FIGURE 18.10 The new constraint for the Contract Agreement action in the Constraints node of the HWS admin console.

Constraint Evaluation

In designing the set of constraints that will govern your system, it is important to understand how the constraints and their individual clauses interact with each other.

For a constraint to be satisfied, the users involved in the activation (the initiator, the target, and enacted users) must satisfy all the clauses for their specific role in the constraint. For example, if a constraint contained two initiator clauses, one specifying the username must equal Michael and the other specifying the Day of Week must not equal Wednesday, and Michael tried to activate the action on a Tuesday, the constraint would not be satisfied.

Only one system constraint must be satisfied, however, for an action to be authorized by the system. In our preceding example, if another constraint existed that had a single initiator clause specifying that the Day of Week must equal Tuesday, then even though Michael's action would fail to satisfy the first constraint, it would satisfy the second constraint and the action would be authorized.

Adding Constraint Properties

By now you've noticed that there are a limited number of properties available to compose constraint clauses with. If you wanted to allow users only within a particular organization in your company to activate a certain action, you would have to add an initiator clause for each of those users.

It is possible to add more constraint properties to your system by creating your own fact retriever. In HWS, each constraint property is supplied by a fact retriever. The initial properties available are all supplied by the intrinsic HWS fact retriever.

To implement your own fact retriever, follow these steps:

1. Create an assembly that exposes a public object that implements the Microsoft.BizTalk.Hws.Runtime.IFactRetriever interface.
2. Install the assembly into the GAC.
3. Using the HWS Administration MMC, expand the root node, right-click the Fact Retrievers node, and select Add Fact Retriever.
4. Fill in the required information about your Fact Retriever object and click OK.

TIP

More detailed information about creating a fact retriever can be found in the BizTalk help topics, and a sample fact retriever is in the `Samples/Hws/HwsFactRetriever` directory in your install directory.

Using the HWS Web Service

The HWS Web service is the only API a client application interacting with HWS will need to communicate with. The Web service provides methods for various categories of interaction, including a set of methods for creating activity flows and composing actions to those activity flows, a set of methods for querying the system and retrieving historical information about an activity flow, a method to send responses to tasks, and a method to interrupt an action or workflow while it is running.

NOTE

One important note before we start using the Web service: The HWS Web service does not allow anonymous connections, so whenever you access the Web service, you must supply Windows credentials to the connection. Even if you modify the virtual directory of the Web service to allow anonymous connections, the security model of HWS will cause all calls to the Web service methods to fail because an anonymous user has no authority in HWS.

All the activity flows created in this section are commonly referred to in HWS as ad-hoc or dynamic workflows. They are called this because the activity flow evolves dynamically at runtime. This differs from a predefined workflow, called an activity model in HWS. Predefined workflows and their interaction with ad-hoc workflows are discussed later in this chapter.

Creating Activity Flows Using the HWS Web Service

Listing 18.4 shows how to create a new activity flow in HWS using the Web service:

LISTING 18.4 Creating a New Activity Flow

```
HWS.HwsService hwsService = new HWS.HwsService();
hwsService.Credentials = CredentialCache.DefaultCredentials;

Guid activityFlowId = hwsService.GetNewActivityFlowID();

HWS.Activity contractAgreementAction = null;
HWS.Activity[] activities = hwsService.GetActivityList(activityFlowId,
➥Guid.Empty, Guid.Empty, "", null);
foreach( HWS.Activity activity in activities )
{
 if( activity.Name == "Contract_Agreement_Action.Action" )
 {
  contractAgreementAction = activity;
 }
}

HWS.ActionParameters actionParams = hwsService.GetActionParameters(
➥contractAgreementAction.ActionTypeID, null);
XmlDocument paramsDoc = new XmlDocument();
paramsDoc.Load("ContractAgreementActivationMsg.xml");
paramsDoc.SelectSingleNode("//ActionSection/ContractApprover").InnerText =
```

LISTING 18.4 Continued

```
➥"DOMAIN\\user";
paramsDoc.SelectSingleNode("//ActionSection/Contract").InnerText =
➥"Enter contract text here";
actionParams.ParametersDoc = paramsDoc.OuterXml;

hwsService.AddActionToActivityFlow(activityFlowId, Guid.Empty,
➥Guid.Empty, false, actionParams, null);
```

The first lines create an instance of a proxy object for the Web service and set the credentials of the proxy to the current user. The credentials are required so that the connection is not made anonymously.

After we have a reference to the Web service, the first thing required to create a new workflow is to create a new workflow ID by calling the `GetNewActivityFlowId` method. This method returns a guid that will uniquely identify our activity flow in the system. At this point, though, the activity flow does not exist in the system. It will be created only when the first action is composed into the activity flow.

Next you will need to find the system information about the action you want to compose to start your workflow. To obtain a list of all actions a user can perform, we make the call to `GetActivityList` and pass in the ID of our new workflow for the `activityFlowID` parameter. (The remaining guid parameters can be set to the empty guid because they are used only in continuing an activity flow. The result of this method is an array of Activity objects, each of which contains the details of an activity the user can compose into the activity flows. The code then loops through the possible activities to find our contract agreement action. The name of the action is created at compile time by prepending the Default Namespace property of the project with .Action. To build an action with the name used in the code sample in Listing 18.4, you should change the Default Namespace property of your action project to Contract_Agreement_Action.

After we have a reference to the `Activity` class that represents the action we want to compose, we need to retrieve the `ActionParameters` object that describes the parameters sent into the Web service to activate the action. To obtain an instance of this class for our desired action, we call the `GetActionParameters` method.

Most of the properties of this object are informational, providing context information about the activity. The most important property of the class is the `ParametersDoc` property, which needs to contain the activation message to be sent to the action. When the `ActionParameters` instance is returned from the Web service, this parameter is set to null. The easiest way to populate the parameter is to load from file an XML document which contains a template instance of the desired action's activation message. To generate this template instance file, follow these steps:

1. Right-click the activate message xsd file in the action solution developed earlier in the chapter, and then choose the Properties option.
2. Fill in a filename for the Output Instance Filename property.
3. Close the Properties panel, right-click the xsd file again, and choose the Generate Instance option. The file you specified in step 2 will be created with an XML instance that conforms to the Activations schema.
4. Edit the generated XML file. Remove all child elements of the HwsSection/ActivityFlowProperties, HwsSection/ActionProperties, and Payloads elements in the instance doc (the BizTalk XML generator supplies default values for those unbounded fields, but you don't want those).

Only the parameters in the `ActionSection` (and optionally any payload data in the `Payloads` section) need to be completed prior to action activation because the elements in the `HwsSection` will be automatically filled out and/or replaced by the system. You'll remember previously that we defined two parameter elements in the activation schema for the contract agreement action, so we need to add data to those elements. You should modify the code in Listing 18.4 so that your username is the target of the action.

Now that we have the parameters prepared to activate the action, we call the `AddActionToActivityFlow` method on the Web service to compose the action into the activity flow. Because this is the first action in the activity flow, this call will cause the creation of the activity flow. Note that because this is the first action composed into the activity flow, the parent guid parameters are set to the empty guid. These parameters will be explained shortly. Also, because this is the first action in the activity flow, it cannot be dependent on a parent action, so the `isDependentComposition` parameter is false.

The Acting User Parameter

As you probably noticed, almost all methods exposed by the Web service include an `actingUser` parameter, which was set to null in all the calls in Listing 18.4 (and will be null in all calls made in this chapter to the Web service). The acting user parameter is used by a client to take advantage of the HWS Trusted User feature. As we discussed earlier, HWS security is based on authenticating the calling users via NTLM and then verifying that the users have the required authorization to perform the action they are attempting. Such actions are not limited to composing an action into an activity flow, but also include querying activity flow information and responding to task messages.

In some cases, the calling user may not actually be the user authorized to perform the action, but is calling on behalf of the authorized user. If the calling user is a trusted user (see the BizTalk 2004 help files for more information on adding trusted users), then the calling user can specify the username of the user being acting for in the `actingUser` parameter, and the system will behave as if the call came from that user.

Querying Activity Flow Information

Now that an activity flow has been created in the HWS system, the Web service provides a number of methods to retrieve information about the current state and historical data of the workflow.

There are two main methods of obtaining information about an activity flow from the Web service. The first way can be used if the client knows the guid ID of the workflow it is interested in. If so, the client can call the `GetActivityFlowInfo` method on the Web service and pass that ID as the `activityFlowId` parameter. The `detailLevel` parameter specifies how much information should be retrieved about the activity model and has the following possible values:

- `ActivityFlowLevel`—Retrieves only the basic level of information about the activity model. This is the least expensive call.
- `ActionInstanceLevel`—Retrieves information about the activity flow, as well as information about each action that has been composed, into the activity model.
- `TaskLevel`—Retrieves all available data about the activity model, including all tasks that have been sent by every action instance within the activity flow and all responses to those tasks. Although retrieving this information from the tracking system is computationally not too expensive, the bandwidth required by this data tends to be much higher than the other two detail levels, and so this detail level should be used with caution.

Listing 18.5 shows the code required to find the task sent out by the action composed into the workflow in Listing 18.4.

LISTING 18.5 Retrieve the *Task* Instance Created by the Action Added in Listing 18.4

```
HWS.ActivityFlow flow = _HwsService.GetActivityFlowInfo(flowId,
➥HWS.ActivityFlowDetailLevel.TaskLevel, null);

HWS.Task desiredTask = null;
foreach( HWS.ActionInstance rootActionInstance in flow.RootActionInstances )
{
  foreach( HWS.Task task in rootActionInstance.Tasks )
  {
    if( task.Target == "REDMOND\\cwhytock" )
    {
      desiredTask = task;
    }
  }
}
```

The second method of determining information about an activity flow can be used in a situation where the flow ID is unknown. In this case, a user can query the Web service to find any activity flows the user is involved in, as in Listing 18.6. After that information has been obtained, the code in Listing 18.5 can be used to find the task sent out by the contract agreement action.

LISTING 18.6 Querying the HWS Web Service for All Activity Flows a Particular User Is Participating In

```
HWS.ActivityFlowFilter filter = new HWS.ActivityFlowFilter();
filter.StartTimeEnd = DateTime.MaxValue;
filter.StartTimeStart = DateTime.MinValue;
filter.UseStatusFilter = false;

HWS.ActivityFlow[] flows = _HwsService.GetAllActivityFlowsForUser(filter, null);

HWS.Task desiredTask = null;
foreach( HWS.ActivityFlow flow in flows )
{
}
```

Often the goal of retrieving activity flow information is to determine if there are any incomplete tasks assigned to a user. Although the previous two code listings can be combined with some loop logic to determine this, there is a more efficient way, by making use of the `GetAllTasksForUser` method on the Web service. This method retrieves all task messages assigned to the calling user, filters those tasks based on the `TaskFilter` structure passed into the method call, and returns those tasks that successfully pass the filter criteria. Listing 18.7 shows how we can use this method to find the task from the contract agreement action with much less code.

LISTING 18.7 Retrieve All Tasks for a Particular User

```
HWS.TaskFilter filter = new HWS.TaskFilter();
filter.StartTimeEnd = DateTime.MaxValue;
filter.StartTimeStart = DateTime.MinValue;
filter.UseStatusFilter = false;

HWS.Task[] tasks = _HwsService.GetAllTasksForUser(filter, null);
```

Responding to Task Messages

Back when we covered action development, I said that if you expect a response to a task from a target user, you must create a Receive shape and receive port, and that port must be bound at deployment to the HWS Interrupt port. The reason is that to maintain the security model that allows only the target of a task to respond to the task, HWS must route the task response message itself.

To do this, the HWS Web service exposes a `SendTaskResponse` method, which accepts a message, verifies that the calling user has the authority to respond to the task, and forwards the message to the action that sent the task. Often the user or client may not have the exact form of the task message, so the Web service also provides the `GetTaskMessage` method that will retrieve the XML form of the task message the client wants to respond to. Listing 18.8 shows how these methods would be used in our scenario to send an affirmative response to the contract agreement task sent by our first action.

LISTING 18.8 Sending a Task Response

```
string taskMessage = _HwsService.GetTaskMessage(myTask.TaskID, null);

XmlDocument taskResponseDoc = new XmlDocument();
taskResponseDoc.LoadXml(taskMessage);
taskResponseDoc.SelectSingleNode("//ActionSection/ContractApproved").
➥InnerText = "true";
taskResponseDoc.SelectSingleNode("//ActionSection/Comments").
➥InnerText = "Looks good";
taskResponseDoc.SelectSingleNode("//HwsSection/TaskStatus").
➥InnerText = "Completed";
taskResponseDoc.SelectSingleNode("//HwsSection/PercentageComplete").
➥InnerText = "100";

_HwsService.SendTaskResponse(taskResponseDoc.OuterXml, null);
```

Continuing Activity Flows

After an activity flow has been created by composing the first action into the flow, more actions will likely be composed into the activity flow to complete the workflow. Although this process is much like the process of composing the first action into the activity flow, the major difference is the use of the parameters that were left empty when we composed the first action.

To continue an activity flow with a new action instance, you must first gather the required information about the point in the activity flow where you want to compose a new action instance. Remember that at each point in an activity flow, only certain users can perform actions. These are

- Action Instance—Only the initiator of the previous action instance can compose a new action as a child.
- Task message—Only the target of the task message can compose a new action as a child.

Using the various query method discussed earlier, you've seen how to obtain the detailed information about each of these points in an activity flow. In Listings 18.9 and 18.10 you can see how we can add a second instance of the contract agreement action into the activity flow, first as the initiator of the first instance and then in Listing 18.10 as the target of the first instance.

LISTING 18.9 Adding an Action to an Activity Flow as the Initiator of the Parent Action

```
HWS.Task myTask = QueryFlowById(activityFlowId);

HWS.Activity contractAgreementAction = null;
HWS.Activity[] activities = _HwsService.GetActivityList(activityFlowId,
➥myTask.ActionInstanceID, Guid.Empty, "", null);
foreach( HWS.Activity activity in activities )
{
 if( activity.Name == "Contract_Agreement_Action.Action" )
 {
  contractAgreementAction = activity;
 }
}

// Fill in properties as in Listing 18-4

_HwsService.AddActionToActivityFlow(activityFlowId, myTask.ActionInstanceID,
➥Guid.Empty, false, actionParams, null);
```

In the preceding listing, you'll notice that the call to `AddActionToActivityFlow` is slightly different from Listing 18.4. The `parentActionInstanceID` parameter is no longer the empty guid. This is because we want to add the new action instance as a child of an existing action instance, and we therefore need to tell the Web service which existing instance should be the parent of this new instance. Note that the `parentTaskId` parameter is still the empty guid, because we are appending the new action as a child of the previous action instance, not the previous task instance. In reality, there is no appreciable difference at runtime; however, the HWS security check would fail if the client attempted to supply a non-empty guid value for the `parentTaskId` and the specified task was not assigned to the calling user.

LISTING 18.10 Adding an Action to an Activity Flow as the Target of a Task of the Parent Action

```
HWS.Task myTask = QueryFlowById(activityFlowId);

HWS.Activity contractAgreementAction = null;
HWS.Activity[] activities = _HwsService.GetActivityList(activityFlowId,
```

18

LISTING 18.10 Continued

```
➥myTask.ActionInstanceID, myTask.TaskID, "", null);
foreach( HWS.Activity activity in activities )
{
 if( activity.Name == "Contract_Agreement_Action.Action" )
 {
  contractAgreementAction = activity;
 }
}

// Fill in properties as in Listing 18.4

_HwsService.AddActionToActivityFlow(activityFlowId, myTask.ActionInstanceID,
➥myTask.TaskID, false, actionParams, null);
```

In Listing 18.10, again the call to `AddActionToActivityFlow` is changed from the call in Listing 18.9 (and Listing 18.4). Here, because we assume the client is acting under the authority of the user targeted by the first action in the activity flow, that user can continue the flow by composing the new action as a child to the task the user received from the first action. To do so, the client supplies the queried value for the task's ID to the `parentTaskId` parameter of the `AddActionToActivityFlow` method call.

Interrupting a Running Action or Activity Flow

Have you ever sent an email and then followed it up two minutes later with an email that has a subject of "Please Ignore: <Last subject>"? Or how about resending an email because you typed it up with the wrong date in the body? Of course, we all have. People make mistakes, in emails and certainly in workflow actions. HWS realizes this, and the Web service supports a method that allows users to revert such mistakes, the `InterruptAction` method.

The `InterruptAction` method has three levels of interrupt capability: It can interrupt a single action, an entire activity model, or an entire activity flow. The capability to perform these interrupts is highly restricted in HWS security, so that only the user who initiated the action, model, or flow can interrupt it (that is, only the initiator of an action can interrupt a single action, and only the initiator of the root action in an activity flow can interrupt the entire activity flow). The level of interrupt is specified by the `interruptLevel` parameter.

Listing 18.11 shows the code that would be involved for the initiator of the workflow created in Listing 18.4 to interrupt and roll back the entire activity flow. The semantics of a rollback are entirely up to the action receiving the rollback interrupt. The action may send cancellation tasks or it may revert database changes; there are no requirements for what the action can or cannot do in this case.

LISTING 18.11 Interrupting an Action

```
_HwsService.InterruptAction(actionInstanceId,
      HWS.InterruptLevel.ActionInstance, HWS.InterruptType.Abort);
```

MECHANICS OF INTERRUPT

Earlier in this chapter I described the various sections of the HWS template action orchestration; one section was responsible for receiving interrupt messages from the HWS system. This section of the orchestration is activated when a user calls the Interrupt Action method. Also remember that there are two specifically defined exceptions which will be caught inside the orchestration if an interrupt occurs: eAbortException and eRollbackException. The type of exception thrown and caught will depend on the interruptType parameter supplied by the caller. In the case of a rollback exception, the action should attempt to undo any changes it has made to the system, such as database updates, and can even go as far as sending messages to users telling them their tasks have been canceled. Abort is a harsher exception, indicating that the action should terminate as quickly as possible.

Developing Activity Models

Up to this point, we've been discussing how to create ad-hoc workflows in HWS. In many cases, though, you may already know how your workflow process should unfold, and you want to enforce that process. Perhaps the process is very complicated, and you need to guide your users through it. In either case, you have a well-known, predefined process that you want to translate into HWS. HWS supports predefining the ordering of multiple actions with the activity model construct.

The base concept of activity models in HWS is to allow a designer to define which actions will occur and define an ordering to those actions. Additionally, because the process is modeled at design time instead of runtime, activity models provide additional benefits, including predefining action activation properties and a finer-grained constraint model.

Activity Model Design

At its core, an activity model is a collection of steps that are ordered by transitions. A step in an activity model represents the occurrence of a specific type of action at runtime. A transition in an activity model links two steps in a parent/child relationship, indicating that the parent step must be activated before the child step is activated. The transition also requires that only a user who is at the parent step in the process can activate the child step of the transition. So the transition implies both an order to the process and imposes a security restriction to prevent unauthorized users from continuing a process.

As a concrete example of this, imagine the process a sales associate in a software company might go through to negotiate a contract with a customer. The sales associate must first negotiate the contract with the customer; then the sales associate must get his manager, and the VP for larger contracts, to agree to the contract. Finally, the sales associate must contact the customer to let the customer know the contract has been agreed to. The final process would look something like Figure 18.11.

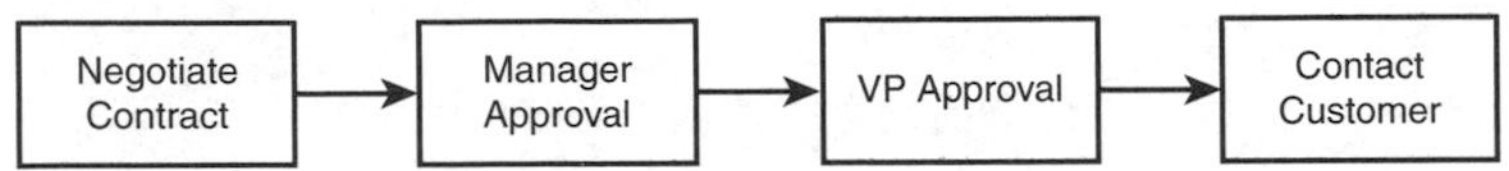

FIGURE 18.11 The contract negotiation process.

After you understand the process you want to model, you are ready to create the process definition in HWS.

Creating an Activity Model

Unlike for orchestrations, there is no visual design environment for activity models. Activity models are created programmatically by using the activity model designer object model. The object model is contained in the `Microsoft.BizTalk.Hws.WorkflowDesign` namespace, exposed in the `Microsoft.BizTalk.Hws.ActivityModelDesignerAPI.dll` file located in the Developers Tools directory under the root install directory for BizTalk.

The activity model object model is quite simplistic and straightforward. Only four major classes are involved in designing any activity model:

- `DesignManager`—The `DesignManager` class is intended as an application environment provider. It is the only class that communicates with your HWS system, and it supplies all the details about the HWS components (actions, other activity models, constraint facts) that are used in the construction of activity models.
- `ActivityModel`—The `ActivityModel` class represents a single activity model. It provides the properties that specify behavior across the entire activity model, it contains the metadata for the activity model, and it serves as a container for all the steps and transitions in the activity model.
- `Step`—The `Step` class represents a single step in the activity model. It maintains the relationship between the activity model step concept and the action type associated with that particular step, including default parameters and constraints.
- `Transition`—The `Transition` class represents a transition from a parent step to a child step in an activity model.

Listing 18.12 utilizes the activity model designer object model to create an activity model that models the business process detailed in Figure 18.11. For the code to work, you must have created the contract agreement action discussed earlier in the chapter and have built and deployed the HWS SDK sample actions (see the help topic Actions in the BizTalk Server Sample for instruction regarding the SDK sample actions).

LISTING 18.12 Creating an Activity Model to Model the Contract Negotiation Process

```
DesignManager designManager = new DesignManager();
designManager.Connect(Environment.MachineName, "BizTalkHwsDb");

ActivityModel activityModel = null;
designManager.CreateActivityModel(out activityModel);

ActionInfo assignAction = null;
ActionInfo contractAgreementAction = null;
ActionInfo[] actions = null;
designManager.GetActionCatalog(out actions);
foreach( ActionInfo action in actions )
{
 if( action.Name == "Contract_Agreement_Action.Action" )
  contractAgreementAction = action;
 else if( action.Name == "Microsoft.Samples.BizTalk.Actions.Assign" )
  assignAction = action;
}

Step negotiateContract, managerApproval, vpApproval, contactCustomer = null;
activityModel.AddStep(assignAction.Id, out negotiateContract);
activityModel.AddStep(contractAgreementAction.Id, out managerApproval);
activityModel.AddStep(contractAgreementAction.Id, out vpApproval);
activityModel.AddStep(assignAction.Id, out contactCustomer);

Transition tempTransition = null;
activityModel.AddTransition(negotiateContract.Id, managerApproval.Id,
➥false, "", "", out tempTransition);
activityModel.AddTransition(managerApproval.Id, vpApproval.Id,
➥false, "", "", out tempTransition);
activityModel.AddTransition(vpApproval.Id, contactCustomer.Id,
➥false, "", "", out tempTransition);

activityModel.Name = "Negotiate Sales Contract Process";
activityModel.Description = "This is the process used to negotiate"
➥+ " and obtain approval of a sales contract";

designManager.SaveActivityModelToSystem(activityModel);
```

The two lines of the code in Listing 18.12 create a new instance of the `DesignManager` class and connects it to a local HWS installation. This is a required first step whenever using the activity model object model, because nothing else will work without a connected

DesignManager. After the connection is made, the code calls the GetActionCatalog method to retrieve a list of all registered actions from HWS and maintains that information in a map keyed to each action's display name.

After the initial setup is done, the code creates the ActivityModel object that will represent the sales contract business process. The metadata (display name and description) values are then updated to identify this activity model to a user.

Next, four Step objects are created in the activity model, corresponding to the four steps identified in Figure 18.11, using the AddStep method of the ActivityModel class. This method creates a new step, associates the action type specified in the parameters to that step, and adds the step to the activity model. After each step is created, the metadata for that step is updated. The metadata supplied at design time gets presented to the client user through the HWS Web service at runtime to give the client more context and information regarding the step.

After all the steps required in the activity model are created, the code creates the transitions specified in Figure 18.11, using the AddTransition method of the ActivityModel class. The first three transitions created are straightforward, each linking the previous step to the next step in the process.

Finally, after the activity model is designed in memory, the last section of the code utilizes the SaveActivityModelToSystem method of the DesignManager class to upload the activity model into the HWS system. After that method is called, the activity model is available for use at runtime.

Executing Activity Models

After the activity model exists in the HWS system, it will be available for any user of the system to activate, with one restriction. Activity models are still subject to the security model of HWS, which means if a user attempts to activate a step in an activity model that is associated with action type A, and the user does not have the authority from system constraints to execute action type A, the user will not be able to activate the step of the activity model. Therefore, the only users who will be able to activate the new activity model will be those users who have constraint authority to activate the action associated with the first step of the activity model.

Executing an instance of an activity model at runtime is very similar to creating a dynamic activity flow, and I will discuss later how the two can intertwine. Listing 18.13 shows a simple program that executes the first two steps of the sales contract business process at runtime.

LISTING 18.13 Executing the First Two Steps of the Contract Negotiation Activity Model

```
HWS.HwsService hwsService = new HWS.HwsService();
hwsService.Credentials = CredentialCache.DefaultCredentials;

Guid activityFlowId = hwsService.GetNewActivityFlowID();
```

LISTING 18.13 Continued

```
// Find the activity we want to initiate
HWS.Activity salesContractProcess = null;
HWS.Activity[] activities = hwsService.GetActivityList(activityFlowId,
➥Guid.Empty, Guid.Empty, "", null);
foreach( HWS.Activity activity in activities )
{
 if( activity.Name == "Negotiate Sales Contract Process" )
  salesContractProcess = activity;
}

// Load the properties for the first step of the activity model
HWS.ActionParameters[] parameters =
➥hwsService.GetActivityModelParameters(salesContractProcess.
➥ActivityModelTypeID, salesContractProcess.ActivationBlockID, null);

XmlDocument paramsDoc = new XmlDocument();
paramsDoc.Load("AssignActionActivationMessage.xml");
paramsDoc.SelectSingleNode("//ActionSection/Task/Target").InnerText =
➥"DOMAIN\\user";
parameters[0].ParametersDoc = paramsDoc.OuterXml;

// Initiate the first step of the activity model
Guid activityModelInstanceID = hwsService.AddActivationBlockToActivityFlow(
➥activityFlowId, Guid.Empty, Guid.Empty,
➥Guid.Empty, false, parameters, null);

System.Threading.Thread.Sleep(5000);

// Find the task assigned by the first activity model step and respond
HWS.TaskFilter filter = new HWS.TaskFilter();
filter.StartTimeEnd = DateTime.MaxValue;
filter.StartTimeStart = DateTime.MinValue;
filter.taskStatus = HWS.TaskStatus.InProgress;
filter.UseStatusFilter = true;
HWS.Task[] tasks = hwsService.GetAllTasksForUser(filter, null);
HWS.Task desiredtask = null;
foreach( HWS.Task task in tasks )
 if( task.ActivityFlowID == activityFlowId )
  desiredtask = task;

XmlDocument taskResponse = new XmlDocument();
taskResponse.LoadXml(hwsService.GetTaskMessage(desiredtask.TaskID, null));
```

LISTING 18.13 Continued

```
taskResponse.SelectSingleNode("//HwsSection/TaskStatus").InnerText =
➥"Completed";
hwsService.SendTaskResponse(taskResponse.OuterXml, null);

// Find the activity we want to initiate
HWS.Activity nextStep = null;
activities = hwsService.GetActivityList(activityFlowId,
➥desiredtask.ActionInstanceID, desiredtask.TaskID, "", null);
foreach( HWS.Activity activity in activities )
{
 if( activity.ActionIndex == 2 )
  nextStep = activity;
}

// Load the properties for the first step of the activity model
parameters = hwsService.GetActivityModelParameters(nextStep.
➥ActivityModelTypeID, nextStep.ActivationBlockID, null);

paramsDoc = new XmlDocument();
paramsDoc.LoadXml(parameters[0].ParametersDoc);
paramsDoc.SelectSingleNode("//ActionSection/ContractApprover").InnerText =
➥"DOMAIN\\user";
paramsDoc.SelectSingleNode("//ActionSection/Contract").InnerText =
➥"Insert contract here";
parameters[0].ParametersDoc = paramsDoc.OuterXml;

// Initiate the next step of the activity model
hwsService.AddActivationBlockToActivityFlow(activityFlowId,
➥activityModelInstanceID,desiredtask.ActionInstanceID,
➥desiredtask.TaskID, false, parameters, null);
```

The preceding code is markedly similar to the code in Listings 18.4 through 18.11, where we created an ad-hoc workflow; but two major differences exist.

First, you can see that a different method is used to compose steps of an activity model into a workflow. `AddActivationBlockToActivityFlow` is used in place of `AddActionToActivityFlow`. The difference between the two methods is that the activity model method requires an additional parameter to specify the instance of the activity model in the activity flow you are activating the next step on, and that the activity model method accepts an array of `ActionParameter` objects. The reason for the latter difference is that at runtime you actually don't activate a specific step in an activity model; you activate what HWS calls an activation block. The activation block concept is explained in the next section.

Dependent and Independent Transitions in Activity Models

I talked briefly about the difference between dependent and independent action activation in HWS earlier when describing sync messages, with the basic idea that a dependently activated action waits for a sync message from its parent action before doing any processing.

In activity models, it is possible to design dependent action activation into your activity model at design time. When you create a transition in your system by calling the `AddTransition` method on the Activity model class (as in Listing 18.12), the third parameter specifies whether the transition is dependent or independent. A dependent transition will cause the child action of the transition to be dependently activated at runtime. Also remember from earlier in the chapter that a dependently activated action must still be manually added to an activity model via the `AddActionToActivityFlow` method. This behavior is slightly different when activating steps in an activity model at runtime. Because it is known ahead of time which steps will be activated dependently or independently, HWS requires that whenever a step is activated, all of its dependent children (and their dependent children, and so on) must be activated at the same time. HWS refers to this group of steps being activated at the same time as an *activation block*. In fact, every step in an activity model is contained in a activation block, but if the step has no dependently linked child steps, the activation block contains only the one step.

Now that you understand the definition of an activation block, the `GetActivityModelParameters` and `AddActivationBlockToActivityFlow` methods should make more sense. Because activating a step may require activating other steps at the same time, these methods have parameters for arrays of `ActionParameter` objects, and for each action that will be activated, there will be one `ActionParameter` object.

Constraints in Activity Models

Activity models introduce three new extensions of the constraint system describe earlier in this chapter, which allow for more fine-grained restrictions for activity models: step constraints, role constraints, and system activity model constraints.

Step Constraints

Step constraints allow the activity model designer to restrict the users who can be chosen as targets or a step when the step is activated. Normally, when a user activates an action, either as a step in an activity model or an ad-hoc action, the set of users the activating user can select as targets of the action is restricted by the system constraints. In some steps of an activity model, though, the designer may want to impose further restrictions on who can be chosen as a target of the step. To do this, the designer would add a step constraint to the step when designing the activity model. Listing 18.14 shows how the code from Listing 18.12 could be changed to enforce a restriction that only the user "Mike" could be chosen as the target of the second step in the sales contract process.

LISTING 18.14 Adding a Step Constraint to an Activity Flow

```
ConstraintFact[] facts = null;
designManager.GetConstraintFacts(out facts);
ConstraintFact usernameFact = null;
foreach(ConstraintFact fact in facts)
        if( fact.Name == "IntrinsicUserName" )
                usernameFact = fact;
clause.FactRetrieverId = usernameFact.FactRetrieverId;
clause.PropertyId = usernameFact.Id;
clause.Operator = 0;
ClauseValue clauseValue = new ClauseValue();
clauseValue.Value = "Mike";
clause.Values.Add(clauseValue);
stepConstraint.AddClause(clause);
managerApproval.AddTargetConstraint(stepConstraint);
```

The preceding code introduces the other two classes exposed in the activity model designer object model: the Constraint class and the Clause class. These classes were designed to programmatically mimic the constraint interface exposed in the HWS administration console. The class properties match the data values required on the dialog boxes in the console. When designing activity models, Constraint classes must be created, initialized with data, have Clause classes constructed and added to them, and then be added to a step via the `AddConstraint` method exposed by the Step class.

Role Constraints

Beyond the individual users who will activate and become targets of the steps in an activity model, there are other users who may need to interact with the activity model at runtime. Again, because the activity model is designed before execution, it is possible to identify such users before the model is executed in runtime.

Activity models use the same constraint system to authorize users in activity model roles as we have seen before. There are three roles defined for an activity model: Initiator, Observer, and Owner. The Initiator role is used to further restrict the user who may activate the activity model. Only the users who satisfy both the initiator role constraints and the system-level constraints for the actions in the root activation block may activate the activity model. Users authorized in the observer role are allowed to query the HWS Web service for the tracking information for that activity model. Normally only participants of an activity flow can query the Web service for this information. The Owner role is the most powerful role. Users authorized in the Owner role can act for any user participating in the activity model. Essentially, an owner is a trusted user within that activity model.

Listing 18.15 shows how we could add the user "Mary" as an observer of the sales contract process activity model.

LISTING 18.15 Adding a Role Constraint to an Activity Model

```
ConstraintFact[] facts = null;
designManager.GetConstraintFacts(out facts);
ConstraintFact usernameFact = null;
foreach(ConstraintFact fact in facts)
 if( fact.Name == "IntrinsicUserName" )
  usernameFact = fact;
clause.FactRetrieverId = usernameFact.FactRetrieverId;
clause.PropertyId = usernameFact.Id;
clause.Operator = 0;
ClauseValue clauseValue = new ClauseValue();
clauseValue.Value = "Mary";
clause.Values.Add(clauseValue);
stepConstraint.AddClause(clause);

Role[] roles = null;
Role observerRole = null;
designManager.GetRoles(out roles);
foreach(Role role in roles)
 if( role.Name == "Observer" )
  observerRole = role;

activityModel.AddRoleConstraint(observerRole.Id, stepConstraint);
```

System Activity Model Constraints

When I first discussed constraints in HWS, I talked about system constraints constraining the initiators, targets, and enacted users for all instances of that action type. Now that we've covered the concept of predefined workflows with activity models, you might have thought about how difficult it becomes to define those constraints properly. In some workflows, you may want a certain action very highly restricted, but in other less-important workflows, you may want anyone to use the action. Because system constraints apply across all workflows and activity models, this would be impossible.

18

To handle such a situation, HWS supports the capability to create system activity model constraints. These are defined exactly like system constraints, using the same process, except that you select an activity model from the activity model drop–down list.

The existence of a system activity model constraint overrides all system constraints for the specified action type in that activity model. They allow you to specify more or fewer restrictions on a specific action type when users are activating that action in the context of an activity model.

Interaction Between Activity Models and Ad-Hoc Actions

One of the most important features of HWS is that it does not restrict you to choose either dynamic or predefined action composition in an activity flow; you can use both methods of composition in the same activity flow. For example, you could start an activity flow with an activity model, and then halfway through the steps defined in the activity model compose, in an ad-hoc manner, actions that weren't defined as part of the activity model into the activity flow. Likewise, you could start off an activity flow with a bunch of ad-hoc action compositions and then compose an activity model into the activity flow.

The first situation just described commonly arises when an activity model does not completely capture a process, or the current instance of the process is an exception to the rule, in which case a participant user needs to dynamically extend the process. The second situation commonly occurs when a loosely defined process contains a well-defined subprocess, so the subprocess has been designed as an activity model that will occur somewhere in the dynamically created process.

Summary

After reading this chapter, you should be able to develop workflow actions and activity models and define workflow constraints. You should also be able to integrate the HWS workflow model with client applications using the HWS Web service API.

Developing workflows in HWS consists of decomposing the business scenario into a set of actions and composing them either a priori into an Activity Model or Activity Flow at runtime. HWS workflows can be made available in any client application using the HWS Web Service API, which provides a mechanism to query and dynamically modify the workflow.

TIP

Microsoft InfoPath 2003 SP1 provides out-of-box support for composing and viewing HWS workflows within InfoPath and is well suited to form-based workflow scenarios.

CHAPTER 19

Business Activity Services

IN THIS CHAPTER

- Business Scenarios for BAS
- Development of a Sample BAS Project
- Deployment of a BAS Project
- Configuring Sample Trading Partners and Business Process
- Executing and Interacting with the Sample Business Process
- Monitoring the Sample Business Process

BizTalk Server 2004 was developed with the goal of providing the right tools for the right users. Business Activity Services (BAS) enables business users to manage trading partners and associated business processes. To address the needs of these business users, BAS is built on business user-friendly Microsoft Windows SharePoint Services and leverages Microsoft Office technologies, including Microsoft InfoPath 2003 and Microsoft Excel 2003, which are familiar to the business user.

NOTE

Because of the dependency on Microsoft Windows SharePoint Services, BAS can be installed only on Windows Server 2003, which includes Microsoft Windows SharePoint Services.

The BAS feature is centered on a Microsoft Windows SharePoint Services intranet site, the BAS site. This site provides a centralized place for business users to collaborate with each other to manage their business. The site includes two major groups of functionality: Trading Partner Management and Business Process Management.

- The Trading Partner Management tool enables business users to define Trading Partners and the Agreements that specify how these Trading Partners participate in business processes. These definitions are used to configure the BizTalk Server runtime to execute the processes that integrate with these Trading Partners. The BAS site also enables business users to interact with business processes by using Microsoft InfoPath 2003 to view and edit message document instances associated with these business processes.

- The Business Process Management tool enables business users to monitor business processes by providing access to Business Activity Monitoring (BAM) views via an interactive BAM query wizard hosted in the Windows SharePoint Services site and via Microsoft Excel 2003.

The steps required to enable business users to use BAS to manage their business include several distinct phases: Development, Deployment, Configuration, Interaction, and Monitoring. Although this chapter focuses on enabling the business user, it is important to note that the development and deployment of these business processes is performed by developers and IT professionals.

NOTE

This chapter assumes the reader has a technical understanding of BizTalk Server Orchestrations, including the use of parties and role links.

Business Scenarios for BAS

BAS can be applied to a number of business scenarios. BAS is primarily targeted toward trading partner integration scenarios, but can easily be leveraged for interdepartmental integration. Because BAS provides simple, manageable interaction with business users, it can also be used for business-level exception management or any scenario in which a business user needs to view business process data and provide input into a running business process.

Trading Partner Integration

Companies can benefit from integrating with their trading partners to reduce transaction processing costs, reduce errors, increase operational efficiency, and increase the timeliness and accuracy of information about business transactions. Classic examples of these interactions include data synchronization for product, pricing, and customer information, and business transaction and status information around supply-chain management transactions.

Interdepartmental Integration

These same scenarios can also apply for interactions between branches or subsidiaries of a single company. Companies often have the same challenges communicating across departments as they do with external trading partners.

Business User Interaction

Not all processes can be automated end to end. Frequently, business processes require input from a business user. Examples include approval processes, data entry, and exception management. BAS provides the infrastructure to easily add business user input into a business process. This applies to points of interaction known at design time. For ad hoc human workflow, see Chapter 18, "Human-based Workflow."

Development of a Sample BAS Project

The first step in enabling business users to manage their business processes is to develop and deploy the process itself. BizTalk Server 2004 defines business processes using orchestrations. For business users to manage these business processes with BAS, the orchestrations must be designed in a way that allows the BAS Trading Partner Management tool to discover and configure them.

In this section, we will walk step-by-step through the development of a sample BAS project.

Sample Scenario

The sample project included with this chapter implements a business process that receives a purchase order from a trading partner and responds back to the trading partner with an invoice after fulfilling the order. The first step in the process is the automated electronic receipt of the purchase order message from the trading partner. This purchase order is received and then submitted to a Line of Business (LOB) accounting application and the BAS site. In this sample scenario, integration with the LOB accounting application is automated, but the fulfillment of the order is a manual process performed by a business user. To enable the inclusion of the business user in this process, the business user opens the purchase order on the BAS site in InfoPath and manually fulfills the order. After the order has been fulfilled, appropriate entries are made in the accounting application that exports an invoice. The business user reviews the invoice to ensure that it matches the order fulfilled and then submits the invoice to the BAS site, which sends it back to the BizTalk Server. The BizTalk Server correlates the invoice with the appropriate purchase order based on the order's reference number and then sends it back to the trading partner to complete the Order to Invoice process. Business processes vary greatly from one business to another, so this example is intended to be just that—an example.

> **NOTE**
>
> The sample BizTalk project included in the code download for this chapter includes an orchestration, document schemas, InfoPath templates, and document instances needed to deploy, run, and demonstrate the use of a BAS-enabled BizTalk project.

Getting Started with the Sample BizTalk Server Project

BAS-enabled projects are built using an Empty BizTalk Server Project template in Microsoft Visual Studio .NET. You can also modify any existing orchestration in a BizTalk project to make it BAS-enabled.

To get started using the sample BAS project for this chapter, open the `OrderMgmt.sln` solution in Visual Studio .NET.

Document Schemas

Similar to other BizTalk projects, you'll need to include XSD schemas for the message documents involved in the process along with any required maps.

The following schemas have already been added to the project:

- PurchaseOrderSchema.xsd
- InvoiceSchema.xsd

The following properties have been promoted in these purchase order and Invoice schemas:

- The `chargeTo` property will be used to determine which trading partner sent the originating purchase order message.
- The `referenceNumber` property will be used for correlation.
- The `ShippingMethod` property will be used to demonstrate how Agreement-level parameters can be used within the orchestration.

InfoPath Forms

BAS helps enable business users to view the previously defined message documents in InfoPath forms. You can create these InfoPath forms using the same XSD schemas used in the BizTalk Server project. To do so, open the InfoPath application in the Design mode, click New from Data Source, and point to the XSD schema created in Visual Studio .NET. You can then drag and drop elements from the schema onto the form surface, including controls, and then customize as needed.

NOTE

See InfoPath documentation for more information on designing InfoPath forms.

When you've finished creating the InfoPath form, you then need to Publish the form. This InfoPath Publishing process decorates the form with a reference to the location to which it is being published. Because you will later upload this form to a location on the BAS site, you should not enter a location when Publishing the form. So, when prompted with the following message, If the Users Require an Alternative Access Path That Points to the Saved Location...Enter It Below, clear the path in the text box, leaving it blank, and then click Finish. When you eventually upload these forms, they will be updated with references to their new location on the Windows SharePoint Services site.

The following InfoPath forms are included in the sample code:

- PurchaseOrder.xsn
- Invoice.xsn

TPPubWS Web Service

The BAS Trading Partner Publishing Web Service (TPPubWS) provides orchestrations with runtime access to parameters configured by the business user in an Agreement. This Web service includes the `GetParameterValue` method for this purpose. Because this Web service includes methods that use complex types that are not supported in this release of BizTalk Server 2004, perform the following steps to point to an alternative WSDL to add a reference to the supported methods on this Web service in your project:

1. Right-click Web References and select Add Web Reference.
2. Enter the following path into the URL text box:

```
[installed drive]\Program Files\Microsoft BizTalk Server 2004\
Business Activity Services\TPM\tppubws.wsdl
```

3. Click Go.
4. After the `GetPararmeterValue` is successfully returned by your search, click Add Reference.

NOTE

If you attempt to add this Web reference to your BizTalk project by browsing to the Microsoft.BizTalk.KwTpm.TPPubWS ASMX page, you will encounter a Request Format Is Unrecognized error. This error is expected and is a result of tightened security on the Web service. You should navigate to the WSDL file specified previously instead of using the ASMX page.

Adding this Web reference adds the following Types to the orchestration properties:

- Port Types
- `TPPubWS` includes the `GetParameterValue` operation.
- Multipart Message Types
- `GetParameterValue_request` includes four strings, which serve as the parameters for the Web services call:
  - `serviceName`—The fully qualified name of the orchestration, using the format namespaceName.OrchestrationName.
  - `serviceLinkTypeName`—The type name of the role link to which it applies in the orchestration, using the format namespaceName.serviceLinkTypeName.
  - `parameterName`—The name extracted from the role link type name, preceding the `"PolicyType"` string. For exemple, a role line type of

19

"DiscountAmountPolicyType" would have a ParameterName of "DiscountAmount."

- partnerID—The organization name of the partner.

- GetParameterValue_response includes a single string returned by the Web service.
    - GetParameterValueResult—Returns the value for the specified parameter.

BAS Port Types

To enable configuration and interaction with these business processes from the BAS site, BAS uses several reserved port types. These BAS Port Types are used in the BAS reserved Role Links defined in the following section. These port types must be created using the following port type names:

- sendToInboxPT—The sendToInboxPT port type is used to send message documents from an orchestration to the Inbox folder of a particular trading partner's document library on the BAS site. Each partner configured on the BAS site will have its own Inbox document library.
- receiveFromOutboxPT—The receiveFromOutboxPT port type is used to receive message documents from the Outbox document library on the BAS site. A single Outbox folder is used to connect the BAS site to the BizTalk Server.
- sendToSentItemsPT—The sendToSentItemsPT port type is used to move the message document from the BAS site Outbox to the SentItems folder of a particular trading partner's document library. Each partner configured on the BAS site will have its own SentItems document library.

NOTE

These Type names are case sensitive and must be created using the specific reserved names.

Figure 19.1 shows the port types listed in the Orchestration view for the sample OrderMgmtProcess.odx orchestration in VisualStudio .NET IDE.

The port types in the sample orchestration were created as follows:

1. In the Orchestration view, Types window, right-click Port Types, click New One-Way Port Type, and then name it **sendToInboxPT** in the identifier field in the Properties window.
2. Expand SendToInboxPT and rename Operation _1 to **SendPurchaseOrder** in the identifier field in the Properties window.

3. Expand the `SendPurchaseOrder` operation and select PO. In the Properties window at the Message Type box, expand Schemas and select `OrderMgmtProcess.PurchaseOrderSchema`.

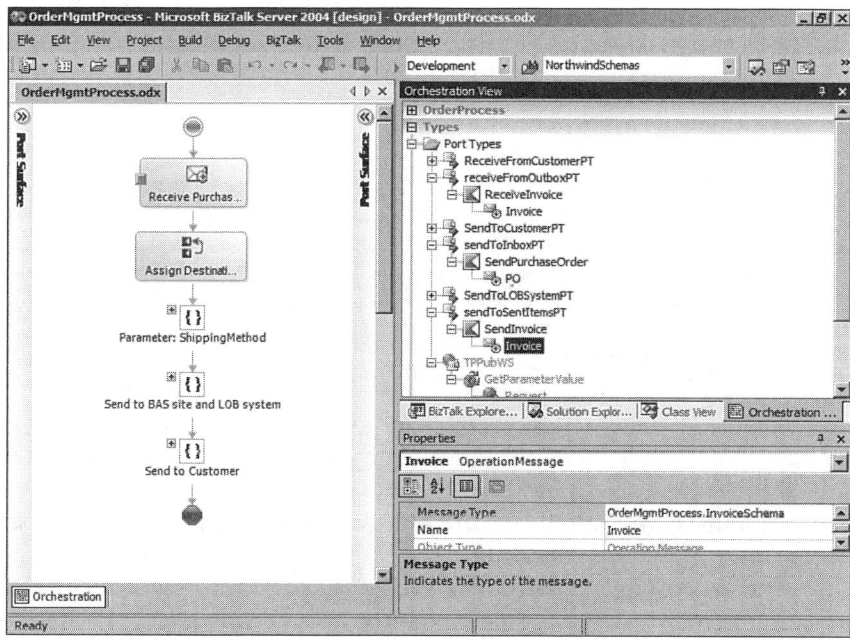

FIGURE 19.1 Orchestration view inside Visual Studio .NET, including configured port types.

The previous steps were used to create all the One-way Port Types listed in Table 19.1.

TABLE 19.1 Orchestration Port Type Configuration

Port Type Name	Operation	Message
`ReceiveFromCustomerPT`	`ReceivePurchaseOrder`	`PO`
`SendToCustomerPT`	`SendInvoice`	`Invoice`
`SendToLOBSystemPT`	`SendPurchaseOrder`	`PO`
`sendToInboxPT`	`SendPurchaseOrder`	`PO`
`sendToSentItemsPT`	`SendInvoice`	`Invoice`
`receiveFromOutboxPT`	`ReceiveInvoice`	`Invoice`

The preceding table includes the `SendToCustomerPT` and `ReceiveFromCustomerPT` used to integrate with the external Trading Partners. Also included is the `SendToLOBSystemPT`, which is used to represent the integration with the internal LOB accounting application.

You will notice that the TPPubWS is also listed with the preceding port types in the Orchestration view. This port type is automatically configured for you when you add the reference to the TPPubWS Web service in the project.

BAS Role Link Types

Similar to the BAS port types, BAS Role Link Types must be created using the following reserved Role Link Type names.

- `sendBusinessDocumentsLT`—The `sendBusinessDocumentsLT` Role Link Type is used to send message documents to the BAS site. This Role Link Type must include a Role named `sender`, which must contain one or both of the following port types:
  - `sendToInboxPT`
  - `sendToSentItemsPT`
- `receiveBusinessDocumentsLT`—The `receiveBusinessDocumentsLT` Role Link Type is used to receive message documents from the BAS site. This Role Link Type must include a Role named `receiver`, which must contain the following port type:
  - `receiveFromOutboxPT`
- `ParameterNamePolicyType`—Orchestrations can contain Agreement-specific parameters using Role Links with a type name ending with the string `PolicyType`. The name of this Role Link Type, excluding the `PolicyType` string, is exposed as the parameter name in the InfoPath Agreement form that is configured by the business user. For example, a Role Link Type defined as `ShippingMethodPolicyType` would expose a parameter named ShippingMethod in the Agreement form. Each PolicyType Role Link implements a Web service which returns a single string. If the orchestration requires multiple configurable parameters, additional PolicyType Role Links can be added to the orchestration.

NOTE

These Type names are case sensitive and must be created using the specific reserved names.

Figure 19.2 shows the role link types listed in the Orchestration view for the sample OrderMgmtProcess.odx orchestration in VisualStudio .NET IDE.

The Role Link Types in the sample orchestration were created as follows:

1. In the Orchestration view, Types window, right-click Role Link Types, create a New Role Link Type, and name it **`OrderToInvoiceLT`**.
2. Expand `OrderToInvoiceLT` and rename Role_1 to **`Customer`**. Right-click the Customer role and select Add Port type. This will bring up the Port Type Wizard.
3. Click Next.
4. Select Use an Existing Port Type and select OrderProcessMgmt.SendToCustomerPT as the port type.
5. Click Next, and then click Finish.

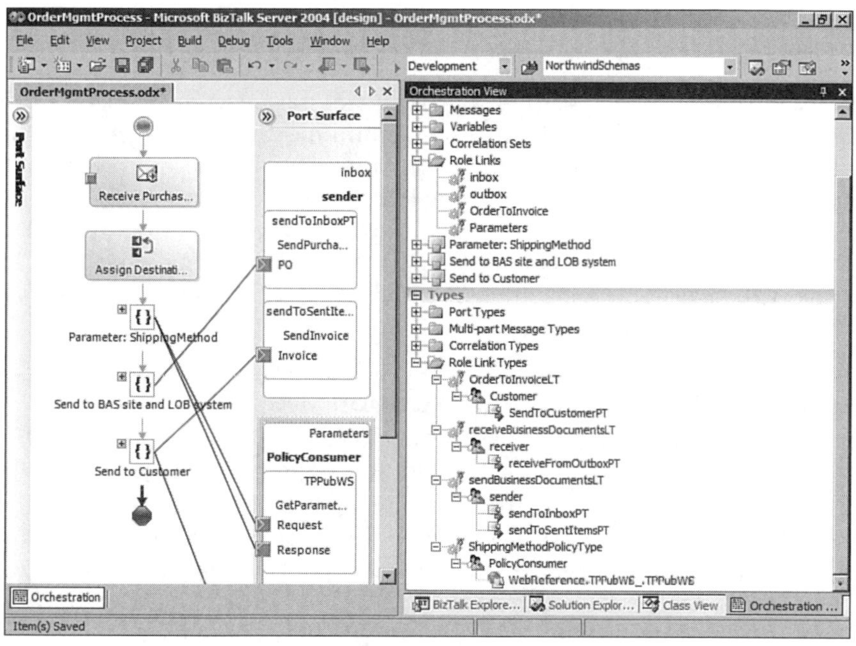

FIGURE 19.2 Orchestration view in Visual Studio .NET, including configured Role Link Types.

Repeat the previous steps to create additional Role Link Types using the parameters as shown in Table 19.2.

TABLE 19.2 Orchestration Role Link Type Configuration

Role Link Type Name	Role	PortTypeRef
`OrderToInvoicePT`	Customer	`SendToCustomerPT`
`sendBusinessDocumentsLT`	sender	`sendToInboxPT`
`sendBusinessDocumentsLT`	sender	`sendToSentItemsPT`
`receiveBusinessDocumentsLT`	receiver	`receiveFromOutboxPT`
`ShippingMethodPolicyType`	PolicyConsumer	`OrderMgmt.WebReference.TPPubWS_.TPPubWS`

Using BAS Types

BAS-enabled orchestrations must include a public Role Link representing the relationship between your business and your trading partners, whether they are vendors, customers, or others. The Role Link is configured by creating Agreements representing how these trading partners participate in these relationships. The reserved BAS Role Link Types will be configured in conjunction with this public Role Link. Only the public, nonreserved Role Link Types are listed as available for configuration by the business user in the Agreement form. The reserved BAS Role Links are configured in conjunction with this public Role

Link. In the BAS site, the business user configures one or more trading partners as Partner Profiles. These Partner Profiles are enlisted to play the Used Role in this Role Link.

BAS defines several Role Link Types for exchanging message documents between an orchestration and the BAS site. Additional Role Link Types are used to retrieve Agreement-specific parameters and make them available as runtime variables to the orchestration. The use of each reserved Role Link Type is optional. If the business process requires only sending message documents to the BAS site but not receiving them from the BAS site, the developer can create a Role Link that implements the `sendBusinessDocumentsLT` Role Link Type and `sendToinboxPT` port type. Implementing any combination of BAS reserved Types is optional based on the requirements of the scenario.

Configuring a BAS-Enabled Orchestration

BAS-enabled orchestrations have a single requirement and many optional add-ons. The single requirement to BAS-enable an orchestration is to implement a public Role Link. The Role Link is the discoverable artifact that is configurable by the BAS Trading Partner Management (TPM) tool. This TPM tool allows business users to create Partner Profiles that are used to automatically create BizTalk Parties. The TPM tool also allows business users to configure Agreements that are used to enlist an associated Partner Profile to play the Role described in the public Role Link. Partner Profiles and Agreements are business user-friendly metaphors used to help business users configure BizTalk Parties and Role Links, respectively. The Activation of an Agreement enlists the associated BizTalk Party in the Used Role in the Role Link being configured, as well as any of the previously described reserved Role Link Types if they exist in the orchestration. Lastly, this Agreement will dynamically create the required Send Ports that are bound to the Ports associated with these reserved Role Link Types in addition to the Send Port associated with the actual public Role Link being configured.

Figure 19.3 shows the Orchestration Designer for the sample OrderMgmtProcess.odx orchestration in VisualStudio .NET IDE.

We will describe the construction of this orchestration in more detail in the following sections as we walk through the design of the sample BAS project.

Receive Documents from Trading Partner

The first step in this sample orchestration is to receive the message document from the trading partner. In the sample, we have used a simple file receive port to receive the message document. Alternatively, this initial receive port can be configured as part of the Role Link, which includes the send port, to the trading partner and take advantage of BizTalk Server's automatic party resolution functionality. This requires the use of a receive port that is configured to use an HTTP receive port in conjunction with the default XML receive pipeline or a custom pipeline. When used with the HTTP receive port, the default XML pipeline performs party resolution based on user context of the HTTP POST. A custom pipeline can also be written to perform party resolution based on other message context for any inbound transport type (for example, filename in a file transport or XML element value in the message document). The use of party resolution sets the Destination Party for the Customer Role in the public Role Link equal to the Party configured for the trading partner that sent the message document. As a result, if a send port is used in that same Role Link later in the orchestration, the Role Link will already be configured to send to that specific destination Party, or trading partner.

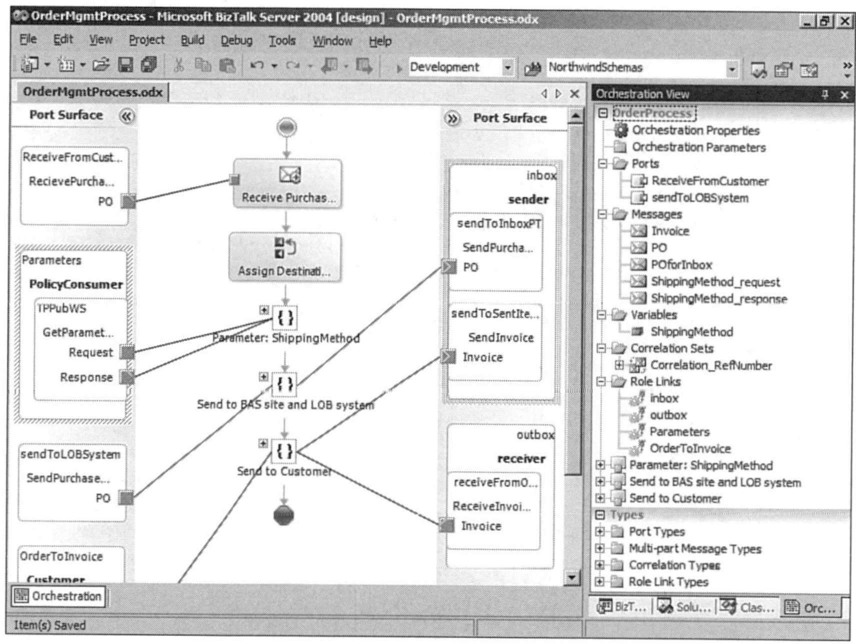

FIGURE 19.3 Sample BAS orchestration in Visual Studio .NET Orchestration Designer.

Assign Parties

For the Role Links in the orchestration that are not configured by party resolution, you'll need to programmatically set the destination Party of each Role.

In the sample orchestration where automated Party resolution is not used, developers must set the destination Party programmatically in an Expression shape. This can be seen in the next step in our sample orchestration, in which the destination Party is set for the externally facing OrderToInvoice Role Link and the internally facing inbox and Parameter Role Links. The code to make this assignment looks like the following:

```
inbox(Microsoft.XLANGs.BaseTypes.DestinationParty) =
➥new Microsoft.XLANGs.BaseTypes.Party(PO
➥(OrderMgmtProcess.PropertySchema.chargeTo), "OrganizationName");
```

The preceding code sets the destination Party for the inbox Role Link to the Party with the `OrganizationName` equal to the value of the `chargeTo` element in the `PurchaseOrder` message. This `OrganizationName` is defined as the Partner Name in the Partner Profile. If automated Party resolution is used, you can alternatively set the destination Party for these Role Links equal to the destination Party already set on the initiating Role Link.

Parameter Web Service

One of the Role Links referenced in the Expression shape described previously is the Parameter Role Link that is used to retrieve a parameter value configured by the business user in the Agreement. This value is retrieved by calling the TPPubWS Web service.

Figure 19.4 shows the parameter Web service configured in the Orchestration Designer and Orchestration view in VisualStudio .NET IDE.

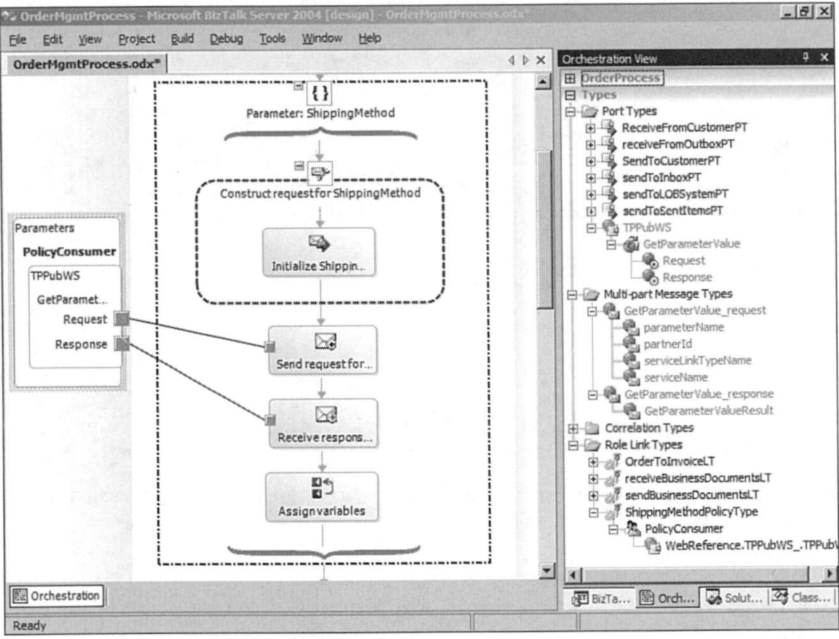

FIGURE 19.4 Orchestration Designer view of call to Parameter Web service.

To call this Web service, we must first construct the multipart message that will be passed to the Web service. The multipart message type was created when we registered the TPPubWS Web service. However, the orchestration Message variable must be created manually as follows:

1. In the orchestration view, right-click Messages and create a New Message. Name it **`ShippingMethod_request`**.
2. In the Properties window at the Message Type box, expand Web Message Types and select

```
OrderMgmtProcess.WebReference.TPPubWS_.GetParameterValue_request
```

Repeat the previous steps to create the other Messages using the parameters shown in Table 19.3.

TABLE 19.3 Orchestration Message Variable Configuration

Message (Name)	Message Type
ShippingMethod_request	WebReference.TPPubWS_.GetParameterValue_request
ShippingMethod_response	WebReference.TPPubWS_.GetParameterValue_response
PO	PurchaseOrderSchema
POForInbox	PurchaseOrderSchema
Invoice	InvoiceSchema

The use of the POForInbox message is described later in this chapter.

The ShippingMethod_request message is constructed by setting values for the four parts of the outbound multipart message as follows:

- parameterName—The parameterName is the name of the Role Link Type minus the string "PolicyType". This is also the parameter name displayed in the Agreement.
- partnerId—The partnerId is the Partner identifier referenced in the Trading Partner Profile. You can set this parameter using the same value used to set the Destination Party in the Assign Destination Party expression.
- serviceLinkTypeName—The serviceLinkTypeName is the Role Link Type configured by the Agreement. Not to be confused with the Role Link Type of the parameter, this Role Link Type is used to configure the interaction with the external trading partner.
- serviceName—The serviceName is the qualified name of the orchestration.

After calling the TPPubWS Web service, the next shape in the parameter scope is a Receive shape, which receives the returned parameter value for the specified Agreement in the ShippingMethod_response message. The TPPubWS Web service essentially queries the TPM database and returns the value stored in the specified Agreement.

The last shape shown in this Parameter scope is an Expression that assigns the returned parameter to an orchestration variable used in the ConstructPOforInbox shape to set the ShippingMethod in the purchase order equal to the value configured in the Agreement. This is an example of how BAS enables the business user to define dynamic business-level configurations of business processes that are made available to the orchestration at runtime.

Send Documents to Trading Partner

Let's look closer at how this message document is sent to the BAS site.

Figure 19.5 shows integration with the BAS Inbox configured in the Orchestration Designer and Orchestration view in VisualStudio .NET IDE.

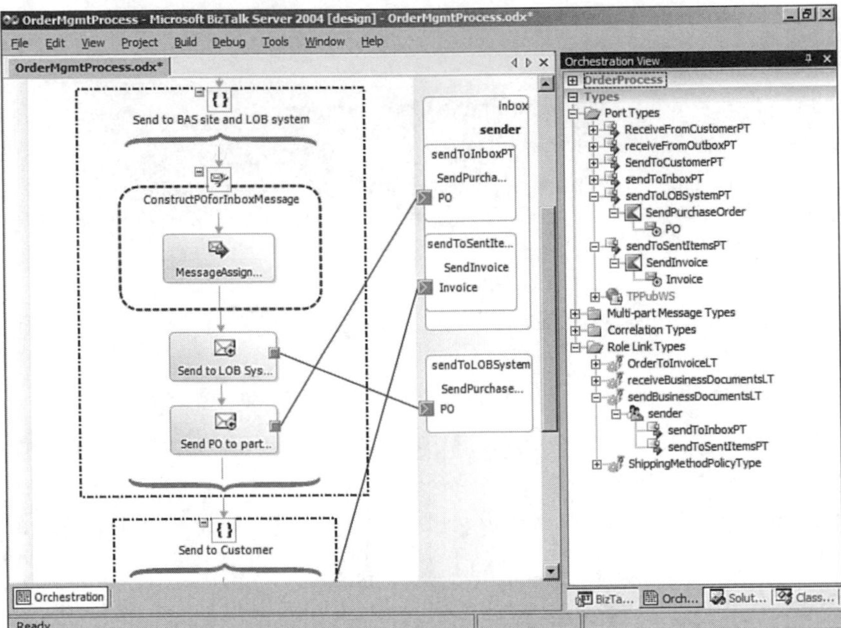

FIGURE 19.5 Orchestration Designer view of Send to inbox and LOB application.

The Construct Message shape is used to create a new instance of the message document to be sent to the "`inbox`" document library on the BAS site. This is an optional step that allows the developer to apply a meaningful filename to the file written to the inbox by setting the filename property for the message in the Message Construction shape. The additional benefit of assigning a specific filename to the file is to prevent writing duplicate copies of this message to the BAS site. This could occur if the send port used to send the message failed after Posting the message to the BAS site but before receiving the HTTP Post acknowledgement, resulting in a retry of the send port. The code in the Message Assignment shape inside the Message Construct shape looks like the following:

```
POforInbox = PO;
POforInbox(Microsoft.BizTalk.KwTpm.StsDefaultPipelines.OutboxFileName)
➥= "PurchaseOrder-"+ PO(OrderMgmtProcess.PropertySchema.referenceNumber);
```

A new message must be constructed because you can only modify message properties in a Message Construct shape. You cannot modify an existing message that has already been constructed.

To set this property, you'll first need to add a reference in the BizTalk project to the `Microsoft.BizTalk.KwTpm.StsDefaultPipelines.dll` assembly located in the `[installed directory]\Program Files\Microsoft BizTalk Server 2004\SEED directory.`

The Send shape is then used to finally send the message document to the BAS site via the `sendToInboxPT` port type in the `inbox` Role Link.

Receive Documents from the BAS Site

The next shape in the sample orchestration is a receive shape that instructs the orchestration to wait for the response from the business user on the BAS site. As this is likely to take a moment, the orchestration will pause until BizTalk Server receives this response message document. The Receive shape is used to receive the message from the BAS site via the "`receiveFromOutboxPT`" port type in the "`outbox`" Role Link. This Receive shape is bound to the `Sts.Outbox` receive port, which is automatically created when the BizTalk Server is registered in the BAS site.

The receive port only transactionally ensures that the message has been received from the BAS site by BizTalk Server. Therefore, the message document is left in the BAS site Outbox document library until BizTalk Server has successfully delivered the message document to the Trading Partner. To communicate to the business user that the message has been delivered successfully all the way to the Trading Partner, developers configure another send port, which writes this message document to the SentItems folder after sending it to the Trading Partner. The Web service that writes this message document into the `SentItems` folder also removes the correlated message from the Outbox document library. This communicates to the business user that this message document has been successfully sent to the Trading Partner and stores a copy of the message document in the SentItems document library for future reference.

Figure 19.6 shows integration with the BAS Outbox configured in the Orchestration Designer and Orchestration view in VisualStudio .NET IDE.

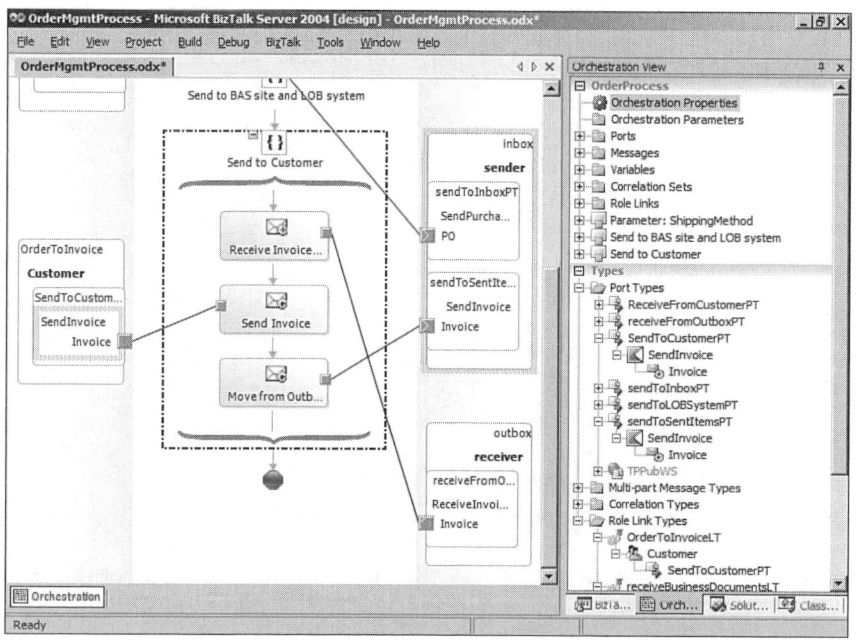

FIGURE 19.6 Orchestration Designer view of Receive from outbox and Send to SentItems.

This is represented in the orchestration by several Send and Receive shapes. A Receive shape is connected to the `outbox` Role Link, followed by a Send shape connected to the pubic `OrderToInvoice` Role Link for the trading partner, and then a final Send shape connecting to the `SendToSentItemsPT` in the `inbox` Role Link. This `SendToSentItemsPT` sends the message document to an ASPX page on the BAS site, which writes the message document to the `SentItems` document library and simultaneously removes the correlated message document from the `outbox` document library on the BAS site.

Deployment of a BAS Project

Deployment of a BAS project is similar to deployment of any BizTalk Server project that includes an orchestration. You'll need to deploy the project and then bind, enlist, and start the orchestration.

The sample BAS-enabled orchestration requires several send ports and receive ports. These ports must be created and then bound to the orchestration. The BAS Trading Partner Management (TPM) tool provides a simplified InfoPath user interface for the configuration of global ports used to send message documents to trading partners. The global port information configured in these forms is then used to automatically create the appropriate send ports for the orchestrations configured in the Agreements. We'll describe global ports in more detail in the "Configuring Partner Profiles" section of this chapter.

The TPM tool also creates all the send ports used by the reserved BAS port types. The TPM tool does not create receive ports. The design assumes that a set of common receive ports can be used by multiple trading partners to receive message documents and pass them to the orchestration. But the send ports used to send message documents to trading partners need to be specific for each individual trading partner.

This section describes how to deploy the BAS project to the BizTalk Server and set up the BAS site.

Set Up the BAS Site

The BAS site is created by the BizTalk Configuration Wizard during setup. You can browse this site by clicking Business Activity Services Site on the Start, Program Files menu under Microsoft BizTalk Server. This BAS site is a generic Microsoft Windows SharePoint Services site that can be configured to include any additional libraries and Web parts you might add to any Microsoft Windows SharePoint Services site. This site is intended to be an internal intranet site.

In the "Configuring Sample Trading Partners and Business Process" section of this chapter, we'll discuss using this site to configure and interact with business processes, but first it needs to be registered to integrate with a specific instance of BizTalk Server. Registering a BizTalk Server on the Business Activity Services site configures a receive port (Sts.Outbox) and receive location, which provide connectivity from the BAS site to the BizTalk Server.

This registration also points the BAS site to locations of other BizTalk resources as described next.

To register a BAS site, complete the following steps:

NOTE

You must be a member of the BizTalk Administrators group to register a BizTalk Server on the BAS site.

1. Start the Business Activity Services (BAS) Site by going to Start, All Programs, Microsoft BizTalk Server 2004, Business Activity Services Site.
2. Under Trading Partner Management Tools, click BizTalkServers to open the BizTalkServers Web page.
3. Click the Register BizTalkServer link to open the BizTalk Servers: New Item Web page.
4. Configure the following properties on the registration page:
   - Registration Name—User-defined name for the BizTalk Server.
   - BizTalk Management Database Server Name—Name of the SQL Server on which the BizTalk Server Management database is deployed.
   - BizTalk Management Database—Name of the BizTalk Server Management database. The default name for this database is BizTalkMgmtDB.
   - BizTalk Server Computer—Name of the computer on which the BizTalk Server is deployed.
   - BAM Query Web Service URL—URL for the BAM Query Web Service. This field is prepopulated with the following local URL: `http://localmachinename/BAMQueryWebSvc/QueryWebService.asmx`

   This URL can be modified if BAM is installed on a remote machine.

The registration step stores this reference information in the Trading Partner Management database and creates the receive port used by BizTalk Server to receive message documents from the BAS site. If the BizTalk Server Computer name defined in the registration is the local machine, BAS will configure a File receive port pointing to the following directory:

```
\Documents and Settings\All Users\Application Data\Microsoft\
➥BizTalk Server 2004\DefaultReceiveLocation\
```

If the BizTalk Server Computer name defined in the registration is not the local machine, BAS will configure an MSMQT receive port on the remote BizTalk Server.

19

The BizTalk SharePoint Messaging Adapter service uses this receive location to send message documents from the BAS site to the BizTalk Server. When a user writes a document to the Outbox document library on the BAS site, Windows SharePoint Services throws an event. The BizTalk SharePoint Messaging Adapter service listens for this event and when it is received, it takes a copy of the message and either writes it to the local file receive location or sends it to the remote MSMQT queue. The status of the file in the Outbox document library is then updated to state that the document has successfully been submitted to BizTalk Server. The orchestration that receives this message should include a send port after the successful reception of the message, which writes a copy of the message sent on to the trading partner back to the BAS site for reference. Writing this message document to the SentItems folder using the specialized Send port type will also delete the associated message from the Outbox document library, thereby transactionally confirming that the message document from the Outbox was successfully received by the orchestration before being removed from the Outbox.

NOTE

This receive port is always named Sts.Outbox, regardless of which transport type is configured.

Registration also stores the location of the BizTalk Server Management Database used by the BAS Web services to configure BizTalk Server.

The BizTalk Server registration also creates the Outbox document library on the BAS site:

```
http:// [BAS machine names]/sites/BASSite/[registration name]_Outbox/
```

Deploying the Sample BizTalk Project

There are no unique requirements around deploying a BAS-enabled project. The project should be built, deployed, bound, enlisted, and started like any other BizTalk orchestration project.

When deploying the sample project for this chapter, you'll need to create and configure the project to point to an Assembly Key File.

You will need to create the send and receive ports not automatically created by the TPM tool. These include any additional receive ports used on the orchestration other than the `Sts.Outbox` and any send port types not reserved by BAS.

To deploy the sample project, create a single File receive port and File send port pointing to local folders.

Bind the sample orchestration to these ports as listed in Table 19.4.

TABLE 19.4 Orchestration Port Binding Configuration

Port Type	Physical Port	Comments
`_outbox_receiveFromOutboxPT`	`Sts.Outbox`	This port is created by the BizTalk Registration process on the BAS site.
`receiveFromCustomerPT`	User Defined (example: File receive port)	This is the port used to receive message documents regardless of trading partner. This receive port could have multiple receive locations.
`sendToLOBSystemPT`	User Defined (example: File send port)	This is the port used to send message documents to the LOB application that processes the orders. In this sample we recommend using a simple File Transport.

Configuring Sample Trading Partners and Business Process

BAS enables developers to design flexible business processes that integrate with various trading partners that play a role in that process. An example of this flexible business process design is the use of Role Links to send a message document to a Vendor role, where the specific vendor is not defined at design time. Instead, the business user defines a Profile for the specific vendor and an Agreement describing how this vendor enlists in this role. This Profile and Agreement configuration is done at runtime and thus enables business users to add, remove, and modify the vendors participating in this business process by playing this role, without making code changes to the orchestration or taking the system offline. There is the additional option of configuring Agreement-specific runtime parameters for the orchestration. In this section, we describe how business users create these Profiles and Agreements and how they are used to configure the underlying BizTalk Server.

After the project has been deployed and started, the business user can configure and use it. Many of the configuration steps described in this section can be performed by an IT professional or developer using the BizTalk Explorer tool. The value of the BAS TPM tool is to provide nontechnical business users with the capability to define Partner Profiles for their trading partners and configure Agreements that define the business relationship between these trading partners and the associated business processes. These simplified Profiles and Agreements hide the technical information from the business user and allow them to configure these partners and processes using terminology and tools they understand.

Security Considerations

Before business users can configure anything, they need to be given permission. The BAS installation by default configures the Windows SharePoint Services site groups and

Windows Local Groups listed in Table 19.5. Ensure that the appropriate users are in the appropriate groups.

TABLE 19.5 BAS User Group Permissions

Site Group (Name)	Local Group (Name)	Permissions
Business User	BizTalk BAS Users	• Create profiles, assign profile classification, view existing profiles, and delete profiles. • Create, send, and browse documents. • Create agreements.
Business Manager	BizTalk BAS Managers	The Business Manager has permission to do everything the Business User can do, plus the following: • Create, edit, deploy, and browse Agreements. • Create, edit, deploy and undeploy, and browse Profiles. • Create and delete Partner Groups.
Business Administrator	BizTalk BAS Administrators	The Business Administrator has permission to do everything the Business Manager can do, plus the following: • Create, edit, and delete BizTalk Server registrations. • Resync and Repair Trading Partner Management Administration.

Configuring Self Profiles

The first step in using the BAS TPM tool is to create a Self Profile used to define identification information representing the business user's company. Users can create multiple Self Profiles to represent themselves differently to different trading partners, for example, if the company wants to have different self profiles for different departments in the company.

To configure a Self Profile in the BAS TPM tool, click the My Profiles link under the Trading Partner Management Administration Tools section of the left navigation toolbar, and then click New Profile. The only required field in a Self Profile is Partner Name. Self Profiles are stored in the TPM database, but are not configured as Parties in the BizTalk Server Management database. My Profiles are used only to identify the business user's company in an Agreement.

To enable the sample project, complete the following steps:

1. Open the BAS site by clicking Start, Programs, Microsoft BizTalk Server 2004, Business Activity Services Site.
2. In the Quick Launch pane (left side) under Trading Partner Management Tools, click My Profiles to open the My Profiles page.

3. Click the New Profile link to start the InfoPath partner template named My Company Profile.
4. Type the following information to create a new Self profile:

   Partner Name: [Enter your company name here]

   All other fields are optional.
5. Click the Submit Profile link.
6. In Internet Explorer, select Refresh to see the new Self profile.

Configuring Partner Profiles

Business users can use the TPM tool to configure their business processes to interact with specific trading partners. Business users must first define the BizTalk parties that will play a role in these processes. The TPM tool enables business users to define these parties using the more business user-friendly metaphor of Partner Profiles. A Trading Partner Profile is like a business card in that it includes information about how to identify and communicate with the partner. The information defined in these Partner Profiles is used to configure the BizTalk Party including aliases, signature certificates, and send ports.

Partner Profiles require a Partner Name to be defined. This name is the primary identifier for the trading partner and configured as Organization Name alias in the BizTalk Party. Additional aliases are configured by adding Custom Properties in the Profile form.

Aliases are used to determine which party is playing a specified role in a role link in the orchestration. This can be done by writing code to set the value of the Destination Party inside the Expression shape or via Party Resolution inside a pipeline component. You can write your own custom pipeline and include the Party Resolution Pipeline Component or use the default XML receive pipeline that includes it. The Party Resolution Pipeline Component uses the WindowsUser and SignatureCertificate message context properties, which can be configured in the Partner Profile, to determine the party.

There are several predefined alias Qualifiers available to choose from, or you can create your own.

The commonly used WindowsUser qualifier is configured as follows:

- Property Name—Partner Identity
- Property Name Qualifier—WindowsUser
- Property value—<ServerName or DomainName>\<UserName>
- Runtime Process Property check box—When unchecked, this value will be stored only in Trading Partner Management database as a property of the Partner Profile. When checked, this property will also be configured as an alias of the BizTalk Party when the Partner Profile is deployed. Configuring this custom property as a Runtime Process Property makes it programmatically available to the orchestration at runtime.

19

TIP

Users can also enter basic Address and Contact information in the Partner Profile.

In the Advanced section of the Trading Partner Profile form, technical users can configure Signature Certificates and Global Ports. Global Ports are used to define one or more ways to communicate with the Trading Partner. Global Ports can be configured for any one of the three out-of-the-box BizTalk Server transports supported by BAS:

- File—Disk-based file exchange
- HTTP—Messages exchanged via HTTP or HTTPS
- SOAP—Messages exchanged via Web services

The Global Ports are analogous to the phone and fax numbers on a business card. They define the way in which you can communicate with a Trading Partner. After they are defined, Agreements can be configured to use these ports when configuring orchestrations to communicate with these specified partners.

The Partner Profile can now be deployed as a Party in the BizTalk Server Management Database by clicking the WSS drop-down menu and selecting Deploy Partner. The Party configured on the BizTalk Server will include an alias with a Qualifier equal to OrganizationName and Value equal to the Partner Name. Additional aliases will be created for each custom property configured in the Partner Profile. Signature Certificates will also be configured in the Party if included in the Partner Profile. However, you will not yet see any of the Global Ports listed as send ports for this Party. These will not be added until the Agreement is activated as described in the "Configuring Agreements with Trading Partners" section.

To enable the sample project, complete the following steps:

1. Click the Partner Profiles link to open the Partner Profiles page.
2. Click the New Partner link to start the InfoPath Partner Profile template form.
3. Type **`Fabrikam`** into the Partner Name box.

NOTE

The spelling must be exact because this will be compared to the "Charged to" element in the PurchaseRequest message document.

4. Click the Insert Custom Property link at the bottom of the form.

5. Click Select to select the WindowsUser property and enter the following information to specify user credentials:

   Property Name—Partner Identity

   Property Name Qualifier—WindowsUser

   Property value—[enter your username including domain]

   Select the Run-time Process Property check box.

6. Click the Advanced tab in the upper-left corner of the form.

   Under Technical Info, click the Insert Global Port link.

   Type (or select) the following information for the Global Port:

   Name: FabrikamSendPort

   Send Pipeline: `Microsoft.BizTalk.DefaultPipeLines.XmlTransmit`

   Retry Count: 3

   Retry Interval: 5

   Transport Type: File

   Destination Location: [local file path]

   This is the path used to configure the send port, which sends the Invoice to the trading partner. To configure this sample trading partner, first create a folder on your local machine and then enter the path to that folder. For example: C:\BizTalkTradingPartners\Fabrikam.

   File Name: `Invoice%MessageID%.xml`

7. Click Submit Profile at the top of the Partner Profile template to upload the information.

8. In Internet Explorer, select Refresh to see the new partner profile.

For each configured Partner Profile, an Inbox, a SentItems, and a Templates folder is created on the BAS site. The Inbox and SentItems folders are used to store message documents sent and received from the Trading Partner. The Templates folder is used to store InfoPath templates for viewing message documents associated with this Trading Partner.

Figure 19.7 shows the BAS Trading Partner Management Tools UI in the BAS site.

You have now configured the sample trading partner in the BAS Trading Partner Management tool, which stores this information in a separate Trading Partner Management database. Perform the following steps to deploy the sample trading partner to the BizTalk Server management database.

1. Point to the Fabrikam Partner Profile and select Deploy Partner from the drop-down list.
2. Click the BizTalk Server Name option button and then click the Deploy link.

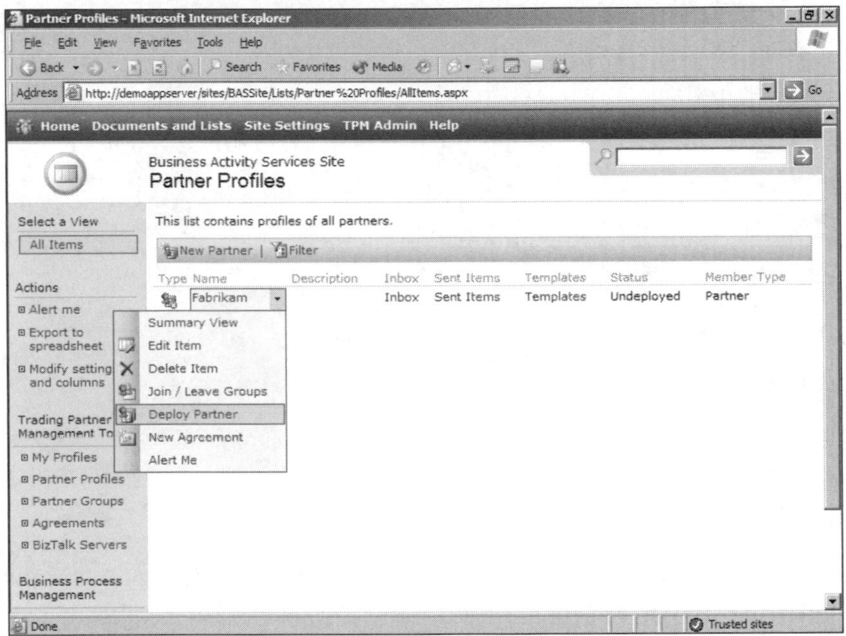

FIGURE 19.7 BAS site Trading Partner Management tool— Partner Profiles.

After completing the preceding steps, refresh and browse the BizTalk Explorer in Visual Studio .NET. You will now see the Fabrikam Party. Double-click the Party and you will see the Custom Properties listed as Party Identifiers.

InfoPath Templates

A Templates folder is created in the document library for each Trading Partner Profile. InfoPath templates are uploaded into this document library with namespaces referenced as a document property. The TPPubWS Web service will use these namespace references to decorate the message documents written to the BAS site with processing instruction references to the associated InfoPath template. Business users can click the message document instance in the BAS site to open them in the appropriate InfoPath template. If the business user is browsing the BAS site from a remote client, the InfoPath template is downloaded to the client. Managing these templates on the BAS site avoids having to manually distribute the InfoPath templates to all clients.

When you upload a template file, the following properties should be configured:

- Name—Required name that will be used to show the document type in the WSS document library
- Namespace—Namespace of the document schema

NOTE

The other fields are descriptive only and are not required.

To enable the sample project, complete the following steps:

1. Click the Partner Profiles link to open the Partner Profiles page.
2. On the Partner Profiles page, click the Templates link to the right of the Fabrikam Partner Profile link.
3. On the Templates page, click the Upload Document link to upload the `PurchaseOrder.xsn` InfoPath template located in the InfoPath Templates folder of the sample code.
4. Type (or select) the following information on the Upload Document page:

   Name: `PurchaseOrder.xsn`

   Namespace:
   `http://schemas.microsoft.com/office/infopath/2003/sample/PurchaseOrder`
5. Click the Save and Close link.
6. On the Template page, click the Upload Document link to upload the `Invoice.xsn` InfoPath template located in the InfoPath Templates folder of the sample code.
7. On the Templates:Upload Document page, type (or select) the following information:

   Name: Invoice.xsn

   Namespace:
   `http://schemas.microsoft.com/office/infopath/2003/sample/Invoice`
8. Click the Save and Close link.

19

Extending Profiles

The Partner Profile and Self Profile data is stored in the Trading Partner Management database using User Profile Management (UPM) services. UPM is a technology originally from Commerce Server that ships with BizTalk Server.

These Profiles use the same Partner Profile schema. The Self Profile uses a different InfoPath template for editing, which does not include the Partner Rating field, Global Ports, or Signature Certificate settings.

You can extend this schema by completing the following steps:

1. Extend Partner, AddressObject, and/or ContactObject tables in the Trading Partner Management database to include new properties.
2. Open MMC and add the Commerce Server 2002 Profile snap-in, add a new data member in Data Objects (Partner, AddressObject, and ContactObject), and then add new properties in Profile Definitions (PartnerObject, AddressObject, and ContactObject) to map new data members.
3. Add new properties into Partner xsd files (`Partner.xsd` and `PartnerNoWsdl.xsd`) under `\Program Files\Microsoft BizTalk Server 2004\Business Activity Services\TPM\Schemas`.
4. Open Partner template (`\Program Files\Common Files\Microsoft Shared\Web Server Extensions\60\TEMPLATE\LAYOUTS\InfoPath\PartnerProfileAdmin.xsn`) in Design mode and choose Extract Form Files. (You can additionally modify the `PartnerProfileStandard.xsn` and `PartnerProfileSelf.xsn` templates located in the same folder.)
5. Add new properties into the `schema.xsd` file (extracted from xsn file).
6. Add new properties into `sampledata.xml` and `template.xml` (extracted from xsn file).
7. Open manifest.xsf file (extracted from xsn file) in Design mode and add new properties.
8. Publish updated manifest.xsf and overwrite `PartnerProfileAdmin.xsn` (in the last page of publish, clear URL to blank).
9. Upload `PartnerProfileAdmin.xsn` from the BAS site.
10. Add new properties into `\Program Files\Common Files\Microsoft Shared\Web Server Extensions\60\template\layouts\1033\BAS\Xml\PartnerObject.xml`.

Configuring Agreements with Trading Partners

An Agreement is used to define a business relationship between the business user's company and a Trading Partner. This Agreement is used to configure the underlying orchestration that implements the business process. Specifically, this Agreement enlists a party in the role defined by a Role Link in that orchestration and configures the Send Ports for integrating with that party and the BAS site.

To configure an Agreement, click the Agreements link under the Trading Partner Management Administration section of the left navigation toolbar, and then click New Agreement.

Configuring Profiles in an Agreement

Role Links are configured to include a Used Role and/or an Implemented Role. A party must be enlisted for each Used Role. Implemented Roles are played by the BizTalk Server itself. Because Parties are represented to the business user in the Business Activity Services site as Partner Profiles, the first pane of the Agreement form prompts users to provide an Agreement Name and select which Profile will play the public Used Role. Clicking the Select Profile button for the Partner Profile returns a list of all Partner Profiles configured in the BAS site. Changing the drop-down list from Partners to Groups refreshes the list to include configured Partner Groups. Similarly, clicking the Select Profile button for My Profile returns a list of My Profiles configured in the BAS site.

Configuring an Addendum in an Agreement

One or more orchestrations must be configured as Addendums to this Agreement. Specifically, the Addendum defines the configuration of a specific Role Link. A Role Link includes one or two roles. In the Addendums pane of the InfoPath form, provide a name for the Addendum. This Addendum name cannot include spaces, but can be given an additional Friendly Name and be further described in the free-text Addendum Terms property. Associate each addendum with the Role Link it will be configuring in the orchestration by clicking the Select Relationship button. Clicking this Select Relationship button returns a list of public Role Links available for configuration in the deployed orchestrations on the BizTalk Server. Only Role Link Types not reserved by BAS are shown in this list.

Configuring Multiple Addendums in an Agreement

You can define multiple Role Links in a single orchestration and then configure them in multiple Addendums in multiple Agreements. Because Role Links represent the interaction between an orchestration and a specified party, which can include multiple operations, there should be only a single Role Link per unique party relationship in an orchestration. An example of this scenario is if your orchestration needed to communicate with two external trading partners. There would be a single Role Link defining the communication between the orchestration and each trading partner and a single Agreement configuring each of these Role Links. If this orchestration was one of two orchestrations that communicated with one of these trading partners, you would create an Addendum for each orchestration that was involved in the logical business relationship. These groupings are an optional way to organize multiple addenda, but users can also create a separate Agreement for each Addendum.

Activating an Agreement

Configuring the sample Agreement in the BAS Trading Partner Management tool stores this information in the Trading Partner Management database. The Activate operation on an Agreement configures the artifacts associated with the Agreement on the BizTalk Server. When the agreement is activated, the Partner Profile is automatically enlisted in the Used roles for the following BAS types if they exist in the orchestration:

- sendBusinessDocumentsLT
- receiveBusinessDocumentsLT
- Any Role Link Type ending in the string "PolicyType"

Additionally, send ports are created for the Global Ports of the Partner Profile and for the reserved BAS Port Types used in the orchestration associated with the Agreement.

To configure and activate the sample Agreement, complete the following steps:

1. In the Quick Launch pane (left side) under Trading Partner Management Tools, click the Partner Profiles link to open the Partner Profiles page.
2. Point to the Fabrikam Partner Profile and select New Agreement from the drop-down list.
3. On the InfoPath Agreement form, type (or select) the following information to create a new agreement:

   Agreement Name: FabrikamOrderProcessAgreement

   Agreement Date: [today's date]

   My Profile: [Select your company name here]

   Partner Profile: Select Fabrikam
4. Click the Addendums tab in the upper-left corner of the form.
5. Type (or select) the following information for the Addendum:

   Addendum Name: FabrikamOrderProcessAddendum

   Business Relationship Name: `OrderMgmtProcess.OrderToInvoiceLT`

   Type **`Two-day air`** into the Value box.

Figure 19.8 shows the Addendum, including ShippingMethod parameter, configured for the sample Order Management Process.

6. Click the Submit Agreement link to submit the agreement.
7. In the Quick Launch pane (left side) under Trading Partner Management Tools, click the Agreements link to open the Agreements page.
8. Point to the FabrikamOrderProcessAgreement and select Activate Agreement from the drop-down list.

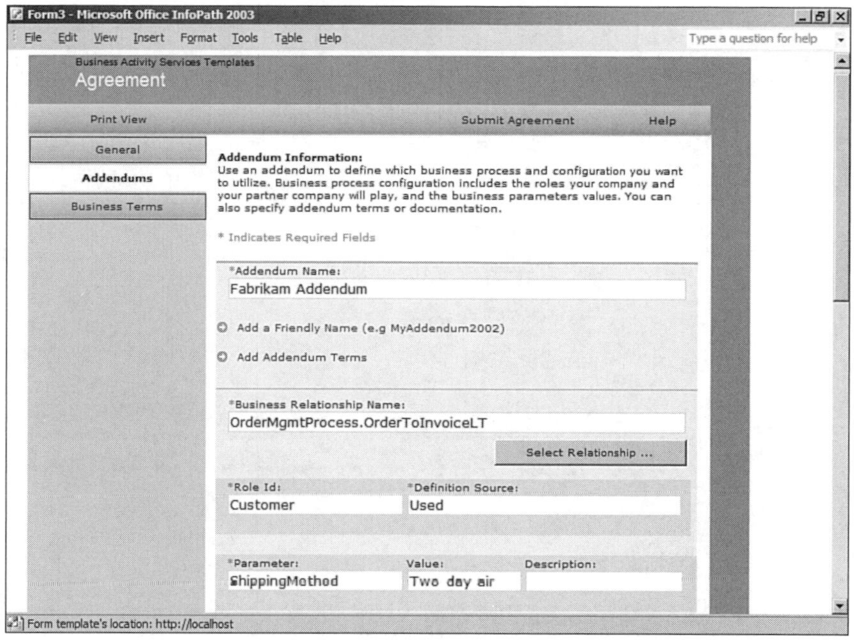

FIGURE 19.8 BAS site Trading Partner Management tool—Agreement Addendum

9. On the InfoPath Agreement Mapping form, select the following information:

   Operation Name: SendInvoice

   Operation Port: FabrikamSendPort

10. Click the Submit Mapping link to submit the Agreement Mapping.

After completing the preceding steps, refresh and browse the BizTalk Explorer in Visual Studio .NET. You will now see the Fabrikam Party enlisted in the various orchestration roles and the newly created send ports.

Figure 19.9 shows the deployed assemblies, orchestrations, roles, parties, and send and receive ports in the BizTalk Explorer in VisualStudio .NET.

Partner Groups

Partner Profiles can be associated into Partner Groups, which can be used in place of a single Partner Profile in an Agreement configuration. This allows users to reduce the number of Agreements they have to manage by creating a single Agreement that applies to all Partner Profiles in the Partner Group.

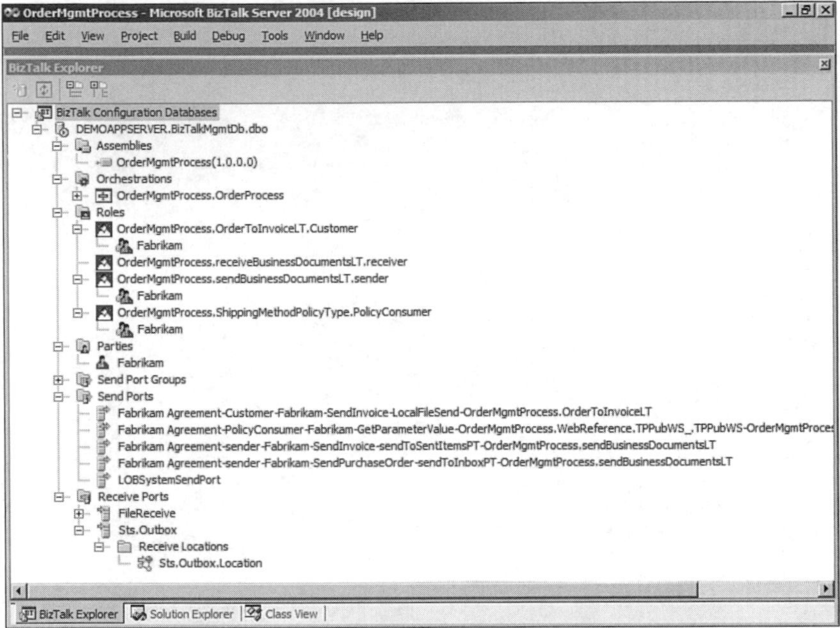

FIGURE 19.9 BizTalk Explorer view after Partner Profile deployment and Agreement activation.

Trading Partner Management Administration

The Trading Partner Management Administration feature supports two functions that can be performed by a BAS Business Administrator: Repair and Resync. Business Activity Services stores BizTalk Server configuration information in the Window SharePoint Services site content database and BizTalk Server Management database in addition to the master record stored in the Trading Partner Management database. These two functions enable administrators to restore the WSS content database and the BizTalk Server Management database if they become out of sync from the Trading Partner Management database.

The Repair function is used to synchronize the BizTalk Server database with the Trading Partner Management database.

The Resync function is used to synchronize the WSS Web portal with the Trading Partner Management database.

Executing and Interacting with the Sample Business Process

BAS enables developers to easily build and manage integration between an orchestration and the BAS site so that business users can collaborate and interact with message document instances associated with the business process. This interaction is enabled by designing orchestrations to include special Role Link Types that send and receive message documents to and from document libraries on the BAS site. The Web service that writes these message documents to the BAS site also decorates the XML message documents with information that instructs Microsoft Windows to open the document in Microsoft InfoPath 2003 using a specific InfoPath template associated with the message document type. Message documents can also be submitted back to the orchestration via a specified document library on the BAS site.

Now that the business process has been developed, deployed, and finally configured, we are ready to execute the sample business process.

Interacting with Documents in Trading Partner's InBox

As described earlier in the chapter, this sample scenario begins with a Trading Partner sending a purchase order to BizTalk. To keep this sample simple and focus on the use of the BAS features, you've bound the initial receive port to `receiveFromCustomerPT` you configured in the "Deploying the Sample BizTalk Project" section of this chapter. To start the process, copy the SamplePurchaseOrder10010.xml file from the Message folder in the sample code and paste it to the File receive location configured for that receive port. You may need to rename this file depending on how you configured the receive location.

This receive simulates receiving a purchase order message from a Trading Partner and instantiates an instance of the orchestration. The orchestration will collect the Shipping Method parameter configured in the Agreement and update the purchase order with this information before writing the purchase order to Fabrikam's Inbox on the BAS site. You can validate that the purchase order was received by browsing the BAS site as follows:

1. In the Quick Launch pane (left site) under Trading Partner Management Tools, click Partner Profiles to open the Partner Profiles page.
2. Click the Inbox link to the right of the Fabrikam Partner Profile link.

   This displays all documents received by your business from the Fabrikam partner. The purchase order document is listed in the New Document column.
3. Click the PurchaseOrder document to open the document in InfoPath and review its contents to see that the Shipping Method has been set to **`Two-day air`** as configured in the Agreement.

Figure 19.10 shows the Fabrikam Inbox document library, including the purchase order documents received from Fabrikam, in the BAS site.

19

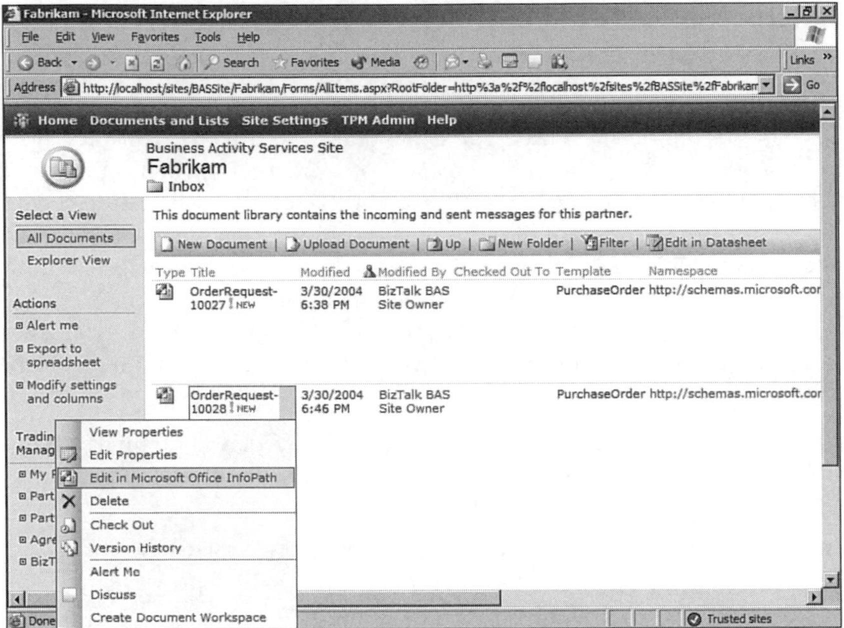

FIGURE 19.10 BAS site Trading Partner Management tool—Partner Inbox

Sending Documents to Trading Partner via the OutBox

The sample scenario states that the next step is for the business user to use the information in this purchase order to manually fulfill the order while the LOB accounting application generates the invoice. The business user exports the Invoice and then uploads it to the BAS site to be submitted back to the Trading Partner via BizTalk. To keep this sample simple, we have provided an associated Invoice document. Perform the following steps to upload the Invoice and send it to the trading partner:

1. In the Quick Launch pane (left side) under Trading Partner Management Tools, click BizTalk Servers.
2. Click the Outbox link to navigate to the Outbox document library.
3. Click Upload Document and browse to the `SampleInvoice10010.xml` in the Message folder in the sample code.
4. Click Save and Close to upload the document.

TIP

You can alternatively write a script or .NET component to programmatically upload a document to the Outbox by saving the file to the WebDAV path for the Outbox. To discover this path, browse the BizTalk Server Registration page on the BAS site. See the Programmer's Reference in the BizTalk Server documentation.

SentItems

BizTalk receives the Invoice from the Sts.Outbox receive port and correlates the Invoice with the orchestration instance that received the original purchase order. The orchestration delivers the Invoice to the Trading Partner and sends the message to the SentItems folder for the Trading Partner on the BAS site, simultaneously removing it from the Outbox. To verify that the Invoice was successfully delivered, perform the following steps:

1. In the Quick Launch pane (left side) under Trading Partner Management Tools, click Partner Profiles to open the Partner Profiles page.
2. Click the Sent Items link to the right of the Fabrikam Partner Profile link.

   This displays all documents sent to the Fabrikam partner from the BAS site. You may need to refresh the browser.
3. Browse to the file location configured for the FabrikamSendPort to verify that the message was also sent to Fabrikam.

TIP

You can rerun this demo by manually editing the two XML documents in Notepad to increment the reference numbers.

purchase order: <ns0:referenceNumber>10010</ns0:referenceNumber>

Invoice: <inv:number>10010</inv:number>

Monitoring the Sample Business Process

The BAS site surfaces Business Activity Monitoring (BAM) information to business users via the Business Activity Search Wizard. This wizard allows business users to easily generate dynamic reports and save the queries for frequent viewing. These reports provide business users with a real-time view of Key Performance Indicators (KPIs) about the health and status of their business processes. The results of the wizard include links to any associated message document instances written to the BAS site. The BAM data can also be viewed in Excel pivot tables and pivot charts stored in the BAS site. BAM is covered in detail in Chapter 20, "Business Activity Monitoring," but we briefly cover how BAM is integrated with the BAS site here.

The Business Activity Search is a wizard hosted in the BAS site that leverages the BAM Query Wizard Web service to enable business users to execute custom queries against live tracking data stored in the BAM database.

NOTE

You will need to have already configured and deployed BAM views to search them from this tool.

To execute a search, perform the following steps:

1. On the BAS site, click Business Activity Search in the Quick Launch pane on the left side of the page.
2. In the View Name drop-down list, select the desired BAM view.
3. In the Available Activities list box, select the activity you want to search against, click Add, and then click Next.
4. In the Available Columns list box, select one or more columns to be displayed in the search results and click Add.
5. To change the relative position of the columns, select a column in the Selected Columns list box and use the Move Up or Move Down buttons as appropriate. This is an optional step.
6. Click Next.
7. Use the drop-down lists on this page to create filters for the search criteria. Use the Add Clause button to add a new blank clause to the end of the query.
8. Click Finish.

The results are displayed on the Business Activity Search Results page. On the Business Activity Search Results page, click the Activity ID of the activity to get a detailed view.

If the BAM view is of an orchestration that used BAS to write message documents to the BAS site, you will also see links to related documents on this page. Click the links to open the related document from the BAS Inbox or SentItems folders.

Summary

In this chapter, we walked through the entire life cycle of a Business Activity Services project. The developer BAS-enabled the orchestration using the BAS reserved port types and role link types. We then registered the BizTalk Server on the BAS site before deploying the project on the BizTalk Server. The business user then configured Partner Profiles and Agreements on the BAS TPM site and interacted with the business process using the Inbox, Outbox, and SentItems folders on the BAS site. Finally, we took a quick look at monitoring the process by accessing the BAM tracking data via the Business Activity Search Wizard on the BAS site.

CHAPTER 20

Business Activity Monitoring

IN THIS CHAPTER

- The BAM Solution
- BAM in BizTalk Server 2004
- Configuring and Deploying BAM Step by Step

Today, the typical organization runs its business using a combination of mission-critical business processes that involve the integration of multiple, disparate applications in combination with more traditional human interactions, such as phone calls and email. The types of applications running in most enterprises range from custom, homegrown applications to traditional "off the shelf" ERP packages. The integration of these systems is sometimes held together with shoestrings, but nonetheless permits data to flow in multiple overlapping directions, making it very difficult to monitor the status of the day-to-day business. This also makes it difficult to gain visibility into the entire business process from start to finish. In most enterprises today, monitoring services that could provide valuable operational data are usually ad hoc and segmented by application. Without real-time visibility into an enterprise's processes, it is almost impossible for the business decisionmaker to determine where the bottlenecks are or to understand what is going on with the business. With increasing market demands, it is often crucial for an organization to make quick decisions to leverage market opportunities or to prevent operational losses. For example, in an order fulfillment process, the Key Performance Indicators (KPIs) may be the time it takes to fill an order from a supplier. If an enterprise does not have the capability to analyze data from heterogeneous event sources and then present that data in a single real-time view so that it can see the current business state and analyze trends and critical conditions, the enterprise may not know that supplier A is twice as slow as supplier B or that supplier A performs poorly when asked to supply part X.

In this chapter we discuss the concept of end-to-end business monitoring known as Business Activity Monitoring (BAM). Specifically, we are going to drill down into how BizTalk

Server 2004's BAM Framework can provide real-time visibility into a running business process with little or no impact on the performance of the process for both BizTalk and non-BizTalk applications. We also discuss how BAM leverages existing Business Intelligence (BI) technologies to aggregate and analyze data from heterogeneous event sources presenting a single real-time view of a business's current state, trends, and critical success factors.

The BAM Solution

The presence of many applications, application owners, business scenarios and business events makes end-to-end visibility into a typical enterprise business process difficult. The implementation of a typical order-management process, for example, is usually much too complex for average business decisionmakers to put their arms around. From a business user's perspective, they want to be able to abstract out this complexity so they can monitor and intercept business events and data about those events to make informed business decisions. BAM provides a way to abstractly define, intercept, collect, and aggregate data tied to specific business events in the context of defined business processes.

BAM's main goal is to connect information workers to the back-end server processes, using familiar desktop tools so that they can monitor performance in as flexible a manner as possible. Its second goal is to provide services to analyze, aggregate and display business event data with as little custom code and impact on the running business process as is possible. The best way to achieve the first goal is to allow the information worker or business expert to define the KPIs, aggregations, and trends needed to monitor a process from a business perspective in a familiar desktop tool. BAM uses an Excel add-in to provide this capability. After these artifacts have been defined, the business experts can use the Excel pivot table created by the BAM Excel add-in to further refine and display multiple views of this data.

To address the second goal, the BAM framework provides the capability to automatically create the database, the analysis, and the event observation SQL asset infrastructure. This allows the aggregations and views of data to be quickly implemented by the developers and IT staff with little or no custom code. The remainder of this chapter will focus on how BAM provides these services as well as how you as a developer can implement them for a sample business process.

BAM in BizTalk Server 2004

BizTalk Server 2004's BAM framework provides an Excel add-in that enables information workers and business experts to define an observation model or wish list of data in the form of Activities and Views in a wizard-driven approach. The data defined is abstractly associated with the business process and is in no way associated with the physical implementation of artifacts or assets. This enables information workers to focus on the business problem, and it abstracts the complexity away from the implementation details by using verbiage that is easy for them to understand. After users complete the definition of the Activities and Views, they are provided with a pivot table and sample data set so they can easily manipulate the views of data as well as leverage the built-in table and charting capabilities found natively in Excel. This part of the process can be done in a completely disconnected state and then emailed, for example, to the IT shop when completed. Figure 20.1 displays the BAM.xls file.

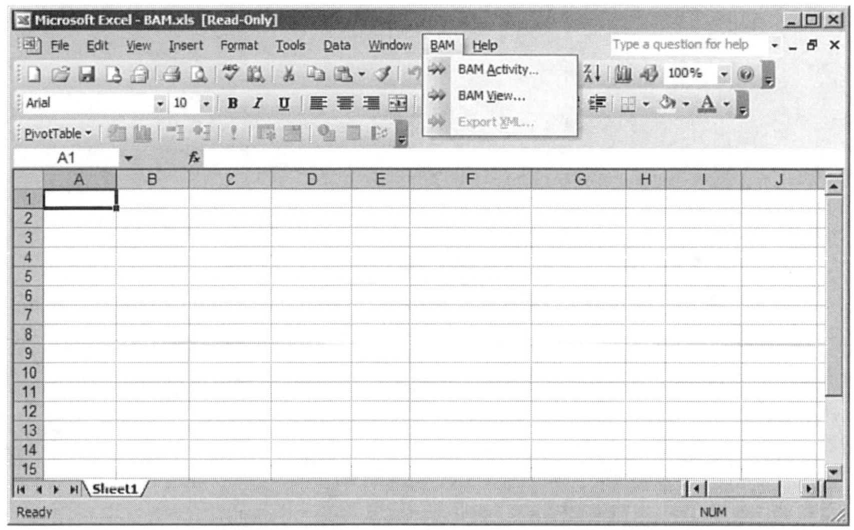

FIGURE 20.1 The BAM Excel add-in.

The provisioning of the SQL assets required to hold the defined data and the mapping of the KPIs to the physical process is done after the information worker is comfortable with the defined Activities, Views, and data aggregations. The BAM Activity and View data, when ready, is exported to a BAM definition XML file using the BAM Excel add-in. The file is then imported by a developer into a tool called the Tracking Profile Editor, shown in Figure 20.2. The Tracking Profile Editor allows developers to map the aggregations and KPIs defined in the Excel add-in to a process defined by an orchestration.

After the data is mapped to the orchestration, the developer then deploys the tracking profile, updating the BizTalk management database with the mappings. The developer may alternatively choose to deploy the Tracking Profile using the btt.exe command-line tool.

The developer or system administrator must also run a command-line tool called BM.exe. This tool accepts the BAM Excel spreadsheet or exported BAM XML so that it can automatically provision the SQL assets required to track the real-time and historical data. If the Excel workbook is provided as the input parameter to BAM.exe the data collected can be viewed using <filename>_livedata.xls. This is a copy of the provided .xls BAM Excel

Workbook created earlier however it is stamped with connection strings to the SQL assets created by BAM.exe when it is provided to the command-line utility.

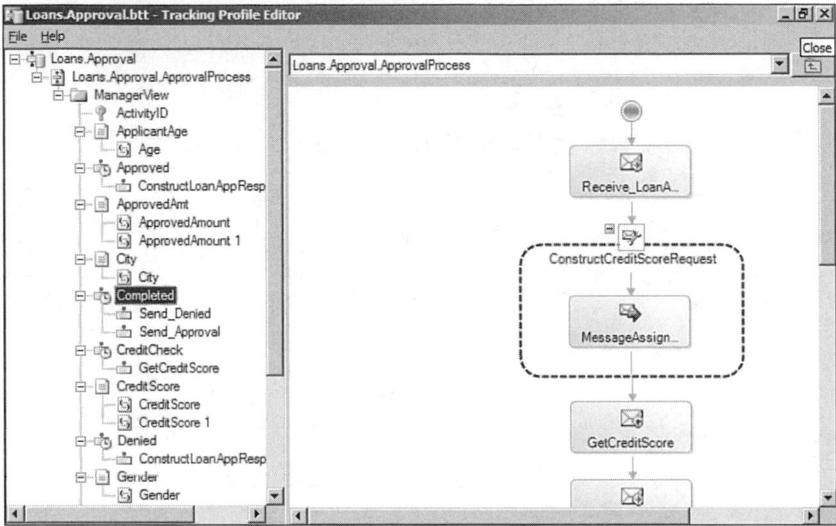

FIGURE 20.2 The Tracking Profile Editor.

In many instances, business processes may include callouts to processes not implemented as BizTalk Server Orchestrations. To accommodate these scenarios, BAM provides an API that enables developers to intercept and track data using the SQL artifacts created with the BAM Excel add-in. In the sections that follow, we discuss BAM user roles, the underlying architecture supporting the BAM framework, and then we walk step by step through the configuration and deployment of BAM aggregations created for a simple orchestration sample application.

BAM User Roles

There are four distinct user personas involved in the creation, deployment, and use of BAM tools and resulting artifacts. They are

- Power Knowledge Worker, Business Expert
- Business User, Knowledge Worker
- Developer
- IT Professional

The first, the power knowledge worker, or business expert, defines the aggregations and data used to monitor the business process using the BAM Excel add-in. The second, the average business user or knowledge worker reviews and queries the data collected to make business decisions. The data collected by BAM can be viewed using several methods. You can use the <filename>_livedata.xls version of the Excel workbook that's created during the deployment of the BAM definition. This enables you to quickly open up the Excel document to view either live or historical information. You can also use the BizTalk Server 2004 Business Activity Services (BAS) site, a Windows SharePoint Services site (WSS) that's provided with the BizTalk Server 2004 product to view and query the information. Finally, BAM provides a Web service interface so that developers can integrate the data with custom application UIs. As far as these two users are concerned, the data is collected "magically" and is then made available to them.

The third persona, the developer, is responsible for constructing the orchestration or business process. After the orchestration is deployed, the developer is also responsible for mapping the orchestration process using the Tracking Profile Editor to the KPIs defined using the BAM Excel add-in. These KPIs are exported into a BAM XML file using the Excel add-in and then imported into the Tracking Profile Editor. The IT professional is responsible for the deployment of the tracking profile created by the Tracking Profile Editor and for deployment of the BAM definition created by the BAM Excel add-in. Deployment of the tracking profile can be done in either the Tracking Profile Editor or by using the btt.exe command-line tool. To deploy the BAM definition file, you must run the BAM.exe command-line utility. This utility generates the SQL assets needed to store the data. A diagram of the flow of information between the user roles is displayed in Figure 20.3.

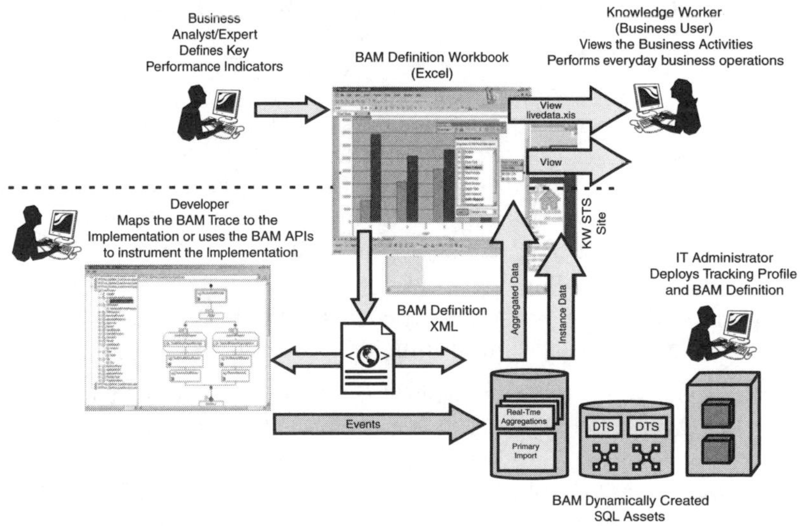

FIGURE 20.3 BAM user roles.

BAM Architecture

In this section we are going to drill down into the BAM architecture diagram displayed in Figure 20.4.

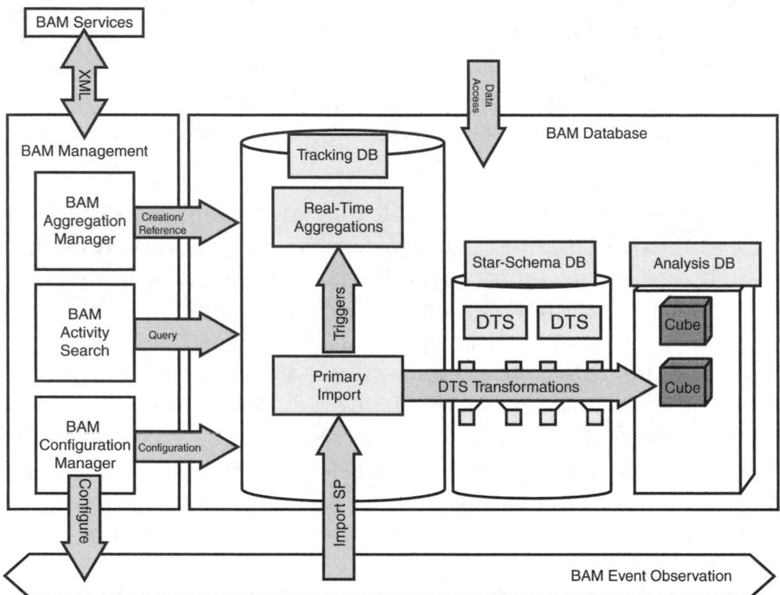

FIGURE 20.4 Overview of BAM architecture.

This diagram depicts the underlying architecture for both real-time and OLAP BAM aggregations. On the left side of the diagram you see the BAM Management object (BM.exe). The BAM Manager is responsible for generating all the SQL assets required for either real-time or OLAP storage. Several of these tables are in a database called the BAM Primary Import (BAMPrimaryImport) or PIT database. The BAM Manager uses the KPIs and aggregations defined in the BAM XML definition file to create these tables as well as the DTS packages required for archival and data maintenance. The BAM Event Observation layer is responsible for collecting the data and routing it to these tables.

So how does this really work? Basically, when the Event Observation layer receives a new event, it creates a new record in the PIT active database (`bam_<ActivityName>_Active`). It then continues to update that record as long as the activity is active. When that activity is complete, it will mark it as Completed and fire a trigger that then moves the record to the `bam_<activity_name>_Completed` PIT database table. This keeps the active instance data tables very clean and greatly improves BAM performance. The completed table, on the other hand, now tends to grow, which could potentially hinder performance. To assist here, rows from the completed table are periodically moved out to new SQL partitions, and the partitioned views are updated for BAM and custom queries. The data in the partitioned table can then eventually be archived using a DTS package created by the

BAM Manager (BM.exe) as shown in Figure 20.5. The DTS archival package in this case must be scheduled to run periodically to archive the data.

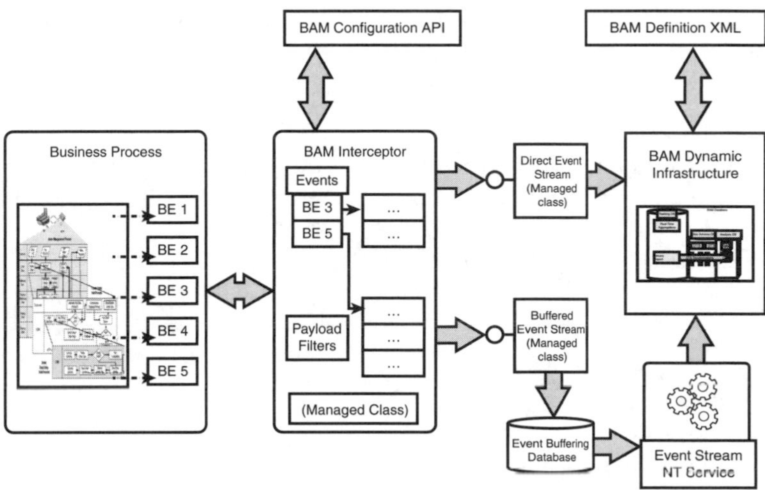

FIGURE 20.5 BAM Data Maintenance.

This underlying architecture is very robust; however, you should be careful to use real-time aggregations (RTAs) only when absolutely necessary. There are a few limitations in SQL Server today that prohibit real-time OLAP cubing in SQL Server. To work around this limitation, BAM is doing some fairly complex SQL tasks to enable you to view aggregations real-time.

OLAP data maintenance and processing activities are similar in concept and are depicted in Figure 20.6.

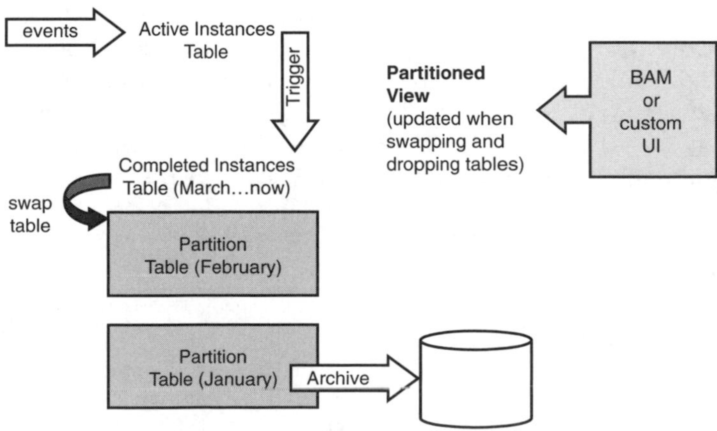

FIGURE 20.6 OLAP Process.

In this case, the data is collected real-time, moved to the completed database, and then data partitions just as real-time aggregations are. To allow the Excel user to view the data in real-time, a snapshot of the active instance is periodically taken and then moved to an active cube using a generated DTS package. The BAM <activityName>_livedata.xls file can then view the snapshot data using a virtual cube. To view the completed activity data in OLAP, you must execute a second DTS BAM Manager generated package that moves the data from the partitioned table to the completed cube.

If the BAM Excel workbook is configured for real-time aggregations, BM.exe creates the following database tables (see Table 20.1) in the BAMPrimaryImport SQL database.

TABLE 20.1 BAMPrimaryImport Database Tables

Table Name
bam_<ActivityName>_Active
bam_<ActivityName>_ActiveRelationships
bam_<ActivityName>_Completed
bam_<ActivityName>_CompletedRelationships
bam_<ActivityName>_Continuations
bam_<Viewname>_<ViewName>_RTA_RTATable
bam_<ViewName>_View<ActivityName>_ActiveInstancesSnapshot

BM.exe will also create the DTS package bam_DM_<ActivityName> for archival purposes.

The BAM Management object accepts one of two parameters: the BAM Excel file or the exported BAM XML definition file. If the Excel file is provided, it will stamp the Excel spreadsheet with a connection string to the BAMPrimaryImport database. Because of the limitations of the current SQL Server OLAP technology, BAM stores the Real-Time Aggregations in SQL materialized views instead of OLAP cubes.

If the Real-Time Aggregations option is not selected in the BAM Excel Workbook, BM.exe generates tables in the BAMPrimaryImport database, tables in the BAMStarSchema database, an OLAP cube for the view, and two associated DTS packages—one to move the data from the PIT to the BAMStarSchema database. The second DTS package moves data from the PIT database to the completed cube. The DTS cube-processing package can be scheduled or manually run to populate the OLAP store. Table 20.2 presents a list of the SQL assets created for a non–real-time aggregation BAM deployment.

TABLE 20.2 BAMPrimaryImport Database Tables Created

SQL Table Name
bam_<ActivityName>_Active
bam_<ActivityName>_ActiveRelationships
bam_<ActivityName>_Completed
bam_<ActivityName>_CompletedRelationships
bam_<ActivityName>_Continuations
bam_<ViewName>_View<ActivityName>_ActiveInstancesSnapshot

Table 20.3 displays a list of tables created in the BAM StarSchema database. The table names created here are specific to the BAM solution you will create later in this chapter and reflect the dimension names defined using the BAM Excel add-in View Definition Wizard.

TABLE 20.3 BAM StarSchema Database Tables Created

SQL Table Name
bam_<ViewName>_Dim_ApplicantAgeDim
bam_<ViewName>_Dim_ApprovalProgress
bam_<ViewName>_Dim_City
bam_<ViewName>_Dim_Gender
bam_<ViewName>_Dim_Status
bam_<ViewName>_Facts
bam_<ViewName>_ViewLoanProcess_Staging

The OLAP cube is created in the Analysis database named BAMAnalysis and is named bam_<ViewName>. The two DTS packages are named BAM_DM_<ActivityName> and BAM_AN_<ViewName>.

When a BAM Excel file is deployed using BM.exe and the real-time option is not selected in the menu options of the BAM Excel workbook, the <filename>_livedata version of the Excel file is stamped with a SQL connection string that points to the OLAP cube as opposed to the real-time database tables. This cube will not be populated until the DTS Cube package for the view has been executed. The data, when collected, is put into the BAMPrimaryImport tables. To move the data into the OLAP cube, you must run the BAM_AN_<ViewName> Data Transformation Services package.

The BAM.EventObservation Object

During the execution of the Business Activity (Business Process), a large amount of data is collected for health-monitoring purposes. This data can be viewed using the BizTalk Health and Activity Tracking (HAT) tool. Most of this data is concerned with implementation logic and very little of it makes any sense to a Business User. BAM's job, on the other hand, is to collect or abstract out the KPI data defined by the business expert using the BAM Excel add-in. The BAM Excel add-in allows the Business User to define the KPIs and then export them to a file called the BAM Definition XML file. This file contains a subset of the information contained in the Excel workbook, focusing on the data points and not the advanced interpretation of information, such as KPI calculations or chart format.

The BAM definition file can be broken into four parts: BAM trace, BAM view, desired aggregation, and real-time aggregation. The manifest that describes the data defined in the BAM add-in is called the BAM Trace. This is a list of data items that must be collected during the Activity execution. A Trace can be thought of as a table with a list of checkpoints or values to look for. The BAM View defines the subset of the data that can be shown to a specific Knowledge Worker. The BAM View also contains some items that represent interpretation of the collected data. On top of the BAM View are multidimensional aggregations and then finally real-time aggregations.

There are basically two ways to trigger a BAM tracking event. You can use the BAM API object BAM.EventObservation or use the BAM Generic Runtime Interceptor interface. Firing explicit events to BAM using the API requires the application to be instrumented in a way that is specific to given BAM Trace(s) or a BAM definition file. This means that the code has to be recompiled and deployed each time a change is made in the BAM definition file. The Generic Runtime Interceptor interface allows applications to be instrumented or monitored in a very generic way. It also allows the extraction of the event data for any given BAM Trace to be driven by metadata configured for the Generic Interceptor.

BizTalk Orchestration's implementation of BAM uses the Generic Interceptor approach. The Orchestration Engine contains a component named the XlangInterceptor. The XlangInterceptor is called at each checkpoint in an orchestration's execution and is really an "Adaptor" between the BAM Generic Interceptor and Orchestration Engine exposing the ITrackingDataExtractor interface. This Generic Interceptor maintains a hashed list of track points (from the deployed Trace data) acting basically as an in-place event filter. At each checkpoint the Interceptor looks at data to decide if the data available needs to be collecting as a tracked event. If the event needs to be tracked, the Interceptor pulls the data it needs and places it in the MessageBox. This allows BAM's implementation within orchestration to hook into and use the standard BizTalk tracking infrastructure. Health and Activity Tracking (HAT) uses a combination of the MessageBox and the Tracking Data Decoding Service (TDDS) service to move data from the MessageBox into the BizTalkDTA tracking database. Just as the TDDS service moves data from the MessageBox to the BizTalkDTA database, it can also evaluate the data in the MessageBox and move the appropriate data to the BAMPrimaryImport database table.

A diagram of the BAM Event architecture is displayed in Figure 20.7.

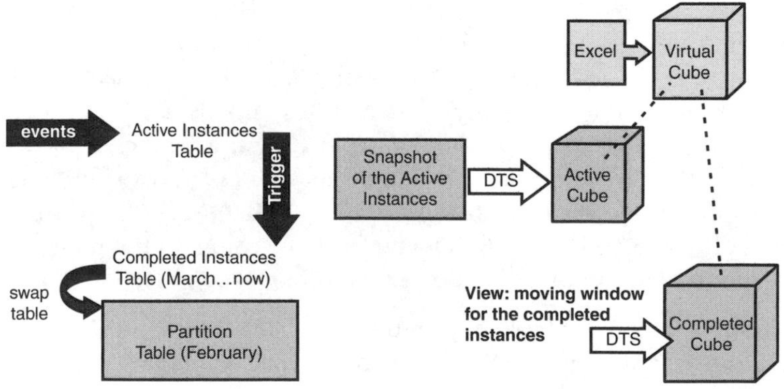

FIGURE 20.7 BAM Event architecture.

BAM.EventObservation assembly contains public classes that the developer can use to collect data for BAM. There are two major interfaces: the `DirectEventStream` and the `BufferedEventStream`. The `DirectEventStream` class implements an in-memory buffered stream for BAM events and is the simplest way to fire events into BAM. Listing 20.1 shows an example of how to accomplish this.

LISTING 20.1 Using the *DirectEventStream* Class

```
// To create an instance of the DirectEventStream, the Application passes
// a Connection String to the BAM Database
EventStream es=new DirectEventStream(connectionString, 1000);

// Initiate the tracing for specific Activity Instance
es.BeginTrace("PurchaseOrder","PO#123");

// Fire event about this Activity Instance
es.Trace("PurchaseOrder","PO#123",
             "POReceived",DateTime.UtcNow,
             "POAmount",100,
             "CustomerName","Joe",
             "CustomerState","WA",
             "CustomerCity","Seattle");

// At some later time, when the PO has been approved
es.Trace("PurchaseOrder","PO#123",
             "POApproved",DateTime.UtcNow,
             "ProductName","Coca-Cola",
             "ProductCategory","Beverages");

// And again when the PO has been shipped
es.Trace("PurchaseOrder","PO#123",
             "POShipped",DateTime.UtcNow);

// Close the Activity Trace - no more events are expected
es.EndTrace("PurchaseOrder","PO#123");

// Now let's save all the events
es.Flush();
```

Each Event is fired in the context of a specific Activity—in this case ("Purchase Order")—and a specific Activity instance ("PO#123"). The Activity Type must match the ID Attribute of a BAM Trace that has been deployed previously. The activity instance can be identified by any unique string up to 128 Unicode characters, such as a GUID.

The second parameter of the `DirectEventStream` specifies how many events it will process before it opens a connection and flushes its in-memory buffer. In the preceding example, the autoflush parameter is set to 1000, and only five events are fired (`BeginTrace` and `EndTrace` are also events), so the `DirectEventStream` will keep everything in memory until the `es.Flush()` statement.

The `BufferedEventStream` class, on the other hand, buffers the event data first in-memory and then writes it to a temporary database (MessageBox) that is used as a source for the Tracking Data Decoding Service (TDDS). The TDDS, also known as the BAM Event Bus Service, moves event data collected by the interceptor from the MessageBox database to the BAM Primary Import database. This service sends a heartbeat to a centralized database and can be monitored using the BAM MMC snap-in. It basically enables you to process the event data without having to call the Primary Import Stored Procedures for each event or `Flush()`. The code that follows demonstrates how to create an object of this type:

```
EventStream es=new BufferedEventStream(connectionString, 1000);
```

Each time a `Flush()` is invoked using the `DirectEventStream`, a call is made to the Primary Import Stored Procedure. So if 100 events were captured and five flushes were performed, it would call the stored procedure five times. The `BufferedEventStream` will make a single stored procedure call that inserts an IMAGE blob as a single row in the Tracking Stream Table. TDDS then processes the events, placing them into the BAMPrimaryImport table.

The BAM Query Web Service

To abstract the complexity of the BAM API from the GUI, a BAM Query Web service is also provided. This Web service hides the specifics of the dynamically generated infrastructure from the user interface. A diagram of the Web service interfaces is displayed in Figure 20.8.

Users can query individual instances through the BAM Query Web service or get connection strings to the BAM database and OLAP Cube to query aggregations. Because of Pivot Table Service limitations, not all data queries can go through the Web services provided. Today the Pivot Table Service works only with SQL and/or OLAP connections.

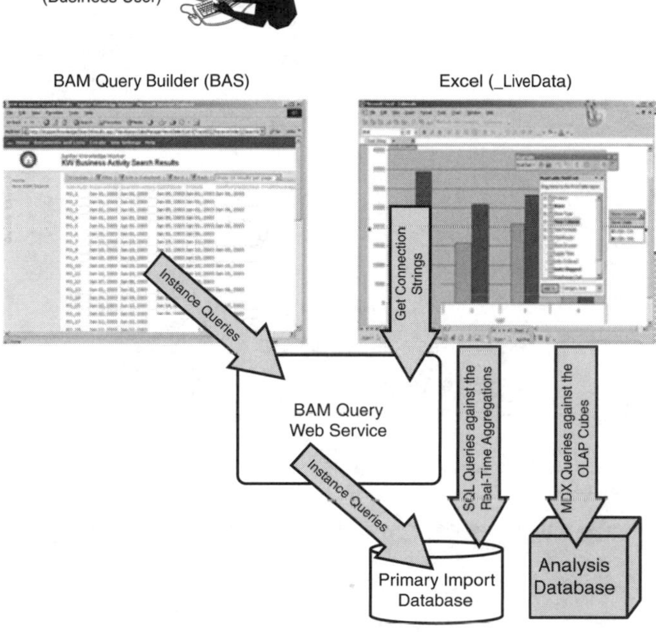

FIGURE 20.8 The BAM Query Web service.

Configuring and Deploying BAM Step by Step

In the next several sections we are going to walk through a step-by-step example of how to configure BAM to monitor an orchestration. The business process modeled by the Loans.Approval project simulates a loan-processing application that accepts an XML loan application request, calls an ASP.NET Web service to retrieve the applicant's credit score, and then evaluates the credit score to determine whether the application should be approved. In this case, the business expert would like to monitor how many applicants are approved and denied by location, age group, credit score, gender, and salary to determine whether the approval business rules should be refined. The orchestration in this example is very simple and uses a decision shape to evaluate an applicant's credit score. In a production scenario, the approval business rules could be implemented using the BizTalk Rules Engine so that they can be tweaked when needed, without having to recompile and redeploy the business process. Based on the BAM KPI data collected, the information worker could then quickly modify the approval rules to ensure that the business meets its monthly loan quota. The schemas for both the loan application request and response are displayed in Figures 20.9 and 20.10.

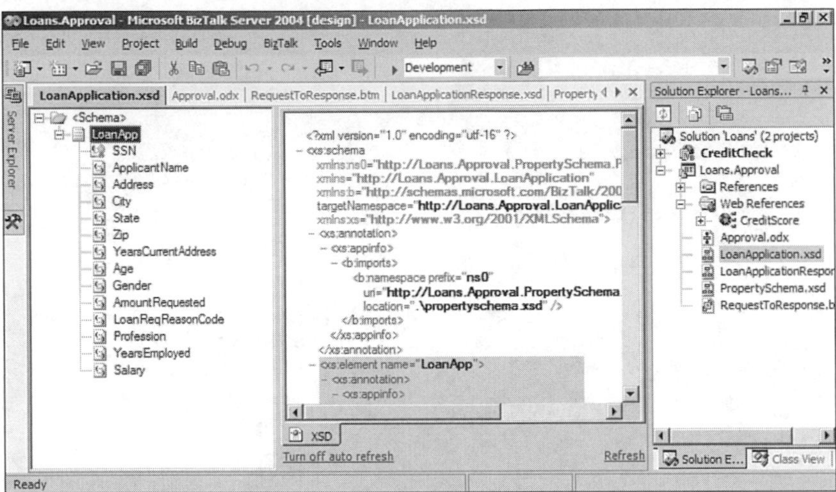

FIGURE 20.9 LoalApplication.xsd XML Request schema.

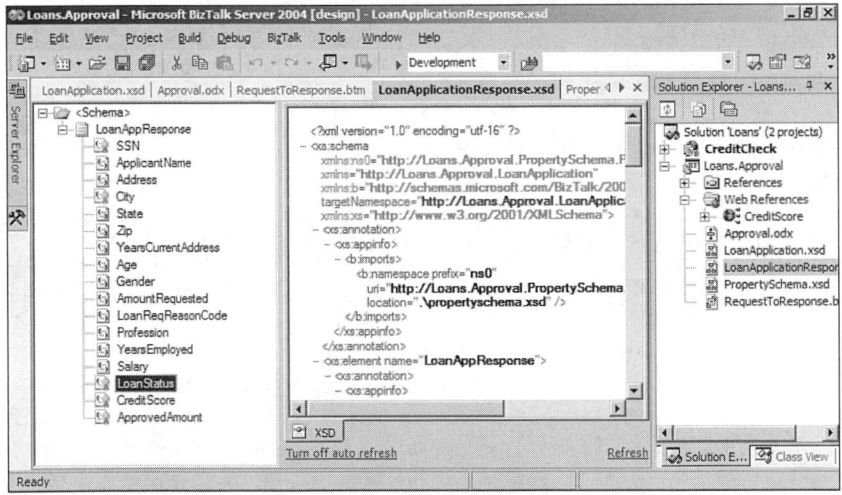

FIGURE 20.10 LoanApplicationResponse.xsd Response schema.

Several steps are involved in the configuration and deployment of the BAM framework and can be slightly different depending on whether you are using real-time aggregations in the BAM Excel Workbook.

NOTE

The Real Time Aggregation button is available only when you are focused on the pivot table in the workbook.

The differences will be discussed in detail later in this section. To configure a typical BAM implementation you must complete the following steps:

1. Use the Excel BAM add-in to construct one or more BAM Activities and one or more BAM Views for the business process.
2. Use the Excel pivot table and pivot table field list created using the data aggregations, measures, and dimensions defined in the BAM wizards to configure the exact view of the KPIs defined.
3. Export the BAM XML using the BAM add-in and save the Excel BAM spreadsheet.
4. Run `BM.exe deploy` on the BAM Excel .xls file to create the SQL assets and stamp the Excel file with the SQL connection stings.
5. Build and deploy the orchestration project.
6. Use the Tracking Profile Editor to map the BAM XML file to the deployed orchestration implementation details.
7. Deploy the Tracking Profile.
8. Run the orchestration.
9. Open the <filename>_livedata version of the BAM Excel file created by the BM.exe command-line tool and refresh the data.
10. If you haven't selected the real-time aggregations option in the BAM spreadsheet, you also then need to run or schedule the DTA package created during the execution of the BM.exe tool to update the OLAP cube for the deployed BAM activity.

We will walk through each one of these steps and discuss in detail how to configure and use the BizTalk BAM framework to monitor the Loan.Approval sample BizTalk application with the real-time aggregations option both on and off.

NOTE

The sample application is complete and can be easily deployed to walk through this example. You must complete the BAM Excel steps prior to deploying and configuring the BizTalk assembly.

Creating BAM Activities

The first step in the BAM definition process requires you to configure a BAM Business Activity that defines the data and milestones you want to track for a given business process. The Business Activities and Views are defined using the BAM Excel add-in. This first step is completely independent and not yet tied physically to the BizTalk application. In this case, the business expert can work independently of the developer. When the data views and aggregations are perfected, the developer can then map them to the orchestration and associated XML inputs and outputs.

There are four types of Activity data items:

- Business Milestone
- Business Data—Float
- Business Data—Integer
- Business Data—Text

A milestone is a simple date or time within the business process. In this example, we define five milestones.

- Completed
- Credit Check
- Received
- Approved
- Denied

We also define several data items of varying types. To begin, make a copy of the BAM.xls spreadsheet found in the BizTalk Tracking folder and rename the copy to Loans.xls. You can find the BAM.xls file in the C:\Program Files\Microsoft BizTalk Server 2004\Tracking directory.

NOTE

The original BAM.xls file is marked as read–only, so make sure you unmark the new file so that you can update it with the BAM artifacts.

Next, open the Loans.xls file in Excel. You should see a blank notebook with a new menu item named BAM. Select the BAM menu's BAM Activity menu item. The Business Activity Monitoring Activity Wizard dialog box should appear. In this example, we are going to create a single activity to describe our process named LoanProcess. To create the new Activity, select the New Activity button. In the New Activity dialog box that appears, name the Activity **`LoanProcess`** and click the New Item button. In the New Activity Item dialog box that appears, name the new item **`Approved`** and select Business Milestone as the item type. Repeat this step for the Milestones and data items listed in Table 20.4.

TABLE 20.4 LoanProcess Activities

Item Name	Item Type
ApplicantAge	Business Data Integer
Approved	Business Milestone
ApprovedAmt	Business Data—Float

TABLE 20.4 Continued

Item Name	Item Type
City	Business Data—Text
Completed	Business Milestone
CreditCheck	Business Milestone
CreditScore	Business Data—Integer
Denied	Business Milestone
Gender	Business Data—Text
Received	Business Milestone
RequestedAmt	Business Data—Float
Salary	Business Data—Integer
Status	Business Data—Text

NOTE

As you are going through this process, it is important to note that the data types for the Business Data items must match the data types of the data you will later map them to.

In our example, these types will map to elements contained in the inbound and outbound loan application and loan application response XML Schemas. If they do not, you may get an error in the Excel <filename>_livedata spreadsheet while viewing the real-time and historical tracking data. The completed view should look like Figure 20.11.

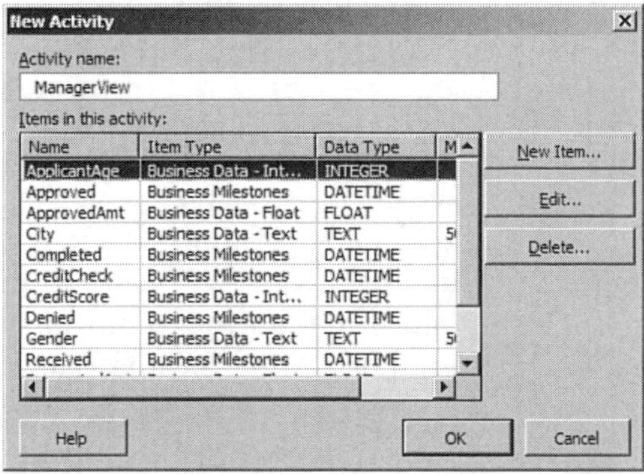

FIGURE 20.11 BAM Activity Wizard.

If the New Activity dialog box is still visible, select the OK button to close the dialog box. You should now see the Business Activity Monitoring Activity Wizard.

You've now defined the data items and milestone information for this example. Next, we need to define a view of this information. In this example we are going to define a single view, the ManagerView. We could, however, define several—one for each Information Worker user group.

Creating BAM Views

You can create a view in one of two ways when using the BAM Excel add-in. You can either select the BAM menu's BAM View menu item or have the BAM Activity Wizard automatically take you to it. If you have not closed the Business Activity Monitoring Activity Wizard dialog box, you can click the OK button. This will automatically bring up the Business Activity Monitoring View Wizard.

Defining the LoanProcess View—Step 1

To begin the definition of the LoanProcess view, select either the BAM View menu option or continue on from the BAM Activity Wizard.

1. In the wizard that appears, click the Next button. In the BAM View dialog box, select the Create a New View option button and click Next. In the New BAM View: Name and Activities dialog box that appears, enter the name **`LoanProcess`** into the name field and select the LoanProcess Activity that we created earlier, and then click Next.
2. In the New BAM View: View Items dialog box that appears, select the Select All Items check box to add all the Activity items to the newly created view, and then click Next.
3. The Edit BAM View: View Items dialog box should appear. This step in the BAM View Wizard enables you to manage the items for the view you just created. At this point you should have all the data items and milestones defined in the activity visible in the items list that is displayed.

Defining the Business Milestones and Durations—Step 2

In addition to the data items and milestones we've created, we want to define three additional items: two durations and one Business Milestone Group. A Business Milestone Group is a collection of milestones that defines a single event in time. In our example we are going to define a Business Milestone Group for the Approval Decision Milestone we created earlier. This milestone can be reached when the application reaches either the Approved or Denied milestone.

1. To create the Business Milestone Group, select the New Group button. In the New Group dialog box that appears, name the group **`DecisionGroup`** and check the LoanProcess.Approved and LoanProcess.Denied milestones.
2. We are also going to define two durations. The first, LoanDecisionDur, will track the time it takes for a loan to complete the decision step in the orchestration. To create this duration, select the New Duration button in the Business Activity Monitoring View Wizard dialog box. In the New Duration dialog box that appears, enter **`LoanDecisionDur`** as the Duration name, select the LoanProcess.Received milestone as

the starting milestone, and select the DecisionGroup Milestone Group as the End Business Milestone; then click the OK button to save the duration.

3. Repeat the same steps for a second duration named ProcessCycleTimeDur. This duration will track the time it takes to process an entire loan application from start to finish. The Start Business milestone should be set to the `LoanProcess.Received` milestone and the End Business milestone should be set to the `LoanProcess.Completed` milestone. Click Next to navigate to the next wizard step.

Defining the Dimensions—Step 3

At this point we are ready to start defining our aggregations. Aggregations are defined as either dimensions or measures. In this example we are going to define five dimensions and six measures.

1. To define a new Dimension, select the New Dimension button on the New BAM View: Aggregation Dimensions and Measures dialog box. In the New Dimension dialog box that appears, name the Dimension **`ApplicantAgeDim`**, select a Dimension type of Numeric Range Dimension, and a Base data item as `LoanProcess.ApplicantAge`.

2. We now need to add three new ranges. Click the New Range button in the New Dimension dialog box and name the range **`UnderTwenty`**. Put 0 in the From (inclusive) data entry box, put 20 in the To (exclusive) data entry box, then click OK. Repeat the same steps, creating two additional ranges—one for FiftyAndOver from 50 to 100 and one for TwentyToFifty from 20 to 50. Your New Dimension dialog box should look as displayed in Figure 20.12.

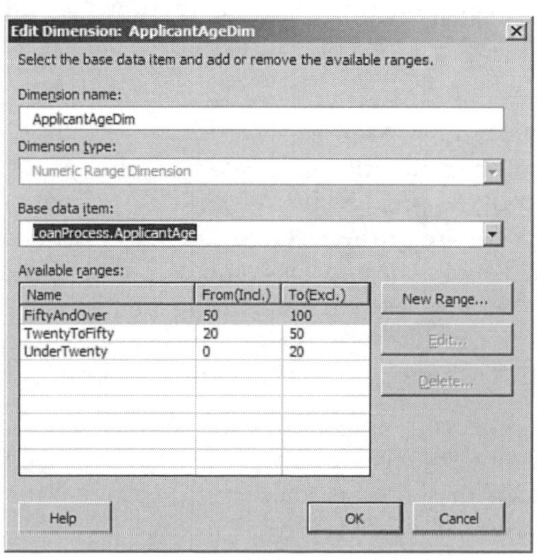

FIGURE 20.12 BAM Applicant Age Dimension.

3. Next, create three new Data Dimensions: City, Gender, and Status. To accomplish this, select the New Dimension button on the New BAM View: Aggregation Dimensions and Measures dialog box. In the New Dimension dialog box that appears, enter City as the Dimension name, select a Dimension type of Data Dimension, and then select the LoanProcess.City data item from the available data items list by selecting it and clicking the Add button, as shown in Figure 20.13.

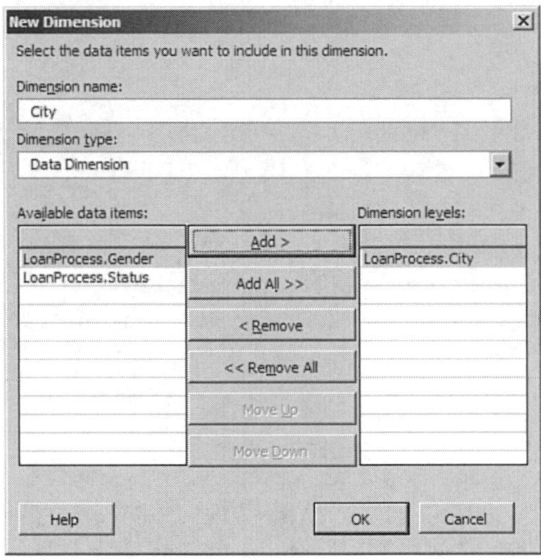

FIGURE 20.13 BAM City Dimension.

4. Click OK to save the new dimension and then repeat the same steps for the Gender and Status data items.

Creating the Progress Duration—Step 4

The final and most complicated duration to create is the Progress duration. A Progress duration collects data about the progress of an executing process. In this example we want to know how many processes are in the received state, how many are in the credit check state, how many are just starting the approved and denied final process stage, and how many are in the completion stage. When configuring a Progress duration, you need to be careful to make sure that the progress steps are all inclusive so that the sum of the processes in each step equals the total number of running processes.

1. To create the new Progress duration, click the New Dimension button from the New BAM View: Aggregation Dimensions and Measures dialog box. In the New Dimension dialog box that appears, name the duration **`ApprovalProgress`** and select the Progress Dimension dimension type.

2. Next, click the New Child button. In the New Progress Stage dialog box that appears, name the stage Requests, select the LoanProcess.Received Business Milestone, and click the OK button to save the stage.

3. Click the New Child button again and name the second stage **`Processing`** with the Business milestone also set to `LoanProcess.Received`, and then save the stage.

4. Next, make sure that the Processing stage is selected in the tree view and click New Child button again to create a new child named CreditCheck with the Business Milestone set to `LoanProcess.CreditCheck`.

5. Next, create two new siblings for the CreditCheck stage—one for Approved and one for Denied—matching the Business Milestones appropriately.

6. Finally, add a last stage by selecting the processing stage in the tree view and clicking the New Sibling button. This stage should be named `Completed` and map to the `LoanProcess.Completed` milestone. When completed, your new progress dimension should look as displayed in Figure 20.14.

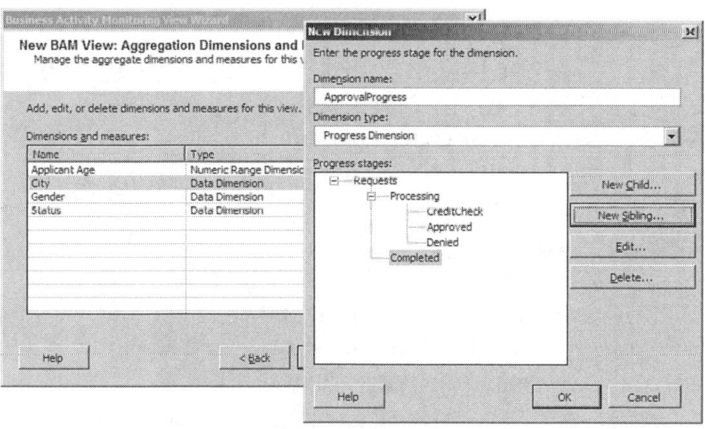

FIGURE 20.14 BAM Loan Progress Dimension.

Adding Measures—Step 5

Next, we need to add a few measures to our view definition. The first measure we are going to add is for the average salary.

To accomplish this, select the New Measure button from the New BAM View: Aggregation Dimensions and Measures dialog box. In the New Measure dialog box that appears, name the measure **`AvgSalary`**, select the base data items type of LoanProcess.Salary, and check the Average option button as shown in Figure 20.15. After you have added this measure, follow the same process to add the measures listed in Table 20.5.

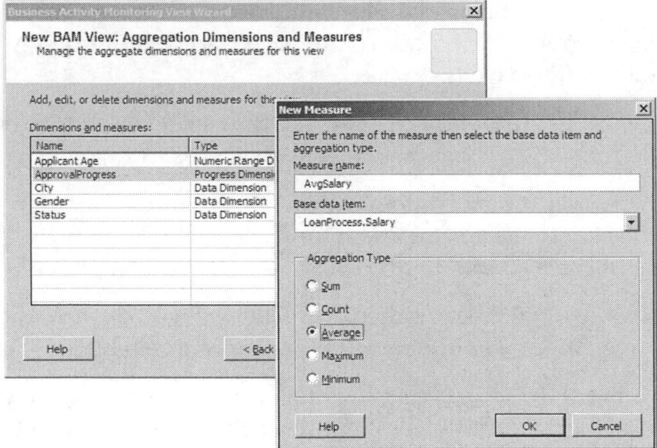

FIGURE 20.15 Creating the AvgSalary Measure.

TABLE 20.5 LoanProcess Measures

Name	Base Data Type	Aggregation Type
AvgCreditScore	LoanProcess.CreditScore	Average
AvgRequestedAmt	LoanProcess.RequestedAmt	Average
Count	LoanProcess	Count
AvgProcessCycleTime	ProcessCycleTimeDur	Average
AvgLoanDecisionDur	LoanDecisionDur	Average

We have now completed the configuration of the BAM Activity and View for our loan process and Loan Manager. Click the Next button twice and an empty pivot table and pivot table file list should appear as shown in Figure 20.16.

In the next section we will walk through the configuration of the pivot table so that the Loan Manager can manipulate the data, dimensions, and measure aggregations we just defined.

Configuring the Pivot Tables and Charts

Configuring the pivot table is fairly straightforward. You drag and drop the PivotTable Field List values from the PivotTable Field List onto the pivot table displayed in the Excel workbook. If a field from the list isn't appropriate for a particular area in the pivot table, you'll be prompted so that you cannot misconfigure the view. If you look at the drop-down list next to the Add To button on the PivotTable Field List pop-up and then navigate through each of the field items, you will notice that it instructs you where to drop the field. Row Area fields can be dropped as either fields or columns and Data Area fields can be dropped in the Drop Data Items Here area.

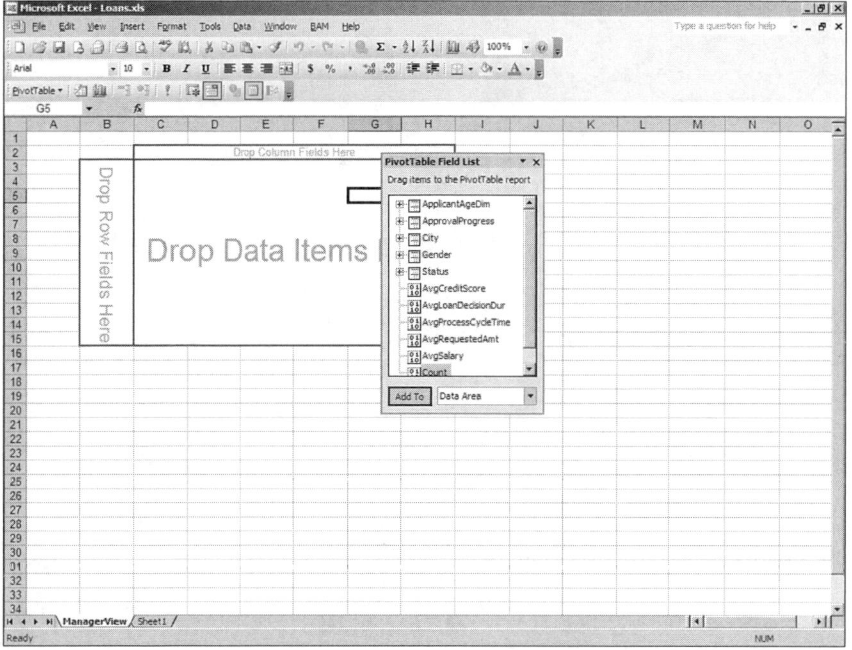

FIGURE 20.16 BAM Pivot Table configuration.

For our purposes, we first want to view by age and gender the number of applications that were approved.

1. To do this, drag the Status field onto the Drop Row Fields Here area.
2. Drag the ApplicantAge and Gender fields to the column heading area, placing the ApplicantAge on top.
3. Now drag the count field onto the Drop Data Items here area followed by these fields: AvgCreditScore, AvgSalary, and AvgProcessCycleTime. You should notice that sample data is provided for you so that you can better tweak and/or play with the pivot table and charting capabilities found natively in Excel.

In a production environment, we would take this to the next step, defining graphs and charts as well as alternative views using multiple pivot tables. For this example we are going to keep it simple and use this single view we've just created, as shown in Figure 20.17.

TIP

To create a second pivot table to drag items onto, highlight the entire pivot table and copy and paste.

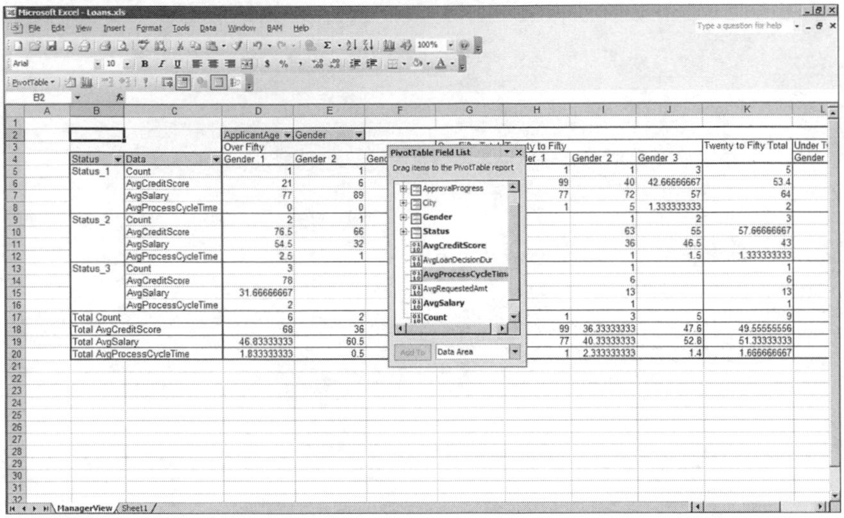

FIGURE 20.17 BAM pivot table configured.

We are now ready to save the Loans.xls BAM spreadsheet and export the BAM XML. Before you save the spreadsheet, select the BAM Real-Time Aggregations button found on the toolbar. This will mark the spreadsheet as requiring real-time in contrast to historical (OLAP) SQL data connections and artifacts when deployed. After you've clicked the Real-Time Aggregations button, save the spreadsheet to the C:\Program Files\Microsoft BizTalk Server 2004\Tracking directory. Next, select the BAM menu's Export XML menu option and save the XML file as Loans.xml on your local desktop. In the next section we will discuss how to run the BM.exe command-line tool to deploy the Loans.xls file creating the BAM SQL assets for this configuration.

The BAM Management Utility

The BM.exe utility is a command-line utility that accepts either the exported XML file or the BAM.xls Excel spreadsheet configured with the Activity and View BAM definitions. If you provide an XML file to the command, it will automatically create the SQL assets for you, but will not stamp an Excel spreadsheet with the SQL connection strings required to retrieve real-time and historical data using the pivot table created by the BAM wizards. In this example, we are going to run the command with the Loans.xls file we just finished creating. To run the command, select the Start menu's Run menu item. In the Run dialog box that appears, type **`cmd`**. Then navigate to the BizTalk tracking directory by typing the following:

```
cd: c:\Program Files\Microsoft BizTAlk Server 2004\Tracking
Type the following to deploy the Loans.xls file:bm deploy loans.xls
```

If all goes well, you should see what's displayed in Figure 20.18 in the command-line window.

```
C:\WINDOWS\system32\cmd.exe
Microsoft Windows [Version 5.2.3790]
(C) Copyright 1985-2003 Microsoft Corp.

C:\Documents and Settings\Administrator>cd c:\Program files

C:\Program Files>cd Microsoft BizTalk Server 2004\Tracking

C:\Program Files\Microsoft BizTalk Server 2004\Tracking>bm deploy loans.xls
Retrieving BAM Definition XML from Excel workbook ... Done!
Deploying PrimaryImportDatabase ... Done!
Deploying StarSchemaDatabase ... Done!
Deploying AnalysisDatabase ... Done!
Deploying ArchivingDatabase ... Done!
Deploying CubeUpdateDTS ... Done!
Deploying DataMaintenanceDTS ... Done!
Updating connection strings in Excel workbook ... Done!
Saving live data copy of the Excel workbook to C:\Program Files\Microsoft BizTal
k Server 2004\Tracking\loans_LiveData2.xls ... Done!

C:\Program Files\Microsoft BizTalk Server 2004\Tracking>_
```

FIGURE 20.18 Deploying the Loans.xls using the BM command-line tool.

> **NOTE**
>
> This assumes that you have saved the Loans.xls file in the tracking directory prior to running the bm command.

To undeploy Loans.xls, first type the following in the same command-line window:

```
bm listchanges
```

This will give you a listing that includes a number for the last change made, in this case the deployment of the Loans.xls file. You use that number to undeploy the Loans BAM data. An example of this is shown in Figure 20.19.

```
C:\WINDOWS\system32\cmd.exe
        Activities: ManagerView
        Views: ManagerView
#39: Deploy loans.xls BamConfiguration.xml
        By DEMOAPPSERVER\Administrator at 6/22/2004 4:36:40 PM (v3.0.4902.0)
        Activities: LoanProcess
        Views: ManagerView
#40: Undeploy #39 BamConfiguration.xml
        By DEMOAPPSERVER\Administrator at 6/22/2004 4:40:43 PM (v3.0.4902.0)
        Activities: LoanProcess
        Views: ManagerView
#43: Deploy loans.xls BamConfiguration.xml
        By DEMOAPPSERVER\Administrator at 6/22/2004 4:45:00 PM (v3.0.4902.0)
        Activities: LoanProcess
        Views: ManagerView
#44: Undeploy #43 BamConfiguration.xml
        By DEMOAPPSERVER\Administrator at 6/22/2004 4:45:31 PM (v3.0.4902.0)
        Activities: LoanProcess
        Views: ManagerView
#45: Deploy loans.xls BamConfiguration.xml
        By DEMOAPPSERVER\Administrator at 6/22/2004 4:52:08 PM (v3.0.4902.0)
        Activities: LoanProcess
        Views: ManagerView

C:\Program Files\Microsoft BizTalk Server 2004\Tracking>bm undeploy #45_
```

FIGURE 20.19 Undeploying BAM configurations.

Now that we've deployed the Activity and associated View, let's take a look at the SQL assets that were created for us automatically behind the scenes. First, if you open up the SQL Server Enterprise Manager, you will see a number of new tables in the BAMPrimaryImport Database, as shown in Figure 20.20.

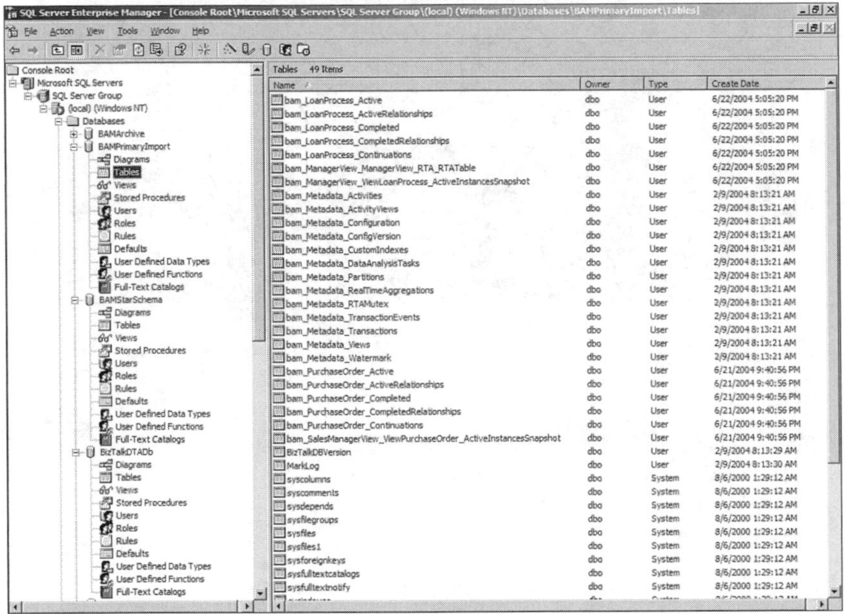

FIGURE 20.20 BAMPrimaryImport Database after Activity and View deployment.

Because we selected the BAM Excel real-time aggregations option, the BM.exe tool did not automatically create the DTS package and OLAP cube for us this time. This allows us to quickly test our aggregations in real-time without having to schedule or automatically run the DTA package. In the section titled "Configuring OLAP," we will undeploy and redeploy the same BAM definition, this time without the real-time aggregation checked, so that we can investigate the DTS package and OLAP cube that's created.

Using the Tracking Profile Editor

The next step in the process is to map the BAM XML file to the orchestration implementation of the loan approval process. To do this, open the BizTalk Server Tracking Profile Editor by navigating to the Start, Programs, Microsoft BizTalk Server 2004, Tracking Profile Editor menu option and select it. The Tracking Profile Editor should appear. To create a new Tracking Profile, select the File, New menu option; the Select Assembly dialog box should appear as shown in Figure 20.21. Select the Loans.Approval assembly and click the OK button.

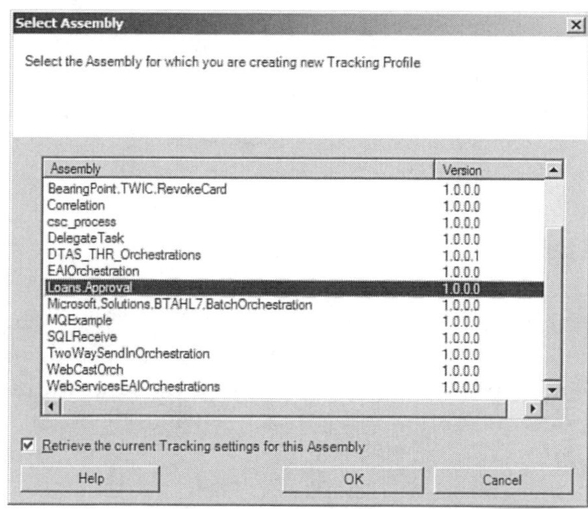

FIGURE 20.21 Creating a new Tracking Profile.

> **NOTE**
>
> This sample comes with a completed version of the Loans.Approval application. If you download the code, go to the C:\Chapter20\Loans\ directory and open up the Loans.sln file. Re-build and deploy the BizTalk assembly, and then run the BizTalk Server Deployment Wizard to import the bindings for the schedule contained in the LoansBinding.xml file. This file can be found in the C:\Chapter20\Loans directory. You must also create a virtual directory for the Web service the orchestration calls named CreditCheck. The source code for this web service can be found in the C:\Chapter20\Loans\CreditCheck directory.

You should now see a simplified version of the Loans.Approval orchestration on the right side. Next you need to import the Activity definition .xml file you earlier exported from the BAM Excel workbook. To do this select the Loans.Approval.ApprovalProcess tree view menu item and right-click. A pop-up menu item named Import Activity Definition should appear. Select the menu option and in the Open dialog box that appears, select the Loans.xml file you created earlier. A tree view depicting the BAM definition file should now be shown on the left.

There are two basic types of bindings that need to be configured. You configure bindings in the Tracking Profile Editor by dragging and dropping items from the right side (schedule) to the left side containing the BAM definitions. The two general types either map to direct shapes in the orchestration or map to the inbound and outbound schema elements. Let's first map all the direct bindings to objects in the orchestration. The first item to map is the ManagerView Received Milestone. You can tell that this is a milestone in the tree view by its clock graphic. To do this, select the Receive_LoanA shape on the Orchestration side and drag it on top of the Received item in the tree view. Repeat the steps for the remaining milestones, as shown in Table 20.6.

TABLE 20.6 Mapping the BAM Milestones

BAM Definition	Orchestration Shape
CreditCheck	GetCreditScore
Approved	ConstructLoanAppResponseApproved
Denied	ConstructLoanAppResponseDenied
Completed	Send Denied
	Send Approval

Next, we need to map the inbound and outbound message schemas to the data items we defined in the BAM definition. To do this, select the Receive_LoanA shape and right-click. In the pop-up menu that appears, select the Message Schema menu item. This will toggle the view on the right side to the inbound message schema. By dragging and dropping, map the BAM definitions as defined in Table 20.7.

TABLE 20.7 BAM Schema Definition Mappings

BAM Definition	Schema Node
ApplicantAge	Age
City	City
Gender	Gender
RequestedAmt	AmountRequested
Salary	Salary

Next, we need to map the remaining BAM definitions to the outbound schema definition. To do this, first select the Loans.Approval.ApprovalProcess menu item from the drop-down menu on the top of the page. Then navigate to the end of the Orchestration, right-click Send Denied, and select the Message Schema menu option. Then map the three schema items to the appropriate BAM definition item, as shown in Table 20.8.

TABLE 20.8 Mapping Denied Output Schema Items

BAM Definition	Schema Item
Status	LoanStatus
CreditScore	CreditScore
ApprovedAmount	ApprovedAmount

Navigate back to the orchestration schedule and repeat these same steps, but this time right-click the Send_Approval shape and select that Message schema. There should be two items for each of the three BAM definitions when you are through. A completed view of the mappings can be seen in Figure 20.22.

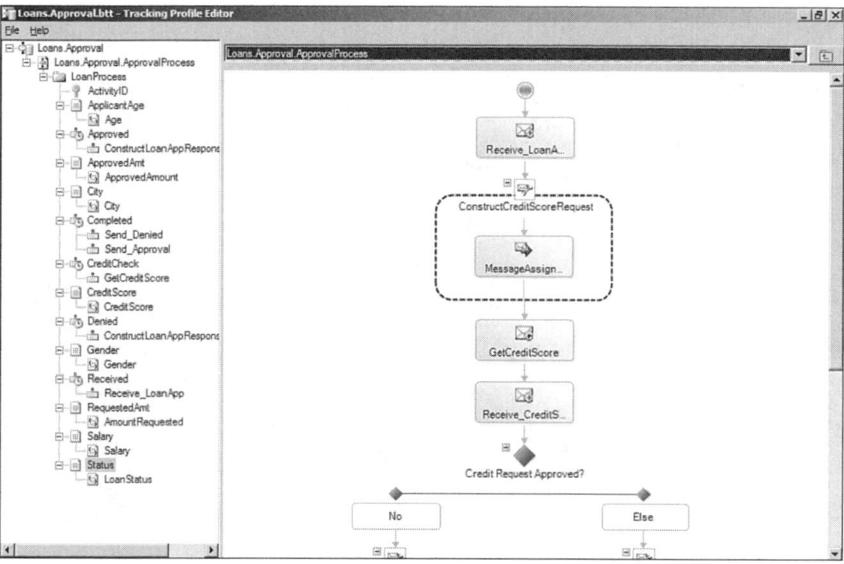

FIGURE 20.22 The completed Tracking Profile.

Now we need to save the Tracking Profile and then deploy it by selecting the Tracking Profile Editor's File, Deploy menu. If everything goes well, you should see a dialog box that tells you that the tracking profile .btt file was deployed successfully. If a tracking profile already exists for this particular assembly, you will be prompted to overwrite the existing profile.

Viewing Real-Time Aggregations

We are now ready to run our Loans orchestration and begin gathering real-time data that we can view in the loans_LiveData.xls spreadsheet that was generated for us when we deployed the BAM definition. This xls should be in the C:\Program Files\Microsoft BizTalk Server 2004\Tracking directory.

To run the orchestration, copy the .xml sample input files found in the C:\Chapter20\loans\filedrop directory into the C:\Chapter20\loans\filedrop\inbox directory. If you've deployed the orchestration correctly, the files should begin to be processed and the output placed into the C:\Chapter20\loans\filedrop\outbox directory. After you've begun processing, open the loans_LiveData.xls file and click the Refresh Data button on the toolbar. You should see real-time information displayed in the spreadsheet, as shown in Figure 20.23.

Configuring OLAP

In the previous deployment we chose to have the BM.exe command-line tool create real-time SQL artifacts for us. We could have just as easily not checked the real-time aggregation BAM Excel add-in button. If we do not check this option, BM will automatically create the OLAP SQL assets, including the DTS package necessary for us to capture and move data into an OLAP cube.

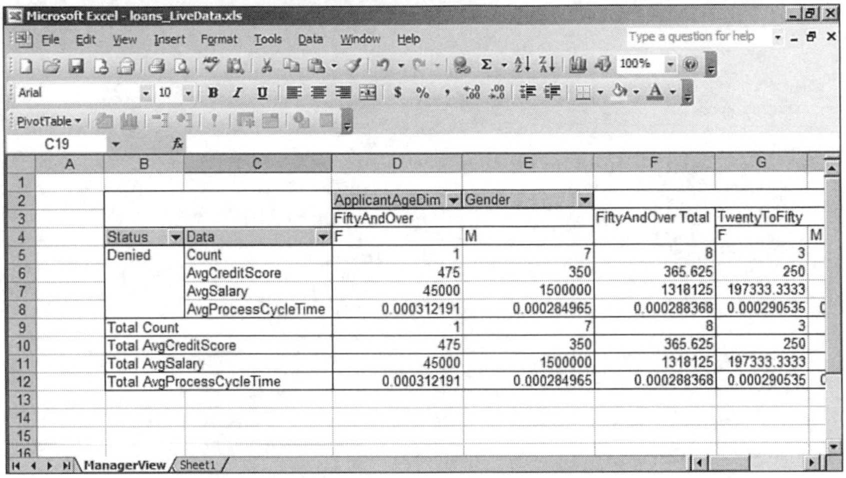
Microsoft Excel - loans_LiveData.xls
C19
ApplicantAgeDim Gender
FiftyAndOver
FiftyAndOver Total
TwentyToFifty
Status Data F M F M
Denied Count 1 7 8 3
AvgCreditScore 475 350 365.625 250
AvgSalary 45000 1500000 1318125 197333.3333
AvgProcessCycleTime 0.000312191 0.000284965 0.000288368 0.000290535
Total Count 1 7 8 3
Total AvgCreditScore 475 350 365.625 250
Total AvgSalary 45000 1500000 1318125 197333.3333
Total AvgProcessCycleTime 0.000312191 0.000284965 0.000288368 0.000290535
ManagerView Sheet1

FIGURE 20.23 The Loans_LiveData.xls file refreshed with real data.

To configure the Loans example to store BAM tracking data in OLAP, open the Loans.xls BAM workbook and unselect the real-time aggregations button on the PivotTable menu.

NOTE

The Real Time Aggregation button is available only when you are focused on the pivot table in the workbook.

Save the Loans.xls file in the C:\Program Files\Microsoft BizTalk Server 2004\Tracking directory. Next we need to undeploy the Loans BAM real-time deployment. To do this, navigate to the Start menu's Run command window and type **`cmd`**. In the command window that appears, navigate to the C:\Program Files\Microsoft BizTalk Server 2004\Tracking directory and type the following:

```
bm listchanges
```

You should see a list of the changes made to the BAM infrastructure along with an associated number. Type **`bm undeploy #`** (the number of the real-time deployment) to undeploy the Loans.xls real-time aggregation. When it's completed, type **`bm deploy Loans.xls`** to redeploy the Loans Activity, this time set for OLAP. A new Loans_livedata.xls file will be created for you; however, this time the SQL connection string will be stamped to pull data using an Analysis MDX query.

CAUTION

If you do not delete the existing Loans_livedata.xls file, BizTalk will name the new _livedata file Loans_lievedata1.xls.

Drop some sample XML files into the C:\Chapter20\Loans\Filedrop\Inbox to run some data through the Loans.Approval orchestration. When it's complete, open the Loans_livedata.xls file stored in the tracking directory. It should tell you that no data is present in the cube and that the cube has not been processed.

To move the data to the cube, you must execute the DTS package named BAM_AN_ManagerView. To run this package, open up SQL Enterprise Manager and navigate to the Data Transformation Services node as displayed in Figure 20.24. Select the package and right-click. In the pop-up menu that appears, select the execute option. After the package has run, you will be able to query the data in the cube from the Loans_livedata.xls Excel workbook by clicking the Refresh Data button in the toolbar.

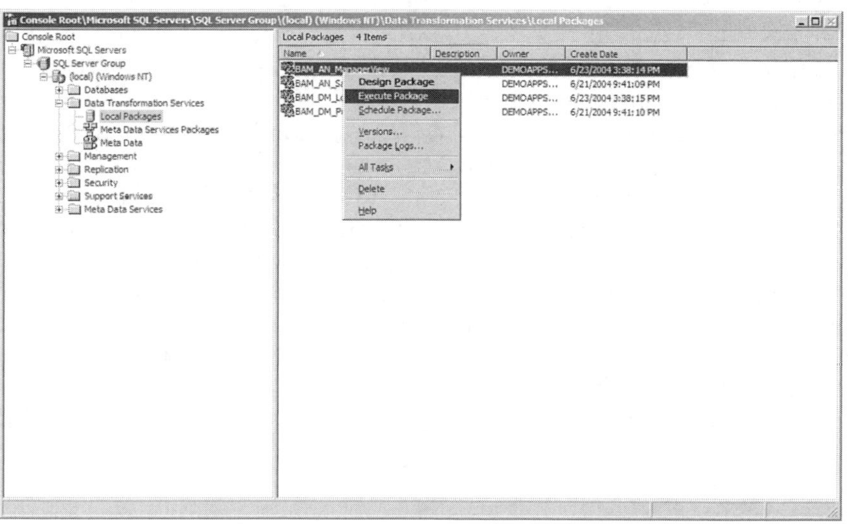

FIGURE 20.24 DTS Packages created by using the command-line tool.

The Analysis database and cubes created for this example can be viewed by opening the SQL Server Analysis Manager as shown in Figure 20.25.

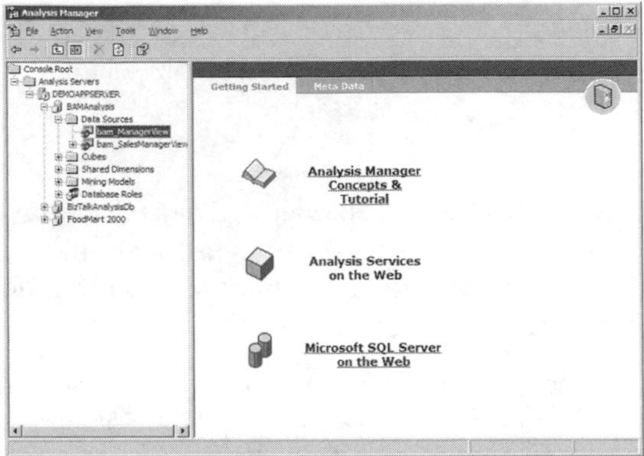

FIGURE 20.25 SQL Analysis Manager and OLAP BAM Loan Activity Cubes.

Summary

As many analysts have recently stated, a new trend in the software industry called Business Activity Monitoring (BAM) is emerging. This new category of services leverages existing business intelligence technologies to concentrate and analyze data for heterogeneous event sources. BizTalk Server 2004's implementation of BAM provides a way to abstractly define, intercept, collect, and aggregate data tied to specific business events in the context of defined business processes. It provides tools that enable the information worker or business expert to define the key performance indicators, aggregations, and trends needed to monitor a process from a business perspective using an Excel add-in. After these artifacts have been defined, the business experts can use Excel's built-in capabilities to further refine them as well as display them in multiple data views. The BAM framework also provides the capability to automatically create the database, analysis, and event observation SQL asset infrastructure. This allows the aggregations and views of data to be quickly implemented by the developers and IT staff with little or no custom code.

PART VII
Appendices

IN THIS PART

APPENDIX A

Installing BizTalk Server 2004

By Purushottam Amradkar

IN THIS CHAPTER

This appendix will cover how to install different components of BizTalk Server 2004. We will also cover the different configurations that are required before you install BizTalk Server.

Hardware Requirements and Recommendations

Microsoft recommends the following minimum hardware for complete installation of BizTalk 2004:

- 450MHz or higher processor
- 512 MB of RAM
- 6GB hard disk
- CD/DVD-ROM drive
- Super VGA monitor or high-resolution monitor
- Mouse or any compatible pointing device

NOTE

For scaling out or scaling up, users may need expensive hardware, depending on the requirements and type of application.

Software Requirements

This section provides information about minimum software requirements for BizTalk Server.

Operating System Requirements

BizTalk Server can be installed on the following:

NOTE

BizTalk Server requires NTFS file system.

- Windows 2000 Advanced Server with Service Pack 4
- Windows XP with Service Pack 1a
- Windows 2003 Standard/Enterprise/Datacenter Server

NOTE

Windows 2003 Server is required for Business Activity Services (BizTalk Component) and Windows SharePoint Services.

Other Software Requirements

Before installing BizTalk Server, you need to install the following software:

- .NET Framework 1.1
- SQL Server 2000 Enterprise/Developer/Standard with Service Pack 3a
- SQL Analysis Service with Service Pack 3a
- SQLXML 3.0 Service Pack 2
- MSXML 3.0 Service Pack 4
- Internet Explorer 6.0 Service Pack 1.0
- Microsoft Office Web Controls 10
- Hot Fixes: Q828748, Q329433, Q821887*, and Q831950**

NOTE

.Net Framework 1.1 must be installed before you install SQLXML 3.0.

SQLXML is required for SQL Adapter.

* This hot fix should be installed only on Windows 2000 Server.

** This hot fix must be installed on the computer(s) where SQL Server 2000 is installed.

You can download hot fixes from `http://support.microsoft.com`.

For some of the hot fixes, you may need to contact Microsoft Support Services.

- Windows SharePoint Services (WSS) 2.0

NOTE

Business Activity Services requires WSS.

- Visual Studio 2003 with Microsoft Visual C# .NET
- Microsoft Internet Explorer 5.01 or later

NOTE

SSO client utility can be installed on Windows XP Professional with Service Pack 1, Windows 2000 with Service Pack 4, or Windows Server 2003.

To install Business Activity Services on a client machine, Microsoft Office InfoPath 2003 and Microsoft Internet Explorer 6 Service Pack 1 should be installed.

Preparing Server for Installing BizTalk Server 2004

Before we can start installing BizTalk Server, we need to install IIS 6.0 on Windows 2003 Server, SQL Server, Analysis Service, Windows SharePoint Services, and Studio 2003 with Microsoft Visual C# .NET.

NOTE

The default installation of Windows 2003 does not install IIS 6.0.

Installing IIS 6.0

The following steps can be taken to install IIS 6.0:

1. Click Start, select Control Panel, and click Add or Remove Programs. This pops up the Add or Remove Programs dialog box.
2. Click Add/Remove Windows Component, which pops up another dialog box for Windows Components Wizard, as shown in Figure A.1.
3. Select the Application Server check box. Then click the Details button. This pops up another window.

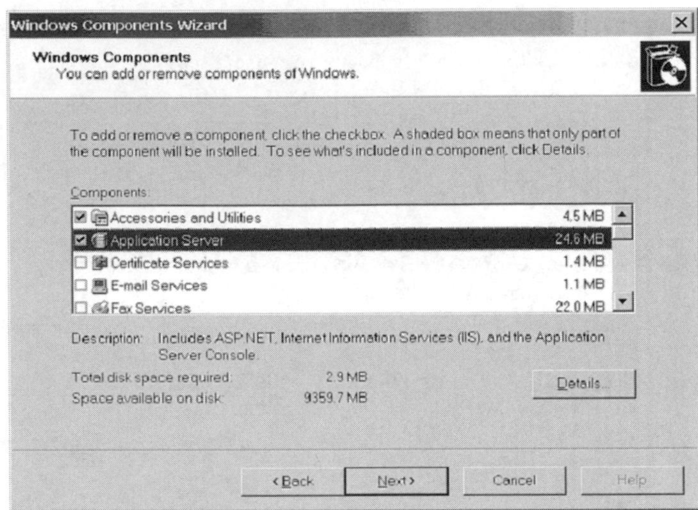

FIGURE A.1 Windows Components Wizard.

4. Select the Application Server Console, ASP.NET, Enable Network COM+, Enable Network DTC access, and Internet Information Services check boxes, as shown in Figure A.2.

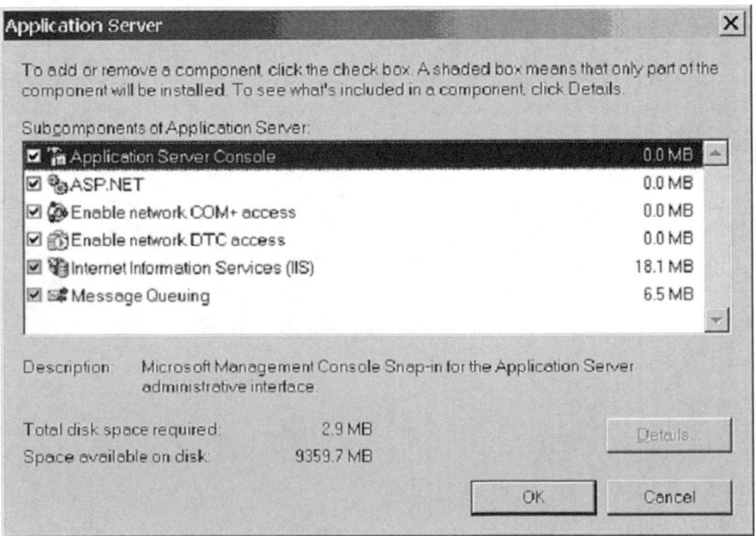

FIGURE A.2 Application Server dialog box.

5. Click OK to install IIS 6.0.

> **NOTE**
>
> To run ASP.NET applications, users need to enable the Web services extension for ASP.NET v1.1.4322 using the Internet Information Services MMC Snap-In. Users will get a "404 Error" if this extension is not enabled.
>
> We also will cover side-by-side installation of MSMQ and BizTalk Message Queuing.

Installing SQL Server 2000

BizTalk Server needs SQL Server to create its databases. SQL Server can be installed remotely. Different databases of BizTalk Server can be installed on different SQL Servers. It is highly recommended that you install the Tracking database and MessageBox on different SQL Servers for high-load scenarios.

To install SQL Server 2000, follow these steps:

1. Do the typical installation of SQL Server.
2. Install Service Pack 3a for SQL Server.
3. Make sure Mixed Mode Authentication is enabled.

> **NOTE**
>
> BizTalk Server requires Windows Authentication.

Installing Analysis Services

BizTalk Server requires Analysis Services for Health Activity Tracking and Business Activity Monitoring (BAM).

Follow these steps to install Analysis Service for SQL Server:

1. Select Typical Installation of Analysis Service.
2. Install Service Pack 3a for Analysis Service.

Enabling Network DTC Access on Windows 2003 Server

If SQL Server is remote to BizTalk Server and if either of them is installed on Windows 2003 Server, users need to enable network DTC Access to create databases on the remote SQL Server. The following steps can be taken to enable Network DTC Access.

1. From the Start menu, select All Programs, Administrative Tools, and Component Services. Then click Component Services. This opens MMC Snap-In for Component Services.
2. Expand the tree and select My Computer.

3. Right-click My Computer and select Properties. The My Computer Properties window opens. Then click the MSDTC tab as shown in Figure A.3.

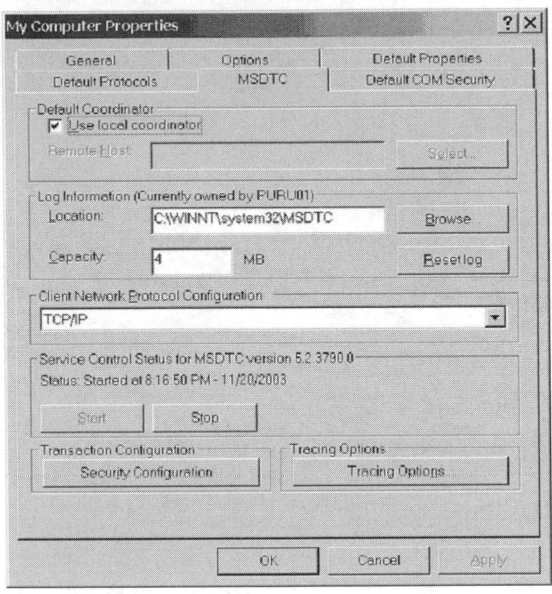

FIGURE A.3 My Computer Properties window.

4. Click the Security Configuration button. This opens the Security Configuration window as shown in Figure A.4.

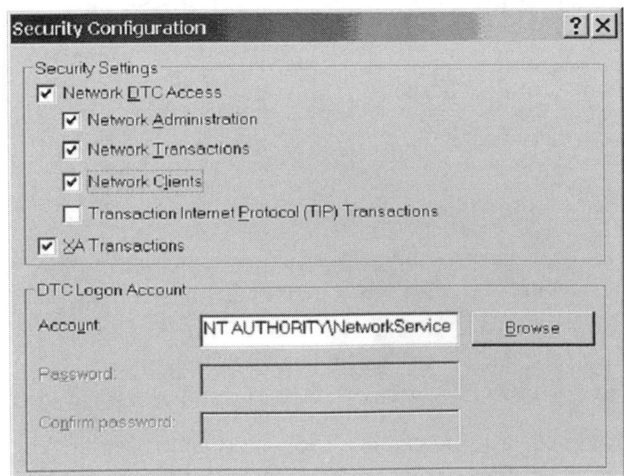

FIGURE A.4 Security Configuration window.

5. Select the check boxes for Network DTC Access, Network Administration, Network Transactions, Network Clients, and XA Transactions. Then click OK.
6. Reboot the machine to enable Network DTC Access.

Installing Windows SharePoint Services 2.0 for BAS

Installation of Windows SharePoint Services is required to work BAS. If you double-click the MSI package of Windows SharePoint Services and select Typical Installation, MSDE will be installed to create and configure WSS databases. If you want to select local/remote SQL Server for WSS databases, you should select the Server Farm option, as shown in Figure A.5.

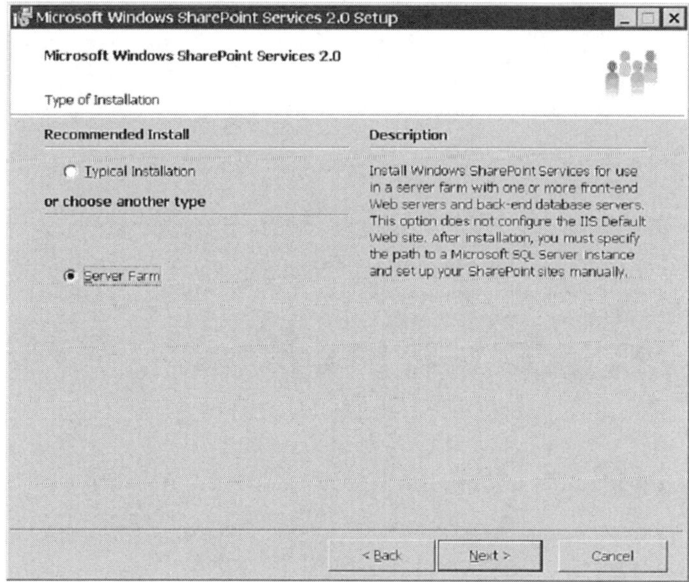

FIGURE A.5 Windows SharePoint Services Setup.

This will not create and configure default configuration and content databases for WSS. After SharePoint setup is finished, it will open the Internet Explorer window to configure SharePoint as shown in Figure A.6.

Take the following steps to create and configure Application Pool.

1. Select Create a New Application Pool.
2. Type **BusinessActivityServicesPool** as the Application Pool Name.

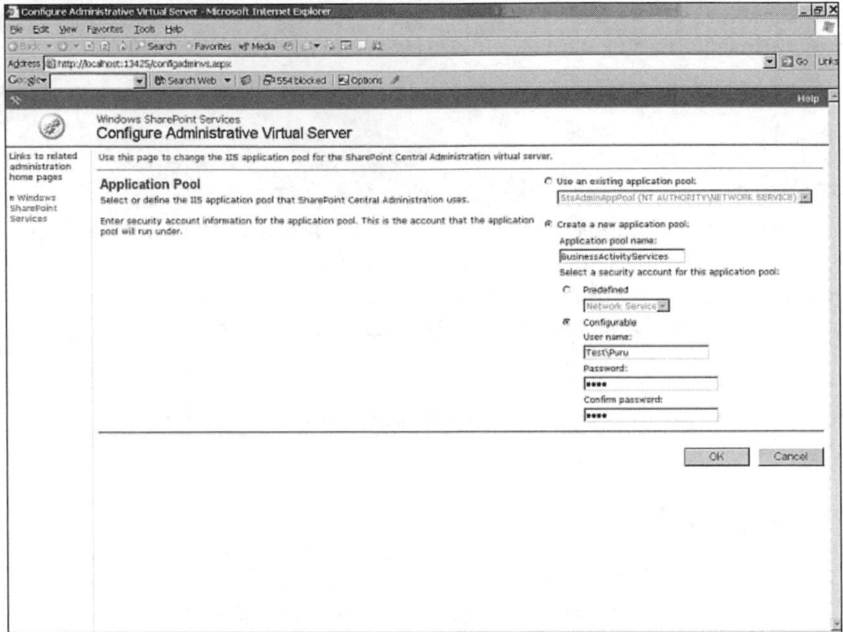

FIGURE A.6 Configure Administrative Virtual Server window.

NOTE

You can provide any name for the Application Pool.

3. Select the Configurable option under Select a Security Account for This Application Pool.
4. Provide the correct username and password and click OK.
5. Reset IIS and then click OK, as shown in Figure A.7.

This opens a window to enable you to configure SharePoint databases, as shown in Figure A.8.

To configure the configuration database, follow these steps:

1. Provide the correct SQL Server as the Database Server.
2. Provide the name of the configuration database as the SQL Server database name.
3. Select the Users Already Have Domain Accounts option. Then click OK. This will take you to another page as shown in Figure A.9.

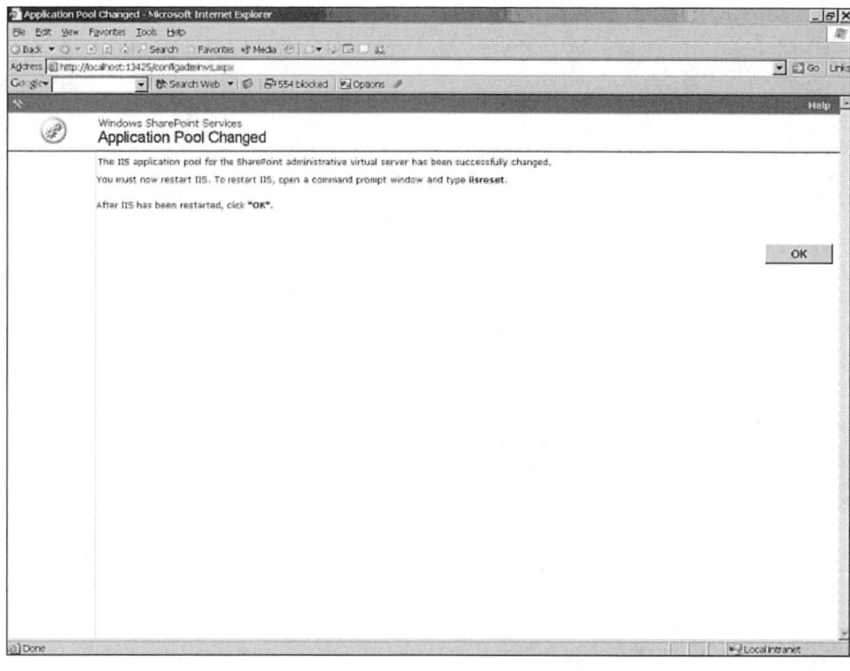

FIGURE A.7 Application Pool changed.

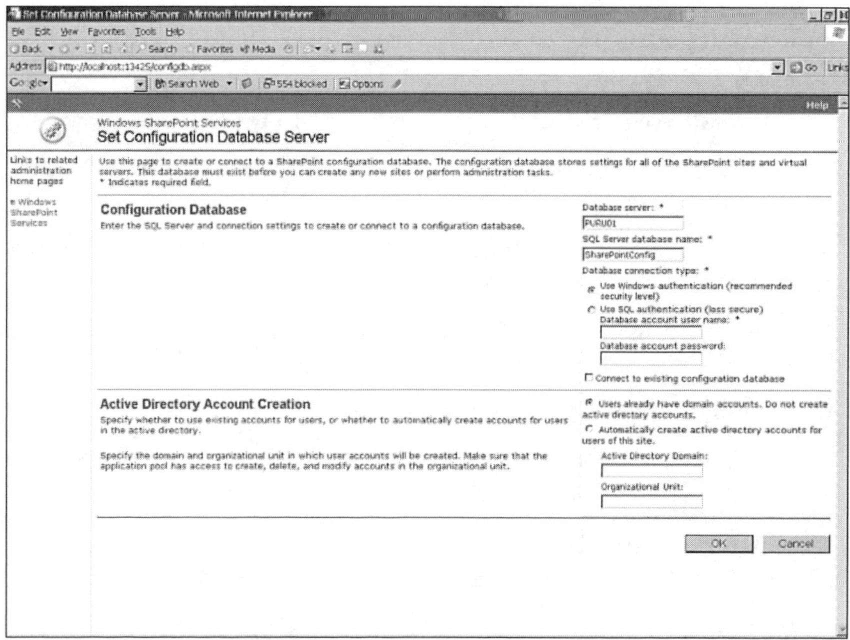

FIGURE A.8 The Set Configuration Database Server window.

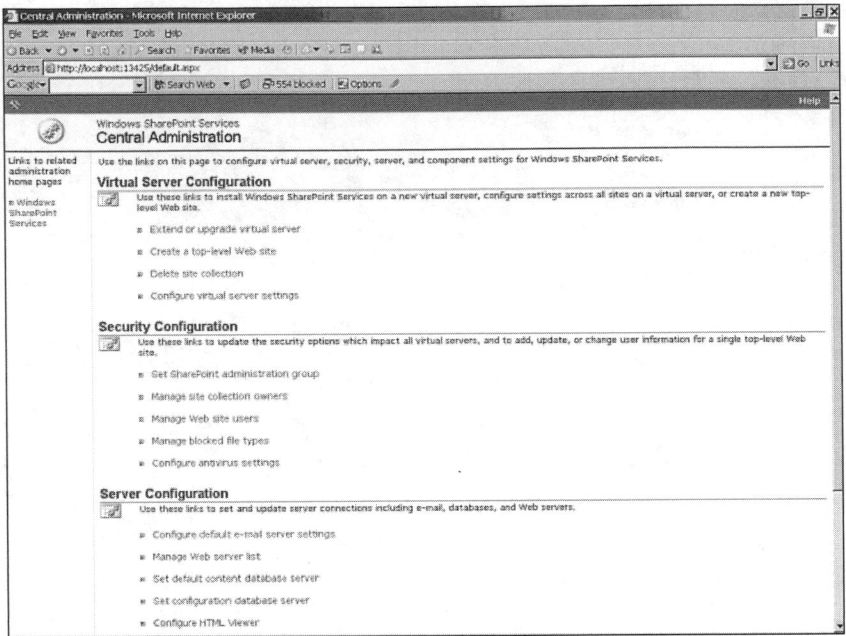

FIGURE A.9 Central Administration window.

To create and configure the content database, follow these steps:

1. Click the Extend or Upgrade Virtual Server link under Virtual Server Configuration. This will open the virtual server list page.
2. Click the Default Web Site link. This will take you to the Extend Virtual Server page.
3. Click Extend and Create Content Database. This will open the Extend and Create Content Database page.
4. Provide the appropriate application pool. You can use the Business Activity Services application pool that you created in the previous step.
5. Provide the correct username and email address as the site owner and then click OK to extend and configure the content database.
6. After the configuration is done, you can test SharePoint configuration by creating a test site.

Testing SharePoint Configuration

To test SharePoint configuration by creating a site, follow these steps:

1. Click Start and select Administrative Tool. Then click SharePoint Central Administration. This opens the Central Administration Web page.

2. Click the Create a Top-Level Web Site link. This takes you to the virtual server list page.
3. Click the Default Web Site link. This opens the Create Top-Level Web Site page as shown in Figure A.10.

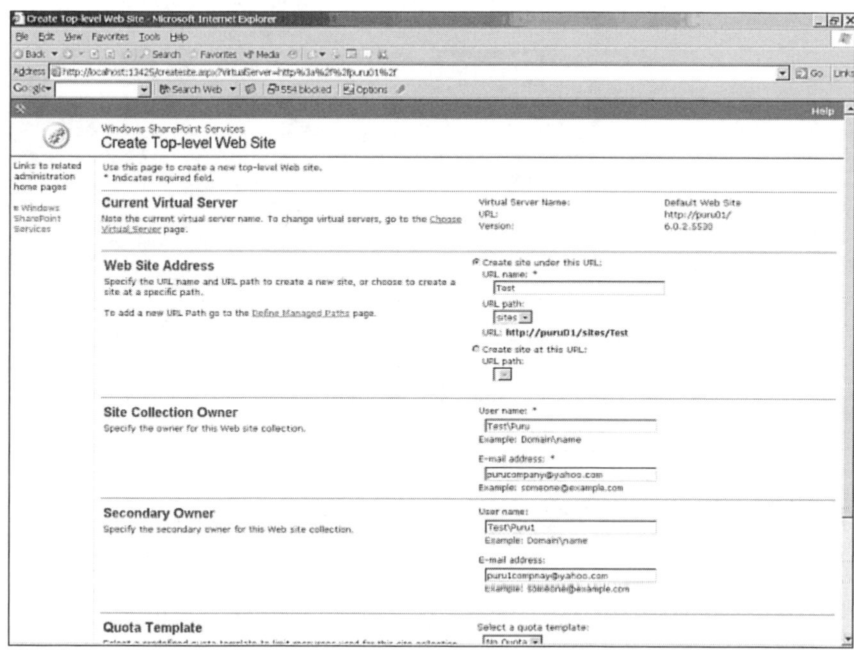

FIGURE A.10 The Create Top-Level Web Site page.

4. Provide an appropriate Web site address, such as Test.
5. Provide a correct username and email address as the site owner; the user may also provide a secondary owner.
6. Click OK to create the Web site. If the site is created successfully, the Top-Level Web Site page opens.
7. You can click the site link to browse the site.

Installing BizTalk Server

Now that you have installed all required supporting software, you can launch the BizTalk setup program from the CD. After the CD is inserted into the CD drive, click the SetUp.exe file, which will start the Installation Wizard as shown in Figure A.11.

Click Install to begin installation of BizTalk Server 2004. In the Customer Information screen, enter your information into the fields, as shown in Figure A.12.

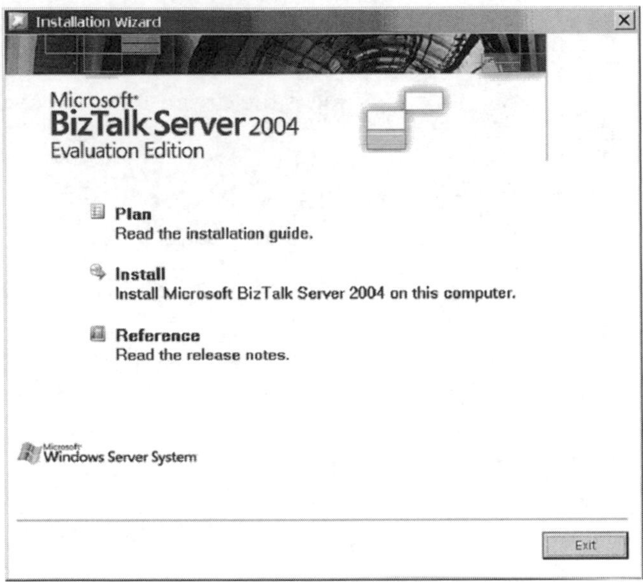

FIGURE A.11 Installation Wizard.

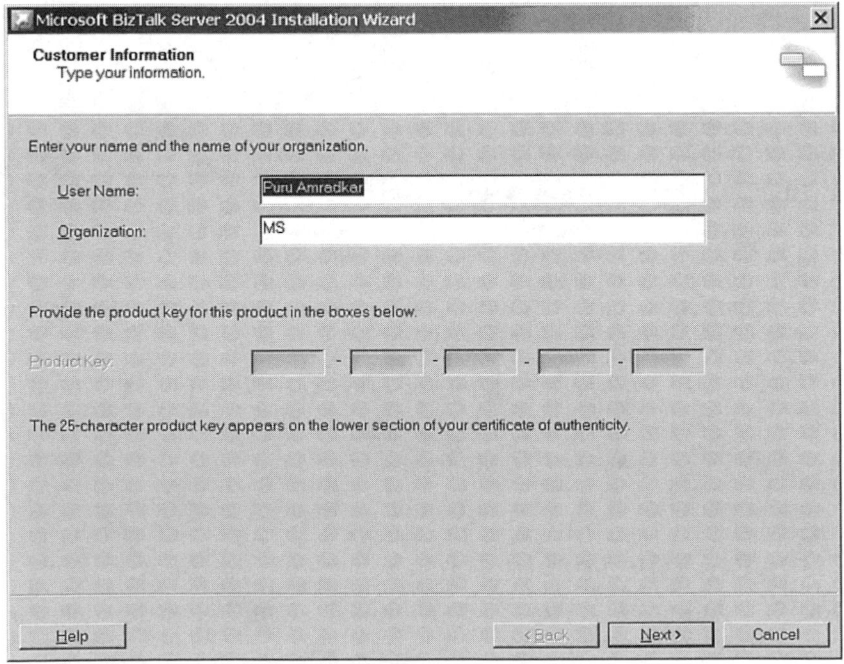

FIGURE A.12 The BizTalk Server 2004 Installation Wizard.

Click Accept to accept the license agreement as shown in Figure A.13. You must read and accept the license agreement to continue setup.

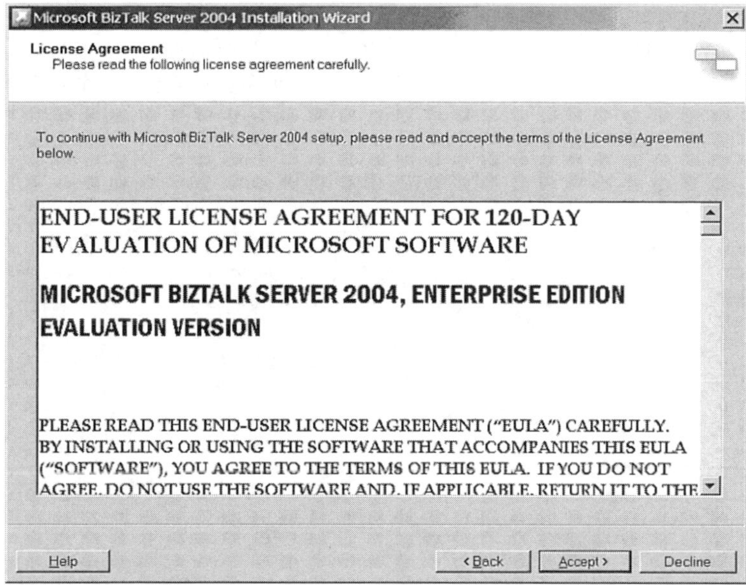

FIGURE A.13 The license agreement.

You have two choices for installation: Complete and Custom, as shown in Figure A.14.

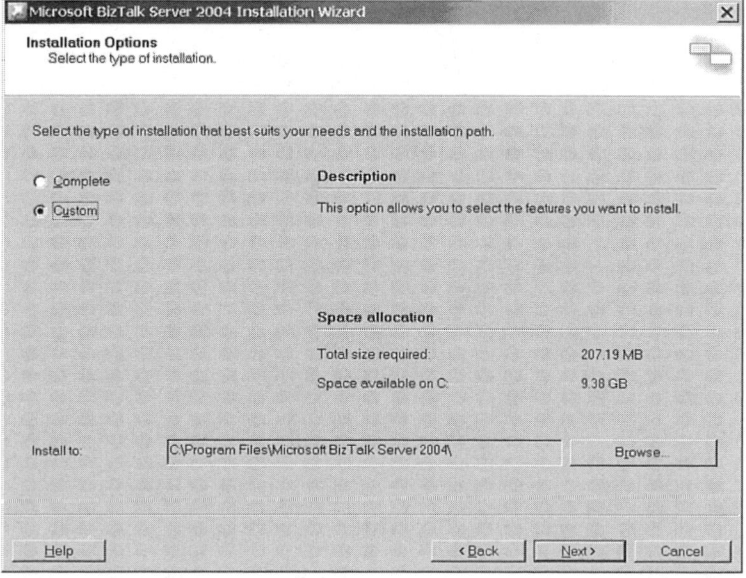

FIGURE A.14 Installation options.

Selecting the complete installation is recommended for development purposes. You also can change the installation directory by clicking the Browse button. You can select the custom installation to select appropriate components. For example, you can unselect components for Information Worker Applications/Portal or for Human Workflow Services. Another good example is installing only development tools by selecting the Development option, which will install the BizTalk project system on the computer. Figure A.15 shows different components that can be installed by selecting the custom installation.

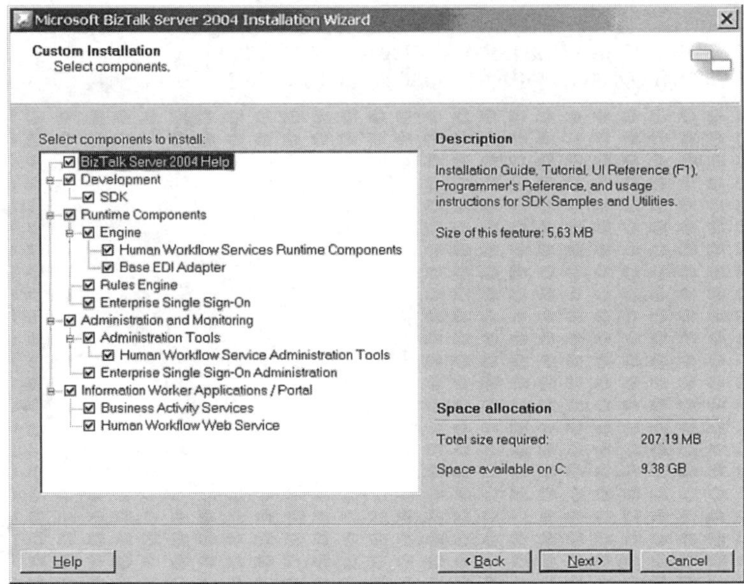

FIGURE A.15 Custom Installation.

> **NOTE**
>
> Business Activity Services will not be installed on Windows 2000 Advanced Server.
>
> Depending on the OS, installation options will differ; therefore, your screen may look different than that shown in Figure A.16.

Click Next to continue to review the components to be installed, as shown in Figure A.16.

Click Install to start the installation process as shown in Figure A.17.

After installation is complete, click Finish to start the Configuration Wizard as shown in Figure A.18.

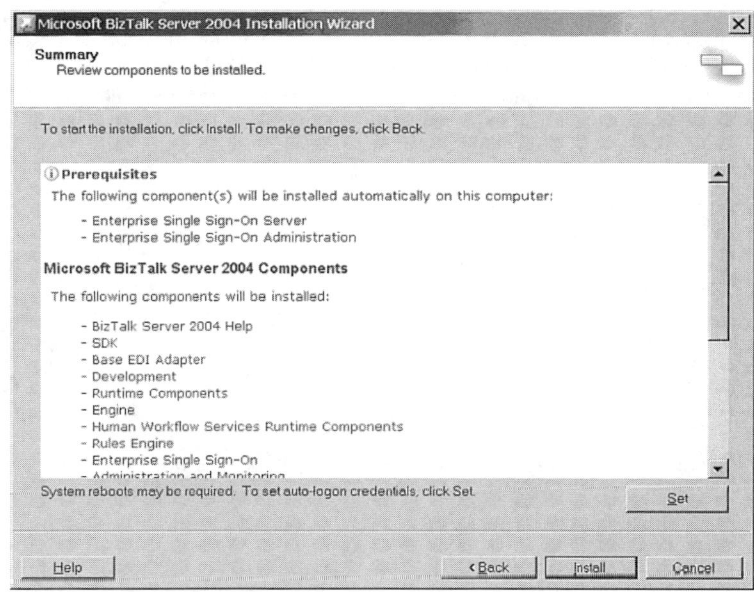

FIGURE A.16 Review components to be installed.

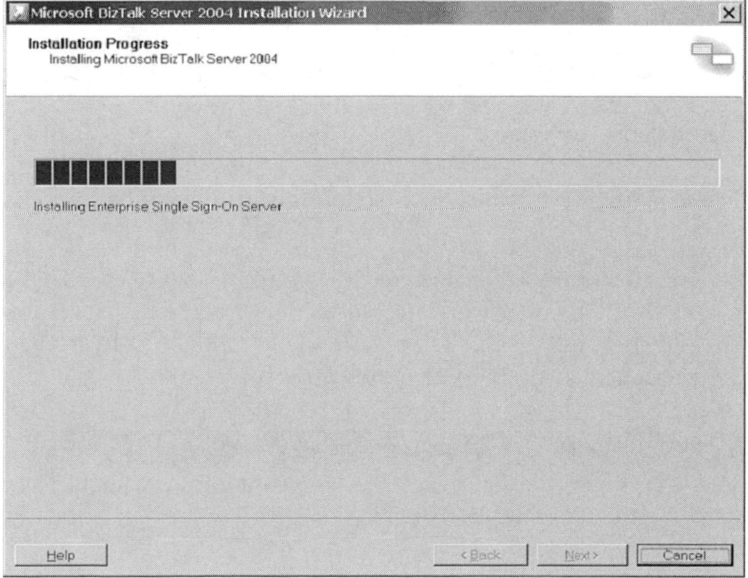

FIGURE A.17 The Installation Progress.

NOTE

If you unselect the check box to launch the Configuration Wizard, you need to launch the Configuration Wizard using ConfigFramework.exe, which is located at C:\Program Files\Microsoft BizTalk Server 2004.

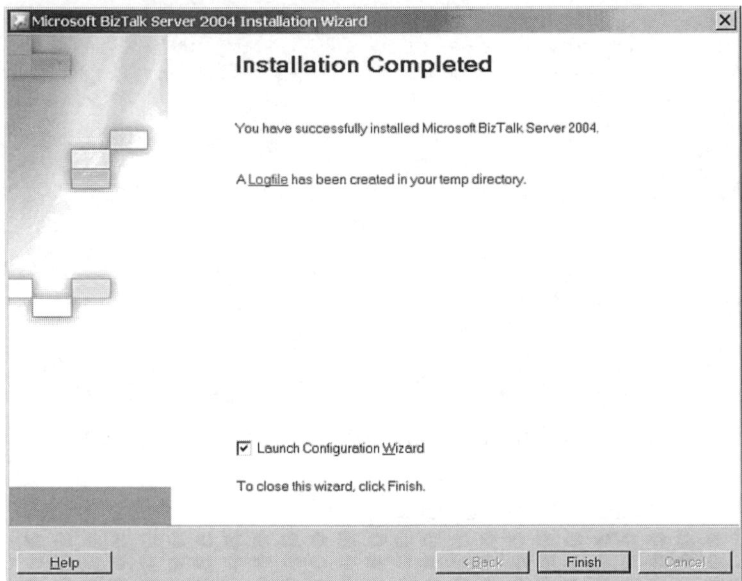

FIGURE A.18 Installation completed.

After installation is finished, click the Next button to start the configuration, as shown in Figure A.19.

You can choose either to create a new BizTalk Server group or join an existing group. If you are choosing to create a new group and Master Secret Server is not set up on another server, you need to select Yes to hold Master Secret key. Click Next to configure Tracking and BAM analysis database as shown in Figure A.21.

NOTE

You can select BizTalk Application Host and Isolated Host as trusted or untrusted; for more information on hosts, read Chapter 17, "Management."

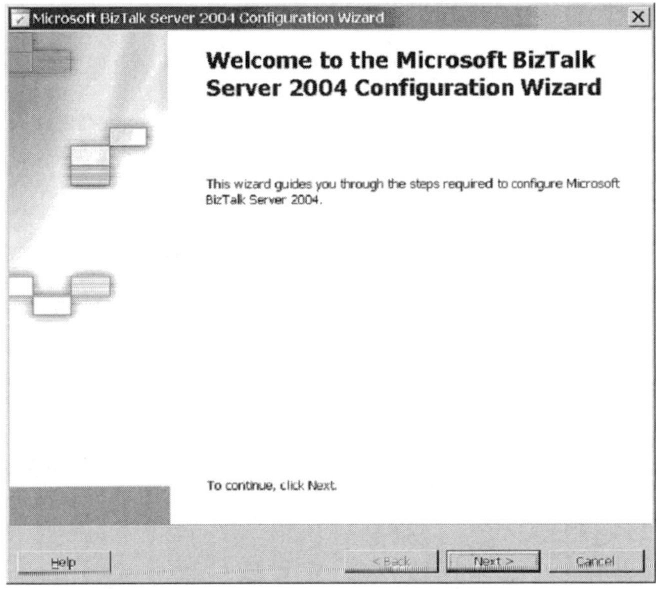

FIGURE A.19 The Configuration Wizard.

Click Next to start the configuration as shown in Figure A.20.

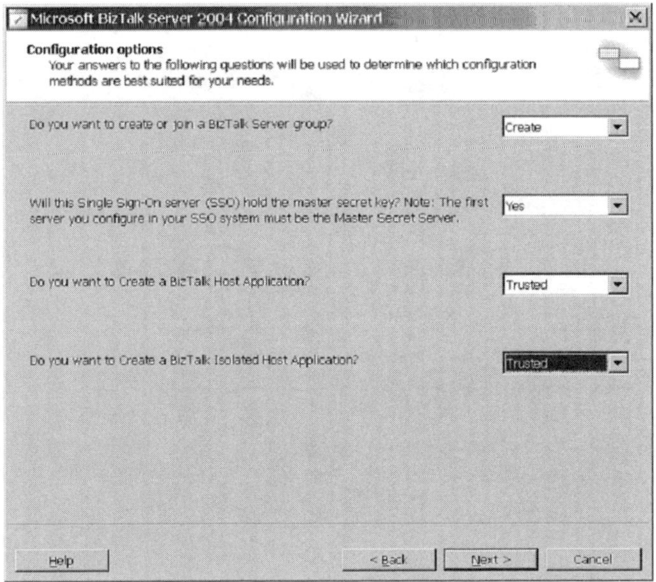

FIGURE A.20 Configuration Options.

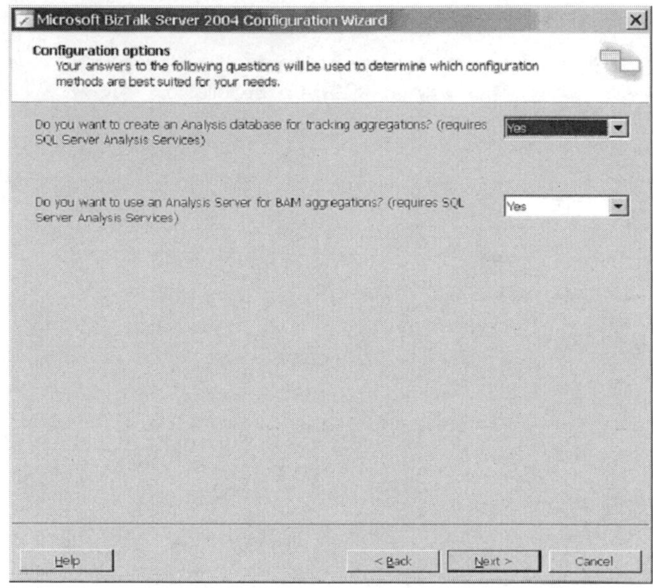

FIGURE A.21 Configure Tracking and BAM Analysis databases.

The tracking analysis database stores business and health monitoring cubes. The BAM analysis database is required for real-time aggregations. Click Next to specify NT credentials for different BizTalk Server Groups as shown in Figure A.22.

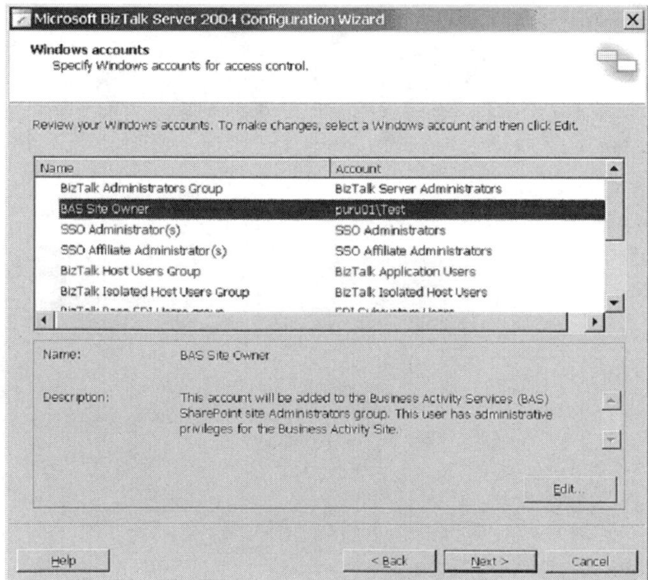

FIGURE A.22 Windows accounts for different BizTalk Server Groups.

NOTE

If SQL Server is remote, you need to create the following groups on the SQL Server machine. If you are using local groups and a remote SQL server, the following BizTalk Server groups must be created on the remote SQL Server:

- BizTalk Application Users
- BizTalk Isolated Host Users
- BizTalk Server Administrators
- SSO Administrators

If you use local groups when configuring Business Activity Services (BAS) on Windows 2003 with Windows SharePoint Services, you must also create the BAS Web Services Group on the remote SQL Server. The service account running the Enterprise Single Sign-On service must be a member of the SSO Administrators group on both computers.

You also can create groups at domain level and use domain groups.

Click Next to configure the BAS Web site as shown in Figure A.23. This screen will be shown only if you are setting up BizTalk Server on Windows 2003 Server.

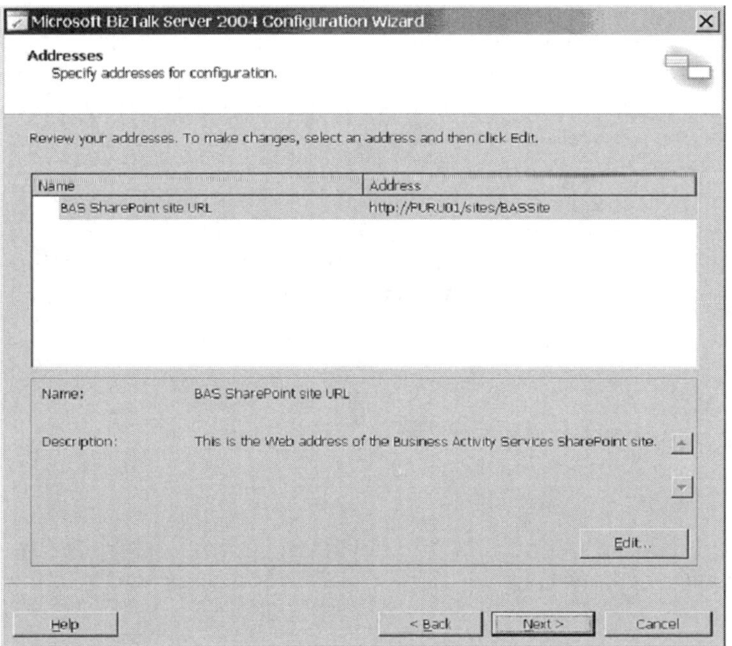

FIGURE A.23 Configure the BAS Web site.

NOTE

The BAS Web site can be configured on only one BizTalk Server in a group.

Click Next to review configuration properties as shown in Figure A.24.

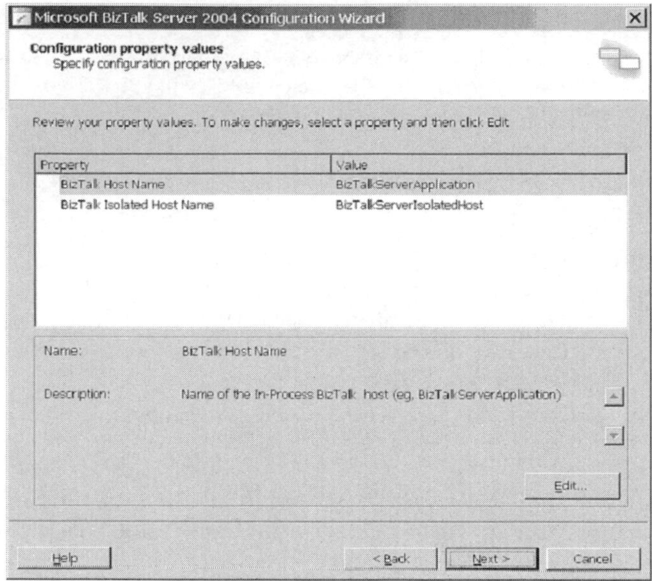

FIGURE A.24 Configuration Property Values.

You can choose a different name for BizTalk Isolated Host and BizTalk Server Application. Click Next to configure the Human Workflow Services Web Site as shown in Figure A.25.

Click Next to select the correct SQL Server for different BizTalk databases as shown in Figure A.26.

To select the appropriate SQL Server, click Edit, Edit Database Configuration. Click Next to select NT credentials for different Windows NT services for BizTalk Server as shown in Figure A.27.

NOTE

It is highly recommended that you not use the Administrative account for configuring BizTalk Services.

You can select the default settings if Windows MSMQ is not installed on the machine. If you want to have side-by-side installation of BizTalk Messaging and Windows MSMQ, take the following steps:

1. You can specify the IP address for binding BizTalk Messaging to a specific IP address. By default, BizTalk Messaging is bound to all IP addresses of the machine.
2. If the machine belongs to the domain, you can select the check box to Register Server in DNS, which will register the server in DNS in the domain.
3. To integrate BizTalk Message Queuing with Active directory, the server must be part of the domain group along with Active Directory Controller. To set BizTalk

Messaging in Active Directory, you need to have privileges to add/remove computer objects from the Active Directory.

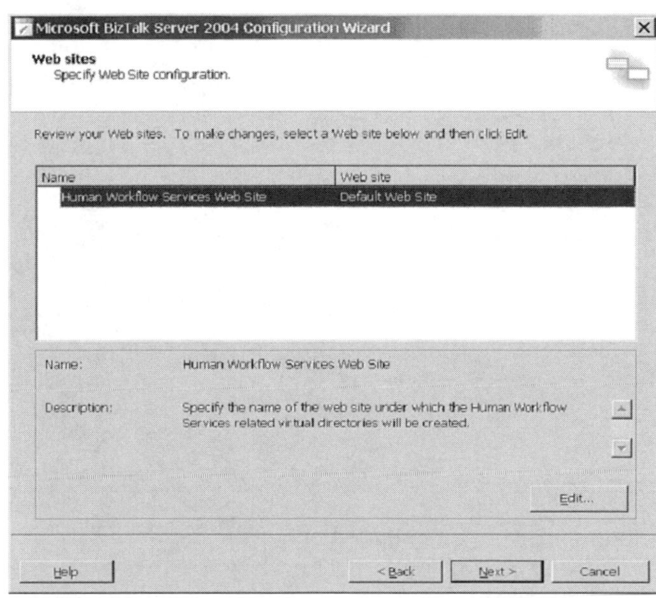

FIGURE A.25 Configure Human Workflow Services Web site.

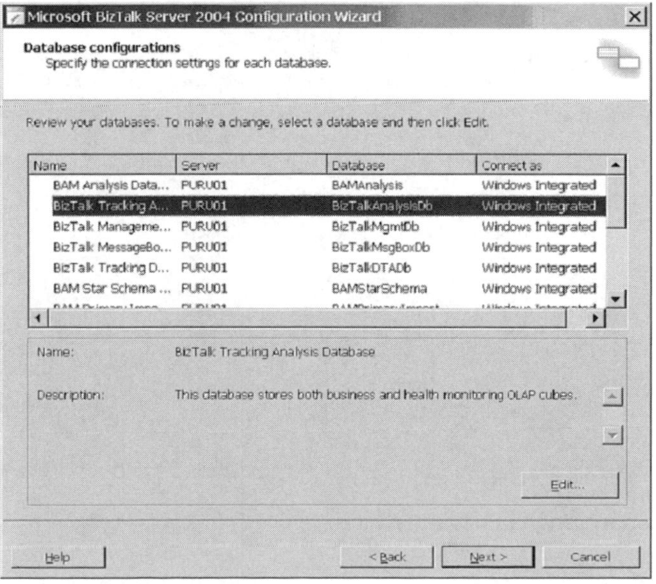

FIGURE A.26 Database Configurations.

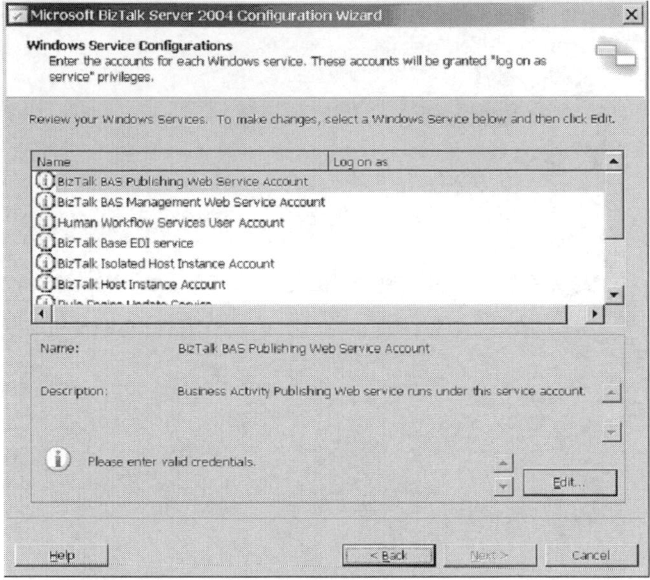

FIGURE A.27 Windows NT Service Configurations.

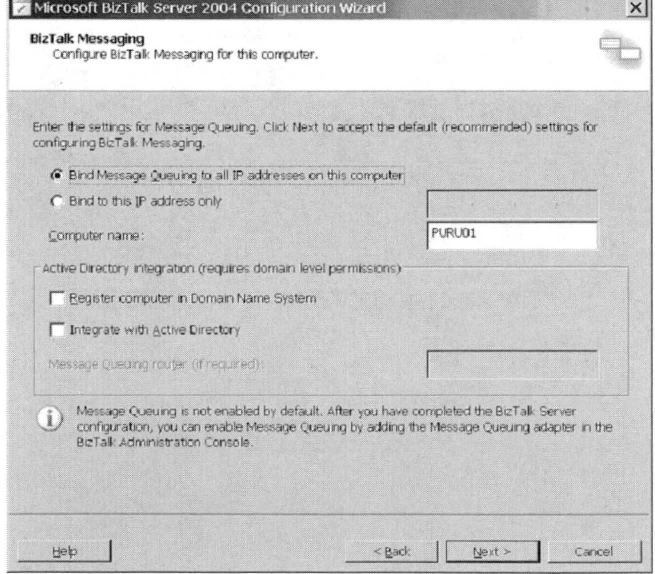

FIGURE A.28 Configuring BizTalk Messaging.

NOTE

If Windows Message queuing is installed, you must disable the service to keep default settings during configuration.

If you are planning to have side-by-side installation of BizTalk Message queuing and Windows Message Queuing, you must configure Windows Message Queuing with a specific IP address.

After BizTalk Messaging is configured, click Next to configure the BAS site, as shown in Figure A.29.

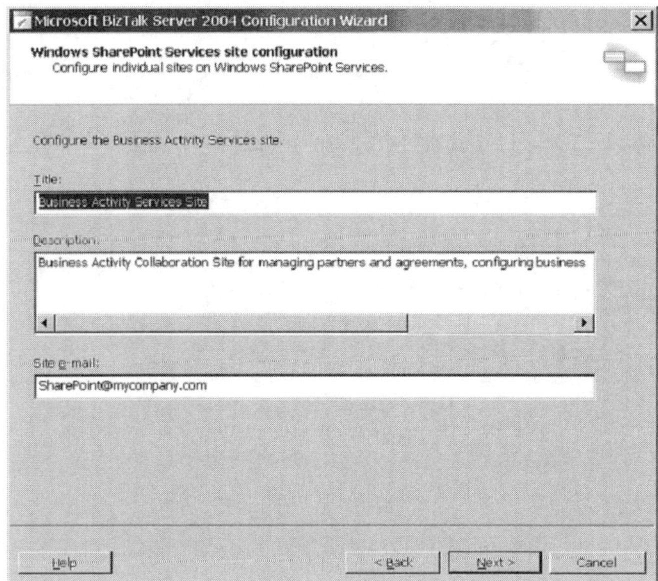

FIGURE A.29 Windows SharePoint Services Site Configuration.

You can specify the title to the site and the email address for the owner of the site. Click Next to review the summary of the components that will be configured during this wizard, as shown in Figure A.30.

You can save the configuration file to the disk, and it can be used later to configure the same machine or different machines with the same configuration. Click Next to start applying configuration settings. When configuration is complete, you will get the Configuration Completed window shown in Figure A.31.

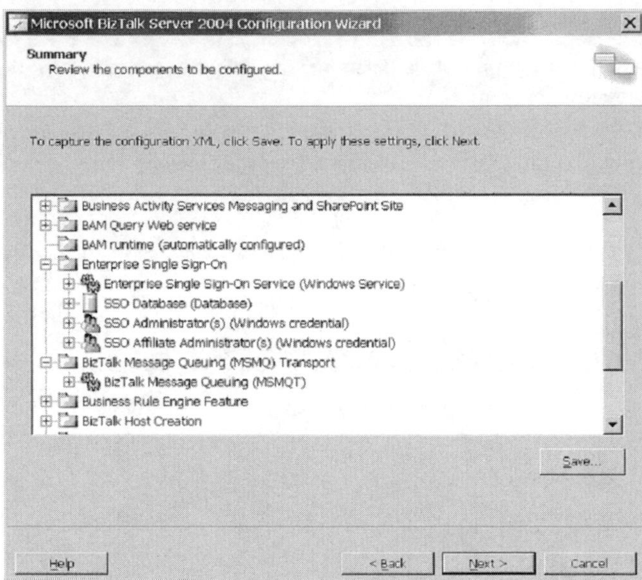

FIGURE A.30 Summary of components to be configured.

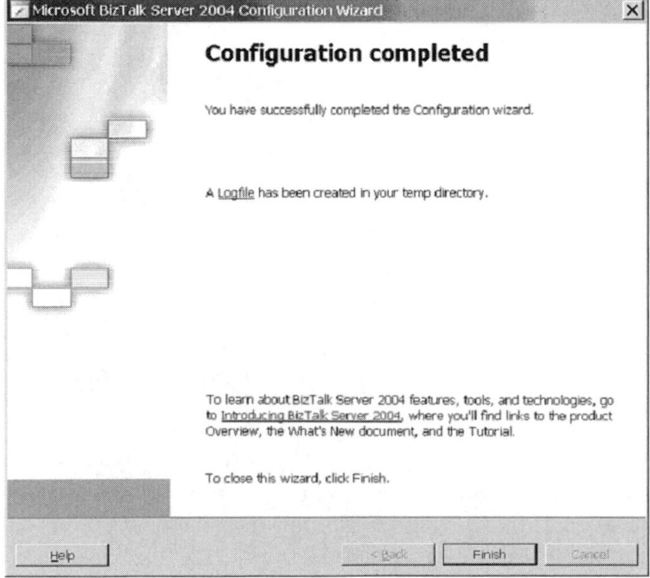

FIGURE A.31 The Configuration Completed window.

APPENDIX **B**

Migration from Previous BizTalk Version

IN THIS APPENDIX

- Planning a Migration Project
- Migrating Messaging Scenarios
- Migrating Orchestration Scenarios
- Migrating Complex BizTalk 2002 Scenarios

When carefully planned and executed, migrating a business application from BizTalk Server 2002 to BizTalk Server 2004 can be a straightforward exercise. After migration, solutions can take advantage of the powerful new features and enhanced performance of the product. The purpose of this chapter is to provide prescriptive guidance on the proper approach to planning and executing the migration of a BizTalk 2002 based solution to BizTalk 2004. Included in this appendix is guidance on the following:

- Planning a migration project
- Migrating messaging scenarios
- Migrating orchestration scenarios
- Complex BizTalk 2002 scenarios made easy with BizTalk 2004

The planning and executing of a migration project section will provide a general methodology for approaching a migration project.

The migrating messaging scenarios section will provide guidance on using the migration tools available for migrating messaging artifacts, including application integration components and preprocessor components.

The migrating orchestration scenarios section will provide guidance on migrating BizTalk 2002 solutions that utilize orchestration.

The last section of this appendix will focus on some typical scenarios that have been greatly simplified with BizTalk 2004, including

- Publish/subscribe messaging
- Large document processing
- Message correlation
- First-in, first-out messaging
- Synchronous orchestration calls

Additionally, this section will provide sample BizTalk 2004 solutions for each of these scenarios.

NOTE

The samples for each of the scenarios contain a Read Me file that explains all the Visual Studio projects provided, how to set up the sample, and how to execute the sample. The samples require that you have a BizTalk Server 2004 environment available.

Planning a Migration Project

This section provides a general approach for planning the functional and technical aspects of a migration project.

Migration Project Scope

As with any information technology project, it is imperative to establish a boundary around the scope of work to be completed. A BizTalk migration project is no different. An early decision for the migration team will be to establish a set of governing design principles to guide the team. Two important areas to decide on are the following:

- How to take advantage of new BizTalk 2004 features
- Whether to add functionality to your solution during the migration effort

BizTalk Server 2004 is a significantly different product than BizTalk Server 2002. It not only provides a rich set of new features, but it provides new ways to do things. For example, imagine you have a business rule that must be invoked from numerous business processes. With BizTalk 2002, you probably solved this challenge in one of two ways. You either implemented a decision shape in each orchestration or implemented the business rule in a custom object that is called from each orchestration. In BizTalk 2004, you may now choose to implement the business rule to execute within the Business Rules Engine that is called from each orchestration. The question then becomes, when I migrate this area of my BizTalk 2002 solution to BizTalk 2004, do I take advantage of the new Business Rules Engine? This question cannot be answered in this appendix. However, it is a recommendation that the team make a decision on how to approach these situations by establishing a set of design principles to be followed by the migration team.

Additionally, there may be a set of outstanding requirements for enhancements to your BizTalk 2002 solution. So the next question becomes, do you implement functionality enhancements to the solution as it is being migrated? Again, this is a question that cannot be answered in this chapter. However, if you plan to add functionality to your solutions as part of the migration project, it is recommended that you complete a "horizontal" migration of the functionality first, and complete a full cycle of regression testing before adding or changing functionality as defined by your requirements.

Migration Planning

When planning the migration of a BizTalk 2002 solution to a BizTalk 2004 solution, it is important to assess the technical architecture requirements as well as plan the migration from a feature perspective. This section provides a detailed look at the planning considerations and recommendations from both perspectives.

Implementing a BizTalk 2004 solution requires architecture planning. Performance and scalability metrics have changed significantly between BizTalk 2002 and 2004 and require you to rethink your infrastructure requirements. In addition, we suggest you define your requirements around security, availability, scalability, and performance. After you define and understand your architecture requirements, we recommend that you create a plan for meeting your architecture requirements. Defining your technical architecture requirements will not be covered in this chapter, but the BizTalk product documentation should be reviewed for additional information.

Feature planning involves a detailed look at the solution and deciding the best way to migrate the functionality. BizTalk 2004 solutions are based on solution projects that must be built and deployed to a BizTalk 2004 environment. As part of the feature migration planning, the following two tasks should be completed:

- BizTalk 2002 Solution Segmentation
- BizTalk 2002 Component Inventory

The first step in feature migration planning is to segment your BizTalk solution by major functional area. The concept is to create a logical grouping of artifacts to facilitate the conversion. Additionally, this segmentation will allow for a phased migration of the BizTalk 2002 solution to minimize the risk and effort.

The proper way to partition a BizTalk 2002 solution for ease of migration depends greatly on the solution being migrated. However, it is recommended that you segment large solutions into smaller, more manageable BizTalk 2004 projects.

To reduce dependencies, you can further split the functional areas of a solution into orchestration and messaging projects. By placing the orchestrations into a separate project, you decrease the number of configuration dependencies and allow for an easier deployment of the migration projects created when you migrate your BizTalk 2002 solution.

NOTE

Visual Studio .NET 2003 contains a BizTalk Server Migration Project template. When selected, a wizard guides you through selecting and migrating components from your BizTalk 2002 solution. How this wizard functions will be explained in more detail later in this appendix.

After your BizTalk 2002 solution has been segmented by functional area, it is important to understand all the components that make up each segment. A component inventory should be developed for each functional area's orchestration and messaging solution. This inventory will prepare the team for the eventual conversion of the components to BizTalk 2004 artifacts. In addition, a common library project must be considered to house schemas, maps, and other components that are identical and common across functional areas. If a common library is necessary, remove these artifacts from the migration projects into a common project and update each migration project to reference this common library. A sample component inventory is shown in Table B.1.

TABLE B.1 Sample Component Inventory

Messaging Object	Name	Purpose
Queue Receive Function	`qrfPlantActualReceive`	Consumes power plant generation data in XML format delivered directly from external sources via HTTP posts.
	`qrfPlantAlarmReceive`	Consumes power plant alarm data in XML format delivered directly from external sources via HTTP posts.
	`qrfPlantScheduleReceive`	Consumes power plant schedule data in XML format delivered directly from external sources via HTTP posts.
File Receive Function	`frfPlantActualReceive`	Consumes power plant generation data in XML format delivered manually for resubmission purposes by a system administrator.
	`frfPlantAlarmReceive`	Consumes power plant alarm data in XML format delivered manually for resubmission purposes by a system administrator.
	`frfPlantScheduleReceive`	Consumes power plant schedule data in XML format delivered manually for resubmission purposes by a system administrator.

TABLE B.1 Continued

Messaging Object	Name	Purpose
Channel	`chlPlantActualToPowerBiz`	Validates XML message against power plant generation schema.
	`chlPlantAlarmToPowerBiz`	Validates XML message against power plant schema.
	`chlPlantScheduleToPowerBiz`	Validates XML message against power plant schedule schema.
Port	`prtPlantDataToPowerBiz`	Delivers power plant XML message to AIC for entry into PowerBiz application.
AIC	`clsPlantAIC`	Class that implements `IBTSAppIntegration` interface for processing inbound plant documents.

After you have determined the architecture requirements of your BizTalk 2004 environment and segmented your BizTalk 2002 solution, you are ready to execute the migration.

Migrating Messaging Scenarios

BizTalk 2004 provides utilities for converting BizTalk 2002 messaging artifacts and BizTalk 2002 integration components to their BizTalk 2004 equivalent. This section will provide guidance on using these utilities.

Using the Migration Wizard

After you have determined how you are going to segment your BizTalk 2002 solution, the BizTalk 2002 artifacts must be migrated to a BizTalk 2004 environment. The first step will be to create migration projects and run the migration wizard. The migration wizard runs automatically when you choose a BizTalk Server Migration Project in Visual Studio .NET 2003. The migration wizard migrates the following messaging objects:

- Document Definitions
- Maps
- Receive Functions (File, HTTP, MSMQ)
- Ports (SMTP, HTTP, MSMQ, File)
- Channels
- Port Groups (Distribution Lists)

Table B.2 shows how these BizTalk 2002 artifacts map to their corresponding BizTalk 2004 artifacts.

TABLE B.2 BizTalk 2002 to BizTalk 2004 Artifact Mapping Table

BizTalk Server 2002 Messaging Item	BizTalk Server 2004 Messaging Item
Document definitions	Schemas
Maps	Maps
Receive functions	Receive locations
Ports and channels	Ports and pipelines
Port groups (distribution lists)	Send port groups

How the Migration Wizard Works

Figure B.1 shows how BizTalk 2002 messaging artifacts are converted by the migration wizard.

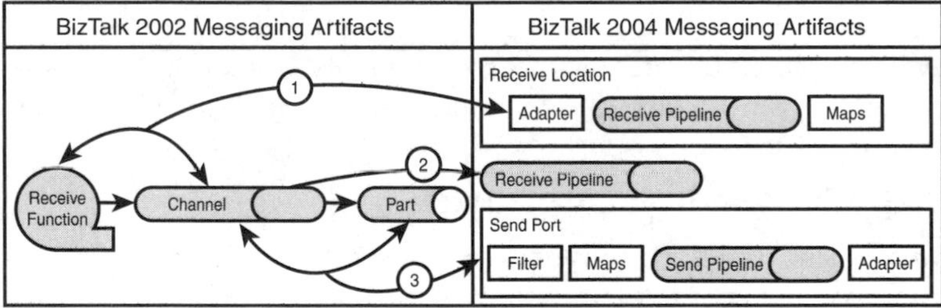

FIGURE B.1 How BizTalk 2002 messaging artifacts map to their BizTalk 2004 equivalent.

As shown in Figure B.1, every BizTalk 2002 receive function that is bound to a channel that is identified during the migration process is converted to a BizTalk 2004 receive location. During this process the following artifacts are also created:

- A binding file that defines the receive location
- Associated BizTalk 2004 maps and schemas
- A receive pipeline

The migration wizard does not add any schemas into the schema validation component of the pipeline. If validation is required, this step must be accomplished manually. Additional information necessary to create the receive location is created within the binding file that is generated, and when the migration assembly is deployed with the binding file, the receive location will be created with the following properties configured:

- The adapter will be set to the transport type of the migrated port (for example, SMTP, HTTP, File, MSMQ).
- Any maps present in the channel will be added to the maps collection of the receive port.
- The created receive pipeline will be selected as the receive locations pipeline.

Furthermore, as shown in Figure B.1, any channel that is not associated to a receive location is migrated to a receive pipeline. During this process, the following artifacts are created:

- Associated BizTalk 2004 maps and schemas
- A receive pipeline

NOTE

For standalone channels, a binding file is not created.

For every channel/port combination selected during the migration process, a BizTalk 2004 send port is created. During this process, the following artifacts are created:

- A binding file that defines the send port
- Associated BizTalk 2004 maps and schemas
- A send pipeline

Additional information required to create the send port is contained within the binding file that is generated. When the migration assembly is deployed with the binding file, the send port will be created with the following properties:

- The adapter will be set to the transport type of the migrated port (for example, SMTP, HTTP, File, MSMQ).
- Any maps present in the channel will be added to the maps collection.
- The created send pipeline will be selected as the send port pipeline.
- Dynamic routing scenarios based on the channel name or a combination of the following properties: source identifier, source id, destination identifier, destination id or document type will have the routing properties promoted and the send port filters configured automatically.

CAUTION

The migration wizard has the following limitations when used to convert BizTalk 2002 messaging artifacts:

- If a custom preprocess is configured on the receive function or an application integration component is associated with a port, the migration wizard will not automatically mig rate it.
- Custom script functoids in maps will not be migrated.
- Custom channel filter expressions will not be migrated.

- Unsupported port protocols will not be migrated.
- Certain properties within XDR schema definitions will not be converted to the equivalent XSD schema definition.

Artifacts that are not migrated will be marked in the task list in Visual Studio .NET for the developer to address.

The proper method for converting custom preprocessors and application integration components is covered in the next section.

Scripting functoids used in BizTalk Server 2002 maps will not be migrated. They must be rewritten to use a .NET language in BizTalk Server 2004, rather than the VBScript and JScript scripting engines. In addition, custom functoids will not be migrated. They also must be rewritten to use a .NET language, in contrast to a COM-based language.

The BizTalk Server 2004 Migration Wizard will not add any custom channel filters, other than the default content-based routing scenario, and will require manual intervention. If you have configured channel filters, you must add those filters yourself to the send or receive ports. To accomplish this, first the appropriate properties must be promoted on the message types defined in the BizTalk migration project. Then, the appropriate send port or send port group must be configured in BizTalk Explorer to filter based on those properties.

Schema Migration Details

When you convert solutions from BizTalk Server 2002 to 2004, it is important to understand the differences in how schemas are described between the two versions of the product. In BizTalk 2002, all message formats are described in XDR, whereas messages in BizTalk 2004 are described in XSD. Because of this difference, it is helpful to note a few key details behind schema migration to ensure a successfully-migrated solution. XDR and XSD use different sets of data types to describe schema data points. To convert schemas from XDR to XSD, data type mappings have been defined. These mappings are described in Table B.3.

TABLE B.3 XDR to XSD Data Type Mappings

XDR Data Type	XSD Data Type
char	xs:string
date	xs:date
dateTime	xs:dateTime
fixed.14.4	xs:decimal
r4	xs:float
time	xs:time
uuid	xs:string
bin.base64	xs:base64Binary
bin.hex	xs:hexBinary
boolean	xs:Boolean

TABLE B.3 Continued

XDR Data Type	XSD Data Type
dateTime.tz	xs:dateTime
entity	xs:ENTITY
entities	xs:ENTITIES
float	xs:float
i1	xs:byte
i2	xs:short
i4	xs:int
i8	xs:long
id	xs:ID
idref	xs:IDREF
idrefs	xs:IDREFS
int	xs:integer
nmtoken	xs:NMTOKEN
nmtokens	xs:NMTOKENS
notation	xs:NOTATION
number	xs:float
r8	xs:double
string	xs:string
time.tz	xs:time
bin.hex	xs:hexBinary
ui1	xs:unsignedByte
ui2	xs:unsignedShort
ui4	xs:unsignedInt
ui8	xs:unsignedLong
uri	xs:anyURI

Of all the message formats supported in BizTalk, flat files involve the most complexity when migrating from 2002 to 2004. This complexity is because of the differences in the parsing and serializing engines between the two versions of the product. These differences are described next.

BizTalk Server 2002

- Allows different delimiters to be specified for the parsing and serializing stages of the document.
- Allows specific directions on how to handle trailing carriage return (Skip Carriage Return, Append New Line) and line-feed (Skip Line Feed) characters in the flat file messages.
- Does not allow multicharacter delimiters. This is why the specific directions outlined previously are necessary.

- For positional flat files, start and end position numbers are used to define the location of data points.

BizTalk Server 2004

- Allows multicharacter delimiters.
- Uses the same character delimiter(s) for both the parsing and serializing of flat-file messages.
- For positional flat files, offset and length numbers are used to define the location of data points.

Based on these differences, the migration of character delimiters is determined by the values of the current delimiter and the Skip Carriage Return and Skip Line Feed directions. The Append New Line direction is ignored.

It is important to note that given the migration path for character delimiters described previously, certain message scenarios cannot be migrated without manual intervention. One of these scenarios involves the use of flexible or multiple character delimiters in BizTalk Server 2002. For example, a flat-file schema in BizTalk Server 2002 may be configured to have a current delimiter set to be a comma, and the Skip Carriage Return and Skip Line Feed directions both set to true. The BizTalk Server 2002 parser would interpret a delimiter as being any character combination of a comma, carriage return, and line feed, so long as the combination began with a comma. This scenario in BizTalk Server 2004 is not supported based on the migration path and the fact that the same character delimiters are used for both the parser and serializer. To successfully convert these scenarios, a custom parser or disassembler would need to be created in BizTalk Server 2004.

Other Helpful Hints When Using the Migration Wizard

When using the migration wizard, be aware of the following:

- The migration wizard must be run on a machine that has BizTalk 2004 and Visual Studio .NET 2003 installed.
- The migration wizard will attempt to log on to the BizTalk 2002 management database using Windows integrated security. Therefore, either the logged-on Windows user must have the appropriate permissions to access the database, or a copy of the database must be made and the appropriate permissions granted on the copy.
- When you select a port during the migration process, all channels associated with the port will be automatically migrated.
- Schemas must have a unique root node/namespace combination for pipelines to resolve the schema. Because the migration wizard places all schemas in the same

namespace, it is important that the migrated schemas have different root nodes, or that the namespace is altered after the migration wizard completes.

Migrating Application Integration Components and Preprocessors

In addition to the migration wizard just covered, an Adapter Migration Toolkit has been provided that allows you to continue to use application integration components and preprocessors from your BizTalk Server 2002 solutions. This toolkit allows you to leverage components that utilize the following interfaces:

- `IInterchange`
- `IPipelineComponent`
- `IPipelineComponentAdmin`
- `IBTSAppIntegration`
- `IBTSCustomProcess`
- `IBTSCustomProcessContext`

In this section, we will explore this toolkit in more detail.

`IInterchange` Migration

In BizTalk Server 2002, the `IInterchange` interface can be used to directly submit documents to BizTalk channels. The two main methods, Submit and SubmitSynch, submit documents asynchronously and synchronously, respectively.

With the exposure of this interface in BizTalk Server 2004, legacy code can be migrated to the new version of the software without any changes. All documents submitted to BizTalk Server 2004 via `IInterchange` will be delivered by way of a single receive port for Submit and SubmitSynch. `IInterchange` has been implemented in BizTalk Server 2004 as a custom receive adapter. After both the Submit and SubmitSynch receive adapters have been created via the BizTalk Administration tool, they are implemented each by a single receive port. When documents are passed through these receive ports and into the messagebox database, legacy properties, such as the channel name, can be used by other BizTalk Server 2004 messaging objects for content-based routing.

`IPipelineComponent` and `IPipelineComponentAdmin` Migration

In BizTalk Server 2002, pipeline components may be associated with ports and allow for custom properties to be set at design time via the `IPipelineComponentAdmin` interface. These components typically serve as application adapters and will house a wide variety of custom-developed functionality.

Pipeline components will be converted to adapters by the Adapter Migration Tool, one of the components included in the toolkit. After registering the component on a BizTalk 2004 Server, the tool can be run against the component. The tool will "wrap" the pipeline component with a .NET assembly that exposes it to the BizTalk Server 2004 environment as an adapter. The tool will also register the assembly with the adapter framework, at which point it can be used to create a new adapter via the BizTalk Administration tool. When creating the new adapter, you must select the ProgID of the pipeline component.

When configuring the adapter on a send port, you must specify the URI property. The pipeline component's properties can then be set by the standard property page that is available when configuring an adapter on a send port.

`IBTSAppIntegration` Migration

The `IBTSAppIntegration` interface has one method, `ProcessMessage`. Unlike pipeline components, there are no custom properties. Components implementing this interface were configured on ports in BizTalk Server 2002 and allowed for custom logic to be applied to a message prior to delivery to the destination system or location.

Application integration components will be converted to adapters by the Adapter Migration Tool, following the same steps as outlined earlier for pipeline components. When these steps have been completed, the new application integration adapter can be selected when you configure send ports in BizTalk Server 2004. At runtime, the adapter will invoke the `ProcessMessage` method on the component and pass the message body to it.

`IBTSCustomProcess` and `IBTSCustomProcessContext` Migration

Via a custom wrapper component provided by the Adapter Migration Toolkit, BizTalk Server 2002 custom preprocessors will be accessible as custom pipeline components. Users can then create custom receive pipelines in BizTalk Server 2004, adding the custom wrapper component in the decode stage and specifying the ProgID of the legacy custom preprocessor component as a configuration option on the pipeline component. At runtime, the shim will do the following:

- Create an `IBTSCustomProcessContext` object. All properties need to exist in the BizTalk Legacy namespace or a pipeline error will occur.
- Instantiate `IBTSCustomProcess`.
- Call the `SetContext` method with the created `IBTSCustomProcessContext` object.
- Call the `Execute` method passing in all the required arguments. All custom developed logic within this method will be executed.

Migrating Orchestration Scenarios

Unlike messaging artifacts, there are no utilities to automatically convert orchestrations from the BizTalk Server 2002 to BizTalk Server 2004 environment. Because of the significant differences between orchestrations in the two versions of the product, these artifacts must be converted manually. The intent of this section is to provide some guidance and hints on how to approach this conversion. When you convert orchestrations, these steps should be followed:

1. Create the orchestration project.
2. Create the orchestration artifact.
3. Define the schemas to be used.
4. Analyze and convert implementation shapes.
5. Implement control shapes.

Creating the Orchestration Project

First, orchestrations should be placed in a separate project from the messaging artifacts (schemas, maps, pipelines, receive and send ports, and so on) that were migrated using the migration wizard. This will create a dependency between the assemblies but will allow the business processes to be modified without worry of inadvertently changing any of the messaging artifacts.

As a brief review, Figure B.2 shows how messaging artifacts are associated with orchestrations.

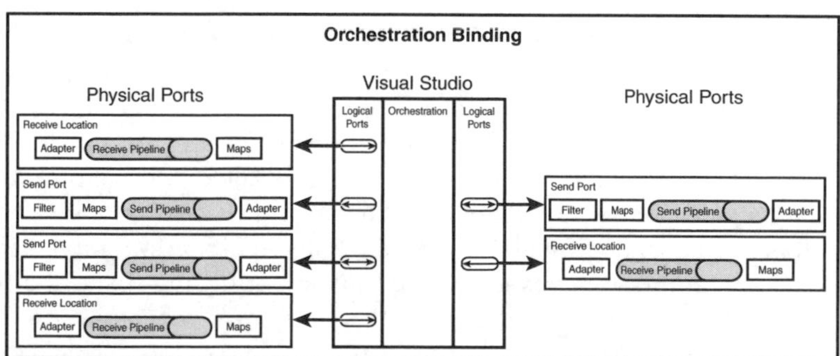

FIGURE B.2 How BizTalk 2004 messaging artifacts are associated with orchestrations.

BizTalk Server 2004 orchestrations no longer rely on a channel/port to receive messages for processing. Instead, orchestrations use the message context data to subscribe to messages for processing. Messages are sent to an orchestration directly from the messagebox and the orchestration returns the message to the messagebox directly when processing is complete. The message is then picked up by one or more BizTalk Server artifacts for further processing (for example, send ports or another orchestration). The orchestration creates a subscription through orchestration binding. Binding enables you to tie logical ports (found on the port surface in orchestrations) to physical ports and create a subscription to messages received through physical receive ports and messages intended for physical send ports. This process can be done at design time through direct binding (that is, specify now logical port property) or at a later time (that is, specify later logical port property). If you choose to bind your logical ports at a later time, you will use the BizTalk Server Explorer tool to create the bindings. After you have bound an orchestration, the necessary subscriptions are created between your orchestration and the receive/send ports it uses.

Creating the Orchestration Artifact

After you have created a project to house the orchestration(s), a blank orchestration should be created. This is done by simply adding a new orchestration to the assembly.

Defining the Schemas to Be Used

Determine which schemas will be used within your orchestration from your completed inventory assessment. For each unique schema, you will need to define a message within the orchestration with a unique name. After you have added a message name and defined the message type, all future references to the message type will be done through the message name. If there are additional required schemas beyond what was converted by the migration wizard, add the schemas to your project or reference an assembly containing those schemas.

Analyzing and Converting Implementation Shapes

Now that you have created an orchestration and added the required schemas to it, the next step is to convert the implementation shapes from the BizTalk Server 2002 Orchestration to the BizTalk Server 2004 Orchestration. There are four possible implementation shapes available in BizTalk Server 2002: the BizTalk Server Messaging shape, the Message Queuing shape, the Script Component shape, and COM Component shape. The suggested approach is to follow the BizTalk Server 2002 Orchestration implementation shapes in a top-down approach, converting and implementing one shape at a time to the BizTalk Server 2004 Orchestration. This ensures that you don't miss anything and is consistent with the linear nature of orchestrations.

Messaging Shape Conversion

BizTalk 2002 had the concept of receive and send messaging shapes. These shapes will become one-way send or receive logical ports within the BizTalk 2004 Orchestration. The migration wizard will have already converted the channel/port combinations that are associated with these shapes into BizTalk 2004 physical ports.

Message Queuing Shape Conversion

BizTalk Server 2004 does not contain an orchestration shape that allows you to post directly to a queue. Instead, it offers the notion of physical/logical send port combinations that point to queues. For each message queuing shape within your BizTalk Server 2002 Orchestration, you will create a new logical send port.

Script Component Shape Conversion

Two options for migrating Windows scripting objects are the following:

- Use the expression shape in BizTalk Server 2004 and recode the script as a BizTalk expression.
- Convert the logic into a .NET assembly and then call the assembly from a BizTalk Server 2004 Orchestration.

If the script functionality is short, static, and relatively straightforward, the expression route should be taken. If the script functionality is long, constantly changing, and complex, or if you prefer to use a .NET language, a .NET assembly should be considered.

COM Component Shape Conversion

BizTalk 2004 is built on the scalable, secure, and dynamic .NET Framework. Being built completely new from the bottom up, it does not natively communicate with older technologies, such as COM. To facilitate .NET to COM interaction, the Framework Class Library (FCL) contains a set of namespaces and tools that greatly simplifies calling COM objects from .NET code and .NET code from COM objects. It does this through the use of Runtime Callable Wrappers (RCW) and COM Callable Wrappers (CCW), respectively. After a COM object has been wrapped in an RCW, it is made available to BizTalk Server 2004 through a reference to the wrapper. It may then be accessed transparently like any other .NET class. Interoperability classes take care of all the plumbing behind the scenes and allow the programmer to focus on object instantiation and method invocation.

Analyzing and Converting Control Shapes

Now that we have completed the necessary preparation, we will systematically convert the BizTalk Server 2002 control shapes to BizTalk Server 2004 shapes. Again, the suggested approach is to follow the BizTalk Server 2002 Orchestration in a top-down approach, converting and implementing one shape at a time to the BizTalk Server 2004 Orchestration.

Furthermore, BizTalk 2004 provides a variety of new shapes. More than likely, logic that was contained within scripting components and/or COM components in your BizTalk 2002 solution could be implemented using shapes available within orchestration. During the conversion process, analysis should be completed to determine if an equivalent implementation can be achieved using the shapes now available to you in orchestration. In this section, we discuss the conversion of the more common control shapes.

Action Connected to BizTalk Messaging Activate

Most BizTalk 2002 Orchestrations begin with an action tied to a BizTalk activate. When a message is sent through a BizTalk channel/port combination tied to that orchestration, the orchestration is instantiated and passed the message. Similar functionality is offered in BizTalk 2004 through the use of physical receive ports, logical receive ports, and orchestration receive shapes.

For each activate receive in your BizTalk 2002 project, you will complete these tasks:

1. Drag a receive shape onto the top portion of the orchestration designer surface.

> **NOTE**
>
> Activate receives must be the top-most shape on the BizTalk 2004 orchestration surface.

2. Choose a message type in the drop-down list.
3. Set the Activate property to `True` in the Properties window.
4. Connect the logical port you created when migrating the BizTalk 2002 receive messaging shape to the BizTalk 2004 receive shape.
5. The final step is to use the BizTalk Explorer to bind the logical ports to the physical ports. This will be completed after the orchestration project is built and deployed.

Action Connected to COM Component When the required COM objects have been wrapped as previously discussed, it will be possible to convert your COM component shapes from BizTalk 2002 to BizTalk 2004. You can accomplish this conversion by taking the following steps:

1. Drag a scope shape onto the design surface and set the transaction to atomic.
2. Declare a variable for each COM object.

> **NOTE**
>
> You must have a reference to your Runtime Callable Wrapper (RCW) to complete this step.

3. Drag an expression shape onto the surface and edit the expression shape to instantiate your object and call your method.

Action Connected to Windows Script Component If you chose to convert your Windows script component code to a .NET language and .NET assembly, you will take the following steps:

1. Add the assembly as a .NET reference.
2. Create a variable to reference the object you want to call.

3. Drag a scope onto the design surface and set the transaction type to atomic.
4. Drag an expression shape to the design surface into the scope shape and edit the expression shape to instantiate your object and call the method.

Through the COM Interop Layer If you chose to register the WSC and call it through the COM interop layer, you will take the following steps:

1. Add the assembly as a COM reference.
2. Create a variable to reference the object you want to call.
3. Drag a scope onto the design surface and set the transaction type to atomic.

> **NOTE**
>
> An atomic scope is not necessary unless you are calling a .NET object that is not XMLSerializable.

4. Drag an expression shape to the design surface into the scope shape and edit the expression shape to instantiate your object and call the method.

> **TIP**
>
> If you chose to convert the script to a BizTalk expression, no additional steps are required.

Decision Shape

BizTalk 2002 Orchestrations frequently made decisions based on incoming XML document nodes using decision shapes. In BizTalk 2004, the decision shape has been renamed "decide" shape, but the functionality is nearly identical. For each decision shape within your BizTalk 2002 project, take the following steps:

1. Drag a decide shape to the BizTalk 2004 Orchestration design surface.
2. Promote any message schema nodes that you want to have access to within the decision shape.
3. Create one or more rules (Boolean expressions) that evaluate to `true` or `false`.
4. Place any shapes you want to execute upon `true` directly below the rule and shapes you want to execute upon `false` under the `else` branch.

Action Connected to BizTalk Messaging Send

Sending messages from a BizTalk 2002 Orchestration is another ubiquitous scenario that can be migrated to BizTalk 2004 as follows:

1. Drag a send shape to the orchestration design surface.
2. Select a message type for the send shape.
3. Connect the send shape to the logical port you created earlier when migrating the BizTalk 200 messaging shape.

Migrating Complex BizTalk 2002 Scenarios

BizTalk 2004 has a new architecture and powerful capabilities that did not exist in BizTalk 2002. For certain scenarios, it would not make sense to simply convert your BizTalk 2002 solution without considering incorporating these features into the solution. Otherwise, you may end up converting artifacts that were custom components in your BizTalk 2002 solution that are no longer necessary. This section describes some prevalent scenarios where a combination of custom components and complex BizTalk 2002 configuration was necessary. In BizTalk 2004, these scenarios are now relatively simple configurations.

Publish/Subscribe Messaging Scenarios

Integration between multiple disparate systems can be accomplished in a variety of ways. The Publish/Subscribe methodology for integration calls for source systems to publish or output messages to a centralized hub. The hub receives these messages, performs any required translation, and delivers them to the appropriate destination, or subscribing, systems. This method of integration has a number of benefits, including a complete decoupling of source and destination systems, easily configurable subscription process on a per-subscriber basis, and insulation of source and destination systems by way of the centralized hub.

The Publish/Subscribe Toolkit was developed for BizTalk Server 2002 to facilitate this style of application integration. The toolkit includes a COM component, called the Publish-Subscribe Framework (PSF), which utilizes BizTalk Server 2002's channel routing and filtering to provide publish/subscribe capabilities. The toolkit also includes a front-end tool for managing publishers, subscribers, and subscriptions.

STOCK QUOTE PUBLISHING SCENARIO

The example that comes with the Publish/Subscribe Toolkit is based on a stock quote publishing scenario. The sample publishing application (PubSample.exe) generates stock quote messages and delivers them to an MSMQ. The subscribing application (SubSample.exe) is used to receive the stock quote messages via a queue receive function. The queue receive function delivers the stock quote messages to the correct subscribers (channels) based on document properties. Specifically, the document definition name and source and destination organizations are used to feed the messages to the correct channels. Optionally, filtering can be applied to the channels, configuring which documents are delivered to the individual subscribers.

In BizTalk Server 2004, publish/subscribe integration methodology has been built into the core of the software. All messages flowing into BizTalk Server 2004 get stored in the messagebox database and are then retrieved by the appropriate BizTalk objects for further processing. To determine which messages should be retrieved, BizTalk objects have a wide array of message properties that can be interrogated. All the configurations necessary to set up publish/subscribe integration solutions can be made through the core BizTalk Server 2004 tools. In this way, the new version of BizTalk simplifies the process for enabling "self-routing" documents.

A very simple example of how this is accomplished with BizTalk Server 2004 involves two orchestrations, which act as subscribing systems. Both of these orchestrations are kicked off by messages published to a distinct file location. The properties of the orchestrations filter which messages are processed by each subscriber. The following BizTalk Server 2004 objects are created for the example:

1. A schema named `Subscription`, representing a published document. This schema includes two elements: `SubType` and `SubName`.
2. An orchestration named `Subscriber1`, representing the first subscribing system. This orchestration has one receive shape and one send shape. The receive shape is attached to a port that is bound to a receive port named `PubSubReceivePort_Start`. The receive shape's Filter Expression properties are set to `SubType = Subscriber1` and `SubType = AllSubscribers`.
3. An orchestration named `Subscriber2`, representing the second subscribing system. This orchestration has one receive shape and one send shape. The receive shape is attached to a port that is bound to a receive location named `PubSubReceivePort_Start`. The receive shape's Filter Expression properties are set to `SubType = Subscriber2` and `SubType = AllSubscribers`.

Figure B.3 shows the design of the `Subscriber1` orchestration.

Sample code has been provided for this scenario.

Large Document Processing Scenarios

Occasionally there are business scenarios that require the processing of large documents. For instance, a quarterly cash flow statement may be sent to BizTalk, mapped into a different format, and distributed to offices around the globe. BizTalk 2002 provided two primary ways to handle this situation: custom preprocessors and envelopes.

With the custom preprocessor scenario, custom code was required that parsed through the document and called the submit method for each instance document in the parent message. Although this method worked, it required development of a custom integration component.

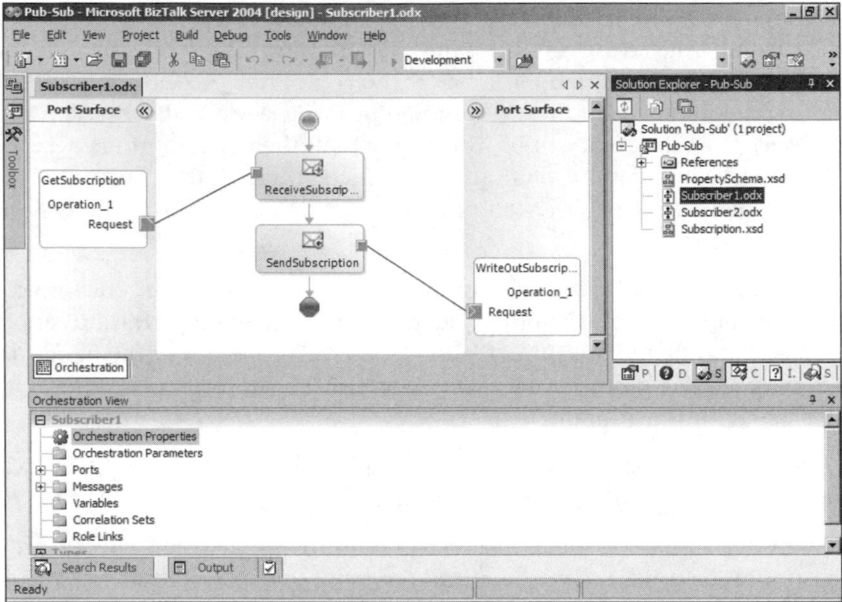

FIGURE B.3 Publish/Subscribe orchestration flow.

The second scenario, envelopes, is still supported and is now the recommended approach for breaking large documents into smaller units for processing. Although BizTalk 2004 now offers more functionality with envelopes, logically the core functionality is still there. In BizTalk 2002 you could create an envelope and specify the Document Container Node dictionary to instruct the XML parser to break apart the document into smaller units. For example, by setting the dictionary property of an envelope to the Body node, the three purchase orders would be split out and processed individually.

```
<POEnvelope>
    <Header>
    </Header>
    <Body>

    </Body>
</POEnvelope>
```

In BizTalk 2004 the technical steps have changed, but the idea is the same. To set up an envelope to process embedded documents, you must take the following steps:

1. Create a new schema and change the envelope property to Yes.
2. Create a root element and then a child record node (along with any nodes you desire in your envelope).

3. Create a child node with a type of any under the child node you just created.
4. Change the Body XPath property of the root node to point to the child record you have just created.

For the XML example we previously provided, you would create an envelope and set the Body XPath property of the `POEnvelope` node to `POEnvelope`/Body. At runtime, the XML Disassembler will resolve the envelope schema and use the Body XPath property to break apart the document and submit each child node to the message box. After it is in the message box, the single Purchase Order document is available for further processing.

Sample code has been provided for this scenario.

Messaging Correlation Scenarios

When you are developing solutions with BizTalk Server, certain scenarios call for the orchestration of long-running processes. These long-running processes often are asynchronous in nature and can involve human interaction where response times are unknown. In these scenarios, the capability to correlate an inbound response message to the initiating delivery process is critical in building a fully functional solution.

An example of this type of business scenario can be found in the BizTalk Server 2002 Software Developer Kit (SDK). In this example, a document requiring approval from a business user is received, which initiates a business process implemented as an orchestration. The document is then delivered to a separate application, where business users review the document and either approve or deny the request. After the document has been either approved or denied, it is submitted back to the long-running orchestration instance that delivered the document to the application.

In BizTalk Server 2002, this correlation process is typically achieved via a number of custom developed objects. In the SDK correlation example, these objects include the following:

- Envelope—Contains information describing an orchestration instance, typically a Global Unique Identifier (GUID). This GUID uniquely identifies the orchestration instance that a message originated from, or the orchestration instance a message is being sent to. The following XML snippet shows how the message looks when wrapped in the envelope:

```
<?xml version="1.0"?>
<SOAP-ENV:Envelope xmlns:SOAP-ENV="http://schemas.xmlsoap.org/soap/envelope/"
xmlns:xsi="http://www.w3.org/1999/XMLSchema-instance">
    <SOAP-ENV:Header xmlns:SOAP-ENV="http://schemas.xmlsoap.org/soap/
➥envelope/">
        …
        <prc:process SOAP-ENV:mustUnderstand="1"
xmlns:prc="http://schemas.biztalk.org/btf-2-0/process">
```

```
<prc:instance>sked://WKSGOELTZBXP.equarius.com!XLANG Scheduler/
{B80A7818-B3CA-4AEA-AA9E-69EC0423FB3B}</prc:instance>
            <prc:detail>
...
            </prc:detail>
        </prc:process>
    </SOAP-ENV:Header>
    <SOAP-ENV:Body>
        <NewApp><Name>Name_1</Name><Limit>Limit_1</Limit></NewApp>
    </SOAP-ENV:Body>
</SOAP-ENV:Envelope>
```

- AIC/Pipeline Component—Handles the retrieval of the existing orchestration instance and the submission of the incoming response message to that orchestration instance. The GUID specified in the message envelope allows this component to retrieve the correct existing orchestration instance. This component also provides the functionality for creating, manipulating, and interrogating the message envelope.

In BizTalk Server 2004, this correlation process has been significantly simplified. Correlation has been built into orchestrations in 2004 by way of Correlation Sets, making the correlation process a configuration task in contrast to a custom development task. The AIC and Pipeline components in the BizTalk Server 2002 SDK example are no longer required. In addition to the general migrations steps, the following changes are made to the SDK correlation solution to successfully convert the process to BizTalk Server 2004:

Correlation Messaging Objects

The following messaging objects are created to implement the correlation sample.

1. A new schema is developed, which is based on the original NewApp message, but with two additional elements containing the orchestration instance GUID and the message status.

2. A new map is created to transform the original NewApp message into the new schema. Within this map, the GUID will be set, uniquely identifying the orchestration instance. The message status will also initially be set to Pending.

NOTE

In the BizTalk 2002 SDK example, the custom envelope was based on the BizTalk Framework SOAP envelope structure. The custom envelope also included an element that contained the orchestration instance GUID. For the purpose of keeping this migration example as simple as possible, the envelope has been removed from the solution because it provided no functionality other than containing the orchestration instance GUID. The orchestration instance GUID and message status are now elements in the new message schema.

Correlation Orchestration Objects

The following orchestration objects are created to implement the correlation sample.

1. Create a new correlation type, named `CorrelationType`. The correlation type is based on the orchestration instance GUID element of the new schema.
2. Create a new correlation set, named `BTFCorrelation`. The correlation set is based on the `CorrelationType`.
3. On the first orchestration shape (`ReceiveDoc`), set the Initializing Correlation Sets property to `BTFCorrelation`.
4. The second orchestration shape (`PrepareDoc`) is no longer needed and can be removed.
5. On the third orchestration shape (`SendDocToApp`), deliver the inbound message to a send port. This send port will deliver the message to the file location. This file location will be monitored by the separate application, where users can either approve or deny the request.
6. Create a new Loop shape called `WaitForResponse` and position it directly below the `SendDocToApp` shape. This shape allows the orchestration to wait until the looping condition is met. In this scenario, after the message that was sent out in the `SendDocToApp` shape is delivered back to the orchestration instance with an Approved or Denied status, the loop completes.
7. Combine the fourth orchestration shapes (Receive Denial and Receive Approval) into a single receive shape and set the Following Correlation Sets property to `BTFCorrelation`. This receive shape will be connected to a receive port shape, which is bound to the file location that the separate application sends response messages to. Because the correlation set is configured with a GUID identifying the running orchestration instance, messages will be fed back into the correct initiating orchestration. Position this shape inside the looping shape.

Figure B.4 shows the design of the Correlation orchestration.

After these changes have been made, the migration of the SDK example is complete.

Sample code for this scenario has been provided.

First-In First-Out Messaging Scenarios

Certain business scenarios require transactions to be submitted and processed in the sequential order of their temporal occurrence. This FIFO (first-in first-out) order must be preserved from start to finish and must be guaranteed to occur only within the FIFO sequence. The second message in a FIFO sequence should not begin processing until the first message is finished without exceptions. A classic example of this requirement is a transactional banking system.

Banking accounts, such as a checking account, must maintain sequential ordering of transactions so that account balances are accurate to a specific point in time. Because banking fees are often assessed for negative balances and fund authorization business rules are based on sufficient balances, transactions against the account that are delivered out of sequence make it possible to have a deposit transaction processed subsequent to a deduction transaction, even though the transaction sequence occurred in the reverse. This situation could cause a negative account balance resulting in the denial of deductions and the assessment of banking fees. By forcing the processing of the transactions in sequence, we can guarantee that the checking account balance is accurate to the time the last message occurred. In short, all negative balances in a FIFO system will be the result of poor account management and not solution inconsistencies.

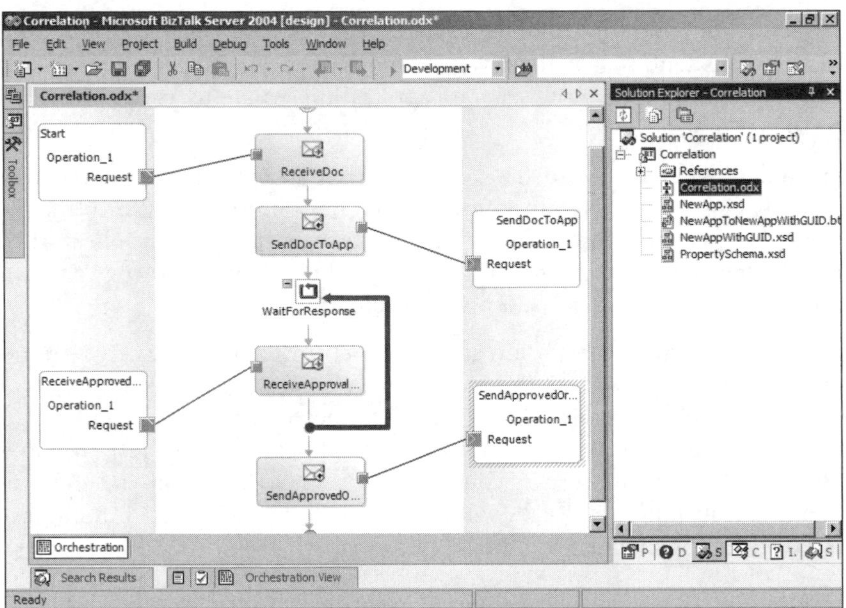

FIGURE B.4 Correlation orchestration flow.

BizTalk 2002 allows FIFO processing by creating a BizTalk application pool in COM+ that allows only a single instance of an orchestration—and using a queue receive function. With this configuration, only a single message at a time will be picked up off the queue and processed. The orchestration must finish its processing before the next message will be received.

BizTalk 2004 still supports first-in-first-out processing. Although you must use queuing, the artifact configuration is simplified. Because BizTalk Server 2004 is built on a publish/subscribe model and both orchestrations and send ports are able to subscribe to messages received in the messagebox, it is now possible to force sequential processing through a single instance of an orchestration.

Setting the ordered delivery property to true for physical send ports or logical orchestration ports, and setting up a sequential convoy in your orchestration, will cause the orchestration instance to process messages in order of receipt to the messagebox. It is important to note, however, that this processing will be sequential in nature only if the receive location that publishes the subscribed document to the messagebox is using the MSMQT adapter. Other adapters do not have the necessary logic to assure that messages are processed and delivered to the message box in the original order. Also, send ports allow ordered delivery only when using the MSMQT adapter.

Sample code for this scenario has been provided.

TIP

To make this sample code as simple as possible, a `send` and `receive` port are created to facilitate getting messages into MSMQT. Because the file adapter doesn't enforce ordered delivery of messages, messages will not be in a true FIFO order. To make this solution a true FIFO solution, create a solution that writes messages directly to MSMQT.

Synchronous Orchestration Calls

The processing of messages between separate systems has traditionally been handled in one of two ways: synchronous or asynchronous. Synchronous processing involves a noninterrupted execution flow, tightly coupling the source and destination systems. Asynchronous processing, on the other hand, allows messages to be stored in predefined locations during the integration. In this manner, the overall integration process is broken up into smaller, self-contained subprocesses. This results in the decoupling of source and destination systems and allows each system to process messages more autonomously.

In BizTalk Server 2002, orchestrations were inherently asynchronous. For example, when a process instantiated an orchestration (either through an XLANG port or a schedule moniker via code), the response would indicate success or failure of the instantiation, as opposed to the actual output of the orchestration.

Certain scenarios call for the use of process orchestration in a synchronous manner. This type of scenario brought about the need for synchronous-on-asynchronous (synch-on-asynch) processing. An example of this type of business solution is found in the BizTalk Server 2002 SDK. In this example, a user makes a request from a Web page, requiring an orchestration to run and a result to be returned. Because a user will be waiting for the response, the underlying process is executed in a synchronous manner to minimize the wait time.

To enable the asynchronous orchestration to process synchronously in BizTalk Server 2002, a Synchronous Orchestration Component (SOC) was developed. This SOC was implemented as an Application Integration Component (AIC), leveraging the `IPipelineComponent` interfaces. The orchestration uses the SOC to block the requesting process while it executes. After it has completed, it sets the response message in the SOC, allowing BizTalk Server 2002 to deliver the response back to the calling process.

In BizTalk Server 2004, exposing asynchronous orchestrations as synchronous processes has been simplified down to a few configuration tasks. No custom components are needed. Orchestrations can easily be exposed as Web services in the new version of BizTalk Server. The BizTalk Web Services Publishing Wizard creates a proxy Web service that allows the orchestration to be called synchronously. By exposing the orchestration as a Web service, BizTalk Server 2004 enables the business process to be leveraged across heterogeneous and remote environments.

An example of how this is accomplished with BizTalk Server 2004 involves a simple orchestration representing a business process that needs to be executed synchronously. Creating the solution includes the following steps:

Synchronous Orchestration Messaging Objects

1. A schema is developed named `SynchMessageIn`, representing the inbound document to be synchronously processed. This schema includes two elements: `SynchType` and `SynchName`.
2. A schema is developed named `SynchMessageOut`, representing the outbound document. This schema includes three elements: `SynchType`, `SynchName`, and `SynchStatus`.
3. A map is developed named `SynchMessageInToSynchMessageOut`. Within this map, the `SynchStatus` will be set to `SynchronouslyProcessed`.

Synchronous Orchestration Objects

An orchestration is developed named SOC, representing the synchronous business process. This orchestration has one receive shape, a transform shape that runs the inbound message through the map, and one send shape. Both the receive shape and send shape are attached to a request/response port, which has the Access Restriction property set to `Public - no limit`.

BizTalk Web Services Publishing Wizard

After the orchestration has been successfully built, the wizard is run to expose the process as a Web service. The public request/response port of the orchestration provides the basis for the Web methods. Specifically, the inbound schema is used to define the input of the Web service, whereas the outbound schema is used to define the output.

Calling Application

A simple ASP.NET application is developed to call the Web service and display results.

Figure B.5 shows the design of the SOC orchestration.

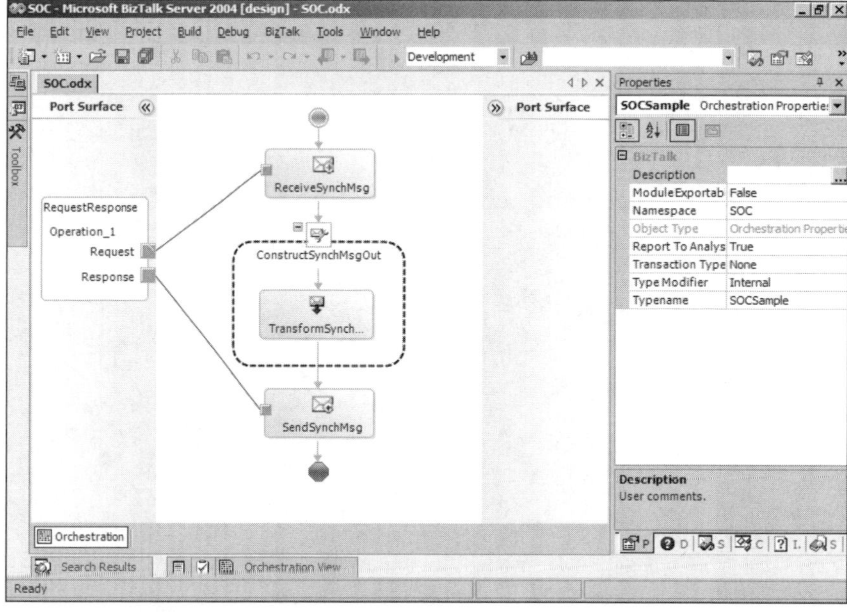

FIGURE B.5 Synchronous orchestration flow.

Sample code for this scenario has been provided.

APPENDIX C
(ONLINE CHAPTER)
Using BizTalk Native Adapters

by Erik Leaseburg

Appendix C, "Using BizTalk Native Adapters" is available on Sams website at http://www.samspublishing.com. Enter this book's ISBN (without the hyphens) in the Search box and click Search. When the book's title is displayed, click the title to go to a page where you can download this element.

Index

Numbers

A

B

C

D

E

F

G

H

I

J-L

M

N

O

P

Q

R

S

T

U

V

W

How can we make this index more useful? Email us at indexes@samspublishing.com

X-Z

How can we make this index more useful? Email us at indexes@samspublishing.com

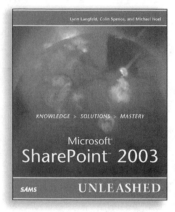

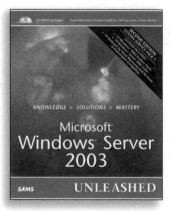

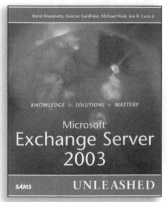

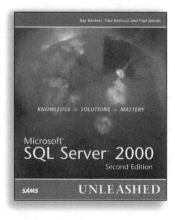